C–V–P Formulas
(X_1 = unit sales and X_2 = dollar sales)

Contribution Margin Technique

$$X_1 = \frac{\text{fixed costs + income}}{\text{CMU}}$$

or

$$X_2 = \frac{\text{fixed costs + inc}}{\text{CM\%}}$$

Income Equation Technique

$$\text{Sales price }(X_1) - \text{VCU }(X_1) - \text{fixed costs} = \text{income}$$

or

$$X_2 - \text{VC\%}(X_2) - \text{fixed costs} = \text{income}$$

Converting Net Income to Income before Tax

$$\text{IBT} = \frac{\text{NI}}{1 - \text{tax \%}}$$

C-V-P Graphs and Profit Graph

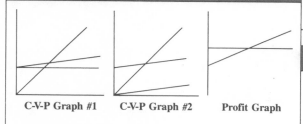

C-V-P Graph #1   C-V-P Graph #2   Profit Graph

A Comparison of Direct and Absorption Costing

	Direct	Absorption
Product costs	DM	DM
	DL	DL
	VFO	VFO
	—	FFO
Period costs	FFO	—
	VS&A	VS&A
	FS&A	FS&A
Income higher when	$Q_s > Q_p$	$Q_p > Q_s$
Breakeven higher when	$Q_p > Q_s$	$Q_s > Q_p$

Income Statement Formats

Contribution Format with Direct Costing	Traditional Format with Absorption Costing
Sales	Sales
− variable costs	− Cost of goods sold
= contribution margin	= Gross profit
− costs	− Selling & administrative
= income	= Net income

Different Approaches to Price Setting: Costs Plus a Markup

	Contribution Margin Pricing Method	Traditional Pricing Method
Costs per unit:	DM	DM
	+ DL	+ DL
	+ VFO	+ VFO
	+ VS&A	+ FFO
Total costs per unit	= Total variable costs	= Total manufacturing costs per unit
Plus the markup per unit	+ CM% (based on TVC) × VCU	+ GP% (based on total manuf. costs) × total manuf. costs per unit
	= Sales price	= Sales price

Multiproduct Firms

$$\text{Sales mix\%} = \frac{\text{sales of individual product}}{\text{total sales of all products}}$$

C-V-P formula

$$X = \frac{\text{fixed costs (for all products) + income (for all products)}}{\text{weighted average CMU (or CM\%) for all products}}$$

$$\text{Weighted average CMU (or CM\%)} = \frac{\text{total contribution margin (all products)}}{\text{total unit (or dollar) sales (all products)}}$$

or

$$= \text{sum of each individual product's CMU (or CM\%) multiplied by each product's respective sales mix \%}$$

Managerial Accounting

Managerial Accounting

Jack L. Smith, Ph.D., C.P.A.
Professor of Accounting, University of South Florida — School of Accountancy

Robert M. Keith, Ph.D., C.P.A.
Professor of Accounting, University of South Florida — School of Accountancy

William L. Stephens, D.B.A., C.P.A.
Professor of Accounting, University of South Florida — School of Accountancy

McGraw-Hill Book Company
New York St. Louis San Francisco Auckland Bogotá Hamburg London
Madrid Mexico Milan Montreal New Delhi Panama Paris São Paulo
Singapore Sydney Tokyo Toronto

MANAGERIAL ACCOUNTING

Copyright © 1988 by McGraw-Hill, Inc. All rights reserved. Printed in the United States of America. Except as permitted under the United States Copyright Act of 1976, no part of this publication may be reproduced or distributed in any form or by any means, or stored in a data base or retrieval system, without the prior written permission of the publisher.

2 3 4 5 6 7 8 9 0 V N H V N H 8 9 2 1 0 9

ISBN 0-07-058990-9

This book was set in Times Roman by Progressive Typographers, Inc. The editors were Michael R. Elia, Robert D. Lynch and Peggy C. Rehberger; the designer was Merrill Haber; the production supervisor was Diane Renda. Drawings were done by J&R Services, Inc. Von Hoffmann Press, Inc., was printer and binder.

Library of Congress Cataloging-in-Publication Data

Smith, Jack L.
    Managerial accounting.

    1. Managerial accounting.   I. Keith, Robert M.
II. Stephens, William L.   III. Title.
HF5657.4.S55   1988   658.1′511   87-17223
ISBN 0-07-058990-9

About the Authors

Jack L. Smith is a professor at the School of Accountancy at the University of South Florida. He received a Ph.D. in accounting at the University of Mississippi and is a CPA. Professor Smith is a member of the American Accounting Association, the AICPA, the Florida Institute of Certified Public Accountants, the National Association of Accountants, and the Florida Association of Accounting Educators, and has been active in a number of state and local professional organizations. Professor Smith was the chamber faculty advisor of the Delta Gamma Chapter of Beta Alpha Psi. He is also active in various local and national professional development programs and has received awards as an outstanding discussion leader. In addition to *Accounting for Financial Statement Presentation,* an MBA-level introductory financial accounting text coauthored with Robert M. Keith, and Accounting Principles, 2d edition, Professor Smith is the author of a number of articles in the *Journal of Accountancy, The Florida CPA,* and the *Financial Executive,* as well as two award winning articles published in the May and July 1978 issues of *Management Accountant.* In addition to his writing activities, Jack Smith is also an experienced teacher. His 20 years of working closely with students make this edition of the principles book one that actively involves students in the learning process.

Robert M. Keith is a professor at the School of Accountancy at the University of South Florida. He received his Ph.D. in accounting from the University of Alabama and holds the CPA certificate. While his research interests center on financial accounting, Professor Keith also has a strong interest in accounting education at both the college and professional levels. He received the first Outstanding Accounting Faculty Award by the Delta Gamma Chapter of Beta Alpha Psi and was voted an outstanding discussion leader four years in a row by CPA participants in continuing professional education seminars sponsored by the Florida Institute of CPAs. In addition to papers presented at regional meetings of the AAA, Professor Keith's research has appeared in the *Journal of Accountancy* and *The Florida CPA.* He was also a coauthor with Jack L. Smith of *Accounting for Financial Statement Presentation,* published in 1979 and Accounting Principles, 2d edition. Professor Keith is a member of the American Accounting Association, the AICPA, and the Florida Institute of Certified Public Accountants, and has served on the editorial board of *The Florida CPA.*

William L. Stephens is a professor at the School of Accountancy at the University of South Florida. He has a DBA from Florida State University and is a CPA. His primary research and teaching interests are in the area of managerial and cost accounting. Active in continuing professional education projects, Professor Stephens is also a member of the American Accounting Association, the National Association of Accountants, and the Florida Institute of Certified Public Accountants. For 13 of the last 14 years, he has been the faculty advisor to the Delta Gamma Chapter of Beta Alpha Psi which has been recognized as a Superior Chapter for 12 straight years. Author of numerous articles in *The Journal of Accountancy,* and *The Accounting Review,* Professor Stephens has also coauthored *Accounting Principles,* 2d edition, a financial accounting text, and a study guide for a financial accounting text.

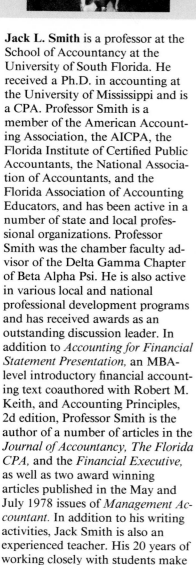

To Diane, Kristie, and Scott

To Leanne and Rob

In memory of my parents, Lois and Lewis Stephens, who raised their children
    To love and respect their parents
    To believe in themselves
    To have empathy for the less fortunate
    To develop a "punnish" sense of humor, and
    To love, honor, and serve the Lord.

CONTENTS

[ix]

PREFACE

This text, along with its companion, *Financial Accounting,* are intended for use in a two-semester or three-quarter sequence by college students who plan a business career, who intend to enter the accounting profession, and who are interested in broadening their business background. While the two books are naturally suited to be used together in the financial accounting–managerial accounting sequence, they are written in such a manner that either may be used in combination with any other financial or managerial accounting textbook.

Our assumption in writing this text is that your students' exposure to business and/or accounting has been limited to a course(s) in financial accounting. Therefore, we have carefully explained and illustrated, where appropriate, all new business terms and practices as they are first introduced.

We view our text as being neither conceptual nor procedural but a balanced blend of the two. Students are informed *why* information is accounted for in a certain manner. The why is reinforced by illustrating *how* the accounting is accomplished. Students can better grasp concepts through sufficient attention to the procedures.

The primary emphasis throughout the text is on (1) the accountant's role in providing management with information to assist in the decision-making process, and (2) the use of that information by management in making both routine and nonroutine decisions. For accounting majors, the text redirects their focus from the external to the internal users. It forces them to think in terms of the meaning of the information they provide management, how the information is to be used, and how to present it in the most concise and understandable manner. In addition, the text provides the accounting major with a solid foundation for the later course in cost accounting. For nonaccountants, the text helps future managers realize how their own success depends substantially on an understanding of accounting information and on the ability to use that information to make good decisions.

IMPORTANT FEATURES IN THIS TEXT

We have incorporated into *Managerial Accounting* numerous pedagogical devices and techniques which we describe in this preface as general or specific. In the general category we include items that are presented in all chapters of the text, while in the pedagogical items we describe as specific are features found only in specific chapters.

GENERAL

■We have written this book in a lively style with extensive use of the active voice which we believe makes the material real and interesting and certainly more helpful to the student in learning and understanding it.

■Each of the six parts of the text is introduced by a section explaining its overall purpose and briefly describing its contents.

[xxi]

- Chapter objectives are given at the beginning of each of the 15 chapters.

- Margin notes are used extensively throughout the chapter to describe text material. Margin notes are also used to briefly indicate the objective of each exercise and problem in the back of each chapter.

- The text contains many well-illustrated charts, diagrams, and figures designed to help the student easily and quickly visualize concepts and relationships, and establish the proper perspectives underlying the material as it is explained.

- Real world examples extracted from sources such as *Forbes, Fortune, U.S. News & World Report,* and *Time,* provide the student with an opportunity to see how the principles of accounting are foundations of much that happens in the business world.

- Appendices are used to cover topics that may not be of interest to all users. The appendices are placed at the end of the chapters they relate to.

- Summaries are included at the end of each chapter.

- Important terms used in the chapter are presented again at the end of each chapter in the format of a glossary which includes references to the page where the term was first introduced.

- There are two different but parallel sets of problems to choose from for users who want to change the problems assigned from one year or term to the next.

- Check figures are located in the margin alongside the exercises and problems where they are most helpful to the student.

SPECIFIC

- Chapter 3 is a comprehensive discussion of variable, fixed, and mixed costs. The different types of variable and fixed costs are discussed in detail, and the accountant's view of these costs is compared to the view of the economist. The three methods of evaluating mixed costs (high-low, visual approximation, and least squares) are explained in a logical step-by-step manner.

- Coverage of cost-volume-profit analysis is divided into two chapters. Chapter 4 introduces the student to the basics of C-V-P analysis with emphasis on the importance of the contribution margin approach. Chapter 5 is concerned with the assumptions underlying C-V-P analysis—what they are, what they mean, and how the analysis has to be revised when the assumptions are no longer valid. Emphasis is placed on the assumptions concerning multiple product firms (the sales mix remains unchanged) and direct versus absorption costing (there is no change in the beginning and ending inventory in finished goods). The application of C-V-P analysis to absorption costing (when the results differ from direct costing) is examined in an appendix.

- Chapter 6 on relevant costing and special decisions is placed after cost-volume-profit analysis—so that students will already be familiar with the contribution margin approach—and before capital budgeting—so that they will have been introduced to short-run decisions before having to deal with the complexities of long-run decisions. EOQ models and the graphical approach to linear programming are included in appendices at the end of this chapter. In addition, the Japanese approaches to inventory management are discussed.

■ Chapter 7 includes a comprehensive discussion of both discounted cash flow and nondiscounted cash flow capital budgeting methods. Taxes are ignored until Chapter 8. The discussion explains what each method is; how each method is used in situations involving both even and uneven cash flows; and how the results of each method are to be interpreted. The chapter includes an introductory explanation of present value for those students who need some review of the basic concepts.

■ Chapter 8 is a comprehensive coverage of the tax considerations in capital budgeting. It includes an up-to-date discussion of the Tax Reform Act of 1986 and how the requirements of the Act affect capital budgeting analysis. Here again, both the discounted cash flow methods and nondiscounted cash flow methods are discussed in detail.

■ Chapters 9 through 11 are organized as a logical package. Chapter 9 contains a comprehensive master budget, fully discussed and illustrated, for both a manufacturer and a retailer. The example for the master budget is carried over to Chapter 10 on flexible budgeting, which compares and contrasts the two types of budgets. A clear and concise development of the relationship between the flexible budget and standard costing is given, contrasting their uses for planning, control, and product costing for cost centers within an organization. In Chapter 11, additional items are discussed concerning the analysis of cost centers, as a natural lead-in to the discussion of profit centers and investment centers. All issues related to this analysis (cost allocation, centralization versus decentralization, transfer pricing, and ROI) are self-contained in a single chapter rather than dispersed among several chapters as is typically the case in other managerial accounting textbooks.

■ Chapter 13 on process costing covers both the weighted average and FIFO methods in detail. The coverage of the two methods is completely independent, so it is not necessary to understand one method in order to cover the other method. In this way, an instructor can cover either or both methods. The discussion of standard process costing is discussed in an appendix.

■ Chapter 14 on financial statement analysis and interpretation is presented as an ongoing analysis of a corporation to make this topic interesting and useful to the student.

■ Chapter 15 on the statement of cash flows provides the student with the procedures for developing this new statement by either the "T-Account" method or the worksheet method. In the Solutions Manual, all problems in this chapter are solved using both methods; the instructor merely needs to indicate which method the student is to use.

SUPPLEMENTARY MATERIALS

Accompanying *Managerial Accounting* is a full array of supporting materials that include:

For the Instructor:

■ *Solutions Manual.* Answers to all the questions, exercises, and problems are contained in this comprehensive manual. The type is extra large and extra bold so that any transparencies made from the manual will be clearly seen by the student in the last row of the classroom.

The questions, exercises, and problems follow closely the textual material and learning objectives. Estimated time, difficulty levels, and descriptions of all exercises and problems are provided as an aid to the instructor in selecting material appropriate for the level of the course being taught.

■ *Teacher's Manual.* Designed to aid primarily graduate teaching assistants, adjuncts, and other part-time instructors, the teacher's manual contains comments, notes, illustrations, and examples that the authors have found useful in teaching managerial accounting. The solutions to the *Tests and Exams* are also included in the *Teacher's Manual.*

■ *Tests and Exams.* Two completely different yet parallel sets are available to provide the instructor with alternative testing options. Each shrink-wrapped package contains 20 copies of each test and each exam.

Both sets include tests that each cover two or three chapters (except for the single-chapter test on Chapter 8) and a final comprehensive examination covering Chapters 1 – 13.

■ *Test Bank.* For those instructors who wish to construct their own examinations, a manual containing nearly a thousand true/false, multiple choice, and short problem test questions arranged by chapter are available. These questions are also available in a computerized test-generation system.

■ *Overhead Transparencies.* An extensive set of teaching transparencies is available for classroom use as an aid in illustrating many of the concepts discussed in the text.

FOR THE STUDENT

■ *Study Guide.* A comprehensive study guide, prepared by Paul Williams from North Carolina State University contains chapter-by-chapter reviews together with an abundance of multiple-choice, fill-in, and true or false questions as well as numerous problems. Solutions to all these self-test items are found in the back of the *Study Guide.*

■ *Practice Set.* A manual practice set for use after chapter four. The practice set will consist of different modules that can be assigned independently. The topics covered will include job order costing, cost-volume-profit analysis, the master budget, standard costing and variance analysis, relevant cost analysis and decision making. This practice set is also available in a computerized format. The solution is available in a separate solutions manual.

■ *Microcomputer Spreadsheet.* Lotus 1-2-3 templates for solving selected exercises and problems at the end of the chapter are available.

■ *Worksheets.* Partially filled-in accounting worksheets for all problems in the text are reprinted with the problem headings and some preliminary facts to help students save time and concentrate on working out the essence of each problem.

ACKNOWLEDGMENTS

We wish to express our sincere appreciation to the many individuals who contributed their efforts to this project. Constructive criticism was gratefully received from David Byrd, Southwest Missouri State University; Dave Greenfield, University of California at Los Angeles; Charles Konkol, University of Wisconsin; Marc Massoud, Claremont McKenna College; Joseph J. Master, Stetson University; Jack Miller, Florissant Valley Community College; Ronald S. Rubin, San Francisco Community College and Robert Zwicker, Pace University.

We are indebted to our students at the University of South Florida — Sandy Chadwick, Lisa Hubbard, Gilda Braddish, Donna Armour, and Lisa Gonzalez — for their diligence in proofreading manuscript, galleys and/or page proofs, and for checking the accuracy of the *Solutions Manual, Test Bank* and *Achievement Tests.* We are also extremely grateful for the continued support of our department Chairman Robert J. West; for the valuable assistance of our colleague Celina Jozsi, who provided innumerable creative ideas and feedback on an "as needed" basis; and to Craig Hubbard who helped us understand the Tax Reform Act even before it became law.

We thank Florida Steel Corporation for letting us use their financial statements. We appreciate the efforts of Thomas G. Creed, Vice-President, for obtaining permission to use the statements.

We were most fortunate to have had the assistance of two outstanding individuals from the McGraw Hill editorial staff, who have become good friends over the years. Mike Elia, our manuscript editor, has become an integral part of our writing team, so integral in fact that we often think of our project as the Smith-Keith-Stephens-Elia book. Peggy Rehberger, our editing supervisor, handled the task of getting our text through production in an efficient, creative, timely, and personable manner.

Managerial
Accounting

Management Accounting and Key Underlying Concepts

The first part of this book lays a foundation for the remaining sections. Chapter 1 introduces the discipline of management accounting, which is the primary emphasis of the course. It explains what we mean by the term *management accounting*; it relates the discipline of management accounting to financial accounting and cost accounting; and it discusses the role of the accountant within an organization and the relationship of the management accountant to the management of that organization. It stresses how everything we do in management accounting and/or cost accounting is done to help management in three main areas: planning, controlling, and product costing. We feel it is important for you to know *why* accountants prepare reports and exactly how management uses the information contained in these reports. Without this understanding you would find the entire course a tedious progression of mechanics and procedures.

The first section also introduces several key cost concepts that are used extensively in this course. Only after you have learned what they are will you be able to use them properly in the many different tools that accountants use to assist management in the decision making process. Chapter 2 distinguishes total costs from average costs and product costs from period costs. Chapter 3 introduces variable, fixed, and mixed costs and explains how the different types of costs can be determined and used by accountants. In later chapters you'll see how important an understanding of these costs terms are to an understanding of many other important concepts.

Management Accounting and Key Underlying Concepts

The first part of this book lays a foundation for the remaining sections. Chapter 1 introduces the discipline of management accounting, which is the primary emphasis of the course. It explains what we mean by the term *management accounting;* it relates the discipline of management accounting to financial accounting and cost accounting; and it discusses the role of the accountant within an organization and the relationship of the management accountant to the management of that organization. It stresses how everything we do in management accounting and/or cost accounting is done to help management in three main areas: planning, controlling, and product costing. We feel it is important for you to know *why* accountants prepare reports and exactly how management uses the information contained in these reports. Without this understanding you would find the entire course a tedious progression of mechanics and procedures.

The first section also introduces several key cost concepts that are used extensively in this course. Only after you have learned what they are will you be able to use them properly in the many different tools that accountants use to assist management in the decision making process. Chapter 2 distinguishes total costs from average costs and product costs from period costs. Chapter 3 introduces variable, fixed, and mixed costs and explains how the different types of costs can be determined and used by accountants. In later chapters you'll see how important an understanding of these costs terms are to an understanding of many other important concepts.

CHAPTER 1

Management Accounting: An Introduction

You will learn the following by studying this chapter:

- What *management accounting* is all about
- How management accounting differs from *financial accounting*
- What *cost accounting* is and how it relates to management accounting and financial accounting
- What *planning* and *control* are
- What accounting tools are used to help management plan its objectives and control its activities
- The difference between line responsibility and staff responsibility and what kind of responsibility the accountant has within the organization.

A basic idea you should have gotten from your financial accounting course is that an organization needs quantitative information to function. Management uses the best available quantitative information to make its organization function in the most effective and efficient manner. This information is provided by the accounting system to management, which uses it primarily to accomplish three broad purposes:

1. To provide financial statements to interested external users

2. To plan the operations of the organization in both the short and the long run

3. To control the results of its operations

FINANCIAL ACCOUNTING AND MANAGEMENT ACCOUNTING

Financial accounting

In *financial accounting* the responsibilities of the accountant are to record, classify, analyze, summarize, and report the results of the activities of the organization to creditors, stockholders and prospective investors, governmental bodies, labor unions, environmental organizations, and others. For corporations, the reports to external users are in the form of four general-purpose financial statements—the income statement, the statement of retained earnings, the balance sheet, and the statement of changes in financial position. These financial statements are used by people who are trying to protect or enhance their investments in the organization as well as by others who have a special interest in it.

Management accounting

This book deals primarily with **management accounting,** also known as **managerial accounting,** and its role in the second and third purposes listed above: planning and control.

In management accounting accountants provide information for use by people within the organization—the managers—rather than for use by people outside the organization. Management uses this information for making decisions concerning the internal workings of the organization.

There are many different types of decisions for which managers need accounting information. Listed below are a few examples of typical questions that regularly confront managers:

1. What price should be set for a product line?

Decisions that need management accounting information

2. Should a product line be dropped?

3. Should old equipment be replaced with new equipment?

4. Has an employee performed well enough to warrant a bonus?

5. Should short-term borrowing be arranged to finance current operations?

In order for managers to make the best decision to resolve each of these questions, the management accountant must provide quantitative information to the managers that is timely and relevant. Only with this information can a manager properly plan and control the organization's operations.

Other Differences between Financial Accounting and Management Accounting

Basic differences

The two most basic differences between financial accounting and management accounting are:

Purposes

1. Financial accounting's purpose is to provide financial statements that will be meaningful to any interested parties; management accounting's purpose is specifically to assist management in planning and control.

Users

2. The people who use financial information are primarily external—that is, outside the organization; the people who use management accounting information are internal—that is, inside the organization.

There are several other differences:

Time orientation

3. The information that financial accountants gather relates primarily to the past; the information that management accountants deal with relates substantially to the future. Whereas financial accounting reports the results of past activities, management accounting often looks to the consequences of planned activities on the future.

Presentation restrictions

4. Much of the information that management accountants provide managers for making internal decisions is never made available to outside users—they never have any idea of what it entails or how it is prepared. As a result—and thankfully so—we don't have to worry about the same restrictions in the presentation of management accounting information as we do with financial accounting information. That is, what we generate only for internal use does not have to be consistent, conservative, objective, historical. For example, many decisions relate to the proper course of action a manager—and thus the firm—should take. Much of the information the manager needs to make these decisions depends on projections of future revenues and expenses. Since these projections are merely estimates—some would say calculated guesses—they need not be based on the actual recorded amounts of past transactions (i.e., they are not historical). Nor can they usually be verified by third parties (i.e., they are not objective). While it might be desirable that the information used for internal decisions fulfill numerous requirements—for example, managers probably wish that accountants' calculated guesses were more objective—the only requirement that internal information must fulfill is that it help managers make the best decisions on a timely basis.

Accounting system required?

5. Publicly held organizations are required by generally accepted accounting principles (GAAP) to provide financial accounting information to the external users—management has no choice. The users have the right to see the financial statements of the organization. Since the users of financial accounting are outside the organization, the main way they learn about how well management is performing is by studying the financial statements of that organization. No one is going to invest in or lend to an organization that has no financial accounting system or is unwilling to distribute its financial statements to interested parties.

On the other hand, whether or not an organization's accounting system produces management accounting information and makes it available to its managers is completely up to management itself. If management foolishly feels that it can make its many decisions without the help of management accounting information, then it does indeed have the option of doing without this valuable input.

Flexibility

6. Closely related to items 4 and 5 is the resulting lack of flexibility in the preparation of financial accounting reports, as compared to the high degree of flexibility that exists in the preparation of management accounting reports. The financial accountant has relatively little flexibility when deciding how much information to include in the financial statements, what the format of the statements will be, and when the financial statements will be prepared for the external users. These decisions are substantially dictated by generally accepted accounting principles. Conversely, the management accountant has a great deal of leeway. He or she can decide on the amount of detail to include in the reports to management, the format of these reports, and the timing of the reports. The only requirement for the management accountant is that the information provided be presented to the decision maker in the most useful format.

View of organization

7. Financial accounting usually takes a condensed view of the organization as a whole; management accounting takes a detailed view of segments of the organization. The management accountant helps managers at all levels of responsibility within an organization; therefore his or her reports are geared to the appropriate managerial level. The report may be for a division, a department, a product line within a department, or for one of several product-line foremen.

These seven differences are certainly not an exhaustive list of the differences between financial accounting and managerial accounting. If we used our imaginations, we could probably come up with quite a few more. The differences we've discussed are simply the ones we feel are the most basic to an understanding of how these two disciplines of accounting differ.

THE FINANCIAL ACCOUNTING MENTALITY

The accounting emphasis within many organizations is often placed primarily on the preparation of general-purpose financial statements for external users; much less emphasis is placed on providing information to management to help in the decision-making process. Financial accounting often takes precedence over management accounting.

"In Europe, many companies have one department to collect and analyze data for internal operations and another to prepare external reports. Some companies, like Phillips in the Netherland, even report to stockholders on the basis used to evaluate internal operations. By contrast, contemporary practice in the United States is to use for internal purposes conventions either developed for external reporting or mandated by such external reporting authorities as the Financial Accounting Standards Board and the SEC."

What some people refer to as the "financial accounting mentality" is the use of financial accounting information for internal purposes, even when that information causes distortions in the internal measurements. For example, when a company measures the performance of one of its divisions with ROI — net income of the division divided by the assets invested in that division — it is very likely that productive assets used by the division but leased from other divisions are included in the denominator only when *Statement #13* of the FASB specifies that they must be capitalized. Naturally, when leased assets are left out of the calculation, the ROI — an internal measurement — will overstate the return that is really being earned by the division. What accountants and financial executives need to do is "redirect their energies — and their thinking — from external reporting to the more effective management of their company's tangible and intangible assets. Internal accounting systems need renovation. . . . Internal accounting practices should be driven by corporate strategy, not by FASB and SEC requirements for external reporting."

Source: Robert S. Kaplan, "Yesterday's Accounting Undermines Production," *Harvard Business Review,* July–August 1984, pp. 95–101. Copyright © 1984 by the President and fellows of Harvard College; all rights reserved. Reprinted by permission of *Harvard Business Review.*

INTERRELATIONSHIP OF FINANCIAL AND MANAGEMENT ACCOUNTING

Financial and management accounting are different, but they are not different

Based upon our discussion of differences, it may seem like financial accounting and management accounting are completely separate disciplines. This would be an improper conclusion, however, because they are actually interrelated. For example, the historical information used in financial accounting is often helpful in evaluating future alternative courses of action that management is considering. Management makes a decision about the best future course based on what happened in the past. Later, when the results of that management decision occur, those results become financial information to be integrated into the financial statements. Financial accounting provides information to be used in management accounting decisions; those management decisions, in turn, yield financial results, which, of course, are of interest to people outside the organization.

A good example of the relationship between financial accounting information and management accounting information is the master budget, which we will cover in Chapter 9. The master budget is a basic tool of the management accountant, yet it depends on information from the income statement, the balance sheet, and the statement of retained earnings.

MANAGEMENT ACCOUNTING AND COST ACCOUNTING

One of the responsibilities of a financial accountant is to keep track of all costs related to the product to be sold by the organization. For many organizations the product (inventory) is a significant asset on the balance sheet and results in a significant expense (cost of goods sold) on the income statement. Therefore, it is important that the costs of the product represented as inventory be properly accounted for. The way an accountant determines the cost of inventory for an organization is by first determining all the costs that went into buying or producing all the units to be accounted for. Then, these costs are split up — or, as accountants like to say, ***allocated*** —

FIGURE 1-1
**Cost Accounting
(Planning, Control, and
Product Costing), Which Is
Part Financial Accounting
and Part Management
Accounting, Is Shown in
the Boxed Area**

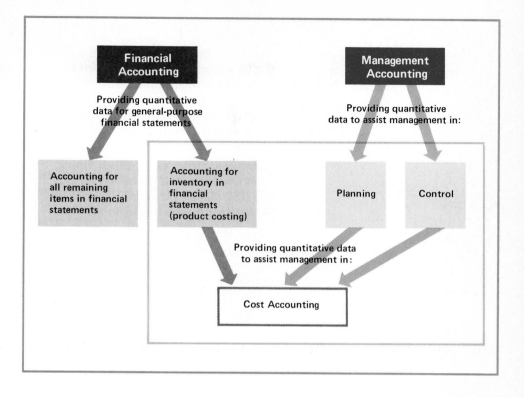

*Assigning costs to
inventory is product costing*

between the units sold and the units not yet sold. If we can (1) collect all the costs that
went into buying or producing all units, (2) calculate a cost for each unit bought or
produced, and (3) determine how many units were sold during a period, and how
many were unsold at the end of the period, then (4) we can determine an expense for
the units sold — commonly referred to as cost of goods sold — and place that amount
on the income statement. The units available for sale, but not yet sold, represent an
asset — the ending inventory — and we can similarly determine the costs to assign to
the inventory that we place on the balance sheet. This process of determining the
costs of the product and then allocating them between the income statement and
balance sheet is referred to as ***product costing.***

*Cost accounting is part
management accounting
and part financial
accounting*

The accountant responsible for product costing is the ***cost accountant.*** The cost
accountant's job, however, is not limited to product costing. The cost accountant is
part financial accountant and part management accountant, involved in a small part
of financial accounting (product costing) plus all of management accounting (assisting management in planning and control). Figure 1-1 distinguishes between financial
accounting and management accounting and shows how cost accounting relates to
the two. The figure shows that ***cost accounting*** includes all of management accounting plus that part of financial accounting known as product costing.

*Terminology is not
consistent for all users,
writers, and teachers.
But — when using our text,
it might be a good idea to
use our terminology*

The terms *management accounting* and *cost accounting* have gradually come to
mean different things to different people. For example, some people's definition of
management accounting embraces the product costing purpose — that is, they include planning, control, and product costing in the definition of management accounting. We refer to this combination as cost accounting. On the other hand, where
we include the product costing purpose as only one of three cost accounting purposes,
some people associate cost accounting strictly with product costing.

In addition, the term *management accounting* recently has been used in an even broader sense. The National Association of Accountants, in a recent pronouncement, included in the term "management accounting" *all* accounting functions performed in private organizations—that is, organizations that aren't CPA firms and aren't the government.[1] In this broadest sense, management accounting includes financial accounting, management accounting as we define it, tax accounting, and internal auditing.

Obviously, the terminology is not consistent among all who teach and practice these areas of accounting. For our purposes, *when we refer to management accounting, we mean assisting managers in planning and control. And when we refer to cost accounting, we mean assisting managers in planning, control, and product costing.*

PLANNING

Planning is setting goals and ways to achieve them

Planning in its most basic form involves the determination of two things: (1) the goals for an organization and (2) the way to achieve the goals. Management should not only know where it hopes to be or what it hopes to accomplish during a future period but should also know how it expects to reach these ends. Planning should take place at all levels within the organization. Because an organization is typically composed of subunits such as divisions, and each division itself is composed of subunits such as departments, the planning of an overall organization is only as good as the planning within each of the divisions, and for each division within each of its departments. Even the smallest subunit of an organization is involved in the planning process, and its plans must be coordinated with the plans of the overall organization.

Accountants use budgets to help managers plan

The tool used by the management accountant to assist management in the planning purpose is the *budget.* The budget is a formal quantitative expression of the goals set by management.

Exhibit 1-1 is a simple budget for a machine maintenance department for August, 1988. It shows, for example, that the maintenance department is expected to spend $43,000 for wages to repair machinery during August and $15,000 for a foreman to supervise the laborers. In total, the maintenance department is expected to spend $81,400 in August in order to efficiently maintain the machines of the production departments.

EXHIBIT 1-1
During August, $81,400 is expected to be spent to maintain machinery.

Machine Maintenance Department Budget August, 1988	
Supplies	$18,000
Utilities	3,400
Supervision	15,000
Rent	2,000
Wages	43,000
Total	$81,400

Budgets as Tools

Throughout this text we will present different types of budgets, each representing a different aspect of the planning process. Some examples follow.

[1] National Association of Accountants Management Practices Committee, *Objectives of Management Accounting,* Statements on Management Accounting No. 1B (New York: National Association of Accountants, 1982), p. 1.

1. The Master Budget (Chapter 9)

The master budget provides management with an overview of the plans for all operations—sales, production, purchasing, financing, etc. The master budget can warn a company of an impending deficiency of cash so that arrangements can be made to obtain short-term financing. Or it might indicate an availability of excess cash that can be profitably invested for a short period.

2. Relevant Cost Budgets for Special Decisions (Chapter 6)

This type of budget helps to evaluate nonrecurring decisions, such as whether or not to drop a product line or to accept a special order. To make decisions like these, budgeted income statements must be prepared for each alternative; the alternative that has the most favorable impact on profits is the one exercised.

3. Capital Budgeting (Chapters 7 and 8)

Organizations are often faced with the need to purchase additional property, plant, and equipment. The investment in such property normally requires a substantial commitment of resources, resulting in a significant increase in the organization's productive capacity and hopefully in the long-run profits as well. Capital budgeting analysis offers several methods to assist management in making these decisions.

CONTROL

After the planning process has been completed, that is, goals and the ways to achieve them have been determined, the next thing to do is put the plans to work. And once those plans are at work, it is necessary for managers to monitor the operation in order to see if they are achieving what they are supposed to. In other words, managers need to exert some control over the operations they manage. ***Controlling*** involves four things:

1. Putting the plans to work.

Control requires implementation, feedback, and corrective action

2. Observing those plans at work and gathering information on how well they are performing. The information collected to assess the performance of the organization in reaching its goals is often referred to as ***feedback.***

3. If the plans are not on track toward attaining the intended goals, as determined by the feedback, management must determine what action is necessary to get those plans back on track.

4. Taking action to remedy whatever may have caused the plans to go astray.

These steps indicate that the control function picks up where the planning function leaves off. The progression of steps from planning through control is shown in Figure 1-2 at the top of the next page.

Once the goals have been set, and the means for attaining them have been determined and the budget representing them has been formulated, it is essential that these plans and the budget be accepted by all personnel within the organization who are affected by them. The personnel affected by the plans should be informed of the purpose of the budget and how the budget can influence the attainment of their own personal goals, their department's goals, as well as the goals of the entire organization. If the personnel who are affected by the plans do not know what they are about or do not accept them, it will be difficult for management to implement the plans. If the plans are implemented by management, but without the support of the affected personnel, it will be difficult to properly control the ineffective plans.

A basic element of the control process is the accumulation of adequate, timely

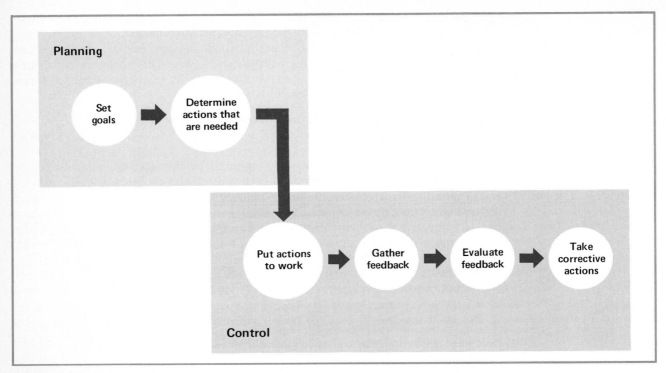

FIGURE 1-2 The Progression of Steps from Planning to Control

Accountants use performance reports to help managers control

information — feedback — reflecting how well the plans are working out at all levels within the organization. With this information, an accountant can prepare a ***performance report,*** which is the principal accounting tool for assisting management in controlling operations. A performance report compares a department's actual results with the budget for that department, and any differences between actual and budget are listed. Exhibit 1-2 portrays a simple version of a performance report for the maintenance department. The original budget for this department was shown in Exhibit 1-1.

EXHIBIT 1-2
The performance report indicates that $85,550 was actually spent during August, 1988, $4,150 in excess of the $81,400 budgeted. The material differences in the third column should be investigated.

Machine Maintenance Department Performance Report August, 1988			
	Budget	**Actual**	**Differences**
Supplies..............................	$18,000	$20,700	$2,700 over budget
Utilities..............................	3,400	5,000	1,600 over budget
Supervision...........................	15,000	14,800	200 under budget
Rent.................................	2,000	2,000	—
Wages	43,000	43,050	50 over budget
Totals	$81,400	$85,550	$4,150 over budget

This performance report offers feedback on how well the maintenance department met its plans — represented by the budget. And this feedback indicates that the department's cost of supplies ($2,700 over budget), utilities ($1,600 over budget), and wages ($50 over budget) were higher than expected; supervision costs ($200 under budget) were lower than expected; and rent was exactly as predicted.

Having received this report from an accountant, a manager can immediately see where the plans are working and where they aren't. It appears from the performance report in Exhibit 1-2 that the only item for which the plans are working is the rent. This does not mean, however, that management should devote considerable time and energy to analyzing the causes of the differences for the remaining four items. Usually, only large differences will warrant investigation.

Management by Exception

Should all differences be investigated?

Investigating differences can be time-consuming and costly, requiring careful attention and evaluation by the manager and workers most closely associated with the operation that did not meet the budget. Unless the benefits from knowing the cause of a difference exceed the costs of determining the cause, investigation is not warranted. The costs of investigating a difference are probably about the same regardless of the size of the difference — it shouldn't take any longer to determine the cause of a large difference than it does for a small difference. The potential benefits, however, from investigating a large difference should be much greater than for a small difference. Therefore, the net effect — benefits from investigation less costs of investigation — will probably be positive for large differences (those considered material in amount), but negative for small differences. Since the net effect is positive only for the differences that are large in relation to the amount budgeted — the **material differences** — these are the ones to receive the time and attention needed to determine their causes. The spotlighting of material differences for investigation is referred to as *management by exception.*

Only material differences should be investigated

Although the accounting profession has long been working on a project to determine specifically what is meant by a material amount, no conclusions have as yet been reached, and many accountants doubt if they can be. What is material to one person may not be to another. Each manager must set his or her own guidelines for determining what is material or significant, and use this guide for spotlighting differences to investigate. For example, the manager of the maintenance department whose performance report is shown in Exhibit 1-2 may decide that any variance that exceeds 10% of the original budget is material and is to be investigated.

In Exhibit 1-2, the differences for supervision and wages would probably both be considered immaterial, since each one represents a very small variation from the budget. On the other hand, the differences for supplies and utilities each represent a substantial variation from the amounts budgeted. Since these differences are material, they would probably be spotlighted for investigation.

Should we investigate favorable differences too?

Both of the differences spotlighted for investigation were over budget — which accountants commonly refer to as *unfavorable differences.* Does this mean that we only investigate unfavorable differences and ignore those that are favorable — that is, under budget? Of course not. Large favorable differences would be examined as well. They might reveal some ways to do things better or for less cost than was originally planned. Once uncovered, they could be instituted as part of the routine.

Cost Benefit

We pointed out above that investigating material differences rather than immaterial differences is more likely to produce benefits that exceed the costs of investigation. We could express this another way by saying that the results of *cost-benefit analysis* indicate that it is *cost-effective* to investigate only material differences.

Cost-benefit analysis is an approach that should be considered in developing any good management accounting system. It is based on the premise that the costs of providing management with information cannot be justified unless the information pays for itself — the benefits must be greater than the costs of preparation. This concept is obviously applicable to the determination of which variances to investigate, but it is also applicable to every other topic in management accounting as well. For example, the only reason that master budgets or capital budgets are prepared in an organization is that management feels that the value of having the information exceeds the costs of getting it.

We feel that every management accounting tool that we introduce in this book is usually cost-effective for an organization to use. However, in a situation where the cost of providing information — or of providing more information or better information — exceeds the benefits of having and using that information, then we feel just as strongly that the information is not needed and should not be prepared.

Responsibility for Differences

Managers can't control unless responsibilities are assigned

It is important that responsibilities are clearly assigned for all activities within an organization. The managers of all departments within the organization need to know exactly what their responsibilities are so that they know for which activities they will be held accountable and for which ones they will not be held accountable. It should then come as no surprise if, for example, the manager of the maintenance department is asked to explain why the cost of supplies, shown in Exhibit 1-2, turned out to be $2,700 over budget.

If the maintenance manager was not informed that he was responsible for spending the budgeted amount for supplies of $18,000, several problems may have occurred: (1) He may not have made a complete effort to make sure the budget was attained; (2) he may have felt that it was unfair when he was blamed for the costs being over the budget; or (3) he may have taken no effort to evaluate the cause of the difference or to take corrective action to prevent recurrence.

Analysis of Differences

Once we have decided which differences are large enough to investigate and who is responsible for them, we next need to determine the cause and corrective action needed for each difference.

For example, referring again to the supplies in Exhibit 1-2, we may learn that the $2,700 difference was due to the following three causes:

1. The purchase price of supplies was higher than anticipated.

2. There was more than normal waste during production because the supplies were of poor quality.

3. The number of times that machines required maintenance was more than usual for the month.

Each of these three causes would be studied to determine if any corrective action need be taken to prevent recurrence. The maintenance department manager may find out from the purchasing agent that the first two causes can be rectified by changing suppliers. A new supplier may agree to sell a better-quality material at a lower price if purchases are made in substantially larger quantities, resulting in significant quantity discounts.

Looking into the third cause, the manager may determine that more maintenance was required than was expected because several machines were run on double rather than single shifts, a situation that was not properly anticipated in the budget. In this case, no corrective action is warranted, but the next budget must be adjusted to reflect the increased maintenance required.

In Chapter 10 we will discuss in more detail how to determine, evaluate, and establish corrective actions for differences found in the performance report.

RELATIONSHIP OF PLANNING AND CONTROL

Planning without control is like a ship without a rudder; control without plans is like a ship without a compass

It is essential that planning and control interact with each other for an organization to reach its goals. However, the interaction between planning and control is not quite as simple as we depicted in Figure 1-2. In that diagram we showed a distinct beginning and end — first there was planning, and then there was control. Although we definitely do need to have plans before we can control, the reverse is also true — we need to control before we can do a good job of making new plans. Unless we have the feedback of the control process, it's not possible to revise our expectations for upcoming periods in order to set new goals and the means of attaining them.

A better way to show the interrelationships of planning and control is presented in the diagram in Figure 1-3.

Although the first step for a new organization must be planning, once initial plans have been implemented there will never again be an abrupt beginning, or ending, of this continuous process. Managers do not postpone the control function while planning is taking place and then cease their planning until the control steps are completed. Instead, the planning function is constantly taking place and being improved upon at the same time that the control procedures are being applied.

FIGURE 1-3 The Interrelationship of Planning and Control

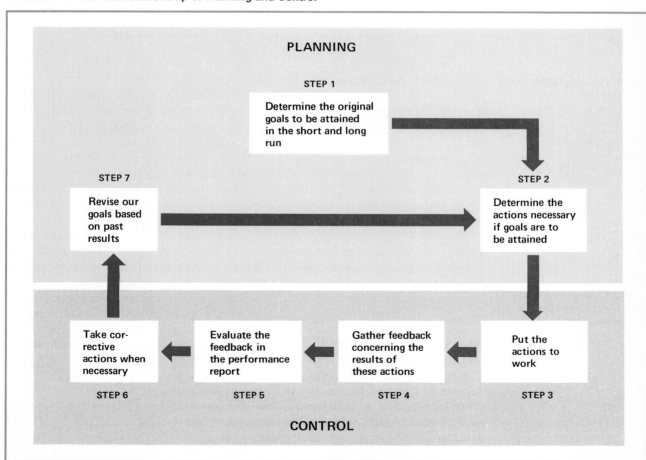

PLANNING

STEP 1
Determine the original goals to be attained in the short and long run

STEP 7
Revise our goals based on past results

STEP 2
Determine the actions necessary if goals are to be attained

STEP 6
Take corrective actions when necessary

STEP 5
Evaluate the feedback in the performance report

STEP 4
Gather feedback concerning the results of these actions

STEP 3
Put the actions to work

CONTROL

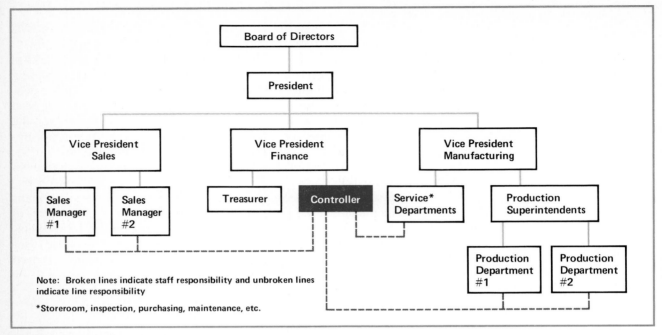

FIGURE 1-4 Organization Chart of a Manufacturer
The organization chart shows that the controller—the chief accounting executive—reports to the vice president for finance. It also indicates that the controller serves in a staff (advisory) capacity to all other departments: sales, production, and service.

ROLE OF ACCOUNTING WITHIN THE ORGANIZATION

Accountants give information and advice to managers—they do not make decisions for managers

The role of the accounting department, and the chief accounting executive, the **controller,** is to provide information that managers need in making decisions. The controller gives managers advice that helps them make decisions; he or she does not make the decisions for managers. The controller is in a position of staff responsibility rather than line responsibility. **Staff responsibility** is the responsibility of giving advice, counsel, or service to other departments; **line responsibility** is the responsibility of making decisions and giving directives that guide the activities toward the organization's goals.

Figure 1-4 depicts a simplified organization chart for a manufacturer. The figure shows that the controller and the accounting department report directly to the vice president of finance. It also shows that the accounting department assists the selling and manufacturing departments in a staff—advisory—capacity.

The controller is responsible for more than the planning and control aspects of management accounting. The controller's responsibilities also include general accounting, internal audit, and taxes, among others. Although the controller is involved in much more than merely management accounting, we will focus primarily on the role of the controller as a management accountant.

The controller's relationship to department managers typically is a staff relationship. However, the controller has line responsibility over subordinate managers within the accounting department itself. The controller gives directives to the managers of general accounting, taxes, and internal audit departments, advising them how to run their respective departments.

The controller also exerts some line responsibility over the managers of nonaccounting departments. Once the controller has determined the accounting procedures and methods for each department to follow, and has recommended to top management that they be followed by the other departments, the president of the organization then delegates to the controller the authority to implement the accounting system. When the controller gives directives to line managers as to their role in generating quantitative information, the controller acts in a line rather than a staff capacity.

Why would anyone resent the accountant?

Because the accounting department provides much of the information management uses in reaching decisions, sometimes it appears that the controller is doing the actual planning and controlling. This is why managers of other departments sometimes resent the accountants and resist their advice. These managers might feel that the accountants are attempting to run their departments and make their decisions. The accountants' role in the organization must be understood and agreed upon by the managers of other departments and the accountants themselves. Only through good communication and cooperation can they together carry out their functions and strive to achieve the goals of the organization.

APPROACH TO REMAINING CHAPTERS

In the following chapters we will tell you about the many types of decisions that managers make concerning planning, control, and product costing. For each decision, we will explain three things: (1) what each tool is, (2) what kind of information is needed to put together each tool, and (3) how each tool assists management.

CHAPTER SUMMARY

The purpose of *management accounting* is to provide the quantitative information that managers need to plan and control the activities of an organization in reaching its goals. In *planning,* managers do two things: determine the goals for the organization and determine how to achieve them. The tool used by accountants to assist managers in the planning function is the *budget* — the quantitative expression of the goals set by management.

In *controlling,* managers do four things: (1) put the plans to work; (2) observe the plans at work and gather information *(feedback)* on how well they are performing; (3) determine if corrective actions are needed so that final results will be in line with the plans; and (4) take the necessary actions to remedy any problems that may exist. The tool used by accountants to assist managers in the control function is the *performance report.* The performance report compares the actual results to the budget so that the material differences can be spotlighted.

Good planning and control are both essential if an organization is to reach its goals. Neither is more important than the other. Effective planning is not possible without good controls and meaningful control cannot come about without thoughtful planning.

The *controller,* as the chief accounting officer within an organization, is in charge of the accounting department. The accounting department's relationship to other departments involves *staff* rather than *line* responsibilities. By providing information to managers, the accounting department gives advice, counsel, and service to the other departments. It does not make the decisions that affect the activities taken by these departments to reach their goals.

IMPORTANT TERMS USED IN THIS CHAPTER

Budget The tool used by management accountants to assist management in the planning function. It is a quantitative representation of the goals set by management. (page 8)

Control A management activity directed toward achieving the organization's goals. It involves the following four steps: (1) putting the plans to work, (2) observing the plans at work and gathering information (feedback) on how well the organization is performing, (3) determining if corrective actions are needed to get the future results back in line with the plans, and (4) taking action to remedy any problems that exist. (page 59)

Controller The chief accounting executive within an organization. (page 14)

Cost accounting An accounting system for providing managers with the quantitative information they need in planning and controlling (management accounting) and in determining the cost of a product (a part of financial accounting). (page 7)

Cost-benefit analysis An approach to developing a good management accounting system that is based on the premise that the costs of providing management with information can be justified only if the benefits to the organization from having and using that information exceed the costs of its preparation. (page 11)

Feedback The information collected to assess the performance of the organization in reaching its goals. (page 9)

Financial accounting The accounting system for providing managers with the quantitative information they need to prepare financial statements for external users. (page 3)

Line responsibility The responsibility of making decisions and giving commands that directly affect the attainment of an organization's goals. (page 14)

Management accounting The accounting system for providing the quantitative information managers need in planning and controlling. Also referred to as managerial accounting. (page 4)

Management by exception Spotlighting the material differences in a performance report as the ones that warrant investigation. (page 11)

Material differences Those differences in a performance report that are large in relation to the amount budgeted. (page 11)

Performance report The principal accounting tool for assisting management in the control function. It displays the budget, the actual results, and any differences between budget and actual. (page 10)

Planning Setting an organization's goals and deciding how to attain them. (page 8)

Product costing The process of determining the costs of a product and then allocating them between the income statement (as cost of goods sold) and the balance sheet (as inventory). (page 7)

Staff responsibility The responsibility of giving advice, counsel, or service to other departments. (page 14)

QUESTIONS

1. What is meant by the term *planning,* and what is the management accountant's role in this function?

2. Discuss several differences in management accounting and financial accounting.

3. Since financial accounting is required for most organizations, it is a much more important accounting discipline than is management accounting, which is purely voluntary. Discuss.

4. "Management accounting is nothing more than a modern term to describe cost accounting." Comment.

5. Discuss what is meant by the term *product costing.*

6. Explain what is meant by the term *management by exception.*

7. When a manager is evaluating the differences between actual and budgeted results on a performance report, the term *management by exception* means that the manager is concerned with *all unfavorable* differences. Discuss.

8. It should be obvious how a performance report assists management in the control function. But how does it help in the planning function?

9. "Planning is a more vital management function than control." Comment.

10. "Accountants assist management by doing the planning and controlling of management's routine decisions." Do you agree? Explain.

11. "The controller does plan in a special sense." Explain what is meant by this statement.

12. Discuss several different types of routine and nonroutine decisions that managers must make and for which accountants can generate relevant information.

13. Explain what we mean by the term *cost-benefit analysis.*

14. A college professor of management accounting was teaching class one night, explaining why a particular approach to making a certain decision was conceptually superior to all others, even though it was probably more complicated, more time-consuming, and more costly than other approaches. One of her students remarked that at his company the same type of decision is usually made with a much more simplistic approach and that the managers at his company feel that the approach must be pretty good because they've been quite successful for several years. The student wanted to know why the class was wasting its time learning something that probably wasn't being used in the real world. If you were the teacher, how might you respond to the student — after you had calmed down?

15. The text discussed a variety of ways that management accounting and financial accounting differ. This was not a completely exhaustive list, however, for there are some other differences, and similarities, that can be mentioned. This question concerns some of those other items that were not discussed in the text.

    For each item below, you are to explain how you think management accounting and financial accounting may be the same and/or may differ, based upon what you have learned so far.

    a. The frequency with which reports are prepared
    b. The timeliness of the information to the user when he or she receives a report
    c. The degree of emphasis on precision and accuracy
    d. The necessity of being audited
    e. The existence of a conceptual framework
    f. The knowledge of who the user is and exactly what the user is doing with the information

16. Does a controller within an organization have line responsibility or staff responsibility? Explain.

17. Generally accepted accounting principles provide guidelines for the preparation of general-purpose financial statements. Do the same principles serve as guidelines for the preparation of reports to management for internal decisions?

18. The controllers of Companies A and B are discussing how they help management control costs with the aid of performance reports. The controller of Company A says that he examines all variances larger than $500. The controller of Company B (which is much larger than Company A) responds that variances as small as $500 are ignored and only those variances greater than $2,500 are investigated. Which controller is correct in the variances he selects for investigation?

19. A performance report has recently been prepared for one of the production departments of the Hi-Tech Company, and the controller and superintendent disagree about which differences to investigate. The superintendent wishes to investigate all unfavorable differences, and the controller expresses apprehension about such a policy. The performance report is shown as follows:

	Budget	Actual	Difference
Materials	$ 50,000	$ 60,000	$(10,000)
Labor	75,000	68,000	7,000
Utilities	6,000	6,100	(100)
Supplies	8,000	7,800	200
Fuel	16,000	16,000	-0-
Totals	$155,000	$157,900	$(2,900)

As the controller, which differences would you recommend be investigated? Why wouldn't you suggest investigation of all differences? Would you suggest investigating favorable as well as unfavorable differences? Why?

20. How would you react to a production manager's criticism to the controller that the accounting department was attempting to run her operation rather than merely keeping records? Instead of providing information for management's use, it sometimes appeared to the manager that the controller was attempting to do the planning and controlling himself.

CHAPTER 2

An Introduction to Cost Accounting Systems

After studying this chapter, you will understand the following:

- The different types of costs that management accountants need to be aware of when preparing reports to management
- What management accountants mean by *activity* and *centers of activity*
- How the concept of activity is used to distinguish between *total costs* and *average costs*
- What a *product cost* is, what a *period cost* is, and how to distinguish them
- How a manufacturing operation basically differs from a retailing operation
- That a retailer has only one type of inventory to be reported, whereas a manufacturer has three types of inventory to be concerned about
- How product costs relate to the inventories for a retailer and for a manufacturer
- How to trace the flow of costs from purchases through to the cost of goods that are sold
- How to prepare an income statement and supporting schedules for a manufacturer

It is the job of the accountant to provide managers with quantitative information. Managers use this information for making a wide variety of decisions. A few examples of the many different decisions regularly confronting managers include:

Different decisions facing managers

- How much should be recognized as the cost of each unit produced and what is the total amount to be expensed when these units are sold?
- What should be the sales price for the units awaiting sale to customers?
- How does a change in the selling price of a product affect the net income generated by that product?
- How many units need to be sold to generate a desired profit for the organization?
- Is a particular product generating sufficient profit? If not, should the firm discontinue making that product?
- Should a special order be accepted?
- Has a manager adequately controlled the costs of operating his or her department during the previous period?
- Should the productive capacity of the firm be enlarged?

DIFFERENT WAYS OF REGARDING THE SAME COSTS

The decision to be made in each of the above examples is based on costs. However, each situation is different, and so may be the cost information that is needed to make the best decision.

Management accountants often use the phrase "different costs for different purposes," meaning that in each decision situation, management has a specific purpose for needing cost information, which differs from the needs for other decisions. And the accountant needs to supply just the right cost information for management to accomplish each purpose.

Because we are going to be concerned with many different kinds of costs, let's begin with the most basic definition of cost:

What is "cost"?

Cost is a measurable sacrifice of resources exchanged for goods or services.

This definition is way too broad to be of any use to us, so we need to tighten it up a bit and begin to examine different ways that costs can be classified. A cost can be classified depending on how you look at it. To see what we mean, consider the following example:

EXAMPLE 2-1

THE JELLYBEAN BUSINESS

Robbie Ragin has just finished his freshman year at State College during which he financed his education by selling gourmet jellybeans which he made at his fraternity house. At the beginning of his freshman year he paid $100 for several mixing bowls and utensils, $750 for 500 bags of sugar, and $5,000 for a special blend of molasses that had a variety of food colors already mixed in. In addition, he paid $130 for 5,500 Ziploc bags that held 1 pound of jellybeans.

During the year Robbie made and sold 5,000 bags of jellybeans and used up all the sugar and molasses (wasting none of what had been purchased) in their production. Of the 5,500 bags that were purchased, 5,200 were used in production (of which 200 were wasted), and the remaining 300 were on hand at the end of the year. In order to sell so many bags of jellybeans, Robbie had to pay $0.25 per bag in commissions to his fraternity brothers to sell the bags door-to-door.

At the end of the year Robbie threw away the worthless bowls and utensils because they were encrusted with dried jellybean mix which had accumulated during the year because the bowls had never been washed. He kept the unused bags, however, just in case he should decide to go into business again at some time in the future.

Now let's look at the various ways of classyifying the costs in this example.

Product costs and period costs

1.a. *Product costs* represent the costs that are assigned—as they are incurred—to the units that are being produced. They become the cost of the units produced and, later, the cost of the units that are sold. For Robbie they amount to $5,973.

Sugar	$ 750
Molasses	5,000
Bowls and utensils	100
Bags used ($130/5,500 = $0.0236 per bag × 5,200 bags)	123
Total product costs	$5,973

The 300 unused bags have a cost of $7 ($0.0236 × 300 bags) and will become a product cost in the future if Robbie ever goes back into business.

b. *Period costs* are those costs that are expensed when incurred. They are not part of the jellybean production process, so they do not become a part of the cost of the jellybeans. For Robbie the only period cost was the $1,250 in commissions that were paid to his fraternity brothers to sell the bags of jellybeans from door to door.

Variable and fixed costs

2.a. *Variable costs* fluctuate in total in response to changes in activity. The cost of molasses, sugar, Ziploc bags, and commissions are variable costs. They changed with the number of 1-pound bags made and sold — the changes in activity.

b. *Fixed costs* remain unchanged in total at all levels of activity. The cost of the mixing bowls would have been $100 whether Robbie had made and sold 1,000 bags of jellybeans or 5,000 bags.

Controllable and noncontrollable costs

3.a. *Controllable costs* are those that can be influenced by a manager during a period of time. Robbie should have been able to influence the amount of molasses, sugar, Ziploc bags, and commissions needed to produce and sell the 5,000 one-pound bags of jellybeans. Since he used 5,200 Ziploc bags in the production and sale of the 5,000 pounds of jellybeans, he wasn't able to influence his operation as efficiently as he might have — he wasted 200 Ziploc bags.

b. *Noncontrollable costs* are those that cannot be influenced by a manager during a period of time. Fortunately, there were not any costs that Robbie was unable to control.

Relevant costs and irrelevant costs

4.a. *Relevant costs* are those that are different for the alternatives being considered. Assume that Robbie considered using a prepackaged jellybean mixture rather than producing the jellybeans from scratch. If the prepackaged mixture had been used, there would have been no need to purchase molasses and sugar. The cost of the ingredients used to make the jellybeans (molasses and sugar vs. the ready-made packages) would have been different — they would have been relevant to the decision of how to make the jellybeans in the least costly way.

b. *Irrelevant costs* are those that are the same for the alternatives being considered. No matter which ingredients Robbie used to make the jellybeans, the same number of bags would have been needed, the mixing bowls would have been the same, and the fraternity brothers would still have been needed to sell the bags. All these items would have been the same regardless of which ingredients Robbie used in the jellybeans — they were irrelevant.

Different costs for different purposes

Depending on the situation to be evaluated, the accountant must decide which type of costs are the ones needed to help a manager make the correct decision. In some cases the accountant must present the costs as product costs or period costs (what is the cost of the jellybeans sold during the summer?); the manager may not need to know if the costs are relevant or irrelevant, variable or fixed. In other cases it may be more helpful for the manager to be aware of which costs are relevant or irrelevant (for instance, should the jellybeans be made with packaged or fresh ingredients?); the manager may not be as concerned with knowing if the costs are product or period, controllable or noncontrollable.

Costs may be classified in many ways

Now, before we finish, let us emphasize one more important point, just in case it isn't clear from our discussion of Robbie's jellybean business. The same cost may be classified in several different ways. For example, a cost may be a product cost, a relevant cost, a controllable cost, and a variable cost—all at the same time. There could be numerous other combinations of cost classifications as well. A cost cannot, of course, at the same time be both variable and fixed, or product and period, or relevant and irrelevant, or controllable and noncontrollable.

For Robbie the cost of jellybeans was a product cost, a variable cost, a controllable cost, and a relevant cost. The sales commission was a period cost, a variable cost, a controllable cost, and an irrelevant cost. Each other cost would have its own combination of cost classifications.

The list of cost classifications in the jellybean example represents only a portion of the many cost terms that will be discussed in this book. Some of them will be discussed in much greater detail in this chapter, while the other cost terms will be introduced at the appropriate time in later chapters of the book.

This chapter emphasizes product costs and period costs

In this chapter our primary emphasis will be on the distinction between product costs and period costs. But first we need to have a good understanding of three basic terms—activity, total costs, and average costs. A clear grasp of what they mean is essential to understanding much of the cost terminology that comes later.

TOTAL COSTS, AVERAGE COSTS, AND ACTIVITY

Making jellybeans is an *activity*. It is an activity that is measurable—by the number of bags of jellybeans that are produced and sold. It is an activity that has a cost—the dollars incurred to produce and sell that number of bags.

Making video games is also an activity—or more specifically, it is the summation of numerous activities needed to produce each of the many different components that make up a computer video game. Each of the activities is measurable in terms of the number of components produced. The costs of each activity can be accumulated and classified as product or period costs, variable or fixed costs, controllable or noncontrollable costs, etc. To properly classify the costs within an organization, you must first develop a good understanding of the term *activity*. We have used this term rather loosely so far, but in such a way that you should have a general feeling of what it means. We will now be more specific.

Activity: a measurement of accomplishment

Management accountants think of activity as something done to produce a result or an output that can be measured. To a management accountant **activity** should be a clear indicator of (1) what was done, (2) in a particular place or environment, (3) during a specific period of time, (4) to produce measurable results.

For example, the firm that manufactures computer video games employs trained technicians who assemble components into a complete game. The number of completed games assembled during a month is a rather good indicator of the activity of the assembly shop. The same firm also employs janitors who clean and tidy the assembly shop as well as other areas within the building. The number of square feet cleaned by the janitors would probably be a good way to measure the activity of the janitorial maintenance department, but it would be a poor way to measure the activity of the assembly shop.

Centers of activity: different types for different organizations

Management accountants regard these as two different **centers of activity**—subunits within an organization that perform a particular function or produce measurable results. In one case, the center of activity is the assembly department; in the other case, the center of activity is the maintenance department.

A manufacturing firm can be considered to be made up of many or perhaps only a few different centers of activity. For example, the production department could be a center of activity, and/or individual specialized groups could each be centers of activity within the production department. Other centers of activity could be the sales department or some large division within the firm. The entire firm itself could be considered a center of activity. However, the larger the center of the activity, the more complex it will be for management accountants to deal with and the less helpful will be the information that accountants provide to managers on a daily basis. For a retailer, the center of activity could be a storeroom; for a hospital, the intensive care wing; for a university, the College of Business Administration.

Activity can be measured in different ways

Activity can be measured in many different ways, depending on the type of organization and the types of centers of activity within that organization. For example, within the production department of a manufacturer, a good measure of activity is the number of units produced or the number of hours worked. For a storeroom, a good measure of activity could be the number of requisitions processed; for an intensive care wing in a hospital, the number of patients treated; for the College of Business Administration, the number of semester hours enrolled by students.

Total Costs and Average Costs

Total costs

The ***total costs*** for a center of activity are simply the sum of all costs related to that center for a specific period of time. For example, for Robbie's jellybean production as a center of activity, the total costs were $5,973; for his selling department as a center of activity, the total costs were $1,250.

Average costs = total costs ÷ activity

An ***average cost*** is simply the center of activity's total costs for the period divided by the activity during the period. For Robbie $5,973, total costs of production, divided by 5,000 bags produced and sold, results in an average cost of $1.19 per bag.

A production department calculates an average cost per unit produced (as in the jellybean example). A hospital might determine an average cost per patient serviced. And a college could compute an average cost per student semester hour enrolled.

The following example shows how an average cost is calculated for different centers of activity. In each case the total cost is the same but the centers of activity and the measure of activity differ.

Be sure you understand how to measure activity

The point of this simple example is that there is no single measure of activity that is applicable to all centers of activity. A meaningful measure of activity for one center might be meaningless for another. A suitable measure of activity for a center is the one that most logically influences the amount of total cost incurred during a period of time. For example, the number of units produced is a meaningful measure of activity for a production department—it has a significant influence on the total costs incurred. On the other hand, the number of units produced would be a silly way to measure the activity of a hospital or a College of Business Administration.

EXAMPLE 2-2

CENTERS OF ACTIVITY

Assume that the total costs for five different centers of activity are each $100,000. The average cost for each center is found by dividing the $100,000 by the measure of activity for that center.

Average Cost for Different Centers of Activity			
Center of Activity	**Possible Measure of Activity**	**Calculation**	**Average Cost**
Production department	50,000 units produced	$100,000 ÷ 50,000 units	$2 per unit
Sales department	$2 million of sales	$100,000 ÷ $2 million sales	5% of sales dollars
Storeroom	50,000 requisitions filled	$100,000 ÷ 50,000 requisitions	$2 per requisition
Intensive care wing	400 patients treated	$100,000 ÷ 400 patients	$250 per patient
College of Business Administration	20,000 student semester hours	$100,000 ÷ 20,000 hours	$5 per semester hour

In the following example, notice how Dan Kirby's confusion over the appropriate measure of activity caused him some financial distress.

EXAMPLE 2-3

DAN KIRBY

Dan Kirby, a student, wanted some tutoring prior to his first accounting exam and wondered how much it would cost. A friend who had been tutored the previous week recommended someone who was very good and who charged only $10. Dan contacted this tutor and arranged for an all-night, 10-hour session the night before the exam. At daybreak Dan was presented a bill for $50. Dumbfounded, he then learned that the rate was $5 per hour and that his friend needed merely 2 hours at this rate while he needed 10.

If Dan had only thought about it logically, he would have realized that tutoring costs are more closely related to the number of hours tutored at $5 per hour than to the number of sessions of unspecified duration at $10 per session. The best measure of activity would have been the number of hours tutored—not the number of tutoring sessions.

Basic Definitions and What's to Come

Many of the concepts to follow in this and later chapters are based on the definitions of total costs, average costs, and activity just presented. Thus, a complete understanding of these terms and how to use them is critical before you proceed.

PRODUCT COSTING

Preparing financial statements and publishing them for interested external parties is the ultimate purpose of financial accounting. For an organization that generates revenue from the sale of a product, the costs of the units to be sold must be fully accounted for and represented in the financial statements.

The Cost of Goods Sold account, found on the income statement, indicates the costs associated with the quantity of units sold during the period. The balance sheet account

PRODUCT COSTS

The heart and soul of a good cost accounting system

"Increased competition, inflation, and greater attention to interim reporting necessitate the revision of many companys' cost accounting systems. . . . The objective of a new cost accounting system should include accurate product costing, cost control, identifying variances, integrity of inventory accounts, and management information."

The starting point in the development of a useful cost system is with the product costs themselves. "From a study of up-to-date material control and profitability reporting systems in several Fortune 500 compa-

nies and many smaller companies, the one overwhelming conclusion that we have is that, in American industry, knowledge of individual product costs is a strategic matter that companies must address to maintain their competitive position. The design and installation of an up-to-date cost system are not trivial undertakings, but if your cost system creaks each time the company moves, action is indicated."

Rather than having an understanding of cost accounting that starts out creaking somewhat, be sure to take all the time you need to completely understand what prod-

uct costs are, and how they flow through a company's cost accounts. Otherwise the topics of job order costing and process costing, direct costing and absorption costing, and standard costing will be more difficult than they need be.

Source: Robert G. Eiler, Walter K. Goletz, and Daniel P. Keegan, "Is Your Cost Accounting Up to Date?" *Harvard Business Review,* July–August 1982, pp. 132–end. Copyright © 1982 by the President and Fellows of Harvard College; all rights reserved. Reprinted by permission of *Harvard Business Review.*

Inventory represents the costs associated with the quantity of unsold units at the end of a period.

It is the responsibility of the cost accountant to determine the costs to assign to cost of goods sold and the costs to assign to inventory.

Product costing: costing inventory and cost of goods sold

The process of determining the costs of all units that can be sold, and then allocating these costs between the units sold during the period (cost of goods sold) and the units unsold at the end of the period (inventory) is referred to as *product costing. Only product costs are used in product costing, not period costs.* Let's now take a closer look at the difference between product costs and period costs and some examples.

Product Costs and Period Costs

Product costs are inventory costs when incurred

Product costs are costs that are closely associated with units produced by a manufacturer or purchased for resale by a retailer or wholesaler.

Examples of product costs are the costs of materials and labor used in production by a manufacturer and the invoice price of merchandise purchased by a retailer. Product costs are assigned to the product when they are incurred and at the same time are classified as an asset, inventory.

Product costs are assets until the units are sold

Product costs are considered assets when incurred, because they are resources that are expected to provide future economic benefits to the firm. When the units to which product costs are assigned are finally sold, these costs then become an expense, cost of goods sold. For example, the costs of molasses, sugar, and bags used in producing bags of jellybeans for Robbie are product costs. In addition, if Robbie were renting and insuring a sales booth, the related insurance and rental costs would also be product costs. These costs are combined in making the jellybeans — an asset — and are considered an asset until the jellybeans are sold. Only at the moment of sale do the costs of molasses, sugar, and bags become an expense — as a part of cost of goods sold.

Your initial instinct may be to think of these costs as expenses instead of assets — which indeed they will become — but not when they are incurred.

Product costs are assets until the product is sold. At the moment of sale, several things happen:

Product costs are expensed when units are sold

1. The economic benefit, sales revenue, is realized. There is no longer any "future" economic benefit to be realized.

2. Thus, the asset expires.

3. No longer recognizing the product cost as an asset, it is now recognized as an expense, cost of goods sold.

4. The cost of goods sold is matched with the sales revenue on the income statement.

To condense the discussion above, we can merely say that ***product costs*** *are (1) assigned to inventory when they are incurred and (2) expensed when the units to which they are assigned are later sold.*

Period costs are expensed when incurred; they are not assets

Period costs *are costs that are recognized as expenses as soon as they are incurred. They are not assigned to the product; instead, they are immediately assigned to the income statement as an expense of that period.* For Robbie the commission of $1,250 given to his friends for selling the jellybeans is a period cost, not a product cost.

Period costs are not assets, for they are not expected to provide any future economic benefits to the organization. *The benefits provided by period costs are realized fully when the costs are incurred and are recognized in the current period.* Examples of period costs include sales representatives' commissions, administrative salaries, and transportation-out costs for units sold.

How to distinguish product costs from period costs

The flow diagram in Figure 2-1 gives a general picture of how to determine whether a cost is a product cost or a period cost, and how and when to account for each.

It is important to classify product costs and period costs correctly. If these costs are classified incorrectly, they will be expensed at the wrong time and the financial

FIGURE 2-1
How to Determine Product Costs and Period Costs

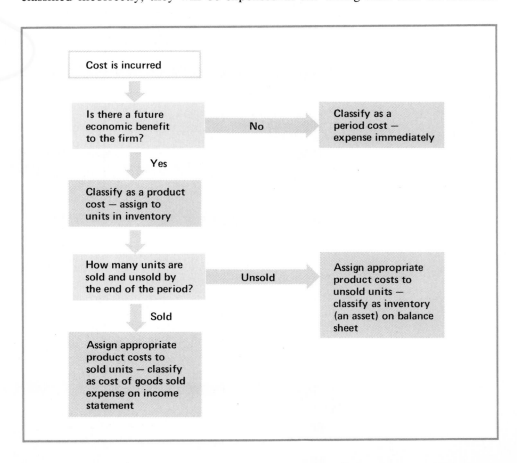

statements for the period will be incorrect. To see what effect an incorrect product cost vs. period cost classification can have on the income statement as well as on the balance sheet, consider the following situation.

Let's assume that a manufacturer incurs $50,000 in some department but is not sure if the costs are product costs or period costs. In addition, 10,000 units are produced but only 2,000 (20%) are sold.

If the costs are product costs, the $50,000, when incurred, would be assigned to the 10,000 units produced, but only $10,000 (20% of the $50,000) of this total would be expensed when the 2,000 units are sold. The remaining $40,000 would be in inventory—an asset on the balance sheet—at the end of the period. On the other hand, if the costs are period costs, then all of the $50,000 would be expensed as soon as the costs are incurred and none of the $50,000 would be in inventory at the end of the period.

Why it's important to distinguish product costs from period costs

If the costs are indeed product costs but are incorrectly classified as period costs, then the expenses will be overstated by $40,000 ($50,000 − $10,000) on the income statement and the inventory will be understated by $40,000 ($0 − $40,000) on the balance sheet. On the other hand, if the costs are actually period costs but are improperly classified as product costs, then the reverse would be true. The expenses would be understated by $40,000, and inventory would be overstated by $40,000.

So you see, the proper distinction between product and period costs is essential in order for the accountant to accurately measure income and value assets.

Noninventoriable Unexpired Costs

Thus far, we may have given you the impression that all costs are classified as either product costs or period costs. But that's not necessarily so. There is a third group into which costs can be classified when they occur: *noninventoriable unexpired costs.*

A third type of cost: noninventoriable unexpired—assets other than inventory

The term *noninventoriable unexpired costs* tells you exactly what these costs are. ***Noninventoriable unexpired costs*** *represent assets when they are incurred, but they are not costs that can be assigned to inventory*—at least not yet. Examples of noninventoriable unexpired costs include expenditures for prepaid insurance, prepaid rent, machinery, and buildings. Each of these costs is an asset (or unexpired cost) other than inventory. Many of these assets are used up or consumed as time passes. As they expire over time, the amount expired can then be classified as a product cost or a period cost.

For instance, assume that a 3-year insurance policy is acquired for $900. At the time of acquisition, the $900 is an asset, but it is not classified as a product cost—it is classified as prepaid insurance, not inventory. At this moment, the $900 of prepaid insurance is a noninventoriable unexpired cost. After the first year of coverage, $300 worth of insurance has been consumed. This $300 of coverage used up must now be classified as either a product cost or period cost. (The proper classification will depend on the type of organization to which the costs apply, i.e., manufacturer or retailer, as we shall see in the next section.) The remaining $600 is still unexpired after 1 year of the policy; it will continue to be classified as an asset (but not as inventory) on the balance sheet until it expires in the next 2 years. In short, the remaining $600 of insurance cost is still a noninventoriable unexpired cost.

A Way to Simplify

In later sections of this chapter and in most homework problems, for simplicity's sake it will be assumed that all costs can be classified as product costs or period costs. Whenever we introduce noninventoriable unexpired costs, they will be specifically identified.

RETAILERS AND MANUFACTURERS

Before we discuss the different types of product and period costs, we first need to compare the different types of organizations that may have product and period costs. For our purposes, we will classify all organizations into one of three categories: service organizations, retailers, and manufacturers.

Service organizations are in business to make a profit from the sale of a personal service (accountants, lawyers, advertising agents, etc.) rather than from the sale of inventory. Since service organizations have no inventories, there are no product costs—all of their costs are period costs.

Retailers sell inventory "as is," but manufacturers change the form before sale

Retailing and manufacturing organizations are both in business to make a profit from the sale of inventory. The difference between them is that the ***retailer*** sells the product in the same form as it was in when purchased, while the ***manufacturer*** converts raw materials into the form of a finished product before it can be sold.

Retailing organizations have only one inventory account—Merchandise Inventory. All costs originally assigned to this account are transferred to cost of goods sold expense at time of sale.

Manufacturers must maintain three different inventory accounts—one for each physical form as the product progresses from its raw to finished state:

Inventories for a manufacturer

1. ***Raw Materials Inventory*** Materials purchased from a supplier and awaiting use in production

2. ***Work-in-Process Inventory*** The unfinished goods in production—the units that are being worked on

3. ***Finished Goods Inventory*** The completed product awaiting sale

When materials are acquired, their costs are first placed in the Raw Materials Inventory account until they are needed in production. Once production begins, all production costs, including raw material costs, are accumulated in the Work-in-Process Inventory account and remain there until the product is completed. Once completed, the cost of these units becomes Finished Goods Inventory. As the units are sold, these costs are transferred to Cost of Goods Sold Expense.

A simple way to picture in your mind this progression of costs through the inventory accounts is with the following T-accounts:

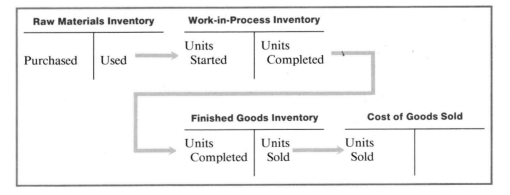

We'll look at this progression of costs in more detail in a few moments.

Now let's see what the different product costs are for the service organization, the retailer, and the manufacturer—that is, what costs are assigned to the respective inventories.

Basic Elements of Product Costs

It is extremely easy to distinguish product costs from period costs for a service-type organization. Since a service rather than a product is sold, there aren't any inventories. And when there aren't any inventories, there are no product costs—all costs are period costs (although the organization could still have noninventoriable unexpired costs).

It's not quite as easy to distinguish product costs from period costs for a retailer as it is for a service organization, but it's certainly a lot easier than it is for a manufacturer.

Product costs for a retailer

Product costs include all costs necessary to get the merchandise inventory from the supplier to the retailer and placed in position for sale. This includes the invoice price of the merchandise and any costs to transport it. Theoretically, there may also be justification for treating the costs of ordering, receiving, and storing the merchandise as product costs. However, since it can be extremely difficult to determine the amount of these costs to assign to different orders purchased, these costs are usually treated as period costs. All other costs for the retailer, such as salaries, expired insurance, expired rent, advertising, utilities, property taxes, and depreciation, are also considered to be related not to the product but to the period and are expensed when incurred.

Are all costs for a manufacturer product costs?

The distinction between product costs and period costs is somewhat different for a manufacturer than it is for the retailer. For a manufacturer the classification of a cost depends on whether it is a cost of a department that is producing a product or of a department that is not producing a product.

To see what we mean, assume that a manufacturing company can be divided into three functional areas: production, sales, and administration. All costs of the selling and administrative departments are period costs; all costs of the production departments are product costs.

Categories of Product Costs

Product costs for a manufacturer—the costs of the production departments—fall into one of the following three main categories.

Direct materials: integral part and easily traceable

1. Direct Materials **Direct materials** are the raw materials that become an integral part of the completed product and that are significant enough to warrant tracing the cost accurately to the finished item. For example, if the production process involves making classroom desks, the direct materials would include wood, formica, and metal legs. Although each desk also includes glue, nails, screws, and varnish, the cost of these raw materials would be insignificant compared to the cost of the major raw materials. The precise cost per desk of each of these minor raw materials might be determinable, but there would be no benefit from having such accurate product costs. You must realize that there is a cost to obtaining information. And as with anything else, you should pay for only as much information as you need.

Nevertheless, we don't forget about the cost of minor raw materials. Such materials as glue, nails, and screws are called *indirect materials.* The cost of indirect materials is one of the costs classified as *factory overhead,* which we will explain shortly.

One more note on direct materials. The cost of direct materials includes not only the purchase price of the materials but also whatever freight costs the buyer has to pay for delivery of the materials, because the freight costs are necessary costs of getting the inventory to the buyer and into a position ready for use.

Direct labor: clearly traceable to the product

2. Direct Labor **Direct labor** is the work that directly converts the raw materials into finished goods. Like direct materials, direct labor costs should be clearly traceable to the product being worked on, from the raw to the finished state. For example, the salaries for those laborers who combine the wood, formica, glue, nails, etc., into a finished desk are direct labor costs. But the salaries of workers who bring raw materials to the direct laborers or of managers who supervise laborers are examples of *indirect labor* costs. Like indirect materials, indirect labor is a component of factory overhead.

Factory overhead: the indirect costs of production

3. Factory Overhead The simplest way to think of what we mean by *factory overhead* costs is this: Combine and add up all the manufacturing costs incurred within a production department. Then subtract from that total the direct materials costs and the direct labor costs. What remains are the factory overhead costs, which are also called *manufacturing overhead* costs. Factory overhead costs represent the indirect costs of production — those that are needed to produce the product, but that cannot be, or for practical reasons (as discussed for indirect materials) shouldn't be, traced directly to the product being worked on. Examples include the following factory costs: indirect materials, indirect labor, expired insurance, expired rent, property taxes, maintenance and repairs, utilities, depreciation, idle time, and overtime premium. (Any of these costs, when incurred in the selling or administrative areas, are period costs. They are expensed as incurred.)

Idle time represents the amount paid to laborers for unproductive time. For example, when a machine breaks down, if the laborers stand around waiting for it to be fixed, the wages paid are considered to be idle time. *Overtime premium* is the amount paid to laborers (above the normal hourly rate) for hours worked in excess of the standard hours for a work period.

For example, assume a machinist is paid $10 per hour for a 40-hour week, works 52 hours this week (including 4 hours of unproductive time and 12 hours of overtime), and is paid time and a half for overtime. The costs of direct labor, idle time, and overtime premium are as follows:

Idle time and overtime premium

Total wages:	
40 hr @ $10/hr.	$400
12 hr @ $15/hr.	180
	$580
Distributed as follows:	
Direct labor [48 (52 − 4) hr @ $10/hr]	$480
Factory overhead:	
Idle time (4 hr @ $10/hr)	$40
Overtime premium (12 hr @ $5/hr)	60 100
	$580

How to assign overhead costs to the product

If factory overhead costs are not traced *directly* to the product being worked on, how do these costs get assigned to the product? That is, how do we determine the factory overhead cost per unit produced? One way is first to determine the total activity for the period — such as the number of desks produced each month — and then to divide that amount into the total actual overhead costs incurred during that same time period. As a result, each desk is assigned an equal part of the total overhead as its product cost. Additional ways of determining the factory overhead cost per unit produced will be discussed in Chapters 10 and 12.

Sometimes accountants find it helpful to combine the terms *direct materials* and *direct labor*. This combination of direct costs they call *prime costs.* Similarly, they sometimes find it helpful to combine the terms *direct labor* and *factory overhead,* a

Prime costs = DM + DL

Conversion costs = DL + FO

cost combination referred to as **conversion costs.**

Prime costs represent the direct costs of manufacturing a product.

Conversion costs represent the costs needed to convert raw materials to a finished product (but not including the cost of those raw materials).

You can use Exhibit 2-1 to practice classifying costs as product costs or period costs. To understand how these costs are classified, keep in mind the following:

Rules for distinguishing product costs from period costs

1. All costs incurred by a service organization are period costs.

2. All costs incurred by a retailer are period costs with the exception of the invoice price and transportation costs of merchandise inventory purchased.

3. The costs incurred by a manufacturer will be classified as product or period costs depending upon the department in which they are incurred:
   a. All costs related to a production department of a manufacturer are product costs.
   b. All costs related to nonproduction departments of a manufacturer are period costs.

EXHIBIT 2-1
Classifications of Product Costs and Period Costs*

			Manufacturer		
Type of Cost	**Service**	**Retailer**	**Administrative Department Cost**	**Sales Department Cost**	**Production Department Cost**
Cost of inventory purchases	†	Pr	†	†	Pr
Transportation-in for inventory purchases	†	Pr	†	†	Pr
Salaries	P	P	P	P	Pr
Expired insurance‡	P	P	P	P	Pr
Expired rent‡	P	P	P	P	Pr
Utilities	P	P	P	P	Pr
Property taxes	P	P	P	P	Pr
Transportation-out for units sold	P	P	†	P	†
Advertising	P	P	†	P	†
Depreciation	P	P	P	P	Pr

* Pr = product costs, P = period costs.
† These costs are not incurred within the respective departments, and their classification would not be applicable.
‡ These are expired insurance and rent, as opposed to the unexpired portions, which are assets in all situations.

Flow of Costs

We have just discussed the types of inventories and the types of product costs for both manufacturers and nonmanufacturers. Now we are going to show how the product costs relate to the inventory accounts—that is, how the product costs flow through the inventory accounts from purchase to ultimate sale.

Cost flow of retailer: directly from purchase to sale

Analyzing a retailer's flow of costs is far simpler than analyzing a manufacturer's cost flow. Because the product sold by the retailer is in the same physical form as it was when purchased, there are very few product costs to keep track of. On the other hand, the manufacturing situation involves a large number of costs to convert the raw materials to a finished product.

Exhibit 2-2 shows with the use of T-accounts how simply a retailer's product costs flow from the initial purchase (assumed to be $200,000) of merchandise inventory to the cost of goods sold ($175,000). All other costs, such as expired insurance ($4,000),

EXHIBIT 2-2   T-Accounts for Cost Flow of Retailer

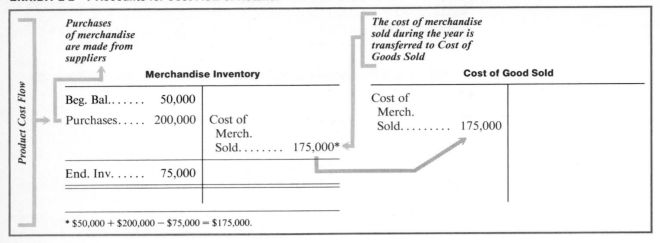

Product Cost Flow

Purchases of merchandise are made from suppliers

The cost of merchandise sold during the year is transferred to Cost of Goods Sold

Merchandise Inventory

Beg. Bal......	50,000		
Purchases.....	200,000	Cost of Merch. Sold.......	175,000*
End. Inv.	75,000		

Cost of Good Sold

Cost of Merch. Sold........	175,000

* $50,000 + $200,000 − $75,000 = $175,000.

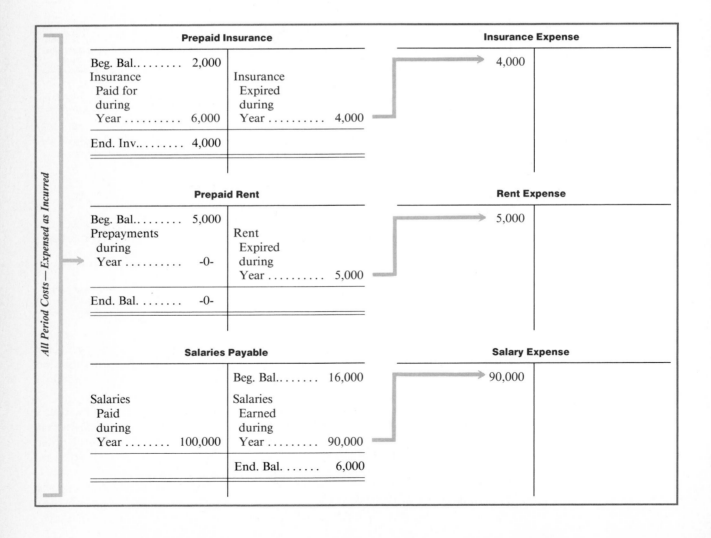

All Period Costs — Expensed as Incurred

Prepaid Insurance

Beg. Bal........	2,000		
Insurance Paid for during Year	6,000	Insurance Expired during Year	4,000
End. Inv........	4,000		

Insurance Expense

4,000

Prepaid Rent

Beg. Bal........	5,000		
Prepayments during Year	-0-	Rent Expired during Year	5,000
End. Bal.	-0-		

Rent Expense

5,000

Salaries Payable

		Beg. Bal.......	16,000
Salaries Paid during Year	100,000	Salaries Earned during Year	90,000
		End. Bal.	6,000

Salary Expense

90,000

expired rent ($5,000), and salaries ($90,000), are expensed as incurred—that is, as they are used up—because they are period costs.

The cost flow for a manufacturer is much longer

The cost flow analysis for the manufacturer is more complex. A manufacturer has many product costs, which flow among three inventories instead of one. We will trace the flow of costs through the three inventory T-accounts of the production department of a manufacturer in a step-by-step manner, using a different exhibit to show each of the following six steps:

1. Purchase and use of raw materials
2. Use of labor
3. Use of factory overhead
4. Transfer of Factory Overhead to Work-in-Process
5. Completion of production
6. Sale of finished goods

Journal entries are in the appendix

If you would like to see the journal entries that accompany the T-accounts for steps 1 through 6, you can find them in the appendix to this chapter. You may want to refer to them as you proceed through the discussion of steps 1 through 6 that follows. On the other hand, if you'd rather limit the analysis to the T-accounts at this time, then simply ignore the appendix when you get to the end of the chapter.

Raw materials: first we buy and then we use

STEP 1: Purchase and use of raw materials   Exhibit 2-3 indicates that the purchases of raw materials are $200,000. When added to the $50,000 on hand at the beginning of the year, there is a total of $250,000 of raw materials available to be used in production during the year. If we find that we still

EXHIBIT 2-3   Purchase and Use of Raw Materials

Purchases of raw materials from suppliers

Raw Materials Inventory

Beg. Bal..	50,000	Raw Materials Used	175,000*
Purchases..	200,000		
End. Bal. ..	75,000		

The cost of direct materials used in production ($165,000) goes directly to Work-in-Process, but the cost of indirect materials ($10,000) goes to Factory Overhead Incurred

* $50,000 + $200,000 − $75,000 = $175,000.

Factory Overhead Incurred

Beg. Bal..	-0-		
Incurred:			
Indirect Materials ...	10,000		
	10,000		

Work-in-Process Inventory

| Beg. Bal.. | 60,000 | | |
| Direct Materials ... | 165,000 | | |

have $75,000 of raw materials on hand at the end of the year, then the amount we must have used during the year is represented as follows:

Total Available for Use	$250,000
Ending Inventory: Raw Materials	75,000
Raw Materials Used during the Year	$175,000

Of the $175,000 of raw materials that were used, assume that $165,000 was for direct materials and that the remaining $10,000 was for indirect materials. Notice in Exhibit 2-3 that the direct materials go immediately — directly — to Work-in-Process Inventory, but that the indirect materials go to an account called Factory Overhead Incurred.

The *Factory Overhead Incurred* account accumulates all overhead costs that are incurred during a period; these are represented by debits in the account. Indirect materials is just the first of many. At the end of the period, when the total overhead costs are accounted for, the account is closed to a zero balance (which it will still have at the beginning of the next period) with a credit. This total is then transferred in one lump sum to Work-in-Process, with a debit to that account. In this way there will be three debits to Work-in-Process each period — one for direct materials (which we already see in Exhibit 2-3); one for direct labor (which we'll see in Exhibit 2-4); and one for factory overhead (which we'll see in Exhibit 2-6).

We see in Exhibit 2-3 that there is a beginning balance in Work-in-Process Inventory of $60,000. This represents the costs of direct materials, direct labor, and factory overhead incurred during last year and assigned to those units that were started but not finished by the end of last year. The total costs so far in Work-in-Process are now merely the beginning balance plus direct materials:

What is a beginning balance in Work-in-Process?

Beginning Balance	$ 60,000
Direct Materials	165,000
	$225,000

Salaries: both product and period costs — both direct and indirect costs

STEP 2: Use of labor During the period the total wages earned by workers are assumed to be $90,000. Of this amount, $70,000 relates to the production department, and $5,000 of these production wages are for indirect laborers. Exhibit 2-4 shows how the payroll is to be distributed. The direct labor ($65,000) goes to Work-in-Process Inventory and the indirect labor ($5,000) goes to Factory Overhead Incurred. Both the direct and the indirect labor costs are product costs, but only the direct labor goes directly to Work-in-Process. Remember from our discussion of direct materials that factory overhead costs will eventually get to Work-in-Process, but in a roundabout manner. The rest of the $90,000 ($20,000) goes to Salary Expense — it is a period cost.

EXHIBIT 2-4 Use of Labor

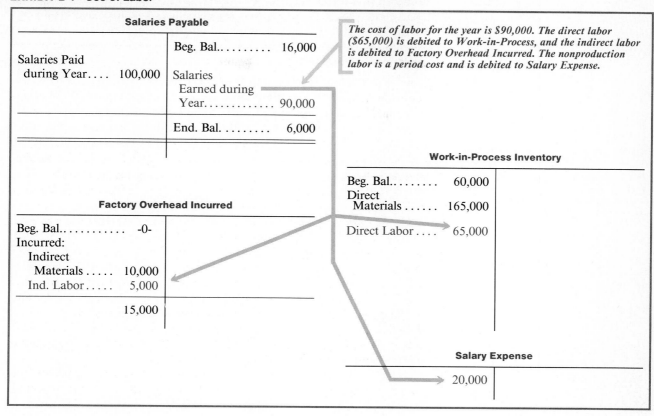

The costs accumulated in Work-in-Process Inventory are now as follows:

Beginning Balance.	$ 60,000
Direct Materials.	165,000
Direct Labor.	65,000
	$290,000

STEP 3: Use of factory overhead The total amounts of insurance and rent that expired during the year were as follows:

The remaining factory overhead costs

	Cost of Production Departments	Cost of Nonproduction (Selling and Administrative) Departments	Total
Insurance	$3,000	$1,000	$4,000
Rent	4,000	1,000	5,000

As shown in Exhibit 2-5, the insurance and rent related to the production departments ($3,000 and $4,000) are classified as factory overhead costs and are debited to Factory Overhead Incurred. The remaining insurance and rent ($1,000 and $1,000) are expensed as incurred, being debited to Insurance Expense and Rent Expense, respectively.

STEP 4: Transfer of Factory Overhead to Work-in-Process   The Work-in-Process account in Exhibit 2-5 is still incomplete. While it is supposed to accumulate all product costs associated with production each period, factory overhead, which is just as much a product cost as direct materials and direct

EXHIBIT 2-5   Use of Factory Overhead

Insurance and rent consumed in the year are determined. The amounts related to production are assigned to Factory Overhead Incurred ($3,000 and $4,000). The remainder is expensed during the period ($1,000 and $1,000).

Work-in-Process Inventory

Beg. Bal. 60,000	
Direct Materials 165,000	
Direct Labor 65,000	

Prepaid Insurance

Beg. Bal. 2,000	

Insurance
  Purchased 6,000
	Insurance
	  Expired. 4,000

End. Bal. 4,000	

Factory Overhead Incurred

Beg. Balance . . . . . -0-	

Incurred:
  Indirect
    Material 10,000
  Ind. Labor 5,000
  Insurance. 3,000
  Rent 4,000	

22,000	

Prepaid Rent

Beg. Bal. 5,000	

Rent Prepaid
  during Year . . . . . .   -0-
	Rent
	  Expired. 5,000

End. Bal. . . . . -0-	

Insurance Expense

	1,000

Rent Expense

	1,000

labor, is missing. Remember that the factory overhead costs have been temporarily stored in the Factory Overhead Incurred account, until they are completely accounted for. Since there are no additional factory overhead costs to account for this period, it is now time to transfer the cumulative overhead costs in Factory Overhead Incurred to Work-in-Process. To do this we simply credit Factory Overhead Incurred, thus closing the account, and debit Work-in-Process. This is shown in Exhibit 2-6.

EXHIBIT 2-6 Transfer of Factory Overhead to Work-in-Process

Factory Overhead Incurred				Work-in-Process Inventory		
Beg. Bal......... -0-				Beg. Bal....... 60,000		*Total manufacturing costs incurred = $252,000.*
Incurred:				Direct		
Indirect				Materials 165,000		
Material.....	10,000			Direct		
Ind. Labor....	5,000			Labor 65,000		
Insurance.....	3,000			Factory		
Rent	4,000			Overhead..... 22,000		
	22,000	22,000		Total Mfg. Costs to Account for 312,000		

The factory overhead that has been accumulated in the Factory Overhead Incurred account is now transferred to Work-in-Process — which now has debits for all three product costs.

Now that there are no additional costs to account for, the total debits to Work-in-Process sum to the following:

<table>
<tr><td>Beginning Balance...</td><td></td><td>$ 60,000</td></tr>
<tr><td>Direct Materials ....</td><td>$165,000</td><td></td></tr>
<tr><td>Direct Labor ....</td><td>65,000</td><td></td></tr>
<tr><td>Factory Overhead................................</td><td>22,000</td><td>252,000</td></tr>
<tr><td>Total Manufacturing Costs to Account for ....</td><td></td><td>$312,000</td></tr>
</table>

Total manufacturing costs to account for

The summation of all debits to Work-in-Process Inventory, $312,000, is referred to as the *total manufacturing costs to account for.*

A large portion of this total will be assigned to units that are completed during the year; the remainder will be assigned to the units that have been started, and worked on, but are not completed by the end of the year.

In this chapter, we are using an actual cost system of accounting for factory overhead. This means that the *actual* factory overhead costs are assigned to Work-in-Process as a product cost. For several reasons, which we will discuss later, many organizations assign something called **applied factory overhead** (rather than actual factory overhead) to the units. We will discuss applied factory overhead in Chapters 10 and 12.

The units are finally finished

STEP 5: Completion of production Throughout the year units in process are being completed; the cost of these units is transferred from work-in-process to finished goods. We assume in Exhibit 2-7 that the cost assigned to units completed during the year is $280,000, and that the amount assigned to the unfinished units remaining in Work-in-Process at year-end is $32,000.

We can see in Exhibit 2-7 that there is a $40,000 beginning balance in Finished Goods Inventory — the amount assigned to units completed last year but not yet sold by the end of the year. When we add this beginning balance ($40,000) to the cost of goods completed in the current period ($280,000), we get $320,000 — the **total goods that are available for sale.**

EXHIBIT 2-7 Completion of Production

Work-in-Process Inventory	
Beg. Bal......... 60,000	
Mfg. Costs Incurred during Period ... 252,000	Cost of Goods Completed during Year.... 280,000*
End. Bal. 32,000	

The cost of units finished during the year is determined to be $280,000. This amount is transferred from Work-in-Process Inventory to Finished Goods Inventory.

* $60,000 + $252,000 − $32,000 = $280,000.

Finished Goods Inventory	
Beg. Bal......... 40,000	
Cost of Goods Completed during Year..... 280,000	
Total Available for Sale........ 320,000	

This means that during the year we had ready for sale finished goods having a cost of $320,000.

The finished goods are sold: product costs are finally expensed

STEP 6: Sale of finished goods The production costs have traveled a long way — starting in raw materials, transferring to work-in-process when the production process began, and coming over to finished goods when production was completed. The costs are still product costs, but they are now in the final stage before they become expenses. All that's left is for the product to be sold.

The cost of the units sold during the year is $310,000, shown in Exhibit 2-8 — this amount being debited to Cost of Goods Sold and credited to Finished Goods. Finally we have an expense — now and only now do the product costs become expenses.

The production costs associated with the unsold units in finished goods are $10,000. These costs are still part of an asset. They will not be expensed until the units to which they are assigned are sold — probably next year.

The cost accountant has now virtually completed his or her product cost responsibilities for the year:

1. The costs for the manufacturer have been classified as product and period costs.

2. The product costs have been accumulated during production and assigned to the units that were completed during the year and are now awaiting sale.

3. The cost of the units available for sale has been allocated between the units that were sold — cost of goods sold — and the units that were not sold — finished goods inventory. The financial statements can now be prepared.

EXHIBIT 2-8 Sale of Finished Goods

Finished Goods Inventory	
Beg. Bal......... 40,000	
Cost of Goods Completed during Period ... 280,000	Cost of Goods Sold during Year.... 310,000*
End. Bal. 10,000	

The cost of the units sold during the year is determined to be $310,000. This amount is transferred to Cost of Goods Sold from Finished Goods Inventory.

* $40,000 + $280,000 − $10,000 = $310,000.

Cost of Goods Sold	
Cost of Goods Sold during Year..... 310,000	

Now let's put it all together

But before we go on to the preparation of financial statements, let's take one last look at the cost flow for our manufacturer shown in Exhibits 2-3 through 2-8. Since these exhibits each showed only a small part of the entire flow, and we also want you to see the complete flow, Exhibit 2-9 on the next two pages combines the six steps discussed in Exhibits 2-3 through 2-8.

FINANCIAL STATEMENTS

Having traced the flow of product costs through the inventory accounts of both retailing and manufacturing organizations, we now come to the final step in the accounting cycle—the preparation of financial statements. In other words, the effects of the flow of costs depicted in the T-accounts shown in Exhibits 2-2 through 2-9 are eventually represented in the income statement and balance sheet.

The Income Statement

The basic format of the income statement is the same for both a retailer and a manufacturer. Using the same facts that were introduced earlier about the cost flows for the retailer (Exhibit 2-2) and the manufacturer (Exhibit 2-9), condensed income statements are shown below (assume that sales revenue is $400,000 and the year is 1988).

The income statements look alike

	Retailer	Manufacturer
Sales...	$400,000	$400,000
Less: Cost of Goods Sold................................	175,000	310,000
Gross Profit	$225,000	$ 90,000
Less: Selling and Administrative Expenses	99,000	22,000
Net Income	$126,000	$ 68,000

EXHIBIT 2-9 Cost Flow of a Manufacturer

Raw Materials Inventory		
Beginning Balance 50,000	Raw Materials	
Purchased . . . . 200,000[a]	Used . . . . 175,000[a]	
Ending Balance 75,000		

Salaries Payable	
	Beginning Balance 16,000
Paid. 100,000	Earned for Year . . . . 90,000[b]
	Ending Balance 6,000

Prepaid Insurance	
Beginning Balance 2,000	
Purchased 6,000	Insurance Expired . . . . 4,000[c]
Ending Balance 4,000	

Prepaid Rent	
Beginning Balance 5,000	
Prepaid in Year . . . . -0-	Rent Expired. . . . . 5,000[c]
Ending Balance . . . . -0-	

[a] Step 1: Purchase and use of raw materials.
[b] Step 2: Use of labor.
[c] Step 3: Use of factory overhead.
[d] Step 4: Transfer of Factory Overhead to Work-in-Process.
[e] Step 5: Completion of production.
[f] Step 6: Sale of finished goods.

Cost of goods sold is simple for the retailer

For the retailer, the determination of cost of goods sold, $175,000, is quite simple. The proper form is as follows:

Merchandise Inventory, Jan. 1, 1988	$ 50,000
Plus: Purchases	200,000
Goods Available for Sale.	$250,000
Less: Merchandise Inventory, Dec. 31, 1988	75,000
Cost of Goods Sold	$175,000

Now look back at Exhibit 2-2 once again. Notice how the organization of the schedule above for cost of goods sold is nothing more than a formal way to show the flow through the Merchandise Inventory T-account.

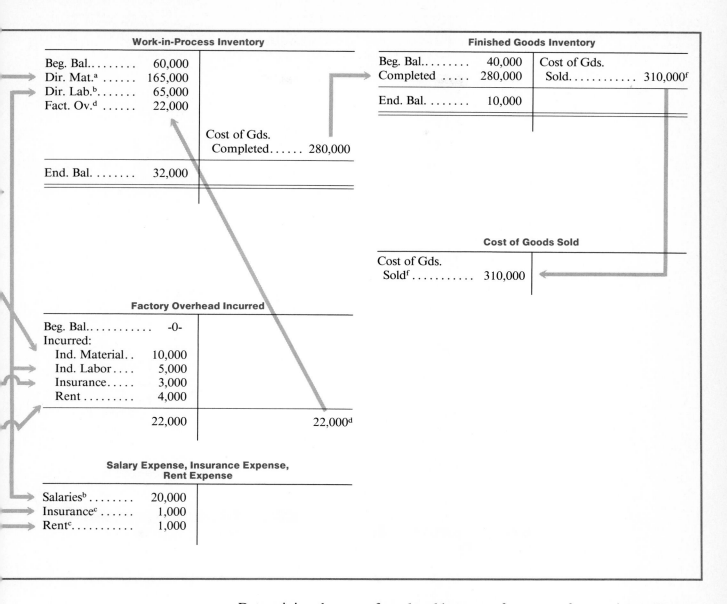

Work-in-Process Inventory		
Beg. Bal.........	60,000	
Dir. Mat.[a]	165,000	
Dir. Lab.[b].......	65,000	
Fact. Ov.[d]	22,000	
		Cost of Gds. Completed...... 280,000
End. Bal.	32,000	

Finished Goods Inventory		
Beg. Bal.........	40,000	Cost of Gds.
Completed	280,000	Sold........... 310,000[f]
End. Bal.	10,000	

Cost of Goods Sold	
Cost of Gds. Sold[f] 310,000	

Factory Overhead Incurred		
Beg. Bal............	-0-	
Incurred:		
Ind. Material..	10,000	
Ind. Labor....	5,000	
Insurance.....	3,000	
Rent	4,000	
	22,000	22,000[d]

Salary Expense, Insurance Expense, Rent Expense		
Salaries[b]	20,000	
Insurance[c]	1,000	
Rent[c]..........	1,000	

There's much more detail for the manufacturer

Determining the cost of goods sold expense for a manufacturer is much more detailed, since it involves the flow of product costs through three inventories rather than one. Often two schedules are used by the cost accountant to calculate the cost of goods sold—these are shown in Exhibit 2-10, which we will explain.

Schedule of Cost of Goods Completed

You should compare the schedules to the T-accounts

The first schedule shows the calculation for cost of goods completed—that is, the cost assigned to all units finished during the year 1988. It is a formal way to show the flow of product costs from raw materials to finished goods. We showed the same flow in a less formal manner with T-accounts in Exhibits 2-3 through 2-7. As you read through schedule 1, it might be a good idea to compare it to the appropriate T-accounts. You will find that the order within the T-accounts and schedule 1 is nearly identical.

EXHIBIT 2-10
Cost of Goods Sold for a Manufacturer

Schedule 1
Cost of Goods Completed
Year Ended December 31, 1988

Raw Materials Inventory, Jan. 1, 1988	$ 50,000	
Plus: Purchases	200,000	
Raw Materials Available for Use	$250,000	
Less: Raw Materials Inventory, Dec. 31, 1988	75,000	
Raw Materials Used	$175,000*	
Direct Materials Used		$165,000
Plus: Direct Labor		65,000
Plus: Factory Overhead		22,000
Total Manufacturing Costs Incurred during 1988		$252,000
Plus: Work-in-Process Inventory, Jan. 1, 1988		60,000
Total Manufacturing Costs to Account for		$312,000
Less: Work-in-Process Inventory, Dec. 31, 1988		32,000
Cost of Goods Completed		$280,000

* Of the $175,000 of raw materials used, $165,000 is direct material and $10,000 is indirect materials (part of the $22,000 of factory overhead).

Schedule 2
Cost of Goods Sold
Year Ended December 31, 1988

Finished Goods Inventory, Jan. 1, 1988	$ 40,000
Plus: Cost of Goods Completed	280,000
Total Available for Sale	$320,000
Less: Finished Goods Inventory, Dec. 31, 1988	10,000
Cost of Goods Sold Expense	$310,000

Cost of goods completed =
DM + DL + FO +
WIP − WIP

It may be helpful to think that there are four basic elements in the calculation of the cost of goods completed: (1) direct materials used, (2) direct labor, (3) factory overhead, and (4) the adjustment for the beginning and ending balances in Work-in-Process.

The first three elements add up to $252,000 — *the total manufacturing costs incurred* during 1988:

Direct Materials	$165,000
Direct Labor	65,000
Factory Overhead	22,000
Total Manufacturing Costs Incurred	$252,000

This is the total of all direct and indirect costs incurred in production, in order to:

1. Complete the units that were unfinished at the beginning of the year

2. Produce fully completed units during the year

3. Start some units that aren't fully completed on the last day of the current year

With the addition of the beginning balance in Work-in-Process, we now have the total manufacturing costs to account for:

Total Manufacturing Costs Incurred	$252,000
Work-in-Process, Jan. 1, 1988...	60,000
Total Manufacturing Costs to Account for.............................	$312,000

When we subtract the ending balance in Work-in-Process ($32,000), we see that the cost of the goods completed is $280,000.

The steps taken to compute the cost of goods completed can also be shown in equation form:

Manufacturing costs incurred (direct material, direct labor, factory overhead)	+	beginning inventory of work-in-process	=	total manufacturing costs to account for	completed units: transfer costs to finished goods
					unfinished units: costs remain in work-in-process
$252,000	+	$60,000	=	$312,000	$280,000
					$ 32,000

Schedule of Cost of Goods Sold

The second schedule in Exhibit 2-10 shows how to calculate the cost of goods sold, once we have determined the cost of goods completed. Schedule 2 traces the progression of costs through Finished Goods Inventory in much the same order as we showed in T-account form with Exhibit 2-8.

Cost of goods sold = cost of goods completed + FG − FG

By adding the beginning balance of Finished Goods to the cost of goods completed, we get the cost of goods available for sale, $320,000. Finally, we see that the ending balance in Finished Goods is $10,000; when this amount is subtracted from $320,000, the difference is the cost of goods sold, $310,000.

We can also represent these calculations in equations, as shown below:

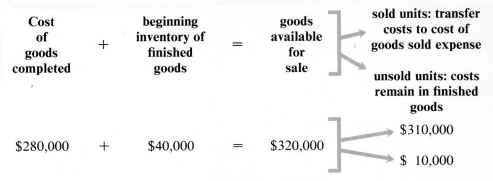

Cost of goods completed	+	beginning inventory of finished goods	=	goods available for sale	sold units: transfer costs to cost of goods sold expense
					unsold units: costs remain in finished goods
$280,000	+	$40,000	=	$320,000	$310,000
					$ 10,000

As an alternative to computing cost of goods sold with the use of two schedules, it would be perfectly acceptable to combine the two schedules into one. As soon as the cost of goods completed, $280,000, was determined in the first schedule, the beginning and ending inventories of finished goods would be immediately added and subtracted respectively.

The Balance Sheet

The balance sheets for the retailer and manufacturer differ in only one respect — the number of inventory accounts found in the current assets section. For the retailer the only inventory account is Merchandise Inventory. For the manufacturer there are the three inventory accounts: Raw Materials Inventory, Work-in-Process Inventory, and Finished Goods Inventory.

A COMPREHENSIVE EXAMPLE

We now present a comprehensive example for an actual manufacturing organization, which covers most of the key concepts discussed in this chapter. Try to work out a complete solution on your own before looking at the one that we provide.

EXAMPLE 2-4

THE FLORIDA STEEL CORPORATION

The Florida Steel Corporation is engaged in the production, fabricating, and marketing of steel products primarily for use in construction. On Oct. 1 of year 1, Florida Steel had the following inventories (in thousands):

Raw Materials (and Supplies)..	$14,012	Finished Goods	$14,645
Work-in-Process	4,200		

Additional cost and revenue information related to operations includes (in thousands):

Purchases	$149,096	Energy Costs...............	$ 46,206
Salaries Accrued and Paid....	61,007	Repairs	11,011
Depreciation...............	9,167	Sales......................	286,108

The purchases of raw materials and supplies are for use in the production, selling, and administrative departments. Of the amount used, $7,262 was an indirect cost of production and $8,338 was used in the selling and administrative areas.

Of the total wages and salaries, $46,038 was a direct cost of production, $11,509 was an indirect cost of production, and the remainder related to selling and administration.

For the remaining costs the breakdown between production and selling and administration is as follows:

	Production	Selling and Administration
Depreciation....................................	$ 8,656	$ 511
Energy costs....................................	43,845	2,361
Repairs	10,413	598

At the end of its year, Sept. 30, the following inventories were on hand:

Raw Materials (and Supplies) ..	$9,533	Finished Goods..............	$22,053
Work-in-Process.............	3,698		

In addition, Florida Steel had the following three items:

Other Income	$ 5,406	Income Taxes	$4,363
Interest Expense	(6,430)		

EXHIBIT 2-11
Income Statement and Supporting Schedules for Florida Steel Corporation

Schedule 1
Cost of Goods Completed
Year Ended September 30, Year 2

Raw Materials (and Supplies) Inventory, Oct. 1, Year 1 ...	$ 14,012	
Purchases	149,096	
Total Available for Use	$163,108	
Raw Materials (and Supplies) Inventory, Sept. 30, Year 2..	9,533	
Raw Materials (and Supplies) Used	$153,575	
Direct Materials Used ($153,575 − $7,262 − $8,338)		$137,975
Direct Labor		46,038
Factory Overhead:		
Indirect Materials	$ 7,262	
Indirect Labor	11,509	
Depreciation	8,656	
Energy Costs	43,845	
Repairs	10,413	81,685
Total Manufacturing Costs Incurred		$265,698
Work-in-Process Inventory, Oct. 1, Year 1		4,200
Total Manufacturing Costs to Account for		$269,898
Work-in-Process Inventory, Sept. 30, Year 2		3,698
Cost of Goods Completed		$266,200

Schedule 2
Cost of Goods Sold
Year Ended September 30, Year 2

Finished Goods Inventory, Oct. 1, Year 1	$ 14,645
Cost of Goods Completed	266,200
Goods Available for Sale	$280,845
Finished Goods Inventory, Sept. 30, Year 2	22,053
Cost of Goods Sold	$258,792

FLORIDA STEEL CORPORATION
Income Statement
Year Ended September 30, Year 2

Sales		$286,108
Cost of Goods Sold Expense (see Schedules 1 and 2)		258,792
Gross Profit		$ 27,316
Selling and Administrative Expenses:		
Salaries	$ 3,460	
Supplies	8,338	
Energy Costs	2,361	
Repairs	598	
Depreciation	511	15,268
Income from Operations		$ 12,048
Other Income and Expenses:		
Other Revenues	$ 5,406	
Interest Expense	(6,430)	(1,024)
Income before Income Taxes		$ 11,024
Income Taxes		4,363
Net Income		$ 6,661

The income statement for Florida Steel (with supporting schedules for cost of goods completed and cost of goods sold) is given in Exhibit 2-11 on the previous page.[1]

Beginning and Ending Inventories: A Simplifying Assumption

In some examples, exercises, and homework problems, we may state specifically that the cost of the ending work-in-process inventory is equal to the cost of the beginning work-in-process inventory, and also that the cost of the ending finished goods inventory is equal to the cost of the beginning finished goods inventory. For example, let's assume that in the Florida Steel example the beginning and ending work-in-process inventories are both equal to $4,200 and that the beginning and ending finished goods inventories are both equal to $14,645. In that case:

When beginning and ending inventories are the same, DM + DL + FO = CGS

Schedule 1 Cost of Goods Completed	
Total Manufacturing Costs Incurred	$265,698
Work-in-Process Inventory, Oct. 1, Year 1 — Beginning	4,200
Total Manufacturing Costs to Account for	$269,898
Work-in-Process Inventory, Sept. 30, Year 2 — Ending	4,200
Cost of Goods Completed	$265,698

Schedule 2 Cost of Goods Sold	
Finished Goods Inventory, Oct. 1, Year 1 — Beginning	$ 14,645
Cost of Goods Completed	265,698
Goods Available for Sale	$280,343
Finished Goods Inventory, Sept. 30, Year 2 — Ending	14,645
Cost of Goods Sold Expense	$265,698

You can see from these schedules that when the balances for the beginning and ending work-in-process inventories are equal (that is, there is no change in inventory from the beginning to the end of the period) and the balances for the beginning and ending finished goods inventories are equal, the cost of goods sold turns out to be equal to the total manufacturing costs incurred. Or:

Total manufacturing costs incurred			=	cost of goods sold
Direct materials used	+ direct labor	+ factory overhead	=	cost of goods sold
$137,975	+ $46,038	+ $81,685	=	$265,698

Although the assumptions that the beginning and ending inventories are equal may not be realistic, they are often made to simplify the mechanics of computing cost

---

[1] A few modifications have been made in the facts concerning Florida Steel's costs for the year. In addition, the format of Florida Steel's income statement has been rearranged in order to make it compatible with the form we have been using.

of goods sold. Whenever we want you to make these simplifying assumptions, we will state so quite specifically in the problem.

THE JOB ORDER COSTING AND PROCESS COSTING METHODS

In this chapter we defined the term *product costing,* and we discussed the different types of product costs as well as the flow of product costs through the inventory accounts of both the retailer and the manufacturer. What we failed to mention was exactly *how* the product costs for a manufacturer are assigned to individual units or batches of units. In order to cover this topic, it is necessary to discuss the two extremes of product costing—job order costing and process costing.

Extremes of product costing

Even though the topics of job order costing and process costing are covered in detail in Chapters 12 and 13, since many of you may not cover these chapters in this course, we would like to give you now just a brief explanation of what each method is all about.

Sometimes a production process is making a rather small number of units (or batches of units)—which we call jobs. Each job is distinctly different from all the rest—probably because the jobs are being made to different customer specifications. Not only is it possible to determine the exact cost of each different job, but it is also usually mandatory that we do so, in order to properly value inventory on the balance sheet and cost of goods sold on the income statement. In this situation the production process would be accounted for with the ***job order costing method*** of product costing.

Characteristics of job order costing

A construction company is a likely candidate to use the job order costing method to account for its different construction projects. In addition, companies in the aircraft and printing industries would also probably use job order costing.

Characteristics of process costing

Process costing is used in those production processes where units are produced continuously in large batches, and each unit is basically the same as every other unit. Not only is it probably impossible to determine the exact cost of each unit—one at a time—but it would also be completely impractical to do so. It would hardly be cost-effective. So instead we determine all the production costs for an entire period and spread them evenly among the "equivalent units" of production during that period. The key to understanding process costing is understanding the concept of equivalent units. In overly simplified terms, the concept of equivalent units represents a way of measuring activity which allows us to combine completed units and incomplete units as if they were all completed. Incomplete units are converted into an equivalent number of completed units.

Typically, industries that are involved in the production of cement, paints, chemicals, and gasoline, among many others, employ process costing.

The basics that you learned in this chapter apply equally well to job order costing and process costing. The flow of product costs through T-accounts and the related journal entries look exactly the same under the two methods. In fact, in most homework problems where we provide you with only total costs for a manufacturer, you will not be able to detect from these facts alone which product costing method is being used. It's not until you have to worry about determining the costs of individual units, or batches of units, that it becomes necessary to distinguish job order costing from process costing.

CHAPTER SUMMARY

It is the job of the management accountant to provide quantitative information to managers to help them make decisions. There are a wide variety of different situations in which managers must make a decision; each situation may require a different type of cost information. It is up to the management accountant to determine and to provide the particular cost information needed to make the best management decision in a particular situation.

Total costs are the sum of all costs incurred within a *center of activity* during a specific period of time. An *average cost* is the total cost for a center of activity during a specific period of time divided by the activity during the period. Management accountants consider *activity* to be something done to produce a result or an output that can be measured. Activity can be measured in many different ways, depending on the type of organization and the types of centers of activity within that organization. For example, within a production department of a manufacturer, activity may be measured by the number of units produced or hours worked. For a storeroom a good measure of activity could be the number of requisitions processed.

In *product costing* we are concerned with determining the cost of the inventory and with the allocation of these costs to units sold and units unsold. In order to accomplish the product costing purpose, we must distinguish between *product costs* and *period costs.* Product costs are assigned to inventory when incurred, and they become an expense when the units to which they are assigned are sold. Period costs are expenses as soon as they are incurred.

There are three types of product costs for a *manufacturer: direct materials, direct labor,* and *factory overhead.* The sum of direct materials and direct labor costs is called *prime costs;* the sum of direct labor and factory overhead costs is referred to as *conversion costs.*

For a manufacturer there are three classifications of inventory — *raw materials, work-in-process,* and *finished goods* — each representing a stage of completion. The flow of product costs through the inventories is as follows. Raw materials are purchased from a supplier and placed in the Raw Materials Inventory account. Direct materials are requisitioned for production and along with direct labor are assigned directly to Work-in-Process. The factory overhead costs (including indirect materials and indirect labor) are first assigned to an account called Factory Overhead Incurred, and the total from that account is then transferred to Work-in-Process. When the units are completed, they are transferred to Finished Goods. As completed units are sold, their costs are transferred to Cost of Goods Sold Expense.

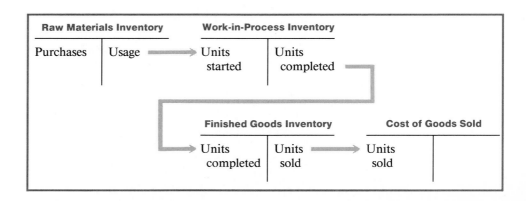

IMPORTANT TERMS USED IN THIS CHAPTER

Activity A clear indicator of (1) what was done or accomplished, (2) in a particular center of activity, (3) during a specific period of time, (4) to produce measurable results. (page 22)

Average cost The total costs of a center of activity for a period divided by the activity during the period. (page 23)

Center of activity A subunit within an organization that performs a particular function or produces measurable results. (page 22)

Conversion costs The sum of direct labor costs and factory overhead costs. (page 31)

Direct labor The labor cost that is needed to convert raw materials into a finished product. For a labor cost to be classified as direct labor, it must be clearly and easily traceable to the units that are being produced. (page 29)

Direct materials The raw materials that become an integral part of the finished product and are significant enough to warrant tracing them from raw materials to finished goods. (page 29)

Factory overhead The indirect costs of production — total production costs less direct materials and direct labor. Also referred to as ***manufacturing overhead.*** (page 30)

Factory Overhead Incurred An account that accumulates the actual factory overhead costs incurred by the production department of a manufacturer. At the end of each period the account is closed to a zero balance, and the total is transferred to Work-in-Process. (page 34)

Finished goods The units that are completed and awaiting sale. (page 28)

Indirect labor The labor needed to keep a manufacturing department running, but not involved directly in converting raw materials into a finished product. In other words, indirect labor costs are the labor costs of a production department that are not classified as direct labor. Indirect labor costs are classified as part of factory overhead. (page 30)

Indirect materials Raw materials that either do not become a physical part of the finished product or become a physical part of the finished good but are not significant enough in amount to justify tracing the cost to the finished product as a direct material. Indirect materials are classified as factory overhead. (page 29)

Job order costing method The method of accounting for the production of identifiable products, often made to customer specifications. The costs of each job are carefully accumulated and kept separate from the costs of any other job. (page 47)

Manufacturer An organization that converts a raw material to a finished product prior to sale. (page 28)

Manufacturing overhead See ***factory overhead.*** (page 30)

Noninventoriable unexpired costs Costs that are assets when incurred, but not assets that can be immediately assigned to inventory. As the asset expires over time, the amount expired can then be classified as a product or period cost. (page 27)

Period costs Costs that are expensed when incurred. (page 21)

Prime costs The sum of direct materials and direct labor costs. (page 30)

Process costing method The method of accounting for the production of a large volume of indistinguishable units in a continuous process. An average cost is determined by dividing the production costs by the equivalent whole units of production. (page 47)

Product costing The process of determining the costs of all units that are to be sold, and then allocating these costs between the units that are sold during the period and the units that are unsold at the end of the period. (page 25)

Product costs Costs that are closely associated with units produced by a manufacturer or purchased for resale by a retailer. Product costs are assigned to inventory when incurred and expensed when the units to which they are assigned are sold. (page 20)

Raw materials inventory The materials purchased from a supplier by a manufacturer to be used in production. When used in production, raw materials will be classified as either direct materials or indirect materials. (page 28)

Retailer An organization that sells a product in the same physical form as it was in when purchased from the supplier. (page 28)

Total costs The sum of all costs incurred in a center of activity for a specific period of time. (page 23)

Work-in-process The unfinished goods in production. (page 28)

APPENDIX 2-1: JOURNAL ENTRIES FOR FLOW OF PRODUCT COSTS FOR A MANUFACTURER

The journal entries to accompany the T-accounts for steps 1 through 6 on pages 33 to 39 are given below.

STEP 1: Purchase and use of raw materials The purchase of raw materials is recorded with a debit to Raw Materials Inventory and a credit to either Accounts Payable (for a credit purchase) or Cash (for a cash purchase).

Raw Materials Inventory	200,000	
Accounts Payable (or Cash)		200,000

The use of raw materials is recorded with a debit to two different accounts — to Work-in-Process Inventory for direct materials and to Factory Overhead Incurred for indirect materials. The credit is to Raw Materials Inventory.

Work-in-Process Inventory	165,000	
Factory Overhead Incurred	10,000	
Raw Materials Inventory		175,000

STEP 2: Use of labor Direct labor is debited to Work-in-Process Inventory; indirect labor is debited to Factory Overhead Incurred; and nonproduction labor is debited to Salary Expense. The credit is to Salaries Payable.

Work-in-Process Inventory	65,000	
Factory Overhead Incurred	5,000	
Salary Expense	20,000	
Salaries Payable		90,000

STEP 3: Use of factory overhead Any other actual factory overhead costs (in addition to indirect materials and indirect labor) are also debited to the account Factory Overhead Incurred. The credits depend upon the type of factory overhead. In this example, the costs relate to insurance and rent. Assuming that they had been first prepaid, the credits would be to Prepaid Insurance and Prepaid Rent. In addition, the insurance and rent that relates to non-producing areas of the company are debited to their respective expense accounts.

Factory Overhead Incurred................................	7,000	
Rent Expense...	1,000	
Insurance Expense	1,000	
Prepaid Rent		5,000
Prepaid Insurance.....................................		4,000

STEP 4: Transfer of Factory Overhead to Work-in-Process The combined costs of factory overhead are closed out to work-in-process with a debit to Work-in-Process Inventory and a credit to Factory Overhead Incurred.

Work-in-Process Inventory................................	22,000	
Factory Overhead Incurred............................		22,000

STEP 5: Completion of production The cost of the units that are completed during the period are transferred to finished goods by debiting Finished Goods Inventory and crediting Work-in-Process Inventory.

Finished Goods Inventory	280,000	
Work-in-Process Inventory		280,000

STEP 6: Sale of finished goods The cost of the units that are sold are expensed by debiting Cost of Goods Sold and crediting Finished Goods Inventory.

Cost of Goods Sold	310,000	
Finished Goods Inventory		310,000

QUESTIONS

1. Define the term *activity* and list the appropriate measure(s) of activity for the following centers of activity of a manufacturer:

a. Production department   **c.** Sales department
b. Storeroom   **d.** Billing department

2. What is the difference between an *average cost* and a *unit cost?*

3. For each center of activity mentioned below, give a possible measure of activity:

a. A school library
b. A computer center
c. A restaurant
d. A maintenance department
e. An assembly department
f. A hospital
g. A telephone company's installation department
h. A personnel department

4. Distinguish between *product costs* and *period costs.*

5. Explain what is meant by *noninventoriable unexpired costs.*

6. "All costs that are treated as assets when incurred are considered product costs." Do you agree? Explain.

7. "All costs of a manufacturer are treated alike." Do you agree? Explain.

8. "Period costs can be defined as costs that are expensed in the current period." Do you agree? Why or why not?

9. Are the following items product or period costs: depreciation, salaries, and utilities?

10. What will be the significance for a firm of not making the proper distinction between product and period costs?

11. Distinguish between the operations of a service organization, a retailer, and a manufacturer.

12. What are the three types of inventories for a manufacturer?

13. What is the difference between *raw materials* and *direct materials* for a manufacturer?

14. Why do you suppose that the combination of direct labor and factory overhead is referred to as *conversion costs?*

15. "Prime costs plus conversion costs equal the total manufacturing costs incurred for a period of time." Do you agree? Explain.

16. "Cost of goods sold is equal to the sum of direct materials, direct labor, and factory overhead." Do you agree? Explain.

17. List five examples of factory overhead.

18. Define the terms *idle time* and *overtime premium,* and state how these costs should be classified.

19. Explain why supervisory labor costs are classified as factory overhead rather than direct labor.

20. A small manufacturer, Rinky Dink, generated a $5,000 profit in 1988, determined as follows:

Sales		$150,000
Cost of Goods Sold		75,000
Gross Profit		$ 75,000
Selling and Administrative:		
Salespersons' Commissions	$15,000	
President's Salary	50,000	
Advertising	5,000	70,000
Net Income		$ 5,000

When a small investor (he was only 4'11" tall) received his annual report, he made the following comments: "Doesn't Rinky Dink have any depreciable assets or production laborers; or haven't the depreciation and salary expenses been recorded? Shouldn't these expenses also be shown on the income statement?" What reply would you give to the small investor's comment?

EXERCISES

**Exercise 2-1
Classifying product costs
and period costs**

The Oregano Company produces spice racks and needs some help in classifying its costs. It has gathered the following list of costs and asks your help in distinguishing between the product costs and the period costs. Place an X under the proper classification for each cost shown below:

Cost	Product Cost			Period Cost
	Direct Materials	Direct Labor	Factory Overhead	
Transportation costs on raw materials purchased	_____	_____	_____	_____
Insurance on factory building	_____	_____	_____	_____
Property taxes on factory building	_____	_____	_____	_____
Depreciation on sales representatives' cars	_____	_____	_____	_____
Salaries of workers putting racks together	_____	_____	_____	_____
Salaries of machine maint. personnel	_____	_____	_____	_____
Sales representatives' commissions	_____	_____	_____	_____
Transportation costs for units sold	_____	_____	_____	_____
Screws connecting shelves to sides	_____	_____	_____	_____
Rent on factory building	_____	_____	_____	_____
Fuel cost to heat administrative offices	_____	_____	_____	_____

Exercise 2-2
Filling in the unknowns in a raw materials used schedule

Fill in the blanks for the raw materials section of the cost of goods sold schedule of the Grant Manufacturing Company shown below:

	1988	1989	1990
Raw Materials Inventory, Jan. 1	$ 16,000	$ 14,000	$?
Purchases	?	200,000	?
Total Available for Use	$176,000	$?	$250,000
Raw Materials Inventory, Dec. 31..................	?	?	?*
Raw Materials Used	$162,000	$190,000	$?

* The ending inventory is $10,000 higher than the beginning inventory.

(Check figure: Raw materials used = $216,000)

Exercise 2-3
Classifying costs as product costs, period costs, or noninventoriable unexpired costs

The Underhill Company has just completed its first year of operation, 1988, and has gathered the following list of costs incurred during the year. Look over the list and additional facts carefully and then prepare three lists, classifying the costs as **(a)** product costs, **(b)** period costs, or **(c)** noninventoriable unexpired costs.

Land..	$75,000
Prepaid insurance (paid on Jan. 1 for 3 years)...............................	3,000
Salaries and wages:	
Production...	35,000
Salespersons' commissions...	27,000
President's salary	40,000
Machinery (10-year life)...	90,000
Utilities:	
Production...	6,000
Selling and administrative	1,200
Purchases of materials and supplies..	80,000

One-fourth of the materials and supplies purchased were used in production in 1988. Another one-fourth was used in the selling and administrative departments. All but $20,000 of the machinery was used in the production department; the remaining machinery was used in the selling and administrative departments.

Two-thirds of the insurance coverage is related to production and the remainder to selling and administration.

None of the units were finished by the end of 1988.

Exercise 2-4
Computing averages for different measures of activity

The Frazer Company wants to determine an average cost for each of its four departments: production departments P and Q; a storeroom; and a sales office.

	Department			
	P	**Q**	**Storeroom**	**Sales**
Operating costs	$200,000	$125,000	$25,000	$65,000
Units produced (or sold where applicable)	40,000	25,000	N/A	65,000
Direct labor hours	60,000	100,000	N/A	N/A
Number of workers	30	50	6	4
Square feet of space	6,000	9,000	1,000	1,500
Number of requisitions filled	N/A	N/A	250	N/A
Sales revenue	N/A	N/A	N/A	$600,000

Compute average costs for each department, using only those measures of activity that are basically related to the costs of that department.

Exercise 2-5
Preparing a cost of goods sold schedule

Based on the list of account balances below for the Xanadu Company, prepare a schedule of cost of goods sold. For simplicity, assume that all beginning and ending inventories are zero.

Raw Materials Added to the Physical Units Produced......................	$120,000
Supplies Used...	6,000
Insurance...	1,000
Utilities	800
Property Taxes..	2,500
Labor Employed Directly in Production................................	67,000
Indirect Labor	9,000
Depreciation..	2,700
Rent...	950
Idle Time...	150

(Check figure: Cost of goods sold = $210,100)

Exercise 2-6
Determining the cost of direct materials used

Compute the cost of direct materials used for the month of July, 1988, based on the following account balances:

Raw Materials Inventory, July 1, 1988	$ 2,200
Transportation Costs of Purchases.....................................	1,000
Transportation Cost of Units Sold	1,200
Invoice Cost of Units Purchased.......................................	37,000
Purchase Returns..	2,700
Raw Materials Inventory, July 31, 1988	1,500

Of the raw materials used, $1,700 was classified as factory overhead.

(Check figure: $34,300)

Exercise 2-7
Determining idle time and overtime premium

The total wages paid to direct laborers in the blending department of the Tropicaine Concentrated Orange Juice Company were $24,000 during March, 1988. Of this total, there were 1,000 overtime hours and 600 idle hours. Overtime hours are paid double time, and the normal wage rate is $6 per hour. Of the total wages paid, specify how much would be classified as direct labor and how much as factory overhead.

(Check figure: Factory overhead = $9,600)

Exercise 2-8
Determining idle time and
overtime premium

Carey Watson was working on the production of some lawn equipment, one Thursday after-noon, when the power went off for 3 hours. Although Carey was unable to work during this idle time, she was still paid her normal wage of $8 per hour. At quitting time the foreman told all the workers that they would have to work overtime that afternoon, as well as on Saturday, in order to make up for numerous short delays (such as the one that had taken place that afternoon) which had occurred over the last several weeks. Carey ended up working 2 overtime hours that same afternoon and all day Saturday (an 8-hour day). All overtime hours are paid time and a half.

Determine the total wages that were earned by Carey during the week. In addition, specify how much of the total represents the cost of overtime and the cost of idle time. How should these costs be classified?

(Check figure: Total wages = $440)

Exercise 2-9
Correcting a schedule of
cost of goods sold

Shown below is a schedule of cost of goods sold expense for the Error Prone Company for 1989. You are to read it over carefully and make any suggestions that you feel are needed to correct it and/or to make it more presentable.

ERROR PRONE COMPANY Schedule of Cost of Goods Sold December 31, 1989		
Direct Materials, Jan. 1, 1989		$ 15,000
Purchases	$100,000	
Freight-Out	5,000	105,000
Total Available for Sale		$120,000
Direct Materials, Dec. 31, 1989		12,000
Direct Materials Used (including Indirect)		$108,000
Labor:		
Direct	$ 65,000	
Indirect	15,000	80,000
Factory Expense:		
Utilities	$ 1,200	
Payroll Taxes	3,000	
Rent	8,000	
Depreciation	6,000	
President's Salary	30,000	48,200
Prime Costs plus Conversion Costs		$236,200
Increase in Work-in-Process		20,000
Cost of Production Finished during Year		$216,200
Finished Goods, Jan. 1, 1989		35,000
Total Available for Sale		$251,200
Finished Goods, Dec. 31, 1989		31,000
Cost of Goods Sold Expense		$220,200

Exercise 2-10
Determining prime costs
and conversion costs

The Axelrod Corporation incurred the following costs during April, 1988:

Direct Materials	$220,000	Direct Labor	$170,000
Indirect Materials	54,000	Indirect Labor	12,000

In addition, the factory overhead costs (exclusive of indirect materials and indirect labor) were $100,000 for the month. Determine **(a)** the prime costs and **(b)** the conversion costs for April.

(Check figure: Conversion costs = $336,000)

Exercise 2-11
Finding the unknowns in an income statement

Incomplete income statements are shown below for 3 years of Kadafy Enterprises. You are to fill in the blanks found in each statement. Beginning and ending inventories are assumed to be zero.

		1988		1989		1990
Sales		$200,000		$260,000		$?
Cost of Goods Sold:						
Direct Materials...	$40,000		$ 48,000		$?*	
Direct Labor......	80,000		100,000		?*	
Factory						
Overhead........	20,000	?	?	?	68,000	220,000
Gross Profit..........		?		$ 60,000		$ 80,000

* Direct materials are one-half of prime costs during 1990.

(Check figure: Direct materials, 1990 = $76,000)

Exercise 2-12
Preparing a simple income statement for a manufacturer with zero inventories

From the list of accounts shown below, prepare an income statement for the Milburn Company for 1988. There are no beginning or ending inventories for 1988.

Direct Materials..............	$ 60,000	Selling and Administrative	
Factory Overhead	75,000	Expenses	$ 85,000
Sales Revenue...............	400,000	Direct Labor................	100,000

(Check figure: Net income = $80,000)

Exercise 2-13
Classifying costs in different ways

The Andros Company, a retailer, sells a single product, and had the following income statement for 1990:

Sales...	$100,000
Cost of Goods Sold......................................	60,000
Gross Margin	$ 40,000
Operating Costs:	
Salaries $30,000	
Rent.. 6,000	
Commissions... 5,000	
Advertising... 10,000	51,000
Net Income (Loss).......................................	$(11,000)

The president of Andros is considering a significant increase in advertising for the following year, 1991, which should double sales. Salaries, which are set by the owner (who is not involved in day-to-day operations) will remain unchanged. Additional space will be rented to accommodate greater storage needs. Commissions will continue to be 5% of sales.

Each cost shown in the income statement above can be classified in several ways:

As a product cost (P) or a period cost (PER)

As a variable cost (V) or a fixed cost (F)

As a relevant cost (R) or an irrelevant cost (I) in the decision of whether or not to stimulate sales with increased advertising

As a controllable cost (C) or a noncontrollable cost (N) for the company president

For each cost listed below, provide the proper classifications by placing the correct letter in the spaces provided.

Item	Product (P) or Period (PER) Cost	Variable (V) or Fixed (F) Cost	Relevant (R) or Irrelevant (I) Cost	Controllable (C) or Noncontrollable (N) Cost
Cost of goods sold	_____	_____	_____	_____
Salaries	_____	_____	_____	_____
Rent	_____	_____	_____	_____
Commissions	_____	_____	_____	_____
Advertising	_____	_____	_____	_____

PROBLEMS: SET A

Problem A2-1
Showing the progression of manufacturing costs through T-accounts

The Johnny Fever Company begins 1989 with the following balances in inventory:

Raw Materials .... $ 40,000
Work-in-Process 130,000
Finished Goods 285,000

During the year the following transactions took place:

1. Raw Materials Purchased .... $ 56,000
2. Raw Materials Used 89,000
3. Direct Labor Accrued........................ 130,000
4. Indirect Labor Accrued 12,000
5. Utilities Paid 2,700
6. Accrued Rent............................... 4,300
7. Insurance Used 1,400
8. Cost of Goods Transferred to Finished Goods ... 306,000
9. Cost of Goods Sold.......................... 511,000

Required

1. Place the beginning balances in T-accounts.
2. Record all transactions that took place in 1989 in T-account form, showing the progression of costs from raw materials to cost of goods sold expense. Indicate the ending balances in the three inventory accounts.

(Check figure: Finished goods inventory = $80,000)

Problem A2-2
Preparing a schedule of cost of goods sold

The Radar Company had the following balances in its general ledger accounts for 1990:

Materials Used:
    Direct...................................... $140,000
    Indirect 14,000
Labor:
    Direct...................................... 135,000
    Indirect.................................... 60,500
Insurance on Factory Building and Machinery... 4,000
Property Taxes on Factory Building 2,300
Rent on Productive Assets.................... 27,000
Utilities on Factory Building. 20,000
Transportation Costs Associated with
    Units Sold.................................. 17,500

Required

1. Assuming no beginning or ending inventories, prepare a schedule of cost of goods sold expense for 1990. How is this schedule simplified by the assumption of zero inventories?

2. Prepare a schedule of cost of goods sold expense for 1990 assuming the following inventories:

Work-in-Process, Jan. 1, 1990...................	$52,000
Work-in Process, Dec. 31, 1990	68,000
Finished Goods, Jan. 1, 1990..................	95,000
Finished Goods, Dec. 31, 1990	87,000

(Check figure: Cost of goods sold expense = $394,800)

Problem A2-3
Determining year-end
inventories

On Dec. 31, 1990, the Pendulum Swing Company gathered the following information related to 1990:

Materials Purchased	$100,000
Direct Materials Used (there were no indirect materials used)................	80,000
Direct Labor...	150,000
Factory Overhead:	
Indirect Labor	23,000
Utilities	1,000
Insurance..	1,500
Depreciation...	2,000
Cost of Units Completed and Transferred	250,000
Cost of Units Sold	280,000

| **Required** |

Determine the Dec. 31, 1990, inventories if the Jan. 1, 1990, inventories were as follows:

Raw Materials	$16,000
Work-in-Process	30,000
Finished Goods	60,000

(Check figure: Work-in-process, Dec. 31, 1990 = $37,500)

Problem A2-4
Distinguishing product
costs from period costs

During 1988 the Coco Manufacturing Company produced 10,000 units, one-half of which were sold at $20 per unit prior to year-end. The direct materials and labor associated with the units produced were $40,000 and $60,000, respectively. The company also incurred an additional $100,000 of costs that had not been classified by year-end. The controller contends that 25% of the costs are for factory overhead and the remainder relate to selling and administration. The vice president of sales argues that 80% of the total relates to production and only 20% is associated with selling and administration. The president says that the income statement for the entire firm will look the same regardless of who is correct.

| **Required** |

1. Do you agree with the assertion made by the president? Explain why or why not.
2. Prepare an income statement for 1988 based upon the controller's contention.

(Check figure: Net loss = $37,500)

3. Prepare an income statement for 1988 based on the contention of the vice president of sales.

(Check figure: Net loss = $10,000)

4. Explain the difference in the results in parts 2 and 3.

Problem A2-5
Preparing a complete income statement for a manufacturer

The Chapman Company was in its first year of operations, 1989, and the head bookkeeper, H. Holman, has gathered the following data for that year:

Sales..	$1,000,000
Sales Returns and Allowances	40,000
Wages and Salaries:	
Direct Laborers..	120,000
Production Supervisors	24,000
Maintenance	16,000
Salespeople..	54,000
Administrators.......................................	120,000
Raw Materials Used:	
Directly Associated with Units Produced........................	150,000
Indirectly Associated with Units Produced	10,000
Supplies Used in Administrative Offices	4,000
Rentals:	
Factory Building.......................................	5,000
Selling and Administrative Building......................	3,400
Depreciation:	
Production Machinery..................................	3,000
Salespeople's Cars....................................	2,000
Utilities*..	7,000
Freight-Out...	50,000

* Allocated on the basis of kilowatt-hours used in each department. The kilowatt-hours used were as follows:
Production departments	24,000 hr
Selling and administrative departments	4,000 hr

In addition, there were no beginning or ending inventories.

Required

1. Prepare a schedule of cost of goods sold expense for 1989.

(Check figure: Cost of goods sold expense = $334,000)

2. Prepare an income statement for 1989.

Problem A2-6
Preparing a detailed income statement for a manufacturer

The controller of the Nellie White Corporation needs to prepare an income statement for the year 1989. She has her head bookkeeper gather the following information for the year:

Revenues
Revenue from the sale of its product totaled $12,000,000, of which $270,000 was returned. Freight costs were $180,000.

Inventory Balances
At the beginning and end of 1989 Nellie White had the following inventory balances:

	Jan. 1	Dec. 31
Raw Materials and Supplies	$450,000	$300,000
Work-in-Process...	540,000	480,000
Finished Goods	660,000	585,000

Materials and Supplies
Purchases of materials and supplies during 1989 were $3,000,000. Of the materials and supplies used, 70% was for raw materials needed for production and 30% was for administrative supplies. Of the raw materials issued to production, 80% was direct and the remainder was indirect.

Salaries and Wages

The total payroll was distributed as follows:

Production:

Direct.....................................	$3,900,000
Indirect	1,200,000
Selling and administrative	900,000

Rent

The building was rented on Jan. 1, 1989, for 2 years. The rent paid in advance for the 2 years was $90,000. The building was used by the different departments in the following proportions:

Production	four-fifths
Selling and administrative	one-fifth

Depreciation

Machinery having a 10-year life, costing $2,000,000, was purchased on Jan. 1, 1989. All the machinery is used in production activities.

Required	Prepare in good form a detailed income statement for the Nellie White Corporation. Also show a supporting schedule for cost of goods sold.

(Check figure: Cost of goods sold = $7,676,000)

Problem A2-7
Determining unknowns on an income statement for a manufacturer

The Philabbott Dental Supplies Company, which manufactures a variety of dental products, produces nothing but dental floss in its Lakeland, Florida, plant. During April, 1989, 12,800,000 feet of dental floss was manufactured, which would subsequently be sold in 400-foot and 800-foot plastic containers.

There are three raw materials—string, floss, and the containers. During April there were the following purchases and usage (for production of 8,000 of the 400-foot containers and 12,000 of the 800-foot containers):

	Purchases		Usage
	Quantity	**Cost**	
String	2,100 lb	$2,100	2,000 lb
Floss	510 lb	765	500 lb
Containers*	20,500	975	20,000

* The 400-foot and the 800-foot containers cost exactly the same amount.

The beginning inventories for string, floss, and containers were $195, $116, and $50 respectively.

The conversion costs for Philabbott for April were the following amounts:

Salaries of direct laborers (120 hours).............	$1,440
Depreciation....................................	75
Insurance.......................................	25
Property taxes...................................	80
Utilities	20
Indirect labor	1,000

The hours for the direct laborers include 20 hours of idle time, and the wage rate averages $12 per hour. The labor cost is the same amount per container regardless of which size container is being produced. In addition, the overhead costs are distributed evenly among the total containers that are produced.

There is no beginning or ending inventory of Work-in-Process for April. The Apr. 1 balance in Finished Goods is:

	Quantity	Cost
400-foot containers	75	$18
800-foot containers	100	35

The cost of finished goods on Apr. 30 was $12 and $28 for the 400-foot and 800-foot containers, respectively.

The Philabbott Company uses the last-in, first-out (LIFO) method to cost all its inventories.

Required

1. Determine the cost of the Apr. 30 inventory of raw materials.

(Check figure: String = $295)

2. Determine the cost per unit for each container produced during April. There will be a different cost per unit for the 400-foot and 800-foot containers.

(Check figure: 400-foot container = $0.265)

3. Determine how many containers were sold in April.
4. Calculate the cost of goods sold for April.

PROBLEMS: SET B

Problem B2-1
Using T-accounts for a manufacturer

Carlson began his company, WARP, Inc., on Jan. 1, 1989. During his second year, 1990, the following things occurred:

Raw Materials Purchased.......	$30,000	Depreciation	$ 1,500
Direct Materials Used..........	27,500	Utilities Used	1,000
Indirect Materials Used	2,500	Property Taxes Accrued........	900
Direct Labor Accrued..........	32,500	Cost of Goods Finished during	
Indirect Labor Accrued.........	12,500	1990	75,900
		Cost of Items Sold in 1990......	95,000

In addition, the controller found the following Jan. 1, 1990, balances in the general ledger:

Raw Materials .... $ 5,000
Work-in-Process 12,500
Finished Goods 25,000

Required

1. Place the beginning inventory balances in T-accounts. Record all transactions that took place during 1990 in the T-accounts, showing the progression of costs from raw materials to cost of goods sold expense.
2. Prepare journal entries for all transactions.
3. Indicate the Dec. 31, 1990, balance in each inventory account.

Problem B2-2
Determining the cost of goods sold, with and without inventories

The controller for the Cinderella Company has gathered information about the following costs for 1988:

Direct Materials Used	$35,000	Insurance on Salespeople's Cars..	$1,500
Indirect Materials Used	2,000	Depreciation on Productive Ma-	
Direct Labor..................	40,000	chinery	5,000
Indirect Labor	15,000	Utilities of Factory	6,200
Sales Labor...................	25,000	Freight Costs for Units Sold	2,400
Insur. on Factory and Machinery	4,000		

Required	1. For this assignment, assume that the beginning and ending inventories for Cinderella had zero balances. Prepare a schedule of cost of goods sold for 1988.

2. Prepare the schedule of cost of goods sold a second time. This time, assume the following inventories for 1988:

Jan. 1, 1988:		Dec. 31, 1988:	
Work-in-Process.............	$10,000	Work-in-Process.............	$12,000
Finished Goods	20,000	Finished Goods	16,000

(Check figure: Cost of goods sold = $109,200)

Problem B2-3
Determining the unknown
inventory values

At the end of 1989, the McLeod Company accumulated the following information:

A Purchase of Raw Materials	$240,000
Materials Used:	
B-1 Direct...	200,000
B-2 Indirect	20,000
C Direct Labor Accrued...	240,000
Other Factory Overhead:	
Indirect Labor	100,000
Utilities Accrued	7,000
Property Taxes Accrued..	12,000
Payroll Taxes	8,000
E Cost of Units Completed in 1989....................................	280,000
F Cost of Units Sold in 1989...	330,000

Assume that the Jan. 1, 1989, inventories were as follows:

Raw Materials	$ 40,000
Work-in-Process	100,000
Finished Goods	160,000

Required	Determine the Dec. 31, 1989, balances in each inventory account.

(Check figure: Finished goods, Dec. 31, 1989 = $110,000)

Problem B2-4
Assigning product vs.
period costs

The Sutton Company manufactured 40,000 units during 1990 and sold 10,000 units at $40 per unit. The prime costs incurred during the year were $100,000 for direct materials and $120,000 for direct labor. The remaining costs incurred by Sutton during 1990 were $400,000, which had not been separated into manufacturing costs vs. selling and administrative costs by year-end. The vice president of manufacturing believes that only $100,000 of the $400,000 is related to manufacturing, while the sales vice president argues that $320,000 of the $400,000 is manufacturing costs. The president has no idea how much of the $400,000 is associated with manufacturing but doesn't think it makes any difference. He contends that the income statement for the firm will be the same regardless of which department gets assigned the most costs.

Required	1. Do you agree with the president's opinion? Explain why or why not.

2. Prepare an income statement for 1990 based on the contention of the vice president of manufacturing.
3. Prepare an income statement for 1990 based on the contention of the vice president of sales.

(Check figure: Net income = $185,000)

4. Explain the difference in the results in parts 2 and 3.

Problem B2-5
Preparing a detailed income statement for a manufacturer

The Elia Pizzeria, which produces 10-ounce pizzas, just completed operations in 1989. Paul Michael, an accountant, has gathered the following data related to the year:

Labor:	
Direct Laborers..	$160,000
Supervisors of Production	60,000
Production Janitors..	32,000
Administrative Employees....................................	40,000
Sales Representatives...	80,000
Raw Materials Used*..	240,000
Depreciation:	
Building†...	16,000
Machinery and Equipment	4,000
President's Orange Computer	2,000
Utilities‡...	14,400
Property Taxes†...	12,000
Shipping Costs of Units Sold..............................	10,000
Sales Discounts..	10,800
Sales	800,000
Interest on Long-Term Borrowing	3,000

* $40,000 of which is for indirect materials.
† One-half relates to factory facilities; the remainder relates to selling and administrative facilities.
‡ Allocated on the basis of kilowatt-hours used in each department. The kilowatt-hours used were as follows:

Production departments	10,000 hr
Selling and administrative departments	2,000 hr

Required

1. Prepare a schedule of cost of goods sold expense. There were no beginning or ending inventories.
2. Prepare the 1989 income statement for Elia Pizzeria.

(Check figure: Net income = $115,800)

Problem B2-6
Preparing a comprehensive income statement for a manufacturer

The Deferral Company has gathered the following information concerning its operations during 1988, and it would like you to prepare a detailed income statement for the year:

Revenues
Sales for 1988 (of which $90,000 was returned) were $4,000,000. The costs of shipping the product were $60,000.

Materials and Supplies
Purchases of materials and supplies for the year were $1,000,000, which was added to a beginning inventory of $150,000. At year-end there was a $100,000 remaining balance in inventory. Of the materials and supplies used, three-fourths was used in production ($650,000 of which was direct materials) and the remaining one-fourth was used in the selling and administrative departments.

Salaries and Wages
The payroll for the year was $2,000,000, broken down as follows:

Direct laborers	$1,300,000
Indirect laborers...........................	400,000
Selling and administrative personnel..........	300,000

Insurance

A 3-year policy was purchased on Jan. 1, 1988, for $30,000. The insurance was related to departments in the following manner:

Production	three-fifths
Selling and administrative	two-fifths

Depreciation

The cost of the depreciable assets used by the company was $2,300,000, and the balances in Accumulated Depreciation on Jan. 1 and Dec. 31 were $950,000 and $1,200,000, respectively. All but 20% of the depreciable assets are used in production.

Inventories

The balances in Work-in-Process and Finished Goods were:

	Jan. 1	Dec. 31
Work-in-Process.	$180,000	$160,000
Finished Goods	220,000	195,000

Other Items

Interest expense for 1988 was $27,000, and income taxes were 40% of income before tax.

Required	Prepare in good form a detailed income statement for the Deferral Company. Also show a supporting schedule for cost of goods sold.

(Check figure: Net income $280,800)

Problem B2-7
Preparing a detailed income statement for a manufacturer

The Sugarsweet Lollipop Company produces nothing but oversized lollipops in its Seffner City plant. During December, 1989, Sugarsweet produced 70,000 lollipops in two sizes—the quarter pound and the half pound.

There are three basic raw materials: lollipop syrup, sticks, and wrappers. The beginning and ending balances of Raw Materials Inventory for December are as follows:

	Dec. 1		Dec. 31	
	Quantity	Cost	Quantity	Cost
Syrup	2,000 lb	$100	7,000 lb	$382
Sticks	5,000	50	2,500	27
Wrappers	15,000	75	500	3
		$225		$412

During the month of December 40,000 quarter-pound lollipops and 30,000 half-pound lollipops were produced. The raw materials purchased in December were:

	Quantity	Cost
Syrup	30,000 lb	$1,650
Sticks	68,000	738
Wrappers	56,000	336
		$2,724

Forty percent of the cost of the syrup used was assigned to the quarter-pound lollipops and the remaining 60% was assigned to the half-pound lollipops. The costs of the sticks and wrappers were allocated to the lollipops in proportion to the number of lollipops produced.

The other production costs incurred during December were as follows:

Direct labor (1,200 hr, split evenly between the two sizes)	$ 8,400
Indirect labor	2,500
Property taxes..	900
Insurance..	200
Payroll taxes	2,600
Other overhead...	800
	$15,400

All overhead costs were split evenly between the two types of lollipops.

There were no beginning or ending balances in work-in-process for December, but the Dec. 1 and 31 balances in Finished Goods were:

	Dec. 1		Dec. 31	
	Number	**Cost**	**Number**	**Cost**
Quarter pound	8,000	$2,240	6,500	?
Half pound	5,000	1,050	2,000	?
	13,000	$3,290	8,500	?

The weighted average method is used to account for all inventories. The lollipops sell for $0.74 apiece for the quarter-pound size and $1.00 apiece for the half-pound size.

Required

Prepare in good form an income statement for the Sugarsweet Lollipop Company. Assume that the selling and administrative costs totaled $8,500. Show all supporting calculations for the two types of lollipops separately and clearly.

(Check figure: Cost of goods sold = $19,140)

Analysis of Cost Behavior: Variable, Fixed, and Mixed

In this chapter you will learn the following:

- What the terms *variable costs* and *fixed costs* mean
- How to represent variable costs and fixed costs graphically
- What a relevant range of activity implies
- How the economist's view of variable costs differs from that of the accountant
- The distinction between *committed fixed costs* and *discretionary fixed costs*, and the distinction between *proportionately variable costs* and *step variable costs.*
- *What a mixed cost* is
- Why it is important to distinguish variable costs from fixed costs
- How to determine the behavioral components of a mixed cost — the variable part and the fixed part
- How to use the high-low, visual approximation, and least squares methods to evaluate mixed costs

In Chapter 2 we first explained what we mean by total costs — the summation of all costs associated with a center of activity — and average costs — the total costs divided by the activity of the center. We then pointed out that we have totals and averages for product costs — those costs that are assigned to inventory when incurred and expensed when the units are sold — as well as for period costs — those costs that are expensed when incurred. In this chapter we will look at the *behavior* of product costs and period costs, that is, how costs respond in total and on the average to changes in activity. We will be concerned with questions such as the following:

1. What is the behavior of a particular cost — variable, fixed, or mixed?
2. Why is it important for a cost to be classified according to its behavior?
3. How can the behavior of a cost be determined when it is not already known?

THE THREE TYPES OF COSTS: VARIABLE, FIXED, AND MIXED

Three types of costs by behavior

There are three types of costs: variable, fixed, and mixed. Which type a particular cost is depends upon how its *total* behaves or responds to changes in activity.

A ***variable cost,*** in total, changes in the same direction and in direct proportion to changes in activity. The costs of direct materials, direct labor, supplies, and sales commissions are a few examples of variable costs.

A ***fixed cost,*** in total, does not change in response to changes in activity. That's the simplest definition. A more complete definition is as follows: For a given period of time and within a relevant range of activity, a total fixed cost does not change in response to changes in activity. Rent, depreciation, property taxes, and certain salaries are examples of fixed costs. We will explain a little later what we mean by *for a given period of time* and *within a relevant range of activity.*

Some costs are a combination of variable costs and fixed costs; these are called ***mixed costs.*** Part of a mixed cost *is not* expected to respond to changes in activity — the fixed cost component — and part *is* expected to respond to changes in activity — the variable cost component. An example of a mixed cost is a utility bill. Part of it is fixed — you will be charged this amount even if you don't turn on the electricity; and part of it is variable — the more kilowatt-hours you use, the higher your cost will be.

Variable and Fixed Costs and Changes in Activity

The next step in understanding the behavior of costs is to see how average variable costs and average fixed costs respond to changes in activity. In the following discussion we will confine ourselves to variable costs and fixed costs. This will prepare us for the analysis of mixed costs that comes later in this chapter.

Total and average variable costs

For variable costs, in order for the total cost to respond in direct proportion to changes in activity, the average variable cost (such as a variable cost per hour or per unit) must remain constant. For example, if the variable cost per unit is $4 when 10 units are produced, it is also $4 per unit when 100 or 1,000 units are produced. Only if the *average* variable cost remains unchanged will the *total* variable costs change in direct proportion — represented by a straight line on a graph — to changes in activity.

Total and average fixed costs

On the other hand, for *total* fixed costs to remain unchanged in response to changes in activity, the *average* fixed costs must be inversely related to activity. That is, the greater the amount of activity, the lower the average fixed cost; and the lower the amount of activity, the higher the average fixed cost.

In Example 3-1 we show you what we mean. Look carefully at the total and average variable and fixed costs and notice how they respond to changes in activity.

In this example we are measuring activity by the number of units produced, and the average is a cost per unit. You may remember that in Chapter 2 we mentioned that activity can be measured in many ways — units, hours, requisitions, or square feet, to name a few — and that an average can be a cost per unit (as shown in Example 3-1), a cost per hour, a cost per requisition, or a cost per square foot.

These total and average variable and fixed costs are represented in graphic form in Figure 3-1. The relationship between activity and total variable costs is shown in graph 1; between activity and total fixed costs, in graph 2. Graphs 3 and 4 depict the relationships between activity and the average costs. For all graphs in this section of the book, the horizontal axis represents activity (units in this example) and the vertical axis represents dollars of cost (or revenue).

In Example 3-1, activity was measured in terms of units of production, and therefore the average cost was a ***cost per unit.*** Remember, however, that activity can be measured in a variety of ways — units, hours, patients treated, requisitions pro-

Example 3-1

THE HARRIS COMPANY

The Harris Company expects its variable costs to be $4 per unit and its fixed costs to be $10,000. Predicted total variable and total fixed costs at several different possible levels of activity are as follows:

Activity (in Units)	×	Variable Cost per Unit	=	Total Variable Costs	Total Fixed Costs
100	×	$4	=	$ 400	$10,000
150	×	$4	=	$ 600	$10,000
500	×	$4	=	$2,000	$10,000
1,000	×	$4	=	$4,000	$10,000
1,200	×	$4	=	$4,800	$10,000
1,500	×	$4	=	$6,000	$10,000

The average for the variable and fixed costs at each of these levels of activity are as follows:

Activity (in Units)	Variable Costs per Unit	Fixed Costs per Unit (Rounded)
100	$4 ($ 400 ÷ 100)	$100 ($10,000 ÷ 100)
150	$4 ($ 600 ÷ 150)	$ 67 ($10,000 ÷ 150)
500	$4 ($2,000 ÷ 500)	$ 20 ($10,000 ÷ 500)
1,000	$4 ($4,000 ÷ 1,000)	$ 10 ($10,000 ÷ 1,000)
1,200	$4 ($4,800 ÷ 1,200)	$ 8 ($10,000 ÷ 1,200)
1,500	$4 ($6,000 ÷ 1,500)	$ 7 ($10,000 ÷ 1,500)

Different ways to define activity

cessed, etc.—depending upon the type of organization and the specific center of activity within the organization. For example, if the Harris Company were Harris Hospital, the activity could be measured in number of patients, and the average variable cost would be $4 per patient instead of $4 per unit.

A Given Period of Time

According to the way we define a fixed cost, the total does not respond to changes in activity. Now, this does not mean that a fixed cost will remain the same indefinitely or that a fixed cost will remain the same regardless of how high or low activity is expected to be. The more complete definition we gave for a fixed cost was that it is not expected to change, in total, in response to changes in activity:

1. For a given period of time

2. Within a "relevant range" of activity

Let's first see what we mean by the phrase *for a given period of time.* Then we will explain what we mean by *within a relevant range of activity.*

CHAPTER 3 Analysis of Cost Behavior: Variable, Fixed, and Mixed
The Three Types of Costs: Variable, Fixed, and Mixed

69

FIGURE 3-1
Graphs for Variable and Fixed Costs

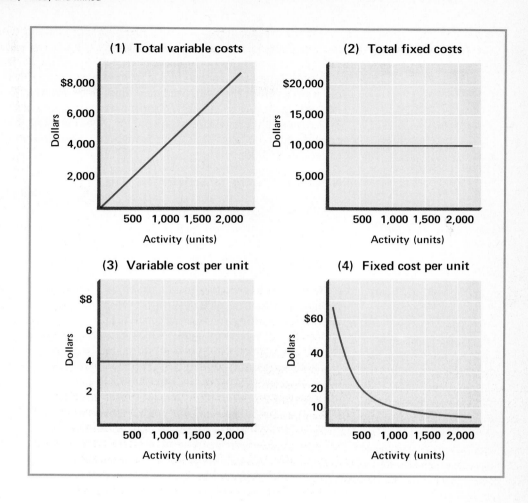

Assume for a moment that you are trying to predict how much three costs (making up part of the $10,000 total in Example 3-1), will be in 1988. During 1987 these costs were as follows:

Property Taxes	$1,500
Insurance	500
Rent	4,000

Fixed costs can change

You know that your property has been appraised at a greater value than it was a year ago, so you expect your property taxes and insurance to increase by 20% in 1988. According to your lease, the rent will automatically drop to $3,500 if you renew for an additional 5 years—and you do plan to renew.

The following are your predictions for 1988:

Property Taxes	$1,800
Insurance	600
Rent	3,500

These costs are all fixed—they just happen to be different in 1988 than they were in 1987: Many fixed costs are fixed only for a single period of time; the fact that they change from one period to another in no way affects their classification as fixed.

Not only can fixed costs change from one period to the next, but they can also be a different amount than you predicted them to be. For instance, if your county government in 1988 started assessing property taxes at 100% of fair market value instead of 80%, you might get a property tax bill for 1988 of $2,250. These property taxes are still considered to be fixed costs even though they are different from the amount that you expected, $1,800.

A Relevant Range of Activity

As you may have already guessed, the ***relevant range of activity*** is a range of activity in which the fixed costs do not respond to changes in activity. Stated in more general terms, it is only within the relevant range of activity that *all* assumptions concerning the behavior of costs are expected to be valid.

Where the cost assumptions are valid

Assume that in Example 3-1 the Harris Company is operating at a full capacity of 1,500 units and wants to increase its production to 2,000 units. Is it reasonable to expect the fixed costs to remain at $10,000 if Harris increases its capacity to accommodate production of 2,000 units? Of course not. Additional machinery must be acquired, resulting in more depreciation, more salaried supervisors for additional workers, more insurance, and additional property taxes. All of these costs combine into a higher fixed cost, corresponding to the higher level of activity.

Assume that the additional fixed costs needed by Harris to increase the capacity would be $5,000, increasing the total fixed costs from $10,000 to $15,000. Assume also that the capacity can now go as high as 3,000 units. If Harris expected to produce from 0 to 1,500 units each year, that would represent one relevant range of activity for which the fixed costs would be only $10,000. But if Harris wants to expand the maximum capacity from 1,500 to 3,000 units, that higher range—from 1,501 to 3,000 units—would represent a higher relevant range of activity, and the total fixed costs for this higher range would be $15,000.

FIGURE 3-2
Graph Depicting the Relevant Range
Fixed costs will change at a new relevant range of activity.

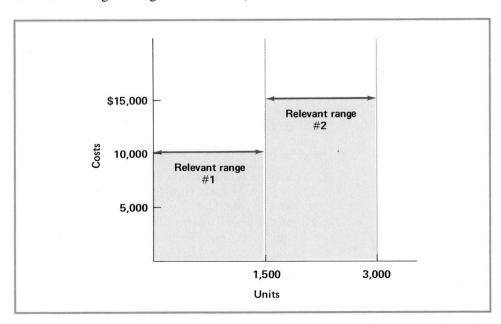

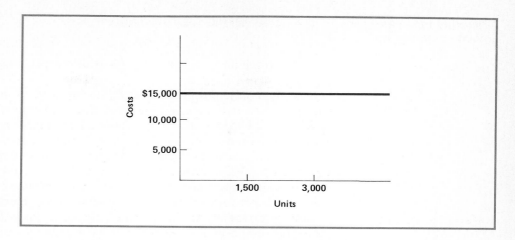

FIGURE 3-3
Simplified Fixed Costs
Graph

The graph depicting these two relevant ranges for the Harris Company is shown in Figure 3-2. Other relevant ranges of activity would also be possible. For example, if Harris increased its maximum productive capacity from 3,000 to 5,000 units, then that range—between 3,001 and 5,000 units—would represent a higher relevant range requiring higher amounts of fixed costs.

Assume that we know that the Harris Company is going to operate in the second relevant range of activity—somewhere between 1,500 and 3,000 units. Rather than showing both ranges as we do in Figure 3-2, we can simplify the graph by merely showing a single horizontal line—representing $15,000 of fixed costs at all levels of activity (shown in Figure 3-3). Of course, this does not mean that Harris can actually produce more than 3,000 units with fixed costs of only $15,000—we merely drew a single horizontal line to simplify the appearance of the graph.

But what if the Harris Company actually produces less than 1,500 units after it has expanded its capacity to accommodate production of 1,501 to 3,000 units. Will the fixed costs still be $15,000, or will they drop back down to the amount for range 1—$10,000? Even though the fixed costs for range 1 are $10,000, they will be that amount only until the capacity is expanded beyond 1,500 units. Once the fixed costs are increased to $15,000, they cannot be later reduced simply because activity doesn't reach the level expected. So once the capacity is expanded and the fixed costs increase, then the fixed costs—at least in the short run—will be $15,000 for production of any amount from 0 to 3,000 units.

It's a lot harder for fixed costs to decrease as activity decreases

Relevant Range and Variable Costs

In the previous section we defined the relevant range as a range of activity in which total fixed costs are not expected to change. The concept of a relevant range doesn't apply only to fixed costs, however. That is why we added to the definition that *all* cost behavior assumptions are valid only within the relevant range—this includes the assumptions for variable costs as well as for fixed costs.

We say that variable costs, in total, change in direct proportion to changes in activity and that average variable costs are constant. Are these statements true no matter how few or how many units we make?

In reality, it is quite possible that the average variable cost is different for different relevant ranges of activity, just as the total fixed costs are different. In basic economics courses you may have already learned—or will soon learn—that economists disagree with accountants' handling of:

*Economists differ with
accounting assumptions*

1. Average variable costs as constant

2. Total variable costs as changing in direct proportion to changes in activity

3. The graph for total variable costs as showing a straight line

Since it is quite possible that you'll be confused by the apparent contradiction between the accountant's and the economist's viewpoints, we want to explain their views and then to show how the accountant's assumptions are not really in conflict with the economist's opinion from a practical point of view.

Economics teachers will tell you that for low amounts of production, the average variable cost is high. But as more and more units are produced, they are made more efficiently and the average variable cost falls. It continues to fall until it reaches a low point—the most efficient level of production in the short run—where the average variable cost is lowest. After that point, units are produced less and less efficiently and the average cost begins to rise, and it will continue to rise at higher levels of production. This view of an average variable cost (AVC) is shown in Figure 3-4.

As you can see, the average starts out at about $6 per unit and drops steadily until it reaches a low of about $3.60 per unit, just below 2,500 units. Then the average begins to rise again as production increases above the point of short-run maximum efficiency.

Since the average variable cost is constantly changing, the total variable costs cannot be a straight line—because the total does not change in direct proportion to changes in activity. Look now at Figure 3-5 for the economist's view of total variable costs (TVC).

When the AVC in Figure 3-4 is falling—between 0 and 2,400 units—the TVC curve in Figure 3-5 is increasing at a decreasing rate. The total continues to increase at a decreasing rate until the AVC in Figure 3-4 reaches the low point—at about 2,400 units. After 2,400 units the AVC begins to rise and the TVC in Figure 3-5 continues to increase—but now at an increasing rate.

Although the views of the accountant and the economist do seem to contradict each other, this doesn't mean, however, that the two views cannot be reconciled. We accountants don't reject the economist's view of curvilinearity, but instead we con-

FIGURE 3-4
**Economist's View of
Average Variable Cost**
The average variable cost
decreases until it reaches a
minimum. Then it increases.

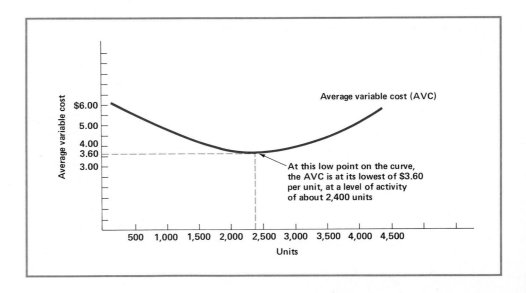

CHAPTER 3 Analysis of Cost Behavior: Variable, Fixed, and Mixed
The Three Types of Costs: Variable, Fixed, and Mixed

73

FIGURE 3-5
Economist's View of Total Variable Costs
Total variable costs increase with activity but are represented by a curve.

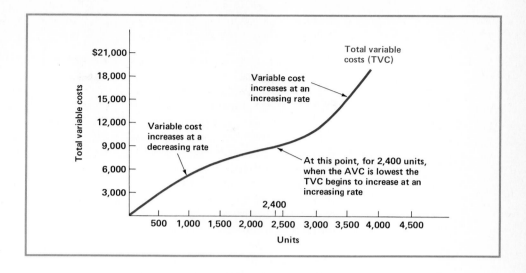

tend that within the relevant range of activity, if the costs are truly curvilinear, any differences between the curve and a straight line are minor. Even if the straight-line assumption isn't completely correct, it certainly is good enough for providing useful information to management.

When we show both the economist's curve and the accountant's straight line on the same graph, as we've done in Figure 3-6, notice how close the two are — but only within the relevant range of activity of 1,501 to 3,000 units.

Of course, at higher or lower ranges of activity the curve and the straight line are further apart. But for different ranges all we have to do is draw new straight lines to closely approximate the curves in each different range.

In the next two sections you will learn that there are different types of variable costs — proportionately variable and step variable. So far, we have only been talking about the proportionately variable. In addition, you'll find out that there are two

Our assumptions are okay within the relevant range of activity

FIGURE 3-6
The Accountant's and the Economists's TVC within the Relevant Range of Activity
The differences are small within the relevant range.

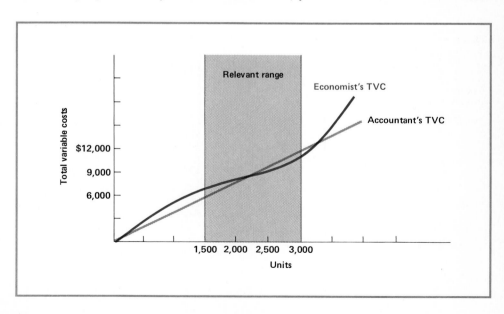

extremely different types of fixed costs—committed fixed and discretionary fixed; but we've only been discussing one of these types—the committed fixed costs.

Types of Variable Costs: Proportionate and Step

The definition we gave for variable costs at the beginning of this chapter is a completely accurate description for only those variable costs that we call ***proportionately variable.*** We explained how the total for these variable costs changes "in direct proportion" to changes in activity. "In direct proportion" means that for each and every increase or decrease in a unit of activity, the total variable cost will increase or decrease by exactly the same amount. This also means that the average cost is exactly the same no matter how many units are produced.

Graphically, the total variable cost is represented by a straight line—showing the connection of a continuous flow of points, coming out of the origin and having a slope equal to the variable cost per unit of activity. For example, if an average variable cost is $5 per unit, then the total cost for 1 unit will be $5; for 2 units, $10; for 3, 4, and 5 units, $15, $20, and $25, respectively, and so on. The graphic representation of this example would be as shown in Figure 3-7.

Materials are a good example of proportionate variable costs

The best example of proportionately variable costs is direct materials. When we purchase materials, the amount we purchase can be stored in inventory and does not have to be used until it is needed in production. When it is needed, it can be used in the exact quantities that are needed for the level of activity worked. Referring to the direct material costs in Figure 3-7, let's assume that each unit of activity requires 1 pound of direct materials at $5 per pound, which totals $5 per unit. If we expect to make 1 unit, we should be able to use 1 pound of direct materials, costing $5. For 5 units, we will use 5 pounds, at a cost of $25. In this example, no matter how many units are produced, the total pounds used should be the number of units produced multiplied by 1 pound per unit, with each pound costing $5.

FIGURE 3-7
Proportionately Variable Costs

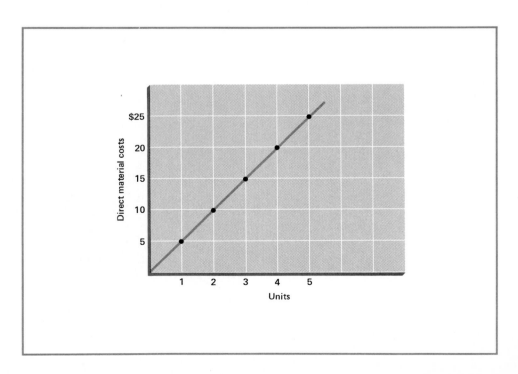

FIGURE 3-8
A Microscopic View of
Step Variable Costs
This picture is for a very small
number of units, so the steps
look bigger than they really are.

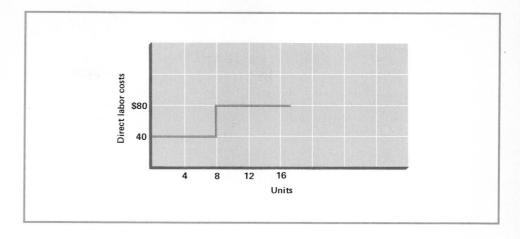

Step variable costs
represent purchases of tiny
chunks of costs

For practical purposes, ***step variable costs*** — the second type of variable costs — are treated like proportionately variable costs although they do not behave in exactly the same manner. For step variable costs, the relationship between changes in costs and changes in activity is represented graphically by a straight line that runs through a series of small steps, rather than by a straight line that connects a series of points. All variable labor costs — direct and indirect — are good examples of step variable costs.

The reason these costs increase step-by-step is that they must be purchased in small chunks which cannot be stored until the time comes for them to be used. Each entire chunk has to be used when purchased, regardless of the number of units produced. No part of a chunk may be stored for use at a later time. For example, assume the variable cost of $5 per unit is for direct labor. Each unit produced requires 1 hour of labor at $5 per hour, or $5 of labor per unit produced. Assume also that because of union agreements or industry conditions, we cannot pay a worker less than 1 day's pay. Therefore, a worker will receive $40 per day (8 hours $\times$ $5 per hour) regardless of how many units are produced. We will not need to hire a second laborer until we expect to produce more than 8 units a day. When that happens, two workers will receive $80 per day for producing any amount between 9 and 16 units. A microscopic graphic view of these labor costs for the first 16 units is represented by the two steps shown in Figure 3-8. There would be a new step for each successive group of 8 units, and each new step would increase the total costs by $40.

After you have looked at Figure 3-8, you may be wondering why we treat direct labor as a proportionately variable cost; when each step is examined individually, it looks more like a fixed cost. The reason is that the two steps in Figure 3-8 are a very small part of a much bigger picture. When we consider the big picture, we realize that the firm is probably making many thousands of units and using hundreds of workers. Looking at the graph in Figure 3-9, for a much larger amount of activity, you can see that the steps are very small, almost blending into a single straight line.

For large amounts of activity, a straight line would be an adequate representation of the many steps. Therefore, we will treat the step variable costs as if they were proportionately variable — at $5 per unit. This is represented by the straight line that is drawn connecting the steps in Figure 3-9. Since the steps are very small, any resulting error that occurs from using the straight line to approximate a point on one of the steps will be immaterial. We'll prove this point on page 77 when we compare step variable costs to step fixed costs.

FIGURE 3-9
Overall View of Step
Variable Costs
Step variable costs can be
treated as proportionately
variable costs.

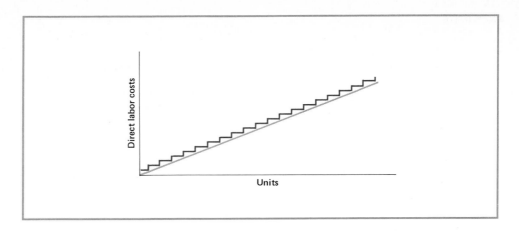

Types of Fixed Costs: Committed and Discretionary

There are two types of fixed costs: *committed fixed costs* and *discretionary fixed costs.* Whether a fixed cost is committed or discretionary depends upon the degree to which management can influence that cost in the short run.

Fixed costs over which management has little influence from one period to the next are committed fixed costs.

Fixed costs that are subject to considerable management influence in the short run are discretionary fixed costs.

Committed fixed costs are costs of capacity and organization

Committed fixed costs represent the costs of (1) establishing the basic organization, (2) maintaining it, and (3) providing its capacity to produce. Examples of committed fixed costs include salaries of key personnel; depreciation on property, plant, and equipment; property taxes; and insurance. If production activity were to cease suddenly, falling to zero output (due to a strike, for example), committed fixed costs would continue to be incurred. If the company did not incur these costs even during such an inactive period, it would not be able to revert to the previous level of productive activity once the interruption was over.

Once management decides upon the level of productive output at which it expects to operate, it commits the organization to incurring the fixed costs necessary to provide that output over an extended period of time. For an established specific level of productive capacity, there is very little that management can do to influence the amount of committed fixed costs from one period to the next. Nevertheless, it is management's responsibility to ensure that:

1. The productive capacity provided by the committed fixed costs is used efficiently.

2. The productive capacity is used at its maximum level before incurring additional committed fixed costs to increase maximum capacity.

There's more flexibility with discretionary fixed costs

Discretionary fixed costs are quite different from committed fixed costs. Discretionary fixed costs are decided upon and funded by management at the beginning of each budget period. The amount funded at the beginning is the amount that can be spent during the budget period. Nevertheless, during the period the amount actually spent can be adjusted at management's discretion. Examples of discretionary fixed costs include the costs of advertising, charitable contributions, research, recruitment, training, bonuses, and company-supported picnics.

Example 3-2

THE SHORTSIGHTED BINOCULAR COMPANY

The Shortsighted Binocular Company funded (or appropriated) $1 million in the 1990 budget for research. On July 1, 1990, after one-half of this amount had been spent, the president of Shortsighted canceled all remaining research projects and laid off its research personnel. The reason he gave for these actions was that the profit picture looked bleak for the entire year and the only way to avoid having a loss was to reduce discretionary expenditures as much as possible.

The president used his discretion to reduce the research costs to salvage some profits for the year. Because of this shortsighted decision, it is possible that the profits of future years will be substantially reduced, since the firm may not be able to remain competitive with firms continuing and eventually benefitting from their research.

Just because a cost may be a discretionary fixed cost does not mean that it is expendable or less important than any other type of cost. Discretionary fixed costs are not nonessential items that can automatically be eliminated whenever profits are low. Discretionary fixed costs are as essential to attaining long-range organization goals as are committed fixed costs. For example, a firm may have the newest, most efficient, and most productive capacity—all a result of committed fixed costs. But if that firm does not promote its product, does not adapt the product to changing tastes and demands, does not recruit and train new personnel—all requiring discretionary fixed costs—it will probably be at a competitive disadvantage relative to firms that see the importance of these discretionary expenditures.

Hybrid Costs: Step Fixed and Discretionary Variable

In the previous sections we used the term *step cost* to indicate a type of variable cost and the term *discretionary cost* to indicate a fixed cost. Sometimes, however, we think of step costs as fixed and discretionary costs as variable.

Step Fixed Costs

If you recall our discussion of the relevant range and how it relates to fixed costs, you'll remember we pointed out that fixed costs may increase with activity—but only as a result of large increases in activity. These increases—or steps—are similar to the steps for direct labor, with a few major differences.

First, a very small increase in activity is enough to result in a new step for step variable costs, but the increase in activity needed to result in a new step for fixed costs is usually quite large. For example, in Figure 3-9, an additional step for direct labor is expected every time 8 additional units are produced. But back in Figure 3-2, we saw that the second step is only expected to occur when production reaches 1,501 units.

Second, the steps themselves—representing the increased costs—are very small for step variable costs but quite large for step fixed costs. For the direct labor costs in Figure 3-9, each step represents an increase of only $40. But for the fixed costs in Figure 3-2, the second step represents an increase of $5,000.

Don't treat step fixed costs as proportionate variable

As a result, it is not only acceptable but also preferable—from a purely practical standpoint—to treat the step variable costs as if they were proportionately variable. Not only is the proportionately variable rate easier to calculate, but the possible error from its use will be very small. For example, if we expect to produce 1,505 units next year, the estimate of direct labor costs arrived at by using the proportionately variable rate of $5 per unit is $7,525 (1,505 units × $5). However, if we worry about the steps, we first have to decide on the number of steps needed to produce 1,505 units and then

FIGURE 3-10
For Step Fixed Costs, You
Must Know Exactly Which
Step You're On

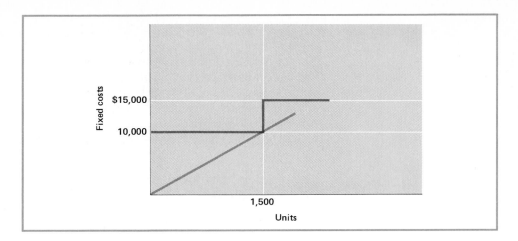

have to multiply each step by $40. For 1,505 units the number of steps needed is:

$$\text{Number of steps} = 1,505 \div 8 \text{ hours per step} = 188.125 \text{ steps}$$

Since we cannot purchase partial steps, we'll need 189 steps, each one costing $40. The estimate of direct labor costs is $7,560 (189 steps $\times$ $40), which is only $35 more than the estimate calculated by using the rate of $5 per unit.

Since the steps are so large for step fixed costs, the approximation of a point on one of the steps—using a straight line connecting the steps—would lead to materially inaccurate predictions. To make good predictions of step fixed costs, we need to know exactly what the level of activity is where a new step is required and exactly what the fixed costs are for each step.

Let's see now what happens when we use the straight line shown in Figure 3-10 to approximate the fixed costs (which we saw originally in Figure 3-2) when 1,505 units are going to be produced. Using the straight line—thereby treating the cost as if it were proportionately variable—we would predict the costs to be a little over $10,000. But—as the second step clearly shows—the costs should actually be at the top of that step—$15,000. The difference between the two approaches to estimating the costs at the 1,505-unit level of activity is nearly $5,000—which is a quite significant error.

Discretionary Variable Costs

Although in most situations discretionary costs are considered fixed costs, in some situations they are treated as if they were variable costs.

Fixed costs as a constant
cost per unit

In this example the discretionary costs of advertising were treated as variable costs since the cost per unit was not affected by the activity. Although discretionary fixed costs may in certain situations be treated as variable costs, throughout this book they are assumed to be fixed costs unless specified otherwise.

Example 3-3

THE THUMBY COMPANY

The Thumby Company has decided that it can afford to spend $2 on advertising for each unit produced, and it budgets the advertising expenditures on this basis for the upcoming year. During each of the first 3 months of 1988, when production is scheduled to be 10,000, 15,000, and 18,000 units per month, respectively, Thumby plans on the following expenditures for advertising:

January	10,000 units × $2/unit	=	$20,000
February	15,000 units × $2/unit	=	$30,000
March	18,000 units × $2/unit	=	$36,000

MIXED COSTS

Mixed = variable + fixed

Some costs are not strictly classified as either variable or fixed, but are a combination of the two. As mentioned previously, a good example of such a cost might be a utility bill, in which a basic fixed charge is paid regardless of the kilowatt-hours used and a variable portion is paid based on the number of kilowatt-hours used. The total of these variable and fixed cost components is a *mixed cost.*

Another example of a mixed cost is the total payment for wages and salaries. Some laborers, such as supervisors, earn a salary that remains the same regardless of the level of activity, while other laborers are hourly workers and their wages are paid according to the level of production.

The total costs for a department or an entire organization include costs that are strictly variable, costs that are strictly fixed, and costs that are mixed. Because the total costs of a department or of the entire organization are the sum of variable costs, fixed costs, and mixed costs, this total is also considered a mixed cost. The list of costs below for Department A includes one of each type of cost — variable (direct materials), fixed (depreciation), and mixed (payroll).

	Department A			
	Variable	**+ Fixed =**	**Total**	
Direct materials	10,000 units × $3/unit +	-0-	= $ 30,000	Variable
Depreciation	-0-	+ $10,000 =	10,000	Fixed
Payroll	10,000 units × $5/unit +	40,000 =	90,000	Mixed
Total	10,000 units × $8/unit +	$50,000 =	$130,000	Mixed

Since the total costs for Department A include costs that are variable (10,000 units × $8 per unit = $80,000) as well as those that are fixed ($50,000), the total ($130,000) is considered to be a mixed cost.

Example 3-1 Revisited

In Example 3-1 the variable and fixed costs are given separately. If the two costs are combined, the resulting mixed costs can be listed as in Exhibit 3-1 and represented graphically as in Figure 3-11.

EXHIBIT 3-1
Mixed Costs at Different Levels of Activity

Activity (in Units)	Variable Costs	+	Fixed Costs	=	Total (Mixed) Costs
100	$ 400	+	$10,000	=	$10,400
150	$ 600	+	$10,000	=	$10,600
500	$2,000	+	$10,000	=	$12,000
1,000	$4,000	+	$10,000	=	$14,000
1,200	$4,800	+	$10,000	=	$14,800
1,500	$6,000	+	$10,000	=	$16,000

FIGURE 3-11
Mixed Costs Graph
The fixed is unchanging and the variable increases with activity.

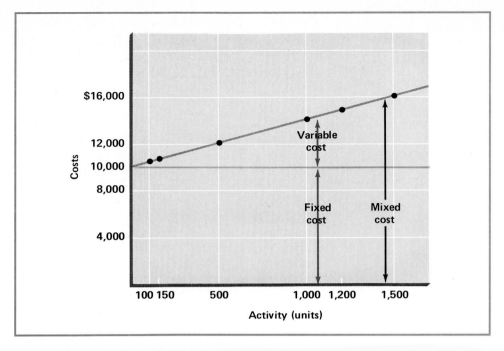

There are three important observations you need to remember about the characteristics of any mixed cost:

Characteristics of a mixed cost

1. The total mixed cost fluctuates with activity.

2. The component of the mixed cost that changes in response to activity is the variable cost.

3. The variable cost component changes proportionately with activity: i.e., there is a constant increase in total costs ($4 per unit in Exhibit 3-1) for each additional unit produced.

In the remaining sections of this chapter we will further discuss these general observations about the characteristics of all mixed costs and explain why it is important to know whether a cost is variable, fixed, or mixed.

Importance of Distinguishing Between Variable and Fixed Costs

Only through an understanding of the behavior of costs can the accountant assist management in making (1) intelligent predictions, (2) rational decisions, and (3) proper performance evaluations.

Notice first, in Example 3-4, how important it is that the accountant understand variable and fixed costs in order to make an ***intelligent prediction*** of utility costs.

Example 3-4

Reason 1: making intelligent predictions

THE PROCRASTINATION COMPANY

The Procrastination Company is preparing a budget on Jan. 1, 1988, for the first 3 months of the year, but it is having difficulty with the estimate for utilities. The bill for December, a month in which 10,000 units were produced, was $800. The company is not sure whether to use a rate of $0.08 per unit ($800 ÷ 10,000) or not. The company controller called the utility company and learned that the December bill involved a $300 fixed charge plus a constant rate per kilowatt-hour. On the basis of an expected number of hours per unit, Procrastination converted the rate per hour to $0.05 per unit. With this knowledge of behavior, the utility costs for the Procrastination Company were predicted as follows:

Month	Expected Activity (in Units)	Expected Utility Bill
January	15,000	$1,050 ($300 + $750)
February	16,000	$1,100 ($300 + $800)
March	17,000	$1,150 ($300 + $850)

Had the Procrastination Company used the $0.08 rate, its predictions would have been $1,200, $1,280, and $1,360 instead.

Now look at Example 3-5. It shows how the ***rational decision*** is made only after the behavior of costs is determined.

Example 3-5

THE DOLL ADOPTION COMPANY

The Doll Adoption Company is considering dropping one of its 10 product lines, the Lettuce Patch doll, after examining the following condensed 1988 income statement:

Sales of Lettuce Patch..	$10,000,000
Total Costs for Lettuce Patch	12,000,000
Net Income (Loss) for Lettuce Patch............................	$ (2,000,000)

Reason 2: making rational decisions

The president wishes to drop Lettuce Patch, hoping to eliminate the $2 million loss. The controller, however, points out that only $7 million of the $12 million of costs were variable. The remaining costs were fixed and the company would incur them whether or not it dropped the Lettuce Patch line. The effect of dropping the product is shown below:

	Do Not Drop Product	Drop Product	Effect on Profits.
Sales	$10,000,000	-0-	$(10,000,000)
Total Costs:			
Variable	$ 7,000,000	-0-	$ 7,000,000
Fixed............................	5,000,000	$ 5,000,000	—
Total Costs........................	$12,000,000	$ 5,000,000	$ 7,000,000
Net Income	$ (2,000,000)	$(5,000,000)	$ (3,000,000)

Sales would be reduced by $10 million and total costs would be reduced by $7 million, resulting in a reduction of $3 million in net income, if the Lettuce Patch line is dropped. Instead of the $2 million loss being eliminated, as the president believes, the loss would be $3 million greater.

Finally, let's see why we can properly *evaluate performance* only after we know which costs are variable and which costs are fixed.

Example 3-6

Reason 3: evaluating performance

THE TIGHT REINS COMPANY

At the beginning of June, 1988, the Tight Reins Company set a production budget of 10,000 units and budgeted its production costs to be $80,000. At the end of June, Tight Reins determined that 12,000 units were actually produced and the production costs actually incurred were $88,000. Since the costs were $8,000 higher than expected, the production supervisor's immediate suspicion was that the operations during June must have been run inefficiently. The controller, however, pointed out to the supervisor that the conclusions would depend upon whether these costs were variable or fixed.

If the entire $80,000 budget was for fixed costs, then regardless of the number of units produced (as long as it was in the same relevant range), the budgeted costs would be $80,000. Since the actual costs were $88,000, the performance report would show an unfavorable variance of $8,000:

Actual Costs	Budgeted Costs	Variance
$88,000	$80,000	$8,000 U

Since the $8,000 unfavorable variance is quite large, an investigation of the variance would probably be warranted.

On the other hand, if the original $80,000 budget was entirely variable, then one would expect each unit produced to cost $8 ($80,000 ÷ 10,000 units). Since 12,000 units were produced in June, the firm would expect the costs to be $96,000 (12,000 units × $8 per unit) for this level of activity, rather than the original budget of $80,000. For this situation the performance report would show the following results:

Actual Costs	Budgeted Costs	Variance
$88,000	$96,000	$8,000 F

Since the $8,000 favorable variance is also quite large, it would probably need to be investigated.

Finally, if the $80,000 that was budgeted at the beginning of 1988 was a mixture of variable and fixed costs, whether or not Tight Reins had any variance would depend upon the breakdown of the $80,000 into its variable and fixed components. If we assume that the controller learned the $80,000 was made up of $40,000 of variable costs ($40,000 ÷ 10,000 units = $4 per unit) and $40,000 of fixed costs, then the costs that would be budgeted for 12,000 units would be:

Variable	12,000 units × $4/unit =	$48,000
Fixed		40,000
Total		$88,000

For this situation the performance report would show a zero variance—the costs are exactly what they should have been:

	Actual Costs	Budgeted Costs	Variance
	$88,000	$88,000	-0-

And, more than likely, there would be no reason to conduct any investigation.

How to Determine the Behavior of Costs

To assist management in making intelligent predictions, rational decisions, and proper performance evaluations, the accountant must first determine which costs are variable, fixed, and mixed.

Thus far we have used examples in which the variable cost rate and the total fixed costs were known. In this section we will discuss how to determine the variable cost rate and the total fixed costs—commonly referred to as the ***behavioral elements***— when only the total mixed costs and their related levels of activity are known.

Example 3-7

THE HARRIS COMPANY

The Harris Company has a new controller, Katy Herrin. Katy suspects that the company's costs are mixed, but she doesn't know how much of the total is attributable to variable or fixed costs. The previous controller, Justin Tyme, had prepared the following budget before he died suddenly from injuries sustained in an accident while hang gliding in the Grand Canyon. Justin left no indication of the variable cost rate and total fixed costs used in the computations.

Katy at first was perplexed. But after she looked at the budget carefully, several key points about the behavior of mixed costs came to mind: (1) The total costs obviously contain some variable costs because the total costs are changing; (2) the variable costs are increasing with respect to the increases in activity; and (3) each additional unit of activity generates the same additional amount of total cost, since

AS MIXED COSTS CHANGE SO DOES THE ROLE OF THE ACCOUNTANT

Critics of the accounting profession contend that the accountant's contributions to management decision making are shrinking significantly, especially in the area of providing short-term performance measures for manufacturers. They associate this declining role primarily with changes in the cost structure of manufacturers who are modernizing their plant facilities. As modernization occurs, manufacturing flexibility has increased with the introduction of technological innovations such as laser machining and robotics—these newly automated systems being referred to as flexible manufacturing systems, or simply FMS.

The result of this trend has been to cause a significant replacement of variable costs with fixed costs, which are less sensitive to changes in short-term decisions. Unfortunately the accountant's contribution to short-term operational decisions and their resulting short-term performance measures is directly proportionate to the percentage of variable costs in the organization. Therefore the tendency to replace variable costs with fixed ones reduces the value of ac-

counting information. This means that as the more highly automated manufacturing process becomes more flexible, so too must the accountant develop a more flexible accounting system that is adapted to the changing corporate structure.

Source: Robert S. Kaplan, "Measuring Manufacturing Performance: A New Challenge for Managerial Accounting Research," *Accounting Review,* October 1983, pp. 686–705.

Activity	Total (Mixed) Costs
100	$10,400
150	10,600
500	12,000
1,000	14,000
1,200	14,800
1,500	16,000

we assume that average variable costs do not change with activity. She noticed that 50 additional units (increasing activity from 100 to 150) brought about an additional $200 of total cost, which on the average is $4 per unit [($10,600 − $10,400) ÷ (150 − 100)]. Likewise, 350 more units of production (increasing activity from 150 to 500) generated a $1,400 increase in total cost, which also averaged $4 per unit [($12,000 − $10,600) ÷ (500 − 150)]. She concluded that the variable cost rate must be $4 per unit. She next figured that if a total cost is made up of variable and fixed cost components, once the variable cost component is known, the fixed cost is easily computed. If 100 units are produced, the variable costs will be $400 (100 × $4). The total at that level of activity is $10,400, so the fixed cost must be $10,000 ($10,400 − $400).

(Naturally, you already knew what the results of Katy's analysis would be, since the variable cost rate of $4 per unit and the total fixed costs of $10,000 were given earlier in Example 3-1. If you had been in Katy's position, however, you would have needed to evaluate the information given in Example 3-7 in a manner similar to the way Katy evaluated it.)

The informal and commonsense approach taken by Katy in this example can be expressed in a formal way. When you know two or more mixed costs and their related levels of activity, you can determine the variable cost rate with the following equation:

Calculating the VC/u

$$\text{Variable cost rate} = \frac{\text{change in total mixed costs}}{\text{change in activity}}$$

If we substitute into this equation some of the numbers used by Katy, we get:

$$\text{Variable cost per unit} = \frac{\$10,600 - \$10,400}{150 - 100}$$

$$= \frac{\$200}{50} = \$4$$

Each of the total mixed costs used in the equation is a combination of a fixed cost plus a variable cost, where the variable cost is the variable cost per unit multiplied by the number of units produced. That means that once we calculate the variable cost for a known total cost, we can determine the fixed cost by the following simple equation:

Total mixed costs = fixed costs + variable costs

= fixed costs + (variable cost rate × activity)

Continuing with the numbers used by Katy:

Calculating total fixed costs

$$\$10,400 = \text{fixed costs} + \$4(100 \text{ units})$$
$$\$10,400 = \text{fixed costs} + \$400$$
$$\$10,000 = \text{fixed costs}$$

Now that the variable cost rate and the fixed costs are known, a prediction of total mixed costs at any level other than the ones already known can be computed by substituting the level of activity into the completed equation:

$$\text{Total mixed costs} = \$10,000 + (\$4 \text{ per unit} \times \text{activity})$$

If Katy is interested in predicting the total costs for 800 units, the calculation would simply be:

$$\text{Total mixed costs} = \$10,000 + \$4(800)$$
$$= \$10,000 + \$3,200 = \$13,200$$

The equation for total mixed costs is often shown more generally in mathematical form by substituting letters into the equation. The equation for total mixed costs is:

The mixed costs equation

$$Y = a + bX \quad \text{(which you may remember from your high}$$
school algebra is also the equation for
a straight line)

where Y = total mixed costs, also known as the ***dependent variable***
$\quad a$ = fixed costs, the point where a straight line crosses the vertical axis of the graph, also called the **Y-intercept** or ***constant***
$\quad b$ = variable cost rate, also called the ***slope of the line***
$\quad X$ = activity, also referred to as the ***independent variable***

This general equation for total mixed costs becomes the following specific equation for the Harris Company:

$$Y = \$10,000 + \$4X$$

The Problem: Oversimplification

Normally, the analysis of cost behavior is not as easily done as Example 3-7 might imply. In that example, the five total mixed costs and their corresponding activity

All costs were on the same straight line

levels can be represented on a graph by a single straight line that goes through each and every point (as shown in Figure 3-12). Because all five points lie on the straight line it does not matter which two mixed costs are used in the equation to calculate the variable cost rate—for any pair of points the result will be $4 per unit. This variable cost rate indicates the slope of the line, and there is only one slope for a straight line. It doesn't matter which two points from a straight line are chosen for this analysis; the slope—or variable cost rate—will always be the same.

However, in actual situations for a firm, the points representing total mixed costs and activity levels won't fall perfectly on a single straight line.

You see, Katy was evaluating a budget prepared by Justin Tyme in which the units were multiplied by $4 to get the total variable costs. The $4-per-unit figure was used because Justin expected each unit to average this amount. So each point on the line represented a different number of units multiplied by $4 per unit, plus $10,000 of fixed costs.

If Katy hadn't been given Justin's budget, she would have had to evaluate the actual results from previous periods. When actual results are plotted on a graph, there

FIGURE 3-12
Simplified Mixed Cost
Graph

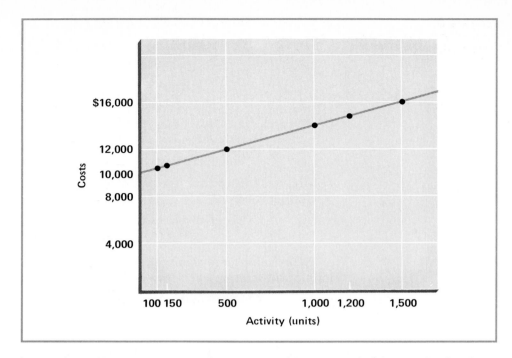

is very little chance that every unit produced will cost exactly $4 per unit of variable cost. Fifty units may take $203 of variable costs ($203 ÷ 50 = $4.06 per unit) instead of $200, and 500 units may require $1,955 of variable costs ($1,955 ÷ 500 = $3.91 per unit) instead of $2,000.

If the units do not average exactly $4 of variable costs, the actual points will not fall perfectly on a straight line. Instead, there will be a distribution of points *about* a line — the line being drawn through the group of points.

Look now at Figure 3-13, and we'll try to explain what we mean.

Assume that Katy did not have access to Justin's budget. So she found out what the costs and corresponding activities were for the past 6 months, and she plotted them on the graph in Figure 3-13. As you can see, no single straight line can be drawn connecting all the points. But observe that there is a distinct upward trend of points as activity increases. And a straight line can be "fitted" to the points to represent this trend.

Assume that Katy goes ahead and fits a line to the points, which is shown in Figure 3-14. Notice that even though none of the points fall on the line, the line is a very good representation of all the points. It is not a precise representation of each point, but it is a sufficiently accurate representation of the group of points to be useful to Katy.

After you have examined the points in Figures 3-13 and 3-14, two questions should come to mind:

1. How do you determine the straight line that should be drawn to the widely dispersed group of points shown in Figure 3-13?

2. When the points are distributed about a line, as they are in Figure 3-14, which two points do you use in the equation

$$\text{Variable cost rate} = \frac{\text{change in total cost}}{\text{change in activity}}$$

for the variable cost rate?

FIGURE 3-13
Costs for the Past 6 Months
Normally, all points won't fall
perfectly on one straight line.

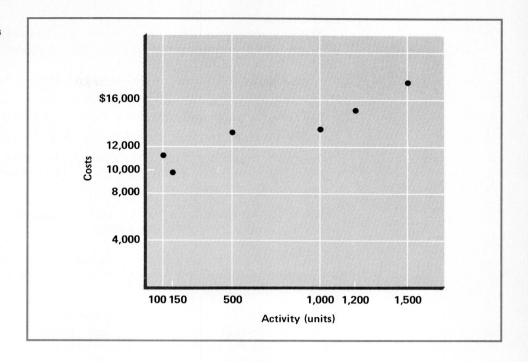

*These are the methods we'll
see later*

The answer to each of these questions depends upon which of three specific methods—high-low, visual approximation, or regression analysis—is used, as we shall discuss in the final sections of this chapter.

FIGURE 3-14
**Fitted Line to Actual
Observations**
There is a line that represents
the general trend of points.

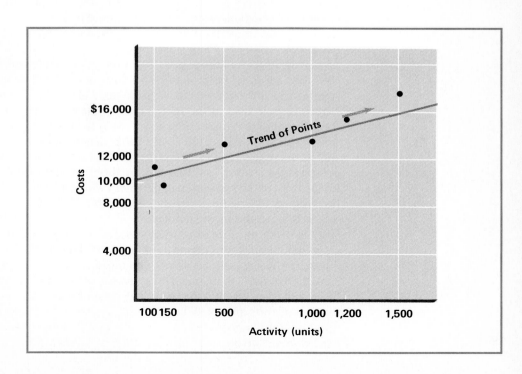

An Overview

There are actually six steps in the evaluation of a mixed cost. They are listed below, and each will be discussed further in the pages that follow.

Six steps to evaluating a mixed cost

1. Identify the dependent and independent variables that are to be evaluated — that is, the mixed cost and the activity.

2. Take a sample of observations for the dependent and independent variables.

3. Plot the observations on a graph called a scatter diagram.

4. Use one of the three methods — high-low, visual approximation, or regression analysis — to determine the variable cost rate and the total fixed costs.

5. Evaluate the results to determine their accuracy.

6. Use the equation $Y = a + bX$ to make intelligent predictions, rational decisions, and/or meaningful evaluations.

The first three steps, as well as the sixth step, are common to all three methods of determining the variable and fixed cost components. The fifth step can be used only with regression analysis.

STEP 1: The Dependent and Independent Variables

Step 1: Y and X

Y = the dependent variable

The first step is to identify the dependent variable and the independent variable, which are the statistical terms we use to represent mixed costs and activity, respectively. We refer to the mixed costs as the ***dependent variable,*** since each mixed cost contains a variable portion which, in total, "depends" upon (thus the name *dependent variable*) the level of activity. As the level of activity changes, so too does the dependent variable — the mixed costs. We use the letter Y to represent the dependent variable in the equation for mixed costs.

X = the independent variable

We refer to activity as the ***independent variable,*** because the value of the independent variable does not depend upon any other variable. It is also referred to as the ***explanatory variable,*** since we need it to help "explain" the behavior of the mixed costs. We use the letter X to represent the independent variable in the mixed cost equation.

The dependent variable is usually pretty easy to identify — it is simply the mixed cost that needs to be broken down into its variable and fixed components. The selection of an independent variable isn't always as obvious, however, and may require a great deal of thought. To see what we mean, let's look at the inspection department of a manufacturer to see what the independent variable might be when we're evaluating the mixed costs of that department.

The purpose of an inspection department is to make sure that each unit produced possesses the required standards of quality that have been set by the company. The mixed costs of the inspection department will obviously be the dependent variable Y. But what should be the independent variable X? Which measure of activity logically seems to have the most significant influence on the variable portion of the mixed cost? Is it the number of units started? The number of units sold? The number of direct labor hours or machine hours worked? The number of miles driven by the sales representatives to sell the units? The number of units inspected?

Although more than one of these measures of activity may have some influence on the mixed costs, the measure of activity that probably has the greatest influence is the number of units inspected. Logically, there should be a close relationship between the number of units inspected and the total costs to inspect those units. Unfortunately, logic may not necessarily provide the best answer. For it's also possible that some unmentioned variable, or even a combination or variation of the several variables that were listed, may be even better than units inspected as the best independent variable.

STEP 2: Taking a Sample

Step 2: a sample is a group of observations for Y and X

To analyze the component parts of a mixed cost, you usually base the analysis on a sample of results that have taken place in the past. A *sample* is a limited collection of observations that provide information about both the dependent variable and the independent variable. For example, each observation for our inspection department would indicate the number of units inspected for some period of time as well as the costs of the inspection department for that same period of time. A sample represents only a portion of the data that is available from a population of data. Our hope is that this small portion is representative of the population as a whole.

Observations in a sample might be collected hourly, daily, weekly, monthly, yearly, or over some other period of time.[1] The appropriate period of time to use depends on two things:

Frequency of sample

1. For what period of time has data been recorded in the past? For example, data may have been recorded and accumulated on a yearly basis or a monthly basis, but not on a weekly, daily, or hourly basis. Consequently, even if you prefer to collect daily observations, you would have to make do with a sample of monthly or yearly observations.

2. How far back in time can observations be taken so that cost-behavior patterns will still be relevant to current and future periods? For instance, if we decide to take a sample of annual observations, was the behavior of costs 5 years ago the same as it is today—or, more importantly, as it will be tomorrow? Probably not. As a result, a sample of monthly observations would be preferable to a sample of annual observations.

Size of sample

Once we decide how frequently to take observations, we then have to decide on the number of observations to take. Should we take 5, 10, 50, 100, or some other number of observations in our sample? Unfortunately, there is no easy answer. We not only want the cost of gathering the sample to be reasonable, but we also want the sample to be a reliable approximation of the population. Unfortunately, we cannot have our cake and eat it too. While the costs are least with a small sample, the statistical reliability of a small sample is questionable. On the other hand, whereas statistical reliability is improved with a large sample, the costs of gathering the sample can become prohibitive.

STEP 3: The Scatter Diagram

Step 3: plot the points

The observations in the sample are now plotted on a graph called a *scatter diagram.* The vertical axis, or *Y* axis, represents the mixed costs; the horizontal axis, or *X* axis, represents activity. A scatter diagram provides a visual representation of the relationship between mixed costs and activity. It can be a useful aid in the analysis in several ways.

Time-series vs. cross-sectional analysis

[1] When we do cost-behavior analysis for a single entity repeatedly, over an extended period of time, we refer to it as time-series analysis. But when we do the analysis for different entities only once, for a specific period of time, we refer to it as cross-sectional analysis. To keep our discussion as simple as possible, we will assume that time-series analysis is being used in our discussion in the text as well as in the exercises and problems for homework.

FIGURE 3-15
Scatter Diagrams
Y and *X* are related in graph
1, but not in graph 2.

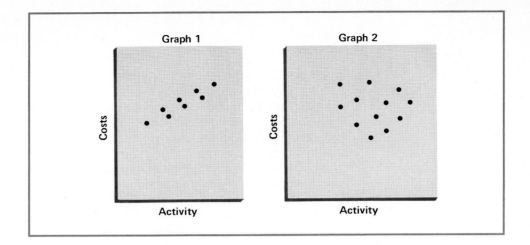

First of all, the scatter diagram can give us a good idea of whether or not mixed costs and activity are related. For example, in graph 1 of Figure 3-15 there is an upward trend of the costs in response to increases in activity, indicating that the costs are somewhat related to activity. On the other hand, graph 2 seems to show that activity has little, if any, effect on the costs. It would make little sense to spend any additional time—that is, doing steps 4 to 6—evaluating the situation presented in graph 2.

Is a curve or a straight line better?

Second, the scatter diagram may also indicate that a curve rather than a straight line will provide a better fit to the observations. This would be the situation represented by the scatter diagram in Figure 3-16, where the trend of points is gradually but continually changing direction. In this situation it may be necessary to fit a curve to the distribution of points—a process that is more difficult than that of using a straight-line approximation. On the other hand, we may find out that the area of analysis actually includes several relevant ranges and that it is necessary to limit the analysis to a single relevant range where a straight-line approximation would be adequate.

Are all points representative?

Third, a scatter diagram shows those points that may not be typical—or representative—of the remaining cost data and therefore should be eliminated from

FIGURE 3-16
Scatter Diagram
Indicating That a Curve Is
Preferable to a Straight
Line

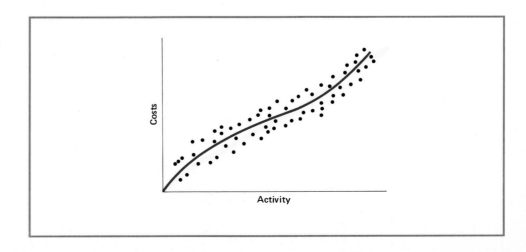

**FIGURE 3-17
Scatter Diagram—
Nonrepresentative
Observation**
**Delete the nonrepresentative
point before analyzing cost
behavior.**

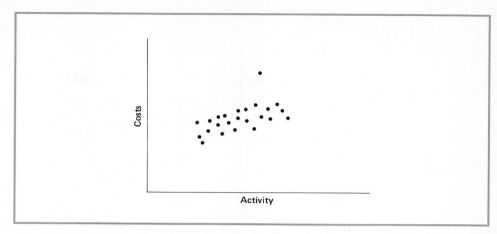

the sample. For example, cost data recorded for a month in which the workers were
on strike may not be typical of the cost data for other months in the sample. In Figure
3-17 you can see that one point is far different from the cluster and trend of the rest. If
this point is left in the sample, it may cause a distortion of the results.

A fourth reason for preparing a scatter diagram concerns the visual approximation
method of analysis in step 4, which we will look at in detail later. With this method
only, it is impossible to determine the variable cost rate and the total fixed costs
without first preparing the scatter diagram.

STEP 4: Determining the Variable Cost Rate and the Total Fixed Costs

*Step 4: use methods to get
b and a*

Once we have evaluated the scatter diagram, we are ready to use one or more of the
three methods (high-low, visual approximation, or regression analysis) to determine
the behavioral components—the variable cost rate and the total fixed costs—of the
mixed costs. In each method we want to fit a line to the points in the scatter diagram
that is representative of the trend and distribution of those points and to determine
the equation for that line, $Y = a + bX$.

STEP 5: Evaluating the Results

*Step 5: how accurate will
predictions be?*

Even though we have determined the equation for predicting mixed costs (step 4),
this does not necessarily mean that we are quite ready to use it, because we don't yet
know such things as:

1. How accurate will the equation $Y = a + bX$ be in providing estimates of the
mixed costs?

2. Is there a statistically significant relationship between the independent variable
X and the dependent variable Y?

Unfortunately, the only method that allows us to answer these important questions is regression analysis. When we use high-low and visual approximation, we have
no objective way of determining how accurate the model will be or how significant
the relationship is between the dependent and independent variables. For this reason
we will discuss this step only after we have discussed regression analysis.

STEP 6: Applying the Results

*Step 6: using the equation
$Y = a + bX$*

The only reason anyone goes to all this trouble to evaluate a mixed cost is that there
is a practical use for the information. As we said earlier, the main reason for knowing
the behavioral components of a mixed cost is to be able to make intelligent predic-

tions, rational decisions, and meaningful evaluations. Assuming we do have a practical use for this information and are satisfied with the answers we got in step 5, we are now ready to use the equation $Y = a + bX$.

METHODS OF ANALYZING COST BEHAVIOR

The information provided for the Big Foot Company in the following example will be used to explain each of the three methods.

Example 3-8

BIG FOOT COMPANY

The Big Foot Company wants to determine the behavior of the costs of its inspection department, which are incurred at the end of the production process. Big Foot wants to predict its costs of operation for the last 6 months of 1988 as part of a budget that management needs to apply for a bank loan. Big Foot has selected the number of units inspected as the best measure of activity and has collected the following historical cost data for the first 6 months of the year.

The sample for Big Foot

Month	Inspection Department Costs (Y)	Units Inspected (X)
January	$41,700	26,500
February	33,500	21,000
March	35,000	25,900
April	37,800	26,000
May	36,000	22,300
June	39,000	28,800

Having gathered these cost data, we have completed steps 1 and 2 of the mixed cost evaluation. The third step for Big Foot is to prepare the scatter diagram shown in Figure 3-18.

FIGURE 3-18
Scatter Diagram for the Big Foot Company
Here is a scatter diagram for Big Foot. Can you see that a straight line could be drawn showing the trend of points?

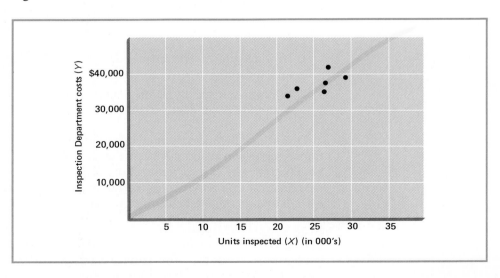

The scatter diagram indicates that although there is no single straight line that can be drawn to connect the six points plotted, the points do indeed display an upward trend as activity increases. Therefore, a straight line can be drawn that, while not exact, presents a reasonable representative relationship between the costs of the inspection department and the number of units inspected.

High-Low Method

The **high-low method** is the easiest of the three methods, consisting of the following steps, once the scatter diagram has been drawn:

STEP 1: A straight line is drawn through the points representing the highest cost, $41,700, and the lowest cost, $33,500, which in this case are for the months of January and February. This line is shown in Figure 3-19.

STEP 2: The variable cost rate b is calculated by substituting into the equation the coordinates for the points having the highest and lowest amount of cost:

$$\textbf{Variable cost rate} = \frac{\textbf{change in total cost}}{\textbf{change in activity}}$$

Using the data for January and February, we get:

Calculating b for Big Foot

$$\text{Variable cost per unit, } b = \frac{\$41,700 - \$33,500}{26,500 \text{ units} - 21,000 \text{ units}}$$

$$= \frac{\$8,200}{5,500 \text{ units}} = \$1.4909$$

STEP 3: The fixed costs a are determined at the high point by substituting the variable cost rate into the equation for total costs:

The a value for Big Foot

$$\textbf{Total mixed costs} = \textbf{fixed costs} + (\textbf{variable cost per unit} \times \textbf{activity})$$

$$\$41,700 = \text{fixed costs} + \$1.4909(26,500)$$

$$\text{Fixed costs} = \$41,700 - \$39,509 = \$2,191$$

FIGURE 3-19
The High-Low Method
For the high-low method, draw a straight line through the point with the highest cost and the point with the lowest cost.

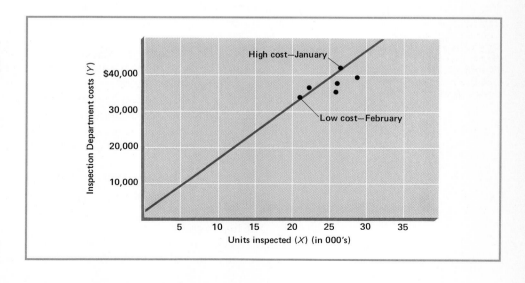

We could have calculated the fixed costs just as easily by substituting b into the equation for total mixed costs and using the low point:

$$\$33,500 = \text{fixed costs} + \$1.4909(21,000)$$

$$\text{Fixed costs} = \$33,500 - \$31,409 = \$2,191$$

This is exactly the same as the result we got using the high point— $2,191. And since the results should come out the same at both the high and low points, it isn't really necessary for you to make both calculations— unless you merely want to double-check your answer. If you do decide to make both calculations, however, be sure to carry out your calculation of b to several places to the right of the decimal point. Otherwise, your two calculations of fixed costs may differ, due only to a liberal rounding for b. For example, if you had rounded the b value of \$1.4909 to \$1.49, then the fixed costs at the high and low points would have been \$2,215 and \$2,210, respectively—different only because of the rounding.

Using the high-low method, the resulting equation for the line is:

$$Y = \$2,191 + \$1.4909X$$

Deficiency of high-low

The high-low method, while the simplest to calculate, is conceptually the weakest of the three methods. That is, although there are six monthly observations plotted on the graph, only two of the six—the highest and the lowest points—were considered in drawing the line to represent the six points. The method assumes that these two points are representative of the entire sample, an assumption which probably is incorrect. If you look at Figure 3-19 again, the distortion introduced by this method should be obvious. Note that the points are not distributed very well about the line—all but one of the points is below the line. As a consequence, the variable cost rate and fixed costs calculated with this method may be substantially different from the variable cost rate and fixed costs calculated with the two methods that follow— each of which considers all—not merely two—of the points in the sample.

Visual Approximation Method

Visual is subjective

The *visual approximation method* is subjective in nature but is preferable to the high-low method because it does consider the entire sample. There are three steps for this method, once the scatter diagram has been drawn:

STEP 1: Draw a straight line through the group of points so that it shows the trend of all points. The trend of the points represents an average relationship—not an exact relationship—between costs and activity. When you draw the line, try to get a good distribution of points about the line—that is, a fairly even number of points above the line and below it and to the left of the line and to the right of it. Look at the three graphs in Figure 3-20. Which do you think satisfies the two characteristics of a good line? That is:

1. The slope of the line represents the trend of points in the sample.

2. It has a good distribution of points about the line.

The line in graph 1 accurately represents the upward trend of points, but there is a poor distribution of points about the line. Most of the points are above and to the left of the line; very few points are below and to the right of

**FIGURE 3-20
Different Visual
Approximations for a
Scatter Diagram**
Graph 3 should show the best
line.

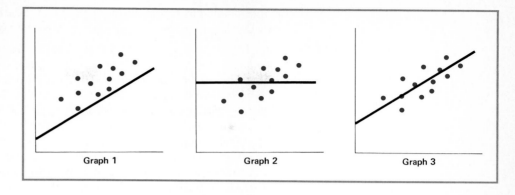

the line. In graph 2 there is an almost equal number of points above and below the line, but the angle of the line does not depict the trend of the points. Finally, we have graph 3. As in graph 1, the angle of the line does represent the upward trend of points. And the group of points is well distributed about the line — a nearly equal number are above and to the left of the line as are below and to the right of the line. Graph 3 is the best visual approximation.

Now let's return to the Big Foot Company example. We will now draw a straight line through the scatter diagram, as shown in Figure 3-21. This line is what *we* perceive to be the best fit to the trend of that scatter of points.

You may perceive and draw a line that is different from ours. That's all right. Remember, we mentioned earlier that this is a subjective method — therefore, different persons may come up with slightly different lines. However, if you understand both the purpose of the line and how to draw it, our line and yours should produce results that, even if not identical, should agree rather closely.

Before we go on to step 2, notice one last thing in Figure 3-21. The line did not go squarely through a single point. This was not our mistake — and it shouldn't be yours. No attempt should ever be made to force the line through any points. The line should represent the trend of all the points, not

**FIGURE 3-21
Visual Approximation —
Authors' View**
After the line has been drawn,
select the coordinates for any
two points that are part of the
line. Do not use points
representing actual costs.

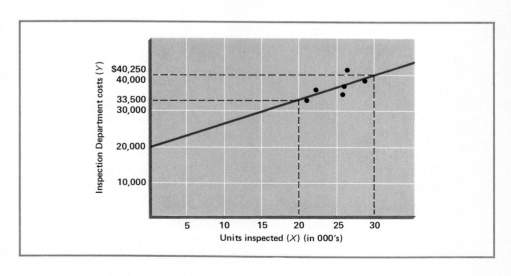

a select few. On the other hand, don't purposely avoid running the line through a point if you feel that the line is the best one you can come up with.

Do not use actual points

STEP 2: Any two *points on the line* are now selected. With the coordinates of these two points, the variable cost rate *b* is computed by using the same equation as the one used for the high-low method. The points chosen *should not be actual sample points, but should be points taken from the line drawn to represent the average relationship of the actual costs to activity.*

For our example, we will use points corresponding to the activity levels of 20,000 and 30,000 units (any other two points could have been chosen as well). The total costs associated with each of these activity levels are found on the vertical axis to be $33,500 and $40,250, respectively. Using these coordinates, *b* is calculated as follows:

Calculating the b value

$$\text{Variable cost per unit, } b = \frac{\$40{,}250 - \$33{,}500}{30{,}000 - 20{,}000} = \frac{\$6{,}750}{10{,}000}$$
$$= \$0.675 \text{ per unit}$$

STEP 3: Fixed costs *a* are calculated by substituting the variable cost rate of $0.675 per unit into the equation for total costs. Using the point having the total cost of $40,250, we get:

Now the fixed

Total costs = fixed costs + (variable cost per unit × activity)

$40,250 = fixed costs + $0.675(30,000)

Fixed costs = $40,250 − $20,250 = $20,000

And finally the mixed cost equation

Using the visual approximation method, the resulting equation for the line representing total, fixed, and variable costs is as follows:

$$Y = \$20{,}000 + \$0.675X$$

Regression Analysis with Least Squares

The third method, *regression analysis,* is a far more analytical approach to evaluating cost behavior than either the high-low method or the visual approximation method. With the use of complex statistical formulas, regression analysis measures the average amount of change in the dependent variable that is related to—or influenced by—a change in one or more independent variables. The formula we use in regression analysis to determine the variable cost rate is a more sophisticated version of the formula (change in mixed costs ÷ change in activity) we used with the high-low and visual approximation methods.

So far in our analysis of the Big Foot Company, we have used the high-low and visual approximation methods to evaluate the relationship between one dependent and one independent variable. When we use regression analysis with such a two-variable model, we call it *simple regression.* Sometimes the behavior of the dependent variable may be influenced by changes in more than one independent variable, in which case we use a multiple-variable model. This means simply that there are two or more independent variables in the regression model and that the analysis is referred to as *multiple regression analysis.* For now we will be concerned only with simple regression; later we will explain in more detail multiple regression.

Least Squares

Least squares is a type of regression method

There are several methods of regression analysis. The easiest to understand and the most commonly used is called the *least squares method.* Use of the least squares method provides the best equation for mixed costs, $Y = a + bX$, and the best graphical representation of that equation. The least squares method of regression analysis guarantees mathematically that the resulting line will have a better overall distribution (a tighter cluster) of points about it than will any other line. This line—which is called the **regression line**—will fit the points better than any other line possibly can. Let's see what this means.

Minimizing the Sum of Squares of Error Terms

Sum of squares of error terms is smallest for least squares

The least squares method results in the best possible line because it **minimizes the sum of squares of the error terms.** To understand what this means, we first need to understand what is meant by an "error term."

Look at Figure 3-22, which shows a line drawn through a group of points. Notice that the line is designated by the notation Y' rather than Y, as it has been previously. This is a way of distinguishing the Y values that are part of the regression line from the Y values that were actually observed and measured. As a rule, from now on whenever we have a line drawn through the trend of a group of points, any point that is a part of that line—the regression line—will be designated Y'. Any point that is an actual observation will be designated Y.

Also notice that for each actual observation, there is a line drawn vertically from the actual point Y to a point Y' on the regression line. This vertical distance, designated $(Y - Y')$, represents the amount of error that was incurred in using the regression line to predict Y at level of activity X. For each observation there will be a unique $(Y - Y')$. Each $(Y - Y')$ is referred to as an **error term.** The least squares method says this: square each of these error terms, $(Y - Y')^2$, then sum all the squared error terms, $\Sigma(Y - Y')^2$, and the result is that the "sum of squares of the error terms" is less than it would be under any other method, resulting in any other line. It has been proven mathematically that the line that minimizes the sum of squares of the error terms represents the line that has the very best fit to the points in the sample.

The Calculations for Least Squares

In the least squares method we substitute all the data from the sample into two equations—one for b (the variable cost rate) and one for a (the total fixed costs). The equation for b is:

The formula for b

$$b = \frac{\Sigma XY - (\Sigma X)\overline{Y}}{\Sigma X^2 - \dfrac{(\Sigma X)^2}{n}}$$

FIGURE 3-22
Error Terms
An error term $= Y - Y'$.

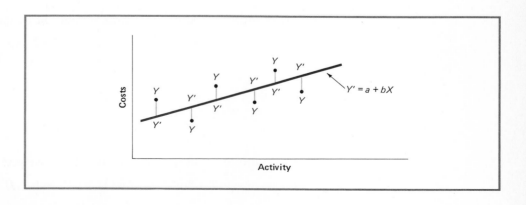

And now for a

And the equation for *a* is:

$$a = \bar{Y} - b\bar{X}$$

The data in Exhibit 3-2 are based on the sample for Big Foot. Zeroes have been dropped from all numbers so that the calculations won't be unnecessarily cumbersome.

Column 1 lists the values for the dependent variable Y, representing monthly inspection costs, the sum of which, (ΣY), is 223. The average Y value, or $\bar{Y}$—$\left(\bar{Y} = \dfrac{\Sigma Y}{n}\right)$—is 37.167.

Column 2 lists the values for the independent variable X, representing the number of units inspected each month. The sum of the X's, (ΣX), is 150.5; and the average X value, or $\bar{X}$—$\left(\bar{X} = \dfrac{\Sigma X}{n}\right)$—is 25.083.

Column 3 lists the values for XY, the multiple of each month's X value times its Y value. For example, for January XY is 1,105.05 (41.7×26.5). The sum of the values in column 3, ΣXY, is 5,623.85.

Column 4 lists the square of each X value. For January X^2 is 702.25 (26.5×26.5). The sum of all the X^2 values, $\Sigma(X^2)$, is 3,816.79.

EXHIBIT 3-2
Values Needed for the Least Squares Formulas

Month	(1) Inspection Costs: Dependent Variable Y (in 000s)	(2) Units Inspected: Independent Variable X (in 000s)	(3) XY (in 000s)	(4) X² (in 000s)
January	41.7	26.5	1,105.05	702.25
February	33.5	21.0	703.50	441.00
March	35.0	25.9	906.50	670.81
April	37.8	26.0	982.80	676.00
May	36.0	22.3	802.80	497.29
June	39.0	28.8	1,123.20	829.44
	$\Sigma Y = 223.0$	$\Sigma X = 150.5$	$\Sigma XY = 5,623.85$	$\Sigma(X^2) = 3,816.79$

$$\bar{Y} = \frac{\Sigma Y}{n} = \frac{223}{6} = 37.167 \qquad \bar{X} = \frac{\Sigma X}{n} = \frac{150.5}{6} = 25.083$$

If we substitute the values in Exhibit 3-2 into the equation for *b*, we get:

$$b = \frac{5,623.85 - 150.5(37.167)}{3,816.79 - \dfrac{(150.5)^2}{6}} = \frac{5,623.85 - 5,593.63}{3,816.79 - 3,775.04}$$

$$= \frac{30.22}{41.75} = .7238$$

$$= \$0.7238 \text{ per unit inspected}$$

And substituting \$0.7238 into the equation for *a*, we get:

$$a = \$37.167 - \$0.7238(25.083) = \$37.167 - \$18.155 = \$19.012$$

The mixed cost equation

If we now add the three dropped zeroes, the fixed costs are $19,012.

Using the method of least squares, the resulting equation for the line is the following:

$$Y' = \$19,012 + \$0.7238X$$

Now that we have the equation for the regression line, we can show you how to calculate an error term. In Exhibit 3-2 you see that the actual observed value for Y for January was $41,700. Using the regression equation, we want to calculate the predicted Y' value for January:

$$Y' = \$19,012 + \$0.7238X = \$19,012 + (\$0.7238 \times 26,500 \text{ units})$$
$$= \$19,012 + \$19,181 = \$38,193$$

The error term for January

And the resulting error term for the 26,500 units of activity is $3,507:

$$(Y - Y') = \$41,700 - \$38,193 = \underline{\underline{\$3,507}}$$

If we did this for the other five months, and then squared each of the six error terms, and finally summed the six squared error terms, we would have the sum of the squares of the error terms. This sum of squares—using the least squares method—would be less than that provided by any other method.

The next thing we need to do is to draw the regression line in the scatter diagram that we saw in Figure 3-18. Using either high-low or visual approximation, we can draw a line before we ever make any calculation of the a and b values. In fact, with the visual approximation method, we must draw the line first. But with least squares, only after we calculate the equation for Y' can we draw the line.

Three steps to drawing the regression line

There are three steps for drawing the regression line on the scatter diagram. They are as follows:

STEP 1: Find the fixed costs on the vertical axis—that will be where the total mixed cost line intercepts the Y axis. This will be $19,012 in Figure 3-23.

STEP 2: Substitute any possible value for X into the equation

$$Y' = \$19,012 + \$0.7238X$$

FIGURE 3-23
Least Squares Graph for Big Foot
The regression line is drawn to the distribution of points for Big Foot. The equation for the line is
$Y = \$19,012 + \$0.7238X$.

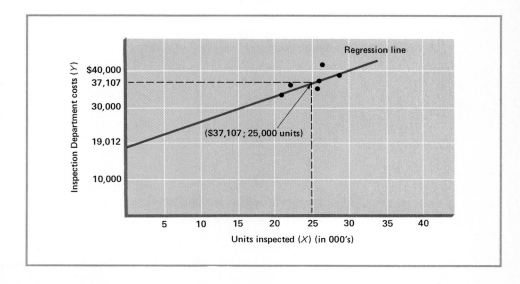

and solve for Y'. Using an X of 25,000 units, the estimate of Y is:

$$Y' = \$19{,}012 + \$0.7238(25{,}000 \text{ units})$$
$$= \$19{,}012 + \$18{,}095 = \$37{,}107$$

Find this point on the graph ($X = 25{,}000$ and $Y' = \$37{,}107$) in Figure 3-23.

STEP 3: With a straight line, connect the Y-intercept ($\$19{,}012$) with the point for $X = 25{,}000$ units and $Y' = \$37{,}107$. This is the regression line.

This line may not appear to be very different from the one we got using the visual approximation method (Figure 3-21). Sometimes we can plot a line by visual approximation that will be pretty close to the regression line; sometimes our approximation differs quite a bit from the regression line. What you must realize is that the regression line found with the least squares method has been mathematically proven to be the best line possible. That is, there is no line that better fits the points or has a tighter distribution of points about the line.

Evaluation of Results

How accurate are the predictions?

Although the least squares method provides the regression line and the equation for the line that best fits the observed points, and thus produces the least error, this does not necessarily mean that the predictions are as accurate or as reliable as we might need them to be. You might say there's some bad news and some good news. The bad news is that it's quite possible for projections made with the regression equation to be way off the mark. Naturally, the user of the least squares method would like to have some warning about this possibility.

The good news is that when the results for the least squares method are obtained with most computer software packages, the user is usually provided with quite a few statistics — without even asking for them — that can help determine the accuracy of the predictions made with the regression equation. The most common statistics provided for the least squares method are the R-square (R^2) and the t-value, which are discussed in the appendix to this chapter. These two, in addition to several other informative statistics, are usually taught in upper-level statistics courses.

Multiple Regression Analysis

There are two or more X's in multiple regression

In the Big Foot Company example, we used one dependent variable and one independent variable. Sometimes, the behavior of the dependent variable can be more accurately described by changes in more than one independent variable. When we have this situation, the only method that can be used to evaluate the relationship between the dependent variable and the multiple independent variables is the least squares method of *multiple regression analysis.*

We cannot use the high-low method or the visual approximation method with multiple independent variables. Moreover, we cannot prepare a scatter diagram to assist in the multiple regression analysis. That's because most of us can depict only two dimensions on a graph, whereas multiple regression requires a multi-dimensional graph.

In some cases there are several independent variables that can each explain different things about the dependent variable. For example, assume that we are evaluating the costs of a shipping department. The costs would naturally be the dependent variable, but there are several independent variables that could each have a different influence on the costs of shipping. The number of units shipped would certainly affect the costs of the shipping department, but so too would the weight of the units shipped, as well as the distance they are shipped, and also the size of the units shipped.

The regression equation for multiple regression

For this situation there would be four different independent variables, and the multiple regression equation for mixed costs would look like this:

$$Y' = a + b_1 X_1 + b_2 X_2 + b_3 X_3 + b_4 X_4$$

where X_1, X_2, X_3, and X_4 are the independent variables and b_1, b_2, b_3, and b_4 are the variable cost rates for the four independent variables.

With additional independent variables we hope to improve the accuracy of the predictions that will be made with this model. Logically, if the weight, size, and distance shipped have an influence on the costs of shipping the package — which is different from the influence of the number of units shipped alone — then the accuracy of the model that uses all four independent variables should be greater than the accuracy of a model that only includes the single independent variable.

Sometimes a user is satisfied with the accuracy of a regression model that includes only a single independent variable, and he or she sees no reason to use additional independent variables. The user may feel that there are no additional independent variables that have an influence on the dependent variable. And even if the user senses that there are other possible independent variables that could be included in the model, he or she may find that the addition of these variables has no significant impact on the accuracy of the model.

Because the mechanics of multiple regression are so complicated and can be performed only with the use of a computer, we will not show you here exactly how a solution is derived, nor do we expect you to be able to do the mechanics by hand.

A REVIEW OF THE DIFFERENT METHODS

Exhibit 3-3 lists the four methods of evaluating cost behavior and briefly describes numerous characteristics of each one. It should be helpful to you in reviewing the main elements of each method, without having to reread the entire chapter.

Two of the columns on the right side of Exhibit 3-3 relate to R^2 and the t-test, which we discuss in the appendix. If the appendix hasn't been assigned as required reading for you, then just disregard these two columns when you get to them.

EXHIBIT 3-3 Summary of Characteristics for Methods

	Description	Preferability	Use of Scatter Diagrams	Use of Statistic		Number of Variables Used
				R^2	t-Test	
High-low	Draws a line connecting points with high and low costs. Uses the formula $b =$ change in mixed cost ÷ change in activity to get variable cost rate. Calculates fixed costs by substituting X values for high or low cost in the formula for mixed costs: $Y = a + bX.$	Objective, but least preferable since only two observations in the sample are considered.	Useful for all reasons described in the text except #4. Line can be drawn before or after a and b values are determined.	No	No	2

continued

	Description	Preferability	Use of Scatter Diagrams	Use of Statistic		Number of Variables Used
				R^2	*t*-Test	
Visual Approximation	Subjectively fits a line to the points in the scatter diagram. The line should display the general trend of points, and there should be a good distribution of points about the line—above and below it and to the left and right of it. Uses same formula as high-low for calculating variable cost rate, and uses any two coordinates of the line (but not actual observations from the sample) in the formula. Also determines fixed costs by substitution into $Y = a + bX$.	Better than high-low because entire sample is considered. Due to subjectivity involved, however, a better approach is still needed. In addition, cannot assess how accurate predictions will be.	Useful for all reasons described in the text. Line has to be drawn prior to determining values for *a* and *b*.	No	No	2
Simple regression	Calculates *b* and *a* by substituting sample values into the following equations: $$b = \frac{\Sigma XY - (\Sigma X)\overline{Y}}{\Sigma X^2 - \frac{(\Sigma X)^2}{n}}$$ $$a = \overline{Y} - b\overline{X}$$ Regression line can only be drawn after the values for *a* and *b* are known.	With least squares method, ensures the very best line. The sum of squares of the error terms will be minimized. Can assess accuracy of predictions.	Useful for all reasons described in the text except #4. Line can only be drawn after values for *a* and *b* are determined.	Yes	Yes	2
Multiple regression	Calculates *b* and *a* by substituting sample values into more complicated versions of the equations above for simple regression. For practical purposes can only be used with assistance of computer. The equation for mixed costs can never be shown graphically.	The same as simple regression, except that analysis can be performed with two or more independent variables. Major drawback is that the scatter diagram cannot be used in conjunction with this method.	Cannot be used with multiple regression.	Yes	Yes	3 or more

CHAPTER SUMMARY

Costs are either variable, fixed, or mixed. *Total variable costs* change in the same direction and in direct proportion to changes in activity. In order for the total to change in direct proportion, the average variable cost must remain unchanged; that is, no matter how low or high the activity is, the average variable cost does not change.

Fixed costs, in total, are not expected to change in response to changes in activity (1) for a given period of time and (2) within a relevant range of activity. Average fixed costs vary inversely with activity — the lower the activity, the higher the average fixed cost, and vice versa.

The *relevant range* is the range of productive activity within which the assumptions of cost behavior are expected to be valid, that is, the range within which the total fixed costs and average variable costs will remain unchanged. The total fixed costs and the variable cost rate may change as you go from one relevant range to another.

A *mixed cost* contains both variable and fixed cost components. To assist management in making intelligent predictions, rational decisions, and proper evaluations of performance, an accountant must be able to separate the variable and fixed cost components of a mixed cost.

The following formula is used to determine the variable component of a mixed cost:

$$\text{Variable cost rate} = \frac{\text{change in total costs}}{\text{change in activity}}$$

The total fixed costs can then be determined by subtracting variable costs from mixed costs, using the following equation for total costs:

$$\text{Total mixed costs} = \text{fixed costs} + (\text{variable cost rate} \times \text{activity})$$

This formula is an integral part of two of the methods we discussed in this chapter: (1) the *high-low method* and (2) the *visual approximation method.* The third method we discussed is called *regression analysis,* which uses a more complicated and mathematically derived formula to determine the variable and fixed elements.

IMPORTANT TERMS USED IN THIS CHAPTER

Committed fixed costs The costs of establishing the basic organization, maintaining it, and ensuring its capacity to produce; the total costs required if production falls to zero activity. Management has very little influence over these costs in the short run. (page 106)

Dependent variable The total mixed costs to be evaluated when the variable and fixed components are not known. It is Y in the equation for total mixed costs, $Y = a + bX$. Its name comes from the fact that total costs are influenced by, or dependent upon, the level of activity X. (page 88)

Discretionary fixed costs Fixed costs decided upon by management at the beginning of a budget period; at management's discretion they can be adjusted as the year progresses. Examples include research costs and advertising expenditures. (page 76)

Discretionary variable costs The same types of costs that are usually treated as discretionary fixed costs. However, rather than a fixed total being set by management at the beginning of a budget period, a fixed amount per unit is budgeted instead. (page 78)

Fixed costs   Costs that in total are expected to remain unchanged in response to changes in activity during a period of time and within a relevant range of activity. (page 67)

High-low method   A method of determining the variable and fixed portions of a mixed cost. The highest cost and the lowest cost (and their related activities) are selected from the sample of points, for use in the equation for the variable cost rate. (page 93)

Independent variable   The level of activity that the variable portion of a mixed cost is related to, or dependent upon. It is the X variable in the equation for total mixed costs, $Y = a + bX$. (page 88)

Least squares method   The method used in regression analysis for determining the variable and fixed components of a mixed cost. The method ensures that the equation for total costs, $Y = a + bX$, resulting from its use is better than that provided by any other method. (page 96)

Mixed cost   A cost that contains both variable and fixed costs. (page 67)

Proportionately variable costs   Total costs which change in direct proportion to changes in activity. For every additional unit of activity, the total variable cost is expected to increase by exactly the same amount. (page 74)

Regression analysis   A statistical approach to evaluating a mixed cost. The specific method usually employed in determining the variable and fixed components is the *least squares method*. (page 96)

Relevant range of activity   The range of activity within which a firm expects to operate and for which the assumptions concerning the behavior of costs are assumed to be valid. (page 70)

R-square   A statistic that measures the percentage of variability in a dependent variable which can be explained by changes in the independent variable(s). (page 107)

Scatter diagram   A graph that contains the plotted points from a sample. It is used in conjunction with all three methods of evaluating a mixed cost. (page 89)

Step fixed costs   Fixed costs which change substantially when activity changes from one relevant range to another. (page 77)

Step variable costs   Variable costs that increase in very small increments as activity increases. The steps are so small and narrow that a straight line can be drawn through the steps so that the cost can be treated as if it were proportionately variable. (page 75)

t-test   A statistical means of determining whether the true slope of a regression line—the variable cost rate—is significantly different from zero (page 107)

Variable costs   Costs that in total change in the same direction and in direct proportion to changes in activity. (page 67)

Visual approximation method   A subjective method of determining the variable and fixed components of a mixed cost. A line is drawn through the plotted points of a sample in such a way that (1) the line appears to represent the trend of the points and (2) there is a good distribution of points about the line. From this line are selected coordinates to be used in the equation for the variable cost rate. (page 94)

CHAPTER 3 Analysis of Cost Behavior: Variable, Fixed, and Mixed
Appendix 3-1: Measures of Accuracy of the Regression Line

105

APPENDIX 3-1: MEASURES OF ACCURACY OF THE REGRESSION LINE

R-Square (R^2)

We would like to think that by using the regression line equation we will be able to predict mixed costs that will be close approximations of the actual mixed costs we will observe in the future. One way to tell if the predictions will be close approximations or not is with the statistic referred to as R^2. But before we explain exactly what we mean by R^2, let's look first at the three diagrams shown in Figure 3-24. Assume that the three graphs represent three different possible samples that we might have taken to get our regression equation. Also assume that each sample resulted in the exact same regression line, having the same slope and the same Y-intercept. Naturally, this would mean that predictions of mixed costs for any given level of activity would be exactly the same, regardless of the sample (in graphs 1, 2, or 3 in Figure 3-24) from which the regression line was derived.

If you could choose the sample that represented the distribution of points from which the regression line in Figure 3-24 had been taken, which sample would you prefer? Would it be the one with all the points on the line (graph 1)? The one with the points closely clustered about the line (graph 2)? Or the one in which the points are quite a distance from the line (graph 3)? Which one would give you the greatest confidence that predictions you make in the future with this line will be close to reality?

If you chose graph 1, you're right. The observed points produced a regression line that precisely intersected each and every observed point in the sample. The fact that all the points are on the regression line means that the actual results in the past were described perfectly by the line. If the relationship between the dependent and independent variables continues to be the same in the future, then we could reasonably assume that any predictions we make in the future with the regression line will also describe perfectly the mixed costs. For example, assume that the slope and intercept for the regression line in graph 1 of Figure 3-24 were $5 per unit and $10,000, respectively. Since the actual observations in the past were all precisely on the regression line, we would then assume that the actual mixed costs in the future will also be on the regression line. If the units of activity were 10,000, then we'd expect the mixed costs to be exactly $60,000:

$$Y' = \$10{,}000 + (\$5 \times 10{,}000 \text{ units}) = \$60{,}000$$

Graphs 2 and 3 both show regression lines that are representative of the points in

FIGURE 3-24
Different Samples Give
Different R^2's
Graph 1 has the best R^2.

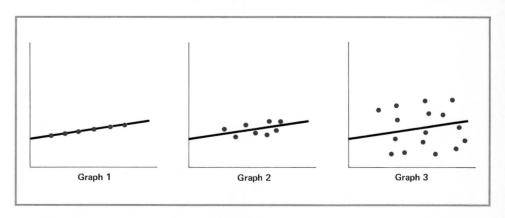

Graph 1   Graph 2   Graph 3

their respective samples. However, since the regression lines in these graphs do not provide exact predictions of the mixed costs in the past, there is no reason to expect the predictions in the future to be any better. Although predictions made with the line in graph 2 will be pretty close to the actual results, predictions resulting from the sample in graph 3 will be way off the mark.

When you first looked at Figure 3-24, it may have been obvious that graph 1 represented the best situation, because it indeed was the perfect situation. In most realistic situations, however, the actual observations are not going to fall exactly on the resulting regression line, and thus the line will not be a perfect reflection of reality. When the situation is not perfect, it is difficult to determine, visually and subjectively, when the line is going to make accurate predictions. So what we need is an objective measure of how closely the regression line will approximate actual results. Such a measure of the predictive accuracy of the regression line is **R-square,** or R^2 (the coefficient of determination).

R^2 is an objective measure of the accuracy of $Y = a + bX$

To begin to understand what R^2 is all about, first consider graph 1 in Figure 3-24. There, R^2 is 100%, which means that 100% of the variation in the dependent variable is explained by the variation in the independent variable. In the Big Foot example, this would mean that 100% of the variation in the mixed costs of the inspection department can be completely explained by changes in the number of units inspected.

$R^2 = 100\%$ for graph 1

What we are trying to do when we analyze a mixed cost is to explain why it behaves, or varies, the way it does. In statistical terms, we want to evaluate how the dependent variable responds to changes in the independent variable. We would naturally like to have the independent variable explain perfectly the variability in the dependent variable so that, by merely knowing the level of activity, we would be able to predict exactly the mixed costs. Such is the situation depicted by graph 1 in Figure 3-24, where R^2 is 100%.

An R^2 of 100% occurs any time all the points in a sample fall perfectly on a nonhorizontal straight line. Since the points in graphs 2 and 3 do not all lie on the lines drawn in the graphs, the R^2 for each of them is less than 100%. Furthermore, we would expect the R^2 for graph 2 to be better than the R^2 for graph 3 because it has a tighter fit of points about the line. But the exact R^2 values for these two graphs cannot be determined without an elaborate formula.

Range of values for R^2: 0–100%

The range of possible values for R^2 is 0 to 100%. We have already seen an example of an R^2 of 100%. But what will an R^2 of 0% look like? It can be shown in several different ways, all of which indicate that the independent variable explains none—0%—of the variability in the dependent variable. An R^2 of zero means that there are no variable costs—all costs are fixed. Both graphs in Figure 3-25 are examples of an R^2 of 0%.

Graph 1 shows a perfectly horizontal string of points, which is obviously a fixed cost; none of the variability in Y is explained by X, because there is no variability in Y. Graph 2 shows a group of points that have been purposely drawn to be completely random. In this situation there is plenty of variability in Y, but none of it can be explained by X. The only line that can be drawn through this distribution of points is a horizontal line, with the value for Y'—all fixed costs—being the average Y value for the sample.

Definition of R^2

All this has been leading up to the basic idea of what R^2 is all about. R^2 is a measure, expressed as a percent, of the variability of a dependent variable that can be explained by, or attributed to, changes in an independent variable.

R^2 for Big Foot = 50.02%

Within this text we will not burden you with the mechanics of calculating R^2. You'll get enough of that in your statistics courses. But we do want you to know what the R^2 is for the Big Foot Company. It is 50.02%, which means that only 50.02% of the

FIGURE 3-25
Examples of $R^2 = 0\%$

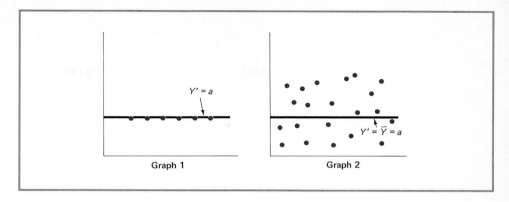

Graph 1   Graph 2

variability in the mixed costs is explained by knowing the number of units inspected. This leaves another 49.98% of the variability in Y that cannot be explained by X.

To what can we attribute this 49.98%? One possibility is that we might need a second independent variable. For example, the costs of inspecting units for Big Foot might also be affected by the nature of the units (size, weight, complexity, etc.) as well as by the number of units inspected. That is why we often use multiple regression instead of simple regression.

It's also possible, however, that the 49.98% could simply be a result of random, or chance, variation in Y that cannot be explained by any other variable.

t-Tests

Another important statistical aid that we can use with the least squares method is the ***t-test***. This helps us to decide whether there is a significant relationship between the dependent and independent variables, based upon the results of the sample.

We found out that the regression coefficient (which is the same as the slope of the regression line and the variable cost rate) determined from the sample given in Exhibit 3-2 was $0.7238 per unit inspected. This means that for every unit inspected, we expect the total costs to increase by $0.7238. We hope that this rate — based upon a sample taken from a much larger population — is a good estimate of the true variable cost rate for the population. We hope further that if we were to repeat the sampling process over and over, we would continue to get a variable cost rate of $0.7238 per unit. More realistically, however, if we did repeated sampling, we would *Repeated samples will give* probably get a somewhat different variable cost rate from each sample taken. It's *different values for b* quite possible that all the variable cost rates from repeated sampling would fall a small distance above and below the value of $0.7238 per unit. If this were to happen, it would give us some confidence that $0.7238 per unit is a good approximation of the true variable cost rate for the population and that it is acceptable to substitute $0.7238 for b in the equation $Y' = a + bX$.

On the other hand, if repeated sampling gave us variable cost rates ranging from, say, $+\$0.73$ to $-\$0.73$, with the highest frequency of rates right around 0.00, then this may indicate that the true value for the variable cost rate is actually the midpoint *Could the true b value = 0?* of this spread — or zero dollars per unit. This would mean that the sample had been taken from a population having a zero variable cost per unit, even though the sample yielded a value for b of $0.7238 per unit. If the true rate is actually zero, then it would naturally be inappropriate to substitute $0.7238 for b in the equation $Y' = a + bX$, because the resulting predictions would consistently misstate the total costs by a significant amount.

Let's stop now for a moment and see graphically how a single sample could come from a population having a zero variable cost rate and yet provide us with a variable

FIGURE 3-26
Nonzero Slopes Resulting from Samples Taken from a Population with a Zero Slope

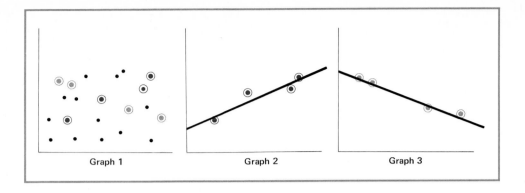

Graph 1   Graph 2   Graph 3

cost rate other than zero. Look at graph 1 in Figure 3-26. Assume that the points plotted on the graph represent the entire population of possible observations and that these observations are completely random. As we saw in Figure 3-25, the regression line for these points is horizontal—meaning there should be no variable costs. Assume next that two different samples of four observations each are taken from this population. The first sample only includes the dark-blue circled points, and the second sample only includes the light-blue circled points. These points and their resulting regression lines are shown in graphs 2 and 3, respectively, of Figure 3-26. See how easily a single sample taken from a population having a zero slope can result in a sample slope that is positive (graph 2) or negative (graph 3).

What we would like to do is to find out whether the true variable cost rate is zero, but without having to take repeated samples. We'd like to find out, with as little trouble as possible, if it's okay to use the variable cost rate we got from the sample in the equation $Y' = a + bX$. We can accomplish this—using only one sample—with the t-test.

The first thing we usually do when conducting a t-test is to state the hypothesis that the true variable cost rate—the slope of the regression line—is actually zero, which implies that the total costs are entirely fixed. We then use the t-test to try to prove that this hypothesis is incorrect.

The t-test helps determine if true slope (b) = 0.

We then calculate a t-value, which in statistical terms represents the distance that the sample statistic ($b = \$0.7238$) is from zero. A t-value greater than 2 is usually regarded as large enough for us to conclude that the variable cost rate is significantly greater than zero.[2] This means that we can reject the hypothesis of a zero variable cost rate. It also gives us pretty good assurance that (1) it is acceptable to use the sample value of $0.7238 as an adequate representation of the true variable cost rate for the population and (2) it is also acceptable to substitute this b value into the equation $Y' = a + bX$ and to make cost projections using the equation.

---

[2] The calculation of t is as follows:

$$t = \frac{b - 0}{s_b}$$

where s_b is the standard error of the regression coefficient. The calculated t-value represents the number of standard deviations that b is from zero. This value needs to be greater than a critical value found in a t-table. The table value is a function of the number of degrees of freedom and the level of confidence desired by the decision maker. The rule of thumb of 2 is actually acceptable only when the degrees of freedom are 30 or more, based upon a 95% level of confidence.

The R^2 and the t-value are just two of many statistics provided by most computer programs for the least squares method. All this information is quite important to the user in fully understanding how to properly use this sophisticated method. We have only discussed these two statistics in order to give you an appreciation of what is available to the informed user when he or she is evaluating cost behavior.

QUESTIONS

1. List and define the three types of costs classified by behavior.

2. "A variable cost can be defined as one that changes." Comment.

3. "If a certain cost changes, it cannot be a fixed cost." Do you agree? Explain.

4. Discuss the importance of *activity* to the definitions of variable and fixed costs.

5. "The more activity increases, the lower the fixed cost per unit will be. Therefore, fixed costs can really be classified as variable costs." Explain why you agree or disagree with these statements.

6. Which of the product costs of a manufacturer would be classified as variable and which would be classified as fixed?

7. Discuss the concept of *relevant range* and how it affects the definitions of variable and fixed costs.

8. Would you agree that the term *discretionary fixed costs* implies that a company can use its discretion, over time, as to whether it should incur these costs, without affecting the attainment of long-range goals? Explain.

9. If you knew that a cost contained both variable and fixed components, but you did not know the variable rate or the amount that was fixed, how would you predict the total cost for some level of activity?

10. What are three reasons for distinguishing between *variable costs* and *fixed costs?*

11. The algebraic equation for total (mixed) costs is $Y = a + bX$. Define each element of the equation.

12. In determining the behavioral components of a mixed cost, what is the purpose of a scatter diagram?

13. "The way to determine if a cost contains a variable portion is to first draw a scatter diagram. If all the points lie on a single, straight line, then the costs are variable." Do you agree? Explain.

14. Discuss what is meant by the *high-low method.*

15. What are the three methods of determining the behavior of costs?

16. Explain how the accountant's view and the economist's view of variable costs differ.

17. Can the high-low, visual approximation, and least squares methods ever have identical results? Explain.

18. Discuss the meaning of the statistic R^2.

19. What are the extreme values for R^2? Draw a scatter diagram that depicts each of these values.

20. Are step costs a type of variable cost or a type of fixed cost? Explain.

21. What are the different categories of variable costs?

22. The Jacobsen Company used regression analysis to evaluate the relationship between sales revenue Y and advertising expenditures X. Its results were as follows:

Behavioral components:
a value... 10,000
b value... 1.50
R-square .... .18
t-value .... .42

How would you evaluate this model in terms of its ability to predict sales revenue?

23. Tampa Bay Cable has recently been granted a license to provide cable service to Paradise Lakes, a small town in Pasco County. The linemen have been laying cable for 6 months and the costs have been much higher than the company controller had expected. She decided to collect a 6-month sample of cost information and try to determine which variables have the most pronounced effect on total costs. She used the least squares method of analysis on a multi-independent variable model. The results of this analysis are presented below.

Independent Variable		Regression Coefficient	t-Value
Feet of cable laid		.450	4.890
Number of new customers		3.780	2.010
Total hookups		.890	.046
Intercept	6,000		
R-square	.886		

Evaluate the results in as much detail as possible.

EXERCISES

Exercise 3-1
Determining *a* and *b* for a mixed cost

From the mixed costs below, determine the variable cost rate, total fixed costs, and resulting equation for mixed costs:

	Mixed Costs	Activity (in Units)
Month 1	$8,100	700
Month 2	7,500	500

(Check figure: Fixed costs = $6,000)

Exercise 3-2
Predicting total mixed costs

During December the McEnroe Company incurred $120,000 in one of its producing departments. The direct labor-hours for that month were 10,000 and the fixed costs were $30,000. Predict the costs for the first 3 months of the next year if the direct labor-hours are expected to be 8,000, 7,000, and 15,000 for January through March, respectively.

(Check figure: March = $165,000)

Exercise 3-3
Classifying costs by
behavior

Listed below are the costs of the assembly departments of the Stenerued Manufacturing Company. Classify each as (1) a product (Pr) or period (P) cost and (2) a variable (V), fixed (F), or mixed (M) cost.

	Product or Period Cost	Variable, Fixed, or Mixed Cost
Direct materials	_____	_____
Direct labor	_____	_____
Indirect materials	_____	_____
Indirect labor	_____	_____
Utilities on factory	_____	_____
Property taxes on factory	_____	_____
Rent on salespeoples' cars	_____	_____
Depreciation of equipment	_____	_____
Insurance on all company assets	_____	_____
Overtime premium	_____	_____
Payroll taxes on factory workers' salaries	_____	_____
Janitorial supplies (services entire company)	_____	_____
Bad debts	_____	_____
Advertising	_____	_____
Machine maintenance	_____	_____
Idle time	_____	_____
Freight-out	_____	_____
Entertainment costs (of salespeople)	_____	_____
Lubricants for machines	_____	_____

Exercise 3-4
Identifying characteristics
of different methods

Following is a list of descriptions about one or more of the methods of evaluating a mixed cost. You are to indicate which method(s) is (are) being described by placing the number for the correct answer(s) in the spaces provided.
1. High-low
2. Visual approximation
3. Least squares
_____ **a.** Uses only two observations from a sample.
_____ **b.** Results in the best estimates of the variable cost rate and fixed costs.
_____ **c.** Uses all observations from a sample.
_____ **d.** Is a subjective approach.
_____ **e.** The mixed cost line *must* be drawn before the variable cost rate and fixed costs can be determined.
_____ **f.** The mixed cost line can only be drawn after the variable cost rate and fixed costs are determined.

Exercise 3-5
Drawing graphs for
different types of costs

For each description below, draw the graph that best depicts the cost behavior being described. The horizontal axis is activity and the vertical axis is total costs.
a. Direct materials costs.
b. Straight-line depreciation.
c. Payroll taxes based on wages and salaries of all workers in a production plant.
d. A distribution of actual costs indicating that no relationship exists between costs and activity.
e. A distribution of actual costs indicating that a positive relationship exists between costs and activity.

f. A mixed cost that increases continuously up to the point in production at which the total costs reach a maximum.

g. Property taxes—a fixed charge if the company operates under a certain level of productive activity. If the activity is above that level, no property taxes will be paid.

h. Average fixed costs.

i. Direct labor costs.

j. Cost of lubricants, computed as follows:

First 100,000 lb	$2.00/lb	Next 100,000 lb	$1.40/lb
Next 100,000 lb	$1.80/lb	etc.	etc.
Next 100,000 lb	$1.60/lb		

k. Utilities—a fixed charge plus a variable portion based upon a constant rate per kilowatt-hour used.

l. Rent—a fixed charge plus a variable portion only after a certain level of productive activity is reached.

m. Salaries of supervisors—a supervisor can supervise only a limited number of employees. After that number has been reached, a new supervisor must be hired.

n. Sum-of-the-years'-digits depreciation.

Exercise 3-6
Predicting mixed costs

During the month of January, 1988, the Puffer Company produced 100,000 units and incurred the following costs:

Direct Materials..............................	$200,000
Direct Labor................................	350,000
Factory Overhead	400,000
Total	$950,000

The company controller expected the production for February, 1988, to double, and he asked a staff accountant to estimate the expected costs for February.

a. Prepare an estimate for February (the staff accountant does not know if the factory overhead is variable, fixed, or mixed).

b. Prepare an estimate for February (assume the January factory overhead is all variable).

c. Prepare an estimate for February (assume the January factory overhead is one-half variable).

(Check figure: $600,000)

Exercise 3-7
Filling in the blanks for an income statement

Fill in the blanks below for the income statement of Rhett Butler Company for 1988 and 1989. Assume no beginning or ending inventories.

	Situation			
	1988		**1989**	
Sales...................................	$200,000		$400,000	
Cost of Goods Sold:				
Direct Materials..............	$40,000		$ 80,200	
Direct Labor................	60,000		120,000	
Variable Overhead...........	20,000		40,000	
Fixed Overhead	50,000	170,000	50,000	290,000
Gross Profit		$ 30,000		$110,000
Selling and Administrative:				
Variable....................	$10,000		$20,000	
Fixed........................	10,000	20,000	10,000	30,000
Net Income		$ 10,000		$ 80,000

(Check figure: Net income, 1989 = $80,000)

Exercise 3-8
Classifying variable and fixed costs

For each cost listed below, indicate its correct classification by placing a V (variable cost), a D (discretionary fixed cost), or a C (committed fixed cost) in the space provided.

	Classification
a. Research	_____
b. Direct labor	_____
c. Insurance	_____
d. Utilities (based entirely upon a per-kilowatt charge)	_____
e. Direct materials	_____
f. Sales vice president's salary	_____
g. Consulting fees from outside adviser	_____
h. Depreciation on equipment	_____
i. Sales commissions	_____
j. Advertising	_____
k. Purchasing agent's salary	_____
l. CPA audit fee (required by the Securities and Exchange Commission)	_____
m. College education paid for employees with 10 or more years of employment	_____
n. Rent on factory building	_____
o. Shipping costs	_____

Exercise 3-9
Determining income based on a higher level of activity

The Packer Corporation sold 12,000 units in 1988 and had the following income statement:

Sales...		$132,000
Variable Costs	$ 96,000	
Fixed Costs..	25,000	121,000
Net Income..		$ 11,000

The fixed costs will be 50% higher for production in excess of 20,000 units, and the variable cost rate will be $0.50 per unit lower for all units when production is in excess of 20,000. If production and sales double in 1989, what will be Packer Corporation's net income.

(Check figure: Net income = $46,500)

Exercise 3-10
Determining the *b* value with least squares

The Bennett Company is attempting to predict its utility costs for December. The controller realizes that they are mixed in nature and that regression analysis is needed. The following sample has been taken:

	Utility Costs	Machine-Hours
July	$420	8,000
August	388	7,200
September	460	9,000
October	480	9,500
November	500	10,000

a. What would be the equation for utility costs ($Y = a + bX$) with the least squares method? Answer the question, however, without using the least squares formulas.

(Check figure: b = $0.04)

b. What would be the R^2 for the regression model? Explain what the R^2 indicates?

Exercise 3-11
Determining the elements of a mixed cost based on averages

The operating costs for Krispy Dunk Donut Shoppe averaged $0.2875 per donut in 1986, but they fell to an average of $0.2750 per donut in 1987. The number of donuts sold in 1986 and 1987 were 700,000 and 800,000, respectively. Determine the total operating costs for 1988 if the sales increase to 900,000 donuts.

(Check figure: $238,750)

Exercise 3-12
Determining the gross profit percentage at two levels of activity

An income statement for July, 1988, is presented below for Spencer Ski Equipment Corporation. Assume there are no beginning or ending inventories.

Sales		$250,000
Cost of Sales:		
Direct Materials......................................	$60,000	
Direct Labor..	50,000	
Factory Overhead*	40,000	150,000
Gross Profit..		$100,000
Operating Costs†		20,000
Net Income		$ 80,000

* One-half of total is fixed.
† Three-fourths of total is fixed.

The sales in August are expected to increase by $100,000.
a. Calculate the gross profit percentage for July.
b. Determine the income that is projected for August.

(Check figure: $126,000)

c. What is the gross profit percentage for August? Why is it different from the gross profit percentage for July?

Exercise 3-13
Determining the effect of the relevant range on cost predictions

The variable and fixed costs for Merrill Corporation depend upon the relevant range of activity, as shown below:

Range of Activity	Total Fixed Costs	Variable Cost per Unit
0–20,000	$15,000	$2.00
20,001–40,000	25,000	2.20
40,001 and above	30,000	2.30

You are to determine the total costs for Merrill Corporation for 20,000 units, 40,000 units, and 60,000 units.

Exercise 3-14
Comparing error terms for different methods

The Condo Company has collected the following sample in order to evaluate the behavior of a mixed cost:

Observation	Mixed Cost	Activity (in Units)
1	$ 700	100
2	1,300	200
3	1,200	300

a. Determine the equation for the mixed costs ($Y = a + bX$) using the high-low, visual approximation, and least squares methods.

(Check figure: b, for least squares = $2.50)

b. Determine the sum of squares of the error terms based upon the results of each method in part **a**.

c. Which method had the lowest sum of squares of the error terms?

Exercise 3-15
Evaluating results for *a*, *b*,
and *R*²

The shipping department of a large department store has recently finished using regression analysis to evaluate the relationship of shipping costs to the number of shipments made each week. A sample was selected from the results of the first 40 weeks of 1989. The results of the analysis are given below:

Intercept $70,000
Regression coefficient $1.75
R-square 85

a. Express these results in equation form ($Y = a + bX$).

b. On a graph, draw the line that represents the equation in part **a**. Make it as close to scale as possible.

c. Assume that the shipments made in week 1 of 1989 totaled 20,000 and that the actual costs of the shipping department were $110,000. Determine the error term for week 1.

(Check figure: $5,000)

d. Assume that the R^2 was 1.00 instead of .85. What would the actual costs and related error term have been in week 1, for part **c**?

Exercise 3-16
Comparing methods when
results are identical

The accountant for Watson's Beauty Supply outlet is preparing a budget for the first quarter of 1988, but he is unsure of the behavioral components of the costs of Watson's selling department. He has decided to gather a sample of observations from the last 3 months of 1987.

	Dollar Sales (X)	Total Costs (Y)
October	$50,000	$22,500
November	70,000	23,500
December	95,000	24,750

a. Using the high-low method, determine the equation for the total costs of the selling department, $Y = a + bX$. First, do it for the months of October and November. Then do it again for the months of November and December.

b. Without making any calculations or plotting a scatter diagram, determine the equation for total costs, $Y = a + bX$, with the visual approximation and least squares methods. Why is it that you can get the answers for these two methods without doing any additional work?

(Check figure: b = .05)

c. What will the R^2 be for this sample?

Exercise 3-17
Evaluating results of
regression analysis

The following scatter diagram has been prepared for an operating department of Gung Ho Model Cars, Inc. Examine it carefully and then look at the results that supposedly relate to the sample depicted in the scatter diagram.

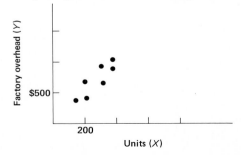

Results:

Intercept....................................	$1,200
Regression coefficient	−$3.50
R-square....................................	1.00
t-value....................................	.00

In what ways are the results inconsistent with the impression you get from the scatter diagram?

PROBLEMS: SET A

Problem A3-1
Preparing income statements having mixed costs

On January 1, 1988, the controller of Cheers Corporation, S. Maloney, prepared budgeted income statements for the first 2 months of 1988, when production and sales were expected to be 12,000 and 15,000 units, respectively. They are shown below:

	January		February	
Sales Revenue		$156,000		$195,000
Cost of Goods Sold:				
Direct Materials	$36,000		$45,000	
Direct Labor	48,000		60,000	
Factory Overhead..............	56,000	140,000	65,000	170,000
Gross Profit		$ 16,000		$ 25,000
Selling and Administrative		17,000		20,000
Net Income (Loss)		$ (1,000)		$ 5,000

Required

If the production and sales for March are expected to be 20,000 units, prepare a budgeted income statement for that month.

(Check figure: Net income = $15,000)

Problem A3-2
Determining losses from fire

The Berns Safety Match Company is trying to determine the amount of inventory lost in a recent fire. It has gathered the following data concerning the inventories at the beginning of the year (when the last complete inventory was taken) and on the morning following the fire.

	Beginning of Year, Jan. 1, 1988	Undamaged Inventory Morning after Fire, Mar. 12, 1988
Work-in-Process...........................	$30,000	$7,000
Finished Goods............................	$44,000	$12,000
Additional information, 1/1/88–3/12/88:		
Sales		$450,000
Gross Profit (%)		60%
Direct Materials Used		$50,000
Direct Labor (percentage of prime costs)		$66\frac{2}{3}$%
Variable Overhead (percentage of variable conversion costs)		$16\frac{2}{3}$%
Fixed Factory Overhead		$40,000
Cost of Goods Completed		$205,000

| **Required** | Determine the amount of estimated loss for Work-in-Process and Finished Goods. |

(Check figure: Loss of work-in-process = $28,000)

Problem A3-3
Using two different
approaches to an income
statement

The Annaheim Company produced and sold 10,000 units in October, 1988, at $25 per unit. Its cost of goods sold averaged $15 per unit broken down as follows:

Direct Materials.....................................	$ 4
Direct Labor.......................................	5
Factory Overhead ($\frac{2}{3}$ of which is variable)	6
Total	$15

Its selling and administrative costs averaged $4 ($\frac{1}{2}$ of which was variable). Annaheim expects to double production and sales in November.

| **Required** | 1. If the cost-behavior assumptions are unchanged, prepare an income statement (in total dollars) for November, 1988. |

(Check figure: Gross profit = $220,000)

2. Now prepare the income statement using a different format. For this part, first group all the variable costs together and subtract their total from sales, and then subtract the total for the fixed costs. This is referred to in Chapter 4 as the contribution margin format.

Problem A3-4
Using all three methods to
evaluate mixed costs

The Perriere Car Wash is trying to estimate its cost of operations for January, 1988. Its controller, Hal Culligan, points out that its operating costs are mixed and one of several approaches will have to be employed in order to determine the behavioral components. Hal proceeds to take a sample of eight observations from May to December, 1987. The sample is given below:

	Total Operating Costs (Y)	Number of Customers (X)
May	$5,100	3,000
June	6,200	4,000
July	5,700	2,500
August	5,800	4,500
September	6,700	3,250
October	7,000	5,000
November	5,200	3,500
December	6,100	4,200

| **Required** | 1. Prepare a scatter diagram. |
| | 2. Using the high-low method, determine the equation for total costs, $Y = a + bX$. |

(Check figure: b = $0.95)

3. Using the visual approximation method, determine the equation for total costs.
4. Using the least squares method, determine the equation for total costs.

Problem A3-5
Using the high-low and
visual methods on the
basis of a given scatter
diagram

The Bowzer Canine Hospital is studying the behavior of its intensive care unit and wants to determine the variable cost rate and fixed costs. A sample was taken of the costs of the intensive care unit and the related measure of activity — patients — over a 10-week period. The observations were then plotted in the scatter diagram below.

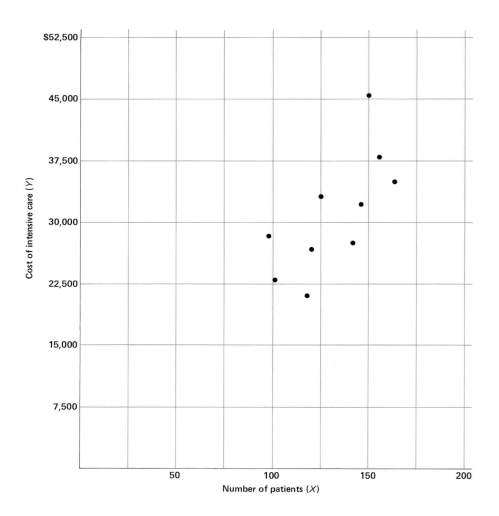

Required

1. Using the high-low method, determine the equation of the line, $Y = a + bX$.

(Check figure: a = −$33,900)

2. Using the visual approximation method, determine the equation of the line, $Y = a + bX$.
3. Using the results in part 2, predict the costs of the intensive care unit if the number of patients increases to 200.
4. Evaluate the high-low method in regard to the results in part 1.

Problem A3-6
Predicting mixed costs
based upon the results of
the least squares method

The R4-D4 Robot Company, which produces miniature robots for use in the home, attempts to control the quality of its product with an intensive inspection by the inspection department. The costs and units inspected during the last 6 weeks are given below:

Week	Costs	Units
1	$4,100	12
2	3,850	14
3	4,500	17
4	4,000	20
5	3,200	9
6	3,700	10

The controller, L. Moonwalker, is trying to predict the costs for the inspection department in week 7 when 25 robots are scheduled to be produced.

Required

Using the least squares method, project the total costs of the inspection department for week 7.

(Check figure: b = 70.03)

Problem A3-7
Deciding on the best
measure of activity based
on a scatter diagram

The Bailey Company is trying to budget its indirect labor costs for January, 1989, but it is not sure of their behavioral nature. The controller collected a sample of observations for the last 6 months and asks your assistance in analyzing indirect labor.

Observation	Indirect Labor Costs	Measures of Activity	
		Units Produced	**Labor-Hours**
1	$20,000	1,400	4,200
2	32,000	2,400	8,400
3	24,900	1,800	5,760
4	30,000	3,000	8,250
5	52,500	3,400	12,920
6	23,000	2,000	5,200

Required

1. Prepare two scatter diagrams: For the first one use units produced as the independent variable, and for the second one use labor-hours as the independent variable.
2. Which measure of activity would be the better independent variable—units produced or labor-hours? Explain.
3. Using the preferable measure of activity, determine the equation $Y = a + bX$ for indirect labor costs with the least squares method.
4. Repeat part 3, but exclude from your sample the fifth observation. Comment on the differences in your results in parts 3 and 4.

Problem A3-8
Evaluating a scatter
diagram

The Kayfred Precision Laser Company manufactures laser equipment for use in surveying and runs a repair shop for the equipment sold to its customers. It is attempting to determine a billing rate and wants to base it upon the variable costs of operating the repair shop. The problem is that the operating costs have not been separated into their variable and fixed components. A sample of the costs of this department has been collected for the last 27 months, and the resulting scatter diagram is shown below. The controller plans to use the least squares method of analysis, but first wants to evaluate the scatter diagram for any relevant information that may be helpful.

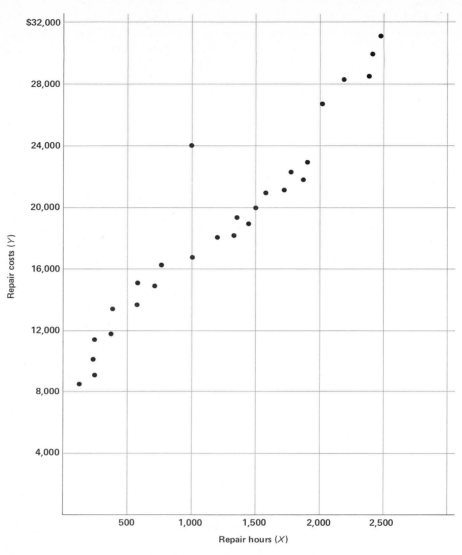

| | **Required** | Entirely on the basis of the scatter diagram, specify as many different relevant bits of information as possible that you think may be helpful in evaluating the relationship between the dependent variable and the independent variable. |

Problem A3-9
Using least squares when
a behavioral assumption
has changed

During the first 3 months of the year Hurts Truck Rental had exactly the same fixed costs in each month. During the next 3 months an expansion project resulted in an $8,000 increase in the fixed costs per month. The total costs for each month and their related activity levels are shown below:

	Total Costs (Y)	Miles Driven (X)
January	$31,500	13,000
February	32,500	15,000
March	37,000	24,000
April	45,500	25,000
May	48,000	30,000
June	50,500	35,000

Required	1. Using the least squares method, determine the equation $Y = a + bX$ for the total costs. 2. Prepare a scatter diagram, and place the line determined in part 1 on the diagram. 3. Now subtract the additional fixed costs of $8,000 from the total costs for April through June, and redo the analysis with the least squares method. 4. Prepare a new scatter diagram, this time using the total costs from part 3. Place the line that you determined in part 3 on the diagram. 5. Which results do you feel are more meaningful? Why?

PROBLEMS: SET B

Problem B3-1
Preparing income
statements that have
mixed costs

The Victorio Corporation has just completed operations for July, 1988, and has prepared the following comparative income statements for June and July:

	June		July	
Sales.		$200,000		$240,000
Cost of Goods Sold:				
Direct Materials	$40,000		$48,000	
Direct Labor	50,000		60,000	
Factory Overhead.	45,000	135,000	51,000	159,000
Gross Profit		$ 65,000		$ 81,000
Selling and Administrative		15,000		18,000
Net Income		$ 50,000		$ 63,000

The selling price in each month was $10.

Required	Victorio anticipates producing and selling 18,000 units during August. Prepare the income statement that Victorio would expect for that month.

(Check figure: Net income = $43,500)

Problem B3-2
Determining losses from
theft

The Precious Metals Manufacturing Company has been in operation just a short time and is concerned that it is having as much inventory stolen as it sells. The accounting department took a physical inventory last night and found the following balances in each inventory account:

Raw Materials	$ -0-
Work-in-Process	12,000
Finished Goods	4,000

There was no inventory of any kind when the company began business. Since beginning production, $40,000 of raw materials have been purchased. The following conversion costs were incurred during production:

Direct Labor ($\frac{1}{2}$ of prime costs and $\frac{2}{3}$ of variable
conversion costs) $30,000
Fixed Factory Overhead. 8,000

Sales totaled $80,000 and cost of goods sold averaged 70% of sales. The cost of units completed was $71,000.

Required	Calculate the amount of inventory stolen from raw materials, work-in-process, and finished goods.

(Check figure: Raw materials stolen = $10,000)

Problem B3-3
Using a new format in preparing an income statement

In March, 1988, the Underhill Coffin Company manufactured and sold 14,000 coffins. Its controller, Ron Kelly, prepared the following income statement, given in total as well as on a per-unit basis:

Sales...	$3,500,000	$250/coffin
Cost of Goods Sold:		
Direct Materials...............................	$1,400,000	$100/coffin
Direct Labor....................................	1,400,000	100/coffin
Variable Overhead	112,000	8/coffin
Fixed Overhead................................	70,000	5/coffin
Total	$2,982,000	$213/coffin
Gross Profit	$ 518,000	$ 37/coffin
Selling and Administrative:		
Variable.......................................	$ 126,000	$ 9/coffin
Fixed	14,000	1/coffin
Total	$ 140,000	$ 10/coffin
Net Income	$ 378,000	$ 27/coffin

Required

Prepare an income statement (showing total dollars and dollars per coffin, as given above) for April if 16,000 coffins will be produced and sold.

(Check figure: Net income = $444,000)

Problem B3-4
Using all three methods to evaluate mixed costs

The controller, Beth Moon, of the Chattanooga Choo Choos Softball Team (one of the new teams in the women's professional softball league) has gathered a sample of six monthly observations for the team's operating costs. Beth wants to project operating costs for the upcoming months and feels that the variable component of its mixed costs fluctuates directly with the number of fans attending its games. The sample taken by Beth is given below:

Week	Operating Costs (Y)	Number of Fans (X)
1	$36,000	1,920
2	40,500	3,300
3	37,500	1,550
4	34,500	2,700
5	32,100	1,200
6	42,600	2,550

Required

1. Prepare a scatter diagram.
2. Using the high-low method, determine the equation for total mixed costs, $Y = a + bX$.

(Check figure: a = $22,766)

3. Using the visual approximation method, determine the equation for total mixed costs, $Y = a + bX$.
4. Using the method of least squares, determine the equation for total mixed costs, $Y = a + bX$.

(Check figure: b = $3.052)

Problem B3-5
Using the high-low and
visual approximation
methods to evaluate a
scatter diagram

The Webster & Robertson Law Office is evaluating the behavior of costs in its Temple Terrace office; the costs are thought to be mixed. The controller, Anne Daveys, has collected a sample of 12 observations from 1989. The scatter diagram for this sample is shown below:

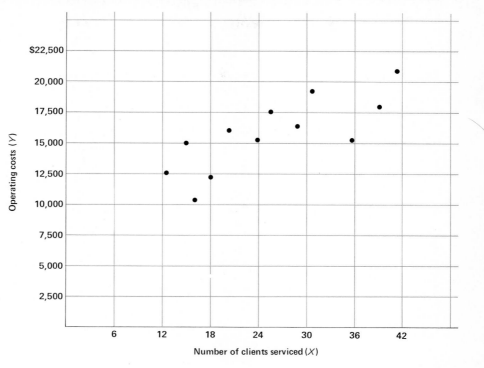

Number of clients serviced (X)

Required

1. Using the high-low method, determine the equation of the line, $Y = a + bX$.

(Check figure: b = $420 per client)

2. Using the visual approximation method, determine the equation of the line, $Y = a + bX$.
3. Using the results from requirements 1 and 2 predict what the firm's operating costs would be if the firm expected to service 45 clients in the upcoming month.

Problem B3-6
Comparing results of least
squares to visual
approximation

P. Holder, controller of Kenny's Exports, is using the least squares method to evaluate the costs of its shipping department. A sample taken from the last 8 weeks of operations is given below:

Week	Costs of Shipping Department	Number of Units Shipped
1	$6,250	1,500
2	7,600	2,400
3	5,800	1,200
4	5,200	800
5	4,900	600
6	6,400	1,600
7	6,700	1,800
8	7,150	2,100

Required

1. Using the least squares method, determine the equation for the mixed costs, $Y = a + bX$.

(Check figure: b = $1.50)

2. Repeat part 1, but use the visual approximation method.

3. Compare the results in parts 1 and 2 and explain why they are so similar.

Problem B3-7
Deciding on the best
measure of activity based
on a scatter diagram

The Gearey Corporation is trying to budget the costs of its inspection department for 1988. The controller is sure that the total costs contain both variable and fixed components, but he is not sure of the correct breakdown between these two groups of costs. In addition, he is not sure of the best measure of activity to use for the independent variable. He has collected a sample of observations for the two possible measures of activity given below and asks your assistance in analyzing the costs of the inspection department.

| | | Measures of Activity | |
| | Inspection Department Costs | Units Inspected | Labor-Hours |
Observation			
1	$25,000	1,750	5,250
2	40,000	3,000	10,500
3	31,120	2,250	7,200
4	37,500	3,750	10,310
5	65,620	4,250	16,150
6	28,750	2,500	6,500

Required

1. Prepare two scatter diagrams: For the first one use units inspected as the independent variable, and for the second one use labor-hours as the independent variable.

2. Which measure of activity would be the better independent variable—units inspected or labor-hours? Explain.

3. Using the preferable measure of activity, determine the equation $Y = a + bX$ for inspection department costs with the least squares method.

4. Repeat part 3, but exclude from your sample the fifth observation. Comment on the differences in your results in parts 3 and 4.

Problem B3-8
Evaluating a scatter
diagram

The Florida Fried Chicken Company sells nothing but chicken wings at county fairs and is attempting to set a price to charge for each wing. The owner, Colonel Cinders, has been told that the price should be based upon the variable costs of operating the stall, but he has absolutely no idea what variable and fixed costs are. He asks his son who has just finished studying regression analysis at school, to help him. The first thing his son did was to take a sample of 30 daily observations. He then plotted the observations from the sample on the scatter diagram shown below. The son felt it might be helpful to examine the scatter diagram for any relevant information before he performed the regression analysis.

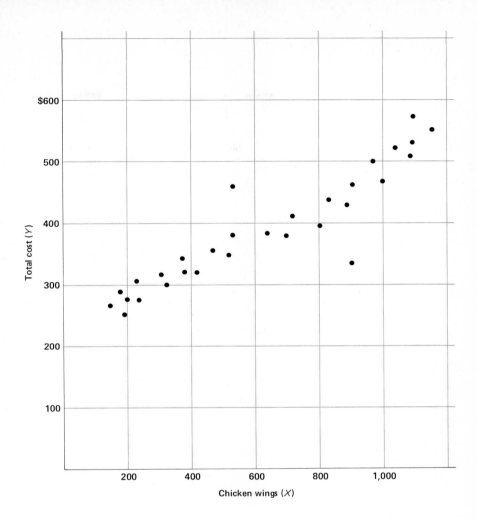

| **Required** | Entirely on the basis of the scatter diagram, specify as many different relevant bits of information as possible that you think may be helpful in evaluating the relationship between the dependent variable and the independent variable. |

Problem B3-9
Using least squares when
a behavioral assumption
has changed

ABM Corporation is a small computer company that makes most of its sales through its outside sales force. The salespeople are reimbursed for their traveling expenses at a fixed amount per day plus a fixed amount per mile driven. In April, 1989, the company increased the mileage reimbursement by $0.05 per mile, and it paid this new rate for the next 3 months.

The total travel reimbursements and related miles driven for the first 6 months of 1989 are given below:

	Total Costs (Y)	Miles Driven (X)
January	$36,500	100,000
February	39,500	115,000
March	40,500	120,000
April	44,000	110,000
May	49,000	130,000
June	39,000	90,000

Required

1. Using the least squares method, determine the equation $Y = a + bX$ for the total costs.
2. Prepare a scatter diagram, and place the line determined in part 1 on the diagram.
3. Now subtract the additional variable costs at $0.05 per mile times the miles driven in April through June from the total costs for April through June. Then redo the analysis with the least squares method.
4. Prepare a new scatter diagram, this time using the total costs from part 3. Place the line that you determined in part 3 on the diagram.
5. Which results do you feel are more meaningful? Why?

Cost-Volume-Profit Analysis and Short-Run Decisions

Once you have mastered the key cost terms and concepts in Chapters 2 and 3, you will be ready to learn about the first of many accounting tools that depend upon the concepts introduced in those chapters. You will learn a new format to an income statement — called the contribution margin format — which is based upon a behavioral breakdown of costs on the income statement. You'll see how this concept of contribution margin can be used to provide management with a great deal of useful information about its operations. For example, in Chapters 4 and 5 you'll learn about a level of activity called the breakeven point and the way it is determined for a firm. In addition, you'll find out how to determine the level of activity needed to generate a desired amount of profit and what effect a change in the sales price, variable cost per unit, or total fixed costs will have on an organization's profits. You'll also learn about the multi-product firm— what it is, what a sales mix is for this type of firm, and how the specific sales mix affects the profits and breakeven point for a multi-product firm.

In Chapter 6 we introduce the concept of relevance, and we show you how to use this concept, in conjunction with the contribution margin concept, to assist management in making a wide variety of decisions that affect primarily the short run. You'll see how easy it is to make such decisions as:

1. Whether or not to accept a special order
2. When to drop or add a product line
3. How to maximize the profits of a multi-product firm
4. Whether to manufacture raw materials or buy them from an outside supplier
5. Whether to sell a product at a split-off point or to process it further
6. Whether to scrap defective units or rework them

CHAPTER 4

The Contribution Margin Approach to Cost-Volume-Profit Analysis: Part I

In this chapter you will learn the following:

- What the *contribution margin income statement* is and how it is different from the *traditional income statement*
- The many terms that are used in cost-volume-profit analysis
- What a *breakeven point* is and how to calculate it
- How to integrate income taxes and dividends into cost-volume-profit analysis and graphs
- What is meant by the *margin of safety*
- How to show graphically the many variables that are involved in cost-volume-profit analysis
- What the simplifying assumptions are for cost-volume-profit analysis

In Chapter 3 we discussed the different ways that costs respond to changes in activity. You learned that variable costs change in direct proportion to changes in activity and that fixed costs do not change in response to changes in activity (that is, within the relevant range of activity). We also discussed, in general terms, several situations in which accountants use this knowledge about the behavior of costs to help managers plan and control their operations.

In this chapter we are going to explain in detail a tool used by accountants to help managers plan for the short run—a tool that can be used only if the accountant knows which costs are variable and which costs are fixed. We refer to this tool as *cost-volume-profit analysis.*

COST-VOLUME-PROFIT ANALYSIS

C-V-P analysis of interacting variables

In cost-volume-profit analysis accountants recognize that there are many interacting variables that affect an organization's profits—such things as the sales price of a product, the variable costs per unit, the fixed costs, and the volume of production and sales. *Cost-volume-profit (C-V-P) analysis* evaluates the relationships among these

PART TWO   Cost-Volume-Profit Analysis and Short-Run Decisions
The Contribution Margin Format to the Income Statement

130

interacting variables and the effect that changes in these variables have on an organization's profits.

A simple example

For example, assume that a new publisher, Prentiss Hill, has just signed its first author to write a fundamentals of accounting textbook. The company has determined that its variable costs will average $30 per book and its fixed costs will total $65,000. Since Prentiss Hill expects the book to be far superior to those of its competitors, it plans to sell the book for a whopping price of $50 per book. The president is naturally concerned with making a profit in the first year, and asks the controller, Cindy Kinsey, to figure out how many books the company will have to sell to break even.

An hour later Cindy reports back to the president with what she has learned:

1. If the company can sell at least 3,250 books, it will do no worse than break even.

2. On the basis of the sales manager's projections for the first year of sales of 8,000 books, the company can expect to show a profit of $95,000.

Just how Cindy was able to make these calculations—and many more—will be explained in the remainder of this chapter. First, however, let's explain what a breakeven point is and how she calculated it.

The Breakeven Point

Breakeven means zero profit

The **breakeven point** is the number of units sold (or dollars of sales) that will guarantee a zero profit for the firm. Cindy found this point—in units—by starting with the following general equation:

$$\textbf{Total sales} - \textbf{total costs} = \textbf{net income}$$

Since total costs will be made up of variable costs and fixed costs, the equation becomes:

$$\textbf{Total sales} - \textbf{variable costs} - \textbf{fixed costs} = \textbf{net income}$$

And now, taking it a little bit further, we get:

The unknown in this equation is the number of units sold

$$\left(\begin{array}{c}\textbf{Sales}\\\textbf{price}\end{array} \times \begin{array}{c}\textbf{units}\\\textbf{sold}\end{array}\right) - \left(\begin{array}{c}\textbf{variable}\\\textbf{cost per}\\\textbf{unit}\end{array} \times \begin{array}{c}\textbf{units}\\\textbf{sold}\end{array}\right) - \begin{array}{c}\textbf{fixed}\\\textbf{costs}\end{array} = \begin{array}{c}\textbf{net}\\\textbf{income}\end{array}$$

Since Cindy did not know how many units would have to be sold in order to break even, she substituted the letter X in the equation for units sold, let net income = 0, or breakeven, and solved the equation in the following manner:

When $X = 3,250$ units, income = $0

$$\$50X - \$30X - \$65,000 = \$0$$
$$\$20X = \$65,000$$
$$X = \$65,000 \div 20 = 3,250 \text{ units}$$

THE CONTRIBUTION MARGIN FORMAT TO THE INCOME STATEMENT

The next thing we want to do is prove that 3,250 units is indeed the breakeven point. In order to do this, we need to prepare an income statement using a format that emphasizes the behavior of costs. The income statement typically used with cost-volume-profit analysis is called the **contribution margin format income statement** (also known as the **behavioral format income statement**). It looks like this:

The contribution margin format takes a behavioral approach to cost classifications

Sales

Less: Total Variable Costs

Equals: Total Contribution Margin

Less: Total Fixed Costs

Equals: Net Income

For this format we add up all the variable costs (production, selling, and administration) and subtract this total from sales. We call the difference the *total contribution margin,* which is why this format is referred to as the *contribution margin format income statement.* We then add together all fixed costs (production, selling, and administration) and subtract them from the contribution margin to get net income.

Now let's look back at the Prentiss Hill Company, but in somewhat more detail. We will use the expanded set of facts in Example 4-1 to explain the contribution margin format income statement.

**Example 4-1
The simple example expanded**

THE PRENTISS HILL COMPANY

The Prentiss Hill Company sells a new book for $50 per book. Variable and fixed costs are expected to be:

Variable Costs:	
Direct Materials	$10/unit
Direct Labor	15/unit
Variable Overhead	3/unit
Variable Selling	2/unit
Total	$30/unit
Fixed Costs:	
Factory Overhead	$40,000
Selling	25,000
Total	$65,000

There were no beginning or ending balances in work-in-process or finished goods.

The contribution margin income statement for the Prentiss Hill Company at the breakeven point of 3,250 units is shown in Exhibit 4-1.

$TCM = total\ sales - TVC$

The key item in the contribution margin statement is the *total contribution margin (TCM),* which is the dollar amount of sales remaining after the total variable costs (TVC) have been subtracted. In Exhibit 4-1 the total contribution margin is $65,000 ($162,500 − $97,500). If the total contribution margin is greater than the fixed costs, there is a profit; if it is less than the fixed costs, there is a loss; and if it is equal to the fixed costs, the firm is breaking even. Notice in Exhibit 4-1 that the total contribution margin is exactly equal to the fixed costs—therefore, 3,250 units must be the breakeven point.

If you recall, when Cindy Kinsey calculated the breakeven point, she also found out that the sales personnel were predicting sales for the year of 8,000 units—well in excess of the breakeven point of 3,250 units. Let's see now, in Exhibit 4-2, what the income statement looks like if the sales personnel are correct.

EXHIBIT 4-1
Contribution Margin Format Income Statement — At Breakeven
Total contribution margin is total sales less total variable costs, or $65,000. This is the amount contributed to the coverage of fixed costs. In this situation the TCM is exactly equal to the fixed costs, so there is no profit.

PRENTISS HILL COMPANY Income Statement Year Ended December 31, 1989			
Sales Revenue (3,250 books × $50)			$162,500
Total Variable Costs:			
Direct Materials (3,250 books × $10)	$32,500		
Direct Labor (3,250 books × $15)	48,750		
Variable Overhead (3,250 × $3)	9,750	$91,000	
Variable Selling (3,250 books × $2)		6,500	97,500
Total Contribution Margin			$ 65,000
Fixed Costs:			
Fixed Factory Overhead		$40,000	
Fixed Selling		25,000	65,000
Net Income			$ -0-

EXHIBIT 4-2
Contribution Margin Format Income Statement — At a Profitable Level of Sales
Total contribution margin is now $160,000 ($95,000 in excess of the fixed costs of $65,000).

PRENTISS HILL COMPANY Income Statement Year Ended December 31, 1989			
Sales Revenue (8,000 books × $50)			$400,000
Total Variable Costs:			
Direct Materials (8,000 books × $10)	$ 80,000		
Direct Labor (8,000 books × $15)	120,000		
Variable Overhead (8,000 books × $3)	24,000	$224,000	
Variable Selling (8,000 books × $2)		16,000	240,000
Total Contribution Margin			$160,000
Fixed Costs:			
Fixed Factory Overhead		$ 40,000	
Fixed Selling		25,000	65,000
Net Income			$ 95,000

TCM exceeds TFC by $95,000—the net income

As you can see, when the sales are 8,000 units, the total contribution margin is $160,000, which is far in excess of the total fixed costs (TFC) of $65,000. The excess of $95,000 is, of course, the net income. So you can see that the key to generating a profit is to sell enough units so that the resulting total contribution margin is greater than the fixed costs.

ADDITIONAL TERMS USED IN COST-VOLUME-PROFIT ANALYSIS

We know from Exhibit 4-2 that the total variable costs for Prentiss Hill were $240,000 and that the total contribution margin was $160,000. Before we go any further into cost-volume-profit analysis, we also need to know what the variable costs and contribution margin are, expressed in two different ways:

1. On a per-unit basis

2. As a percentage of sales dollars

We will look first at the per-unit figures and then at the percentage figures for the variable costs.

Variable Cost per Unit (VCU)

Although we were actually given the variable cost per unit in Example 4-1, if it had not been given we still could have calculated it based only on the totals from Exhibit 4-1 or 4-2. Using Exhibit 4-2, we could have applied the following reasoning: Since Prentiss Hill incurs $240,000 of variable costs to produce and sell 8,000 units, the average variable cost per unit (VCU) must be:

$$VCU = \frac{TVC}{units}$$

$$\text{Variable cost per unit (VCU)} = \frac{\text{total variable costs}}{\text{units sold}}$$

$$= \frac{\$240,000}{8,000 \text{ units}}$$

$$= \$30$$

For each additional unit produced and sold, Prentiss Hill's total costs increase by $30.

Look now at Exhibit 4-3. You can see that it is the same as Exhibit 4-2 except that we've added columns for units, per unit, and percentage, in addition to the column for total dollars. The $30-per-unit cost is simply the $240,000 divided by the 8,000 units.

EXHIBIT 4-3
Contribution Margin Format Income Statement — Showing Totals, Units, Per Units, and Percentages

The $240,000 of variable costs averages $30 per unit and 60% of sales. The $160,000 of contribution margin is $20 per unit and 40% of sales.

PRENTISS HILL
Income Statement
Year Ended December 31, 1989

	Total Dollars	Units	Per Unit	Percentage
Sales Revenue......................	$400,000	8,000	$50	100%
Variable Costs:				
Direct Materials...........	$ 80,000		SP	
Direct Labor..............	120,000			
Variable Overhead	24,000		VCU	VC%
Variable Selling...........	16,000			
Total Variable Costs.............	240,000	8,000	30	60%
Total Contribution Margin	$160,000	8,000	$20	40%
Fixed Costs:				
Fixed Factory Overhead ...	$ 40,000		CMU	
Fixed Selling.............	25,000	65,000		CM%
Net Income........................	$ 95,000			

Variable Cost Percentage (VC%)

The *variable cost percentage* (or *variable cost ratio*) represents the portion of total sales that is needed to cover the variable costs; it is the percentage that variable costs are to sales dollars. The variable cost percentage (VC%) for Prentiss Hill is 60%, which can be determined several different ways. The first way uses total dollars:

$$VC\% = \frac{TVC}{sales\ dollars}$$

$$\text{Variable cost percentage (VC\%)} = \frac{\text{total variable costs}}{\text{total sales dollars}} \times 100\%$$

$$= \frac{\$240,000}{\$400,000} \times 100\% = .60 \times 100\%$$

$$= 60\%$$

If you look at the income statement in Exhibit 4-3, you can see the 60% in the percentage column. This means that the variable costs average 60% of sales dollars, or that 60% of the sales dollars are needed to cover the variable costs.

Before we show you a second way to calculate the VC%, look again at the last step of its calculation above. It was:

$$.60 \times 100\% = 60\%$$

When the VC% is expressed in decimal form, as .60, we should actually call it the *variable cost ratio.* And when this ratio is multiplied by 100% to get 60%, we should call it the *variable cost percentage.* From a practical standpoint, however, it really doesn't matter which one of the forms you use — .60 or 60% — or which name you use — variable cost ratio or variable cost percentage — as long as you know how to use it, which is all that is really important. Therefore, for simplicity we will use one notation — VC% — to represent the variable cost ratio (.60) or the variable cost percentage (60%).

The second way to calculate the VC% uses the variable cost per unit and the sales price (SP), as follows:

$$VC\% = \frac{VCU}{SP}$$

$$VC\% = \frac{\text{variable cost per unit}}{\text{sales price per unit}}$$

$$= \frac{\$30}{\$50} = .60 \times 100\%$$

$$= 60\%$$

There is a third way to calculate the VC%; it relates to an understanding of the contribution margin percentage (CM%), which we discuss in a later section.

Contribution Margin per Unit (CMU)

In Exhibit 4-2 Prentiss Hill had a total contribution margin of $160,000. We can determine the amount that each unit contributes — the ***contribution margin per unit (CMU)*** — in two different ways. In the first way we merely subtract the variable cost per unit from the sales price per unit:

$$CMU = SP - VCU$$

Contribution margin per unit (CMU) = sales price per unit − variable cost per unit

$$= \$50 - \$30 = \$20$$

This means that each time a unit is sold, it provides, or contributes, the difference between the sales price and the unit variable costs toward covering the fixed costs needed to produce and sell all the units. In this case, each unit sold contributes $20 toward paying for the fixed costs. Furthermore, once the total fixed costs are covered, then the $20 represents the amount that each unit sold contributes to net income — that is, every time a unit is sold, the profits increase by $20.

Notice now where the $20 per unit is in Exhibit 4-3. It is right below the $30 in the per-unit column of the income statement ($50 − $30 = $20).

The second way to calculate the CMU is to divide the total contribution margin by the number of units sold:

$$CMU = \frac{TCM}{units}$$

$$CMU = \frac{\text{total contribution margin}}{\text{units sold}}$$

$$= \frac{\$160,000}{8,000 \text{ units}}$$

$$= \$20 \text{ per unit}$$

If 8,000 units contribute $160,000, then each unit must contribute $20.

Contribution Margin Percentage (CM%)

The *contribution margin percentage* (or *contribution margin ratio*) represents the portion of total sales that remains after the variable costs have been subtracted. It can be determined in three ways.

The first way is to divide the total contribution margin by total sales dollars. For Prentiss Hill, it would be as follows:

$$CM\% = \frac{TCM}{dollar\ sales}$$

$$\text{Contribution margin percentage (CM\%)} = \frac{\text{total contribution margin}}{\text{total sales dollars}} \times 100\%$$

$$= \frac{\$160,000}{\$400,000} \times 100\% = .40 \times 100\%$$

$$= 40\%$$

Look closely at how we calculated the CM%, because it relates to our discussion of the VC% in the previous section. The result of the first calculation,

$$\frac{\$160,000}{\$400,000} = .40$$

is in decimal form, and it should actually be called the *contribution margin ratio*. When this ratio is multiplied by 100% to get 40%, the proper terminology is then *contribution margin percentage*. But once again, from a practical standpoint, it really doesn't matter which one of the forms you use — .40 or 40% — or which name you use — contribution margin ratio or contribution margin percentage — as long as you know how to use it, which is what's most important. Therefore, for simplicity we will use one notation — CM% — to represent the contribution margin ratio (.40) or the contribution margin percentage (40%).

Now look one last time at Exhibit 4-3, and notice where the contribution margin percentage of 40% is. You'll find it directly below the 60% in the percentage column of the income statement.

Forty percent of the sales dollars remain after the variable costs have been subtracted; this means that 40% of the sales are contributed to the coverage of fixed costs.

A second way to calculate the CM% involves the contribution margin per unit and the sales price per unit:

$$CM\% = \frac{CMU}{SP}$$

$$CM\% = \frac{CMU}{\text{sales price per unit}} \times 100\%$$

$$= \frac{\$20}{\$50} \times 100\% = .40 \times 100\%$$

$$= 40\%$$

Finally, we can calculate the CM% by subtracting the variable cost percentage from 100%, or the variable cost ratio from 1:

$$CM\% = 100\%\ (or\ 1) - VC\%$$

$$CM\% = 100\% - VC\% \quad \text{or} \quad CM\% = 1 - VC\%$$

$$= 100\% - 60\% \qquad\qquad = 1 - .60$$

$$= 40\% \qquad\qquad\qquad = .40$$

If the CM% = 1 − VC%, then conversely the VC% = 1 − CM%. For Prentiss Hill, its VC% can be calculated this third way:

VC% = 100% (or 1) − CM%

$$\textbf{VC\% = 100\% − CM\%} \qquad \text{or} \quad \textbf{VC\% = 1 − CM\%}$$
$$= 100\% − 40\% = 60\% \qquad\qquad = 1 − .40 = .60$$

We have shown you several ways to calculate the variable cost per unit, the variable cost percentage, the contribution margin per unit, and the contribution margin percentage. Although it will not be necessary for you to use all of these approaches in any one situation, it is likewise improbable that you can use a single approach in all situations. The easiest (and sometimes the only) way to determine the variable cost percentage, the contribution margin per unit, or the contribution margin percentage may depend on the exact information you are given. Therefore, it is probably a good idea for you to try to understand each of the approaches we discussed, rather than just the one that seems to be the easiest to calculate for Example 4-1. The easiest way for Example 4-1 may not be the easiest way in another situation.

TECHNIQUES OF COST-VOLUME-PROFIT ANALYSIS

In the previous section we calculated the breakeven point for Prentiss Hill. At that time, however, you were not familiar with many of the relevant terms used in C-V-P analysis, so we did not point out to you several things:

1. There are two different techniques for doing C-V-P analysis; we presented only one of them.
2. The techniques can be used to determine the level of sales needed to generate any desired amount of profit, not just the breakeven point.
3. The techniques can be used to calculate the answer in either unit sales or dollar sales; we only showed you how to calculate the answer in unit sales.

We will now show you *both* methods of calculating (in *both* unit and dollar sales) the level of sales needed to generate *any* desired income.

Income Equation Technique

Sales − TVC − TFC = net income

The first technique is referred to as the ***income equation technique.*** This approach is the one you learned in the earlier section. It derives its name from the format for the contribution margin income statement. It is:

$$\left(\begin{matrix}\text{Sales} \\ \text{price}\end{matrix} \times \begin{matrix}\text{units} \\ \text{sold}\end{matrix}\right) - \left(\text{VCU} \times \begin{matrix}\text{units} \\ \text{sold}\end{matrix}\right) - \begin{matrix}\text{total} \\ \text{fixed} \\ \text{costs}\end{matrix} = \text{net income}$$

Let X be the number of units to be sold

Since we are looking for the number of units to be sold, we designate that unknown quantity as X. Substituting X into the income equation for units sold and substituting zero for net income, we have a breakeven point of 3,250 units, just as we did before:

$$\$50X − \$30X − \$65,000 = \$0$$
$$X = \frac{\$65,000}{\$20}$$
$$= 3,250 \text{ units}$$

Just substitute net income for zero in the income equation

Let's assume for a moment that Prentiss Hill has greater aspirations than merely breaking even, and wants to know how many units need to be sold to show a profit of $95,000. The only difference now is that we substitute $95,000 (instead of zero) for net income in the equation. We now get an answer of 8,000 units:

$$\$50X - \$30X - \$65,000 = \$95,000$$
$$\$20X = \$160,000$$
$$X = \frac{\$160,000}{\$20}$$
$$= 8,000 \text{ units}$$

We can get dollars by multiplying X times SP

Once we know how many *units* we have to sell, we can get the total sales revenue by multiplying the units times the sales price. At breakeven the sales dollars are:

$$3,250 \text{ units} \times \$50 = \$162,500$$

And for a profit of $95,000 the sales dollars are:

$$8,000 \text{ units} \times \$50 = \$400,000$$

Or we can let X = sales dollars in the equation

Or we can solve for the total sales dollars directly, without first calculating the answer in units. We do this with the following equation:

Sales dollars − (VC% × sales dollars) − fixed costs = net income

In this equation sales dollars is the unknown and is designated as X. Solving for the equation, we first get the breakeven point:

$$X - \text{VC\%}(X) - \textbf{fixed costs} = \textbf{net income}$$
$$X - .60X - \$65,000 = \$0$$
$$.40X = \$65,000$$
$$X = \frac{\$65,000}{.40}$$
$$= \$162,500$$

If Prentiss Hill desires a profit of $95,000, then sales have to be $400,000, determined as follows:

$$X - .60X - \$65,000 = \$95,000$$
$$.40X = \$160,000$$
$$X = \frac{\$160,000}{.40}$$
$$= \$400,000$$

Contribution Margin Technique

The second approach that we can use for cost-volume-profit analysis is called the **contribution margin technique.** If we designate X to represent unit sales, then our solution will be in units, using the following equation:

$$X = \frac{\textbf{total fixed costs} + \textbf{net income}}{\textbf{CMU}}$$

By substituting zero for net income, once again we get a breakeven point of 3,250 units:

$$X = \frac{\$65,000 + \$0}{\$20} = 3,250 \text{ units}$$

If we desire a \$95,000 profit, we get an answer of 8,000 units:

$$X = \frac{\$65,000 + \$95,000}{\$20}$$

$$= \frac{\$160,000}{\$20} = 8,000 \text{ units}$$

The contribution margin technique is a variation of and superior to the income equation technique

Notice that the next to last step in the income equation technique is identical to the only step in the contribution margin technique. This is because the contribution margin technique is a variation of the income equation technique. There are two advantages of using the contribution margin technique: (1) It involves fewer steps, and (2) it can be employed when the CMU is given but the sales price and VCU are not individually known.

If you want your solution to be in dollar sales rather than unit sales, let X represent the dollar sales and use the following formula:

$$X = \frac{\textbf{total fixed costs} + \textbf{net income}}{\textbf{CM\%}}$$

In order to break even, Prentiss Hill's dollar sales must be \$162,500:

$$X = \frac{\$65,000 + \$0}{.40} = \$162,500$$

And in order to show a profit of \$95,000, dollar sales will have to be \$400,000, determined as follows:

$$X = \frac{\$65,000 + \$95,000}{.40} = \$400,000$$

In the numerator, TFC + NI = the TCM at the unknown level of sales X

In each of the calculations above we added together the fixed costs plus net income in the numerator of the formula. But do you know what the numerator of this formula represents? Refer once more to Exhibit 4-2 and look at the bottom of the income statement. Going from the bottom up, add the net income and fixed costs together—what do you get? The \$95,000 plus \$65,000 totals to \$160,000, which is the total contribution margin. This means that the numerator represents the amount of total contribution margin that must be generated by some level of sales that will be just enough to cover the fixed costs and leave the desired profit remaining.

Income Stated as a Percentage of Sales

So far, when we calculated the level of sales needed to generate a certain amount of income, the income was stated in absolute terms. In the case of Prentiss Hill, the desired income was \$95,000. The desired income can also be stated as a percentage of sales. In this situation the calculations are a little more difficult, because neither the income nor the sales they are a percentage of are known until the cost-volume-profit formula is completed.

For example, assume that Prentiss Hill hopes to sell enough textbooks to have an income equal to 15% of total sales, and it is wondering what the total sales (and number of textbooks sold) will have to be.

When we were using the C-V-P formulas to calculate an answer in terms of the number of units to be sold, you might remember that the total sales were represented by $50X, where X was the unknown number of units to be sold and $50 was the sales price. In that situation, if the desired income is 15% of total sales, then the income can be expressed with the following equation:

$$\text{Income} = \textbf{15\% of total sales}$$
$$= 15\% \times \$50X = \$7.50X$$

If we substitute $7.50X into the C-V-P formula, the resulting number of units to be sold is 5,200, determined as follows:

The C-V-P formula when X = unit sales

$$X = \frac{\textbf{fixed costs} + \textbf{net income}}{\textbf{CMU}}$$

$$= \frac{\$65,000 + \$7.50X}{\$20}$$

$$\$20X = \$65,000 + \$7.50X$$

$$\$12.50X = \$65,000$$

$$X = \$65,000 \div \$12.50 = 5,200 \text{ units}$$

The total sales dollars are easily determined by multiplying 5,200 units times $50, or $260,000. If we had wanted to calculate the total sales dollars without first determining the number of units, we would have simply used the alternative form of the C-V-P formula, which determines sales dollars directly:

$$X = \frac{\textbf{fixed costs} + \textbf{net income}}{\textbf{CM\%}}$$

In this formula total sales are represented by X, and the desired profit is 15% of X. The total sales needed to generate a 15% profit are $260,000, determined as follows:

The C-V-P formula when X = dollar sales

$$X = \frac{\$65,000 + 15\%(X)}{40\%}$$

$$= \frac{\$65,000 + .15X}{.40}$$

$$.40X = \$65,000 + .15X$$

$$.25X = \$65,000$$

$$X = \$65,000 \div .25 = \$260,000$$

For proof that these results are correct, look at the income statement presented in Exhibit 4-4. Notice that the number of units sold is 5,200, the total sales are $260,000, and the net income of $39,000 is exactly 15% of $260,000.

EXHIBIT 4-4
Income Statement for a Profit of 15% of Sales
$$\frac{\$39,000}{\$260,000} = 15\%$$

Sales Revenue (5,200 units $\times$ $50)	$260,000
Total Variable Costs (5,200 units $\times$ $30)	156,000
Total Contribution Margin	$104,000
Fixed Costs	65,000
Net Income (15% $\times$ $260,000)	$ 39,000

Margin of Safety

A firm is said to have a *margin of safety (MS)* when its sales are in excess of breakeven. We calculate a margin of safety by subtracting the breakeven (BE) sales from the actual or budgeted sales for the period. Prentiss Hill expected its sales to be 8,000 units ($400,000) during its first year of operation and determined its breakeven point to be 3,250 units ($162,500). For these data the margin of safety (in units) is:

MS = actual sales − BE sales

$$\begin{matrix} \text{Margin} \\ \text{of} \\ \text{safety} \end{matrix} = \begin{matrix} \text{actual or} \\ \text{budgeted} \\ \text{sales} \end{matrix} - \begin{matrix} \text{breakeven} \\ \text{sales} \end{matrix}$$

$$= 8{,}000 - 3{,}250 = 4{,}750 \text{ units}$$

We can also measure the margin of safety in terms of sales dollars with the following calculation:

$$\begin{matrix} \text{Margin} \\ \text{of} \\ \text{safety} \end{matrix} = \$400{,}000 - \$162{,}500 = \$237{,}500$$

Or we can calculate it by multiplying the margin of safety, in units, by the sales price:

$$4{,}750 \text{ units} \times \$50 = \$237{,}500$$

The margin of safety expresses the amount that a firm's sales can decrease without experiencing a loss. For Prentiss Hill sales can drop by as much as 4,750 units (or $237,500) before the company has to worry about a loss for the year.

Effect of Income Taxes

Thus far, we have ignored a very significant expense that appears on the income statement of many organizations: income taxes. Let's now look briefly at that expense and see how it affects the cost-volume-profit analysis.

Taxes = tax % × income before tax

If we add the complication of income taxes (at 40% of income before tax) to the income statement of Prentiss Hill, the expanded income statement (for 8,000 units) appears as shown in Exhibit 4-5.

EXHIBIT 4-5
Income Statement—
Income Tax Effects
Considered
What we called net income in Exhibit 4-2—$95,000—is actually income before tax when we have income tax to consider.

	8,000 Units
Sales Revenue.	$400,000
Total Variable Costs	240,000
Total Contribution Margin	$160,000
Fixed Costs	65,000
Income before Tax	$ 95,000
Income Tax @ 40%.	38,000
Net Income.	$ 57,000

Notice in Exhibit 4-5 that what we've been calling "net income"—the $95,000—is actually "income before tax" for an organization that has to pay taxes. And what we will now properly refer to as "net income"—the $57,000—is "income after tax."

Now let's suppose further that you were asked: "How many units must Prentiss Hill sell in order to have a net income of $57,000?" Naturally your answer would be 8,000 units. But in order to get that answer, which amount of income would you place in the numerator of the C-V-P formula—net income or income before tax? As we showed previously, it has to be $95,000, and that amount is the income before tax. Therefore, whenever we deal with a company that pays taxes, the C-V-P formula is

Income in the numerator is income before tax

$$X = \frac{\text{fixed costs} + \text{income before tax}}{\text{CMU}}$$

where X represents unit sales.

What do you do if you don't know the amount of income before tax — what if you have only net income? In that case you need to convert the net income to income before tax. You make this conversion with the following formula:

Converting net income to income before tax

$$\text{Income before tax} = \frac{\text{net income}}{1 - \text{tax rate}} \qquad 26000 = \frac{15,600}{1-x}$$

If the net income is $57,000 and the tax rate is 40%, then the income before tax is determined like this:

$$\text{Income before tax} = \frac{\$57,000}{100\% - 40\%} = \frac{\$57,000}{1 - .40}$$

$$= \frac{\$57,000}{.60} = \$95,000$$

Finally, all of this discussion might naturally prompt you to ask: "When I see the term *net income,* how will I know if it means income before tax or income after tax?" That's a good question.

If you first accept the fact that the last item on an income statement is the only item that should ever be called *net income,* then we can answer your question with the following rule:

When there are no taxes

If there is no mention of income taxes in the problem, then net income *means income before tax — because the income before tax is the last item on the income statement.*

But:

When there are taxes

If income taxes are being considered in the problem, then net income *means income after tax.*

In most of the problems at the end of the chapter, there is no mention of income taxes, so the term *net income* will usually mean income before tax.

Income after Tax as a Percentage of Sales

If the desired income is after tax and if it is stated as a percentage of sales, then the aftertax income percentage will have to be divided by 1 minus the tax rate, just as the dollar amount of net income was when it was stated in absolute terms. For example, look back at the net income of $39,000 in Exhibit 4-4, which is now the income before taxes, since there are taxes to pay. If the tax rate is 30%, then the resulting net income (after taxes) is $27,300, or 10.5% ($27,300 ÷ $260,000) of sales.

PTI% = ATI% ÷ (1 − T%)

If the desired profit had been stated in terms of an aftertax rate of 10.5%, the first step would be to determine the pretax rate with the following calculation:

$$\begin{array}{c}\text{Pretax income} \\ \text{as a \%} \\ \text{of sales}\end{array} = \frac{\text{aftertax income as \% of sales}}{1 - \text{tax rate}}$$

$$= \frac{10.5\%}{100\% - 30\%} = \frac{.105}{1 - .30}$$

$$= \frac{.105}{.70} = .15, \text{ or } 15\%$$

Now we can use the 15% figure in calculating the number of units and/or sales dollars that will generate a 15% pretax return and a 10.5% aftertax return. And, of course, we already know from a previous section that these amounts will be 5,200 units and $260,000, respectively.

ADDITIONAL INCOME STATEMENTS

In Exhibit 4-2 we showed you a detailed contribution margin income statement based on sales of 8,000 units. In Exhibit 4-6, the income statement is repeated, but this time in a more condensed form.

EXHIBIT 4-6
Comparative Income Statements—A More Direct Approach to the Contribution Margin
This exhibit calculates TCM for 15,000 units directly: units sold × CMU.

	8,000 Units	15,000 Units
Sales Revenue....................................	$400,000	
Total Variable Costs	240,000	
Total Contribution Margin	$160,000	$300,000
Fixed Costs	65,000	65,000
Net Income	$ 95,000	$235,000

Two new ways to determine income

We are now going to prepare two additional income statements using the contribution margin format. The first one—based on 15,000 units—is shown in Exhibit 4-6, alongside the statement for 8,000 units. The second one—based on 25,000 units—is given in Exhibit 4-7, next to the income statements for both 8,000 units and 15,000 units. As you can easily see, we are determining the net income for each of these two new levels of sales in a slightly different manner. We are doing this in order to provide you with some additional insights into the contribution margin approach.

You see, when you use a contribution margin approach to solve a problem, you have a great deal of flexibility—that is, there are usually several ways to come up with the correct answer. So when you look at Exhibits 4-6 and 4-7, think of them as providing you with more flexibility when calculating income, rather than merely adding more things for you to learn.

When we discussed the contribution margin per unit, we found that each unit sold by Prentiss Hill contributes $20 ($50 − $30) to the coverage of fixed costs. For 8,000 units we see in Exhibit 4-6 that we have $160,000 (8,000 units × $20 per unit) of total contribution margin; so for 15,000 units our total contribution margin is $300,000 (15,000 × $20). We could also have determined the $300,000 in the same way as we determined the total contribution margin for the 8,000 units, that is:

	15,000 Units
Sales (15,000 × $50)..	$750,000
Total Variable Costs (15,000 × $30)................................	450,000
Total Contribution Margin	$300,000

It is more direct to merely multiply the 15,000 units by $20 per unit.

Additional TCM means additional net income

Let's now look a little closer at Exhibit 4-6. Notice that the increase in net income, when the sales are increased from 8,000 to 15,000 units, is identical to the increase in the total contribution margin—$140,000. What brought about this increase of

$140,000 was the additional 7,000 units (15,000 − 8,000) that were sold — with each one contributing an additional $20 per unit. This means that each additional unit sold not only increased the total contribution margin by $20 but also increased net income by the same amount (assuming fixed costs remain the same). If we now assume that the units sold increase to 25,000, we can calculate the net income at that level in a new way, as shown in Exhibit 4-7.

EXHIBIT 4-7
Incremental Approach to Net Income
Now we get net income by adding the additional contribution margin (CMU × additional units) to the old net income.

	8,000 Units	**15,000 Units**	**25,000 Units**
Sales Revenue...................	$400,000		
Total Variable Costs	240,000		
Total Contribution Margin	$160,000	$300,000	
Fixed Costs	65,000	65,000	
Net Income	$ 95,000	$235,000	$435,000

10,000 Additional Units

10,000 units × $20/unit = $200,000

Additional Net Income

You can see in Exhibit 4-7 that we are now selling 10,000 additional units (25,000 − 15,000). Since each additional unit sold adds $20 to net income, the net income should increase by $200,000 (10,000 × $20) — from $235,000 to $435,000.

A Final Way to Determine CMU

Now let's assume that you know exactly the opposite of what you knew in Exhibit 4-7, where you calculated the increase in income by multiplying the CMU times the increase in sales of 10,000 units. This time, assume that you know that the income has increased by $200,000 due to additional sales of 10,000 units and that you are trying to determine the CMU. The calculation will be just the reverse of the one we used in Exhibit 4-7. All you need to do is divide the increase in income by the increase in units sold:

$$\text{CMU} = \$200,000 \div 10,000 = \$20$$

You need to use this approach to calculating CMU only when the information provided is limited to the amount of income for two or more levels of sales.

The general form of the equation used above looks like this:

$$\text{CMU} = \frac{\text{difference in incomes (before tax)}}{\text{difference in units sold}}$$

When only incomes and unit sales are known

Look now at Exhibit 4-8, and pretend for a moment that you do not know the CMU for Prentiss Hill. Nor do you know the sales price, the variable cost per unit, or the total fixed costs. The only information that you have is the income when 10,000 units are sold ($135,000) and the income when 30,000 units are sold ($535,000). By selling an additional 20,000 units, Prentiss Hill can increase its income by $400,000, which averages $20 per unit. This $20-per-unit figure is the firm's contribution margin per unit:

EXHIBIT 4-8
Incomes for Two Levels of Activity
For each additional unit income increases by CMU.

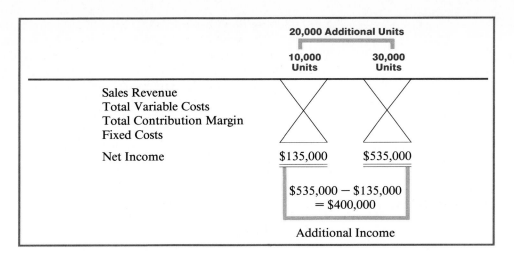

$$CMU = \frac{\text{difference in incomes}}{\text{difference in units sold}}$$

$$= \frac{\$535,000 - \$135,000}{30,000 - 10,000} = \$20 \text{ per unit}$$

The Alternative Format to an Income Statement

In Chapter 2 we prepared income statements using an alternative format. They looked like this:

The traditional format income statement

Sales

Less: Cost of Goods Sold

Equals: Gross Margin

Less: Selling and Administrative Expenses

Equals: Net Income

Traditionally the income statement used in published financial statements follows this format and that is why we call this statement the ***traditional format income statement.*** When we use this format, we group costs within the income statement according to the *function* of each cost—i.e., production, selling, and administration. That is why it is also referred to as the ***functional format income statement.***

Superiority of the Contribution Margin Format

The contribution margin format is better suited for evaluating the effect on profits of a change in a variable

Although it is possible to determine the same income using either the traditional format or the contribution margin format, we recommend that the contribution margin format be used primarily within this course. It may not yet be obvious to you, but the contribution margin format is much more naturally suited to analyzing the many interacting variables that make up net income. For example, none of the procedures that we've performed in this chapter could be carried out with the same ease—if done at all—with the traditional format approach.

You see, whichever method we use, we still need to know which costs are variable and which costs are fixed. Since the contribution margin format uses a behavioral approach to grouping costs on the income statement, it is extremely easy to keep track of how each group of costs responds to a change in activity. Because the traditional format groups costs according to their function, each group is a combination of variable and fixed costs. As a result it is more difficult, and sometimes impossible, to predict accurately how each group will respond to a change in activity.

Our recommendation of the contribution margin format has to do with helping managers make decisions—not with publishing financial statements for external parties. For financial reporting purposes you must use the traditional format in order to comply with generally accepted accounting principles (GAAP).

We will discuss both formats again in the next chapter, when we compare the direct costing and absorption costing methods of product costing.

GRAPHIC APPROACH TO COST-VOLUME-PROFIT ANALYSIS

Up to this point we have used income statements and equations to analyze the relationships among revenue, costs, volume, and profit. Now we will use a graphic approach to analyze these interacting variables.

Figures 4-1 and 4-2 present two similar, yet different, approaches to a cost-volume-profit graph for Prentiss Hill. In both graphs the horizontal axis represents activity (unit sales) and the vertical axis measures dollars of revenues, costs, and profits. Figure 4-3 represents a variation of Figure 4-2, but it is called simply an *income graph.*

FIGURE 4-1
Cost-Volume-Profit Graph:
Variable Costs on Top of
Fixed Costs
The horizontal axis is unit sales and the vertical axis is dollars. The total costs line is derived by adding the variable costs to the fixed costs line. The breakeven point is 3,250 units ($162,500).

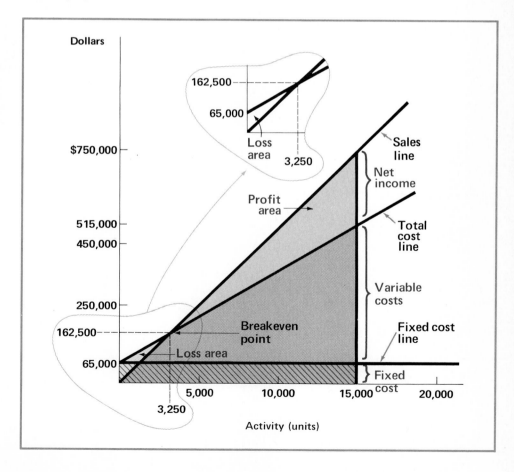

FIGURE 4-2
Cost-Volume-Profit Graph:
Fixed Costs on Top of
Variable Costs
The total costs line is derived
by adding the fixed costs to
the variable costs line. Total
contribution margin is the
distance from the sales line to
the variable costs line.

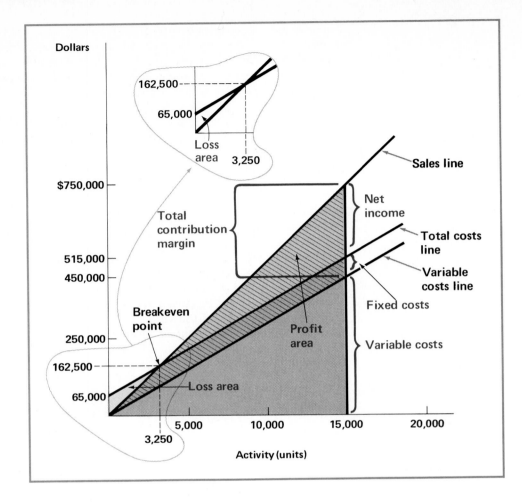

FIGURE 4-3
Income Graph
The slope of the line is the
CMU.

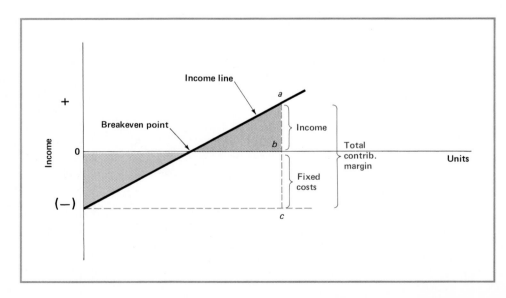

In cost-volume-profit graphs the sales line is traditionally drawn having a 45° angle extending from the origin upward and to the right. The total costs line begins at $65,000 (the fixed costs) on the vertical axis and also extends upward and to the right—but with a smaller slope than that of the sales line. The intersection of the sales line and the total costs line is the breakeven point (3,250; $162,500).

At levels of activity above the breakeven point of 3,250 units, the firm will have a profit, as shown by the gray-shaded *profit area* in both graphs. But for levels of activity below 3,250 units, the firm will experience a loss, as shown by the light-blue-shaded *loss area.*

The graphs differ in how the total costs line is derived

The main difference between Figures 4-1 and 4-2 is the manner in which the cost lines are drawn. In Figure 4-1 the fixed costs line ($65,000) is drawn first. The variable costs line is not shown, but the total costs line represents the addition of the variable costs to the fixed costs. Thus the variable costs are said to be graphed above the fixed costs. In Figure 4-2 the variable costs line is drawn first, to which are added the fixed costs, resulting in the total costs line. In Figure 4-2 the fixed costs are graphed above the variable costs.

Does it make any difference which graph we use? Do both graphs show the same relevant information—but in different ways?

Look carefully at the graph in Figure 4-2 and see if you can find anything important that is missing from Figure 4-1—something that we have been emphasizing throughout this chapter.

How about the total contribution margin?

It's easy to see TCM in Figure 4-2

Remember, total contribution margin is the difference between total sales and total variable costs. Since the variable costs line is drawn in Figure 4-2, it is easy to see the total contribution margin—it is the vertical distance from the sales line to the variable costs line. By reading the dollars from the vertical axis, you can see in Figure 4-2 that the total contribution margin for 15,000 units is as follows:

Total Sales	$750,000
Total Variable Costs	450,000
Total Contribution Margin	$300,000

You can also easily see in Figure 4-2 what the total contribution margin would be for any level of activity from 0 to 15,000 units—it is represented by the dashed area between the sales line and the variable costs line.

Because it is so easy to visually determine the total contribution margin in Figure 4-2, we often refer to such a graph as the *contribution margin cost-volume-profit graph.*

You can't see TCM in Figure 4-1

It is much more difficult to find the total contribution margin in Figure 4-1. At 15,000 units there is no vertical distance from one line to another representing total contribution margin, and there is no way to show a dashed area for total contribution margin in the range of activity from 0 to 15,000 units.

Therefore, we feel that the graph in Figure 4-2 is the better of the two graphs, because of its emphasis on contribution margin. However, the emphasis on contribution margin is even greater in the graph in Figure 4-3. Called an *income graph,* this graph shows basically three things—total contribution margin, fixed costs, and net income.

The horizontal axis represents unit sales; the vertical axis measures net income, which is positive for any point above the horizontal axis, negative below the horizontal axis, and zero on the horizontal axis. The diagonal line is the income line, which is zero where it intersects the horizontal axis—the breakeven point. The vertical distance between any point on the income line and the corresponding point on the horizontal axis represents the amount of income (or loss) at the specific level of activity represented by that point on the horizontal axis.

The dashed lines in Figure 4-3 are not part of the graph. They serve to help us visualize what is represented by certain vertical and horizontal distances within the graph. See, for example, the vertical dashed line that extends from the income line to the horizontal dotted line that runs parallel to the horizontal axis:

The dashed lines help visualize distances

The line segment from point a *to* b *indicates the amount of income at the level of activity represented by point* b.

Fixed costs = loss at zero activity

The line segment that runs from point *b* to *c* represents the fixed costs. This distance represents the fixed costs because it is the same distance as the line segment that runs from the horizontal axis at zero activity to the intersection of the income line with the vertical axis. This distance represents the amount of loss at zero activity—which is the fixed costs.

Income + TFC = TCM

Finally, the line segment from point *a* to *c*, which is the sum of line segments *ab* and *bc*, is the total contribution margin at the level of activity *b*. Remember, as we discussed earlier in this chapter, the sum of income (line segment *ab*) plus fixed costs (line segment *bc*) is total contribution margin.

This graph may appear somewhat unusual at first, but it is really quite simple to prepare and easy to use. To construct it:

Rules for preparing income graph

STEP 1: Find the point on the vertical axis representing the amount of loss at zero activity. This amount is the total fixed costs.

STEP 2: Calculate the breakeven point, and plot this point on the horizontal axis.

STEP 3: Draw a straight line connecting the two points in steps 1 and 2. This is your income line.

Determining income for a level of sales

We have used these three steps to construct the income graph for Prentiss Hill, shown in Figure 4-4. The income line starts at negative $65,000—the amount of fixed costs—which would be the loss at zero activity. The income line intersects the horizontal axis at 3,250 units—the breakeven point. In addition, notice that the incomes for the 5,200-unit and 8,000-unit levels of activity are $39,000 and $95,000, respectively—exactly as we determined in Exhibits 4-4 and 4-2, respectively.

Determining unit sales needed to generate a desired income

The income graph can also be used to quickly determine the number of units that need to be sold to generate a desired profit. This means that with the income graph you can do C-V-P analysis without the formulas. For example, say we want to have an income of $55,000. Find $55,000 on the vertical axis; draw a line horizontally over to the income line; and from that point of intersection drop a vertical line to the horizontal axis. The vertical line should hit the horizontal axis at 6,000 units, which is the same as the result achieved with the C-V-P formula:

$$X = \frac{\$65,000 + \$55,000}{\$20} = \frac{\$120,000}{\$20} = 6,000 \text{ units}$$

FIGURE 4-4
Income Graph—Prentiss Hill
The line starts at the amount of loss at zero activity— $65,000—and it intersects the horizontal axis at the breakeven point.

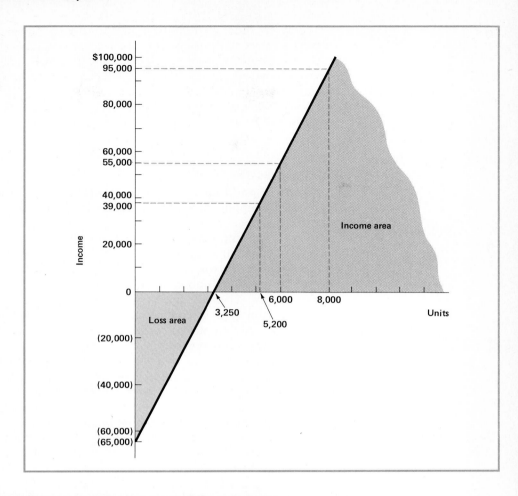

ASSUMPTIONS UNDERLYING COST-VOLUME-PROFIT ANALYSIS

When we use the cost-volume-profit model, our projections for an organization are reliable only if the assumptions we make about the model are valid. The assumptions we make relate to the interacting variables in the model—each of which is assumed to remain unchanged during the period that the model is used. We make five assumptions about the cost-volume-profit model. They are as follows:

No Δ in SP

1. All units can be sold at the same price; and this price stays the same throughout the period of and within the relevant range of the cost-volume-profit analysis.

No Δ in VCU

2. The variable cost per unit is the same for all units produced and sold throughout the period of and within the relevant range of the cost-volume-profit analysis.

No Δ in TFC

3. The total fixed costs remain the same throughout the period of and within the relevant range of the cost-volume-profit analysis.

No Δ in sales mix

4. The analysis involves a firm that sells a single product or a multi-product firm in which the sales mix remains the same.

No Δ in inventories

5. There is no significant difference between the beginning and ending inventories of finished goods—that is, the number of units produced equals the number of units sold.

(There are other assumptions, but they are the substance of a discussion in an upper-level cost accounting course.)

If we find that any of the variables just mentioned do not remain constant, then the projections we made with the C-V-P model will be incorrect, and the model must be revised to accommodate the changes.

Each of the assumptions, and the effect of changes in the assumptions on C-V-P analysis, will be discussed in the next chapter.

CHAPTER SUMMARY

Cost-volume-profit analysis is used by management to analyze and evaluate the relationships among interacting variables — prices, costs, and activity — and the effect that a change in these variables has on profits. Our approach to cost-volume-profit analysis emphasizes the separation of costs based on their behavior. The income statement that separates the variable and fixed costs is called the *contribution margin format income statement.* Within this statement, all variable costs are grouped together and subtracted from sales; the difference is called the *total contribution margin.* Then the fixed costs are combined and subtracted from the total contribution margin, leaving net income. Although the *traditional* (or *functional*) *format* is usually employed in financial statements issued to external users, the contribution margin approach is considered superior for internal decision making.

One way that we can use cost-volume-profit analysis involves the determination of a level of sales that will generate a desired amount of profit. One such level of sales is the *breakeven point,* where the income is zero, because the sales and total costs are equal. We use two techniques in cost-volume-profit analysis: the *contribution margin technique* and the *income equation technique.*

When an organization operates above its breakeven point, it is said to have a margin of safety. The *margin of safety* is simply the excess of the actual or budgeted sales over the breakeven sales.

For an organization that pays income taxes, the income referred to in the C-V-P formulas is the income before tax. If the desired income for the organization is stated in terms of "net income" instead of "income before tax," it is necessary to determine the income before tax before the C-V-P formulas can be used. When only net income and the tax rate are known, income before tax is found by dividing the net income by 1 minus the tax rate.

There are five assumptions underlying C-V-P analysis. Each of these assumptions must be correct in order for the results of the C-V-P analysis to be valid. If any of the assumptions change, then the C-V-P model will have to be revised in order to accommodate the change.

IMPORTANT TERMS USED IN THIS CHAPTER

Breakeven point   The level of sales (measured in units or dollars) for an organization at which net income is zero. At breakeven, total costs equal total sales dollars. (page 130)

Contribution margin format income statement   An income statement in which variable costs are separated from fixed costs. The variable costs are subtracted from sales to get the total contribution margin. Fixed costs are subtracted next, resulting in net income. Also known as the *behavioral format income statement.* (page 130)

Contribution margin percentage (CM%) The percentage of total sales that remains after the variable costs are subtracted. (page 135)

Contribution margin per unit (CMU) The sales price less the variable costs per unit. The CMU is the amount that each unit sold contributes to the coverage of fixed costs and to the accumulation of profits. It is the amount that is added to net income every time an additional unit is sold. (page 134)

Contribution margin technique A method used in cost-volume-profit analysis. The level of sales that will generate a desired profit is determined by dividing the fixed costs plus net income by the contribution margin per unit (or contribution margin percentage). (page 137)

Cost-volume-profit (C-V-P) analysis A tool used by accountants to assist managers in the analysis and evaluation of the relationships among prices, costs, and activity and of the effect that changes in these variables have on profits. (page 129)

Income equation technique A method used in cost-volume-profit analysis. The level of sales needed to generate a desired profit is determined by substituting X (for unit sales or dollar sales) into the equation for net income: sales − variable costs − fixed costs = net income. (page 136)

Margin of safety The excess of actual or budgeted sales above the breakeven level of sales. It can either be measured in units or dollars of sales. (page 140)

Total contribution margin Total sales revenue less total variable costs. It is the amount contributed by sales to the coverage of fixed costs. If the total contribution margin is greater than the fixed costs, there is a profit; if the reverse is true, there is a loss. (page 131)

Traditional format income statement An income statement format that separates costs on the income statement according to their functions — production, selling, and administration. The cost of goods sold is subtracted from sales to get gross profit; and net income remains after the selling and administrative expenses are subtracted from gross profit. Also called the *functional format income statement.* (page 144)

Variable cost percentage (VC%) The percentage of total sales needed to cover the variable costs; the percentage that total variable costs are to sales revenue. (page 133)

Variable cost per unit (VCU) The amount by which total costs increase for each additional unit produced and sold. (page 133)

APPENDIX 4-1: DIVIDENDS AND C-V-P ANALYSIS

There's only one other thing that we can integrate into the C-V-P analysis, and that's dividends — when they are paid as a percentage of net income. Let's assume now that Prentiss Hill makes a habit of distributing 30% of its net income to its stockholders in the form of dividends. If we pick up with the bottom part of the income statement in Exhibit 4-5, the amount distributed and the addition to retained earnings will be:

Income before Tax	$95,000
Income Tax ($95,000 × 40%)	38,000
Net Income	$57,000
Dividends ($57,000 × 30%)	17,100
Increase in Retained Earnings	$39,900

Based upon a net income of $57,000, dividends of $17,100 can be distributed, leaving an undistributed net income—the increase in retained earnings—of $39,900.

Now suppose that the firm had specified that it wanted to sell enough units during the year to pay dividends of $17,100. Or, put another way, how many units must be sold to increase retained earnings by $39,900? How would we work our way back from this objective?

The first step, which is the only new step in the procedure, is to determine the net income that will be needed to pay dividends of $17,100 and increase retained earnings by $39,900. How we do this depends upon whether we are given the amount of dividends or the increase in retained earnings.

If the amount of dividends we hope to pay is given, the net income is calculated in the following manner:

$$\textbf{Dividends} = \textbf{net income} \times \textbf{dividend \%}$$

$$\textbf{Net income} = \frac{\textbf{dividends}}{\textbf{dividend \%}}$$

$$= \frac{\$17,100}{30\%} = \frac{\$17,100}{.30} = \$57,000$$

On the other hand, if the increase in retained earnings—the undistributed net income—is given, the net income is determined in the following manner:

$$\textbf{Net income} - (\textbf{net income} \times \textbf{dividend \%}) = \textbf{increase in retained earnings}$$

$$\textbf{Net income } (100\% - \textbf{dividend \%}) = \textbf{increase in retained earnings}$$

$$\textbf{Net income} = \frac{\textbf{increase in retained earnings}}{100\% - \textbf{dividend \%}}$$

And for our example the net income would again be $57,000:

$$\textbf{Net income} = \frac{\$39,900}{100\% - 30\%} = \frac{\$39,900}{1 - .30}$$

$$= \frac{\$39,900}{.70} = \$57,000$$

Now that we have net income, the next step is to calculate income before tax, which we know from a previous section is:

$$\textbf{Income before tax} = \frac{\textbf{net income}}{100\% - \textbf{tax \%}}$$

$$= \frac{\$57,000}{100\% - 40\%} = \frac{\$57,000}{1 - .40}$$

$$= \frac{\$57,000}{.60} = \$95,000$$

And the final step is to calculate the number of units that need to be sold to generate $95,000 of income before tax. As we learned previously, it is 8,000:

$$X = \frac{\textbf{fixed costs} + \textbf{income before tax}}{\textbf{CMU}}$$

$$= \frac{\$65,000 + \$95,000}{\$20}$$

$$= \frac{\$160,000}{\$20} = 8,000 \text{ units}$$

APPENDIX 4-2: AN EXPANDED SET OF GRAPHS

Now that we have discussed the effects of both income taxes and dividends on C-V-P analysis, we are ready to see how these items can be analyzed in the C-V-P graph and the income graph. The first thing that we need to realize is that the income areas shown in the graphs in Figures 4-1, 4-2, and 4-3 all represent income before tax. We want to show two things within this section of the graph:

1. That portion of the income-before-tax area which represents the part of income to be paid in taxes; the remaining area represents the net income.

2. That portion of the net income area which represents the amount of income distributed as dividends; the remaining area represents undistributed net income.

The contribution margin C-V-P graph is shown in expanded form in Figure 4-5; the income graph is shown in expanded form in Figure 4-6. In both graphs a dashed

THE BREAKEVEN POINT IN MOTION

It was back in the 1982 recession, and the numbers at Bayer A. G.'s Mobay Chemical Company were bad—sales down by nearly 10% to $1.1 billion and net income plunging from $57.7 million to a loss of $8.3 million. Howard Martin, Mobay's manager of strategic planning, wanted better information—some historical perspective to see if profits were really keeping up with costs.

"Accountants tend to be interested in comparisons with this year's budget or last year's actual, but they're not interested in much more history than that," Martin says. He wanted to know things like: How much had so-called fixed costs changed over time? How had the company's breakeven point changed? How did 1982 earnings compare with the last time Mobay had a comparable level of capacity utilization? What level of profitability could Mobay expect at full capacity?

Most strategic planners rely on a snapshot approach that illustrates breakeven points for each individual unit or on an an-

nual basis. Unfortunately, key variables like inflation, total capacity, and fixed costs keep changing, and that means the corporate breakeven point does, too. What was needed, Martin decided, was a motion picture instead of a snapshot.

Armed with a hand-held Texas Instruments calculator, Martin spent several months developing what he called "profit geometry" analysis of the entire company's breakeven history.

The key to Martin's analysis is the way he adjusts fixed costs by weight-averaging sales of products per unit of capacity utilization; using sales dollars to adjust for inflation; adjusting for capacity additions; and so forth. These enabled him to come up with adjusted numbers for gross margins and operating results that are consistent over time.

First he developed two maximum performance curves representing breakeven gross margins and operating results at various levels of capacity utilization. Then he

plotted Mobay's actual results for the previous ten years against those curves. He could compare current performance against prior years' records and conceivably the projected performance of competitors.

Later, Martin, a chemical engineer and Harvard M.B.A., extended his profit geometry chart to take into account the cost of capital, thinking ahead to when Mobay would need replacement funds. Here the news is not so pleasant. Even in 1984, when revenues were up to $1.55 billion and net income was $73.1 million, Mobay came nowhere near breakeven at 12% or even 10% interest, a target cost of capital.

Martin remains confident that profit geometry can make a useful contribution, particularly in tough economic times and for capital intensive companies like his.

line is dropped vertically from the highest line to the horizontal axis to help us identify what each different line segment represents. In each graph the income before tax is represented by line segment *ad*. In Figure 4-5 *ad* represents the difference between total sales and total costs (variable plus fixed). In Figure 4-6 distance *ad* is simply the height of the income-before-tax line when income is positive.

Notice also that in both graphs the lines representing the effects of income taxes and dividends have their origins at the breakeven point. Obviously, when there is zero income before tax, there must be zero income tax and zero net income. Likewise, when there is zero net income and dividends are paid as a percentage of net income, the dividends must also be zero.

The income-before-tax segment *ad* consists of the following component parts in both graphs:

Line Segment	Representation
cd	Income taxes
ac	Net income
bc	Dividends
ab	Increase in retained earnings (undistributed net income)

One last thing: Notice also in each graph that the lines representing the effects of taxes and dividends do not extend through the breakeven point into the loss area. For one thing, we will not be concerned with the possibility of tax refunds on operating loss carrybacks; and for another, we don't think an organization is going to have its stockholders return some of their past dividends when it suffers a loss.

FIGURE 4-5
C-V-P Graph with Income Tax and Dividends
The sales line is drawn with a slope of 45°. The variable costs are plotted first, and the fixed costs are added to the variable costs. Next, the income tax effect is shown, followed by the effect of dividends.

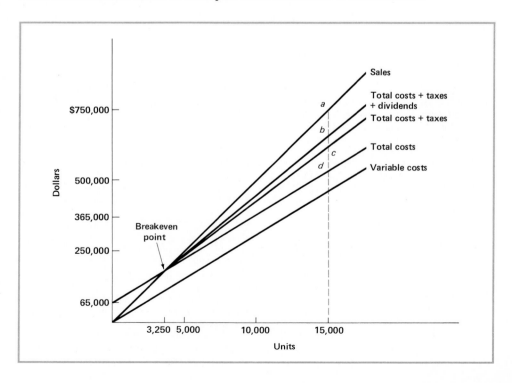

FIGURE 4-6
Income Graph with
Income Taxes and
Dividends
The line segment *ad* is income
before tax. After the income
taxes *(cd)* and dividends *(bc)*
are subtracted, the remainder
(ab) is undistributed net
income.

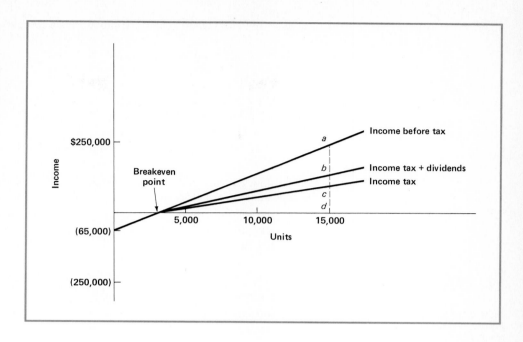

QUESTIONS

1. Explain the differences between the *contribution margin format* and the *traditional format* income statement.

2. "The terms *total contribution margin* and *total gross margin* are synonymous." True or false? Explain.

3. The increase in net income generated by an increase in activity is identical to the increase in total contribution margin, as long as which assumption underlying cost-volume-profit analysis is valid?

4. Define the term *breakeven point*. Is the term *breakeven analysis* identical to the term *cost-volume-profit analysis?* Explain.

5. If a firm's sales are expected to increase by 50% in an upcoming period, what will happen to the breakeven point? Explain.

6. Given the formula for the cost-volume-profit relationship

$$X = \frac{\text{fixed costs} + \text{income}}{\text{CMU}}$$

is the income before or after taxes?

7. "The income taxes for a firm operating at its breakeven point of 2,000 units are twice those for a firm operating at its breakeven of 1,000 units." Do you agree? Explain.

8. Define the term *margin of safety*. What does it measure for a firm?

9. "As long as a firm has a positive margin of safety, it will definitely also have a profit." Explain why this statement is correct or incorrect.

10. A firm has just increased its advertising expenditures, causing its sales to improve substantially. Unfortunately, the firm's profits have dropped off during the same period. How do you explain this situation?

11. The following profit graph depicts the situation in a company prior to the changes men-

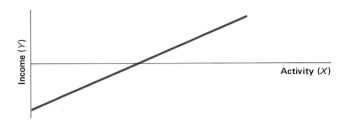

tioned below. For each of the independent changes below, indicate what would happen to the appearance of the profit line:

a. The sales price increases.
b. The variable cost per unit is reduced.
c. The total fixed costs increase.

EXERCISES

Exercise 4-1
Filling in the missing blanks in a contribution margin income statement

Fill in the blanks for each of the income statements below. The sales price in each situation is $10.

	A	B	C
Sales Revenue	$200,000	$?	$?
Variable Costs	100,000	?	?
Total Contribution Margin	$?	$100,000	$120,000
Fixed Costs	30,000	50,000	?
Net Income	$?	$?	$?
Units Sold	?	40,000	30,000
Breakeven (in units)	?	?	10,000

(Check figure: Net income, C = $80,000)

Exercise 4-2
Finding the unknown variables

For each independent situation below, fill in the missing spaces for the unknown items:

	I	II	III
Sales Price	$150	$?	$?
Variable Cost per Unit	120	24	?
Contribution Margin per Unit	$?	$?	$60
Variable Cost Percentage	?	20%	?
Contribution Margin Percentage	?	?	40%

(Check figure: Sales price, III = $150)

Exercise 4-3
Doing C-V-P analysis for a single product

The Macho-Man Exercise Studio sells units of exercise classes for $250 per unit. Its variable costs average $100 per unit, and the fixed costs are $4,000 per month.
a. How many units would need to be sold for Macho-Man to break even each month?

(Check figure: 27 units)

b. How many units would have to be sold each month if a $36,000 profit is desired?

c. What would be the margin of safety (in units) for Macho-Man if 40 units are sold each month?

d. Using a contribution margin format, prepare an income statement for a month in which 40 units are sold.

Exercise 4-4
Doing C-V-P analysis with and without tax effects

The Tobacco-Free Institute produces and sells a single-size carton of smokeless cigarettes for $20 per carton. Its expected costs are as follows:

Variable Manufacturing Costs. . . . . $8 per carton
Variable Selling Costs . . . . $4 per carton
Fixed Manufacturing Costs $60,000
Fixed Selling Costs. $20,000
Tax Rate 40%

a. Using a contribution margin format, prepare an income statement (after tax) for the company if 200,000 cartons are sold in 1988.

(Check figure: Net income = $912,000)

b. Compute the breakeven point (in dollars).

c. If 200,000 cartons are sold, determine the margin of safety in units and in dollars.

d. Determine the number of cartons that must be sold in order to generate an aftertax net income of $80,000.

(Check figure: 26,667 cartons)

Exercise 4-5
Determining breakeven for different situations

The Disco Beat Company used to sell records, but it was unable to make any money, so now the company sells computer diskettes for $25 per package of 10 diskettes. Disco Beat is trying to decide whether to purchase an automatic or a semiautomatic machine. If the automatic is purchased, the company's variable and fixed costs will be $15 and $20,000, respectively. However, if the semiautomatic machine is acquired, these costs will be $18 and $16,000.

a. Determine the firm's breakeven point (in units) for each different situation described above.

b. Determine the net income for each situation if 1,300 packages are sold and if 3,500 packages are sold.

c. Determine the level of sales (in units) at which the net income for the two situations will be the same.

(Check figure: 1,333 units)

d. Discuss whether the automatic or the semiautomatic machine should be bought.

e. Answer part **c** again, but this time assume that the variable cost per unit for the automatic machine is $19 rather than $15.

Exercise 4-6
Determining the margin of safety

The Diana Leonard Skin Cream Company sells a 10-ounce bottle of skin cream called Soft-as-a-Baby for $50 per bottle. The variable and fixed costs of producing and selling each bottle are $8 and $65,000, respectively.

If the company sells 2,200 bottles of Soft-as-a-Baby in 1989, what will be its margin of safety in both units and dollars.

(Check figure: $32,619)

Exercise 4-7
Identifying line segments
for C-V-P graphs

Presented below are two graphs depicting different views toward cost-volume-profit analysis.

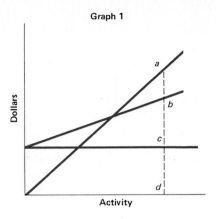

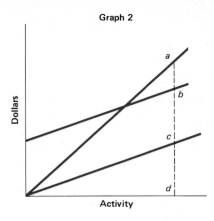

The one on the left we explained in the book, but the one on the right we did not explain. For each graph, you are to identify the items described by placing the appropriate letters for the line segments in the spaces provided below:

	Graph 1	Graph 2
Example: Sales revenue	*ad*	*ad*
a. Total variable costs		
b. Total fixed costs		
c. Total contribution margin		
d. Net income		

Exercise 4-8
Drawing a C-V-P graph
including taxes and
dividends

Draw a cost-volume-profit graph in which the variable costs are drawn first and the fixed costs are then added to the variable. Include within the graph a line that represents the effect of taxes on income, assuming that there is no tax impact when losses occur. Also include a line to represent dividends when paid as a constant percentage of net income (after tax).

Exercise 4-9
Doing C-V-P analysis with
a profit graph

At the beginning of 1988 the Nelson Bible Company prepares the following profit graph based upon the expectations for the year:

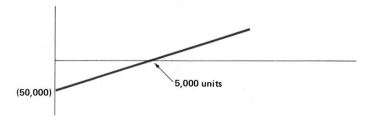

a. What is the contribution margin per unit and the total fixed costs for Nelson?
b. If Nelson expects an income of $35,000 in 1988, what is the anticipated margin of safety?

(Check figure: 3,500 units)

Exercise 4-10
Doing C-V-P analysis before and after income taxes

The Jimmy Moon Company had the following income statement for 1989:

Sales Revenue............................	$320,000
Variable Costs...........................	240,000
Total Contribution Margin	$ 80,000
Fixed Costs	54,000
Income before Tax......................	$ 26,000
Income Tax.............................	10,400
Net Income	$ 15,600

a. If Moon expects to have an income before tax of $56,000 in 1990, how great must its sales revenue be?

b. If Moon desires an aftertax net income of $40,000 in 1990, how many dollars of sales must

(Check figure: $482,668)

Exercise 4-11
Evaluating mixed costs in C-V-P analysis

The Bull Durham Company manufactures and sells chewing tobacco in tin cans. Each tin sells for $1.80. During the last 2 months of 1988 Durham sold 500,000 and 650,000 tins, respectively. The related costs for this period of time were as follows:

	November	December
Cost of Sales......................................	$350,000	$395,000
Commissions......................................	45,000	58,500
Executive Salaries	50,000	50,000
Advertising.......................................	100,000	100,000

a. Determine the variable cost per tin and the total fixed costs.

b. If the sales for January, 1989, are expected to be 720,000 tins, what should Durham's income be for January?

(Check figure: $665,200)

Exercise 4-12
Integrating dividends into C-V-P analysis

Steamy Hots Hot Dog Carts incorporated its operations in 1988. During 1989 the owner wanted his franchise to earn enough to distribute a dividend of $15,000, but he would never withdraw more than 60% of its net income from operations. The corporation pays taxes at a 45% rate. Each hot dog sells for $1.00, and the variable and fixed costs are $0.70 and $35,000, respectively (based upon a constant number of carts in operation throughout the year).

How many hot dogs will have to be sold in 1989?

(Check figure: 268,183)

Exercise 4-13
Doing C-V-P analysis with income taxes and income as a % of sales

LeRoy's Automotive is a one-man repair shop. LeRoy, the owner, bills his services at $15 per hour. He figures that his variable operating costs average 40% of his revenues and that his fixed costs are $1,000 per month. LeRoy's tax bracket is 30%.

a. If LeRoy wants to earn an income before tax of at least $800 per month, how many hours of repair time must he work?

b. If LeRoy wants his income before tax to be 20% of his revenues, what must be LeRoy's total monthly revenues?

c. LeRoy wants his monthly net income to average $600. How many hours would LeRoy have to spend repairing cars each month?

d. Assume now that LeRoy would be satisfied if his aftertax income was 7% of revenues. How many hours would he need to work each month?

(Check figure: 133.33 hours)

Exercise 4-14
Determining CMU using incomes at two levels of activity

During the first 2 months of 1988 the Bates Motel had incomes of $750 and $1,100, respectively. The number of rooms rented in each month was as follows:

	Rooms Rented
January	150
February	200

Bates expects to be at full occupancy of 240 rooms during March. What should its income be for that month?

(Check figure: $1,300)

Exercise 4-15
Determining variables on the basis of breakeven level of sales

The Risque Business Video Tape Rental broke even during 1988 with revenues of $100,000. The fixed costs for Risque are $60,000 per year.

a. What is the contribution margin percentage for Risque?
b. If the variable cost per tape rented is $0.80, what is the rental per tape?
c. If Risque expects to rent 67,000 tapes in 1989, what will be its margin of safety (in units)?

(Check figure: 17,000 tapes)

PROBLEMS: SET A

Problem A4-1
Integrating taxes and dividends into C-V-P analysis

During 1988 the Pinella Company produced and sold 10,000 baseball batting gloves. On the basis of this level of activity, the following cost-per-unit statement was prepared:

Sales Price		$150
Variable Manufacturing Cost	$40	
Fixed Manufacturing Cost	10	50
		$100
Variable Selling Costs	$20	
Fixed Selling Costs	4	24
Income before Taxes.		$ 76
Income Tax.		38
Net Income		$ 38

In addition, 40% of the net income was paid out to stockholders as dividends.

| **Required** |

1. If 15,000 gloves are produced and sold during 1989, prepare an income statement using the contribution margin format.
2. If the company desires an income before tax of $600,000 in 1989, how many gloves must be sold?
3. If the company wants to increase its retained earnings (after dividends are paid at 40%) during 1989 by $660,000, how many gloves would have to be sold?

(Check figure: 26,000 gloves)

**Problem A4-2
Determining VCU and total
fixed costs from two
mixed costs**

The Horshack Newspaper Company prepared the following budgeted income statements for the first quarter of 1988:

	January	February	March
Sales	$60,000	$70,000	$100,000
Total Costs	32,000	34,000	40,000
Net Income	$28,000	$36,000	$ 60,000

The sales price during each of the months is expected to be $25.

| **Required** |

Consider each part below independently:

1. Determine **(a)** the variable cost per unit and **(b)** the total fixed costs.
2. Determine the income for April if the sales are $200,000.

(Check figure: Income = $140,000)

**Problem A4-3
Doing C-V-P analysis with
changing assumptions**

Donald Reagen starts a small manufacturing company that will produce and sell gourmet jelly beans for $5 per jar. The company controller, David Stockman, estimates the following data concerning activity for its first year of operation, 1989:

Expected Sales	150,000
Direct Materials............................	$1.00 per jar
Direct Labor...............................	$0.75 per jar
Variable Overhead	$0.25 per jar
Fixed Overhead............................	$80,000
Variable Selling............................	$0.20 per jar
Fixed Selling...............................	$60,000

There are no beginning or ending inventories of finished goods.

| **Required** |

1. How many jars would have to be sold in 1989 in order to show a profit of $200,000?
2. If the company is to generate a profit of 25% of sales, what must be its dollar sales?
3. Looking ahead to 1990, Reagen plans to increase the sales price by $1. In addition, he expects the fixed manufacturing costs to increase by 10%. How many jars will he have to sell in 1990 to have the same income he expects for 1989?

(Check figure: 112,632 jars)

**Problem A4-4
Doing C-V-P analysis with
different relevant ranges**

The Leaded Bottoms Company manufactures kewpie dolls for carnivals and sells them for $2 per kewpie. The variable costs of manufacturing and selling are $1.00 and $0.25 per kewpie, respectively. The fixed costs are based upon the following ranges of activity:

Range of Activity	Fixed Costs
0– 40,000 kewpies	$35,000
40,001– 75,000 kewpies	50,000
75,001–125,000 kewpies (maximum capacity)	70,000

During 1988 Leaded Bottoms produced and sold 45,000 kewpies.

| **Required** |

1. Determine the net income for Leaded Bottoms for 1988.
2. How many additional units (above the 45,000) would Leaded Bottoms need to sell in order to break even if the additional units will be sold for only $1.90?

3. Answer part 2 again but assume that the company wishes to generate a profit of $6,000.

(Check figure: 110,000 units)

4. What is the maximum profit that could be earned by Leaded Bottoms (disregard parts 2 and 3)?

5. Leaded Bottoms wanted to produce and sell 85,000 units but did not want to incur any additional fixed costs. The company production supervisor decided to pay double time for labor in order to produce the 10,000 kewpies above the second range of activity. If the labor costs are three-fourths of the variable manufacturing costs, determine the profit that the company should earn.

(Check figure: $6,250)

Problem A4-5
Doing C-V-P analysis with
changing variables

During 1988 Horngren Paperback Book Company manufactured and sold 500,000 books; its income statement for the year was as follows:

Sales.		$1,250,000
Cost of Sales:		
Prime Costs.	$500,000	
Factory Overhead	250,000*	750,000
Gross Profit		$ 500,000
Operating Costs:		
Salaries.	$100,000	
Commissions	50,000	
Advertising	100,000	
Royalties	100,000†	350,000
Income before Tax		$ 150,000
Income Tax		60,000
Net Income		$ 90,000

* Of which $100,000 is fixed.
† The variable royalty is 6% of sales.

Required

Each part below is independent:

1. How many books have to be sold in order to break even?

2. If the current variable royalty is maintained for all books sold up to the breakeven point but is increased by $0.05 for all books sold in excess of the breakeven point, how many books have to be sold in order to have a net income of $150,000?

(Check figure: 619,883)

3. If the sales commissions in 1989 are discontinued in exchange for additional salaries of $60,000, how many books would have to be sold to have the same amount of net income in 1989 as in 1988?

Problem A4-6
Calculating breakeven
and income as a % of
sales and taxes

Sonny Springsteen is a promoter of rock concerts in Tampa, Florida, and is currently considering booking the group "The What" for a summer date. He has made the following estimates concerning his revenues and costs:

Ticket price.	$20
Average concession	
revenue per customer.	$15
Advertising	$15,000
Concession costs	50% of concession revenues
Security	$5,000

Cleanup.................. $0.75 per customer
Rental .... $25,000 plus 5% of ticket
revenues
Fee for "The What" $50,000

Required

1. How many fans would have to attend the concert in order for Springsteen to break even?

(Check figure: 3,689 fans)

2. If Springsteen wanted to generate an income of 40% of total revenues, how many fans would have to attend the concert?
3. If Springsteen's tax bracket was 35%, how many fans would have to attend in order for him to have a net income of $78,000?

**Problem A4-7
Calculating C-V-P for a
firm in different relevant
ranges**

Floyd Mayberry owns and operates a three-chair barber shop that is open 6 days a week. The only service that is offered is haircuts at $8 a clip. The number of barbers (in addition to himself) that Mayberry employs depends on the number of estimated haircuts for the year. The compensation for each barber (other than Mayberry) is $5,000 per year, 25% of the revenues from his or her own customers, and 100% of his or her tips. Mayberry takes no salary for his work but does keep all his tips, which average about 15% of the revenues from his customers.

As long as Mayberry expects fewer than 4,000 customers in a year, he will operate the shop by himself. He will hire additional barbers to meet the following yearly demands:

Number of Additional Barbers	Expected Haircuts for Year
1	4,001 – 8,000
2	8,001 – 15,000

The other costs of operating the shop are $6,000 per year and $2 per haircut.

Required

1. If the number of haircuts in 1988 was less than 4,000, determine Mayberry's breakeven point.
2. If the number of haircuts is expected to increase in 1989 to 9,000 (due to a contract to do all the haircuts for the nearby Marine base), what will be the income for Mayberry? Assume that the barbers (including Mayberry) share all work equally.

(Check figure: $29,600)

PROBLEMS: SET B

**Problem B4-1
Integrating taxes and
dividends into C-V-P
analysis**

During 1988 Delorean Miniatures produced and sold 20,000 miniature car kits at $50 per kit. Based upon this level of activity, the average costs per kit were as follows:

Variable Manufacturing Costs $15.00
Variable Selling 5.00
Fixed Manufacturing 10.00
Fixed Selling.................................. 2.50
Income Taxes (at 40% of income before tax)....... 7.00

In addition, 30% of income is paid out as dividends each year.

Required

1. If 30,000 kits are produced and sold in 1988, prepare a contribution margin format income statement.
2. If the company desires a profit in 1988 of $220,000 (before tax), how many kits need to be sold?
3. If the company wants $150,000 of profits to remain after the payment of dividends, how great must the dollar sales be in 1988?

(Check figure: $1,011,900)

Problem B4-2
Determining VCU and total fixed costs for mixed costs

The Baxter Corporation sold 10,000 units and 15,000 units in March and April, respectively, at $10 apiece. The total mixed costs in these 2 months were $60,000 and $85,000, respectively.

Required

1. Using the high-low method we discussed in Chapter 3, determine the variable cost per unit and the total fixed costs.

(Check figure: Fixed costs = $10,000)

2. If the sales in May fall to 4,000 units, what will be the income for that month?
3. How many units have to be sold in a month to have a profit of $45,000?

Problem B4-3
Doing C-V-P analysis in different ways to express desired income

The Galaxy Video Arcade estimates that each of its customers spends an average of $10 per visit. On the basis of past experience the owner, Pac Boy, estimates his costs to be as follows:

Variable Operating . . . .$6.50 per customer
Salaries . . . .$30,000 per year
Rent and Machine Leasing . . . .$20,000 per year
Advertising . . . .$10,000 per year

Required

1. How many visits by customers will Galaxy need in order to have a profit of $25,000?
2. What will the total revenues have to be in order to show a profit of 30% of sales?
3. If Galaxy wants to generate a profit of $1 per customer, how many customer visits must it have during the year?

Problem B4-4
Doing C-V-P analysis with different relevant ranges

The Hubbard & Annaheim CPA Firm bills its services to customers at $50 per billable hour and estimates that the variable costs of running the office average $30 per billable hour. The level of fixed costs depends upon the number of employees working for the firm. All fixed costs, other than salaries, will be the same no matter how much business the firm can attract. The total fixed costs will be as follows:

Number of Employees	Fixed Costs
One (for 0–2,000 billable hr).	$60,000*
Two (for 2,001–3,600)	75,000
Three (for 3,601–6,000)	95,000

* Includes costs of insurance, advertising, rent, etc., in addition to salaries.

During the past year the firm employed two staff employees and was able to charge customers for 3,500 billable hours.

Required

1. Determine the income for last year.
2. How many billable hours must Hubbard & Annaheim have in order to break even?
3. What is the maximum profit possible for Hubbard & Annaheim?

**Problem B4-5
Doing C-V-P analysis with
changing variables**

During 1988 the Larry Seffner Publishing Company manufactured and sold 2,000,000 magazines. The company had the following income statement for the year:

Sales		$10,000,000
Cost of Sales:		
Direct Materials	$4,000,000	
Conversion Costs	2,000,000*	6,000,000
Gross Profit		$ 4,000,000
Operating Costs:		
Salaries.....................................	$ 800,000	
Shipping.....................................	400,000	
Advertising	800,000	
Royalties	800,000†	2,800,000
Income before Tax..		$ 1,200,000
Income Tax		480,000
Net Income		$ 720,000

* Of which $1,200,000 is variable.
† Of which $200,000 is fixed.

Required

Each part below is independent:

1. How many magazines have to be sold in order to have an income before tax of $500,000?
2. If the current variable royalty is maintained for all magazines sold up to the breakeven point but is increased by $0.05 for all magazines sold in excess of the breakeven point, how many magazines have to be sold in order to have a net income of $600,000?

(Check figure: 1,908,962)

3. If the magazine contributors agree to accept an all-variable royalty of 10%, instead of a royalty that guarantees a fixed payment as a minimum, how many magazines would have to be sold in 1989 to have the same income as in 1988?

**Problem B4-6
Calculating breakeven
and income as % of sales**

Johnny Reunitis has observed the success of the oldtimers' games in baseball and basketball, and he is considering putting on such a game with retired USFL football players on the day preceding the Super Bowl. He has received permission from the commissioner of the USFL and has lined up quite a few players who need the money and weren't famous enough to do light-beer commercials. He is now trying to figure out whether the game can be profitable, and he has compiled the following information:

✓Ticket price.........	$20
✓Average concession revenue per customer..........	$10
Advertising.........	$75,000
Concession costs	60% of concession revenues
Health insurance....	$50,000
MVP awards........	$25,000
Rental of stadium ...	$100,000
Fee for players......	$200,000 plus 10% of ticket revenues

Required

1. How many fans would have to attend the game in order for Reunitis to break even?
2. If Reunitis wanted to generate an income of 30% of ticket revenues, how many fans would have to attend the game?
3. If Reunitis has to pay 20% of his net income to the players' pension fund, how many fans will have to attend in order for the pension fund to receive $60,000? *(Check figure: 23,864)*

Problem B4-7
Calculating C-V-P within different relevant ranges

Wella Paulson owns a shop, located in a prestigious shopping mall, that provides only one service: makeup applications for women. The cost of each application is $50. The number of applicators (who do 100% of the applications) employed by Paulson depends on the number of estimated applications for the year. The compensation for each employee is $20,000 per year, plus 5% of all revenues from her or his own customers and 100% of her or his tips. The number of employees is based upon the following yearly demands:

Number of Employees	Expected Applications for Year
1	Less than 1,500
2	1,501–3,500
3	3,501–6,000

The other costs of operating the shop are $12,000 per year and $20 per application.

Required

1. If the number of applications in 1988 was less than 1,500, determine Paulson's breakeven point.
2. If Paulson desires an income of $20,000, how many applications must the shop make in the year?

(Check figure: 2,618)

CHAPTER 5

The Contribution Margin Approach to Cost-Volume-Profit Analysis: Part II

After you have completed this chapter, you should understand the following:

- The assumptions underlying the mechanics of cost-volume-profit analysis
- The assumptions that accountants make concerning the sales price and variable cost per unit for each product produced and sold, and how these assumptions compare to the ones made by economists
- How a change in either the sales price, the variable cost per unit, or the total fixed costs will affect the accountant's cost-volume-profit analysis
- What is meant by *sensitivity analysis* and how it relates to the changes that are discussed in this chapter
- What is meant by *sales mix* and what effect a change in the sales mix has on the accountant's cost-volume-profit analysis
- The difference between the *direct costing method* and the *absorption costing method* and how to calculate each when the quantity produced is equal to the quantity sold, when it is greater than the quantity sold, and when it is less than the quantity sold
- How to apply cost-volume-profit analysis to absorption costing

In Chapter 4 we explained the fundamentals of cost-volume-profit analysis under a somewhat limiting set of assumptions. We pointed out what the common assumptions were, but we postponed discussing them. We will now examine the significance of each assumption in great detail. In addition, we will explain how a change in each assumption affects the accountant's cost-volume-profit analysis.

The assumptions are listed on page 149

Return to page 149 in Chapter 4 to review the five assumptions underlying cost-volume-profit analysis.

THE UNCHANGING SALES PRICE

No Δ in SP

The first assumption accountants like to make when using cost-volume-profit analysis actually consists of two parts.

Part 1

First, we assume there is only one price for our product, no matter how many units we sell. For example, the product we evaluated in the previous chapter sold for $50 per unit. Regardless of the number of units we sell, we assume that the price will remain at $50 per unit. A change in the number of units we sell will not affect the price we charge.

Part 2

Second, we assume this price will not change during the period of analysis. Referring to the same example, we expect the price to remain the same throughout the year — $50.

[167]

FIGURE 5-1
The Accountants' View of Total Sales
An unchanging sales price results in a linear total.

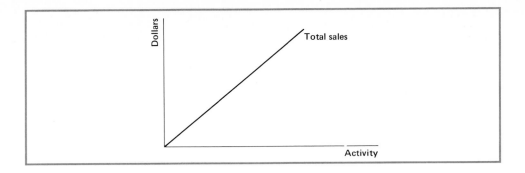

On the basis of the first part of this assumption, the accountant perceives the relationship between total sales and the quantity sold to be represented graphically by a straight line, as shown in Figure 5-1.

See Appendix 5-2 for the economists' view

Economists disagree with this assumption and normally prefer to represent total sales (which they refer to as total revenue) as curvilinear rather than linear. If you'd like to learn more about economists' assumptions, see Appendix 5-2 at the end of this chapter.

The second part of the assumption concerning the sales price is that the price will remain the same throughout the period of analysis. Whether or not this is a valid assumption depends greatly on inflation. In years with little or no inflation, it is probably a valid assumption. But in years of high inflation, like the seventies, the sales price might change several times during a year.

Revise C-V-P if △ in SP

If the sales price is different from what it was predicted to be in the original C-V-P calculations (and all other variables are unchanged), the difference will change the contribution margin per unit, the breakeven point, and the income for any level of sales. The accountant needs to be aware of this change so that he or she can make the necessary adjustments to the C-V-P model.

THE UNCHANGING VARIABLE COST PER UNIT

The second assumption underlying C-V-P analysis also consists of two parts:

No △ in VCU

1. The variable cost per unit is the same for all units produced and sold within the relevant range of cost-volume-profit analysis.

2. The variable cost per unit remains unchanged within the period of analysis.

For example, if the variable cost per unit is $30, we assume that it does not matter whether 2,000 or 10,000 units are produced and sold. We expect each and every unit to cost an additional $30 of variable cost. And we assume that the variable cost per unit at the end of the period will be exactly what it was at the beginning and throughout the period—$30. The graphic representation of the VCU and its related total costs is shown in Figure 5-2.

For the economists' view see Appendix 5-2

Economists also disagree with the accountants' assumption concerning the variable cost per unit. If you'd like to know about their opposing view, you will find it discussed in Appendix 5-2, along with the discussion concerning the sales price.

The second part of the assumption concerning the VCU is that it will remain unchanged throughout the period of analysis. Once again, as long as there is no significant inflation, this assumption will probably be acceptable. However, if the economy is experiencing a significant amount of inflation, it really wouldn't be

FIGURE 5-2
Accountants' View of VCU
and Total Variable Costs
When the VCU is constant,
the total is linear.

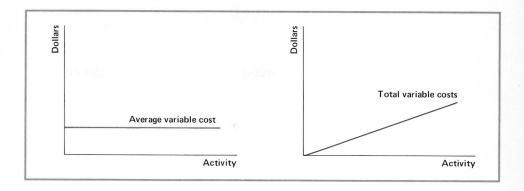

realistic to expect the variable costs per unit to remain unchanged for any extended
period of time.

Effect of Δ on C-V-P   If the variable cost per unit is different from what it was predicted to be in the
original C-V-P calculations (and all other variables are unchanged), the difference
will change the contribution margin per unit, the breakeven point, and the income
for any level of sales. Once again, the accountant needs to be aware of this change and
must adjust the C-V-P model accordingly.

THE UNCHANGING TOTAL FIXED COSTS

No Δ in TFC   The third assumption is that total fixed costs remain unchanged in response to
changes in activity, within the relevant range of activity, and during the period of
analysis. Since we discussed this assumption in great detail in Chapter 3, we will not
discuss the meaning or significance of this assumption any further. However, we do
need to be concerned with the possibility of a change in the fixed costs and with the
effect that this change will have on C-V-P analysis.

If the total fixed costs are different from what they were predicted to be in the
original C-V-P calculations (and all other variables are unchanged), the difference
will change the breakeven point and the income for any level of sales—but it will
leave the contribution margin (per unit and total) unchanged. The accountant once
again needs to adjust the C-V-P model to accommodate a change in this key variable.

UNCERTAINTY AND SENSITIVITY ANALYSIS

When we did C-V-P analysis in Chapter 4, we assumed that all our key variables, such
as the sales price, the variable cost per unit, and the total fixed costs, were known with
certainty. That is, we felt certain that these variables would be exactly as they were
predicted to be.

For instance, in the Prentiss Hill example in Chapter 4 we treated the $50 sales
price, the $30 variable cost per unit, the $65,000 of fixed costs, and the production of
8,000 units as if we knew with certainty that they represented the exact value for each
variable.

Things aren't always what   However, we should realize that we live in a world of uncertainty, where we can
we think they'll be   never be entirely sure that our predicted values are going to be correct. So what do we
do if there is a good chance that the predictions will be incorrect? Do we scrap the
analysis? Of course not. But, as we pointed out in the preceding sections on the sales
price, variable cost per unit, and total fixed costs, the accountant will certainly want

to know the consequences that might occur if our predictions are wrong, so that the C-V-P model can be adapted to accommodate the changes.

The Effects of Uncertainty

Living with uncertainty

For example, let's see now what will be the effect of changes in the sales price, the variable cost per unit, and the total fixed costs, using the data in the example we introduced in Chapter 4:

Sales Price	$ 50
Variable Cost per Unit	30
Contribution Margin per Unit	$ 20
Fixed Costs	$65,000

Assume that because of an increase in direct material prices, the variable cost per unit is expected to increase to $33, which in turn prompts a $2 increase in the sales price. In addition, the fixed costs are going to increase to $70,000 as a result of a bigger advertising campaign than was originally planned.

In Chapter 4, on the basis of early estimates, we made these original calculations:

Breakeven point (in units)	3,250
Net income for sales of 8,000 units	$95,000

When values for key variables change, so do our results

Now, as a result of the changes specified, we must revise the calculations for breakeven and net income. Because of the changes in the sales price and the variable cost per unit, the contribution margin per unit falls to $19 ($52 − $33 = $19). The new breakeven point will be 3,684 units:

$$X = \frac{\text{fixed costs} + \text{income}}{\text{CMU}}$$

$$= \frac{\$70,000 + \$0}{\$19} = 3,684 \text{ units}$$

It will now take more units to break even, which makes sense because of the lower CMU and the higher fixed costs.

If the same number of units is sold — 8,000 — as originally expected, the income will fall from $95,000 to $82,000:

Total Contribution Margin (8,000 × $19)	$152,000
Total Fixed Costs	70,000
Net Income	$ 82,000

Hopefully, however, the $5,000 increase in the advertising budget will stimulate sales far enough beyond the 8,000-unit level to increase the income or at least to keep it from falling.

Sensitivity Analysis

Sensitivity analysis deals with "what if" questions

What we have just been doing in our analysis of the effects of these changes is something called sensitivity analysis. **Sensitivity analysis** evaluates the effect that a change in the value of an input to a decision model will have on the results of using that model. It basically is interested in "what if" situations. What if the sales price or variable cost per unit or fixed costs change by such and such? What will happen to the breakeven point? To the net income? To the amount of dividends that we can pay?

In the example above the effect of the changes was an increase in the breakeven point from 3,250 to 3,684 units—an increase of 434 units, or 13.4%. You could certainly say that the breakeven point was "sensitive" to the changes in the values of these three variables. If the sales were still 8,000 units, the income would go from $95,000 to $82,000—a drop of $13,000, or 13.7%. Again, you could say that income is "sensitive" to the changes in the three variables.

Conversely, we might think of sensitivity analysis as a way of determining what a value of a variable will have to be in order to achieve a certain result. For instance, the firm in our example is currently producing and selling 8,000 units; it would like to generate a profit of $125,000, but it does not feel that it can sell any additional units. The managers of the firm want to know what the sales price would have to be to generate this profit, assuming that all other variables remain the same. That is, the VCU is still $30, the fixed costs remain at $65,000, and the quantity sold remains at the 8,000-unit level.

We can approach this version of sensitivity analysis by using the C-V-P formula in the following manner, determining first what the CMU would have to be:

$$X = \frac{\text{fixed costs} + \text{income}}{\text{CMU}}$$

Filling in all but the CMU, we get:

$$8,000 = \frac{\$65,000 + \$125,000}{\text{CMU}}$$

Solving for CMU, we find that the contribution margin would have to be $23.75:

$$8,000\text{CMU} = \$65,000 + \$125,000 = \$190,000$$

$$\text{CMU} = \frac{\$190,000}{8,000} = \$23.75$$

In order for the contribution margin to be $23.75, with a variable cost per unit of $30, the sales price would have to be raised to $53.75 ($30 + $23.75). This would represent an increase of $3.75 ($53.75 − $50.00 = $3.75), or 7.5% ($3.75 ÷ $50.00) of the original price.

THE UNCHANGING SALES MIX

The fourth assumption underlying C-V-P analysis is that the analysis either involves a firm that sells a single product or a multi-product firm in which the sales mix remains the same.

In this section we will discuss how the analyses for a single-product and a multi-product firm differ, what a sales mix means for a multi-product firm, and what the significance is of the assumption concerning the sales mix.

We only worry about sales mix for multi-product firms

Up to this point we have assumed that Prentiss Hill (first introduced in Example 4-1) planned to sell just one product—the fundamentals of accounting textbook. Realistically, however, most firms in the real world sell numerous products—which explains why we refer to them as multi-product firms. The C-V-P analysis for the multi-product firm is nearly the same as that for the single-product firm, but the differences that do exist are significant enough to warrant our attention.

We will now assume Prentiss Hill decides to publish an intermediate accounting text as well as the fundamentals text, which will make Prentiss Hill a multi-product firm. The facts concerning the two products are presented in Example 5-1.

Example 5-1

A firm with two products

THE MULTIPLE PRODUCTS OF PRENTISS HILL

Assume now that Prentiss Hill plans to produce and sell two accounting textbooks in its second year of operation. The marketing editors for Prentiss Hill assure the president that they will continue to sell 8,000 copies of the fundamentals text and, in addition, will sell 2,000 copies of the new intermediate text.

Relevant data pertaining to the two texts is as follows:

	Funda-mentals Text	Inter-mediate Text
Sales Price..	$50	$55
Variable Cost per Unit...............................	30	40
Contribution Margin per Unit	$20	$15

The two products will be produced at the same production facility, so the total fixed costs will continue to be $65,000 no matter how many units of each text are produced. These fixed costs are split evenly between the two products in determining product-line net incomes.

Based upon the facts in Example 5-1, three income statements are shown in Exhibit 5-1—two for the individual product lines (fundamentals and intermediate) and one for the organization as a whole.

EXHIBIT 5-1
Product-Line Income Statements
The sales of fundamentals are 80% of the total unit sales. The sales of intermediate are 20%.

	Funda-mentals (8,000 Units)	Inter-mediate (2,000 Units)	Total (10,000 Units)
Sales Revenue...........................	$400,000	$110,000	$510,000
Total Variable Costs.....................	240,000	80,000	320,000
Total Contribution Margin	$160,000	$ 30,000	$190,000
Fixed Costs (allocated ½ to each)...........	32,500	32,500	65,000
Net Income............................	$127,500	$ (2,500)	$125,000

Looking at the combined income statements in Exhibit 5-1, you can see that Prentiss Hill should be able to earn a total of $125,000 during its second year if it can sell 10,000 textbooks. But how many must it sell in order to break even; or to have a profit of $95,000 or any other desired amount? The answers to these questions can be supplied by the same C-V-P formulas we've been using all along—with just a few modifications.

Sales Mix

The first thing we need to do is to introduce a new term—sales mix—a term that has meaning only for a multi-product firm. The *sales mix* for a multi-product firm represents the percentage of total sales that is distributed to each product line. We might also think of the sales mix as the percentages that the sales of each product line

Sales mix is measured in relative terms

are to the combined sales for all product lines of the firm. The sales mix percentages for any multi-product situation can be determined with the following equation:

$$\text{Sales mix \%} = \frac{\textbf{sales of individual product line}}{\textbf{sales of all product lines combined}}$$

The sales mix for a firm can be measured in terms of unit sales or dollar sales. For Prentiss Hill the sales mix in unit sales is calculated as follows:

Sales mix based on unit sales

Product	Unit Sales	Sales Mix %
Fundamentals.....................................	8,000	.80 (8,000/10,000)
Intermediate	2,000	.20 (2,000/10,000)
	10,000	1.00

The fundamentals text represents 80% of total unit sales, and the intermediate text represents 20% of total unit sales.

The sales mix in dollar sales for Prentiss Hill would be:

Sales mix based on dollar sales

Product	Dollar Sales	Sales Mix %
Fundamentals..............................	$400,000	.784 ($400,000/$510,000)
Intermediate	110,000	.216 ($110,000/$510,000)
	$510,000	1.000

For each sales mix there's a different weighted average CMU

As we shall see in a moment, the sales mix for an organization has an effect on the contribution margin per unit (CMU) or contribution margin percentage (CM%) that we use in the C-V-P formulas. When the sales mix changes we get a new CMU (or CM%), and a new CMU (or CM%) requires that we revise the C-V-P model. In the example that follows we will use only the sales mix that is measured in terms of units and will show how it affects the C-V-P analysis that uses CMU. The analysis with CM% would be done in a similar manner.

Sales Mix and C-V-P Analysis

There are four steps in doing C-V-P analysis for a multi-product firm.

Step 1: Determine the Sales Mix

This we have already done.

Step 2: Calculate the Weighted Average Contribution Margin per Unit

This we can do in one of two ways. The first way is to divide the total contribution margin for all products combined by the total unit sales. For Prentiss Hill it would be:

$$\text{Weighted average CMU} = \frac{\textbf{total CM (all products)}}{\textbf{total units (all products)}}$$

$$= \frac{\$190,000}{10,000} = \$19 \text{ per unit}$$

A second way to calculate the average CMU is to multiply each individual CMU by its respective sales mix percentage and then add together the individual multiplications. We can do this for Prentiss Hill as follows:

See how the sales mix affects the weighted average CMU

Product	Individual CMU	×	Sales Mix %	=	Average CMU
Fundamentals	$20	×	.80	=	$16
Intermediate	$15	×	.20	=	3
					$19

Either way we do it, we get an average CMU of $19 per unit.

Step 3: Use the Traditional C-V-P Formula

Place total fixed costs and desired income for all products combined in the numerator and average CMU in the denominator. For Prentiss Hill the breakeven point (in units) for both products combined is:

Calculate an answer in total first

$$X = \frac{\$65,000 + \$0}{\$19 \text{ per unit}} = 3,421 \text{ units}$$

And the level of sales needed to generate a profit of $95,000 is:

$$X = \frac{\$65,000 + \$95,000}{\$19 \text{ per unit}} = 8,421 \text{ units}$$

Step 4: Allocate the Total between the Product Lines

Allocate the answer from step 3 between the different product lines by multiplying each product's sales mix percentage times the total unit sales. For Prentiss Hill the allocation of the breakeven units of 3,421 would be:

Always determine the sales for individual products on the basis of the total for all products

Product	Total Sales	×	Sales Mix %	=	Allocation to Product
Fundamentals	3,421	×	.80	=	2,737
Intermediate	3,421	×	.20	=	684
					3,421

We would allocate the 8,421 units in exactly the same manner in order to determine the unit sales for the two products that are needed to generate a profit of $95,000 for the firm.

Income statements at the breakeven level of activity are shown in Exhibit 5-2. They are similar to the breakeven statement in Exhibit 4-1, except that the individual statements for the fundamentals and intermediate texts are shown in Exhibit 5-2 in addition to the income statement for the entire organization. Also, the breakeven point is no longer 3,250 units, as it was for the single-product situation in Chapter 4.

EXHIBIT 5-2
Income Statements at Breakeven
(Sales mix: 80:20)
The key is that the bottom line for the total is zero

	Fundamentals (2,737 Units)	Intermediate (684 Units)	Total (3,421 Units)
Sales Revenue	$136,850	$ 37,620	$174,470
Total Variable Costs	82,110	27,360	109,470
Total Contribution Margin.	$ 54,740	$ 10,260	$ 65,000
Fixed Costs	32,500	32,500	65,000
Net Income	$ 22,240	$(22,240)	$ -0-

Notice in Exhibit 5-2 that net income for the entire firm is zero but that neither of the incomes for the individual product lines is zero. Is there something wrong, or is our answer correct as it stands?

There is nothing wrong with our answer or with the income statements. You see, when we calculate the breakeven point for the entire firm, we have no guarantee that the net income for each product line will also be zero. Even though the intermediate text shows a loss and the fundamentals text shows a profit, the fact that the combined income is zero is evidence that this is the correct breakeven point for the entire organization.

Why Aren't Both Products Breaking Even at Breakeven?

It's quite possible that the individual product lines won't have zero profits

You may be wondering why the individual products don't also have a zero income. It has to do with how we distribute the fixed costs between the individual products. Since fixed costs are not directly associated with the specific product, the allocation of fixed costs among product lines is usually an arbitrary process.

Even though Prentiss Hill divided the fixed costs evenly, assigning 50% ($32,500) to each product line, the allocation could have been made with many other possible proportions—each combination as arbitrary as any other.

Both product lines could have shown a zero income only if, coincidentally, $54,740 of the $65,000 of fixed costs had been assigned to the fundamentals text and the remaining $10,260 had been assigned to the intermediate text. Then—and only then—would we have all zeroes across the bottom of the income statements, like this:

	Fundamentals	Intermediate	Total
Total Contribution Margin	$54,740	$10,260	$65,000
Fixed Costs	54,740	10,260	65,000
Net Income	$ -0-	$ -0-	$ -0-

What about a Shortcut?

Don't do it this way

Some of you may also be wondering why we don't calculate the breakeven points more directly—and possibly more simply. Why don't we just divide each product's individual fixed costs by its individual CMU—like this:

$$X \text{ (fundamentals)} = \frac{\$32,500 + \$0}{\$20} = 1,625 \text{ units}$$

and
$$X \text{ (intermediate)} = \frac{\$32,500 + \$0}{\$15} = 2,167 \text{ units}$$

Then we could combine the individual answers for the two products to get the breakeven for the entire organization:

$$X \text{ (entire organization)} = 1,625 + 2,167 = 3,792 \text{ units}$$

If we then prepared income statements for the individual products and the entire organization, all three statements would show zero incomes.

Although this approach might be quicker—and it would indeed give us *a* breakeven point—unfortunately, it would not give us *the correct* breakeven point. So don't do it this way.

To understand why we shouldn't do the analysis this way, let's first refresh our

If you do it this way, the sales mix will change

memories about the cost-volume-profit assumption we are evaluating. Remember: Assumption 4 says that the sales mix for a multi-product firm remains the same. We are assuming that no matter how many textbooks Prentiss Hill sells, 80% of them will be fundamentals and 20% of them will be intermediate—whether the sales are 8,000 units, 3,421 units, or 3,792 units.

The correct breakeven point cannot be 3,792 units because that answer is based on a sales mix which is different from 80:20:

Product	Sales	Sales Mix %: Individual Sales Divided by Total Sales	Assumed Sales Mix %
Fundamentals....................	1,625	.43 (1,625/3,792)	.80
Intermediate	2,167	.57 (2,167/3,792)	.20
	3,792	1.00	1.00

In order for 3,792 units to be the correct breakeven point, the sales mix would have to be 43:57 instead of 80:20.

A Change in the Sales Mix

Our predictions of a breakeven point of 3,421 units and a net income of $125,000 (based on sales of 10,000) will be correct only as long as the sales mix remains the same—that is, only as long as we expect the total sales to be distributed to the fundamentals and intermediate texts in an 80:20 ratio. As soon as the sales mix changes from 80:20 to any other combination, our predictions will have to be revised. This is true because the average contribution margin per unit we use will no longer be $19.

A Δ in mix changes weighted average CMU

We calculated the $19 average CMU for Prentiss Hill by weighting each individual CMU by its respective sales mix percentage. The CMU of $20 for fundamentals was multiplied by 80%, and the CMU of $15 for intermediate was multiplied by 20%. Any change in the sales mix changes the weights that we multiply by $20 and $15. If, for example, the sales mix changes from 80:20 to 20:80, then a much smaller proportion of total unit sales is now contributing $20 per unit—so a much smaller weight is multiplied by $20. And now a much larger proportion of total unit sales is contributing $15 per unit—thus a larger weight is multiplied by $15. As a result, the weighted CMU will go down—it will decrease to $16 for Prentiss Hill, as shown by the following calculations:

Product	New Sales Mix %	×	Individual CMU	=	Weighted Average CMU
Fundamentals	.20	×	$20	=	$ 4
Intermediate	.80	×	$15	=	12
					$16

Effects of Δ in weighted average CMU

When we have a smaller CMU, two changes take place:

1. Our income for the same level of total sales (10,000 units) decreases.

2. Our breakeven point rises.

Let's first see what happens to Prentiss Hill's net income when 10,000 texts are still being sold but the sales mix is 20:80 rather than 80:20. Look at Exhibit 5-3.

EXHIBIT 5-3
Income Statement
(Sales mix: 20:80)
With a Δ in mix the total
income is different even
though total unit sales are
unchanged

	Fundamentals (2,000 Units)	Intermediate (8,000 Units)	Total (10,000 Units)
Sales Revenue	$100,000	$440,000	$540,000
Total Variable Costs	60,000	320,000	380,000
Total Contribution Margin.	$ 40,000	$120,000	$160,000
Fixed Costs	32,500	32,500	65,000
Net Income	$ 7,500	$ 87,500	$ 95,000

The 10,000 units now contribute — on the average — $16 rather than $19 per unit. Therefore, the total contribution margin is now $160,000 (10,000 units × $16 per unit), down from $190,000 (10,000 units × $19 per unit). As a result, the income decreases from $125,000 to $95,000.

With a smaller weighted average CMU, Prentiss Hill will also have a higher breakeven point. Whereas the breakeven point is 3,421 units when the weighted average CMU is $19, it will be 4,062 units when the weighted average CMU falls to $16:

We now have a new breakeven point

$$X = \frac{\$65,000 + \$0}{\$16} = 4,062.5 \text{ units}$$

Of this total, 812.5 units (4,062.5 × 20%) will be fundamentals texts and 3,250 units (4062.5 × 80%) will be intermediate texts.

THE UNCHANGING INVENTORY LEVELS

No Δ in FG

The fifth assumption underlying cost-volume-profit analysis is that there are no significant differences in the beginning and ending inventories of finished goods (FG). Stated another way, the assumption is that the number of units produced during the period equals the number of units sold. Since only manufacturers produce the units they sell and, therefore, have a finished goods inventory, this assumption concerns only manufacturing organizations. It does not concern retailers, wholesalers, or any other types of organizations.

CHANGE IN SALES MIX FOR THE RECORD INDUSTRY

The scene is familiar to anyone who has visited a record store lately: Customers swarm like locusts over the compact-disc bins; meanwhile, the aisles in the vinyl-LP section look like a no-man's land. . . . "It's a marketplace decision, a case of the consumer telling us what he wants." Russ Solomon, president of Tower Records, the country's biggest record chain, agrees. "Consumer acceptance of CD's is phenomenal. The best word is 'total,'" says Solomon.

To underline the point, RCA records recently announced that it will shut down its last vinyl-record pressing plant at the end of 1987 because its Indianapolis facility "no longer makes economic sense when vinyl represents less than 25 percent of our sales." . . . Prerecorded tape cassettes still account for about half of the industry's revenues, with CD's now even with vinyl sales, at about 25 percent for each.

But CD's are expected to make even bigger inroads in the months ahead.

"There's a strong possibility that CD's will represent half our dollar volume in 1987, including cassettes," says Jerry Shulman, vice president for marketing development at CBS records, the biggest U.S. record company.

Source: "The Stunning Success of CD's," *U.S. News & World Report,* Feb. 23, 1987, pp. 41–42.

To understand the meaning of this assumption, let's first remind ourselves of the two income statement formats that we have used in this course:

Different formats for an income statement

Contribution Margin Format	Traditional Format
Sales	Sales
Less: Total Variable Costs	Less: Cost of Goods Sold
Equals: Total Contribution Margin	Equals: Gross Margin
Less: Total Fixed Costs	Less: Selling and Administrative
Equals: Net Income	Equals: Net Income

The one on the left is the one we've used primarily in Chapter 4 and this chapter. It is the *contribution margin format* (or *behavioral format*). The one on the right was used in Chapter 2 and is the one most often used in financial statements issued to the public. It is called the *traditional format* (or *functional format*).

The contribution margin format for an income statement is used whenever a firm is employing the ***direct costing (DC) method*** (also called the ***variable costing method***) of product costing. The traditional method is used whenever a firm is employing the ***absorption costing (AC) method*** (also called the ***full costing method***) of product costing.

Definitions of Direct Costing and Absorption Costing

Absorption costing: fixed factory overhead is a product cost

Under absorption costing the product costs are direct materials, direct labor, variable factory overhead, and fixed factory overhead. Remember, as product costs, all these costs, as they are incurred, are assigned to inventory when units are produced, and they become expenses (as part of cost of goods sold expense) only when the units to which they are assigned are sold. All costs that are assigned to the unsold units remain as an asset on the balance sheet. All selling and administrative costs are period costs and as such are expensed when incurred.

Direct costing: fixed factory overhead is a period cost

For direct costing the product costs include direct materials, direct labor, and variable factory overhead — the sum of all these comprises the variable manufacturing costs. We assign only the variable manufacturing costs to the units produced. The variable manufacturing costs are expensed (as part of variable cost of goods sold expense) only when the units to which they are assigned are sold. And nothing but the variable manufacturing costs is assigned to the unsold units that remain on the balance sheet as an asset. Fixed factory overhead is not a product cost; it is a period cost which, like the variable and fixed selling and administrative costs, is expensed when incurred.

The difference between absorption costing and direct costing is that fixed factory overhead is a product cost under absorption costing but a period cost under direct costing.

The classification of costs for a manufacturer under absorption costing and under direct costing is shown in the income statements in Exhibit 5-4.

A Simple Example

We will start with a simple example that completely explains why the income for direct costing is different from the income for absorption costing when the number of units produced and sold are different. Then we will graduate to a detailed example, where we will compare entire statements under the two approaches.

FFO = $40,000

Q_p = 8,000

Assume for now that all you know about Prentiss Hill is that its fixed factory overhead (FFO) is $40,000 and that it expects to produce 8,000 units of a single product, which averages $5 per unit of fixed factory overhead.

traditional   *cm. Format*

EXHIBIT 5-4
A Comparison of Product and Period Costs for Absorption and Direct Costing

Absorption Costing			Direct Costing		
Format of Statement		**Type of Cost**	**Format of Statement**		**Type of Cost**
Sales			Sales		
Cost of Goods Sold Expense:			Variable Costs:		
Direct Materials		Product	Direct Materials		Product
Direct Labor		Product	Direct Labor		Product
Variable Overhead		Product	Variable Overhead		Product
Fixed Overhead		Product	Variable Selling and Adm.		Period
Gross Margin			Contribution Margin		
Selling and Adm. Expenses:			Fixed Costs:		
Variable		Period	Factory Overhead		Period
Fixed		Period	Selling and Adm.		Period
Net Income			Net Income		

$Q_p > Q_s$

Quantity Produced Q_p Exceeds Quantity Sold Q_s We'll assume first that only 6,000 of the 8,000 units that are produced in the current period are sold, leaving 2,000 in the ending inventory of finished goods.

For absorption costing, since the fixed factory overhead is a product cost, the $40,000 is assigned to the 8,000 units when it is incurred during production. The units—when finished—and the $40,000 of product costs as well, are represented in the Finished Goods Inventory account. When the 6,000 units are sold, $30,000 (6,000 × $5 per unit) of the fixed factory overhead is expensed (along with direct materials, direct labor, and variable factory overhead) as part of cost of goods sold expense. The remaining $10,000 stays in finished goods inventory as an asset at year-end.

For direct costing, since fixed factory overhead is a period cost, all $40,000 is expensed as incurred, and none of it remains in finished goods at year-end.

Some of the $40,000 stays in FG for AC

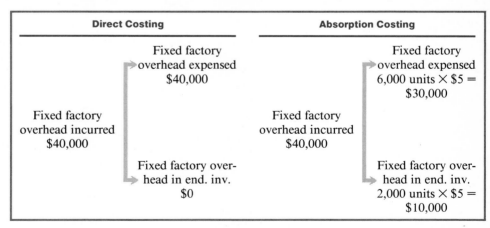

The amount of fixed factory overhead expensed is $10,000 greater for direct costing than for absorption costing; therefore, the income will be $10,000 higher for absorption costing than for direct costing. It's as simple as that.

When we later examine complete income statements for direct and absorption costing, you'll see that there are many other items to keep track of besides the fixed factory overhead. But no matter how complicated the statements may appear, the difference in the incomes for direct and absorption costing can be explained entirely by the different accounting for fixed factory overhead. All other items in the two income statements will be exactly the same—even though they may be placed in different sections of the statements.

Quantity Produced Q_p *Equals Quantity Sold* Q_s We'll now assume that all of the 8,000 units that are produced are also sold in the same time period. Since the quantity produced equals the quantity sold, the finished goods inventory at the end of the period is the same as it was at the beginning of the period. This is the fifth assumption underlying C-V-P analysis, so let's now see what the consequence is when this assumption is valid.

$Q_p = Q_s$

For absorption costing the $40,000 is assigned to the 8,000 units when it is incurred during production; these units and costs are transferred to finished goods as soon as the units are completed. When the 8,000 units are sold, all $40,000 (8,000 × $5 per unit) of the fixed factory overhead is expensed as part of cost of goods sold expense. None of the $40,000 remains in finished goods inventory as an asset at year-end, because there is no ending inventory.

For direct costing, since fixed factory overhead is a period cost, all $40,000 is expensed as incurred.

FFO expensed is $40,000 for AC and DC

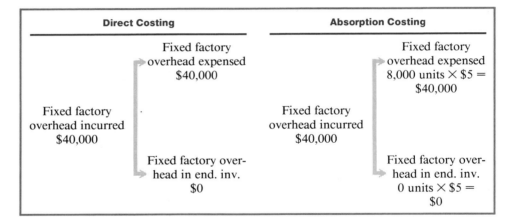

The amount of fixed factory overhead expensed is now the same—$40,000—for both absorption costing and direct costing. Therefore, the incomes will also be the same for absorption costing and direct costing. Once again, it's as simple as that.

In this situation the amount of fixed factory overhead expensed was the same under the two methods. ***It is extremely important, however, for you to realize that the way in which it was expensed was entirely different under the two methods.***

For absorption costing the $40,000 flowed through the production accounts—as a product cost—in the following manner:

Work-in-Process Inventory		Finished Goods Inventory		Cost of Goods Sold Expense	
$40,000	$40,000 ⟶	$40,000	$40,000 ⟶	$40,000	

When $Q_p = Q_s$, FFO incurred is all expensed for AC

The $40,000 of fixed factory overhead starts in work-in-process inventory; when the units are completed, all $40,000 is transferred to finished goods inventory. Because

—and only because—all 8,000 units were sold, the entire $40,000 was also expensed.

For direct costing the fixed overhead costs do not flow through the production accounts because they are not product costs. Since fixed factory overhead is a period cost, it is expensed as soon as it occurs—regardless of the number of units produced or sold.

$Q_s > Q_p$

***Quantity Sold* Q_s *Exceeds Quantity Produced* Q_p** Finally, we'll assume that the quantity sold is greater than the quantity produced. To consider this possibility, it is necessary to introduce a beginning inventory. If we assume that 8,000 units are going to be produced and that 10,000 units are now going to be sold during the period, we will need to have a beginning inventory of at least 2,000 units. For simplicity, we will also assume that the fixed costs assigned to the beginning inventory (from last period's production) also averaged $5 per unit.

For AC more FFO is expensed than incurred

For absorption costing the $40,000 incurred in the current period is assigned to the 8,000 units as they are produced. And these costs—when the units are completed—go to finished goods. When the 8,000 units are sold, all $40,000 (8,000 × $5 per unit) of the fixed factory overhead incurred is expensed as part of cost of goods sold expense. In addition, $10,000 (2,000 × $5 per unit) of fixed factory overhead that was incurred last period, and deferred as an asset in inventory, is expensed when the 2,000 units in beginning inventory are sold. The total fixed factory overhead expensed is the sum of these two parts:

$$(8,000 \times \$5) + (2,000 \times \$5) = 10,000 \times \$5 = \underline{\$50,000}$$

For direct costing, since fixed factory overhead is a period cost, all $40,000 is expensed as incurred.

For AC some FFO is expensed from last year

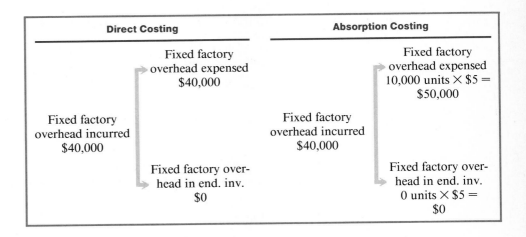

In this example the amount of fixed factory overhead expensed is now $10,000 greater for absorption costing than it is for direct costing ($40,000 + $10,000 = $50,000, vs. $40,000). Therefore, the income for direct costing will be $10,000 greater than it will be for absorption costing.

The Relationships Summarized The three situations (and associated assumptions) that we have just looked at can now be summarized in the following chart:

Summary of relationships for Q_s and Q_p

Assumption Concerning Production and Sales	Finished Goods Inventory	Fixed Overhead Expensed	Net Income
Units produced exceed units sold ($Q_p > Q_s$).	Ending inventory is higher than beginning inventory.	More expensed for direct costing	Higher for absorption costing
Units produced equal units sold ($Q_p = Q_s$).	Beginning and ending inventories are the same.	Same for both methods	Same for both methods
Units sold exceed units produced ($Q_s > Q_p$).	Ending inventory is lower than beginning inventory.	More expensed for absorption costing	Higher for direct costing

A Comprehensive Example of Direct and Absorption Costing

Now that we have a basic understanding of the difference between direct and absorption costing and why they may have different amounts of income, we are ready to begin a comprehensive example. For this example we will present complete statements for direct and absorption costing under the same three situations we just discussed in the previous section. The different situations are (1) quantity produced equals the quantity sold; (2) quantity produced exceeds the quantity sold; and (3) quantity sold exceeds the quantity produced. We will also show how to determine the difference in net incomes without even preparing the statements. We will use the same facts we presented in Example 4-1. These facts are:

The facts for a detailed example

Sales Price.		$50/unit
Variable Costs:		
Direct Materials.	$10/unit	
Direct Labor.	15/unit	
Variable Overhead	3/unit	
Variable Selling	2/unit	
Total Variable Costs.		$30/unit
Fixed Costs:		
Factory Overhead	$40,000	
Selling	25,000	
Total Fixed Costs		$65,000

The Product Costs

First, we determine the product costs per unit for the two methods. For absorption costing they are:

Product Costs— Absorption Costing

AC—FFO is a product cost

Direct Materials	$10
Direct Labor	15
Variable Factory Overhead	3
Fixed Factory Overhead ($40,000/8,000 units)	5
	$33

The only thing we need to explain concerns the fixed factory overhead cost per unit of $5. What a company typically does to get this rate under absorption costing is to estimate at the beginning of the year its production quantity for the entire year. We will assume that Prentiss Hill planned on producing 8,000 units for the year. Next, this quantity is divided into the predicted fixed factory overhead for the year to get a fixed factory overhead cost per unit. Every unit produced during the year will be assigned this same amount of fixed overhead as a product cost. If we assume that Prentiss Hill expected its fixed factory overhead for the year to be $40,000, its fixed overhead cost per unit would be $5, calculated as follows:

Determining FFO per unit for AC

$$\text{Fixed factory cost per unit} = \frac{\$40,000}{8,000 \text{ units}} = \$5 \text{ per unit}$$

When the year is over, if 8,000 units have actually been produced, with each one assigned $5, then the total units produced will cost $40,000 (8,000 × $5 per unit) of fixed factory overhead. This amount would then be equal to the actual amount of fixed factory overhead for the period that we have been assuming all along. When everything happens exactly as planned—that is, producing the quantity we expected and incurring the fixed overhead costs we expected—we avoid the complications of having a volume variance and a spending variance, which have not yet been discussed. In the current examples and in all homework assignments, we will assume for simplicity that everything we planned on actually took place. The complications of volume variances and spending variances will not be discussed until Chapter 10, which is on standard costs.

The product costs for direct costing are given below:

Product Costs—Direct Costing
DC—FFO is not a product cost

Direct Materials.........................	$10
Direct Labor............................	15
Variable Factory Overhead	3
	$28

Notice that the product costs for direct costing include all the variable manufacturing costs, but exclude the variable selling costs. Variable selling costs are not product costs because they are not associated with the production department. All costs that are not part of production are period costs.

The Solution

Exhibit 5-5 gives the results for absorption costing for 3 consecutive years, assuming production of 8,000 units and three different levels of sales:

$Q_p = 8,000$

Three different values for Q_s

1. $Q_s = 8,000$ units in year 1

2. $Q_s = 6,000$ units in year 2

3. $Q_s = 10,000$ units in year 3

Exhibit 5-6 gives the results for direct costing for the same 3 years.

EXHIBIT 5-5
Income Statements —
Absorption Costing

	Year 1	Year 2	Year 3
Units Sold.	8,000	6,000	10,000
Sales.	$400,000	$300,000	$500,000
Cost of Goods Sold Expense:			
Beginning Inventory.	$ -0-	$ -0-	$ 66,000
Costs of Production:			
Direct Materials	$ 80,000	$ 80,000	$ 80,000
Direct Labor	120,000	120,000	120,000
Variable Overhead	24,000	24,000	24,000
Fixed Overhead.	40,000	40,000	40,000
	$264,000	$264,000	$264,000
Total Costs Available for Sale	$264,000	$264,000	$330,000
Less: Ending Inventory of Finished Goods	-0-	66,000	-0-
Cost of Goods Sold Expense.	$264,000	$198,000	$330,000
Gross Margin.	$136,000	$102,000	$170,000
Selling Expenses:			
Variable Selling.	$ 16,000	$ 12,000	$ 20,000
Fixed Selling	25,000	25,000	25,000
	$ 41,000	$ 37,000	$ 45,000
Net Income	$ 95,000	$ 65,000	$125,000

EXHIBIT 5-6
Income Statements —
Direct Costing

	Year 1	Year 2	Year 3
Units Sold.	8,000	6,000	10,000
Sales.	$400,000	$300,000	$500,000
Total Variable Costs:			
Beginning Inventory.	$ -0-	$ -0-	$ 56,000
Variable Costs of Production:			
Direct Materials	$ 80,000	$ 80,000	$ 80,000
Direct Labor	120,000	120,000	120,000
Variable Overhead	24,000	24,000	24,000
	$224,000	$224,000	$224,000
Total Variable Costs Available for Sale	$224,000	$224,000	$280,000
Less: Ending Inventory of Finished Goods	-0-	56,000	-0-
Variable Cost of Goods Sold Expense	$224,000	$168,000	$280,000
Variable Selling Expenses	16,000	12,000	20,000
Total Variable Expenses	$240,000	$180,000	$300,000
Total Contribution Margin.	$160,000	$120,000	$200,000
Total Fixed Costs:			
Fixed Factory Overhead	$ 40,000	$ 40,000	$ 40,000
Fixed Selling	25,000	25,000	25,000
	$ 65,000	$ 65,000	$ 65,000
Net Income	$ 95,000	$55,000	$135,000

Explanation of Exhibits 5-5 and 5-6

In year 1 we're assuming that there is no beginning inventory of finished goods and that all units produced are sold. As a result, there is no ending inventory of finished goods.

Year 1   For absorption costing the costs of production, which include the fixed costs of $40,000, are added to the zero beginning inventory to get total costs available for sale of $264,000. Since the ending inventory is zero, the cost of goods sold is the entire $264,000. Remember, this includes all $40,000 of fixed factory overhead. When the cost of goods sold is subtracted from the sales of $400,000, we have a gross margin of $136,000, which is more than enough to cover the variable and fixed selling costs of $41,000. The net income is $95,000.

For direct costing we start with the same zero balance in inventory, and we add to it the variable manufacturing costs to get the variable costs available for sale of $224,000. Because of the zero balance in the ending finished goods inventory, $224,000 is also the variable cost of goods sold. When the variable selling costs of $16,000 are added, we have total variable costs of $240,000, which, when subtracted from the sales, leave a total contribution margin of $160,000. After the $65,000 of fixed costs — which include the $40,000 of fixed factory overhead — is subtracted, we have the exact same income as we have under absorption costing — $95,000 — a situation we expect to have whenever the units sold equal the units produced.

When $Q_s = Q_p$, FFO expensed is the same for AC and DC

Remember: The reason that the incomes are the same is that the amount of fixed factory overhead expensed, $40,000, is the same under the two methods.

In the second and third years, when the quantity produced does not equal the quantity sold, the fixed overhead expensed is not the same, so the incomes are not the same either.

Year 2   In year 2 we sold only 6,000 of the 8,000 units that we produced; therefore, some of the production costs remain in the ending inventory of finished goods.

$Q_p > Q_s$ — some of FFO stays in FG for AC

For absorption costing the costs available for sale are still $264,000, but not all of this amount is expensed since there are 2,000 units remaining in finished goods at year-end. And since the cost of this ending inventory is $66,000 (2,000 units × $33 per unit), the cost of goods sold is only $198,000 ($264,000 − $66,000). Included in the cost of goods sold total is $30,000 of fixed factory overhead (6,000 units × $5). This means that the remaining $10,000 (2,000 units × $5) of the $40,000 of fixed factory overhead is a part of the total of $66,000 in the ending inventory of finished goods.

For direct costing the variable costs available for sale are $224,000. But since there is an ending inventory of $56,000, the variable cost of goods sold is only $168,000. The $56,000 in the ending inventory includes only the variable costs of production (2,000 units × $28); the $168,000 in the variable cost of goods sold also includes only the variable costs of production (6,000 × $28). The fixed factory overhead costs of $40,000 are not part of the cost of goods sold or the ending inventory since fixed overhead is not a product cost for direct costing. Because fixed factory overhead is a period cost, all $40,000 is expensed in the year it is incurred.

The $40,000 of fixed factory overhead that is expensed under direct costing is $10,000 higher than the amount of fixed overhead that is expensed under absorption costing. This $10,000 difference in the amount of fixed overhead expensed in year 2 is the reason that the income of $55,000 for direct costing is $10,000 less than the income of $65,000 for absorption costing.

When $Q_s > Q_p$, FFO in FG at the beginning of the year is expensed in the current year

Year 3   In year 3 we have a beginning inventory. This is because 2,000 units were left unsold from the production of year 2. Under absorption costing the cost of this beginning inventory is $66,000 (2,000 units × $33 per unit); for direct costing it is $56,000 (2,000 units × $28 per unit). In year 3 we continued to produce 8,000 units, but we sold 10,000 — which includes everything we produced during year 3 plus the beginning inventory.

The cost of goods sold under absorption costing in year 3 is $330,000. This includes the costs of production for year 3 of $264,000 plus the cost of the beginning inventory of $66,000. Included in the $330,000 for the cost of goods sold is $50,000 (10,000 units × $5 per unit) of fixed factory overhead. This is composed of two parts — the $40,000 that was incurred in year 3 and assigned to the 8,000 units that were eventually sold (8,000 units × $5 per unit) and the $10,000 of fixed overhead that was incurred in year 2 and assigned to the beginning inventory (2,000 units × $5 per unit) of year 3.

Under direct costing the same $40,000 of fixed factory overhead is expensed in year 3, $10,000 less than the amount expensed under absorption costing. For this reason — and for this reason alone — the direct costing income of $135,000 is $10,000 greater than the income of $125,000 for absorption costing.

Reconciliation of Incomes under Direct and Absorption Costing

On the basis of our initial discussion of direct and absorption costing, and prior to looking at the income statements in Exhibits 5-5 and 5-6, you should have known which net income would have been higher in each of the 3 years. You would have realized this by knowing no more than the number of units produced and sold in each year.

Now we are going to explain how you could have known what the difference in the net incomes would be each year without going to the trouble of preparing statements. For example, by merely looking at the basic facts for Prentiss Hill, you could have quickly indicated that net income under direct costing would be $10,000 lower than absorption costing income in year 2, $10,000 higher in year 3, and the same in year 1 — without preparing a single line of either statement.

The explanation is simple, for it has to do with two basic facts that you already know about each year. The first is the difference in the number of units sold and produced, $Q_s - Q_p$. The second is the $5 fixed overhead cost per unit. With these two facts, the difference in profits each year can be calculated as follows:

An easy way to determine the difference in incomes for DC and AC

$$\frac{\text{Difference}}{\text{in profits}} = \frac{\text{difference in units sold}}{\text{and produced}} \times \frac{\text{fixed overhead}}{\text{cost per unit}}$$

$$= (Q_s - Q_p) \times \$5 \text{ per unit}$$

or

$$\frac{\text{Difference}}{\text{in profits}} = \frac{\text{increase (or decrease)}}{\text{in finished goods}} \times \frac{\text{fixed overhead}}{\text{cost per unit}}$$
$$\text{inventory}$$

Based upon the facts related to Prentiss Hill for each of the 3 years, the application of the first approach yields the results shown in Exhibit 5-7. When you compare the results in Exhibit 5-7 to those in Exhibits 5-5 and 5-6, you can see that the formula perfectly explains the differences in income under the two methods.

EXHIBIT 5-7 Reconciliation of Incomes for Direct and Absorption Costing

Situation	$(Q_s - Q_p)$	×	Fixed Overhead rate	=	Difference	Direct Costing Income	Absorption Costing Income	Difference
1	(8,000 – 8,000)	×	$5	=	-0-	$ 95,000	$ 95,000	-0-
2	(6,000 – 8,000)	×	$5	=	$(10,000)	55,000	65,000	$(10,000)
3	(10,000 – 8,000)	×	$5	=	10,000	135,000	125,000	10,000

Why the reconciling formula works

You may be wondering why the formulas above work so simply. Let's look at year 2 to explain it.

Remember first that for absorption costing each unit produced has $5 of fixed factory overhead assigned to it. If a unit is later sold, then the $5 is expensed at that time as part of cost of goods sold expense. On the other hand, if a unit produced is not sold during that period, then the $5 of fixed factory overhead remains in finished goods inventory as an asset. It is not expensed.

Remember next that for direct costing every dollar of fixed factory overhead is expensed as incurred. None of the fixed overhead is ever an asset. Therefore, whenever a single unit is produced but not sold, absorption costing treats the $5 as an asset, whereas direct costing treats it as an expense. If a single unit produced is not sold, direct costing has $5 more expensed than does absorption costing; therefore, the direct costing income will be $5 less. In addition, if a number of units produced are not sold, the direct costing income will be $5 less for each one of them. In year 2, 2,000 of the units produced were not sold in the same period; therefore, the income under absorption costing is higher than under direct costing by $5 for each of the 2,000 units. Thus the difference in profits is:

$$\text{Difference in income} = 2,000 \text{ units} \times \$5 = \underline{\underline{\$10,000}}$$

Reasons to use the reconciling formula

There are several situations in which you might want to use the reconciling formula for determining the difference in profits. First, you may not need to know the net income under either method, but merely how much higher one method is than the other. Using this reconciling approach is much quicker than preparing two complete sets of statements.

Second, you may need to know the incomes for both methods, but may not need complete statements. All you have to do is calculate the results for one method and then either add or subtract the difference in profits, determined by the reconciling formula.

And third, you can use the reconciling formula to check your accuracy when preparing complete statements. If the difference in the two income statements does not match the results of the reconciling formula, then quite likely you've made an arithmetic error that you need to find and correct.

CHAPTER SUMMARY

Accountants make a variety of assumptions that underlie C-V-P analysis. Several of these were evaluated in this chapter. The first assumption is that all units can be sold at the same price and that this price remains the same throughout the period. This unchanging price results in total sales which are linear with respect to activity. Economists disagree with this assumption and contend that total sales should be represented by a curve rather than a straight line. The accountant points out that from a practical standpoint, even if the curve is the better representation, the straight-line assumption is certainly acceptable within the relevant range of activity.

The second assumption is that the variable cost per unit is the same for all units produced and sold throughout the period. On the basis of this assumption of an unchanging VCU, the resulting total variable costs are represented by a straight line, extending out of the origin. Economists contend that the VCU is constantly changing with respect to activity and that total variable costs should be represented by a curve. Once again, the accountant contends that even if the curve is the better representation of total variable costs, within the relevant range the straight-line approximation of total variable costs is certainly good enough for practical purposes.

The third assumption is that the total fixed costs remain the same in response to changes in activity, during the period of analysis, and within the relevant range of activity.

The fourth assumption is that the analysis is either for a single-product firm or for a multi-product firm in which the sales mix remains the same. The *sales mix* for a firm represents the percentage of total sales that is distributed to each different product line. Different products usually have different contribution margins per unit. Therefore, the weighted average contribution margin per unit (for all products) depends upon the proportion that each product's sales are to the total sales. And since the C-V-P formulas use a weighted average CMU, the results of the analysis depend upon the assumed sales mix. For the C-V-P predictions to be correct, the sales mix that actually comes about must be the same as the sales mix originally assumed in the C-V-P model.

The final assumption of C-V-P is that there is no significant difference between beginning and ending inventories of finished goods. Or, put another way, the quantity of units produced equals the quantity of units sold. Only when this assumption is true will the net income for direct costing equal the net income for absorption costing.

Direct costing defines product costs as the variable manufacturing costs. Fixed factory overhead is a period cost and as such is expensed when incurred.

Absorption costing defines product costs as the variable and fixed manufacturing costs. The fixed factory overhead costs are expensed when the units to which they are assigned are sold rather than when the costs are incurred. The income under absorption costing is higher than under direct costing whenever production exceeds sales. When production exceeds sales, some of the fixed overhead costs that have been incurred and expensed under direct costing are deferred in finished goods under absorption costing.

When sales exceed production, income under direct costing is higher than the income under absorption costing. For absorption costing not only are the fixed costs that are incurred in the period expensed (when the units that are produced are sold), but in addition some fixed overhead incurred in a previous period (and deferred in beginning inventory) is also expensed. For direct costing only the fixed factory overhead incurred in the current period is expensed.

To determine the difference in incomes under direct and absorption costing without having to prepare both sets of income statements, use the following calculation:

$$\text{Difference in incomes} = \left[\left(\begin{matrix} \text{quantity} \\ \text{sold } Q_s \end{matrix} \right) - \left(\begin{matrix} \text{quantity} \\ \text{produced } Q_p \end{matrix} \right) \right] \times \begin{matrix} \text{fixed overhead} \\ \text{rate per unit} \end{matrix}$$

The fixed overhead rate is determined at the beginning of the year with the following calculation:

$$\begin{matrix} \text{Fixed overhead rate} \\ \text{per unit} \end{matrix} = \frac{\text{predicted fixed overhead for the year}}{\text{expected production for the year}}$$

IMPORTANT TERMS USED IN THIS CHAPTER

Absorption costing method A product costing method that assigns variable and fixed manufacturing costs to the units produced. The product costs include direct materials, direct labor, variable factory overhead, and fixed factory overhead. The costs are expensed only when the units to which they are assigned are sold. (page 178)

CHAPTER 5 The Contribution Margin Approach: Part II
Appendix 5-1: Cost-Volume-Profit Analysis with Absorption Costing

189

Direct costing method A product costing method that treats only the variable manufacturing costs as product costs. These costs include direct materials, direct labor, and variable factory overhead. Fixed factory overhead is a period cost and is expensed when incurred. (page 178)

Normal profit The fair return that an investor could have earned on his or her money if the money had been invested elsewhere. To the economist this is a cost (just like direct materials and direct labor) of doing business — a cost that has to be covered by the firm's revenues before there is any profit. (page 193)

Sales mix For a multi-product firm, the percentage of total sales that is distributed to each product line. (page 172)

Sensitivity analysis The evaluation of the effect that a change in the value of an input to a decision model has on the results of using that model. (page 170)

APPENDIX 5-1: COST-VOLUME-PROFIT ANALYSIS WITH ABSORPTION COSTING

If $Q_s = Q_p$, C-V-P analysis is the same for DC and AC

In the C-V-P analysis we presented in Chapter 4, we assumed that the quantities of units produced and sold were the same. The significance of the assumption is that the net income under direct costing will be the same as the net income under absorption costing. If this assumption is valid, the C-V-P analysis will also yield the same results — the breakeven point will be the same and the level of sales needed to have a desired income will also be the same — for direct and absorption costing.

If the assumption is not valid — that is, the number of units produced is not equal to the number of units sold — then the breakeven points under the two methods will be different. In addition, the level of sales needed to have a desired income will be different for the two methods.

The C-V-P analysis we learned in Chapter 4 works best with DC

The C-V-P analysis we explained in Chapter 4 will be satisfactory for both direct and absorption costing only when the units produced equal the units sold. When the units produced and units sold are different amounts, the approach we learned in Chapter 4 will still provide reliable results for direct costing but not for absorption costing.

For example, in Chapter 4 when we assumed that the units produced equaled the units sold, we calculated the breakeven point of 3,250 units for Prentiss Hill. At this level of sales Prentiss Hill would be expected to break even under both product costing methods. If we assume that the units produced and units sold are different amounts, however, the answer of 3,250 units is still the breakeven point with direct costing, but it is no longer the breakeven point under absorption costing.

C-V-P analysis for absorption costing is very similar to that for direct costing. You need to know two basic things that you have already learned.

First, you need to remember the contribution margin C-V-P formula, presented in Chapter 4, that is used with direct costing. Instead of using X to represent unit sales, however, the notation Q_s will be used. The formula is:

The C-V-P formula for DC

$$Q_s = \frac{\text{fixed costs} + \text{net income}}{\text{CMU}}$$

The second thing you need to remember is the reconciling formula for determining the difference in the net incomes for direct and absorption costing.

Plus the reconciling formula

$$\text{Difference in net incomes} = (Q_s - Q_p) \times \text{fixed overhead cost per unit}$$

To make the C-V-P calculation under absorption costing, simply add the reconciling formula to the numerator of the direct costing C-V-P formula. When we do this, we get the following formula for C-V-P analysis under absorption costing:

Equals the C-V-P formula for AC

$$Q_s = \frac{\text{fixed costs} + \text{net income} + (Q_s - Q_p) \times \text{fixed overhead cost per unit}}{\text{CMU}}$$

Based upon production of 8,000 units, the number of units that must be sold to break even under absorption costing is 1,667 units (rounded), determined as follows:

When $Q_p > Q_s$, breakeven for AC is less than for DC

$$Q_s = \frac{\$65,000 + \$0 + (Q_s - 8,000)\,\$5}{\$20}$$

$$\$20Q_s = \$65,000 + \$5Q_s - \$40,000$$

$$\$15Q_s = \$25,000$$

$$Q_s = \frac{\$25,000}{\$15} = 1,666.67 \text{ units}$$

Just in case you're not convinced, the following income statement proves that this is the breakeven point under absorption costing. And remember, this is only the breakeven point if the number of units produced is 8,000. Under absorption costing there would be a different breakeven for any other level of production.

If $Q_p = 8,000$ and $Q_s = 1,667$, AC will break even

Sales (1,666.67 units × $50)...		$83,333
Cost of Goods Sold:		
Direct Materials......................................	$ 80,000	
Direct Labor.......................................	120,000	
Variable Factory Overhead	24,000	
Fixed Factory Overhead............................	40,000	
	$264,000	
Ending Inventory (6,333.33 × $33)...................	209,000	
Cost of Goods Sold (1666.67 × $33)		55,000
Gross Margin		$28,333
Selling Expenses:		
Variable (1,666.67 × $2)	$ 3,333	
Fixed	25,000	28,333
Net Income		$ -0-

What would you expect the net income to be for direct costing at this level of sales? Profit or loss? Well, based upon the direct costing breakeven point of 3,250 units, net income will actually be a loss at 1666.67 units—this sales quantity is below the direct costing breakeven point.

When $Q_s = Q_p$

Let's now use both direct costing and absorption costing C-V-P formulas one more time to prove an important idea. We want to show that if the units produced and units sold are the same, the breakeven points will be the same for direct costing and absorption costing. To show this, let's assume that we are going to produce only 3,250 units. The breakeven point for direct costing is still 3,250 units:

Breakeven for DC

$$Q_s = \frac{\$65,000 + \$0}{\$20} = 3,250 \text{ units}$$

It makes no difference how many units we actually produce with direct costing—the breakeven point is still the same.

We can now calculate the breakeven point for absorption costing:

$$Q_s = \frac{\$65,000 + \$0 + (Q_s - 3,250)\ \$12.31}{\$20}$$

$$\$20Q_s = \$65,000 + \$0 + \$12.31Q_s - \$40,000$$

$$\$7.69Q_s = \$25,000$$

When $Q_s = Q_p$, breakeven points for DC and AC are the same.

$$Q_s = \frac{\$25,000}{\$7.69} = 3,250 \text{ units}$$

An important difference in the equation above and the one used when 8,000 units were produced is the fixed overhead rate. It is now $12.31 instead of $5.00, because the number of units produced is going to be 3,250, not 8,000. We assume that the production of 3,250 units had been predicted at the beginning of the year when the rate was determined. The rate was calculated in the following manner:

$$\frac{\text{Fixed overhead}}{\text{cost per unit}} = \frac{\$40,000}{3,250 \text{ units}} = \$12.31 \text{ per unit}$$

Only now, when the units produced are equal to the units sold — 3,250 — is the breakeven level for both methods 3,250 units.

Naturally, if we desire to have a profit instead of merely breaking even, we simply add the desired net income to the numerator, in place of the zero in the previous calculations.

APPENDIX 5-2: DIFFERENCES IN ACCOUNTANTS' AND ECONOMISTS' ASSUMPTIONS OF COST-VOLUME-PROFIT ANALYSIS

Several of the assumptions accountants make when using cost-volume-profit analysis differ from the assumptions made by economists. We mentioned briefly two of these differences in the text of this chapter. One of the differences concerned the sales price (and related total sales), and the other concerned the variable cost per unit (and related total variable costs).

The Different Assumptions Concerning the Sales Price

Accountant: SP is unchanging

Accountants assume there is one price for the product, regardless of the number of units sold. Therefore, total sales are represented by a straight line (see Figure 5-1).

Economists feel that total sales (which they call total revenue) should be curvilinear rather than linear. That is, economists argue that to sell additional units, the sales price must be lowered. As the price is reduced, the units sold will increase and the total sales dollars will also increase — not proportionately — but only to a point. At that point, represented by X in Figure 5-3, the total sales dollars will be at a maximum. Any further reduction in the sales price will continue to generate additional demand for units, but the total sales dollars will start to decrease.

Economist: SP is changing

The Different Assumptions for VCU

Accountant: VCU is constant

Accountants assume that the variable cost per unit is the same for all units produced and sold. Because of this assumption, total variable costs (see Figure 5-2) and total costs (variable costs plus fixed costs) are represented by a straight line.

Economist: VCU is constantly changing

As you will recall from Chapter 3, economists believe that the variable cost per unit is constantly changing. At low amounts of production the VCU is very high; as more

FIGURE 5-3
Economists' View of Total Sales
The total revenue is at a maximum at *X*. Above *X*, total revenue starts to fall.

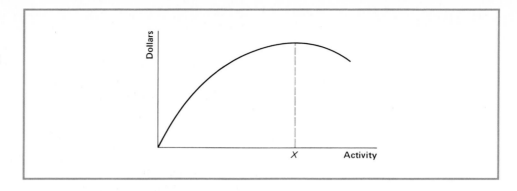

and more units are produced, the VCU falls—because increasingly large quantities can be produced more and more efficiently. As the VCU is falling, it does so more and more slowly, until it reaches a minimum point—the level of activity where average VCU is the lowest. Beyond that point the VCU begins to rise as the units are produced less and less efficiently. The economists' representation of the VCU, total variable costs as a function of sales activity, and total costs is shown in Figure 5-4.

Within the relevant range, accountants' assumptions are acceptable

Although accountants' and economists' assumptions concerning the sales price and VCU don't agree, the two approaches can be reconciled for practical purposes within the concept of the relevant range. Remember, we accountants don't necessarily reject the economists' view of curvilinearity. But we do argue that within the relevant range of activity any curves in the lines are minor and the use of straight lines to depict the behavior of total sales, total variable costs, and total costs is certainly good enough, even if it is not always strictly theoretically valid.

Other Differences

The graphic representations of total sales and total costs are combined for both accountants and economists in the two cost-volume-profit graphs in Figure 5-5. In addition to the differences relating to sales and total costs, two other differences can be seen in the graphs:

FIGURE 5-4 Economists' View of VCU, Total Variable Costs, and Total Costs
The addition of TFC to the middle graph gives us the third graph.

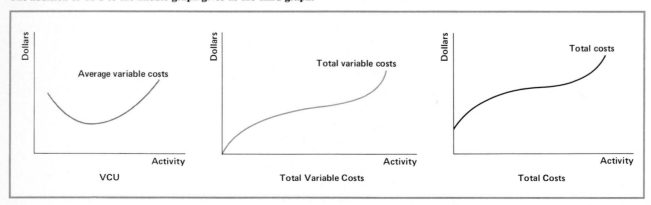

**FIGURE 5-5
Accountants' and
Economists' Versions of
CVP Graphs**

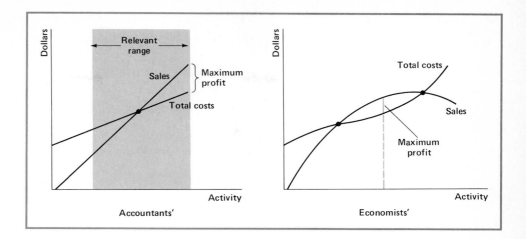

One vs. two BE points

1. The accountants' graph shows only one breakeven point (BE). The economists' graph indicates that there are two breakeven points.

2. The economists' graph indicates that there is a point of maximum profit between the two breakeven points. The activity at which profit is maximum is at the point where the vertical positive distance between the sales curve and the total costs curve is the greatest. The accountants' graph seems to indicate that unlimited profits are possible; that is, as long as production and sales are increasing, profits will rise. However, this is incorrect. What the accountant assumes is that profits are at a maximum, within the relevant range of activity, at the maximum point within that range.

Maximum profit

There is one additional difference in accountants' and economists' assumptions for C-V-P analysis. This one, however, is not evident from the graphs alone. It involves the economists' concept of *normal profit.*

Normal profit

3. Included in the total costs for economists is a ***normal profit,*** or normal return. This represents the fair return that the investors could have gotten on their investment if they had invested elsewhere. For the owner-manager it also represents the fair wage that the owner would have earned by working in someone else's business. Economists do not acknowledge having any profit—which they call a "pure" profit—until all costs, including this normal return, are covered by the sales. On the other hand, accountants do not include the normal return as one of the costs that have to be covered by sales. Instead, the normal return is simply an indistinguishable part of accounting profit.

QUESTIONS

1. Discuss three differences between the accountants' and the economists' view of cost-volume-profit analysis.

2. Each of the five accounting assumptions underlying cost-volume-profit analysis represents something that accountants argue can never change throughout the analysis. Discuss.

3. List the five different accounting assumptions that underlie cost-volume-profit analysis.

4. Discuss the significance of the relevant range to cost-volume-profit analysis.

5. Define the term *sales mix.* What is the assumption made in C-V-P analysis concerning the sales mix?

6. What is the significance of the C-V-P assumption "For a multi-product firm the sales mix remains unchanged"?

7. A firm sells two products, A and B, both of which are expected to be 50% of total sales during the first year of operation. After the first year, it was determined that the sales mix for A and B was 75% and 25%, respectively. Discuss the consequence of this change in the sales mix for the cost-volume-profit analysis of the firm.

8. "If all products of a multi-product firm had the same contribution margin per unit, the sales mix would have no effect on the cost-volume-profit analysis." Explain why you either agree or disagree with the statement.

9. "Total contribution margin and total gross profit will never be the same for a manufacturer." True or false? Explain.

10. Define the terms *direct costing* and *absorption costing.*

11. Explain why the incomes under direct costing and absorption costing are the same when the units produced and units sold are equal.

12. Explain why the income under direct costing is less than the income under absorption costing when the units produced exceed the units sold.

13. Discuss the significance of the cost-volume-profit assumption "There are no significant differences in the beginning and ending inventories."

14. Opponents of absorption costing contend that there are too many ways to manipulate income with this costing method. One way has to do with the level of production. If you wanted to increase income by merely changing the level of production, how would you do it?

15. The only level of activity that affects direct costing income is sales. Is this also true for absorption costing? Explain.

16. If you want to know which income—direct costing or absorption costing—will be higher in a given situation, how do you decide without preparing income statements? How do you determine the difference in incomes without preparing separate income statements?

EXERCISES

Exercise 5-1
Specifying how changes in key variables affect C-V-P analysis

For each situation in the table below, determine the effect on the total contribution margin, the breakeven point, and the net income for the firm. Choose one of the five following effects for each answer:

a. Doubles
b. Increases more than double
c. Increases less than double
d. No change
e. Decreases

Place the correct letter in the spaces provided.

	Effect on:		
	Total Contribution Margin	Breakeven Point	Net Income*
1. Units sold double.	_____	_____	_____
2. Sales price doubles.	_____	_____	_____
3. Variable cost per unit increases by 10%.	_____	_____	_____
4. Sales price and variable cost per unit both double.	_____	_____	_____
5. Fixed costs double.	_____	_____	_____
6. Fixed costs are cut in half.	_____	_____	_____
7. Sales mix changes from 40:60 to 70:30 for products having contribution margins per unit of $20 and $30, respectively.	_____	_____	_____

* Before tax.

Exercise 5-2
Doing straightforward C-V-P analysis for two products

The McEnconnors Company sells two tennis racket models—the Prince and the Pauper. The contribution margins per unit, respectively, are $40 and $20. The fixed costs for the company are $35,000. Sales are expected to be distributed to Prince and Pauper in a 40:60 ratio.

a. Determine the number of units of each product that must be sold in order for McEnconnors to show a $50,000 profit, assuming the sales mix is exactly as expected.
b. If the sales mix changes from 40:60 to 50:50, how many units of each product would now be required to have a profit of $50,000?

(Check figure: Prince = 1,416.5 units)

Exercise 5-3
Doing C-V-P analysis— units and dollars—for a two-product firm

The Paspalakis Company has recently opened a ticket-scalping booth outside Yankee Stadium. The owner purchases his tickets from season-ticket holders who cannot attend games and then resells them at an escalated price for any games that are sellouts. His income statement for the last game is given below:

	Type of Ticket		
	General Admission	Reserved	Total
Number of Tickets..................................	600	200	800
Total Revenue	$6,000	$3,000	$9,000
Cost of Tickets	1,800	1,000	2,800
	$4,200	$2,000	$6,200
Allocated Fixed Costs	400	400	800
Income for Game...................................	$3,800	$1,600	$5,400

a. Determine the sales mix based on (1) the number of tickets sold and (2) the amount of dollar sales.
b. Determine the weighted average (1) contribution margin per unit and (2) contribution margin percentage.
c. Calculate the breakeven point in units (in total and by product line).

(Check figure: 103)

d. Calculate the breakeven point in dollars (in total and by product line).

Exercise 5-4
Doing improper C-V-P analysis for a multi-product firm

The Goodstone Tire & Rubber Company sells two types of tires—firsts and seconds. The firsts have a contribution margin per unit of $6 and the seconds, $2. During last month the sales were 5,000 for the firsts and 20,000 for the seconds. The fixed costs of $50,000 are allocated evenly to each product line.

a. Determine the sales mix for last month.
b. What assumption do we make concerning this sales mix?
c. Calculate the breakeven point for each product line by dividing the product's allocated fixed costs by the product's contribution margin per unit.
d. Using your answer in part c, determine the new sales mix.
e. Why is your answer in part c wrong, in light of your answer in part b.

Exercise 5-5
Working backward to get the sales mix

The Petrocelli Pizza Parlor sells two types of pizzas—large and extralarge. The following relevant information concerning these two products has just been determined by Paula Petrocelli, the daughter of the owner:

	Large	Extra-large
Sales price	$8	$12
Cost per pizza..................	$3	$4
Pizzas sold in April	2,000	1,500

The total fixed costs are $12,000 per month.

If all variables except the sales mix are expected to remain the same in May, what would the sales mix have to be in order to increase the income to $12,500?

(Check figure: Weighted average CMU = $7)

Exercise 5-6
Determining two variations for VCU and TFC—breakeven and indifference points

The following facts relate to the operations of the Cosby Company in 1989:

Units Sold..		15,000
Sales Price...		$80/unit
Variable Costs:		
Manufacturing	$20/unit	
Selling...	10/unit	
Total Variable Costs...............................		$30/unit
Fixed Costs:		
Manufacturing	$250,000	
Selling...	180,000	
Total Fixed Costs		$430,000

In 1989 Cosby expects to reduce its selling price by $5 because of a 20% decrease in the variable costs of production. In addition, a salesperson who is currently on commission (5% of total sales) will switch to a fixed salary of $5,000 per month.

a. Determine the breakeven points under the old and new plans.
b. Determine the incomes under the old and new plans for sales of (1) 12,000 units and (2) 24,000 units.
c. Determine the indifference point (i.e., the level of sales at which the incomes under the old and new plans are equal).

(Check figure: Income = $570,000 at indifference point)

Exercise 5-7
Determining breakeven, income, and indifference points for different plans

The Hilman Publishing Company sells two products—a textbook and a study guide. Because of the market for used books, sales of new books drop substantially during each year of the three-year life of a book, even if the number of adoptions remain virtually unchanged. The budgeted sales for the sixteenth edition of the text are as follows over the next three years:

Year	Sales
1988	50,000 books
1989	30,000 books
1990	10,000 books

The percentage of total sales represented by the study guide increases in each of the three years since there is very little of a used book market for them. In 1988, the study guide sales are expected to be equal to the textbook sales (in terms of unit sales, not dollar sales). In 1989, the unit sales for the study guide will be 50% higher than the sales for the text; and in 1990 the study guide sales will triple the sales of the text.

Additional relevant data related to each product are as follows:

	Products	
	Textbook	**Study Guide**
Sales price...	$45	$15
Variable cost per unit..............................	30	5
Contribution margin per unit........................	$15	$10
Allocated fixed costs...............................	$400,000	$300,000

a. Determine the sales mix for each year.
b. Determine the incomes for 1988 and 1989.
c. Determine the breakeven point in 1988 and 1989 (in total units and by product line).
d. How many total units would have to be sold in 1989 to have the same income as Hilman expects to have in 1988?

Exercise 5-8
Determining sensitivity of results to changes in variables

The Pace Company sells a single product called New Spice Deodorant. The Pace Company's 1989 income statement is shown below:

Sales (10,000 jars @ $3 per jar)................	$ 30,000
Variable Costs...............................	(13,500)
Fixed Costs (advertising).....................	(12,000)
Net Income	$ 4,500

a. Determine the breakeven point (in dollars).
b. How many units need to be sold in order to show a profit of $20,000?
c. A 25% increase in advertising, accompanied by a 6% reduction in the sales price, is expected to increase unit sales by 30%. What will be the new net income? *(Check figure: $4,110)*

Exercise 5-9
Doing breakeven and sensitivity analysis

The Sibbald Nursery sells all its plants for $5.00 per plant. Its variable costs average $1.50 per plant, and its fixed costs are $10,000. In 1988 Sibbald sold 9,000 plants.

a. How many plants have to be sold so that Sibbald will have a net income of 20% of sales?
b. Sibbald is going to reduce its price from $5.00 to $4.80 since the variable costs are expected to drop by $0.40 per plant. How many plants will have to be sold in 1989 in order to have the same net income as in 1988? *(Check figure: 8,514 plants)*

Exercise 5-10
Computing different incomes for DC and AC

The Mitchell Company plans to produce and sell 10,000 units in 1988 and expects the following costs for the year:

Direct Materials...........................	$10 per unit
Direct Labor..............................	$15 per unit
Variable Overhead.........................	$3 per unit
Variable Selling	$2 per unit
Variable Administrative....................	$1 per unit

Fixed Factory Overhead.................... $100,000
Fixed Selling............................. $60,000
Fixed Administrative $30,000

The sales price is $50 per unit.

a. Compute the product cost per unit for the absorption costing method.

(Check figure: $38)

b. Compute the product cost per unit for direct costing.

c. Prepare an income statement for the Mitchell Company using (1) direct costing and (2) absorption costing.

Exercise 5-11
Determining different
incomes from differences
in inventory

The Iacocca Cola Company had fixed costs of $100,000 ($60,000 of the total relates to manufacturing) in 1988. During the same year it produced 80,000 cases of soda, exactly what it had expected to produce at the beginning of the year. The variable costs are $3.50 per case ($0.50 of which relates to the distribution of the product). The sales price is $9.00 per case.

a. If 75,000 cases are sold, which income method (direct or absorption) will have the highest income? How much higher will the income be?

b. Answer part **a** again, assuming this time that 90,000 cases are sold.

Exercise 5-12
Specifying which is
higher—DC or AC

For each situation below concerning the production and sale of a product, fill in each blank with the letter D (direct costing), A (absorption costing), or N (no difference):

	Which Method Has the Highest:			
	Sales	**Cost of Ending Inventory**	**Income**	**Breakeven Point**
Quantity produced > quantity sold	_____	_____	_____	_____
Finished goods inventory decreases	_____	_____	_____	_____
Quantity sold = quantity produced	_____	_____	_____	_____

PROBLEMS: SET A

Problem A5-1
Determining sensitivity of
results to changing
variables

Lisel Gonzalez starts a small manufacturing company that will produce and sell silk honors sashes for college graduates. The company controller, Jeannie Us, estimates the following data concerning activity for its first year of operation, 1989:

Sales Price............................. $5.00 per sash
Expected Sales .... 150,000 sashes
Direct Materials........................ $1.00 per sash
Direct Labor........................... $0.75 per sash
Variable Overhead .... $0.25 per sash
Fixed Overhead $80,000
Variable Selling .... $0.20 per sash
Fixed Selling.......................... $60,000

There are no beginning or ending inventories of finished goods.

Required

1. How many sashes would have to be sold in 1989 in order to show a profit of $200,000?
2. If the variable manufacturing costs can be reduced by 10%, and the fixed costs reduced by $5,000, what would the sales price have to be in order to break even?
3. Based on the original facts, assume that Lisel is considering eliminating the fixed selling costs (all salaries) in favor of increasing the commission paid to salespeople by $0.50 per

sash. How many sashes would have to be sold in order for the income to be the same under the fixed salary and the increased commission situations? *(Check figure: 120,000 sashes)*

Problem A5-2
Using the formula CMU =
change in income ÷
change in activity

The Citrus Rich Vitamin Company produces two types of vitamin C tablets: chewable and nonchewable. At the end of its first year of operations, Citrus Rich sold 45,000 cases of the chewable vitamins and 55,000 cases of the nonchewables. The product-line income statements showed a profit (before tax) for the chewables of $1,750,000 and a profit (before tax) for the nonchewables of $1,700,000. On the basis of projections made by its sales force, Citrus Rich foresees much better results for its second year of operations:

| | Budgeted Results for Year 2 | | |
	Chewables	Nonchewables	Total
Unit sales (in cases)......................	67,500	82,500	150,000
Projected income before tax	$2,875,000	$2,800,000	$5,675,000

The fixed costs are allocated 50:50 to the two products and will be the same amount as long as total production never exceeds 200,000 cases. Once production reaches 200,000 cases, it will be necessary to add to the productive capacity. Each increase of 100,000 cases of capacity will cost approximately an additional $200,000.

Required

1. Determine the contribution margin per unit for each product line and the total fixed costs.
2. Determine the breakeven point, in total and by product line.
3. How many cases of each product line would have to be sold in order to have a net income of $10,800,000? The income tax rate is 40%. *(Check figure: 440,449)*

Problem A5-3
Doing C-V-P analysis for a
multi-product firm

Jackson's T-Shirt Emporium sells two types of t-shirts: the Michael and the Group. A condensed income statement is shown below for the company's first year of operation:

	Michael	Group	Total
Shirts Sold......................	100,000	150,000	250,000
Total Contribution Margin	$1,000,000	$600,000	$1,600,000
Fixed Costs	400,000	250,000	650,000
Net Income.....................	$ 600,000	$350,000	$ 950,000

Required

1. Determine the sales mix for the two products.
2. Determine the weighted average contribution margin per unit.
3. Determine the breakeven point for the firm as a whole. How many shirts of each type would be sold? *(Check figure: 40,625 Michael shirts)*
4. Prepare income statements for the firm as a whole and for each product line, based upon your answer in part 3.

Problem A5-4
Analyzing the effect of
changing variables

During 1988 the Gustavo Company produced and sold 10,000 units of its product line, which resulted in a profit of $100,000. Its fixed costs were $200,000, which was $25,000 less than they were expected to be in 1988. Gustavo plans to revise its sales price in such a way as to increase the contribution margin per unit by $2 during 1989.

Required

1. Gustavo would like to double the 1988 profit in 1989; how many units would the company have to sell in order to accomplish this goal?

2. Assume that the fixed costs in 1989 are going to remain the same as they were in 1988 but that the contribution margin is still going to increase by $2 per unit. How many units would Gustavo have to sell in 1989 in order to have as much income in 1989 as in 1988?

3. Assume now that the fixed costs are going to increase by $50,000 and that the contribution margin per unit is going to change, but we're not sure what it is going to be. Finally, assume that the 1989 sales are expected to be 15,000 units. What will the contribution margin per unit have to be in 1989 in order to earn a profit of $150,000?

(Check figure: $26.67)

Problem A5-5
Preparing income statements for DC and AC when $Q_p \neq Q_s$

During 1989 the Billy Martin Company produced and sold 15,000 boxing punching bags and prepared the following income statement:

Sales Revenue		$600,000
Cost of Goods Sold:		
Direct Materials	$ 80,000	
Direct Labor	100,000	
Variable Overhead	40,000	
Fixed Overhead	60,000	280,000
Gross Profit		$320,000
Selling and Administrative:		
Variable	$130,000	
Fixed	70,000	200,000
Net Income		$120,000

At the beginning of 1989 Billy Martin had used an expected production level of activity to determine the fixed factory overhead rate. There were no beginning or ending inventories of finished goods.

Required

1. Reconstruct the income statement using the contribution margin format.
2. Assume that 15,000 units were produced but that the unit sales were only 14,000. Prepare income statements for both direct costing and absorption costing.
3. Assume now that there were 2,000 units on hand in finished goods at the beginning of 1989. Billy Martin continued to produce 15,000 units, but 17,000 units were sold. The cost per unit in beginning inventory is the same as it is in 1989. Prepare income statements for direct and absorption costing.

(Check figure: Absorption net income = $145,333)

Problem A5-6
Doing C-V-P analysis — DC and AC — when $Q_p \neq Q_s$

During 1988 the Cardigan Water Softener Company produced and sold 6,000 water softeners at $400 apiece. Its income statement is below:

Sales		$2,400,000
Total Variable Costs:		
Manufacturing	$840,000	
Selling	120,000	960,000
		$1,440,000
Total Fixed Costs:		
Manufacturing	$900,000	
Selling	300,000	1,200,000
		$ 240,000

At the beginning of 1988 Cardigan expected to produce 6,000 water softeners.

| Required |

1. What was Cardigan's income for 1988 under the absorption costing method?
2. What is the breakeven (in units) for (a) direct costing and (b) absorption costing?
3. If Cardigan produces 6,000 units in 1989 but sells 7,000 units, what will be the income for each method?

Problem A5-7
Determining the effect of changing inventories on C-V-P analysis for absorption costing

The Larouche Company produces strait jackets. At the beginning of 1990 the controller made the following projections for the upcoming year:

Expected Production and Sales...... 250 strait jackets
Sales Price...................... $800 per strait jacket
Variable Manufacturing Costs....... $250 per strait jacket
Fixed Manufacturing Costs $45,000
Variable Selling Costs .... $50 per strait jacket
Fixed Selling Costs................. $5,000
Tax Rate 45%
Dividend Rate..................... 70%

When the year was over, the controller determined that 250 strait jackets were actually produced and that 200 were sold.

| Required |

1. Before you prepare an income statement for direct or absorption costing, indicate which method will have the most income before tax. What will be the difference in the incomes before tax for the two methods?
2. Prepare income statements (after tax) for both direct costing and absorption costing.
3. How many strait jackets will need to be sold in order for Larouche to pay out dividends of $35,000? Dividends will be paid out based on the income reported in the financial statements issued to stockholders.

(Check figure: 300)

Problem A5-8
Doing sensitivity analysis

Mr. Hyper is an emotional wreck. He started a new business on the basis of his accountant's projections concerning Hyper's first year of operation. The accountant indicated that Hyper could earn $45,000 (after tax) in the first year, basing his projections on the following assumptions:

Sales Price..................................... $80
Variable Cost per Unit......................... $55
Total Fixed Costs.............................. $50,000
Tax Rate 25%

The accountant waited until Hyper had made his investment before he told Hyper that the projections and assumptions were basically calculated guesses and that the projected income would come about only if all the assumptions were valid. The accountant pointed out that the results could be significantly different if the original assumptions were incorrect. Hyper then hired a new accountant and asked him the questions presented below.

| Required |

Consider each part below independently:

1. By how much would the unit sales have to fall below the original "calculated guesses" before the company would experience a loss?
2. If the contribution margin was actually $5 higher than expected, what would be the difference between the actual net income and the original projection of $45,000?
3. If the unit sales are 5,000 higher than predicted by the first accountant, what will be the correct breakeven point?

4. Which of the changes below will have the greatest percentage impact on net income?
   a. A 5% increase in the sales price
   b. A 5% decrease in the variable cost per unit
   c. A 5% decrease in fixed costs
   d. A 5% decrease in the tax rate (5% × .25)

PROBLEMS: SET B

Problem B5-1
Determining the effect of changing variables on C-V-P results

Merrick Merry Minstrels specializes in performing "surprises" for unsuspecting people on momentous occasions such as birthdays and anniversaries and at any other good time. Merrick charges the same price no matter what the occasion is or who the unsuspecting person is. The income earned by Merrick in 1988 was $25,000, based on 250 surprises during the year. The fixed costs of running Merrick Merry Minstrels are $5,000 per year.

Required

1. How many surprises does Merrick have to perform each year in order to break even?
2. Merrick plans to increase its fee next year by $25 per surprise. How many surprises will it have to perform in order to show a profit in 1989 equal to that in 1988?
3. Disregard the change in part 2. Instead, assume that the fixed costs are going to increase by 20% in 1989 but that Merrick still expects the income for the year to double. What will be Merrick's margin of safety in 1989?

(Check figure: 417)

Problem B5-2
Doing C-V-P analysis for a multi-product firm — change in income and relevant ranges

Wood Products is a company that manufactures and sells two types of swing sets. The basic model is called Swingalong and the deluxe model is called Jungle Gym. The fixed costs (allocated evenly between the two products) for Wood Products depend upon the relevant range of activity:

Relevant Range	Total Fixed Costs
1. 0–1,000.....................................	Lowest
2. 1,001–2,000.....................................	$20,000 higher than range 1
3. 2,001–3,000.....................................	$50,000 higher than range 1

Any increase in fixed costs that is needed to go to a higher range of activity is divided evenly between the two products.

In both 1988 and 1989 the two products were sold in a 70:30 ratio. Total unit sales were 800 in 1988 and 1,200 in 1989; the net incomes (net of taxes at 40%) for these 2 years were $89,200 ($52,200 for Swingalong and $37,000 for Jungle Gym) and $190,400 ($121,800 for Swingalong and $69,000 for Jungle Gym), respectively.

Required

1. Determine the contribution margin per unit and total allocated fixed costs for each product line.

(Check figure: CMU, Swingalong = $450)

2. Determine the breakeven point, in total and by product line.
3. How many units of each swing set would have to be sold in order to have a net income of $480,000?

Problem B5-3
Doing C-V-P analysis for a multi-product firm

The Napa Valley Wine Stand sells bottles of wine on the side of the road. Its motto is "We sell our wine just in time." Napa sells two types of wine — Chipper Chablis and Rosé Red — both of which are bought at the back door of local wineries. During 1988 Napa sold 2,000 bottles of Chipper Chablis and 3,000 bottles of Rosé Red. The income statement for Napa for 1988 is 'as follows:

	Chipper Chablis	Rosé Red	Total
Sales	$4,000	$9,000	$13,000
Variable Costs................................	1,000	3,000	4,000
Total Contribution Margin	$3,000	$6,000	$9,000
Fixed Costs	500	1,000	1,500
Net Income	$2,500	$5,000	$7,500

Required

1. Determine the sales mix for Chipper Chablis and Rosé Red.
2. Compute the weighted average contribution margin per unit.
3. Using your answer to part 2, determine the breakeven point for the entire firm. How many bottles of each type of wine would be sold in order to break even?

(Check figure: Chipper Chablis = 333 bottles)

4. Prepare the income statements for each product line and the firm as a whole on the basis of the answers to part 3.

Problem B5-4
Doing C-V-P analysis —
income stated as % and
per unit

The Calgary Oilers hockey team estimates that each fan spends $4 per game for refreshments in addition to the $6 price of admission. Its controller estimates further the following costs based upon a 40-game home schedule:

Variable operating costs	$6.50 per fan
Salaries...........................	$3,000,000 per year
Arena rental	$250,000 per year
Advertising	$750,000 per year

Required

1. How big would the arena have to be in order for Calgary to show a $500,000 profit, assuming all games are sellouts?
2. If the variable operating costs are overstated by 20%, how much smaller could the arena be in order to have the same profit as in part 1?
3. Using the arena size determined in part 1, by what amount would income be reduced if the arena is sold out 50% of the time, and averages 80% of full capacity for the remaining home games?

(Check figure: $449,982)

Problem B5-5
Preparing income
statements for DC and AC
when $Q_p \neq Q_s$

Charlie Moore Farms produced and sold 800,000 packages of eggs during 1988, incurring the following revenues, expenses, and income:

Sales		$200,000
Cost of Goods Sold:		
Direct Materials.......................................	$50,000	
Direct Labor..	25,000	
Variable Overhead.....................................	12,500	
Fixed Overhead	37,500	125,000
Gross Profit		$ 75,000
Selling and Administrative Expenses*		30,000
Net Income		$ 45,000

* $15,000 of this total is fixed.

At the beginning of 1989 Moore, the owner, estimates that he will produce 800,000 packages but will sell only 750,000.

Required	1. Assume that in 1989 the results turned out as planned. Prepare new income statements for direct costing and absorption costing.
	2. Assume now that 800,000 packages were produced in 1989 and that all of these were sold. In addition, however, another 100,000 packages were sold from the beginning inventory. Prepare income statements for direct and absorption costing. Assume there were only 100,000 units in beginning inventory. The cost per unit is the same as it is in 1989.

Problem B5-6
Doing C-V-P analysis — DC
and AC — when $Q_p \neq Q_s$

The 1988 income statement for the Seduzzi Company is given below. Seduzzi is a manufacturer of hot tubs.

Sales (800 hot tubs)		$1,200,000
Cost of Goods Sold:		
Variable Manufacturing.....................................	$420,000	
Fixed Manufacturing	60,000	480,000
		$ 720,000
Operating Costs:		
Variable..	$450,000	
Fixed	150,000	600,000
		$ 120,000

Seduzzi produced 800 hot tubs during 1988, exactly the number it predicted at the beginning of the year when the fixed overhead rate was determined.

Required	1. What was Seduzzi's income for 1988 under the direct costing method?
	2. What is the breakeven point (in units) for **(a)** direct costing and **(b)** absorption costing?
	3. If Seduzzi produces 800 units in 1989 but sells 1,000 units, what will be the income for each method? Assume Seduzzi had a beginning inventory of 300 units and that the fixed overhead rate in 1989 is the same as in 1988.
	4. Assume that Seduzzi's fixed overhead rate is still $75 per tub and that the unit sales will not exceed 800 in 1989. How many units would Seduzzi have to produce in order to have an income for the year of $180,000 under absorption costing?
	5. Using your answer in part 4, determine the income for direct costing.

Problem B5-7
Doing C-V-P analysis — AC
and DC — when FG
changes

The Decoded Satellite Dish Company produces a state-of-the-art satellite dish. What makes this company's product so special is that it will automatically unscramble the scrambled reception of all movie channels without having to purchase a decoder box. At the beginning of 1990, the controller prepared the following projected income statement for the upcoming year. It was based upon expected production of 200 dishes and sales of only 180 dishes.

Sales (180 dishes)...		$540,000
Cost of Goods Sold:		
Finished Goods, Jan. 1, 1989 (30 dishes).....................	$ 54,000	
Cost of Goods Manufactured		
(200 dishes)	360,000	
Total Available for Sale......................................	$414,000	
Finished Goods, Dec. 31, 1989 (50 dishes)	90,000	324,000
Gross Margin		$216,000
Operating Expenses:		
Variable..	$ 36,000	
Fixed	20,000	56,000
Income before Tax		$160,000
Income Tax...		48,000
Net Income..		$112,000

The fixed factory overhead that was budgeted for the year was $60,000.

Required	

1. Without preparing an income statement, determine the projected net income under direct costing.
2. Assume that the production for 1990 was actually 180 dishes and that all the dishes on hand during the year were sold. Prepare income statements for both direct costing and absorption costing.
3. Still assuming that 180 dishes were produced in 1990, how many dishes would have to be sold in order for Decoded to pay out dividends of $35,000? Dividends will be paid at 60% of absorption costing net income.
4. Assume that Decoded is fairly certain that 180 dishes will be sold in 1990. In addition, the controller realizes that the only way net income can be increased above the amount shown in the projected income statement is by increasing production. How many dishes would have to be produced if Decoded desires an income before tax of $200,000?

(Check figure: 333 dishes)

Problem B5-8
Doing a sensitivity analysis

As a student, Sandra Bedford suffered from test anxiety whenever she took an accounting exam. After going through several years of analysis and switching her major from accounting to psychology, she was finally cured. Knowing that many students suffer from the same problem, she has decided to conduct seminars for accounting majors at different universities. Each seminar, called "How to Lick Test Anxiety — Getting to Know Your Phobias," will last 8 hours and will cost $50 per student. She estimated her variable costs for materials and lunches to be $15 per student and her fixed costs for room rentals to be about $300 per seminar. In addition, she feels that 25 students on the average will attend each seminar. She realizes that each of these variables might be different from what she's estimated and wonders how a change in each variable might affect her results.

Required	

1. On the basis of her original estimates, how many students would have to attend the seminars in order for Bedford to break even? What is the projected income if all estimates are correct?
2. Three possible errors in estimating key variables in the C-V-P model are given below. Which of the three will have the most significant effect on net income?
   a. An overestimate of 10% for the variable cost rate
   b. An underestimate of 10% for the student demand
   c. An overestimate of 10% for the fixed costs
3. Assume that the fixed costs at Bedford's first seminar are actually $500 and that the variable costs are 10% higher per unit than she expected. What would the price for the seminar have to be in order for Bedford to have the income she originally projected, based on 25 students attending?
4. Assume the same changes that were listed in part 3. Also assume that promotional flyers have already been sent out, listing the price of the seminar as $50. How many students would have to register in order for the seminar to generate the same income as Bedford's estimate based on the original projections?

Relevant Information for Special Decisions

After you have finished studying this chapter, you will understand:

- What we mean by the term *relevant information*
- How to determine the normal price for recurring sales
- When it is appropriate to accept a special order
- How to maximize the profits in a multi-product firm
- When an organization should produce its raw materials internally rather than buy them from an outside supplier
- What we mean by a *joint product;* and what happens to the joint product at the stage in production called the *split-off point*
- How to decide if a joint product should be sold at the split-off point or processed further
- Whether to scrap or rework defective units
- How to use the graphic method of linear programming
- How to determine the economic order quantity for a firm's inventory

The profits that a firm reports in a particular year are a reflection of the decisions that its managers made in that year and in preceding years. And the decisions that managers make today will have an impact on next year's profits, and maybe on the profits for many years after that. Decisions such as the price at which to sell a product, whether to accept a special order at a price that is lower than the regular price, and whether to drop an apparently unprofitable product line all put managers in a position of choosing between at least two, and perhaps more, alternatives. In each case the manager is expected to select the alternative that is the most profitable for the firm as a whole.

This is where the accountant comes in. The manager depends on the accountant to provide complete and pertinent information concerning each alternative. Only with all the facts can the manager make the correct choice. The information that accountants provide managers to help them make these decisions must have a special quality: The information must be *relevant.* In this chapter we will be concerned with

[206]

those decisions that primarily affect the organization's short-run profit picture and with the information that is relevant to the short-run decision alternatives. In Chapters 7 and 8 we will direct our attention to those decisions that have an impact on long-run profits.

THE CONCEPT OF RELEVANCE

Two criteria for relevance

In order for information (costs or revenue) to be ***relevant*** to a decision, the information must meet two criteria. It must (1) relate to the future and (2) be different for each alternative being considered. Information that fails to meet either one of these two criteria is considered to be ***irrelevant.***

First, the information must relate to the future — because all decisions relate to the future. Managers are concerned with what they are going to do today and tomorrow; it is too late for them to dwell on what they could have done yesterday or last year. Since the alternatives under consideration involve possible future courses of action, the information that accountants gather should also be about the future. *The past is irrelevant.*

In order for information to be relevant, it must also be different for the alternatives being considered. Otherwise, there is no quantitative basis for a decision. If the facts are the same concerning different courses of action, how can we decide if one course of action is better than any other?

Assume for a moment that you are trying to decide where you want to go for dinner, and you are considering only two possibilities — McDonald's and Burger King — both of which are on University Avenue. The last time you went to McDonald's, a hamburger, fries, and a cola cost you $1.59; the same dinner cost you only $1.49 at Burger King. You've heard, however, that a hamburger, cola, and fries now costs $1.79 at McDonald's and $1.85 at Burger King. You figure that it will cost $0.50 for gas no matter which place you go. Assuming that you like the meals at McDonald's as much as you do those at Burger King, where would you go for dinner in order to keep your costs as low as possible?

The key to any decision — whether it is as simple as where to go for dinner or extremely complex — is to first decide what information is relevant to the decision and what information is irrelevant. For the situation above the only information that is relevant is the cost that you will pay today for dinner — $1.79 at McDonald's and $1.85 at Burger King. These are the only costs that both (1) relate to the future and (2) are different for the two alternatives. The amounts you paid the last time you went to dinner are irrelevant, because they relate to the past. The cost of gasoline is irrelevant, because it is the same amount whether you go to McDonald's or Burger King. Therefore, if you want to minimize the cost of dinner, go to McDonald's and save $0.06 ($1.85 − $1.79).

As you might expect, the decision situations that we are going to discuss later in this chapter are a bit more complicated than the one above. However, the concept of relevance never changes — if you know the two criteria for relevance, you should be able to apply the concept to any situation. Unfortunately, some students have trouble with the concept of relevance because they confuse it with other concepts discussed earlier in the text.

Just in case you might be one of these students, let's see how you answer the following questions. Are relevant costs the same as variable costs? Must information be accurate to be relevant? Is information that relates to the past *ever* relevant? Is information that relates to the past *always* useless? The correct answer to each of these questions is definitely *no.* If you answered *yes* to any of them, be sure to read the next three sections very carefully—because there is probably still something missing in your understanding of this important concept.

Relevance vs. Variable and Fixed Costs

Is relevant the same as variable?

A common mistake is to conclude that relevant costs and variable costs mean the same thing or that irrelevant costs and fixed costs mean the same thing. Variable and fixed costs are defined in terms of how total costs respond to changes in activity, not in terms of whether or not the totals are different for alternative courses of action.

Variable costs can be relevant or irrelevant; fixed costs can be relevant or irrelevant. Whether or not each cost is relevant depends on the alternatives being considered. For example, assume that a firm is considering the purchase of two new machines, each having a 4-year life. Each machine produces the same product and each product requires the same amount of direct materials—$36,000 per year. Machine 1 costs $100,000 and machine 2 costs $200,000. The direct labor costs for machine 1 are much higher than those for machine 2—$50,000 vs. $32,000 per year. The supervisor who is currently employed by the firm is capable of overseeing the operations of either machine. His annual salary is $25,000.

In this example there are both (1) relevant and irrelevant variable costs and (2) relevant and irrelevant fixed costs, as shown below:

	Relevant Cost	**Irrelevant Cost**
Variable cost	Direct labor of $50,000 vs. $32,000 per year	Direct materials of $36,000 per year
Fixed cost	Depreciation of $25,000 per year ($100,000 ÷ 4 years) vs. $50,000 per year ($200,000 ÷ 4 years)	Supervisor's salary of $25,000 per year

Although the direct materials and supervisor's salary do relate to the future, they are irrelevant because they will be the same amount regardless of which machine is purchased. Both direct labor and depreciation relate to the future and are different for the alternatives being considered—therefore, they are both relevant.

Relevance vs. Usefulness

Is the past always irrelevant?

The first of the two criteria for relevance is that the information must relate to the future. Since information about the past does not meet this requirement, all past information is irrelevant. Past (or historical) information relates to events that have already occurred—there is nothing that can be done to change that fact, regardless of the alternatives being considered.

Does the fact that past information is always irrelevant also mean that past information is always useless? Definitely not! Being irrelevant does not necessarily mean being useless.

Information about the past can help us to predict the future. In this way the past is useful even though it isn't relevant. Assume that we are trying to predict the labor costs for one of two new projects. Last year the labor costs were $40,000 (8,000 hours at $5 per hour) for an old project. We know that the labor rates are going to increase

CHAPTER 6 Relevant Information for Special Decisions
Quantitative vs. Qualitative Factors

209

by 20% and that the labor-hours will be 10% less than they were in the past. The prediction of future labor costs of $43,200 (7,200 hours at $6 per hour) is relevant, as long as it is also different from the labor costs of the other project under consideration. The past labor costs (8,000 hours and a $5 rate) helped us to predict the relevant costs—they were useful, but they were not relevant.

Relevance vs. Accuracy

Relevant is not the same as accurate

Another common mistake is to confuse being accurate with being relevant. These concepts, however, are not the same. Accurate information is information that is precise or exact; relevant information is information that relates to the future and is different for the alternatives being considered.

Accuracy is indeed a desirable characteristic—we would like the information that we as accountants provide managers to be accurate. Unfortunately, that is not always possible. Since relevant information must relate to the future, it involves predictions. Predictions are estimates—and estimates are, more often than not, inexact.

If it was necessary for information to be accurate in order to be relevant, there would be very little information that accountants could give managers to help them make decisions about the future.

QUANTITATIVE VS. QUALITATIVE FACTORS

Qualitative factors are important too

When a manager makes a decision, he or she needs to consider both the quantitative and the qualitative factors involved in the decision. Quantitative factors are those that can be measured with some reasonable degree of precision in dollars and cents. The fact that dropping a product line will eliminate a supervisor's salary of $20,000 is a quantitative factor.

Qualitative factors are those that cannot be expressed with a reasonable degree of precision in dollars and cents, yet many still have a significant influence on a manager's decision. For example, if a firm is considering moving its manufacturing facilities from Delaware to Mexico, a qualitative factor may be the effect on morale of the employees who are forced to move. If a firm is considering the installation of safety equipment in its mines, a qualitative factor would be the health and protection of its employees.

It's not that qualitative factors have no financial effect on a decision; it's just that the financial effect cannot be measured. Obviously, if a move to Mexico causes the employees to become disgruntled, then operating profits will be lower than they would be otherwise. However, if no one knows for sure whether the move will affect morale—or what effect low morale will have on the profits—then there is no objective way in which a manager can integrate these factors—in dollars and cents—into the analysis.

It will be up to the individual manager to assess subjectively the importance of a qualitative factor in a decision situation. Qualitative factors may be given very little weight in some situations but may be the determining factor in others.

Since the accountant is involved primarily with the quantitative factors in a decision situation, the quantitative factors are the ones that we emphasize in this chapter. However, if the accountant is to be of real assistance to managers, he or she should attempt to quantify as many qualitative factors as possible, thereby reducing the amount of subjectivity in a manager's decision.

TYPES OF DECISION SITUATIONS

We will discuss eight different types of decision situations. Each situation requires that a manager decide the course of action that will maximize his or her firm's short-run profits.

Managers face many more decisions in their day-to-day operations than the ones we will present; our eight are merely a representative sample. However, by the time you have finished studying this chapter, you should be able to adapt what you have learned to many other decision situations as well.

The eight decision situations we will discuss are:

1. Accepting the special order
2. Setting the normal price
3. Dropping a product line
4. Maximizing profits in a multi-product firm
5. Making vs. buying raw materials
6. Evaluating joint products—sell or process further
7. Scrapping or reworking defective units
8. Determining the economic order quantity

The Special Order

The special-order situation

Imagine that you are a manufacturer of volleyballs and are currently producing at 80% of full capacity. Your customers have always been exclusively American companies, but last week you were approached by a representative of the Chinese government. The Chinese are some of the finest volleyball players in the world, but they have temporarily run out of quality balls in their preparation for the 1988 Summer Olympics. They hope that you will use your idle capacity to produce a special order of volleyballs. The catch is that the price they are offering is below your regular price. You'd certainly like the business, but you'd really hate to reduce your price. What should you do?

The first thing you *shouldn't* do is to reject the offer simply because the price is lower than you would normally like it to be. You need to evaluate the offer in a great deal more depth. Manufacturers are often receptive to accepting a special order at a reduced price—but only if the conditions are right. The necessary conditions are as follows:

1. There must be excess productive capacity.
2. The order must be from a customer in a market different from the one in which the manufacturer normally sells—an unrelated market.

Idle capacity is necessary for a special order

It is important that there is excess capacity available; otherwise, you would have to reduce production and sales to regular customers to make sales to one-time customers. Not only would you have to sell the same units at a lower price, but your regular customers would be forced to find other suppliers and their business might be permanently lost to the firm. It's one thing to reduce the price in order to sell units that you wouldn't otherwise sell and quite another to reject the business of a regular customer in order to accept one-time business at a lower price.

Special orders should come from a special market

Also, it is usually important that special orders be accepted only when they come from an unrelated market. You could accept the special order from the Chinese government, because your regular customers would probably be unaware of the arrangement. On the other hand, you should reject the same offer from an American buyer, since your regular customers could easily learn about the reduced price you were offering a competing company and demand that similar concessions be granted to them. This could result in either reduced prices to all customers or a loss of regular customers. Either way, if you accept a special order in a related market as a temporary use of excess capacity to boost short-run profits, you may seriously affect your long-run pricing structure and long-run net income.

For this reason it is always necessary for the accountant and the manager to consider the impact that a special order might have on long-run profits, as well as on the profits in the short run. As a matter of fact, this is an important consideration in all the short-run decision situations we will discuss in this chapter. To simplify matters, however, we will always assume — unless we specifically state otherwise — that the long-run profit picture will not be affected by the decision to maximize short-run profits.

We will now look in depth at the special order for volleyballs from the Set and Spike Athletic Equipment Company. The facts are provided in Example 6-1.

Example 6-1

An example of a special order

THE SET AND SPIKE ATHLETIC EQUIPMENT COMPANY

The Set and Spike Athletic Equipment Company produces a wide range of athletic equipment, but it specializes in nets, balls, and shinguards for volleyball teams. Set and Spike normally sells its top-grade volleyball — called Olympic Gold — for $100 per box (each box contains four balls). Set and Spike is currently considering a special order from the Chinese government for 1,000 boxes at $78 per box. Since the deal is quite hush-hush — only Set and Spike, the Chinese government, and the CIA are aware of it — production and sales of volleyballs to Set and Spike's regular customers will not be affected in any way. The income statement for Set and Spike, without the special order, was budgeted for 1988 as follows:

Sales (5,000 boxes)	$500,000
Cost of Goods Sold	400,000
Gross Margin	$100,000
Operating Expenses	110,000
Net Income	$(10,000)

The cost of goods sold includes both variable costs ($40 per box) and fixed costs ($200,000 per period). This is also true for the operating costs ($10-per-box sales commission and $60,000 fixed). If the special order is accepted, Set and Spike will not pay a sales commission to its own sales representatives, but a CIA agent will receive $5,000 for arranging the deal. Should Set and Spike accept the order?

Faulty Reasoning

At first glance, you might be tempted to reason that the order should be rejected because the $78 price is less than the cost of producing each box:

$$\frac{\text{Cost of goods}}{\text{sold per box}} = \frac{\$400,000}{5,000 \text{ boxes}} = \$80 \text{ per box}$$

The gross margin is a negative $2 per box ($78 − $80). If a 1,000-box order is accepted, then won't the gross margin be a negative $2,000? And since the gross margin is negative, won't net income also be negative?

We hope you do not agree with this line of reasoning, because it can lead to serious mistakes in the decisions you may make in this chapter. The fact of the matter is that the order should be accepted, because the profits for the firm can be substantially improved. You may wonder how this can be true, since the cost of goods sold per unit is greater than the sales price. The problem is that the income statement in Example 6-1 has been prepared using the traditional format — that is, sales — cost of goods sold = gross profit − operating expenses = net income.

Included within the cost of goods sold for Set and Spike is $200,000 of fixed factory overhead. When we calculated the cost per box of $80, we concluded that each additional box would cost an additional $80 to produce. This is not true, however, because the total fixed overhead is not expected to increase with additional production — it is assumed to remain the same. Therefore, the cost of goods sold will not increase by $80,000 (1,000 boxes × $80), but will instead increase by only $40,000 — which is just the variable portion of cost of goods sold:

Additional Variable Manufacturing Costs (1,000 boxes × $40)	$40,000
Additional Fixed Manufacturing Costs	-0-
Additional Cost of Goods Sold	$40,000

So you see, the additional sales of $78,000 will be greater — not less — than the additional cost of goods sold of $40,000 by $38,000, or $38 per unit ($78 − $40).

The type of reasoning error we just discussed concerning the special order can be a problem any time the traditional format is used. Since cost of goods sold is often mentioned on a per-unit basis, it is a simple mistake to forget that some fixed costs have gone into that per-unit calculation. It is also easy to forget that the cost of goods sold cannot be calculated by simply multiplying the average cost per unit by the number of units sold — the variable and fixed costs must be calculated separately.

Unit costs can lead you astray

Warning: Beware of unit costs — when they include a fixed portion.

The easiest way to avoid this problem is to use the ***contribution margin format*** for an income statement, which requires that variable costs and fixed costs be evaluated separately. The contribution margin format, in case you've forgotten, is as follows:

Sales

Less: Total Variable Costs

Equals: Total Contribution Margin

Less: Fixed Costs

Equals: Net Income

A Better Approach

We will now analyze the situation correctly, this time using the contribution margin format for the income statement. First of all, we will revise the original budgeted income statement for Set and Spike given in Example 6-1:

Sales (5,000 boxes at $100/box)...................................		$500,000
Variable Costs:		
Manufacturing (5,000 boxes at $40/box)	$200,000	
Operating (5,000 boxes at $10/box)......................	50,000	250,000
Total Contribution Margin (5,000 boxes at $50/box)...................		$250,000
Total Fixed Costs:		
Manufacturing	$200,000	
Operating...	60,000	260,000
Net Income		$ (10,000)

Next, we will present the facts about the special-order decision in a three-column decision format. As you can see in Exhibit 6-1, the first column shows Set and Spike's loss ($10,000) if it rejects the order—the status quo. The second column shows Set and Spike's expected income if it accepts the special order. And the third column reports the differences in columns 1 and 2—only relevant items appear in the difference column.

EXHIBIT 6-1
Contribution Margin
Format for Solution

	Alternatives		
	(1) **Reject Order**	**(2)** **Accept Order**	**(3)** **Difference**
Sales.....................................	$500,000	$578,000	$ 78,000
Variable costs:			
Manufacturing.........................	$200,000	$240,000	$(40,000)
Operating—Sales Commissions	50,000	50,000	-0-
Total Variable Costs................	$250,000	$290,000	$(40,000)
Total Contribution Margin.................	$250,000	$288,000	$ 38,000
Fixed costs:			
Manufacturing.........................	$200,000	$200,000	$ -0-
Operating	60,000	65,000	(5,000)
Total Fixed Costs	$260,000	$265,000	$ (5,000)
Net income.............................	$(10,000)	$ 23,000	$ 33,000

The sales are expected to increase by $78,000 (1,000 additional boxes $\times$ $78 per box), more than enough to offset the additional variable costs of $40,000 (1,000 additional boxes $\times$ $40 per box). There are no additional variable operating costs because sales commissions are not to be paid on the special order—the variable operating costs are irrelevant. The additional contribution margin of $38,000 ($78,000 − $40,000) exceeds the additional fixed operating costs (the CIA agent's fee) of $5,000 by $33,000—which is the increase in net income from accepting the special order. The fixed manufacturing costs are irrelevant because they are expected to be $200,000 with or without the special order.

As you can see, the special order should be accepted—because profits are expected to increase by $33,000.

We recommend the
contribution margin format

Although we strongly recommend that you use the contribution margin format in order to minimize the likelihood of errors, this doesn't mean that it is impossible to get the correct answer with the traditional format. As long as you properly separate the variable and fixed costs within each functional cost grouping of the traditional format, you can get the same answer as we showed in Exhibit 6-1 for the contribution margin approach.

Although the same solutions can be obtained with the traditional approach, we will use the contribution approach exclusively throughout this chapter. The contribution approach is more easily adapted to any type of analysis, and it is less likely to lead to improper conclusions such as those we made with the traditional approach.

Excluding irrelevant items has no impact on the decision

Irrelevant Items Can Be Excluded   Notice in Exhibit 6-1 that the variable operating costs and the fixed factory overhead costs were included in the solution even though they were irrelevant to the decision. It is acceptable to include irrelevant items in an analysis as long as you show them to be the same amount under both alternatives.

In most situations, if you prefer to delete the irrelevant items and if there is nothing specified in the problem to the contrary, then it is acceptable for you to do so. Sometimes, however, you don't have a choice. For example, if the requirements of a problem specifically indicate that all items — relevant and irrelevant — must be included, then of course you must include them. Or if a problem requires that complete income statements be prepared, then as long as an item is a component of income — relevant or not — it must be included in the analysis.

Setting the Normal Price for a Product

Whereas a firm such as Set and Spike may be willing to accept a special order at a price far below the normal price, this does not mean that this special price is appropriate for all the other units that Set and Spike expects to sell throughout the year. The price of $78 was acceptable for the single, nonrecurring event because the only costs that had to be covered by the sales were the variable manufacturing costs and the additional fixed operating costs. Since the other costs (fixed factory overhead and variable operating) were unaffected by the order, they were ignored.

When a normal price is being set for the vast majority of units to be sold during a year, none of the costs can be ignored. All costs must be considered in setting the best price — the variable and fixed costs, the manufacturing and nonmanufacturing costs.

Don't use the special-order price for all units

The normal price for Set and Spike is $100 per box. At this price each box sold contributes $50 to the $260,000 of fixed costs. Even with sales of 5,000 boxes, the total contribution margin of $250,000 (see the income statement on page 213) is inadequate to cover the total fixed costs — resulting in a $10,000 loss. Imagine how much worse the results would have been if the sales price were $78 for each of the 5,000 boxes, and not just for the special order of 1,000 boxes. The contribution margin per box for the 5,000 boxes would be $28 ($78 − $50); the total contribution margin would fall to $140,000 (5,000 boxes × $28); and the loss would be a much larger $120,000 ($140,000 − $260,000). Even if the lower price did stimulate greater sales, the increase in sales would have to be substantial in order for Set and Spike to do only as well as it did with the $100 sales price.

Cost-Plus-a-Markup

Cost + (Cost × markup %)

A common approach to setting a price for a product is called *cost-plus-a-markup.* With cost-plus pricing an appropriate group of costs is combined — on a per-unit basis — and a desired markup is added to the costs. The markup is found by multiplying a desired markup percentage times the costs per unit. This combination — of costs plus the markup — represents the sales price that will provide the desired markup percentage when the product is sold.

In practice, the actual price may depend upon the relationship of the cost-plus-a-markup price to a prevailing market price — if one exists. For example, assume that a company desires a 50% markup over its costs of $10 per unit. A strict application of the cost-plus-a-markup approach leads to a price of $15. If there is an established market price of $14, the company may have to set its price at that figure rather than at $15. It would then need to direct its efforts to reducing costs through better controls, if the desired markup of 50% is to be achieved. If the prevailing market price is higher than the cost-plus-a-markup price, say, $18, then a favorable gap exists between the cost-plus-a-markup price and the market price. In this case the firm has some flexibility in the price it sets, since any price between $15 and $18 will provide a markup of at least 50%.

Cost-Plus-a-Markup Pricing Methods

There are two different methods of determining a price on the basis of costs—one for each of the product costing methods we discussed in Chapter 5. They are the traditional pricing method (used with absorption costing) and the contribution margin pricing method (used with direct costing). The two methods differ in their definition of *costs* and in their definition of *markup.*

The traditional pricing method

With the ***traditional pricing method*** a combined cost per unit is determined for all the items included in cost of goods sold expense (direct materials, direct labor, variable factory overhead, and fixed factory overhead). Next, a desired gross profit per unit is found by multiplying the desired gross profit percentage times the combined cost of goods sold per unit. The gross profit per unit is then added to the cost of goods sold per unit to get the sales price. With this sales price the resulting total gross profit, based on the number of units sold, must be great enough to cover the selling and administrative expenses—leaving an acceptable net income.

The contribution margin pricing method

With the ***contribution margin pricing method*** the combined variable costs per unit are determined (direct materials, direct labor, variable factory overhead, variable selling, and variable administrative). Next, a desired contribution margin per unit is found by multiplying the desired contribution margin percentage times the combined variable costs per unit.[1] The contribution margin per unit is then added to the variable costs per unit to get the sales price. With this sales price the resulting total contribution margin, based on the number of units sold, must be great enough to cover the total fixed costs (factory overhead, selling and administrative)—and hopefully generate an acceptable net income.

Determining the Sales Price

Each of the two pricing methods will now be demonstrated, using the facts given in Example 6-2.

Traditional Pricing Method The cost of goods sold is expected to average $40 per unit, which includes $10 of fixed factory overhead. The fixed factory overhead per unit is determined exactly as it was in Chapter 5 for absorption costing. You simply divide the expected overhead for the year by the expected production for the year.

We get an average fixed manufacturing cost for pricing purposes only

The sales price—using the traditional pricing method—is $50, determined as follows:

$$\text{Selling price} = \frac{\text{cost of goods}}{\text{sold per unit}} + \left(\frac{\text{cost of goods}}{\text{sold per unit}} \times \frac{\text{desired gross}}{\text{profit \% per unit}} \right)$$

$$= \$40 + \$40(.25) = \$40 + \$10 = \$50$$

---

[1] Up to this point, the contribution margin percentage represented the percentage of contribution margin to sales dollars. For pricing purposes, however, the contribution margin percentage represents the percentage of contribution margin to variable costs.

Example 6-2

THE FONTAN COMPANY

The Fontan Company expects to produce 20,000 units during 1989, but it has not yet set the price for its main product. The president of Fontan, Gilda Braddish, requests your help. The expected unit costs are as follows:

Manufacturing:		
Direct Materials	$15.00	
Direct Labor	10.00	
Variable Overhead	5.00	$30.00
Fixed Overhead ($200,000/20,000 units)		10.00
		$40.00
Selling and Administrative:		
Variable	$ 3.33	
Fixed	3.00	6.33
		$46.33

Gilda wants a price that will provide a gross profit of at least 25% of cost of goods sold and a contribution margin of at least 50% of variable costs.

Contribution Margin Pricing Method   Variable costs are expected to average $33.33 ($30.00 + $3.33) per unit, and the company wants to have a contribution margin of at least 50% of variable costs. The sales price is $50, just as it was with the traditional pricing method:

$$\text{Selling price} = \frac{\text{variable costs}}{\text{per unit}} + \left(\frac{\text{variable costs}}{\text{per unit}} \times \frac{\text{desired contri-}}{\text{bution margin percentage}} \right)$$

$$= \$33.33 + \$33.33 \, (.50) = \$33.33 + \$16.67 = \$50$$

Pros and Cons   Proponents of the traditional pricing method contend that the contribution margin pricing method ignores fixed costs, since the price provides a markup over the variable costs only. By ignoring fixed costs, the price can easily be set too low, resulting in large losses which will eventually run the company out of business.

Does contribution margin ignore fixed costs?

Proponents of contribution margin pricing might counter this argument in the following manner. If the contribution margin approach ignores some costs, then so too does the traditional approach. The traditional pricing method ignores the selling and administrative costs, because the price provides a markup over the cost of goods sold only. As a result, the price will be too low, and eventually the company will price itself out of business.

Each of these arguments is deficient in its reasoning, because each implies that top management wears blinders when setting prices and that it will forget that a significant group of costs need to be covered before the company can show a profit. The manager using the contribution margin approach most likely does not ignore fixed costs. He or she simply considers them in a different way than the variable costs. The manager realizes that in setting the price, the total contribution margin based on the sales generated by that price must be great enough to cover the total fixed costs.

The manager using the traditional approach is no more likely to ignore selling and administrative costs. He or she simply considers them in a different way than the cost of goods sold. The manager realizes that in setting the price, the total gross profit based on the sales generated by that price must be great enough to cover the selling and administrative costs.

Both approaches can lead to the same price

The bottom line is that the same sales price can probably be determined under either approach. As long as management realizes that the demand for the product must be great enough for the total contribution margin to cover the fixed costs, or for the total gross profit to cover the selling and administrative costs, then it shouldn't make too much difference which method is used.

Dropping a Product Line

Changing a firm's sales mix

Firms are referred to as ***multi-product*** firms when they sell more than a single line of products. We first introduced the idea of a multi-product firm in Chapter 5—in cost-volume-profit analysis. At that time we defined ***sales mix*** as the proportion of total sales that is distributed to each product line. We showed how to calculate the breakeven point for a multi-product firm, and we discussed the significance of a change in the sales mix on a firm's profits. In this section we are going to talk about dropping entire product lines—decisions that can result in rather abrupt changes in the sales mix. You need to be able to determine when a product line is no longer profitable and should be eliminated.

Let's look at the situation of The Gas Glow Grill Company in Example 6-3 and see if any changes are advisable for its product lines.

THE GOULD ELECTRONICS APPROACH TO PRICING

In case you've wondered how the costs of so many products purchased by so many agencies and departments of the federal government cost so doggone much money, this example is for a $436 hammer that was manufactured for the U.S. Navy by Gould Electronics. Notice that the materials were only $7; the mechanical subassembly took only .3 hour and cost approximately $3.58 ($\frac{.3\ hr}{7.8\ hr} \times \$93$); and that a wide assortment of other non-direct items cost the remaining $425.42.

This is an example of the "cost plus the kitchen sink" method of pricing. And to think that the Navy could have bought one from Sears for less than $20.

Source: Proceedings & Debate of the 98th Congress, Second Session, *Congressional Record,* Vol. 130, No. 63, p. H3923, March 15, 1984.

Purchased Item		Amount
Direct material		$7.00
Material packaging		1.00
Material handling overhead (19.8%)		2.00
Engineering support:		
Spares/repair department	1.0 hr	
Program support/administration	0.4	
Program management	1.0	
Secretarial	0.2	
	2.6 hr	37.00
Engineering overhead (110%)		41.00
Manufacturing support:		
Mechanical subassembly	0.3 hr	
Quality control	0.9	
Operations program management	1.5	
Program planning	4.0	
Manufacturing project engineering	1.0	
Quality assurance	0.1	
	7.8 hr	93.00
Manufacturing overhead (110%)		102.00
		283.00
General and administrative expenses (31.8%)		90.00
Negotiation fee		56.00
Interest charge		7.00
Total Price		$436.00

Example 6-3

THE GAS GLOW GRILL COMPANY

The Gas Glow Grill Company sells three models of barbeque grills: Super Deluxe, Deluxe, and Matchless. Its income statement for 1988 showed a profit for the firm as a whole. However, one of the three product lines reported a loss as shown below:

| | Model | | | |
	Super Deluxe	Deluxe	Matchless	Total
Sales	$200,000	$240,000	$200,000	$640,000
Variable Expenses (and % of Total Sales)	120,000 (.60)	180,000 (.75)	160,000 (.80)	460,000 (.72)
Total Contribution Margin (and % of Total Sales). .	$ 80,000 (.40)	$ 60,000 (.25)	$ 40,000 (.20)	$180,000 (.28)
Fixed Expenses. .	60,000	50,000	50,000	160,000
Net Income	$ 20,000	$ 10,000	$ (10,000)	$ 20,000

The controller, Neon Propane, thinks that Matchless should be dropped. Not only does it have the smallest contribution margin percentage of the three products ($40,000 ÷ $200,000 = 20%), but it is the only product line showing a loss. Neon says, "If we drop Matchless, we can improve our profits by the $10,000 loss that we eliminate."

Neon is partially right about Matchless—that is, it does have the smallest contribution margin percentage of the three product lines, and it is the only product line with a loss. Neon is wrong, however, in his conclusion—that Matchless should be dropped.

Before we explain why Neon is wrong, we want to first point out two important assumptions that we are making—assumptions that you must also make until we tell you differently. They are as follows:

Fixed costs don't change and excess capacity is not used in an alternative manner

1. The total fixed costs are not affected by the decision and will remain the same.

2. The excess capacity will not be used in any other productive manner, such as producing more of another product line or renting it to an outsider.

The solution is really quite simple, because the only thing that changes for Gas Glow if Matchless is dropped is its total contribution margin. Since Matchless has a contribution margin of $40,000, if it is dropped, the contribution margin for the entire firm will fall by $40,000. And when the contribution margin falls by $40,000 — with no change in the fixed costs—the profits will also fall by $40,000. The profits will not improve by $10,000, as Neon believes they will.

Don't drop Matchless, because it does make a contribution to fixed costs

Is this the same conclusion that you reached when you first read the example, or did you agree with Neon Propane's reasoning for dropping the product line? Neon thinks that the entire loss of $10,000 will be eliminated if Matchless were dropped by Gas Glow. For this to be true, not only would the contribution margin of $40,000 have to be eliminated, but the fixed costs of $50,000 would have to be eliminated as well. Remember, however, that we assumed that the total fixed costs aren't affected by the decision. So if Matchless is dropped, the fixed costs of $50,000 are not eliminated but are instead distributed to Deluxe and Super Deluxe.

If you look now at the three-column format in Exhibit 6-2, you can see that the fixed costs are $160,000 whether or not Gas Glow drops Matchless. Also, notice that the profits will continue to be $20,000 if Gas Glow leaves well enough alone (column 1) but will fall to a negative $20,000 if it drops the line (column 2)—resulting in a reduction in net income of $40,000 (column 3).

**EXHIBIT 6-2
Comparative Analysis—
Drop Matchless**

	Totals		
	(1) **Keep Matchless**	**(2)** **Drop Matchless**	**(3)** **Difference**
Sales.....................................	$640,000	$440,000	$(200,000)
Variable Expenses.....................	460,000	300,000	160,000
Total Contribution Margin............	$180,000	$140,000	$ (40,000)
Fixed Expenses	160,000	160,000	-0-
Net Income	$ 20,000	$ (20,000)	$ (40,000)

Utilizing Excess Capacity

Now let's use excess capacity productively

Let's now assume a slightly more complicated situation for The Gas Glow Grill Company. First, we'll assume that of the $50,000 of fixed costs for Matchless $20,000 is for a supervisor's salary that can be eliminated if the line is dropped. Second, the productive capacity that had been used for Matchless will now be used to produce additional Deluxe models, increasing the sales of Deluxe from $240,000 to $340,000. The solution to the revised example for Gas Glow is shown in Exhibit 6-3. We now see that Matchless should be dropped.

**EXHIBIT 6-3
Comparative Totals—
Drop Matchless, Produce
Additional Deluxe**
By dropping Matchless and increasing Deluxe, the net effect on contribution margin is a reduction of $15,000. The reduction of $20,000 in fixed costs, however, offsets the negative contribution margin by $5,000.

	Totals		
	(1) **Keep Matchless**	**(2)** **Drop Matchless**	**(3)** **Difference**
Sales.....................................	$640,000	$540,000*	$(100,000)
Variable Expenses.....................	460,000	375,000†	85,000
Total Contribution Margin............	$180,000	$165,000	$ (15,000)
Fixed Expenses	160,000	140,000	20,000
Net Income	$ 20,000	$ 25,000	$ 5,000

* Super Deluxe + Deluxe = $200,000 + $340,000 = $540,000.
† Super Deluxe + Deluxe = $200,000(.60) + $340,000(.75)
$$= \$120,000 + \$255,000 = \$375,000$$

The total sales will be $540,000 if Matchless is dropped and Deluxe is expanded. This is a reduction of $100,000 in the total sales. The variable expenses will also be lower—by $85,000, resulting in a reduction of $15,000 in the contribution margin for Gas Glow. Since a product-line supervisor will be terminated, the $20,000 savings in fixed costs is great enough to offset the reduced contribution margin. The net effect is an increase of $5,000 in net income.

Adding a Product Line

Another possibility that might be considered by The Gas Glow Grill Company if Matchless is dropped is adding a new product line rather than expanding the production of Deluxe. However, since the analysis of this alternative is very similar to that of expanding the production of Deluxe, it is not necessary to discuss it separately.

Maximizing Profits in a Multi-Product Firm

In the previous section we discussed how The Gas Glow Grill Company tried to improve its profits by dropping and/or expanding product lines. Of the three possibilities that Gas Glow considered—(1) continue to produce and sell all three lines, (2) drop Matchless, and (3) drop Matchless and increase the sales of Deluxe—the most profitable alternative was number 3. If Matchless is dropped and the sales of Deluxe are increased, the net income should increase from $20,000 to $25,000.

Is there a maximum profit? Is there a best sales mix?

Even though $25,000 is the maximum net income for the three alternatives that were mentioned, is it also the maximum net income that Gas Glow could possibly earn? Might there be any other combination of product lines that could increase the net income above $25,000? For example, since Super Deluxe has the highest contribution margin percentage—40% (see Example 6-3)—maybe the excess capacity from dropping Matchless should be used to increase production of Super Deluxe; or maybe both Matchless and Deluxe should be dropped and the entire capacity of Gas Glow should be used to produce and sell nothing but Super Deluxe.

Already we have mentioned a half-dozen possibilities, and we could probably come up with a half-dozen more. Even then, however, we might not have stumbled upon the optimum combination of product lines—the optimum *sales mix*—that would maximize the profits of Gas Glow.

Is it even possible to determine an optimum sales mix for a multi-product firm without doing exactly what we are doing now—that is, trying as many possible combinations as we can think of? Yes, it is possible, but first it is necessary to answer three important questions:

Key variables for finding the best sales mix

1. What is the contribution margin per unit (or contribution margin percentage) for each product line?
2. What resources (capacity, labor, materials, customers) does the firm possess for the production and sale of its product lines?
3. What restrictions (constraints) are placed upon the use of the firm's resources in the production and sale of each product line?

Unless we find the answers to these questions, there is no way to determine an optimum sales mix for Gas Glow. At first, it might seem reasonable to conclude that all the firm's resources would be utilized best by producing nothing but Super Deluxe—after all, it does have the highest contribution margin percentage.

Suppose, however, that when we answer questions 2 and 3 above, we find out the following facts about Super Deluxe:

The product with the best contribution margin per unit or percentage may not be the best product

1. The demand from customers for Super Deluxe is currently at a maximum.
2. It takes longer to produce Super Deluxe than either of the other models, and the total hours of machine time are limited.
3. More highly qualified laborers are required to work on Super Deluxe than on the other models, and qualified laborers are scarce.
4. Super Deluxe requires a raw material that is nearly impossible to acquire in greater amounts.

Constraints are restrictions on production and sales

Each of these facts represents a restriction, or *constraint,* on Gas Glow's ability to produce and sell what at first glance appears to be its most profitable product line.

Should Gas Glow shift all its productive capacity to Super Deluxe in light of this information? Because of these constraints, it would be foolish for Gas Glow to produce and sell nothing but Super Deluxe. In fact, the constraints could be so restrictive that it might be better if Super Deluxe were not produced at all.

Maximum Profits for Gas Glow

More details for Gas Glow

On the basis of the original facts presented for Gas Glow in Example 6-3, let's assume that you are now given a more detailed set of facts related to the income statement of Gas Glow for 1988:

	Super Deluxe	Deluxe	Matchless
Sales Price	$ 400	$ 240	$ 100
Variable Cost per Unit	240	180	80
Contribution Margin per Unit	$ 160	$ 60	$ 20
Unit Sales	500	1,000	2,000
Total Contribution Margin	$80,000	$60,000	$ 40,000
Fixed Expenses.	60,000	50,000	50,000
Net Income.	$20,000	$10,000	$(10,000)

We also find out that it takes 10 hours to make one Super Deluxe; 4.8 hours for one Deluxe; and 1 hour for each Matchless. The total available production hours are 11,800.

Production constraint: hours per unit and limited total hours

For now, we are going to consider only one constraint for Gas Glow — the number of hours that it takes to produce each grill. When there is only one constraint, the solution can be derived quite simply — the solution will always be to produce and sell a single product. Do you have any idea which product it will be?

What we need to do is to convert the contribution margin per unit to a contribution margin per hour — the product with the highest contribution margin per hour will be the best.

Contribution margin per unit of the constraining factor: contribution margin per hour

$$\text{Contribution margin per hour} = \frac{\text{contribution margin per unit}}{\text{number of hours per unit}}$$

$$\text{CM per hour (Super Deluxe)} = \frac{\$160}{10 \text{ hours}} = \$16 \text{ per hour}$$

$$\text{CM per hour (Deluxe)} = \frac{\$60}{4.8 \text{ hours}} = \$12.50 \text{ per hour}$$

$$\text{CM per hour (Matchless)} = \frac{\$20}{1 \text{ hour}} = \$20 \text{ per hour}$$

Lo and behold, Matchless has the highest contribution margin per hour — and this is the product we kept wanting to dump! For every one of the 11,800 hours, Matchless contributes $20 toward the coverage of fixed costs, while Super Deluxe contributes $16 and Deluxe contributes $12.50. If the full 11,800 hours of production are used to produce only one product line, the income statements for each line would be as follows:

Maximize profits with Matchless

	Super Deluxe	Deluxe	Matchless
Contribution Margin per Hour	$ 16.00	$ 12.50	$ 20.00
Total Hours of Capacity	× 11,800	× 11,800	× 11,800
Total Contribution Margin	$188,800	$147,500	$236,000
Fixed Costs	160,000	160,000	160,000
Net Income	$ 28,800	$(12,500)	$ 76,000

The most profit that Gas Glow can possibly earn is $76,000 — when Matchless is the only product that is produced and sold.

You may say, "How can this be true? Matchless looks like such a loser. Super Deluxe contributes eight times as much per unit as Matchless does — $160 vs. $20."

The key point is that Matchless is not a loser once you consider how many hours it takes to make a unit of each product line. Although Matchless has a much lower contribution margin per unit than either of the other two products, the fact that it takes so little time to produce — 1 hour — makes up for its deficiency.

Notice below how many more units of Matchless can be produced each year than can be produced of Super Deluxe or Deluxe:

Fewer hours per unit means that more units can be produced

	Super Deluxe	Deluxe	Matchless
Total Hours of Capacity	11,800	11,800	11,800
Hours per Unit	÷ 10	÷ 4.8	÷ 1
Maximum Units That Can Be Produced	1,180	2,458*	11,800
Contribution Margin per Unit	× $160	× $60	× $20
Maximum Contribution Margin	$188,800	$147,500	$236,000
Fixed Costs	160,000	160,000	160,000
Maximum Net Income	$ 28,800	$(12,500)	$ 76,000

* Rounded.

Gas Glow can produce 11,800 units of Matchless but only 2,458 units of Deluxe or 1,180 units of Super Deluxe. Matchless may have a much smaller contribution margin per unit than either of the other two products — but because of its significant advantage in the number of units that can be produced, the total contribution margin and net income for Gas Glow are highest when Matchless is produced.

More than One Constraint

We will now introduce a second constraint for each product line. Now there will be not only a maximum number of units that can be produced but also a maximum number of units that can be sold.

Maximum Units That Can Be Sold	
Super Deluxe	500
Deluxe	1,100
Matchless	4,000

Don't produce more than you can sell

In the previous section profits would be maximized by producing and selling 11,800 units of Matchless—that was when the only constraint concerned the number of units that could be produced. Now we see that only 4,000 units of Matchless can be sold. We would be foolish to produce 11,800 units when we can sell only 4,000. What we need to do is produce and sell 4,000 units of Matchless and then let the remaining productive capacity be used to produce the other two products.

The solution in Exhibit 6-4 indicates that the maximum profit for Gas Glow is $34,980 if it produces and sells the following combination of units:

4,000 units of Matchless,

500 units of Super Deluxe

583 units of Deluxe

EXHIBIT 6-4
Determining Maximum Profits for a Multi-Product Firm: Two Constraints
The middle column shows the production capacity available and the right-hand column gives the contribution margin from each product sold. The order of product lines that are sold is based on their contribution margins per hour: high to low—until you run out of capacity.

Production and Sales	Productive Capacity (in Hours)	Total Contribution Margin
Total hours of capacity	11,800	
1. Produce and sell 4,000 units of Matchless:		
4,000 units × 1 hr/unit	(4,000)	
4,000 units × $20/unit.....................		$ 80,000
Remaining hours............................	7,800	
2. Produce and sell 500 units of Super Deluxe:		
500 units × 10 hr/unit.....................	(5,000)	
500 units × $160/unit		80,000
Remaining hours............................	2,800	
3. Produce and sell 583 units (2,800 hr ÷ 4.8 hr/unit) of Deluxe:		
583 units × 4.8 hr/unit	(2,800)	
583 units × $60/unit		34,980
Remaining hours............................	-0-	
Maximum contribution margin..................		$194,980
Fixed expenses...................................		160,000
Maximum net income..........................		$ 34,980

Steps to solution for multi-products and two constraints

There were eight steps in calculating the solution for Exhibit 6-4. They are as follows:

1. Select the product with the highest contribution margin per hour. This was Matchless ($20 per hour).

2. Considering both the production and sales constraints, determine the maximum number of units that can be produced and sold for the product with the highest contribution margin per hour. The maximum number of Matchless that can be produced is 11,800 (11,800 hours ÷ 1 hour per unit) and the maximum that can be sold is 4,000. The smaller amount is 4,000 units, so this number will be produced and sold—having a contribution of $80,000.

3. Subtract the number of hours used (4,000 units × 1 hour per unit) to produce Matchless from the total hours available (11,800). This leaves 7,800 hours available for the other two products.

4. Select from the remaining products the one with the higher contribution margin per hour. This would be Super Deluxe ($16 per hour).

5. Consider both the production and sales constraints and determine the maximum number of units that can be produced and sold. The maximum number of Super Deluxe that can be produced is 780 (7,800 remaining hours ÷ 10 hours per unit), and the maximum number that can be sold is 500. The lower of these two, 500, will be produced and sold — its contribution is $80,000.

6. Subtract the number of hours used to produce Super Deluxe (500 units × 10 hours per unit) from the total hours available (7,800) — the difference of 2,800 hours (7,800 − 5,000) will be used to produce Deluxe.

7. Determine the maximum number of units of Deluxe that can be produced and sold. Although 1,100 units can be sold, only 583 units (2,800 remaining hours ÷ 4.8 hours per unit) can be produced. The remaining hours will be used to produce 583 units, which will contribute $34,980 when they are sold.

8. Add up the three contribution margins and subtract the fixed costs. This is the maximum profit of $34,980.

Linear programming is discussed in Appendix 6-1

When The Gas Glow Grill Company had only one constraint, the solution was calculated very quickly. By adding the sales constraint, the analysis became much more tedious and analytical. If we were to add a third constraint, the analysis would become too complicated to perform without the aid of a quantitative tool called **linear programming.** This technique is briefly discussed in Appendix 6-1.

Make or Buy

Reasons to make: cost, quality, and availability

A manufacturer is often faced with an interesting option: It can buy the raw material that goes into its finished product, or it can produce its own raw material. Sometimes it is more economical to produce the raw material internally. Also, the manufacturer is able to maintain better control over the quality and availability of a raw material if it is made internally. On the other hand, the main problem with producing one's own raw materials is that this may require that some of the firm's productive capacity be taken away from the production of the finished product. What good does it do to produce one's own raw materials if there is little remaining capacity for producing the main product? The main product might cost less, but the firm may not be able to make and sell enough of its main product line to be profitable.

Reasons to buy: lower cost and better use of productive capacity

To be complete, any analysis of making vs. buying raw materials must be concerned with utilizing all of the productive capacity in the most effective manner. In order for a manufacturer even to consider making its own raw materials, there must be productive capacity that is idle — and therefore available for an alternative use.

The Analysis

The analysis of a make-or-buy decision simply determines the relevant costs of making the material and compares that amount to the relevant costs of buying it from an outsider. A typical make-or-buy situation is presented in Example 6-4 for The Frankensense Company.

Example 6-4

To make or buy Roo Myrr

THE FRANKENSENSE COMPANY

The Frankensense Company produces a perfume called Breathless. The company is also currently producing 100,000 ounces of one of the ingredients, Roo Myrr, for the following costs:

Direct Materials...	$600,000	$6.00/oz
Direct Labor...	100,000	1.00/oz
Variable Overhead	50,000	0.50/oz
Fixed Overhead..	50,000	0.50/oz
	$800,000	$8.00/oz

Frankensense is considering purchasing the 100,000 ounces from the CinDi Lauder Company for $7.25 per ounce plus shipping costs of $0.40 per ounce. The productive capacity that is currently being used to manufacture Roo Myrr will be used to produce additional units of another product line—After Dark. The additional contribution margin that can be generated from After Dark is $20,000.

The solution for Example 6-4 is given in Exhibit 6-5. The first column shows the total costs of making Roo Myrr; the second column shows the total costs of purchasing Roo Myrr; and the third column shows the difference between the costs of making and buying Roo Myrr.

Total fixed costs are assumed to remain the same

For the variable items the costs of buying are $15,000 higher than the costs of making ($765,000 − $750,000). And the fixed overhead is $50,000 regardless of Frankensense's decision. Remember: For all the decision situations that we evaluate in this chapter, the total fixed costs are assumed to remain the same regardless of activity, unless we give you specific information to the contrary. It is possible, for example, that in a situation such as this one, the fixed costs could change, possibly because of a reduction in the number of supervisors needed. However, we are not assuming a change of that sort for Frankensense.

EXHIBIT 6-5
A Comparison of Make or Buy Roo Myrr
Frankensense is $5,000 better off by buying Roo Myrr. The additional contribution margin of $20,000 from After Dark is an opportunity cost.

	Alternatives		
	(1) **Make** **Roo Myrr**	**(2)** **Buy** **Roo Myrr**	**(3)** **Difference**
Variable Costs:			
Direct Materials	$600,000	-0-	$ 600,000
Direct Labor	100,000	-0-	100,000
Variable Overhead	50,000	-0-	50,000
Shipping Costs...............................	-0-	$ 40,000	(40,000)
Purchase of 100,000 oz	-0-	725,000	(725,000)
	$750,000	$765,000	$ (15,000)
Fixed Overhead................................	50,000	50,000	-0-
Total Actual Costs	$800,000	$815,000	$ (15,000)
Additional Contribution Margin for After Dark ...	-0-	(20,000)	20,000
Net Costs	$800,000	$795,000	$ 5,000

The final item in Exhibit 6-5 concerns the additional contribution margin that Frankensense can generate from After Dark if Roo Myrr is purchased. If this item were left out of the analysis, Frankensense would probably decide to continue making Roo Myrr—because the costs of buying it are $15,000 higher than the costs of making it. However, since Frankensense can increase its contribution margin by $20,000 on After Dark only if it buys Roo Myrr, the additional contribution is relevant to the decision. And the net effect is an increase of $5,000 in its profits ($20,000 − $15,000) by purchasing Roo Myrr from an outside supplier.

Opportunity Costs

The additional contribution margin of $20,000 that is listed at the bottom of Exhibit 6-5 is called an opportunity cost.

Opportunity costs are foregone profits

An ***opportunity cost*** is the profit foregone or lost by a firm in taking one course of action rather than another. It relates to an opportunity that is given up, or sacrificed. It is not an actual cash outlay as other costs usually are. Instead, it is a cash inflow that the firm sacrifices by accepting one alternative over another. If Frankensense decides to continue making Roo Myrr, it is giving up $20,000 of additional profit from After Dark.

In Exhibit 6-5 we've shown the opportunity cost as additional income in column 2; this reduces the total costs of the purchase alternative from $815,000 to $795,000. The $5,000 balance at the bottom of column 3 indicates that the buy alternative is preferable.

Another good example of an opportunity cost that could relate to the Frankensense Company is rent income. Ceasing production of Roo Myrr might release floor space that could be rented to outsiders. The rent foregone by making Roo Myrr would be an opportunity cost, and it, too, would be relevant to the decision.

Joint Products

There are many production processes that begin with a single raw material and end up with two or more final products. A prime example involves the many final products that come from a single steer—hides, hamburger, steaks, pet food, etc. Another is a barrel of crude oil that ends up being kerosene, regular and unleaded gasoline, and other petroleum products. Other examples can be found in the lumber and chemicals industries.

Joint products: a single product splits into two or more products

The raw material is treated as a single product up until a point in production called the ***split-off point.*** At this point the single product divides into two or more products called ***joint products.*** The joint products are not individually identifiable until the split-off point.

The costs of producing the single product up to the split-off point are the ***joint product costs.*** These costs are common to all the units produced and cannot be associated directly with the units once they split into the individual products. Take, for example, the costs of raising a herd of cattle. The costs of buying, feeding, caring for, and transporting each cow to market are the joint product costs. When the cows are slaughtered—the split-off point—there really is no way to tell how much of the joint costs were costs of the hide, the hamburger, or the steaks.

This processing of cattle is depicted in the simplified diagram at the top of the next page.

Choices at split-off

Sometimes we can sell a joint product immediately after the split-off point. In other situations we may have to process the joint product beyond the split-off before it can be sold. We may even have the option of selling at split-off or processing further.

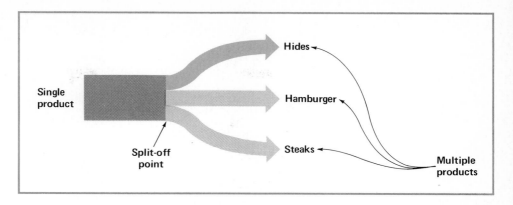

A Useful Diagram

A more elaborate diagram for joint products is given below. It shows both the sales at split-off and any additional processing that may be needed for two joint products, product A and product B.

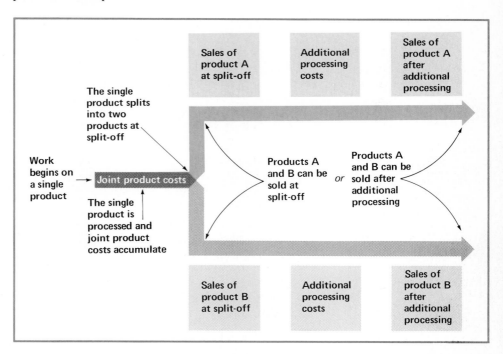

This type of diagram can be very useful when you do your homework. If you place the key facts from a problem into the appropriate positions in the diagram, you can get a complete overview of what you are about to evaluate. We'll do this for you in a moment in our example on joint products.

Sell at Split-Off or Process Further

When a firm has the option of selling a joint product at the split-off point or processing it further, it will naturally select the option with the more favorable effect on profits. The key to making the correct decision is knowing which information is relevant and which information is irrelevant.

Let's look at such a situation in Example 6-5. Although Jimmy Joe is a farmer rather than a manufacturer, the concepts still apply.

Example 6-5

JIMMY JOE'S PEANUT FARM

Jimmy Joe James has recently purchased substantial farmland in Georgia and is currently growing peanuts. At harvest time the crop is divided into nuts and shells. The nuts can be sold immediately to a grocery store chain or processed into vegetable oil. The shells can be burned or ground into a powder. The powder can be sold to a drug company, which uses it in a new medicine for acne.

The costs of growing the crop, harvesting it, and separating it into the two products are $400,000. At harvest the following information pertains to Jimmy Joe's choices:

	Sales at Harvest Time (Split-Off)	Additional Processing Costs	Sales after Additional Processing
Nuts	$750,000	$500,000	$1,200,000
Shells	-0-	50,000	100,000

What actions should Jimmy Joe take to maximize profits?

Before you can evaluate Jimmy Joe's alternatives, you must get an overview of the situation. This overview is provided in the diagram below, in which all the numbers given in Example 6-5 are presented in the general format that we discussed on the previous page.

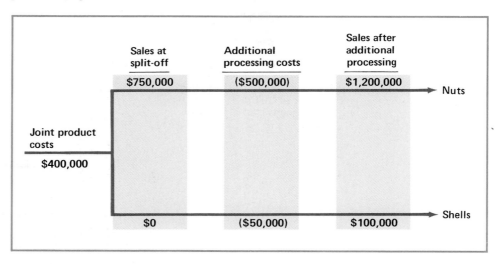

All the facts for Jimmy Joe are in this diagram

Notice in this diagram that the only way Jimmy can produce nuts and shells is to spend $400,000 developing the crop up to the split-off point. No matter what you decide he should do with the nuts and shells—that is, sell at split-off or process further—he first has to spend the $400,000. Since the joint product costs are not affected by the decision you make, they must be irrelevant to the decision.

For nuts, it's better to sell at split-off

The items that are relevant to the decision of selling at split-off or processing further are those that come after the single product splits into two or more joint products. Let's look now at the relevant items, first for the nuts and then for the shells.

For the nut crop, you can see in the diagram that there are two choices. Jimmy can sell it at split-off for $750,000 or he can process it further. If he spends $500,000 to process the nut crop further, he can then sell it for $1,200,000, a net of $700,000 ($1,200,000 − $500,000). If you were Jimmy Joe, would you rather have the $750,000 or the $700,000? Assuming that you'd like to make as big a profit as possible, we feel sure that you would rather have the $750,000 — you would sell the nuts at the split-off point.

For shells: sell after processing

Although technically you have two choices for the shells, telling Jimmy to dispose of them at split-off would probably be the last resort. By processing them further, Jimmy can increase his profits by $50,000 ($100,000 − $50,000). Since this is obviously preferable to receiving zero at the split-off, the shells should be processed further.

The format that accommodates this evaluation of nuts and shells is presented in Exhibit 6-6. It shows that the maximum profit before subtracting the joint costs is $800,000 — if the nuts are sold at split-off and the shells are processed further. After the joint costs are deducted, the maximum profit for Jimmy Joe's farm is $400,000.

EXHIBIT 6-6
Sell at Split-Off or Process Further — An Incremental Approach
What to do depends on this: Is incremental profit from processing further less than or greater than sales at split-off?

	Sales at Split-off	Process Further					Best Decision
		Sales after Processing	−	Additional Processing Costs	=	Net	
Nuts	$750,000	$1,200,000	−	$500,000	=	$700,000	$750,000 Sell at split-off
Shells	-0-	$ 100,000	−	$ 50,000	=	$ 50,000	50,000 Sell after processing

Maximum profits before joint product costs.....................$800,000
Joint product costs.. 400,000
Maximum profits $400,000

Product Costing vs. Special Decisions

The main issue concerning joint products is what to do with them — sell them at split-off or process them further. A second issue concerns the distribution of joint product costs to the joint products. The joint product costs are ***product costs*** — costs that are assigned to inventory when incurred and that are expensed (to cost of goods sold) when the units to which they are assigned are sold. The joint product costs of $400,000 for Jimmy Joe were incurred to produce both nuts and shells. In order to make income statements for the nuts and the shells, we need to know the amount of the joint product costs that is assigned to each.

Income statement for joint products

The problem is, how do we tell exactly how much of the joint product costs was incurred because of the shells and how much was incurred because of the nuts, so that we can assign to each joint product the amount of joint cost that is related to it? The answer is that there is no way to tell exactly how much cost relates to each joint product. So what do we do? We use one of two methods to rather arbitrarily allocate the joint costs to the joint products.

Methods of allocating joint product costs

One method allocates the joint product costs on the basis of the quantity of each joint product — the ***physical volume method.*** For instance, assume that we determine the number of pounds of nuts and shells at the split-off point. If the nuts represent three-fourths of the total weight, then we allocate three-fourths of the joint costs ($\frac{3}{4} \times \$400,000 = \$300,000$) to nuts and the remaining one-fourth ($\frac{1}{4} \times \$400,000 = \$100,000$) to shells. The net income for nuts would be $450,000 ($750,000 − $300,000) and for shells would be a loss of $50,000 ($100,000 − $50,000 − $100,000), combining to a total of $400,000 — which is the maximum profit possible for Jimmy Joe — just as we proved in Exhibit 6-6.

At this point you may be tempted to suggest that Jimmy not sell shells at all because of the $50,000 loss. However, remember that the joint costs of $400,000 are irrelevant to any decision concerning what should be done with each product. There-fore, the amount of joint costs we allocate to each product — and the resulting income for that product — is also irrelevant to this decision. We concluded from Exhibit 6-6 that the very best Jimmy can do is a $400,000 profit, and that's exactly what he has: $450,000 + $(50,000) = $400,000. If Jimmy stopped selling shells alto-gether, the full $400,000 of joint costs would still be incurred and would be assigned completely to the nuts. Consequently, its net income, and the income for the farm as a whole would drop to $350,000 ($750,000 − $400,000).

The other method allocates the joint product costs to the joint products on the basis of the relative sales value of each product at the split-off point. This method is called the ***relative sales value method.*** If a product has no sales value at the split-off point, but can be sold after further processing (which is the situation we have for the shells), the net of (1) the sales after further processing less (2) the additional processing costs is substituted for the sales at split-off. For example, we allocate the $400,000 of joint costs for Jimmy Joe between nuts and shells in the following manner:

Product	Sales Value	Fraction	×	Joint Cost	=	Allocation of Joint Cost
Nuts	$750,000	750/800	×	$400,000	=	$375,000
Shells	50,000*	50/800	×	$400,000	=	25,000
	$800,000					$400,000

* Since there is no sales value at split-off for the shells, the net of $100,000 − $50,000 = $50,000 is substituted.

When we prepare individual income statements for the nuts and shells, we assign $375,000 of the joint costs to nuts and the remaining $25,000 to shells, leaving us with an income for nuts of $375,000 ($750,000 − $375,000) and for shells of $25,000 ($100,000 − $50,000 − $25,000). The combined income once again is $400,000, the maximum profit possible for Jimmy Joe.

Defective Units

Defective units do not meet production standards

When a manufacturer produces finished goods for sale, it is important that the product meet all quality and dimensional (size and shape) standards. When an unsatisfactory unit — a ***defective unit*** — is sold, there is a good chance that the cus-tomer will either return it for a good one, ask for a refund, or stop purchasing from the company altogether. When a bad unit is returned by a customer or is detected as bad before it is sold, the manufacturer can dispose of it for a minimal value or rework it so that it can be sold at close to the regular price. As you might expect, the existence of defective units can seriously erode a manufacturer's profit margin.

Can Defective Units Be Avoided?

Don't try to eliminate all defective units

What would you do if you had defective units? Would you make every effort to produce 100% of your output without a single bad unit? Or would you simply not worry about the problem because there is nothing that you could do about it? Your answer is, hopefully, somewhere between these two extremes.

Most companies are aware that some units will be defective and even expect a certain amount of bad units to accompany the good units. A reasonable number of defective units is considered a normal or acceptable part of continuing efficient operations, given the current quality of materials, laborers, machinery, and supervision. If you attempted to eliminate all defective units, you would have to incur substantial additional costs to improve the overall quality of the production process. The additional costs are often greater than the benefits of eliminating a small amount of defective units. As a result, most organizations look upon this small quantity of defective units as a necessary evil.

Whenever the number of defective units exceeds an acceptable level (probably set as a percentage of total production), every effort must be made to find the cause and eliminate the problem. Defective units in excess of an acceptable level are not a part of continuing efficient operations. Based on the current quality of materials, laborers, machinery, and supervision, there is no reason to have excess defective units — they are not a necessary evil. The system of controls will have to be tightened.

JIT assumes no defects

This attitude toward defective units — as a necessary evil — is quite a bit different from the attitude taken by the Japanese in an approach to inventory control called ***just-in-time (JIT) material control.*** An integral part of JIT is a commitment to 100% quality — zero defects — through constant improvement of the production process. Every person in the production line is given the responsibility for the quality of the total product. Both operators of equipment and their supervisors are educated so that they can detect quality problems as they arise. They become so familiar with the entire production process that they recognize a problem even if it relates to the work of other employees. At this point — when a defect is observed — work rules require that the production process be stopped and corrections be made, even though the units are still technically acceptable. Immediate feedback concerning the existence of and nature of the defect is then relayed to operators and supervisors at the point where the defect occurred. This immediate feedback not only assists managers in correcting the problem in a timely manner but also helps them to anticipate problems before they occur — thus reducing the number of work stoppages.[2]

Scrap or Rework

As long as we're going to have defective units, let's make the best of the situation

Accepting the fact that some defective units will probably occur, what should a firm do with them — sell them as is when they are detected, or correct their deficiencies and then sell them at a price much closer to the regular price? Let's look at Example 6-6 and its solution in Exhibit 6-7.

---

[2] Robert W. Hall, "Zero Inventory Crusade — Much More than Inventory Management," *Production and Inventory Management,* 3d quarter 1983, pp. 1–4.

Example 6-6

THE CASAROJO CEILING FAN COMPANY

At the beginning of 1988 The Casarojo Ceiling Fan Company budgets production of 100,000 fan blades, of which it expects 10% to be defective. At the point of inspection defective units can be sold for $3 per blade as irregulars or reworked so that they can be sold for the normal price of $10. The costs assigned to each blade up until the inspection point are as follows:

Direct Materials.	$1.50
Direct Labor.	1.20
Variable Overhead.	1.00
Fixed Overhead ($30,000 ÷ 100,000 blades).	0.30
	$4.00

The additional costs of reworking each blade so that it can be sold as a regular are as follows:

Direct Materials.	$0.90
Direct Labor.	0.60
Variable Overhead.	0.50

The selling costs average $1 per blade, whether the units are sold as regulars or irregulars. Should the defective units be sold at $3 per blade or reworked and sold at $10 per blade?

Let's first see which items are irrelevant to the decision.

Casarojo expects to produce 100,000 blades in 1988—10,000 of which are expected to be defective. Since Casarojo doesn't know which blades are defective until the inspection point, it must produce all 100,000 units at least until they are inspected. At that point the 10,000 defective blades are withdrawn from production and the 90,000 good ones continue on.

The production costs up to inspection occur no matter what you do later: they're irrelevant

The cost of making 100,000 blades up to the point of inspection is $4 per unit—a total of $400,000. Look what happens to the $400,000 in the diagram below:

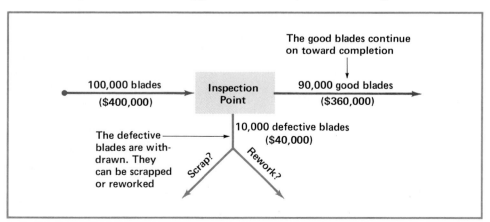

The $40,000 assigned to the defective blades could not be avoided — the costs had to be incurred in order to get the blades to the inspection point. They are the same amount whether the defective blades are scrapped or reworked. Since these costs are not different for the alternatives being considered — scrap or rework — they are irrelevant to the decision. The only production costs that are relevant are the additional costs to rework the defective blades.

The other item that is irrelevant to the decision is the $1-per-blade selling cost. It costs the same amount to scrap a blade as it does to sell a reworked one.

The solution to Example 6-6 is shown in Exhibit 6-7. In column 1 you can see the sales and the costs if we sell the 10,000 defective blades at the inspection point. The sales are 10,000 blades at $3 per blade, and the costs are the 10,000 blades multiplied by the original per-unit costs given in Example 6-6. In column 2 we show the consequences of reworking the 10,000 defective units and selling them for $10 per blade. The production costs shown in column 2 are a combination of the costs of producing the blades up to the inspection point at one cost per unit plus the costs to rework the blades at different costs per unit. For example, the direct materials in column 2 are:

Costs to produce up to inspection point (10,000 blades × $1.50).............	$15,000
Costs to rework (10,000 blades × $0.90).................................	9,000
	$24,000

**EXHIBIT 6-7
Defective Units — Scrap or
Rework — Irrelevant
Production Costs Included**

	(1) Sell at Inspection Point	(2) Rework	(3) Difference
Sales...	$ 30,000	$100,000	$ 70,000
Variable Costs:			
Direct Materials	$ 15,000	$ 24,000	$ (9,000)
Direct Labor	12,000	18,000	(6,000)
Variable Overhead	10,000	15,000	(5,000)
Variable Selling.............................	10,000	10,000	-0-
	$ 47,000	$ 67,000	$(20,000)
Contribution Margin	$(17,000)	$ 33,000	$ 50,000
Fixed Costs..................................	3,000	3,000	-0-
Income from Defective Units..................	$(20,000)	$ 30,000	$ 50,000

Notice also that the items we pointed out as being irrelevant to the decision — the variable selling and the fixed costs — are the same amounts in column 1 as they are in column 2. As a result, there are zeroes for these two in column 3 — the difference column.

In the difference column we see that the revenues are $70,000 higher if we rework the blades, and the costs are $20,000 higher for reworking. The net, $50,000, means that we will have an additional $50,000 of income if we rework the defective blades rather than sell them at the inspection point.

If you prefer to delete the irrelevant items from the analysis, the solution in Exhibit 6-8 could be used instead.

EXHIBIT 6-8
Defective Units—Scrap or Rework
This approach leaves out all irrelevant production costs. We're $50,000 better off if we rework.

	(1) Sell at Inspection Point	(2) Rework	(3) Difference
Sales.............................	$30,000*	$100,000*	$ 70,000
Additional Costs to Rework:			
Direct Materials	$ -0-	$ 9,000	$ (9,000)
Direct Labor	-0-	6,000	(6,000)
Variable Overhead	-0-	5,000	(5,000)
Incremental Costs...........................	$ -0-	$ 20,000	$(20,000)
Incremental Income.........................	$30,000	$ 80,000	$ 50,000

* 10,000 blades at $3 and $10 per blade, respectively.

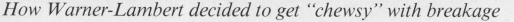

DOING AWAY WITH DEFECTIVE CHICLETS
How Warner-Lambert decided to get "chewsy" with breakage

Although some companies may look upon defective units as a necessary evil, others go to great expense to eliminate all they can. Take for example the case of Warner-Lambert's Adams division which produced Chiclets chewing gum and had been receiving a lot of complaints about damage to its product. "A management team found that the most breakage was occurring at the high-speed filling machines to which the gum went after the candy coating process. Its inspectors compared weights of coated and uncoated gum to see if enough coating had been applied. They didn't test for length, width, or thickness. As a result, lots of malformed Chiclets were pouring into filling machines designed to accept Chiclets of just the right shape. Nonconforming morsels were mashed or broken. When the gum-making machines were adjusted to tighter tolerances, and when the Chiclets were then inspected for length rather than weight, damage fell 60% and output increased 10%. The greater reliability enabled the plant to shrink inventories by 18%."

Source: Steven Flax, "An Auto Man Tunes Up Warner-Lambert," *Fortune,* March 4, 1985, pp. 72–73.

CHAPTER SUMMARY

Managers face a variety of decisions that affect both long-run and short-run profits. Accountants have the responsibility to assist management in the decision-making process by providing them with information that is relevant to the decision at hand. In order for information to be *relevant,* it must meet two criteria: First, it must relate to the future. Second, it must be different for the alternatives being considered. Past information cannot be relevant, but it may be useful in projecting relevant information. Although we prefer relevant information to be as *accurate* as possible, information does not have to be accurate to be relevant.

Managers need to consider both quantitative and qualitative factors when making a decision. *Quantitative* factors are those that can be measured in dollars and cents. *Qualitative* factors cannot be measured in dollars and cents but may still have a significant effect on a decision.

An organization is often receptive to accepting a *special order* at a reduced price from a customer in an unrelated market. Two important considerations in a special order are (1) that excess capacity is available and (2) that the reduced price for a special order will not hurt the firm's pricing structure with regular customers.

There are two different ways to determine the normal price for a product, when the price is based on the costs associated with the product. These methods are referred to as *cost-plus-a-markup* pricing methods. The first method is the *traditional pricing method.* This method adds a desired gross profit per unit to an expected cost of goods sold per unit. The second method is called the ***contribution margin pricing method.*** With this method, the price is determined by adding a desired contribution margin per unit to the variable costs per unit.

Multi-product firms attempt to maximize profits by determining an optimum *sales mix* for their many products. This may involve dropping an entire line or merely revising slightly the percentage of total sales distributed to different products. In order to determine the optimum mix, consideration must be given to each product's contribution margin per unit, the resources of the firm, and the constraints imposed on those resources by each product.

Many organizations produce the raw materials needed for a finished good as well as the finished good itself. However, they may find it more economical to purchase the raw materials from an outsider, and they may wish to free productive capacity for more profitable uses. In this case consideration needs to be given to the most effective use of idle capacity.

Joint products come about when a single product divides into two or more products at a ***split-off point.*** An important decision for a firm with joint products is whether to sell them at split-off or process them further. The joint product should be processed further if the incremental revenue (sales after processing less additional processing costs) exceeds the sales at split-off. ***Joint product costs*** are always irrelevant to the decision.

Defective units are items that fail to meet quality or dimensional standards of production. They can be scrapped when detected as defective or reworked and sold at a price close to the regular price. Defective units should be reworked whenever the incremental profit (sales after reworking less additional costs of reworking) from reworking is greater than the scrap value (sales at the inspection point).

IMPORTANT TERMS USED IN THIS CHAPTER

Accuracy A quality of information; exactness, or preciseness. (page 209)

Carrying costs The costs of maintaining—or carrying—an item in inventory. (page 245)

Constraints Restrictions on a firm's ability to produce and sell an unlimited amount of different product lines. (page 220)

Contribution margin format An income statement format in which variable costs are subtracted from sales and fixed costs are subtracted from the difference (the total contribution margin). (page 212)

Contribution margin pricing method A method of determining the normal price for a product. The price is determined by adding a desired contribution margin per unit to the variable costs per unit. (page 215)

Defective units Units that do not meet dimensional or quality-of-production standards and that can be either scrapped when detected as defective or reworked and sold at a price closer to the regular price. (page 230)

Economic order quantity (EOQ) The size of an inventory order that will minimize the combined costs of ordering and carrying inventory. (page 245)

Graphic method A method for solving linear programming problems in which the constraints for a two-variable model are plotted on graph paper, indicating the point on the graph that will maximize profits or minimize costs. (page 237)

Joint product costs The costs associated with a single product up until the split-off point in a joint product situation. (page 226)

Joint products Multiple products that result from the division of a single product at a split-off point in production. (page 226)

Linear programming A sophisticated mathematical tool for determining the best way to utilize a fixed amount of productive capacity when constraints exist upon the use of that capacity. (page 236)

Opportunity cost The measurable sacrifice (or lost profits) of rejecting one alternative in order to accept another. (page 226)

Ordering costs The costs of ordering, receiving, and handling purchased goods. (page 245)

Relevant Information Information that (1) relates to the future and (2) is different for the alternatives being considered. (page 207)

Reorder point The level of inventory that signals the need to purchase additional inventory. (page 248)

Safety stock The excess inventory—a cushion—that a firm carries to ensure against running out of an item in inventory during lead time. (page 249)

Sales mix For a multi-product firm, the percentage of total sales distributed to each product line. (page 217)

Simplex method A quite rigorous method for solving linear programming problems that can be employed no matter how many variables or constraints there are. (page 237)

Split-off point A point in production at which a single product divides into two or more joint products. (page 226)

Traditional format An income statement format in which the cost of goods sold is subtracted from sales, leaving the gross margin; operating costs are then subtracted from the gross margin. (page 213)

Traditional pricing method A method of determining the normal price for a product. The price is determined by adding a desired gross profit per unit to the cost of goods sold per unit. (page 215)

APPENDIX 6-1: LINEAR PROGRAMMING

Uses of linear programming

Linear programming is a mathematical tool that enables us to determine the best way to use a fixed amount of productive capacity within a number of constraints upon that capacity. What this tool actually does is help us determine exactly how to use the productive capacity to maximize profits or to minimize costs. There are many decision situations in which linear programming, known simply as *LP*, can be used. Examples are determining the optimum mix of different product lines, determining the most efficient mix of raw materials, calculating the most powerful blend of gasolines, and establishing the best way to route a product through a multi-step production process.

We already covered how to determine the optimum mix of different product lines in the text of this chapter, but we will explain this application further in this appendix.

We showed you with Example 6-3 on The Gas Glow Grill Company that when there are only one or two constraints, the best sales mix — the sales mix that ensures maximum profits for the firm — is easily determined. We also pointed out that if there are three or more constraints, it would not be possible to determine the optimum sales mix in the same simple, logical progression of steps. Instead, we would need to use linear programming.

Simplex method

There are basically two approaches to LP. One, called the ***simplex method,*** can be used with any number of constraints and for any number of product lines. However, it is quite rigorous and would require an extensive explanation, which is far beyond the scope of this book. You will probably cover this method in an upper-level quantitative methods course.

Graphic method

The other LP method, called the ***graphic method,*** can be used with multiple constraints, but its application is limited to two product lines (since there are only two axes on the graph). This is the method we will explain here. But in order to do so for the Gas Glow example, we will need to assume that one of the product lines is dropped. With only two product lines the two-dimensional graph can accommodate a fairly complicated situation.

The Graphic Method

Refer to the situation of The Gas Glow Grill Company presented in Example 6-3, and assume that the Deluxe model has been dropped. Also assume the following slightly revised facts:

	Super Deluxe	Matchless	Total
Contribution Margin per Unit.............	$160	$20	
Hours needed to produce each unit........	10	1	
Total machine-hours available			11,800
Maximum demand for each product (in units)........................	1,000	8,000	
Maximum sales of both products combined (in units).............................			7,000

All the constraints for Gas Glow

The contribution margins per unit ($160 for Super Deluxe and $20 for Matchless), the hours needed to produce each unit (10 for Super Deluxe and 1 for Matchless), and the total machine-hours that are available (11,800) are the same as they were originally. Now, however, the maximum demand for Matchless is 8,000 units, and the maximum demand for Super Deluxe is 1,000 units. In addition, a completely new constraint has been added to the analysis. The total combined sales for Super Deluxe and Matchless are not expected to exceed 7,000 units.

What will be the number of units of each model that can be produced and sold to maximize profits for Gas Glow? Let's now look to the linear programming graphic method to find out.

Steps in LP Analysis

There are four basic steps in the LP graphic approach:

Four steps in the graphic method

1. Determine the objective for the firm and express it in a mathematical formula called the *objective function.*

2. Determine the constraints for the firm and express each as a mathematical formula.

3. Draw the constraints on the graph and determine the possible solutions to the analysis.

4. Substitute the values for the different possible solutions into the objective function and select the best result — the optimum solution — as the correct answer.

Let's now explain each step in detail.

Step 1

The objective function

The first step is to be sure of the firm's objective in doing the analysis. Usually, the objective can be expressed in terms of either maximizing profits or minimizing costs. Since Gas Glow is trying to determine its optimum sales mix, its objective is to maximize its profits. The formal expression of this objective in mathematical (or algebraic) form is called the **objective function.** For Gas Glow it is:

Maximize profits

$$\text{Maximum profits} = \$160X + \$20Y$$

where

X = number of Super Deluxe units to be produced and sold (graphed on the X axis)

Y = number of Matchless units to be produced and sold (graphed on the Y axis)

$\$160$ and $\$20$ = coefficients of X and Y; the CMUs for Super Deluxe and Matchless, respectively

An important point to remember is that when you are determining maximum profits, you are doing so by maximizing the total contribution margin. This is because the productive capacity is fixed, which means the total fixed costs are not expected to change. No matter how the capacity is used — no matter which sales mix is the best — total fixed costs remain the same. Therefore, the fixed costs are always irrelevant to the determination of the optimal sales mix. So, when we label the objective function "maximum profit," we could just as well refer to it as "maximum contribution margin."

Step 2

The constraints

The next step is to identify all relevant constraints — the restrictions or limitations on the firm's use of its resources. Once we know the constraints, we need to express them in algebraic form.

The first constraint we have concerns the number of machine-hours needed to produce each unit. It would be expressed algebraically as:

Production constraint

Production constraint: $10X + Y \leq 11{,}800$

According to this equation, the total hours required to produce Super Deluxe and Matchless combined cannot be greater than 11,800 hours. Stated another way, the total combined hours must be less than or equal to 11,800. The symbol $\leq$ indicates "less than or equal to."

The total hours required for any combination of units of X and Y are found by first substituting the number of units to be produced of X and the number of Y into the left side of the constraint equation. Then the number of units are multiplied by the respective number of hours that are required to produce each unit. For example, if 100 units of X (Super Deluxe) and 5,000 units of Y (Matchless) are to be produced, the total hours required would be

$$10(100) + 1(5{,}000) = 1{,}000 + 5{,}000 = 6{,}000 \text{ hours}$$

which certainly satisfies the constraint of being less than or equal to 11,800 hours. On the other hand, if 1,000 units of X and 5,000 units of Y are to be produced, the total hours required would be

$$10(1{,}000) + 1(5{,}000) = 10{,}000 + 5{,}000 = 15{,}000 \text{ hours}$$

which exceeds the 11,800-hour constraint.

The next constraint is the first of two sales constraints. It specifies the maximum possible demand for each individual product. Sales of X (Super Deluxe) are not expected to exceed 1,000 units, and sales of Y (Matchless) are not expected to exceed 8,000 units. This constraint is expressed algebraically for each product as follows:

Individual sales constraints

Sales constraint (individual sales): $X \leq 1,000$

$Y \leq 8,000$

Another constraint is actually the second of the two sales constraints. This one indicates a limit on the total unit sales for the entire firm. Regardless of the demand for individual units (the previous constraint), the firm may feel that its sales force is not big enough to generate maximum unit sales for both products combined of more than 7,000 units. This constraint is expressed in the following manner:

Combined sales constraint

Sales constraint (combined): $X + Y \leq 7,000$

We have one final constraint, one that wasn't even mentioned in the given information. As a matter of fact, it will probably never be explicitly given; you will just have to remember it. This constraint isn't mentioned because it is a constraint in every single LP situation and may seem to be rather obvious. However, it is still necessary to specify this constraint in order for the LP analysis to be completely correct. It involves the simple assumption that the production and sales of each product cannot be negative. That is, we will produce some number of units that is greater than or equal to ($\geq$) zero:

Nonnegativity constraints

Nonnegativity constraint: $X \geq 0$

$Y \geq 0$

Now we are ready to use the graph.

Step 3

Each of the mathematical constraints is graphically represented in Figure 6-1. We will now explain each one.

Plotting the constraints

Nonnegativity Constraint The nonnegativity constraint states that the number of units produced and sold cannot be negative — that is, the number produced and sold must be zero or greater. To represent this constraint within the graph, all we have to do is draw the X and Y axes. Any point on the Y axis or to the right of it satisfies the constraint that X (Super Deluxe) must be positive or equal to zero. And any point on or above the X axis satisfies the constraint that Y (Matchless) must be positive or equal to zero. Therefore, any point within the graph bounded by the X and Y axes represents a level of activity that is greater than or equal to zero for both products.

The X and Y axes provide a boundary

Production Constraint The production constraint equation is:

$$10X + Y \leq 11,800$$

To draw the line representing this constraint, you must first find the point from the equation that falls on the Y axis and the point that falls on the X axis. Then draw a line connecting these two points. The point on the line that falls on the Y axis represents the number of units of Y (Matchless) that could be produced if none of the hours of productive time are used to produce X (Super Deluxe). To find this point, set $X = 0$ in the equation, and solve for Y:

FIGURE 6-1
Constraints for Graphic
Approach to Linear
Programming

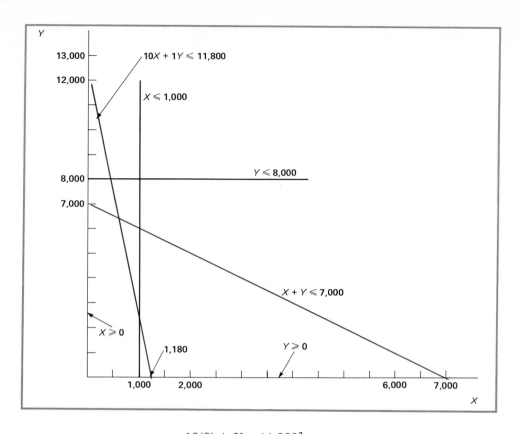

$$10(0) + Y \le 11,800^3$$

When X = 0, Y = 11,800

$$Y = 11,800 \text{ units}$$

When none of the 11,800 hours are going to be used to produce X, all 11,800 are available to produce Y. Thus, at 1 hour per unit for Y, 11,800 units of Y could be produced.

The point on the line that falls on the X axis represents the number of units of X that could be produced if none of the hours of productive time are used to produce Y. Using the same equation but now setting $Y = 0$, we get:

$$10X + 0 \le 11,800$$

When Y = 0, X = 1,180

$$X = 1,180 \text{ units}$$

When none of the 11,800 hours are going to be used to produce Y, all 11,800 are available to produce X. At 10 hours per unit for X, 1,180 units of X could be produced.

These two points ($X = 0$, $Y = 11,800$ and $X = 1,180$, $Y = 0$) represent the extremes — the ends — of the line that connects them. You should now draw the line between these two points.

Once the line is drawn, it is extremely important for you to realize that every point on this line — and any point in the space below and to the left of this line (but not below or to the left of the X and Y axes) — satisfies the 11,800-hour constraint.

---

[3] Any mathematical expression that has an inequality sign rather than an equals sign is solved in the same way as an equation that has an·equals sign.

Sales Constraint — Demand for Individual Products

The next constraint indicates the sales vice president's estimate of the maximum possible sales demand. (You should be aware that a sales manager's estimate of sales is not limited by the number of units that can be produced.) The individual sales constraint on each product is:

$$X \leq 1,000 \text{ units}$$
$$Y \leq 8,000 \text{ units}$$

We can sell no more than 1,000 of X and 8,000 of Y

There is no single line that represents both of these constraints together as there was for the production constraint. Instead, there is a separate line drawn in the graph for each individual constraint. The vertical line labeled $X \leq 1,000$ and drawn parallel to the Y axis in Figure 6-1 represents the constraint for product X. Any point on the line or in the space to the left of the line (but not to the left of the Y axis) represents a value for X that is less than or equal to 1,000 units.

Similarly, the horizontal line labeled $Y \leq 8,000$ and drawn parallel to the X axis represents the constraint for product Y. Any point on or below this line (but not below the X axis) represents a value for Y that is less than or equal to 8,000 units.

Sales Constraint — Total Sales of Products Combined

The final constraint relates to the total unit sales that Gas Glow perceives as possible with the limited sales force that it currently employs. Gas Glow estimates that regardless of the type of product sold, the sales force will not be able to generate sales in excess of 7,000 units. The equation for this constraint is:

X and Y combined can't exceed 7,000

$$X + Y \leq 7,000$$

Even though the individual demands for the two products may total 9,000 units (1,000 plus 8,000 from the previous constraint), the sales force has enough time and ability to generate combined sales of only 7,000 units.

We determine the line for this combined sales constraint in a manner similar to the procedure used for the combined production constraint. First, we find the points representing the quantity of each product sold when the sales of the other product are zero. Doing this mathematically for the combined sales constraint equation, we get:

When one variable = 0, the other = 7,000

$$0 + Y \leq 7,000 \text{ units} \qquad X + 0 \leq 7,000 \text{ units}$$
$$Y = 7,000 \text{ units} \qquad\qquad X = 7,000 \text{ units}$$

When none of the effort of the sales force is used to sell X, all the effort can be exerted to sell Y; the quantity of Y that could be sold (if there is a corresponding demand) is 7,000 units. Conversely, when all the effort is used to sell X and none is used to promote Y, then the sales force could sell 7,000 units of X.

These two points ($X = 0$, $Y = 7,000$ and $X = 7,000$, $Y = 0$) and the line connecting them are represented by the line labeled $X + Y \leq 7,000$ in the graph in Figure 6-1. Any point that lies on this line or to the left of and below this line (but not to the left of or below the X and Y axes) satisfies the constraint of $X + Y \leq 7,000$.

The best answer is in the feasible solution space

Now that we know how to represent graphically all the constraints, we need to identify the area within the graph that satisfies these constraints. Within this area will be the point representing the units of X and Y which, if produced and sold, will maximize profits. This area — which we call the ***feasible solution space*** — is shown by the shaded section of the graph in Figure 6-2. This area is bounded by segments of the sales and production constraints and has corners (labeled 1 to 5) where these segments intersect.

FIGURE 6-2
Linear Programming Graph
The feasible solution space is
bounded by corners 1 through
5. One of these five is the
point of maximum profits.

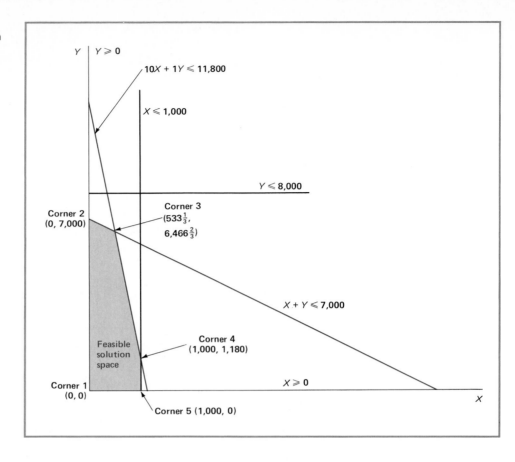

*There are five corners to
the feasible solution space*

The corners of the feasible solution space are the following:

Corner	Value for X	Value for Y
1	-0-	-0-
2	-0-	7,000
3	$533\frac{1}{3}$	$6,466\frac{2}{3}$
4	1,000	1,180
5	1,000	-0-

Every point within this area (which includes the line segments that connect the points) represents a combination of X and Y that satisfies all the constraints. Any point outside the feasible solution space represents a combination of X and Y that violates at least one of the constraints.

Although every point within the feasible solution space satisfies all the constraints, the single point that ensures maximum profits is always on one of the corners. Maximum profits will never be at a point that falls between the lines of the feasible solution space. (It is also possible that the same optimum combination will be found on two adjacent corners. In this unusual situation the optimum will be either of the two corners as well as any point on the line connecting these corners.)

Before we find out which of the five corner points represents the optimum combination, we'll first try to explain how we got the coordinates of corners 3 and 4, which are not as obvious as the coordinates of corners 1, 2, and 5.

Although you can get a rough estimate of the coordinates by merely reading the graph, the better approach is to use simultaneous equations (and substitution, where applicable) to solve for the intersection of the two lines that form a corner.

The third corner represents the point of intersection for the following constraint equations:

Solving for corner 3

$$X + Y = 7,000 \quad \text{and} \quad 10X + Y = 11,800$$

Solving for X and Y with simultaneous equations goes like this:

$$X + Y = 7,000$$
$$10X + Y = 11,800$$

We can solve for X by subtracting the second equation from the first equation:

$$
\begin{aligned}
X + Y &= 7,000 \\
-10X - Y &= -11,800 \\
\hline
-9X \quad &= -4,800 \\
-X &= -4,800 \div 9 \\
X &= 4,800 \div 9 = 533\tfrac{1}{3} \text{ units}
\end{aligned}
$$

When we substitute $533\tfrac{1}{3}$ into the first equation for X, we get the corresponding value of Y:

$$533\tfrac{1}{3} + Y = 7,000$$
$$Y = 7,000 - 533\tfrac{1}{3} = 6,466\tfrac{2}{3} \text{ units}$$

The fourth corner is at the intersection of the two lines representing the following two constraint equations:

And now for the fourth corner

$$10X + Y = 11,800 \quad \text{and} \quad X = 1,000$$

This corner can be found in a simpler manner than that used for corner 3, because the value $X = 1,000$ is already known. By substituting $X = 1,000$ into the following equation, we can get the value of Y:

$$10X + Y = 11,800$$
$$10(1,000) + Y = 11,800$$
$$Y = 11,800 - 10,000 = 1,800 \text{ units}$$

The point of intersection of the two lines—the fourth corner—is $X = 1,000$ and $Y = 1,800$.

Step 4:

Now we are ready to find out which of the five corners has the combination of X and Y values that leads to maximum profits for Gas Glow. We simply substitute the values of X and Y at each corner into the objective function, which, as you know, is:

$$\text{Maximum profits} = \$160X + \$20Y$$

The total contribution margin, as shown below, is highest at corner 3.

Corner	Coordinates	$160X	+	$20Y	=	Total Contribution Margin
1	0; 0	-0-	+	-0-	=	-0-
2	0; 7,000	-0-	+	$140,000	=	$140,000
3	$533\frac{1}{3}$; $6,466\frac{2}{3}$	$ 85,333	+	$129,333	=	$214,666
4	1,000; 1,800	$160,000	+	$ 36,000	=	$196,000
5	1,000; 0	$160,000	+	-0-	=	$160,000

Corner 3 has the most profit

When X is $533\frac{1}{3}$ units and Y is $6,466\frac{2}{3}$ units (or more realistically, $X = 533$ and $Y = 6,467$), the maximum total contribution margin for Gas Glow is $214,666. When the fixed costs of $160,000 are subtracted, we find that the maximum profit is $54,666.

APPENDIX 6-2: INVENTORY PLANNING AND CONTROL MODELS

Planning and controlling inventories is an important process for any company that sells a product. How much merchandise inventory for a retailer (or raw materials inventory for a manufacturer) should be on hand at any point in time? How much inventory should be purchased? What should be the size of each purchase? When should each purchase be made? These are a few of the crucial questions that a firm must answer in order to be profitable in both the short run and the long run. Having too much or too little of any asset — not just inventory — can be costly. For example, having too little cash often results in the loss of cash discounts that are available for early payment on account. However, having too much cash means the loss of interest income that could have been earned from investment opportunities. As another example, not extending credit to customers, which means having no accounts receivable, probably reduces total sales. But extending too much credit can result in large losses from uncollectibles. In the case of inventory, having too little on hand leads to lost sales for a retailer or postponed production runs for a manufacturer when the company is out of stock. On the other hand, having too much in inventory leads to excessive costs of insurance, property taxes, and interest, among other costs of maintaining inventory.

We don't want to have too much or too little of any asset

The Costs of Inventory

There are three groups of costs associated with inventory:

The costs of the purchase itself

The costs of ordering the inventory

The costs of carrying the inventory

The first group includes the invoice price and the transportation costs for the purchased inventory. These costs are considered to be product costs. The second and third groups of costs — the ordering costs and the carrying costs — are period costs.

It is probably obvious that maintaining good control over purchasing costs is important. What may not be so obvious is that the planning and control of ordering costs and carrying costs can be just as important. For the total costs associated with

We want an average balance in inventory that minimizes the inventory costs

any inventory system to be as low as possible, management needs to maintain an average balance in inventory that minimizes the combined costs of purchasing, ordering, and carrying inventory. To minimize this combination, it is necessary to purchase just the right amount of raw materials for a manufacturer or merchandise for a retailer or wholesaler each and every time a purchase is made. This "right amount" is known as the ***economic order quantity (EOQ).*** To understand how we determine the economic order quantity, we first need to understand the types and nature of ordering costs and carrying costs. We no longer need to be concerned with the amount we pay to purchase the inventory, because that total annual cost normally will not be affected by the size of each order. In effect, the total cost of the purchases for the year is assumed to be irrelevant.

EOQ

Ordering and Carrying Costs

Ordering costs (OC) are the costs associated with ordering, receiving, and handling purchased goods. Examples of ordering costs include:

Ordering costs

Clerical costs of preparing and processing the purchase order

Supplies used in the preparation of a purchase order

Costs of unloading, inspecting, and placing the inventory on the storeroom shelves

When we evaluate ordering costs in EOQ analysis, we must first determine the average cost of preparing an order. To do this, we calculate the incremental—the additional—costs of preparing a group of orders during some period of time, and then we divide the incremental costs by the additional orders. The resulting cost per order is assumed to be constant; therefore, the total ordering costs are small when there are just a few extremely large orders made during the year. Conversely, the total ordering costs are large when there are numerous small orders made during the year.

High ordering costs occur when there are many small orders, and vice versa

As you can see in the graph in Figure 6-3, the yearly total ordering costs are very high when the order size is small—since there are a lot of orders. But as the order size increases—and thus the number of orders falls—the total ordering costs get smaller and smaller.

Carrying costs (CC) are the costs of maintaining, or carrying, an item in inventory. These costs include:

Total carrying costs are high when there are just a few large orders

Insurance costs	Obsolescence and theft
Personal property taxes	Storage
Interest costs	Breakage and deterioration

The relevant carrying costs are usually specified in terms of the cost of carrying a single unit in inventory for an entire year. This per-unit cost is assumed to be constant regardless of the number of units purchased per order. Total carrying costs are directly related to the size of the purchase order. Notice in Figure 6-3 the relationship between order size and total carrying costs. When the order size is small, the average investment in inventory is also small; thus the costs of carrying very little inventory are minor. As the order size increases, the related average investment in inventory also increases; thus the resulting total costs of carrying larger amounts in inventory are higher.

As you can see in Figure 6-3, the total ordering and total carrying costs run at odds with each other—as one is increasing the other is decreasing. As a result, the total for the two groups combined has the appearance of a parabola—the top curve in the graph. First, it falls as the order size increases; next, it reaches a low point—which,

The lowest combined costs are found where OC = CC

FIGURE 6-3
Ordering Costs and
Carrying Costs for
Inventory
The combined costs of
ordering and carrying
inventory are lowest when the
ordering costs equal the
carrying costs.

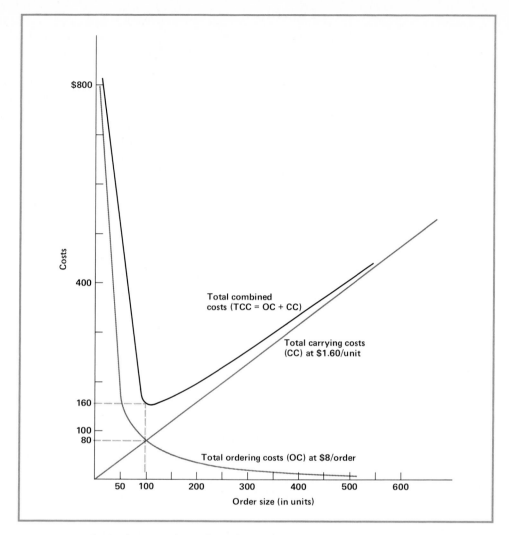

you can see, is the intersection of the lines for total ordering costs and total carrying costs; and then it begins to rise. Naturally, our objective is to determine the low point of the curve for the total combined costs. This minimum point is the EOQ.

Trial and Error

One way to find this minimum point is through trial and error. This involves repeatedly calculating the combined costs for different order sizes until we have found the one with the lowest cost. To do this, we need to use the following formulas to determine the combined costs of ordering and carrying inventory. First, the formula for ordering costs:

Ordering costs = total
orders × cost per order

$$\text{Total ordering costs (OC)} = \frac{\text{number of orders}}{\text{per year}} \times \frac{\text{cost per}}{\text{order made}}$$

$$= \frac{\text{annual demand}}{\text{order size}} \times P$$

$$= \frac{A}{E} \times P$$

where A = total units to be purchased for the year
E = size of each order
P = cost per order placed

Now, the formula for carrying costs:

$$\text{Total carrying costs (CC)} = \text{average investment in inventory} \times \text{cost per unit carried in inventory}$$

Carrying costs = average inventory × carrying cost per unit

$$= \frac{\text{order size}}{2} \times C$$

$$= \frac{E}{2} \times C$$

where C equals the cost of carrying a unit in inventory for an entire year.

And, finally, the formula for the combined costs of ordering and carrying inventory:

Total costs = OC + CC

$$\textbf{Total combined costs (TCC)} = \textbf{OC} + \textbf{CC}$$

$$= \left(\frac{A}{E} \times P\right) + \left(\frac{E}{2} \times C\right)$$

Let's now see how to use these formulas, using the facts given for The Huxtable Company in Example 6-7.

Example 6-7

THE HUXTABLE COMPANY

The Huxtable Company, a retailer, sells a product called Award. Huxtable is trying to decide on the size of each order it will place during the year in order to minimize its combined costs of ordering and carrying inventory. Each unit costs $200 and sells for $300. The costs of ordering and carrying inventory are $8.00 per order and $1.60 per unit, respectively. Huxtable expects its total sales demand to be 1,000 units for the year. The costs for a variety of different order sizes are shown in Exhibit 6-9.

EXHIBIT 6-9   Total Combined Costs of Ordering and Carrying Inventory
Trial and error approach

Symbol		Order Size (E)							
		10	**25**	**50**	**100**	**200**	**400**	**500**	**1,000**
A/E	Number of orders	100	40	20	10	5	2.5	2	1
OC	Ordering costs ($A/E \times$ $8)	$800	$320	$160	$ 80	$ 40	$ 20	$ 16	$ 8
$E/2$	Average investment	5	12.5	25	50	100	200	250	500
CC	Carrying costs ($E/2 \times$ $1.60)	$ 8	$ 20	$ 40	$ 80	$160	$320	$400	$800
TCC	Total combined costs (OC + CC)	$808	$340	$200	$160	$200	$340	$416	$808

The order size that has the smallest combined costs is 100 units, where the ordering costs and the carrying costs are exactly equal. Below 100 units the total combined costs become progressively higher as the order size decreases from 100 to 10. Above

100 units the total combined costs also become progressively higher as the order size increases from 100 to 1,000. This behavior of costs is consistent with the total combined costs curve in Figure 6-3.

Since we used the trial and error approach for only eight different order sizes, you may be wondering whether the total combined costs might be lower at one of the levels we didn't try. Let us assure you that no matter which order size we might have tried, the total combined costs would never be any less than $160, resulting from an order size of 100 units.

The Formula Method

Rather than using trial and error to determine the EOQ, we can use an easier method known as the *EOQ formula.* This approach, which uses square roots, determines the EOQ with a single calculation. The EOQ formula is as follows:

EOQ formula

$$\text{EOQ} = \sqrt{\frac{2AP}{C}}$$

where EOQ = economic order quantity

A = total units to be purchased for the year

P = cost per order placed

C = cost of carrying a unit in inventory for an entire year

We need to order 100 units per order

Using the facts presented for the Huxtable Company, we can determine the EOQ with the following calculation:

$$\text{EOQ} = \sqrt{\frac{2(1,000)(\$8)}{\$1.60}} = \sqrt{10,000} = 100 \text{ units per order}$$

As you can see, this is the same as the solution we got by using trial and error — but it required a lot less work.

Reorder Point

Now we figure when to order

Now that we know what the best order size is for an item in inventory, a related concern is when to make the order. Normally, when EOQ models are employed, the order is made when the inventory balance reaches a certain minimum level. The minimum level that triggers the need to make the order is referred to as the *reorder point.*

In order to determine the reorder point for a firm, we need to know three things:

1. The lead time

2. The average usage during lead time

3. The amount of safety stock

Lead time

The *lead time* is the number of days from the date we place an order to the date we receive the goods. Obviously, we need to have enough inventory on hand to satisfy our needs during this period of time. The amount of inventory we need to have on hand during the lead time is called the *average usage during lead time.* It is determined by finding the average daily usage and then multiplying this amount by the lead time. If we assume constant daily usage, then the daily usage should be the total demand for the year divided by the number of working days in the year.

Average usage during lead time

Naturally, any estimates we make can be wrong. If our estimate of lead time is too short or that of daily usage is too low, then the amount of actual usage during the

We need a safety stock to be sure we don't have stock-outs

actual lead time may be far greater than we anticipated. In this situation we may find ourselves running out of inventory, resulting in lost sales, lost goodwill, and lost customers. To protect themselves against such occurrences, firms often carry more inventory than they need in most lead-time situations. The excess inventory is called the ***safety stock.*** The safety stock serves as a buffer, or cushion, against the chance of stock-outs.

The amount of inventory a company maintains as safety stock should be reasonable. Naturally, the level of safety stock shouldn't be too low, or stock-outs will occur frequently and the related lost sales will be high. On the other hand, it's not wise to have such a large safety stock that the company is ensured of never having a stock-out, because the carrying costs associated with a large safety stock are excessive.

Determining the right amount of safety stock can involve some difficult calculations, which we will not go into. Instead, for all situations in which a safety stock is required, we will tell you what the amount is.

The reorder point for a firm is simply the sum of the average usage during lead time plus the safety stock. If we assume, for Huxtable Company, that the lead time is 10 working days, that there are 250 working days in the year, and that the safety stock is 32 units, then the reorder point would be determined as follows:

We order when inventory falls to 72 units

$$\text{Reorder point (RP)} = \frac{\text{average daily usage}}{\text{during lead time}} + \text{safety stock}$$

$$= (\text{average daily usage} \times \text{lead time}) + \text{safety stock}$$

$$= [(1{,}000 \div 250 \text{ days}) \times 10] + 32$$

$$= (4 \text{ units per day} \times 10) + 32 = 40 + 32 = 72 \text{ units}$$

If everything goes as planned

When the inventory balance falls to 72 units, the order will be placed. If everything goes as planned, 40 units will be used during the 10-day lead time and the inventory balance will be at the safety stock level of 32 when the order comes in. The inventory level increases to 132 units (32 + 100) when the order is received. This is the maximum balance in inventory as long as everything goes as planned. This situation is depicted in the diagram in Figure 6-4.

FIGURE 6-4
Usage during Lead Time as Expected
We order at 72 units. We expect the order to be received in 10 days, when inventory is at 32 (the safety stock). The balance increases to 132, and the process starts again.

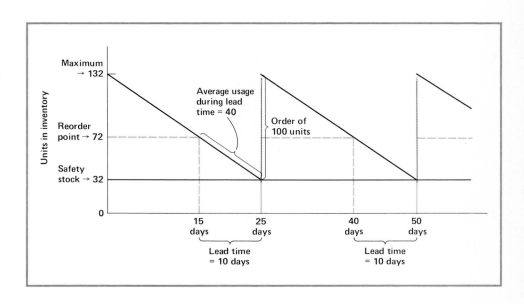

If things don't go as planned

If things don't go as planned and we need more than 40 units during lead time, we have the 32 units in the safety stock to absorb the excess. For example, the lead time might actually be longer than 10 days, or the average usage during lead time might be more than 4 units per day. The idea is for the order to come in before the safety stock is fully depleted and we are forced to turn away customers.

The diagram in Figure 6-5 shows what would happen if the lead time was 12 days instead of 10. First of all, the order would be received on day 27 instead of day 25. During this lead time the usage would be 48 units (12 days × 4 units per day). On day 27 the balance in inventory will have fallen to 24 units (72 units − 48 units) — 8 units lower than the safety stock level of 32, due to the 2 extra days of lead time at 4 units per day. When the 100-unit order is received, the balance will increase to 124 instead of 132, and the process will begin once again. The next reorder point will be on day 40, and if the average usage is as expected — during the lead time expected — the order will be received when the inventory balance falls to the safety stock level of 32 units.

Application of EOQ to Production Runs

In the previous sections we explained how the EOQ formulas can be used to determine the size of each purchase order of merchandise for a retailing concern or of raw materials for a manufacturer. These formulas can also be used to determine how many units to produce in each production run for a manufacturer. For this situation, however, there would be setup costs rather than ordering costs. **Setup costs** include the labor costs associated with preparing machines for the production of a different product, the costs of reorienting workers, and the costs of any necessary paperwork.

Production runs have setup costs instead of ordering costs

Material Requirements Planning (MRP)

A weakness of using EOQ and reorder point methodology with a manufacturer is that it is often used in situations in which it may not be appropriate. Although we did explain how the EOQ can be used for determining the order size of raw materials and the size of production runs, its use should really be limited to those situations in which there is production of *independent demand items* rather than *dependent demand items*.

Independent demand is the demand from customers for finished products. **Inde-**

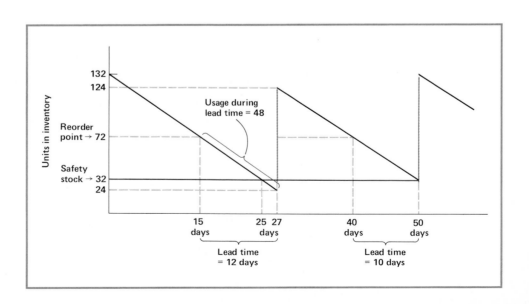

FIGURE 6-5
Usage during Lead Time Greater than Expected
If lead time is longer than expected, our inventory drops into the safety stock before the order comes in.

EOQ is OK with independent demand

pendent demand items are finished goods that need to be produced. **Dependent demand items** are component parts and raw materials that are produced and/or assembled into finished products. All these items depend upon the demand from customers.

For example, a simple file cabinet is constructed from a variety of materials and parts, such as sheet metal, plastic, paint, and handles, and is then packaged for shipping. The finished and packaged file cabinet is the independent demand item. The dependent demand items are the sheet metal, plastic, paint, handles, and packaging.

When the EOQ is used, the need for one inventory item is assumed to be independent of the needs for every other item. For finished goods this assumption is correct, but for raw materials and component parts that go into the finished goods, the assumption is incorrect. If the EOQ is used for each different dependent demand item, there will be separate order quantities and reorder points. This often leads to poor coordination in timing the receipt and usage of the items, which in turn results in excessive safety stocks for some items and stock-outs for others.[4]

EOQ shouldn't be used with dependent demand

Use MRP when there is dependent demand

For manufacturing situations involving dependent demand, the material requirements planning (MRP) technique is recommended. MRP starts with a master schedule for the independent demand items—the finished goods to be sold to the customer. On the basis of these production needs, the requirements of each raw material or component part needed to make or assemble the finished goods can be determined. MRP identifies when a job needs to be done, how much raw material needs to be purchased, and when the raw material is needed. By recognizing the independent-dependent relationship between finished goods and their component parts, MRP is better able to coordinate all manufacturing activities. As a result, the firm is able to maintain a smaller average balance in inventory, while also reducing the number of stock-outs it experiences.[5]

Just-In-Time Inventory

The EOQ and MRP inventory models both assume that it is necessary to maintain some minimum investment in inventory in order to satisfy the maximum needs for that inventory during a planning period. The critical issues are which raw materials or parts should be ordered, how many are needed, and when they are needed. In contrast, the Japanese approach to inventory planning is to have no inventory at all.

The Japanese approach

The Japanese consider space to be one of their most precious commodities. The use of space to store inventory is seen as a terrible waste. In an effort to use all available space in the most productive manner possible, and with their ability to reduce the costs of placing an order (and/or setting up a new production run) to a bare minimum, the Japanese developed an inventory system called **just in time (JIT)**. The philosophy of just in time is that having idle inventory (raw materials, work-in-process, and finished goods) on hand is a waste of resources and that every effort should be made to reduce the investment in inventory to as close to zero as possible. They feel that it is not necessary to have inventory on hand until the very moment it is needed—until it is "just in time" to be used. By managing the timing of the receipt of raw materials and the flow of manufactured parts through the factory, inventory arrives in very small lots on nearly a continuous basis—often only hours or even minutes before it is needed.

For JIT the ideal is zero inventory

[4] Thomas E. Hendrick and Franklin G. Moore, *Production/Operations Management,* 9th ed. (Homewood, Ill.: Richard D. Irwin, Inc., 1985), pp. 207–230.

[5] James J. Chrisman, "Basic Production Techniques for Small Manufacturers: II. Inventory Control Methods and MRP," *Production and Inventory Management,* 3d quarter 1985, p. 58.

With JIT the OC and CC are near zero

By holding very small amounts in inventory at any time, carrying costs are reduced to a minimum. In addition, since the Japanese have been able to reduce the time required to order raw materials (and the time required to set up new production runs) to only a fraction of what it takes in U.S. industry, the related costs of placing an order (or setting up a new production run) are likewise kept to a minimum. The Japanese, in essence, have been able to minimize the combined costs of ordering and carrying inventory by reducing these costs almost to zero.[6]

QUESTIONS

1. Explain what is meant by the term *relevant information.*

2. "Information must be accurate in order to be relevant." Comment.

3. All differential costs relate to relevant items. Why?

4. What is an *opportunity cost?*

5. "Opportunity costs are always relevant." Do you agree? Explain.

6. Since past costs are irrelevant, is it possible for them to be useful? Explain.

7. "A special order should be accepted only if the gross profit for the special order is positive." Comment.

8. "In a multi-product firm, the firm can maximize profits by producing and selling only that product with the highest contribution margin per unit." Comment.

9. Explain several reasons why a firm would make a raw material needed in production rather than buy it from an outside supplier.

10. Why are joint product costs irrelevant to the decision of whether to sell at split-off or process further?

11. What is a *defective unit?* Why would a firm be willing to accept the occurrence of defective units rather than try to completely eliminate them?

12. Give some examples of both quantitative factors and qualitative factors in a make-or-buy decision and for a decision regarding whether to accept or reject a special order.

13. Discuss completely whether the following statements are true or false:

    a. A product should always be dropped by a firm when its product-line income is negative.
    b. As long as a product line is showing a profit, it should never be dropped.
    c. It's not that important whether a product line has a positive or negative contribution margin. What's important is whether or not it has a favorable amount of net income.

14. Explain what is meant by the term *economic order quantity.*

15. "The relevant costs associated with an economic order quantity for a firm are the ordering costs, the carrying costs, and the purchase price of the inventory." Do you agree? Explain.

16. A common financial ratio used to evaluate the profitability of a firm is the number of inventory turnovers. Many people feel that a firm should have as many turnovers as possible. How does this attitude relate to the use of an EOQ inventory model? Is it always best to maximize the number of inventory turnovers? Why?

17. What are the types of inventory costs that are relevant to the determination of an EOQ? How do these costs relate to increases in the size of the inventory order?

---

[6] Hendrick and Moore, p. 310.

18. Define the term *linear programming,* and give some business applications for this quantitative model.

19. What assumptions do we make concerning the amount of fixed costs when doing linear programming.

20. Describe the steps that are taken in the graphic approach to linear programming.

EXERCISES

Exercise 6-1
Deciding whether to accept or reject a special order

The General Electronics Corporation sells cordless phones that double as Strideman radios for $100 apiece. The per-unit costs for the phones are shown below (based on normal sales of 20,000 per year):

Cost of Goods Sold (including $20 for fixed factory overhead) $60
Selling Costs (including $10 of fixed selling costs; the remaining costs are shipping costs) 30

The sales vice president is offered a unit price of $56 for a special order of 3,000 phones by an Eskimo village. The village representative will pick up the order at the door, since shipments to his remote village take 6 months for delivery. The vice president suggests that the order be rejected when he learns that it costs $60 to produce each phone.

What would you suggest? How much more (or less) income will General Electronics have if it accepts the order?

(Check figure: $48,000)

Exercise 6-2
Determining whether an unprofitable product should be dropped

The Upbeat Company sells three products, but is considering dropping at least one of them because it looks like a couple are losing money for the firm. Income statements for the three products are shown below:

	Product		
	A	**B**	**C**
Sales.	$100,000	$60,000	$ 55,000
Variable Costs	55,000	50,000	60,000
	$ 45,000	$10,000	$ (5,000)
Fixed Costs.	15,000	15,000	15,000
Net Income	$ 30,000	$ (5,000)	$(20,000)

a. Should any product line be dropped? Why? Show calculations to support your conclusion.
b. Prepare income statements for all three products if the $45,000 of fixed costs is distributed to A, B, and C in a 60:20:20 ratio. Compare the total income to the income in the original situation. Should any product be dropped now?

(Check figure: $5,000)

Exercise 6-3
Determining whether a new product line will improve profits

Currently the Bruno Company has only one product line, but it is considering the addition of a second line in 1988. Information related to the new product line is as follows:

Sales Price. $25
Variable Costs per Unit $20
Unit Sales 8,000
Fixed Costs Allocated to New Product Line $40,000

The projected income statement for Bruno, if the new line is not added, is shown below:

Sales (8,000 units)............................	$525,000
Variable Costs	260,000
	$265,000
Fixed Costs..................................	80,000
Net Income..................................	$185,000

Should Bruno add the new line? Why or why not?

(Check figure: Net income if added = $225,000)

Exercise 6-4
Maximizing profits in a
multi-product firm with
one constraint

The O'Donohue Company sells two products, A and B, that have contribution margins per unit of $6 and $4, respectively. It takes 3 hours to produce A and 1 hour to produce B. The company can sell all the units it produces, and the fixed costs are $17,000.

Which product should be produced? Why?

Exercise 6-5
Deciding whether to
purchase a part or
produce it internally

The Reeves Corporation is currently producing 10,000 units of a part that is used in the production of its main product line. The costs of producing this part are:

Direct Materials	$1.50
Direct Labor	0.75
Total Overhead.................	1.25*
	$3.50

* 60% is for variable overhead.

The vice president of production is considering buying the part from a supplier at $3.15 per unit and discontinuing internal production. He determines that four-fifths of the fixed overhead will exist regardless of the decision. The remainder will occur only if the part is produced.

Determine whether the part should be purchased or produced internally. Provide supporting computations for your answer.

(Check figure: Produce is preferable by $500)

Exercise 6-6
Deciding whether it's
better to sell a joint
product at split-off or to
process further

The Banana Split Fruit Company makes a product that breaks into three products at a split-off point. Information concerning the three products is as follows:

1. Product X can be sold at the split-off point for $90,000 or processed further (additional processing costs are $35,000) and sold for $115,000.

2. Product Y can be sold only after further processing (additional processing costs are $40,000) for $70,000.

3. Product Z can be sold only at the split-off point for $60,000.

The joint product costs are $135,000.

Determine whether each product should be sold at the split-off point or after additional processing. What are the maximum profits possible for Banana Split?

(Check figure: Maximum profits = $45,000)

Exercise 6-7
Maximizing profits in a joint product situation

In 1989 the Energetics Company produced two chemicals, Oxydol and Pectic, from a single compound. The following income statement relates to that year:

	Oxydol	Pectic	Total
Sales..............................	$150,000	$220,000	$370,000
Additional Processing Costs	$ 60,000	$180,000	$240,000
Allocated Joint Product Costs	45,000	50,000	95,000
	$105,000	$230,000	$335,000
Net Income	$ 45,000	$ (10,000)	$ 35,000

a. Energetics is considering dropping Pectic (because of its reported loss and the fact that it cannot be sold at split-off). Prepare a new income statement to reflect this action. Is it a good idea to drop the product?

b. Assume instead that Energetics can sell Oxydol and Pectic at the split-off point for $100,000 and $35,000, respectively. When should each product now be sold in order to maximize profits? What are the maximum profits possible?

(Check figure: Maximum profits = $45,000)

Exercise 6-8
Deciding whether to scrap or rework defective units

The Huff Corporation expects 2,000 units to be defective during the next month out of a total production of 30,000 units. The cost of producing each unit is $15 (including $2 of fixed overhead). The defective units can be scrapped for $4 per unit or reworked so that they can be sold for $16 each. The regular sales price is $24, and the variable costs of reworking the defective units are $13 per unit.

Should the defective units be scrapped or reworked?

(Check figure: Difference in alternatives = $2,000)

Exercise 6-9
Calculating EOQ and minimum OC + CC

Goodday Tire Supply sells tires that cost $20 apiece for $50. The costs of placing an order average $6.25 per order, and the carrying costs are 25% of the cost of tires carried in inventory. The total purchases for the year are estimated to be 16,000 tires.

What will be Goodday's economic order quantity? What will be the minimum combined costs of ordering and carrying inventory?

(Check figure: EOQ = 200)

Exercise 6-10
Determining the reorder point

The Supercharge Company expects to purchase 3,000 batteries during the coming year at $20 per battery. The batteries will later be sold at a markup of 75% of cost. The company has determined its EOQ to be 1,000 batteries per order. There are 250 working days during the year for Supercharge, and it normally takes 14 working days for an order to be received. The company maintains a constant safety stock of 150 batteries.

a. What will be the company's reorder point?
b. How many units will typically be in inventory when an order is received?
c. How many days' supply will be carried in safety stock?
d. What will be the balance in inventory when the order arrives if the order arrives 3 days late?
e. Answer part **d** again, but this time assume the order arrives 3 days early.

Exercise 6-11
Maximizing profits with graphic LP

The In Pursuit Company sells two versions of its new board game, "Significant Pursuit." They are the adult's version and the child's version. The contribution margin per unit for the adult's version is $12, for the child's version $15. The total fixed costs for the company are $80,000 regardless of how many units of each version are sold. The total productive capacity of the printing process is 20,000 hours, and it takes 1 hour and $1\frac{1}{2}$ hours to produce the adult's and child's versions, respectively. The sales manager estimates total demand for the two versions to be 15,000 units for the first year. In addition, she estimates that the maximum sales for the two products individually will be 8,000 for the adult's version and 9,000 for the child's version.

In order to maximize profits for the firm, how many units of each version should be produced? Use the graphic approach to linear programming to determine your answer. What will be the maximum profits for the firm?

(Check figure: $118,000)

Exercise 6-12
Maximizing profits with
two constraints

Sexy Spa Associated produces two models of spas. The following facts relate to the production and sale of each model:

	In-Ground	Portable
Contribution margin per unit...................	$450	$600
Hours per unit to produce	9	15
Maximum unit sales................................	1,500	800

The total hours of machine time available for the year are 20,000. The fixed costs are $300,000.
Determine the number of units that must be sold to maximize profits. Use the graphic approach to linear programming to get your answer. What will be the maximum profits for the firm?

(Check figure: $874,800)

PROBLEMS: SET A

Problem A6-1
Deciding whether a
product line should be
dropped

The Patriotic T-Shirt Corporation, an official sponsor of the 1984 Olympics, is continuing to sell 1984 Olympic T-shirts in 1988, before they become out of date with the 1988 Olympics. After looking at the 1987 income statement presented below, the president feels that the USA '84 shirt is the only profitable line. He insists that the Gold Rush '84 and LA '84 lines be dropped.

	Product			
	USA '84	Gold Rush '84	LA '84	Total
Sales.........................	$450,000	$300,000	$ 500,000	$1,250,000
Cost of Goods Sold:				
Variable....................	$200,000	$180,000	$ 300,000	$ 680,000
Fixed	45,000	40,000	50,000	135,000
	$245,000	$220,000	$ 350,000	$ 815,000
Gross Profit	$205,000	$ 80,000	$ 150,000	$ 435,000
Selling and Administrative:				
Variable....................	$ 50,000	$ 60,000	$ 210,000	$ 320,000
Fixed	30,000	30,000	40,000	100,000
	$ 80,000	$ 90,000	$ 250,000	$ 420,000
Net Income....................	$125,000	$ (10,000)	$(100,000)	$ 15,000

Required

1. Assuming that the total fixed costs will not be affected by the decision, should any product line be dropped? Why? By what amount will income change?
2. Assume that Gold Rush '84 and LA '84 are being dropped and that the fixed overhead costs reduced by dropping each line are $30,000 and $25,000, respectively. By how much will the deletion of these products increase or decrease the net income for the firm?

(Check figure: $5,000)

Problem A6-2
Preparing income statements and maximizing profits for joint products

The Generic Component Company produces a liquid in a heating process which, at 525 degrees, splits into two products that can be sold to drug manufacturing companies. The first product, TR3, can be sold at the split-off point for $2,400,000, or processed further. The product's additional processing will cost $450,000 but will increase sales to $3,600,000.

The second product, SX100, can also be sold at split-off or processed further. Sales at split-off would be $1,800,000; after additional processing, $2,250,000. The additional processing costs will be $600,000. The joint product costs are $3,000,000.

| Required |

1. Draw a diagram depicting the situation described above.
2. Assume that the joint costs are allocated $1,050,000 to TR3 and $1,950,000 to SX100. If both products are sold at split-off, what would be the income for the firm as a whole as well as for each product?
3. Answer part 2 again but assume that both products are sold after additional processing.
4. In order to maximize profits for the firm, should each product be sold at split-off or processed further?
5. Using the answer to part 4 and assuming the same cost allocation as in part 2, determine the income for the firm as a whole as well as for each product line.

(Check figure: Net income = $1,950,000)

Problem A6-3
Maximizing profits in a two-product firm with constraints

The Toysuki Company produces two models of television sets. The following information relates to the production and sale of each model:

	Portable	Console
Sales price....................................	$400	$500
Variable cost per unit............................	$320	$300
Allocated fixed costs............................	$1,620,000	$3,580,000
Hours needed to produce	2	10
Maximum unit sales	100,000	20,000

The total hours of productive capacity are 250,000. The controller is trying to decide how to distribute the productive capacity to the two products in order to maximize profits, and she asks for your advice.

| Required |

Determine the number of units of each product that should be produced and sold in order to maximize profits. What are the maximum possible profits for Toysuki?

(Check figure: Maximum profits = $3,800,000)

Problem A6-4
Determining the effect of accepting a special order

The Stickney Stuffing Company produces and sells cases of bread-crumb stuffing. During 1988 Stickney had the following operating results:

Sales ($25 per case)		$75,000
Cost of Goods Sold:		
Variable.......................	$25,000	
Fixed	5,000	30,000
Gross Profit		$45,000
Selling and Administrative:		
Variable.......................	$15,000*	
Fixed	3,000	18,000
Net Income		$27,000

* 40% for sales commissions and the remainder for shipping.

Stickney is considering a special order from Golden Fresh Poultry, during a slow month, for 1,000 cases at $15 per case. If the order is accepted, there will be no sales commissions on the transaction. Since it is a one-time deal, Stickney figures it can cut variable production costs by 20% per unit (by using cheaper materials).

| **Required** |

Determine whether or not the special order should be accepted. What will be the effect on profits of the firm if the order is accepted?

(Check figure: Change in profits = $5,333)

Problem A6-5
Determining whether profits will improve by making instead of buying a raw material

The Impredrin Corporation produces and sells an aspirin called Tylenun. In the past one of the raw materials, Buffer, was purchased from a supplier, but Impredrin is now considering producing it internally. During 1989 Impredrin will require 10,000 pounds of Buffer for production; if purchased externally, it will cost $5.25 per pound. The costs of receiving and handling purchases of Buffer average $0.60 per pound.
   The costs per pound of producing Buffer internally are given below:

Direct Materials...............................	$1.00
Direct Labor....................................	4.00
Variable Overhead..............................	0.50
Fixed Overhead	0.75
	$6.25

The fixed overhead for the company in total will not change. Some of the total is assigned to the production of Buffer, since it does utilize some of the productive capacity.

| **Required** |

Determine whether Buffer should be produced internally or purchased from an outside supplier.

(Check figure: Difference in profits = $3,500)

Problem A6-6
Determining whether improvements should be made that can eliminate defective units

Each year the Moody Blues Company produces 25,000 record players, of which 2,000 are found to be defective prior to their sale. A record player regularly sells for $75, but a defective unit can only be scrapped for $25. The chief engineer, Ray Virginian, feels that the process can be improved enough to eliminate all defective units, but the controller, Regina Christy, is doubtful that the changes can be cost-effective. Regina determines the following per-unit cost relationships expected for the coming year, with and without the proposed changes:

	Without Improvements	With Improvements
Direct Materials............................	$20	$22.50
Direct Labor................................	10	11.00
Variable Overhead	5	5.00
Fixed Overhead.............................	4	4.20
Fixed Selling...............................	3	3.00

| **Required** |

Should Ray Virginian be allowed to implement his proposed improvements? Support your answer with computations in good form.

(Check figure: Difference in profits = $7,500)

**Problem A6-7
Making decisions
concerning multiple
products**

The controller of Sonymax Electronics has prepared the following product-line income statements for 1988, and the president is extremely dissatisfied with the profits from his SR25 and SR100 lines.

	SR25	SR50	SR100
Units Produced and Sold............	12,500	15,000	8,000
Sales	$500,000	$300,000	$250,000
Variable Costs:			
Production	$300,000	$105,000	$110,000
Selling	100,000	45,000	40,000
	$400,000	$150,000	$150,000
Fixed Costs (allocated by set ratio):			
Production	$ 75,000	$ 60,000	$ 70,000
Selling	50,000	40,000	50,000
	$125,000	$100,000	$120,000
Income...........................	$ (25,000)	$ 50,000	$ (20,000)

Required

Answer each *independent* question below:
1. What will be Sonymax's profits if SR25 or SR100 is dropped? Would you recommend that either one be dropped?
2. Assume that Sonymax is considering a special order of 2,000 SR50 units at $14 per unit. It will not be necessary to incur any additional shipping costs (shipping costs are two-thirds of the variable selling costs). If Sonymax accepts the special order, the variable production costs will be $3 higher per unit because higher labor rates must be paid for overtime work. Should the order be accepted? Show all work.
3. Sonymax is hoping to shift some of the production and sales from SR25 to SR100. It wants to have a sales mix of 20:40:40 for SR25, SR50, and SR100, respectively. How many units would the firm have to sell to generate a profit of $75,000 if the desired sales mix can be attained? (See "Unchanging Sales Mix" section in Chapter 5.)
4. Assume that it takes 1 hour to produce SR25, 2 hours for SR50, and 4 hours for SR100 and that the total hours of machine time available are 74,500 per year. In addition, the maximum demand for each product is estimated to be the following:

Maximum Sales	
SR25	25,000
SR50	30,000
SR100	19,000

How many units of each product line should be sold in order to maximize profits? What are the maximum profits possible for Sonymax?

**Problem A6-8
Using the EOQ model with
different values for C and P**

Chic Jean Apparel uses an EOQ model to help in the planning and control of its inventory. One of the best-selling items for Chic is its line of Saswhom Designer Jeans, which are sold to the irrational public for $60 per pair (at a markup of 400% of cost). Chic expects to buy and sell 12,000 pairs of Saswhom in 1988. The relevant costs are:

Ordering costs......................... $2.50 per order
Carrying costs:
  Insurance........................... 1% of cost
  Property taxes...................... 2% of cost
  Interest............................ 12% of cost

1. Determine the EOQ and calculate the total ordering costs and carrying costs at this level.

(Check figure: TCC = $328.66)

2. Do part 1 again, but this time assume the ordering costs are 40% higher than they were in the original information.
3. Do part 1 again, but this time assume the carrying costs are 40% higher than they were in the original information.
4. Evaluate the significance of the different results obtained in parts 1 through 3.

Problem A6-9
Determining the values to use for *C* and *P* in EOQ

Radio Hut is a retailer that sells a variety of electronic devices. One very popular item is the Smokey the Bandit Fuzz Buster, which retails for $110 (at a 100% markup over cost). Radio Hut plans to buy 8,800 Fuzz Busters in the coming year and to sell them continuously throughout a 312-working-day year. Radio Hut has gathered the following information concerning the costs of ordering and carrying inventory.

Ordering Costs

During the 2 months representing the high and low activity levels for last year, the total costs for the receiving, purchasing, and accounts payable departments, and the related orders made, were as follows:

	Low	High
Total costs...	$14,000	$17,000
Number of orders for all inventory items...............	200	500

Desired Rate of Return

Radio Hut expects to earn a 15% return on the cash that will be tied up in inventory.

Theft

Radio Hut estimates that it loses about .1% of its inventory each year from employee theft.

Storeroom Costs

Radio Hut leases a warehouse in which it stores inventory until the items are shipped out to the retail store. The rental is based primarily on the square feet of space used for storage. A fixed charge of $1,000 per month has to be paid even if no inventory is stored during a particular month. The relevant rental information for December of last year was:

Square feet rented	10,000 feet
Inventory stored...........................	18,000 units
Total rent	$6,000

For simplicity, assume that all inventory items take up the same amount of space in storage.

The remaining carrying costs average $2,500 per month plus 2% of the average investment in inventory.

Radio Hut maintains a minimum balance in inventory great enough to ensure that it is never out of stock. The time it takes for an order to be processed and later received from the supplier averages 12 working days. The longest time it ever took to receive an order was 15 working days.

1. Determine the ordering cost per order, and the carrying cost per unit carried in inventory for a full year.
2. Determine the economic order quantity.
3. Calculate the total ordering costs and carrying costs.
4. Determine the reorder point.

(Check figure: 762)

**Problem A6-10
Using graphic LP with
several constraints**

The Whirleybird Fan Company produces two types of ceiling fans that pass through two production departments (A and B) before they are completed. The production time per unit and the total capacity of each production department were determined to be:

	Production Time per Unit	
Total Capacity	Model A281	Model B564
Department A 100,000 hr	6 hr	3 hr
Department B 30,000 hr	2 hr	1 hr

In addition, the raw material needed for model B564 is in scarce supply. Whirleybird's supplier indicates that he can guarantee only enough raw material to produce 25,000 units.

The company has a contract to sell a buyer at least 5,000 units of model A281. The buyer is an important customer, so Whirleybird realizes the contract must be honored.

Both models sell for the same price, $250, but the variable costs per unit differ:

	Variable Costs per Unit	
	Model A281	Model B564
Department A..................................	$55	$ 63
Department B..................................	44	48
	$99	$111

Whirleybird wants to maximize its profits.

| *Required* |

1. What is the objective function for Whirleybird?
2. What are the constraints for Whirleybird? Show them in equation form.
3. Using the graphic approach to linear programming, determine the number of units of each product that must be produced and sold in order to maximize profits for the firm.

(Check figure: 5,000 of A281)

**Problem A6-11
Using graphic LP for
Problem A6-7**

Refer to part 4 of Problem A6-7 on Sonymax Electronics. This time, however, the problem will be solved by using the graphic approach to linear programming. We will continue to assume that it takes 1 hour to produce SR25, 2 hours for SR50, and 4 hours for SR100 and that the total machine time available is 74,500 hours. We will now, however, add a few new wrinkles to the problem. Assume that Sonymax has a contract to sell 5,000 units of SR100 to one of its customers and that there are no other customers for this product line. In addition, assume that Sonymax has binding contracts to sell at least 3,000 units of SR25 and 4,000 units of SR50. However, for these two products, there is a great potential for additional sales beyond those guaranteed by the binding contracts. The maximum sales for SR25 and SR50 are estimated to be 25,000 units and 30,000 units, respectively.

| *Required* |

(Hint: Since the graphic approach can be used with only two product lines, you need to deal with only the two products whose total sales are not fixed by binding contract.)
1. What is the objective function for Sonymax?
2. What are the constraints for Sonymax?
3. Using the graphic approach, determine the maximum contribution margin and the number of units of each product line that need to be sold in order to maximize the contribution margin.

(Check figure: SR25 = 25,000)

PROBLEMS: SET B

Problem B6-1
Increasing profits by
dropping or adding
product lines

The Jordan Company sells three products and has prepared the following income statements for 1988:

	Product			
	S	**F**	**U**	**Total**
Sales	$100,000	$ 80,000	$150,000	$330,000
Cost of Goods Sold	65,000	75,000	70,000	210,000
Gross Margin........................	$ 35,000	$ 5,000	$ 80,000	$120,000
Operating Expenses	40,000	35,000	35,000	110,000
Net Income	$ (5,000)	$(30,000)	$ 45,000	$ 10,000

The fixed costs included in Cost of Goods Sold and Operating Expenses are as follows:

	Fixed Costs Included in:	
	Cost of Goods Sold	**Operating Expenses**
Product S	$25,000	$20,000
Product F........................	15,000	10,000
Product U	20,000	25,000
	$60,000	$55,000

Required

1. Reconstruct the income statements in the contribution margin format.
2. Should any of the product lines be dropped? Why?
3. Assume in this part that products S and F are dropped and that the fixed overhead costs which can be reduced by dropping each line are $10,000 and $8,000, respectively. By how much would the profits for the firm be reduced or increased?

(Check figure: $17,000)

4. Disregarding part 3, assume that product N is added, having sales of $90,000 and a variable cost ratio of 35%. Assume also that the total fixed overhead and fixed operating costs will not change but that $25,000 ($15,000 of factory overhead and $10,000 of operating expenses) of the total will be allocated to this new line. By how much will the net income change with the addition of product N?

(Check figure: $58,500)

Problem B6-2
Preparing income
statements and
maximizing profits for
joint products

The Stockstill Lumber Company incurs costs of $200,000 in cutting and transporting trees to the sawmills, at which time the trees are split into three products: wood, pulp, and sawdust. Wood can be sold immediately for $170,000 or processed further in order to be sold for $185,000. Pulp can be sold at split-off for $120,000 or after processing for $130,000. Sawdust can be sold only at split-off for $40,000. The additional processing costs are $10,000 for wood and $20,000 for pulp.

Required

1. Draw a diagram depicting the situation described above.
2. Assume that the joint costs are allocated as follows: $80,000 to wood, $70,000 to pulp, and $50,000 to sawdust. If all products are sold at split-off, what would be the income for each product and for the firm as a whole?

3. Answer part 2, but assume that wood and pulp are sold after additional processing.
4. Should each product be sold at split-off or processed further? Determine the maximum profits for the firm.

(Check figure: $135,000)

Problem B6-3
Maximizing profits in a multi-product firm

The Cuomo Corporation is about to introduce two new product lines that will share the facilities of a single plant. Estimates concerning the potential per-unit revenues and costs are given below:

	Product X	Product Y
Sales Price	$100	$200
Cost of Goods Sold:		
Variable	$ 20	$ 80
Fixed	10	15
	$ 30	$ 95
Gross Profit	$ 70	$105
Operating (all variable)	10	20
Income	$ 60	$ 85

In addition, it will take 2 hours to make one unit of product X and 4 hours to make one unit of product Y. The total productive capacity is 100,000 hours, and Cuomo can sell all the units it produces.

Required

1. How many units of each product need to be produced and sold in order to maximize profits for Cuomo?
2. Assume now that the maximum demand for X and Y is 15,000 and 20,000 units, respectively. How many units of each product should be produced and sold in order to maximize profits? What is the maximum total contribution margin for Cuomo?

(Check figure: Product Y = 17,500 units)

Problem B6-4
Deciding whether to accept or reject the special order

The Winfield Corporation produces baseball batting helmets priced to sell for $16 per helmet, but it is considering a special order for 5,000 helmets at only $14 per helmet. In 1989, 25,000 helmets were produced and sold, 6,000 below full capacity. The income statement for 1989 is shown below:

Sales		$400,000
Cost of Goods Sold:		
Direct Materials	$40,000	
Direct Labor	30,000	
Variable Overhead	25,000	
Fixed Overhead	12,500	107,500
Gross Profit		$292,500
Operating Expenses:		
Variable Selling	$50,000	
Fixed Selling	20,000	70,000
Net Income		$222,500

The additional information relates to the special order. The materials used will be of an inferior quality, costing $0.20 less per helmet. Direct labor will require 10% fewer hours, and variable overhead fluctuates with direct labor hours. Shipping costs of $0.25 per helmet will not have to be paid by Winfield since the helmets will be picked up by the customer at the factory door. Finally, if the deal goes through, the sales representative will receive a bonus of $1,000.

| **Required** | Should the special order be accepted or rejected? Show details to support your answer. |

(Check figure: Difference = $43,350)

Problem B6-5
Determining whether profits will be better by making or buying a part

The Amplex Radio Company makes its own circuit boards for use in the production of its radio lines. One circuit board, FX12, was used in 10,000 radios last year. The costs of producing FX12 were:

Direct Materials...............................	$ 8,000
Direct Labor..................................	12,000
Variable Overhead	4,000
Fixed Overhead	16,000
	$40,000

Amplex is considering purchasing the 10,000 circuit boards from Beta Electronics for $2.70 per board (plus shipping costs of $0.10 per board).

If the boards are purchased, the released capacity can be used to produce 500 additional radios, bringing total production to 10,500 radios. The contribution margin per radio is expected to be $10, and the fixed costs of producing the 10,000 radios are $60,000. The fixed overhead of $16,000 represents the salary of a supervisor who will be used to supervise additional production of the major product line if the boards are purchased.

| **Required** | Determine whether the circuit boards should be purchased or produced internally. |

(Check figure: Difference = $1,000)

Problem B6-6
Deciding whether defective units should be completely eliminated

The Murray Corporation is operating at full capacity of 20,000 units per year. The costs of production for 1988 were the following:

Direct Materials ($10/unit)....................	$200,000
Direct Labor ($9/unit).........................	180,000
Variable Overhead ($4/unit)...................	80,000
Fixed Overhead	200,000
	$660,000

Murray's selling costs were $100,000, all of which were fixed. Each year 10% of production is found to be defective, leaving only 18,000 units to be sold at the regular price of $50 per unit. The defective units are scrapped for only $12 per unit.

Murray is considering making improvements in the production department in order to eliminate the occurrence of defective units. This will entail the following: (1) Paying an extra $1 per unit for better-quality materials; (2) spending additional labor time on each unit, which will increase the cost per unit by 15%; (3) hiring an additional supervisor for $20,000 per year; and (4) providing additional maintenance on machinery, which will cost $4,000 per year.

Assume that variable overhead is closely related to the number of direct labor hours.

| **Required** | Determine whether Murray should make the improvements in order to eliminate the occurrence of defective units. |

**Problem B6-7
Making decisions
concerning multiple
products**

The Longex Watch Company produced and sold a total of 72,000 digital watches in 1988. This total is broken down by product line in the 1988 income statement:

	Product Line		
	Luxury	**Diver**	**Sports**
Unit Sales..................	20,000	2,000	50,000
Sales Revenue...............	$ 5,000,000	$2,000,000	$8,000,000
Cost of Goods Sold:			
Variable	$ 4,000,000	$1,500,000	$3,500,000
Fixed.....................	800,000	600,000	1,000,000
	$ 4,800,000	$2,100,000	$4,500,000
Gross Profit	$ 200,000	$ (100,000)	$3,500,000
Operating:			
Variable	$ 1,100,000	$ 300,000	$ 500,000
Fixed.....................	500,000	100,000	500,000
	$ 1,600,000	$ 400,000	$1,000,000
Net Income	$(1,400,000)	$ (500,000)	$2,500,000

Required

Consider each part below independently:
1. Which product(s), if any, should be dropped? Support your answer with organized calculations.
2. Assume now that Longex is considering a special order from the Russian Sports Federation for 5,000 Sports watches at a price of $90 per watch. Longex salespeople usually work on a fixed salary, but if this order is accepted, the salesperson who arranged the deal will receive a $2,000 bonus. Since production of Diver watches is rather slow, one of the supervisors for this product line (who is paid $25,000 per year) will supervise production of the special order. Longex figures that it can reduce the variable production costs by 20% per unit, due to the substitution of questionable materials for the ones usually used. By what amount will Longex's income change if the special order is accepted?
3. Assume now that Longex is going to drop Luxury and attempt to sell Diver and Sports in a 50:50 ratio. If this sales mix can indeed be achieved, how many watches (in total) must Longex sell in order to show a combined profit of $1,000,000?
4. Assume finally that there are two constraints on Longex's production and sale of watches. The constraints are shown below:

	Hours to Produce per Unit	Maximum Sales Demand
Luxury	4	25,000
Diver	2	20,000
Sports	1	100,000

In addition, the total hours of machine capacity are 134,000. How many units of each product line should be sold in order to maximize profits? What are the maximum profits possible for Longex?

(Check figure: $6,200,000)

**Problem B6-8
Using EOQ when the
values for *C* and *P* are
changing**

An extremely popular item for the Sun and Fun Summer Clothes Shop are shorts called "Jammers." Due to the unbelievable demand for these shorts, Sun and Fun expects to be able to sell 25,000 pairs at $30 per pair during 1988. Sun and Fun uses an EOQ model to help in the planning and control of this inventory item, and its accountant has gathered the following information:

Purchase price	$12 per pair
Ordering costs	$10 per order
Carrying costs:	
Shoplifting	4% of cost
Property taxes.........................	3% of cost
Interest...............................	14% of cost

| **Required** |

1. Determine the EOQ and calculate the total ordering costs and carrying costs at this level.

(Check figure: EOQ = 445.44)

2. Do part 1 again, but this time assume the ordering costs are twice what they were in the original information.
3. Do part 1 again, but this time assume the carrying costs are twice as high as they were in the original information.
4. Evaluate the significance of the different results obtained in parts 1 through 3.

**Problem B6-9
Using EOQ after
determining the values for
P and *C***

The Door Emporium is a wholesale distributor of decorative stained-glass doors for the home. Each door costs $200 from the manufacturer and is marked up to sell for $500. During 1988 the Emporium plans to buy 10,000 doors, but it isn't sure how many doors to include in each order. The Emporium wants to maintain a safety stock of 1,000 doors at all times to hedge against the possibility of running out of inventory while waiting for an order to arrive. On the average it takes 16 working days for an order to arrive from the manufacturer. The Emporium expects to be open 6 days per week, 52 weeks per year.

The costs associated with placing an order relate to the purchasing, receiving, and accounts payable departments. Since some of the costs of each department are fixed and will not fluctuate with the number of orders placed, the accountant decides to use the high-low method to determine the variable portion of the total costs of each department. The accountant collected the following results for the appropriate two months from last year:

	High Month	Low Month
Total costs:		
Receiving......................	$4,090	$4,042
Purchasing	$3,243	$3,108
Accounts payable...............	$2,612	$2,554
Total orders placed	54	24
Total orders received and paid for ...	60	28

The Emporium determines the following costs related to carrying the doors in inventory:

Property costs (depreciation, property taxes, etc.).........................	$3,000 per month
Insurance and interest on inventory ...	20% of invoice cost

The Emporium pays freight on all orders received. These costs average 5% of the cost of each order.

Required

1. Determine the ordering costs per order, and the costs of carrying one unit in inventory for an entire year.
2. Determine the economic order quantity. *(Check figure: 142.12)*
3. Calculate the total costs of ordering and carrying inventory for the year, based upon the EOQ determined in part 2.
4. Determine the reorder point.

Problem B6-10
Using graphic LP with several constraints

The Sesayou Doll Company makes two types of dolls for its only customer—Foster Doll, Inc. The two dolls are called Patsy Punk and Rambo Rodney. Both dolls sell for $100, but the variable costs for each type differ. The total variable costs for Patsy Punk are $35 per unit and for Rambo Rodney are $45 per unit. Each doll goes through four steps in the production process—cutting, sewing, stuffing, and packaging. The cutting and sewing are done by machine, but the stuffing and packaging are done manually. The total time available in each production step and the time required to work on each type of doll are given below:

	Times per Unit (in Minutes)		Total Available Time (in Minutes)
	Patsy Punk	Rambo Rodney	
Cutting	30	45	60,000
Sewing	60	50	70,000
Stuffing	10	15	15,000
Packaging	5	5	8,000

Since the foster-doll concept has caught on so tremendously, Sesayou feels that everything it can produce can also be sold. The fixed costs of $50,000 are allocated evenly between the two product lines.

Required

1. What is the objective function for Sesayou?
2. List all the relevant constraints for Sesayou.
3. Using the graphic approach to linear programming, determine the maximum profits for Sesayou. How many units of each doll will have to be produced and sold in order to maximize profits?

(Check figure: Patsy Punk = 750)

Problem B6-11
Using graphic LP for Problem B6-7

Refer to part 4 of Problem B6-7 on the Longex Watch Company. This time, however, the problem will be solved by using the graphic approach to linear programming. We will now assume the following facts concerning the production and sale of the three products. Notice that the maximum sales for Sports are only 6,000 units now.

	Hours per Unit	Maximum Unit Sales
Luxury	4	25,000
Diver	2	20,000
Sports	1	6,000

The total machine time available is still 134,000 hours. In addition, we will now assume that Longex has signed a binding contract to sell 5,000 units of Luxury, 10,000 units of Diver, and 6,000 units of Sports to the Bogus Watch Company.

Required	

(*Hint:* Since the graphic approach can be used with only two product lines, you need to deal with only the two products that have a sales potential greater than the amount agreed to in the binding contract.)

1. What is the objective function for Longex?

2. What are the constraints for Longex?

3. Determine the maximum profits and the number of units of each product line that need to be sold in order to maximize profits. Use the graphic approach to linear programming.

(Check figure: Luxury = 23,500)

PART THREE

Applying the Concept of Relevance to Long-Run Decisions

In Part Two of this book we introduced the concept of relevance and explained how to use this concept to make a variety of decisions that affect primarily the short run. In Part Three we will see how the same concept can be used to help management make decisions that affect the long run—decisions such as whether or not to invest in new productive fixed assets, whether to keep an old productive asset or to replace it with a new productive asset, and whether or not to rearrange machinery within a plant in order to improve the flow of a product through the different stages of production.

Planning for the commitment of a firm's resources to such investment opportunities is called *capital budgeting.* There are two broad categories of capital budgeting methods — discounted cash-flow methods and nondiscounted cash-flow methods — and there are different methods within each of the two categories. You'll learn how to use these methods, how to interpret the results of each method, and what the deficiencies and strengths are of the different methods.

In Chapter 7 we'll explain how to calculate each method, assuming for the moment that there is no income tax law to worry about. Although it may be impractical to make such an assumption in today's business environment, it is far better to learn the basic mechanics of each capital budgeting method before you study the complicating tax effects. Once you have mastered the basics in Chapter 7, you can then go on to Chapter 8, in which we discuss several income tax considerations that affect the calculations and results of each capital budgeting method.

Capital Budgeting: An Introduction to the Discounted and Nondiscounted Cash-Flow Methods

After you have completed studying this chapter, you should understand the following things:

- What is meant by the term *capital budgeting*
- The steps to be taken by an organization in the capital budgeting process
- The difference between *discounted cash-flow methods* and *nondiscounted cash-flow methods,* and which specific methods belong to each group
- How to compute the net present value and internal rate of return for a project, and the criteria for accepting or rejecting a project when these methods are used
- How to compute the nondiscounted cash-flow methods—payback and accountant's rate of return—and how to evaluate the results of each of these methods
- The weaknesses of the nondiscounted cash-flow methods, and why the methods are popular in spite of these weaknesses
- What we mean by the term *sensitivity analysis,* and how this analysis can be helpful in evaluating a proposed capital outlay

In Chapter 6 we discussed many types of decisions that managers make in running their day-to-day operations. A common element of each was the use of current productive capacity; that is, it was not necessary to purchase or build additional fixed assets in order to implement the decision. In our role as accountants we tried to help managers determine the most profitable way to use that productive capacity. Each decision primarily affected short-run profits—1 year or less.

Changes in productive capacity have long-run consequences

Once the decision is made to change productive capacity, the impact on profits will be felt for many years into the future. For instance, managers might consider increasing the size of a factory, replacing old productive assets with new ones, or substituting machinery for labor.

For every decision that a manager makes, whether the decision affects the short run or the long run, it is naturally very important that careful consideration be given to all the relevant factors that are involved. Few decisions, however, require the same amount of time-consuming and diligent attention as do those that involve changes in an organization's productive capacity. This is true because:

1. The decision usually involves a significant outlay of resources, which commits the organization to a project for an extended period of time.

2. The success or failure of the project depends on a future that is unknown, or uncertain at best.

3. The possible losses that can result from a poor decision concerning a single project might be so great that they threaten the continued existence of the organization.

4. If the future proves that a poor decision has been made, it may be too late to avoid much of the impact of that decision.

Since changes in productive capacity can have such a significant effect on the long-run profits of an organization, accountants have to be able to help managers make the right decision. Therefore, accountants need to have reliable evaluation methods at their disposal. There are, in fact, quite a few evaluation methods that are available to accountants — they are called *capital budgeting methods* — and some are more reliable than others.

THE CAPITAL BUDGETING PROCESS

Capital budgeting:
—planning
—acquisition and financing
—long-term investments

Capital budgeting is a process that helps managers plan for the acquisition and financing of long-term investments — primarily in fixed assets.[1] The capital budgeting process involves eight steps, which must be taken one step at a time.

The eight steps in the capital budgeting process are:

Steps in the capital budgeting process

1. Determine the investment needs of the organization.

2. Determine the investment opportunities that meet the needs of the organization.

3. Gather the relevant information concerning the investment opportunities to be evaluated.

4. Determine the method(s) to be employed in evaluating the investment proposals.

5. Calculate the results for the method(s), using the relevant information.

6. Determine the criteria to be used for deciding whether an investment proposal is to be accepted or rejected.

7. Determine which investments meet the criteria for acceptance.

8. Determine a means of financing these investments.

Steps 1 and 2: determine investment needs and alternative opportunities

In the first two steps management needs to take a good hard look at the organization and decide what it has to do now, in order to reach its objectives for 5, 10, and 15 years down the road. What changes are needed in the current and future productive

---

[1] Although our emphasis is placed primarily on investments in fixed assets, the concepts and tools involved in capital budgeting apply equally well to investments that do not involve changes in an organization's productive capacity. We discuss these other applications on page 301 at the end of this chapter.

capacity in order to be on the right track? Once the needs of the organization have been determined, then all alternative ways of satisfying these needs must be specified.

For example, assume that the management of Home Video, Inc., which currently has a 2% share of the home video market, predicts that the firm will maintain that share over the next 10 years and that the total market will quadruple. In order to meet this explosive demand, Home Video's capacity will have to be doubled within the next 2 years. Should the present capacity be maintained, and double and triple work shifts be started; should additional space be rented when needed and more machinery purchased; or should a second factory be constructed? If Home Video is sure that there are no other practical ways to meet its needs, then it could go on to step 3 in the capital budgeting process—the gathering of relevant information concerning the alternatives to be evaluated.

Remember that in Chapter 6 we learned that ***relevant information*** represents that information which (1) relates to the future and (2) is different for the alternatives that are being considered in the decision. Within this chapter all relevant information can be placed in one of two categories. And these two categories—the key factors of step 3—are common to all capital budgeting situations. The two key factors are:

Step 3: gather relevant information—net incremental investment and incremental cash flows

1. The net incremental investment

2. The incremental cash flows

The ***net incremental investment*** represents the outlay of resources made at the very beginning of a new project. The ***incremental cash flows*** represent the additional cash generated by the firm during the life of a project due to the net incremental investment that was made at the beginning of the project.

Now we will explain these two factors in more depth.

Most of the time the term *net incremental investment* means the cash outlay required to obtain a fixed asset and to prepare it for productive use. The incremental investment for the purchase of a fixed asset may be much more than just the purchase price of the new fixed asset, however. Other costs that are also a part of the net incremental investment include transportation costs, receiving and handling costs, set-up costs, costs of testing the new asset prior to its productive use, and investments in a variety of current assets.

The investment includes more than just the purchase price

Net investment = cost of new − disposal of old

When an old fixed asset is sold prior to purchasing a new one, the proceeds from the sale of the old asset are subtracted from the cost of the new asset in determining the net incremental investment.

Constructed fixed assets = DM + DL + FO

Finally, if a manufacturer constructs its own productive assets instead of buying them from someone else, then the net incremental investment is the accumulation of production costs required to prepare the asset for productive use. The production costs of a self-constructed asset are the same as they are for any other manufactured item, that is, direct materials, direct labor, and factory overhead.

You can normally think of the incremental cash flows from the use of an investment in one of two ways. They are either (1) the incremental cash operating receipts in excess of the incremental cash operating costs from the use of newly acquired fixed assets or (2) the cash operating savings that result from the replacement of one fixed asset with a new and more efficient fixed asset. A good portion of the incremental cash flows are the cash flows that are continuous and repetitive in nature. For example, assume that Craig Hubbard is considering buying a new machine—machine A—that will produce 10,000 units per year, all of which are expected to be sold. The cash receipts and the cash disbursements associated with the sale and production of these units occur in a continuous and repetitive manner, year after year.

Nonrepetitive cash flows

There are other types of incremental cash flows that are not repetitive in nature—instead, they may occur only once or twice during the life of a project. As examples, we might have:

1. An extraordinary or major repair
2. An advertising or promotional campaign
3. The disposal of the fixed asset at the end of the project's useful life

The amount of incremental cash flows in any given year depends to a substantial degree on the amount of income tax to be paid in that year. Although a consideration of income taxes is necessary in order for you to get a complete appreciation of the capital budgeting process, we will defer the integration of tax effects into capital budgeting to the following chapter.

Let's now assume that Hubbard finds out that the cost of machine A will be $10,000. Also, the production and sale of 10,000 units will increase the cash receipts and disbursements by the following amounts over an 8-year period:

Total additional cash receipts..	$30,000
Total additional cash disbursements....................................	14,000
Total incremental cash flow...	$16,000

The incremental cash flow of $16,000 exceeds the net incremental investment of $10,000 by $6,000. Does this mean that Hubbard should buy the new machine?

We cannot answer this question until we complete steps 4 to 7 in the capital budgeting process.

Step 4: select a capital budgeting method

The fourth step in the capital budgeting process is the selection of a capital budgeting method that we can use to evaluate the relevant information about a capital budgeting proposal.

We are going to look at four different capital budgeting methods. The four methods are classified as either discounted cash-flow methods or nondiscounted cash-flow methods. They are:

1. Discounted cash-flow methods
   a. Net present value   b. Internal rate of return
2. Nondiscounted cash-flow methods
   a. Payback period   b. Accountant's rate of return

Step 5: calculate results for the capital budgeting method

Once we decide which method (or methods) to use to evaluate the investment proposals, we then do step 5—we calculate the results for each method, using the procedures that are discussed in the remaining pages of this chapter.

As you can tell from the list of steps, step 5 is not the last step. The net present value for a project does not automatically tell us if it is good enough to warrant our investment. That's where the criteria—steps 6 and 7—come in. The criteria are simply guidelines that tell us what is an acceptable answer and what is not. If the results for a project do not meet certain minimum standards, then that project is dropped from further consideration. For example, when we use the net present value

Steps 6 and 7: determine and use criteria for acceptability

CAPITAL BUDGETING

To some an unrewarding experience

At a recent management conference, an upper level executive of a prosperous high-technology company was asked to name his most difficult problem. Instead of citing Japanese competition or the constant need in that business to come up with innovative technology, the executive stated simply "trying to convince my CEO and board to approve an idea for a new investment project."

Many managers will agree that getting a project through a corporate capital appropriations committee can be one of the most frustrating and unrewarding experiences of corporate life. Battles wage against a background of high interest rates, tight budgets, and increasing sensitivity to investment risk. Typically, two sides develop; strategists, who look at a project for what it might accomplish, are pitted against quantitative an-

alysts, who look at it for what it will cost. Often, the only result is a stalemate.

method, the guideline says that the net present value must be greater than or equal to zero or the project is unacceptable.

Step 8: determine the means of financing

Once we decide which project or projects to invest in, the last step in the capital budgeting process is deciding how to finance the investment. Should we finance with debt, or stock, or internally generated funds? The answer to this question is beyond the scope of this text but will likely be discussed in detail in your finance courses.

DISCOUNTED CASH-FLOW METHODS

For discounted cash-flow methods we need to understand present value concepts

The main characteristic of the ***discounted cash-flow methods*** is that they consider the time value of money through the application of present value analysis. You were probably introduced to the concept of present value in your financial accounting course when you were shown how to apply the concept to long-term liabilities. In this chapter we will take the same concept but apply it to capital budgeting. First though, let's review some of what you learned in financial accounting.

The Concept of Present Value

A review of present value

Present value analysis recognizes the time value of money, that is, that cash invested today will accumulate to greater amounts in future periods, due to the compounding of interest. For example, if $1 is invested today (referred to as ***time period zero***) at 10%, the $1 will accumulate in the following manner:

Investment today..	$1.000
Interest in year 1 @ 10%	.100 ($1.000 × .10)
Investment at end of year 1................................	$1.100
Interest in year 2	.110 ($1.100 × .10)
Investment at end of year 2................................	$1.210
Interest in year 3	.121 ($1.210 × .10)
Investment at end of year 3................................	$1.331

By the end of 3 years, interest of $0.331 ($0.100 + $0.110 + $0.121) will have been added to the $1 investment, totaling $1.331.

This accumulation of cash can also be shown by the following diagram:

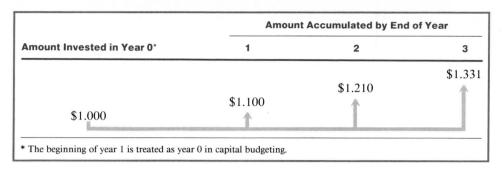

	Amount Accumulated by End of Year		
Amount Invested in Year 0*	1	2	3

$1.000 → $1.100 → $1.210 → $1.331

* The beginning of year 1 is treated as year 0 in capital budgeting.

A lump sum accumulates into the future

Let's assume now that instead of investing $1, you want to invest $10,000. What amount would $10,000 accumulate to in 3 years? One way to find out is to multiply the amount that $1 accumulates to in 3 years, $1.331, by the $10,000 investment:

$$\$1.331 \times \$10,000 = \$13,310$$

Another way is with the diagram:

	Amount Accumulated by End of Year		
Amount Invested in Year 0	1	2	3

$10,000 → $11,000 → $12,100 → $13,310

You would have $13,310 in your account in 3 years.

The value today of a future lump sum

Now let's turn things around just a bit. Assume, instead, that you know you want to have $13,310 in your bank account in 3 years but are wondering how much you have to invest today at 10% to accumulate to $13,310. Naturally, we know from above that the amount is $10,000. But, assuming for a moment that we do not know, we could determine it by reversing the computation above. That is:

$$\$13,310 \div 1.331 = \$10,000$$

An alternative way to show this computation is:

$$13,310 \times \frac{1}{1.331} = \$10,000$$

And one final way is as follows:

$$\$13,310 \times .7513 = \$10,000$$

The number .7513 is merely the decimal form for the fraction 1/1.331. This number, .7513, is called the present value (PV) of $1 in 3 years at 10%, which means that $0.7513 invested today at 10% will accumulate to $1 in 3 years:

Investment	$0.7513
Interest in year 1	0.0751
	$0.8264
Interest in year 2	0.0826
	$0.9090
Interest in year 3	0.0909
Accumulation at the end of 3 years.................	$0.9999 = $1.0000 (rounded)

When we multiply .7513 by $13,310, the $10,000 result represents the present value of $13,310 in 3 years at 10%—meaning that $10,000 invested today at 10% will accumulate to $13,310 in 3 years.

PV of $1 table; little p-n-slash-i: $p_{\overline{n}|}\,i$

If you look at the Present Value of $1 table (Table 7-1 on page 279), you will find the number .7513 (rounded to .751) at the intersection of the 10% column and the 3-year row. The present value of $1 for other combinations of years and interest rates can also be found in Table 7-1. Therefore, any time you need to determine the present value of some lump-sum amount of cash in the future, you merely find the appropriate number (called a ***present value factor***) in Table 7-1 and multiply it by the future lump sum. You will be making quite a few of these present value calculations in this chapter, so be sure you know how to do them.

Another example: should land be purchased?

Let's change our example now to one that obviously involves a capital budgeting situation. Mr. Cincy is looking for a good real estate investment and goes to see Mr. Shotz, a real estate agent. Shotz shows Cincy a piece of land costing $20,000 and assures Cincy that if the land is held for 2 years, it will have a resale value of $24,000—an appreciation of $4,000. Should Cincy buy the land?

Estimating that he can earn 12% interest in a CD, Cincy computes first:

Investment...	$20,000
Interest in year 1 (.12 × $20,000)	2,400
	$22,400
Interest in year 2 (.12 × $22,400)	2,688
Investment at end of year 2	$25,088

If $20,000 is invested in a CD, Cincy sees that he will have $25,088 in 2 years, $1,088 more than he will have if he buys and then resells the land.

Cincy also evaluates the situation a second way—which is very similar to one of the discounted cash-flow methods we will discuss in a moment. He finds the present value of receiving $24,000 in 2 years:

$$.7972 \times \$24,000 = \$19,133$$

The $19,133 is the amount that could be invested today at 12% in order to have $24,000 in 2 years. Given the choice of investing $19,133 in a CD or $20,000 in land, but receiving the same $24,000 in 2 years under both alternatives, Cincy makes the logical choice—turn down Shotz's deal—or get a lower price from him.

Lump sum vs. annuity

In this example Cincy was dealing with the present value of a ***lump sum***—that is, he determined the value today of receiving (or paying) some amount of cash at one point in time in the future. Sometimes, however, the receipt (or payment) of cash occurs in equal amounts per year—this is called an ***annuity.*** Determining the present value of an annuity is actually just a variation of determining the present value of a lump sum, and we will show you how to do it in the section on net present value.

Now we are about ready to discuss the two discounted cash-flow methods — net present value and internal rate of return. The facts we will present in Example 7-1 provide the input for these two methods, as well as for the two nondiscounted cash-flow methods that follow.

The Illustration

Everything is the same for two projects except the timing of cash flows

Example 7-1 involves two machines that cost the same amount of money, have the same life, and generate the same amount of incremental cash flows over their lives. The only difference in the two machines is the timing of the incremental cash flows. One of the machines is expected to generate the same amount of cash flow in each year (an annuity), while the other machine is expected to experience greater cash flows in the early years than in the later years of life.

For each capital budgeting method that we discuss in this chapter, the calculations of the method, and in some cases the usefulness of that method, depend on the timing of the cash flows. In all but one of the methods, the solution is different when the cash flows are the same each year from the solution when the cash flows are not the same each year. When we get different solutions, we know that they are due entirely to the different timing of cash flows — since all other facts about the two machines are identical.

Example 7-1

HUBBARD CONTRACTING

Craig Hubbard, the owner of a local printing company, is considering an investment in one of two projects, A or B. Each project requires a $10,000 incremental outlay for a different machine — which we will call machines A and B. Both machines have an expected 8-year life. The total incremental cash flows over the 8-year life is $16,000 for both machines, but the distribution of this total to individual years is quite a bit different.

Year of Life	Incremental Cash Inflows	
	Project A	Project B
1	$ 2,000	$ 4,000
2	2,000	3,000
3	2,000	3,000
4	2,000	2,000
5	2,000	1,000
6	2,000	1,000
7	2,000	1,000
8	2,000	1,000
Total	$16,000	$16,000

Cash flows are even for project A and uneven for project B

When discounted cash-flow methods are employed, Hubbard will use an interest rate of 10%. This rate, referred to in capital budgeting as the cost of capital or the minimum desired rate of return, will be represented by the letter r. This is the cost of raising funds to finance the project.

Simplifying Assumptions

The present value factors that are found in Table 7-1, Present Value of $1, and in Table 7-2, Present Value of an Ordinary Annuity of $1, are based upon the assump-

$$p_{\overline{n}|i} = \frac{1}{(1+i)^n}$$

n \ i	1%	2%	3%	4%	5%	6%	7%	8%	9%	10%	12%	15%	20%
1	0.990	0.980	0.970	0.961	0.952	0.943	0.934	0.925	0.917	0.909	0.892	0.869	0.833
2	0.980	0.961	0.942	0.924	0.907	0.889	0.873	0.857	0.841	0.826	0.797	0.756	0.694
3	0.970	0.942	0.915	0.888	0.863	0.839	0.816	0.793	0.772	0.751	0.711	0.657	0.578
4	0.960	0.923	0.888	0.854	0.822	0.792	0.762	0.735	0.708	0.683	0.635	0.571	0.482
5	0.951	0.905	0.862	0.821	0.783	0.747	0.712	0.680	0.649	0.620	0.567	0.497	0.401
6	0.942	0.887	0.837	0.790	0.746	0.704	0.666	0.630	0.596	0.564	0.506	0.432	0.334
7	0.932	0.870	0.813	0.759	0.710	0.665	0.622	0.583	0.547	0.513	0.452	0.375	0.279
8	0.923	0.853	0.789	0.730	0.676	0.627	0.582	0.540	0.501	0.466	0.403	0.326	0.232
9	0.914	0.836	0.766	0.702	0.644	0.591	0.543	0.500	0.460	0.424	0.360	0.284	0.193
10	0.905	0.820	0.744	0.675	0.613	0.558	0.508	0.463	0.422	0.385	0.321	0.247	0.161
11	0.896	0.804	0.722	0.649	0.584	0.526	0.475	0.428	0.387	0.350	0.287	0.214	0.134
12	0.887	0.788	0.701	0.624	0.556	0.496	0.444	0.397	0.355	0.318	0.256	0.186	0.112
13	0.878	0.773	0.680	0.600	0.530	0.468	0.414	0.367	0.326	0.289	0.229	0.162	0.093
14	0.869	0.757	0.661	0.577	0.505	0.442	0.387	0.340	0.299	0.263	0.204	0.141	0.077
15	0.861	0.743	0.641	0.555	0.481	0.417	0.362	0.315	0.274	0.239	0.182	0.122	0.064
16	0.852	0.728	0.623	0.533	0.458	0.393	0.338	0.291	0.251	0.217	0.163	0.106	0.054
17	0.844	0.714	0.605	0.513	0.436	0.371	0.316	0.270	0.231	0.197	0.145	0.092	0.045
18	0.836	0.700	0.587	0.493	0.415	0.350	0.295	0.250	0.211	0.179	0.130	0.080	0.037
19	0.827	0.686	0.570	0.474	0.395	0.330	0.276	0.231	0.194	0.163	0.116	0.070	0.031
20	0.819	0.672	0.553	0.456	0.376	0.311	0.258	0.214	0.178	0.148	0.103	0.061	0.026
21	0.811	0.659	0.537	0.438	0.358	0.294	0.241	0.198	0.163	0.135	0.092	0.053	0.021
22	0.803	0.646	0.521	0.421	0.341	0.277	0.225	0.183	0.150	0.122	0.082	0.046	0.018
23	0.795	0.634	0.506	0.405	0.325	0.261	0.210	0.170	0.137	0.111	0.073	0.040	0.015
24	0.787	0.621	0.491	0.390	0.310	0.246	0.197	0.157	0.126	0.101	0.065	0.034	0.012
25	0.779	0.609	0.477	0.375	0.295	0.232	0.184	0.146	0.115	0.092	0.058	0.030	0.010
26	0.772	0.597	0.463	0.360	0.281	0.219	0.172	0.135	0.106	0.083	0.052	0.026	0.008
27	0.764	0.585	0.450	0.346	0.267	0.207	0.160	0.125	0.097	0.076	0.046	0.022	0.007
28	0.756	0.574	0.437	0.333	0.255	0.195	0.150	0.115	0.089	0.069	0.041	0.019	0.006
29	0.749	0.563	0.424	0.320	0.242	0.184	0.140	0.107	0.082	0.063	0.037	0.017	0.005
30	0.741	0.552	0.411	0.308	0.231	0.174	0.131	0.099	0.075	0.057	0.033	0.015	0.004
31	0.734	0.541	0.399	0.296	0.220	0.164	0.122	0.092	0.069	0.052	0.029	0.013	0.003
32	0.727	0.530	0.388	0.285	0.209	0.154	0.114	0.085	0.063	0.047	0.026	0.011	0.002
33	0.720	0.520	0.377	0.274	0.199	0.146	0.107	0.078	0.058	0.043	0.023	0.009	0.002
34	0.712	0.510	0.366	0.263	0.190	0.137	0.100	0.073	0.053	0.039	0.021	0.008	0.002
35	0.705	0.500	0.355	0.253	0.181	0.130	0.093	0.067	0.048	0.035	0.018	0.007	0.001
36	0.698	0.490	0.345	0.243	0.172	0.122	0.087	0.062	0.044	0.032	0.016	0.006	0.001
37	0.692	0.480	0.334	0.234	0.164	0.115	0.081	0.057	0.041	0.029	0.015	0.005	0.001
38	0.685	0.471	0.325	0.225	0.156	0.109	0.076	0.053	0.037	0.026	0.013	0.004	0.001
39	0.678	0.461	0.315	0.216	0.149	0.103	0.071	0.049	0.034	0.024	0.012	0.004	0.001
40	0.671	0.452	0.306	0.208	0.142	0.097	0.066	0.046	0.031	0.022	0.010	0.003	0.000
41	0.665	0.444	0.297	0.200	0.135	0.091	0.062	0.042	0.029	0.020	0.009	0.003	0.000
42	0.658	0.435	0.288	0.192	0.128	0.086	0.058	0.039	0.026	0.018	0.008	0.002	0.000
43	0.651	0.426	0.280	0.185	0.122	0.081	0.054	0.036	0.024	0.016	0.007	0.002	0.000
44	0.645	0.418	0.272	0.178	0.116	0.077	0.050	0.033	0.022	0.015	0.006	0.002	0.000
45	0.639	0.410	0.264	0.171	0.111	0.072	0.047	0.031	0.020	0.013	0.006	0.001	0.000
46	0.632	0.402	0.256	0.164	0.105	0.068	0.044	0.029	0.018	0.012	0.005	0.001	0.000
47	0.626	0.394	0.249	0.158	0.100	0.064	0.041	0.026	0.017	0.011	0.004	0.001	0.000
48	0.620	0.386	0.241	0.152	0.096	0.060	0.038	0.024	0.015	0.010	0.004	0.001	0.000
49	0.614	0.378	0.234	0.146	0.091	0.057	0.036	0.023	0.014	0.009	0.003	0.001	0.000
50	0.608	0.371	0.228	0.140	0.087	0.054	0.033	0.021	0.013	0.008	0.003	0.000	0.000

$$P_{\overline{n}|i} = \frac{1 - \dfrac{1}{(1+i)^n}}{i}$$

n \ i	1%	2%	3%	4%	5%	6%	7%	8%	9%	10%	12%	15%	20%
1	0.990	0.980	0.970	0.961	0.952	0.943	0.934	0.925	0.917	0.909	0.892	0.869	0.833
2	1.970	1.941	1.913	1.886	1.850	1.833	1.808	1.783	1.759	1.735	1.690	1.625	1.527
3	2.940	2.883	2.828	2.775	2.723	2.673	2.624	2.577	2.531	2.486	2.401	2.283	2.106
4	3.901	3.807	3.717	3.629	3.545	3.465	3.387	3.312	3.239	3.169	3.037	2.854	2.588
5	4.853	4.713	4.579	4.451	4.329	4.212	4.100	3.992	3.889	3.790	3.604	3.352	2.990
6	5.795	5.601	5.417	5.242	5.075	4.917	4.766	4.622	4.485	4.355	4.111	3.784	3.325
7	6.728	6.471	6.230	6.002	5.786	5.582	5.389	5.206	5.032	4.868	4.563	4.160	3.604
8	7.651	7.325	7.019	6.732	6.463	6.209	5.971	5.746	5.534	5.334	4.967	4.487	3.837
9	8.566	8.162	7.786	7.435	7.107	6.801	6.515	6.246	5.995	5.759	5.328	4.771	4.031
10	9.471	8.982	8.530	8.110	7.721	7.360	7.023	6.710	6.417	6.144	5.650	5.018	4.192
11	10.367	9.786	9.252	8.760	8.306	7.886	7.498	7.138	6.805	6.495	5.937	5.233	4.327
12	11.255	10.575	9.954	9.385	8.863	8.383	7.942	7.536	7.160	6.813	6.194	5.420	4.439
13	12.133	11.348	10.634	9.985	9.393	8.852	8.357	7.903	7.486	7.103	6.423	5.583	4.532
14	13.003	12.106	11.296	10.563	9.898	9.294	8.745	8.244	7.786	7.366	6.628	5.724	4.610
15	13.865	12.849	11.937	11.118	10.379	9.712	9.107	8.559	8.060	7.606	6.810	5.847	4.675
16	14.717	13.577	12.561	11.652	10.837	10.105	9.446	8.851	8.312	7.823	6.973	5.954	4.729
17	15.562	14.291	13.166	12.165	11.274	10.477	9.763	9.121	8.543	8.021	7.119	6.047	4.774
18	16.398	14.992	13.753	12.659	11.689	10.827	10.059	9.371	8.755	8.201	7.249	6.127	4.812
19	17.226	15.678	14.323	13.133	12.058	11.158	10.335	9.603	8.950	8.364	7.365	6.198	4.843
20	18.045	16.351	14.877	13.590	12.462	11.469	10.594	9.818	9.128	8.513	7.469	6.259	4.869
21	18.856	17.011	15.415	14.029	12.821	11.764	10.835	10.016	9.292	8.648	7.562	6.312	4.891
22	19.660	17.658	15.936	14.451	13.163	12.041	11.061	10.200	9.442	8.771	7.644	6.358	4.909
23	20.455	18.292	16.443	14.856	13.488	12.303	11.272	10.371	9.580	8.883	7.718	6.398	4.924
24	21.243	18.913	16.935	15.246	13.798	12.550	11.469	10.528	9.706	8.984	7.784	6.433	4.937
25	22.023	19.523	17.413	15.622	14.093	12.783	11.653	10.674	9.822	9.077	7.843	6.464	4.947
26	22.795	20.121	17.876	15.982	14.375	13.003	11.825	10.809	9.928	9.160	7.895	6.490	4.956
27	23.559	20.706	18.327	16.329	14.643	13.210	11.986	10.935	10.026	9.237	7.942	6.513	4.963
28	24.316	21.281	18.764	16.663	14.898	13.406	12.137	11.051	10.116	9.306	7.984	6.533	4.969
29	25.065	21.844	19.188	16.983	15.141	13.590	12.277	11.158	10.198	9.369	8.021	6.550	4.974
30	25.807	22.396	19.600	17.292	15.372	13.764	12.409	11.257	10.273	9.426	8.055	6.565	4.978
31	26.542	22.937	20.000	17.589	15.592	13.929	12.531	11.349	10.342	9.479	8.084	6.579	4.982
32	27.269	23.468	20.388	17.873	15.802	14.084	12.646	11.434	10.406	9.526	8.111	6.590	4.985
33	27.989	23.988	20.765	18.147	16.002	14.230	12.753	11.513	10.464	9.569	8.135	6.600	4.987
34	28.702	24.498	21.131	18.411	16.192	14.368	12.854	11.586	10.517	9.608	8.156	6.609	4.989
35	29.408	24.998	21.487	18.664	16.374	14.498	12.947	11.654	10.566	9.644	8.175	6.616	4.991
36	30.107	25.488	21.832	18.908	16.546	14.620	13.035	11.717	10.611	9.676	8.192	6.623	4.992
37	30.799	25.969	22.167	19.142	16.711	14.736	13.117	11.775	10.652	9.705	8.207	6.628	4.994
38	31.484	26.440	22.492	19.367	16.867	14.846	13.193	11.828	10.690	9.732	8.220	6.633	4.995
39	32.163	26.902	22.808	19.584	17.071	14.949	13.264	11.878	10.725	9.756	8.233	6.638	4.995
40	32.834	27.355	23.114	19.792	17.159	15.046	13.331	11.924	10.757	9.779	8.243	6.641	4.996
41	33.499	27.799	23.412	19.993	17.294	15.138	13.394	11.967	10.786	9.799	8.253	6.645	4.997
42	34.158	28.234	23.701	20.185	17.423	15.224	13.452	12.006	10.813	9.817	8.261	6.647	4.997
43	34.810	28.661	23.981	20.370	17.545	15.306	13.506	12.043	10.837	9.833	8.269	6.650	4.998
44	35.455	29.079	24.254	20.548	17.662	15.383	13.557	12.077	10.860	9.849	8.276	6.652	4.998
45	36.094	29.490	24.518	20.720	17.774	15.455	13.605	12.108	10.881	9.862	8.282	6.654	4.998
46	36.727	29.892	24.775	20.884	17.880	15.524	13.650	12.137	10.900	9.875	8.287	6.655	4.998
47	37.353	30.286	25.024	21.042	17.981	15.589	13.691	12.164	10.917	9.886	8.292	6.657	4.999
48	37.973	30.673	25.266	21.195	18.077	15.650	13.730	12.189	10.933	9.896	8.297	6.658	4.999
49	38.588	31.052	25.601	21.341	18.168	15.707	13.766	12.212	10.948	9.906	8.301	6.659	4.999
50	39.196	31.423	25.729	21.482	18.255	15.761	13.800	12.233	10.961	9.914	8.304	6.660	4.999

Most cash flows are treated as if they came at the end of the year

tion that all cash flows occur at the end of a year. Naturally, not all cash flows in a realistic business situation are going to occur at the end of a year. They may take place at some intermediate point in time during the year; they may occur evenly throughout the year; or they may occur on a sporadic basis throughout the year. In each situation, in order to determine the exact present value, we would need to have different present value tables for each different type of cash flow. This would require quite a few more tables than are typically found in accounting and finance textbooks.

What we do — for the sake of simplicity only — is treat most cash flows that occur within a particular year as if they were received or paid at the end of that year. The one exception to this rule is cash that is received or paid in the very early part of a year. In this case the cash flow is treated as if it occurred at the very end of the previous year, which makes the present value factor for the previous year the appropriate one to use in determining its present value.

Net Present Value Method

The first discounted cash-flow method that we discuss is the ***net present value method.*** The steps we take in the net present value method are very similar to those taken by Cincy when he decided not to purchase the land from Shotz for $20,000.

In the net present value method we first calculate the present value of all future cash flows and then compare this amount to the amount of required initial cash outlay (the net incremental investment). If the present value of the net cash receipts exceeds the outlay, the project is acceptable. If the present value is less than the outlay, the project must be rejected. We accept only projects with positive net present values (NPVs) because a positive NPV means that the value of what we get back from the investment — measured by the present value of future cash flows — is greater than what it costs us to invest in the project. And only when we invest in a project with a positive NPV will the value of the firm as a whole be increased.

The steps we take in this process are the same, whether the cash flows are the same amount each year (an annuity) or a different amount each year. They are:

STEP 1: Determine the total present value (TPV) of the future cash flows using the appropriate interest rate r (referred to as the cost of capital or the minimum desired rate of return).

NPV = TPV − investment

STEP 2: Subtract the cash outlay for the net incremental investment from the TPV. This difference is called the ***net present value.***

STEP 3: If the NPV is positive, the project is acceptable. If the NPV is negative, it should be rejected. If it is zero, the decision maker is indifferent to accepting or rejecting.

Using these steps, we will now compute the NPV for project A and then decide if it is acceptable or not.

Project A

When the cash flows in each year are the same amount, we can determine their total present value in one of two ways. We can individually find the present value of each $2,000 receipt for years 1 through 8 using only the Present Value of $1 table (Table 7-1). Or we can use a simpler approach in which we use the Present Value of an Ordinary Annuity of $1 (Table 7-2), and make one calculation instead of eight.

You see, the Present Value of an Ordinary Annuity table is closely related to the Present Value of $1 table. Specifically, any number — a factor — in the Present Value of an Ordinary Annuity table is simply the summation of the numbers — the factors

— from the Present Value of $1 table. For example, at 10% the first eight factors from the Present Value of $1 table are as follows:

PV of $1 @ 10% in 1 year $(p_{\overline{1}\|10\%})$ =	.909
PV of $1 @ 10% in 2 years $(p_{\overline{2}\|10\%})$ =	.826
PV of $1 @ 10% in 3 years $(p_{\overline{3}\|10\%})$ =	.751
PV of $1 @ 10% in 4 years $(p_{\overline{4}\|10\%})$ =	.683
PV of $1 @ 10% in 5 years $(p_{\overline{5}\|10\%})$ =	.620
PV of $1 @ 10% in 6 years $(p_{\overline{6}\|10\%})$ =	.564
PV of $1 @ 10% in 7 years $(p_{\overline{7}\|10\%})$ =	.513
PV of $1 @ 10% in 8 years $(p_{\overline{8}\|10\%})$ =	.466
Summation of PV of $1 factors, at 10%, for years 1–8 =	5.332

PV of Ordinary Annuity table: big P-little n-slash-i: $P_{\overline{n}\|i}$

The summation of present value factors for 8 years at 10% equals 5.332. If you now look at the Present Value of an Ordinary Annuity table for 8 years at 10%, you will see the same number: 5.334. (The difference between the 5.332 above and 5.334 is due to rounding in the calculations of present value factors.)

Using this annuity factor of 5.334 $(P_{\overline{8}\|10\%})$, the steps in computing net present value are:

STEP 1: TPV = PV of $2,000 @ 10% for 8 years
$$= P_{\overline{8}\|10\%} \times \$2,000$$
$$= 5.334 \times \$2,000 = \$10,668$$

NPV for project A is positive: it's acceptable

STEP 2: NPV = TPV − net incremental investment
$$= \$10,668 - \$10,000 = \$668$$

STEP 3: Since the NPV of $668 is greater than zero, or positive, the project is acceptable.

Notice that in step 3 we used the term "acceptable" rather than "accepted." Since only one of the two projects, A or B, will be undertaken, the two are referred to as being ***mutually exclusive*** — the acceptance of one project automatically results in the rejection of the other. Even though the NPV of $668 for project A is acceptable, we will accept project A over project B only if the NPV of project B is not higher than $668.

If we were not comparing projects A and B for the same purpose, then they would not be mutually exclusive, and the acceptance of one would not automatically preclude the acceptance of the other. If this were the case, then whether or not we do accept all acceptable projects (NPV > 0) depends on the availability of funds. It might be that we accept all projects with a positive NPV. However, if the funds budgeted for capital projects are limited, then we would have to rank the projects according to the NPVs, and we would accept the projects with the highest NPVs until the available funds for investment purposes are exhausted.

Project B

The cash inflows expected for project B are not the same amount each year — they do not represent an annuity — thus we cannot determine the TPV with the PV of an Ordinary Annuity of $1 table. Instead, we need to use the PV of $1 table and separately compute the present value of each cash inflow. The steps are:

STEP 1: TPV

PV of $4,000 @ 10% in year 1 = $4,000 × .909 = $ 3,636
PV of $3,000 @ 10% in year 2 = $3,000 × .826 =   2,478
PV of $3,000 @ 10% in year 3 = $3,000 × .751 =   2,253
PV of $2,000 @ 10% in year 4 = $2,000 × .683 =   1,366
PV of $1,000 @ 10% in year 5 = $1,000 × .620 =   620
PV of $1,000 @ 10% in year 6 = $1,000 × .564 =   564
PV of $1,000 @ 10% in year 7 = $1,000 × .513 =   513
PV of $1,000 @ 10% in year 8 = $1,000 × .466 =   466

TPV = $11,896

NPV for project B is positive: it's acceptable, and higher than NPV for project A

STEP 2: NPV = TPV − net incremental investment
$$= \$11,896 - \$10,000$$
$$= \$1,896$$

STEP 3: The NPV of $1,896 is greater than zero, so it is acceptable.

Not only is project B acceptable, but since its NPV is also greater than the NPV for project A, it is probably the one we would choose — if only the two projects are being compared.

Without making any computations, you might have expected the NPV for project B to be greater than the NPV for project A. Both projects A and B are expected to generate the same total amount of cash inflows, $16,000, during the same 8 years of useful life, for the same amount of investment, $10,000. Since the total cash inflows are the same, $16,000, the timing of the cash inflows is the clue to which project is the better of the two. Project B promises greater cash inflows than project A in years 1 to 3 but less cash inflows than project A in years 5 to 8. By looking at the factors in the Present Value of $1 table for years 1 through 8, you can see that the present value of early-year cash flows is more valuable than the present value of later-year cash flows. Therefore, the present value of the $16,000 distributed to the 8 years of project B has to be greater than the same $16,000 distributed to the 8 years of project A.

An Adaptable Format for NPV

An easy-to-use format for NPV — especially for harder problems

The calculations for project B were a little more cumbersome than they were for project A because of the uneven stream of cash inflows for project B. Even so, they were still rather simple and straightforward, when compared to what they can be in some capital budgeting problems. So let's now make project B somewhat more complicated so that we can show you a useful format for calculating NPV which is really needed only when the problems get a little more difficult.

Example 7-2

ADDITIONAL FACTS FOR HUBBARD CONTRACTING

Assume that in Example 7-1 the machine required for project B will also necessitate an investment in current assets of $1,000 at the beginning of the project, all of which will be recovered at the end of the useful life of the project. Also, a major overhaul will be needed at the beginning of year 6. In addition, the acceptance of project B will involve the use of building space that is currently being leased to the Apex Company for $200 per year. Finally, the machine can be sold for $2,500 at the end of the project's useful life.

In addition to the cash receipts from operations, we must now consider an investment in current assets, a major overhaul, a disposal, and some lost rentals.

The new solution for project B is presented in Exhibit 7-1. What we want to emphasize in this solution is the format that we are using to compute the NPV — a format that can be easily adapted to any NPV situation, no matter how simple or detailed the situation may be.

The key to the format is in the headings that run from left to right across the top of the page:

Description	PV Factor	Present Value	Yearly Sketch of Cash Flows								
			0	1	2	3	4	5	6	7	8

The format organizes your work under easy-to-use headings

The first item in Exhibit 7-1 comes from the original facts in Example 7-1. The initial outlay of $10,000 goes in year 0 (the beginning of year 1), and its present value is $(10,000) — shown in parentheses to represent an outflow. The cash receipts from operations are shown in the sketch of cash flows for years 1 through 8, and eight different present value computations are made.

The remaining items come from the additional complications introduced in Example 7-2. They are discussed below.

The Investment in Nondepreciable Assets Sometimes an incremental investment in depreciable assets is accompanied by an investment in nondepreciable assets. For example, with project B it's quite possible that an increased demand for the product may make it necessary to maintain a larger balance in inventory over the life of the project. In addition, more credit may be extended to customers, causing the average balance in accounts receivable to increase. And the average balance in cash may need to be increased in order to handle the greater volume of business. Each of these increases in current assets — the inventory, the accounts receivable, and the cash — represents an investment in nondepreciable assets.

All investments aren't necessarily depreciable

Investments in nondepreciable assets usually take place at the beginning of a project and are treated in much the same way as the initial outlay for depreciable assets. For Craig Hubbard, the initial investment of $1,000 in nondepreciable assets is shown in Exhibit 7-1 as an outlay in year 0. At the end of the project's useful life, the current assets are fully recovered. Therefore, the $1,000 is shown as a cash inflow in year 8. The difference in the present values of the $1,000 outlay in year 0 ($1,000) and the $1,000 inflow in year 8 ($466) represents the interest that was lost on the $1,000 because it was tied up in non-interest-bearing current assets.

An overhaul

The Major Overhaul Hubbard expects that machine B will need a major overhaul at the beginning of year 6. Since this is not a recurring item, it is not included in the cash receipts from operations. For this reason it's shown separately in Exhibit 7-1 as an outflow. We place it in year 5 rather than year 6 because it comes at the beginning of the year, which is treated the same as the last day of the previous year. The present value of the overhaul is $(310).

EXHIBIT 7-1   Solution to Example 7-2
For each item described: (1) Put the cash in the sketch of cash flows, (2) find the correct PV factor, and (3) multiply to get PV.

Description	10% PV Factor	10% Present Value	Yearly Sketch of Cash Flows								
			0	1	2	3	4	5	6	7	8
Net incremental investment— depreciable	1.000	(10,000)	(10,000)								
Investment in nondepreciable assets...........	1.000	(1,000)	(1,000)								
Recovery of nondepreciable assets...........	.466	466									1,000
Cash receipts from operations:											
Year 1..........	.909	3,636		4,000							
Year 2..........	.826	2,478			3,000						
Year 3..........	.751	2,253				3,000					
Year 4..........	.683	1,366					2,000				
Year 5..........	.620	620						1,000			
Year 6..........	.564	564							1,000		
Year 7..........	.513	513								1,000	
Year 8..........	.466	466									1,000
Major overhaul....	.620	(310)						(500)			
Opportunity cost: lost rentals.......	5.334	(1,067)		(200)	(200)	(200)	(200)	(200)	(200)	(200)	(200)
Disposal of machine.........	.466	1,165									2,500
Net present value..		1,150	(11,000)	3,800	2,800	2,800	1,800	300	800	800	4,300

The numbers in this row represent the summation of each column

An opportunity foregone

The Lost Rentals   The $200 of lost rentals represents an opportunity cost to the firm. Even though the lost rentals are not actually cash outflows, they will still have a negative impact on the firm's cash position. If the space is rented, the cash receipts will be $200 per year. But if the space is not rented, then the cash receipts will be reduced by the $200—the opportunity foregone. The present value of the annuity of reduced rentals is $(1,067).

End-of-life disposal

Disposal Value   The value of most productive assets declines substantially through use, over the assets' useful lives. Hubbard feels that machine B will be worth only $2,500 at the end of 8 years, when he expects to dispose of it. In Exhibit 7-1 the $2,500 is treated as a cash inflow in year 8, and its present value is $1,165.

The NPV for project B—with all the added complications from Example 7-2—is now $1,150.

As long as the facts within a problem are no more complicated than they were originally in Example 7-1, there really is no reason for you to use the format we've just shown you. However, for the more complicated situations we recommend that you use the format shown in Exhibit 7-1, because all the facts in the solution can be easily seen and followed by you or anyone reviewing your work.

Cost of Capital—The Interest Rate Used in Computing NPV

We compute PV using r—the cost of capital

The first step in the NPV method requires that we find the total present value of future cash flows using an interest rate that is considered to be appropriate for our firm. In capital budgeting we refer to this interest rate as the **cost of capital** (or **minimum desired rate of return**), which is the weighted average cost of financing capital projects. In our illustration the cost of capital is 10%—but what exactly is a "cost of capital"?

The cost of capital is the cost of financing long-term investments

You see, when we purchase a fixed asset, we obviously need to have the resources to finance the purchase. To obtain the needed resources, we could borrow from creditors, we could issue stock to investors, or we could use funds that were generated internally through operations. Each of these types of financing has a cost to the organization; that is, creditors require that they be paid interest for the funds that are loaned, and owners expect either to receive dividends or to have some appreciation in the value of their stock as a return on their investment.

The cost of capital is a weighted average; that is, the cost for each type of financing is weighted by the proportion of all financing that is planned for each type of financing. For example: Assume that for Craig Hubbard the cost of financing with debt is 6% and the cost of financing with stock is 14%. Assume also that Hubbard expects to finance all capital projects equally with debt and equity. The cost of capital for Hubbard's organization would be 10%, computed as follows:

Source of Financing	Cost of Financing	×	Proportion of Total Financing	=	Weighted Average Cost of Capital
Debt	.06	×	.50	=	.03
Stock	.14	×	.50	=	.07
					.10

We have already seen how to use the cost of capital in the NPV method. We will now see if, and how, the cost of capital is used in the internal rate of return method.

Internal Rate of Return

Changing rates mean different NPVs

When we determined the NPV for project A from Example 7-1, using a 10% cost of capital, we got an NPV of $668. If we had used any rate other than 10%, the NPV would naturally have been different. Let's see what the NPV would have been if we had used 8% or 12%, rather than 10%:

8%	12%
TPV = $P_{\overline{8}\rvert 8\%} \times \$2,000$ per year	TPV = $P_{\overline{8}\rvert 12\%} \times \$2,000$ per year
= 5.746 × $2,000	= 4.967 × $2,000
= $11,492	= $9,934
NPV = $11,492 − $10,000 = $1,492	NPV = $9,934 − $10,000 = $(66)

After we compare the results for NPV at 8%, 10%, and 12%, we can make the following conclusions:

1. The higher the cost of capital, the smaller the NPV; and the smaller the cost of capital, the higher the NPV.

2. NPV can either be positive or negative, depending on the cost of capital.

When NPV = zero, this rate is the IRR

If the second conclusion is true, then it must also be correct to conclude that there is an interest rate for which the TPV exactly equals the incremental investment — resulting in an NPV of zero. Since NPV is positive at 8% and 10% and negative at 12%, it must be zero for some rate between 10% and 12%. When we have found that rate, at which the NPV of the project is zero, we will have found the ***internal rate of return*** for the project.

The IRR is the effective rate earned on a project

The internal rate of return (IRR) is the actual, effective, or true rate of return that we are earning on a project. So once we have determined the IRR, we then compare this rate to the cost of capital *r* in order to decide whether or not the project is acceptable. If the project is earning a rate of return that is greater than what it costs to finance the project (IRR > *r*), the project is acceptable; if the reverse is true (IRR < *r*), then the project should be rejected; and if the internal rate of return equals the cost of capital (IRR = *r*), then we are indifferent to accepting or rejecting.

Criteria for acceptance with IRR

Project A

We can always determine the IRR by doing what we did in the discussion above. When we calculated the NPV at different costs of capital, we found that the NPV was positive at one rate but negative at the next. We then knew that the IRR must be between the two rates. Although this approach is necessary for projects with uneven cash flows, there is a much easier way to calculate the IRR for projects that have an even stream of cash receipts.

To find IRR — search for the factor

Since cash receipts for project A are the same amount each year — an annuity — why don't you first turn to Table 7-2, Present Value of an Ordinary Annuity. We will be looking for a specific number in that table — a present value of an annuity factor. We want to find that factor which we can multiply by the $2,000 cash receipts per year to give us a TPV of $10,000 and an NPV of zero. The only factor that can do this, of course, is 5.000. Now try to find this factor in the row for 8 years. If you find it, then the interest rate at the top of the column having the factor will be the IRR.

Although you will not find the exact factor that you want, you can get awfully close. As you can see, the factor 5.000 falls between the factors of 5.334, for 10%, and 4.967, for 12%. Therefore, just as we concluded in the previous section, the IRR must be between 10% and 12%. Now that we know approximately where it is, we need to use interpolation to calculate the exact rate. ***Interpolation*** is a procedure used to find an exact number when you know it lies between two other numbers.

The discussion above for determining the IRR *for projects having even cash flows* can be converted into the following list of mechanical steps:

STEP 1: Divide the net incremental investment by the cash flow expected per year. This results in a PV of an annuity factor ($P_{\overline{n}|i}$):

$$\text{Factor} = \frac{\text{net incremental investment}}{\text{cash flow per year}}$$

$$= \frac{\$10,000}{\$2,000} = 5.000$$

The PV of an Ordinary Annuity table is used only when we have an annuity

STEP 2: Go to the PV of an Ordinary Annuity of $1 table and find the row representing the life of the project. Scan across this row looking for the factor determined in step 1. It will probably be between the factors for two other interest rates:

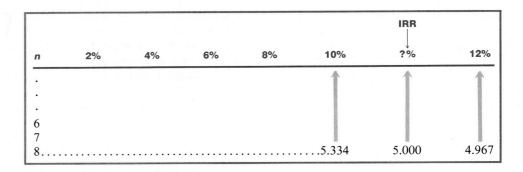

Interpolation — finding an exact IRR

STEP 3: Find the exact IRR by the process of interpolation. This involves first of all finding the ratio of the distance from 5.334 to 5.000 to the distance from 5.334 to 4.967. The distance from 5.334 to 4.967 is .367, which is the subtraction of factors immediately above and below 5.000:

10%	5.334
12%	4.967
	.367

The distance from the factor for 10% (5.334) to the factor for the exact IRR (5.000) is .334.

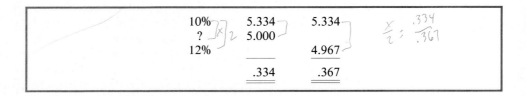

The factor 5.000 is 91% of the way from 5.334 to 4.967:

$$\frac{.334}{.367} = 91\%$$

The exact IRR is 91% of the way from 10% to 12% (the interest rates for 5.334 and 4.967). So the exact IRR is 1.82% above 10%:

$$.91 \times (12\% - 10\%) = 1.82\%$$

When added to 10%, the IRR becomes 11.82%:

$$IRR = 10\% + 1.82\% = 11.82\%$$

STEP 4: Compare the IRR to r, the cost of capital — which, remember, is the cost of the money used to finance the project. If IRR $>r$, the project is acceptable. If IRR $<r$, the project must be rejected. If IRR $=r$, the decision maker is indifferent to accepting or rejecting. Since the IRR of 11.82% $>$ 10%, the project is acceptable.

The reason we consider a project to be acceptable when its IRR exceeds r is that it means that the actual return being earned on the project is greater than the cost of funds that will be used to finance the project. And since we can earn more with those funds than it costs to raise the funds, the value of the firm will increase by investing in the project.

Project B

For uneven cash flows use trial and error for IRR

We will not be able to calculate the IRR for project B in the same way that we did for project A. The only reason that we were able to use the Present Value of an Ordinary Annuity table for project A is that the cash receipts for project A were an annuity. *Since the cash receipts for B are not an annuity, we cannot use the annuity table to calculate the IRR* — we need to find another approach. The other approach is called *trial and error.* First, however, let's remind ourselves of what the IRR represents: The IRR is an interest rate — representing what the project is actually earning for the firm — and when we calculate the TPV of a project at that rate, the TPV equals the incremental investment (the NPV is zero).

IRR isn't 10%, since NPV > 0 — go higher

For project B we are trying to find that rate of interest which will give us a TPV for the future cash flows of $10,000 — exactly equal to the incremental investment. If you look back to the original calculation of the NPV for project B, using the 10% cost of capital, you'll see that the TPV was $11,896 and the NPV was $1,896. The interest rate of 10% cannot be the IRR, because the NPV at this rate is not zero.

If we're going to determine what the IRR is, we need to calculate the NPV at another rate and see if it will be zero. Remember one of our conclusions earlier: A higher interest rate results in a lower NPV. So if we calculate the NPV for project B at a rate higher than 10%, we know that the NPV will drop below $1,896, and possibly as far as zero. Using an interest rate of 14%, we see that the NPV drops to $750:

Year		
1	$4,000 \times p_{\overline{1}|14\%} = \$4,000 \times .877 =$	\$ 3,508
2	$3,000 \times p_{\overline{2}|14\%} = \$3,000 \times .769 =$	2,307
3	$3,000 \times p_{\overline{3}|14\%} = \$3,000 \times .675 =$	2,025
4	$2,000 \times p_{\overline{4}|14\%} = \$2,000 \times .592 =$	1,184
5	$1,000 \times p_{\overline{5}|14\%} = \$1,000 \times .519 =$	519
6	$1,000 \times p_{\overline{6}|14\%} = \$1,000 \times .456 =$	456
7	$1,000 \times p_{\overline{7}|14\%} = \$1,000 \times .400 =$	400
8	$1,000 \times p_{\overline{8}|14\%} = \$1,000 \times .351 =$	351

TPV.....................................$10,750

Less: Incremental investment.............. 10,000

NPV.....................................$ 750

It's not 14% either — go a little higher

Since at 14% the NPV is not zero, then 14% cannot be the IRR. And, since the NPV is still positive, the IRR must be higher than 14%. By repeating the NPV calculation at 18%, we get a negative NPV:

Year		
1	$\$4,000 \times p_{\overline{1}|18\%} = \$4,000 \times .847 =$	\$ 3,388
2	$\$3,000 \times p_{\overline{2}|18\%} = \$3,000 \times .718 =$	2,154
3	$\$3,000 \times p_{\overline{3}|18\%} = \$3,000 \times .609 =$	1,827
4	$\$2,000 \times p_{\overline{4}|18\%} = \$2,000 \times .516 =$	1,032
5	$\$1,000 \times p_{\overline{5}|18\%} = \$1,000 \times .437 =$	437
6	$\$1,000 \times p_{\overline{6}|18\%} = \$1,000 \times .370 =$	370
7	$\$1,000 \times p_{\overline{7}|18\%} = \$1,000 \times .314 =$	314
8	$\$1,000 \times p_{\overline{8}|18\%} = \$1,000 \times .266 =$	266
	TPV.....................................	\$ 9,788
	Less: Incremental investment...............	10,000
	NPV.....................................	\$ (212)

Now NPV < 0, so IRR must be between 14% and 18%

Once again the NPV is not zero. However, since the NPV is greater than zero at 14% and is less than zero at 18%, the interest rate for which NPV equals zero (the IRR) must be between 14% and 18%.

The steps for calculating the IRR, which we have just described, for any situation that involves *uneven cash flows* are:

STEP 1: Select any interest rate and calculate the NPV of the cash flows, using the PV of $1 table

STEP 2: If NPV $\neq$ 0, repeat step 1. If NPV $>$ 0 in step 1, repeat using a higher interest rate. If NPV $<$ 0, repeat using a lower interest rate.

STEP 3: Continue repeating step 2 until you have an NPV $>$ 0 and an NPV $<$ 0.

Once we have an approximate IRR, we then complete the process with steps 4 and 5:

STEP 4: Interpolate to determine the exact IRR.

STEP 5: Compare the IRR to *r* and decide if the project is acceptable or is to be rejected.

Picking up with step 3 for project B, we see that the TPV and NPV at 14% and 18% are as follows:

	14%	18%
TPV..	\$10,750	\$ 9,788
Incremental investment.....................................	10,000	10,000
NPV	\$ 750	\$ (212)

Using interpolation, we find that the exact IRR is 17.12%:

		TPV	TPV	
	14%	$10,750	$10,750	
	?	10,000		
	18%		9,788	
		$ 750	$ 962	

$$\frac{\$750}{\$962} = 78\% \times (18\% - 14\%) = \quad 3.12\%$$

$$14.00\%$$

$$\text{IRR} = 17.12\%$$

Both projects A and B have IRRs that are higher than the cost of capital of 10%—they are both acceptable projects. Since they are mutually exclusive, we will choose project B over project A because of the higher IRR (17.12% > 11.82%).

IRR for Revised Project B

If we wanted to determine the IRR for project B using the revised facts given in Example 7-2, the mechanics would be similar to the calculations above. The only difference would be that there are more items to include in the trial-and-error approach. All the present value calculations that were made in Exhibit 7-1 would be repeated at higher interest rates until we found an interest rate with a negative NPV. Since the NPV at 10% is positive (shown in Exhibit 7-1), we would find the exact IRR by interpolating between 10% and the rate that gives us a negative NPV.

Comparison of Results Using NPV and IRR

Whenever we are evaluating the acceptability of a project, it shouldn't make any difference whether we are using the NPV method or the IRR method—the answer will be the same. If the NPV method indicates acceptability, so will the IRR. If the NPV method dictates rejection, the same will be true for IRR. Exhibit 7-2 may help you keep track of the relationships between the NPV and the IRR:

EXHIBIT 7-2
Relationships of NPV and IRR
The decisions for NPV and IRR should be the same.

When the NPV Is:	The IRR Will Be:	Decision
NPV > 0	IRR > r	Project is acceptable
NPV < 0	IRR < r	Reject project
NPV = 0	IRR = 0	Indifferent to accepting or rejecting

The cost of capital r is an integral part of both the NPV and the IRR methods. It is extremely important for you to realize the exact role it plays in each method.

When the NPV method is used, the value of r represents the interest rate we go to in the present value tables. At that interest rate we find the appropriate present value factors which we use to determine the total present value of future cash flows.

How r is used in IRR and NPV methods

Although it isn't necessary to know the value of r when calculating the IRR, it is necessary to know r when determining whether the IRR is acceptable or not. Any project with an IRR greater than r is acceptable; any project with an IRR less than r is not acceptable—it must be rejected.

An Expanded Meaning of IRR

The IRR is the actual rate of return for a project. It is not only the overall rate of return being earned over the entire life of the project but also the rate being earned in each year of the project's useful life, based upon the amount of unrecovered investment outstanding throughout the year. To see what we mean, look at the simple set of facts given in the next paragraph, and then refer to Exhibit 7-3 as you read the explanation that follows the exhibit.

Assume that a project costing $21,065 has a 3-year life and is expected to generate $10,000 in net cash receipts each year. The IRR is determined to be 20%.

EXHIBIT 7-3
IRR as a Percentage of the Unrecovered Investment

In dollars, IRR = % × unrecovered investment at the beginning of the year

Year	(1) Unrecovered Investment, Beg. of Year	×	(2) IRR	=	(3) (Col. 1 × 2) 20% Return on Investment	(4) Annual Cash Flow	(5) (Col. 4 − 3) Recovery of Investment	(6) (Col. 1 − 5) Unrecovered Investment, End of Year
1	$21,065	×	.20	=	$4,213	$10,000	$ 5,787	$15,278
2	$15,278	×	.20	=	3,056	10,000	6,944	8,334
3	$ 8,334	×	.20	=	1,666	10,000	8,334	-0-
					$8,935	$30,000	$21,065	

In each year of life the profit earned by the project is 20% of the unrecovered investment at the beginning of the year. At the beginning of year 1 the unrecovered investment is the same as the original investment—$21,065. The 20% return is represented by $4,213 ($21,065 × .20) of profit for the year. The remaining $5,787 ($10,000 − $4,213) of cash generated during the year represents the amount of investment recovered during the year. The unrecovered investment at the beginning of year 1 is reduced by $5,787, leaving $15,278 ($21,065 − $5,787) of unrecovered investment at the end of year 1—which is the same as the unrecovered investment at the beginning of year 2.

Recovery of investment = cash − return on investment

In year 2 the project still earns 20%, but now the return is 20% of $15,278, or $3,056. Once again, the remainder of the cash receipts ($10,000 − $3,056 = $6,944) represents the recovery of investment, and the unrecovered investment is reduced by the amount recovered during the year. In year 3 the process is continued until the end of the year, when the unrecovered investment is reduced to zero.

By the end of year 3 the cash receipts (column 4) total $30,000. Of this total $8,935 represents the sum of the profits earned (at 20%) on the unrecovered investment during the 3 years. The remaining $21,065 (column 5) represents the complete recovery of the initial investment.

Depreciation and Discounted Cash-Flow Methods

Does IRR consider depreciation

Students are often confused at this point by the apparent exclusion of depreciation expense in the discounted cash-flow methods. As a result, it is sometimes tempting to reduce the annual cash flows by the depreciation expense for the year prior to calculating the IRR or NPV. There are two reasons why this handling of depreciation is incorrect. First of all, depreciation is not a cash inflow or a cash outflow—it is a noncash expense. Since discounted cash-flow analysis deals with cash items only, the reduction of the cash flows by the depreciation causes the cash flows—and the resulting IRR and NPV—to be understated.[2]

Depreciation is not a cash flow

---

[2] Depreciation does have an indirect effect on cash when taxes are considered. Because it is deductible in determining the total tax bill, it does save taxes—and therefore reduces the amount of cash that needs to be paid in taxes. However, we are not yet considering tax implications, so this tax effect is to be ignored—at least for now.

*Recovery of investment =
depreciation*

The second reason for not reducing the cash flows by the depreciation expense is that depreciation has already been considered rather subtly in the determination of the IRR and NPV. For example, in Exhibit 7-3 look again at column 5, "Recovery of Investment." At the bottom of this column you'll see that the total cost of the investment has been recovered, $21,065 — a little bit in each year. It is this little bit of investment recovered each year that is the same thing as depreciation. Therefore, if you subtract the depreciation from the cash flows, you will have considered the impact of depreciation not once, but twice. You'd be guilty of double counting.

NONDISCOUNTED CASH-FLOW METHODS

*We don't use PV tables for
these methods*

As the name should imply, the distinguishing characteristic of the **nondiscounted cash-flow methods** is that they do not require the use of present value techniques. Accountants usually consider these methods to be inferior to the discounted cash-flow methods, because they do not explicitly consider the time value of money. However, we should still be interested in learning about these methods for the following reasons:

1. Many organizations still use these methods, and it is important for us to understand all the methods that are being used.

2. Some of the methods may be very useful when employed in conjunction with one of the discounted cash-flow methods.

3. In certain circumstances a nondiscounted cash-flow method may be more appropriate than a discounted cash-flow method.

Payback Period Method

*Payback is the number of
years needed to recoup
investment*

The **payback period (PP)** is the number of years needed for a project to accumulate enough cash to pay for the initial cost of the investment. The calculation of the payback period depends on the timing of the stream of cash flows. Are they even or uneven?

Project A

When the stream of cash flows is even, we determine the payback period by dividing the incremental investment by the cash inflows per year. For project A we do the following:

$$\textbf{Payback period (PP)} = \frac{\textbf{incremental investment}}{\textbf{cash flow per year}}$$

$$= \frac{\$10,000}{\$2,000} = 5 \text{ years}$$

For project A it takes 5 years for the accumulation of cash flows at $2,000 per year to pay for the $10,000 investment.

*For a project with even
cash flows, the PP is the
factor for IRR*

If you look carefully at the payback calculation, it should look familiar — the payback for project A is calculated in the same manner as we calculated the factor in the IRR method. In fact, this factor will always be the same — but only for projects having an even stream of cash flows.

Project B

We cannot take the same approach for project B as we did for project A. The reason is due to the fact that project B's cash flows do not represent an annuity. Instead, we need to accumulate the cash flows, 1 year at a time, until the total amount accumulated is equal to the incremental investment. We can do this for project B in the following manner:

Accumulate cash flows until they equal the investment

Year	Cash Flow per Year	Cumulative Cash Flow
1	$4,000	$ 4,000
2	3,000	7,000
3	3,000	10,000

It should take exactly 3 years for the cash flows of project B to accumulate to the $10,000 incremental investment.

Let's assume for a moment that the incremental investment for B is $10,500 instead of $10,000. If this were the case, then the cumulative cash flows at the end of 3 years would not fully pay for the investment. Instead, the payback period would be somewhere in the fourth year, as you can see below:

Payback for uneven cash flows

Year	Cash Flow per Year	Cumulative Cash Flow
1	$4,000	$ 4,000
2	3,000	7,000
3	3,000	10,000
Payback period		10,500
4	2,000	12,000

At some point during the fourth year, the investment of $10,500 will be fully paid for. If we assume that the cash flows are generated evenly throughout the year, the exact answer can be determined by interpolation:

		Cumulative Cash Flows
End of year 3	$10,000	$10,000
Needed to pay for investment	10,500	
End of year 4		12,000
Difference	$ 500	$ 2,000

$$\text{Fraction of year} = \frac{\text{cash flow needed during year to pay for investment}}{\text{cash flow for full year}}$$

$$= \frac{\$500}{\$2,000} = .25 \text{ year}$$

Payback period = 3 years + .25 year = 3.25 years

Now the payback period would be 3.25 years, which places it near the end of March in year 4.

Payback for Revised Project B

If you want to determine the payback for project B using the expanded set of facts that were given in Example 7-2, first look at the last line in Exhibit 7-1. It lists the summation of all cash flows for each year. To determine the payback, you accumulate these cash flows until they add up to the initial investment of $11,000. For example, the cash flow in year 1 is now $3,800 ($4,000 − $200). It will be added to the cash flow in year 2 of $2,800 ($3,000 − $200), which accumulates to $6,600. This process goes on until the cumulative total of $11,000 is reached.

Decision Criteria and Resulting Weaknesses of the Payback Period Method

Is there life after payback?
　　If we accept or reject projects entirely on the basis of the project's payback period, we would naturally select those projects with the shorter payback periods. In the original set of facts in Example 7-1, we would select project B, because it has a shorter payback period (3 years) than does project A (5 years). The choice of project B over project A is consistent with the choice we made when we used the NPV and IRR methods. But is this just a coincidence, or will the payback period method *always* yield results that are consistent with the discounted cash-flow methods?

　　The problem with the payback period method is that it often evaluates projects differently than do the NPV and IRR methods — for two main reasons. First, as the name — nondiscounted cash-flow methods — implies, the payback period method ignores the time value of money. Second, the payback period ignores the useful life of the project. For example, pretend for a moment that the life of project B is only 3.1 years — barely longer than the payback period — and project A still has a payback of 5 years and a useful life of 8 years. The payback period of 3 years for project B is still better than the 5 years for project A. But does this mean we should still choose B over A, simply because B has the shorter payback period? Of course not! For when we calculate the new IRR for project B, we find that it is now approximately 1% (please don't be concerned with how this was calculated), which not only is far below the 11.82% for A but is now less than our *r* of 10% — it is no longer even acceptable.

　　Since the payback method does have some serious weaknesses, you might ask: "Do any firms use this method, and if so, why?" The answer is definitely yes, and for several reasons. These include:

In spite of shortcomings, it can be useful

1. Payback is simple to calculate and understand. The discounted cash-flow methods seem overly complicated to many potential users.

2. Payback can be used in conjunction with the discounted cash-flow methods. If a project has an undesirable payback period, it might be a waste of time determining the IRR or the NPV.

3. A company in a poor liquidity position may be more interested in a project having a quick return of the cost and a short life than in a project having a longer payback period but an extremely long life and high rate of return.

4. A company that is considering a high-risk project, which could cause the company to go out of business if the project fails, once again may prefer the project with the short payback period regardless of the potential long-run profits on alternative opportunities.

Accountant's Rate of Return

The ARR is the only method that uses averages
　　The final capital budgeting method we will look at is the ***accountant's rate of return (ARR),*** which is also known as the *accounting rate of return* or the *unadjusted rate of return.* Rather than emphasizing cash flows as do all the other methods, this method stresses accrual-based accounting income. The ARR is the percentage that the expected average annual income will be of the investment required to generate this income. The ARR is determined with the following equation:

$$\text{ARR} = \frac{\text{average net income}}{\text{incremental investment}}$$

The ARR is an *average rate of return for the entire life of a project*. Since it is an average, it makes no difference if the cash flows are even or uneven. Whenever we calculate an average, we merely divide the total cash flows by the number of years — it makes no difference if the total cash all comes in at the beginning of a project, if it all comes in at the end of a project, or if it is distributed evenly over the life of a project. The fact that the timing of a project's cash flows have no effect on the ARR is a serious weakness of the ARR method.

Is net income the same as cash flows?

We have just been talking about cash flows for a project — the timing, the total, and the average. When you look at the equation for the ARR, however, you see that there is no mention of cash flows. The numerator is average net income, not average cash flows.

Net income and cash flows aren't equal, but they are related

This may be true, but since net income and cash flows are closely related, we have no trouble converting the ARR equation into a form that will better accommodate the facts we have been given. The main difference between the cash flows from operations of an organization and the net income of an organization is depreciation. Therefore, the relationship of cash flows to net income is as follows:

$$\textbf{Cash flows} - \textbf{depreciation} = \textbf{net income}$$

Now we can substitute the phrase *average cash flows − depreciation* for average net income in the numerator of the ARR equation, and we get:

$$\textbf{ARR} = \frac{\textbf{average cash flows} - \textbf{depreciation}}{\textbf{incremental investment}}$$

or

$$= \frac{\text{ACF} - \text{D}}{\text{I}}$$

If a project has a salvage value, don't forget to subtract it in computing depreciation

Depreciation (D) is determined by

$$\textbf{D} = \frac{\textbf{incremental investment} - \textbf{salvage value}}{\textbf{useful life of investment}}$$

or

$$= \frac{\text{I} - \text{S}}{\text{L}}$$

which is the equation for straight-line depreciation.

An important point: The cash flows in the numerator of the ARR equation are cash flows from the operations of the project; they do not include nonoperating cash items such as the salvage value or a recovery of working capital. The cash receipt for salvage is included only in the calculation of depreciation.

Now let's calculate the ARR for projects A and B.

Project A

Since the cash flows for project A are the same each year, $2,000, we do not have to calculate the average cash flows for the numerator of the ARR equation — the annual amount is also the average. The average depreciation for project A is $1,250 per year:

$$\text{D} = \frac{\$10,000 - \$0}{8 \text{ years}} = \$1,250$$

And the ARR for project A is:

$$\text{ARR} = \frac{\$2,000 - \$1,250}{\$10,000} = \frac{\$750}{\$10,000} = 7.50\%$$

Net income should average 7.50% of investment for project A

And here's what an ARR of 7.50% means. For an investment of $10,000, the income earned from this investment, $750 per year, averages 7.50% of the initial cost of the investment over the 8-year useful life. As you might expect, the higher the ARR, the better the project, and in order for a project to be acceptable, the ARR must be higher than the cost of capital r.

Both the ARR and the IRR are rates of return that we expect to be earned by a proposed capital project. The difference is that the IRR considers the time value of money while the ARR assumes that all cash flows received throughout the life of a project are of equal value. Even though we may find that in some situations the ARR and IRR methods may have similar answers, you should use the IRR whenever possible. In many situations the results of the two methods are quite a bit different, and the results of the IRR are always conceptually superior.

Project B

Since this project has an uneven stream of cash flows, the first thing we need to do is compute the average cash flow (ACF). The average cash flow for project B, over its useful life of 8 years, is $2,000, the same as for project A:

$$\text{ACF} = \frac{\text{total cash flows (from operations) for entire useful life}}{\text{useful life}}$$

$$= \frac{\$16,000}{8 \text{ years}} = \$2,000 \text{ per year}$$

The ARR for project B is now

$$\text{ARR} = \frac{\$2,000 - \$1,250}{\$10,000} = \frac{\$750}{\$10,000} = 7.50\%$$

which is identical to the answer for project A.

Similarity of Answers

ARR for project A equals ARR for B because we use averages

The ARR for project A and that for B are both 7.50%. The reason for this is that the calculations involve averages. Since the total cash flows and the useful lives are the same for the two projects, the average cash flows are equal. And since the net incremental investment of $10,000 is also the same for both alternatives, the resulting answers are identical.

It is no coincidence that these two answers are identical. We purposely constructed the example to make this happen so that the weakness of the method would be obvious. If you were the decision maker, would you be indifferent to selecting project A or B? Hopefully not. Instead, wouldn't you select the project that returns the total of $16,000 on the $10,000 investment in the more timely manner? This is what project B does, because of its heavier emphasis on early-year cash flows. Remember: When different projects have different timings of cash flows, the ARR method is not capable of discriminating one project from the other. Only the NPV and IRR methods can do that properly.

Even though the ARR method is inferior to the discounted cash-flow methods, it is still somewhat popular with many decision makers. The reasons are simple:

1. ARR emphasizes net income rather than cash flows; this is more consistent with the accounting model employed in financial accounting.

2. ARR does not require the use of present value tables, which to many users are still confusing and overly complicated.

Effect on ARR of Depreciation Method Used

When we computed the ARR, depreciation was calculated with the equation

$$D = \frac{I - S}{L}$$

which is simply the straight-line method. You may be wondering what effect it would have on the ARR if we used the double-declining-balance method or sum-of-the-years'-digits method instead of straight line. The answer to your question is: It would have no effect whatsoever, since the ARR computation involves an average return over the useful life. It makes no difference how we calculate depreciation for years 1 to 8; the total taken over the 8 years is still $10,000, averaging $1,250 per year. Notice below how the average depreciation for sum-of-the-years'-digits (SYD) is indeed $1,250, the same as for straight line:

ARR is not affected by the depreciation method actually used

Year	SYD Factor	×	I − S	=	Depreciation
1	$\frac{8}{36}$	×	$10,000	=	$ 2,222
2	$\frac{7}{36}$	×	$10,000	=	1,944
3	$\frac{6}{36}$	×	$10,000	=	1,667
4	$\frac{5}{36}$	×	$10,000	=	1,389
5	$\frac{4}{36}$	×	$10,000	=	1,111
6	$\frac{3}{36}$	×	$10,000	=	833
7	$\frac{2}{36}$	×	$10,000	=	556
8	$\frac{1}{36}$	×	$10,000	=	278
Total depreciation...........................					$10,000
					÷ 8 years
Average depreciation per year.................					$ 1,250

If we determined a different ARR for each year, then the depreciation method selected would affect the expected return in each of those years. However, in capital budgeting we do not compute a different ARR for each year; we compute a single ARR which is an average for the full 8 years.

ARR for Revised Project B

For the very last time refer to Exhibit 7-1, and you'll see the expanded set of facts for project B. The ARR calculations for this situation differ in several ways from those we just explained above. First, the initial investment is now $11,000 rather than $10,000, because of the $1,000 investment in current assets. However, since the additional $1,000 does not relate to depreciable assets, it will not be part of the depreciation calculation. In addition, since the $1,000 recovery is not a cash flow from the operations of the project, it will not be part of the ACF calculation.

Denominator includes depreciable and nondepreciable investment

The disposal value of $2,500 represents a reduction in the depreciable base and needs to be subtracted from the $10,000 ($10,000 − $2,500 = $7,500) depreciable investment. This reduces the depreciation from $1,250 to $938 [($10,000 − $2,500) ÷ 8]. Since the cash proceeds from disposal are not generated from the operations of the project, they are excluded from the ACF calculation.

Disposal — part of depreciation calculation only

The average cash flows from operations include the lost rentals of $200 per year and the $500 overhaul, in addition to the eight different operating cash receipts. For example, in year 1 the net cash flow is $3,800 ($4,000 − $200) and in year 5 the net cash flow is $300 ($1,000 − $500 − $200).

There is no disposal in this calculation

The calculations related to the ARR for the revised set of facts for project B are as follows:

$$\text{Average cash flows} = \frac{\begin{array}{c}\$3,800 + \$2,800 + \$2,800 + \$1,800 +\\ \$300 + \$800 + \$800 + \$800\end{array}}{8}$$

$$= \frac{\$13,900}{8} = \$1,738$$

$$\text{Depreciation} = \frac{\$10,000 - \$2,500}{8} = \$938$$

$$\text{ARR} = \frac{\$1,738 - \$938}{\$10,000 + \$1,000} = \frac{\$800}{\$11,000} = 7.3\%$$

The average income of $800 is expected to be 7.3% of the initial investment.

UNCERTAINTY AND SENSITIVITY ANALYSIS

Since we live in a world of uncertainty, all our estimates could be wrong

The variables that we must consider in the capital budgeting methods are the initial outlay, the useful life, the salvage value, the amount and timing of cash flows, the cost of capital, and the relevant tax considerations. If the estimates we make for any of these variables turn out to disagree woefully with actual results, then the decisions we make based on the results of the ARR, IRR, NPV, and payback methods may also turn out to be woefully incorrect. After all, these methods yield results that are sensitive to any error in the estimates of the variables used. What can we do when there is a chance that our estimates will be incorrect and the resulting decisions may not be best for the firm? One thing we can do is use sensitivity analysis to help us assess the possible consequences of incorrect predictions.

Sensitivity analysis deals with "what if" situations

Sensitivity analysis evaluates the effect that a change in the value of an input variable in a decision model will have on the results yielded by that model. Sensitivity analysis deals with "what if" situations. What if the life is 6 years instead of 8? What if the cash flows drop by $1,000? What if the cost of capital is 14% rather than 10%? What might the IRR or any other measure actually be because of these errors?

For example, let's refer to the original projections for project A for Hubbard Contracting. The initial outlay was $10,000; the useful life was 8 years; the cash flows were $2,000 per year; the salvage was zero; and the cost of capital was 10%. On the basis of these projections, the results of the capital budgeting methods were:

NPV $668

IRR 11.82%

Payback . . . . 5 years

ARR 7.50%

Now let's assume that Craig Hubbard is concerned that two of the variables might not be exactly as originally predicted. On the basis of the firm's previous experience, Hubbard feels that the life and cash flows might actually take on the following ranges of values:

Life . . . . 7 to 9 years

Cash flows . . . . $1,500 to $2,500

Hubbard wonders what the most pessimistic and optimistic results might be for project A, and he has the firm's accountant come up with these figures:

	Original Expected Results	Pessimistic Expected Results	Optimistic Expected Results
Life	8 years	7 years	9 years
Cash flows	$2,000	$1,500	$2,500
NPV	$668	$(2,698)	$4,398
IRR	11.82%	1.23%	20.25%
Payback	5 years	6.7 years	4 years
ARR	7.50%	.70%	13.89%

As you can tell, the results of each method are quite sensitive to the changes in the variables. For example, look at the NPV. Our best guess was that it would be $668, which was acceptable. However, it's quite conceivable that it could range from a low of $(2,698)—a loss which is far from acceptable—to a high of $4,398. We might accept the project thinking it will have a positive NPV but find out later that it is actually negative. So what should we do? Reject the project because it might be negative? Or take a chance that it will be as originally projected—or even go as high as $4,398?

There really isn't any single answer that will be satisfactory for all decision makers. The best answer in each case depends on how much risk a decision maker is willing to take that results won't turn out as well as estimated. As accountants, though, we will have done our job. With sensitivity analysis we provide the decision maker with more information than just the best estimate. The range of possibilities that we provide gives the decision maker a better foundation for making a decision.

Other Applications

Sensitivity analysis is used in a direct way to determine how sensitive the output of a decision model is to a change in one of the input variables. However, sensitivity analysis can also be used indirectly to determine how much an input variable must change to obtain a specific result. For example, our original estimate of the NPV for project A was $668, assuming cash flows of $2,000. Since the NPV was positive, it was acceptable. Hubbard, however, might also be interested in how much lower the cash flows could actually be before the NPV would become negative.

To determine this, we need to calculate the amount of cash flows that will give us an NPV of zero. The NPV will equal zero when the TPV equals the initial outlay of $10,000. These cash flows would be:

$$\text{TPV} = P_{\overline{n}|i} \times \text{cash flows} = \$10,000$$

$$\$10,000 = P_{\overline{8}|10\%} \times \text{cash flows}$$

$$= 5.334 \times \text{cash flows}$$

$$\text{Cash flows} = \frac{\$10,000}{5.334} = \$1,875 \text{ per year}$$

If the cash flows fall to no lower than $1,875 per year, a drop of $125 per year from the original estimate, the NPV will be zero or positive. The NPV will not be negative unless the annual cash flows fall below $1,875.

In this example we used sensitivity analysis to determine the cash flows that would ensure an acceptable NPV. We could also use this approach for determining the life, the cost of capital, the salvage, or the tax rate that would yield an acceptable NPV — assuming all other variables remain the same.

We could also use sensitivity analysis in a similar manner with each of the other methods.

ALTERNATIVE USES OF CAPITAL BUDGETING

Capital budgeting isn't only for fixed assets

Early in this chapter we defined capital budgeting as planning for the acquisition and financing of long-term investments, primarily property, plant, and equipment. The four methods that we introduced all dealt with the question of whether or not to acquire a fixed asset, or which fixed asset it would be better to buy. Although the capital budgeting methods have obvious uses in fixed asset decisions, they are not limited to these applications. Quite the contrary, there are numerous other situations that provide opportunities for the use of these methods as well.

As a matter of fact, any situation faced by management that has the same characteristics as the purchase decision for a fixed asset may be ideal for capital budgeting. The key characteristics of a purchase decision that are also found in numerous other decision situations are the following:

1. A large initial outlay of resources at year 0

2. An expectation that the incremental benefits in future years will adequately compensate the organization for its outlay of resources

Each of the decision situations described below has these characteristics — so each could have capital budgeting techniques employed as part of its analysis.

1. Should the plant rearrange its machinery in order to provide a more efficient flow of materials through the different stages of production?

2. Would the advantages of reduced competition offset the cost of purchasing a patent to a new process?

3. Should we undertake a substantial advertising campaign that holds the promise of significantly increasing our sales for several years?

4. Should we develop an in-house training facility to minimize the amount of on-the-job training required for new employees?

These situations are not an all-inclusive list. We merely wanted to give you enough examples so that you won't associate capital budgeting only with fixed asset acquisitions.

FOR YOUR REVIEW

You may now find it helpful to refer to Exhibit 7-4, which summarizes the key items in each of the four capital budgeting methods we have discussed in this chapter. For each method there is a brief (1) definition, (2) description of the required calculation, and (3) explanation of the criteria for accepting or rejecting projects.

EXHIBIT 7-4 Summary of Capital Budgeting Methods

Method	Definition	Calculation	Criteria for Acceptance— Acceptable if:
NPV	The amount of present value of future cash inflows in excess of net incremental investment	$NPV = PV$ of cash flows @ r − net incremental investment (for both even and uneven streams of cash flows).	$NPV > 0$
IRR	Actual rate earned on a project; the rate for which $NPV = 0$	1. Even cash flows: $$\text{Factor} = \frac{\text{investment}}{\text{cash flows}}$$ Find the interest rate that has this factor in the PV of Ordinary Annuity of $1 table. 2. Uneven cash flows: Trial and error—using the PV of $1 table.	$IRR > r$
PP	Number of years needed to recoup the original investment	1. Even cash flows: $$PP = \frac{\text{investment}}{\text{cash flows}}$$ 2. Uneven cash flows: Accumulate cash flows until cumulative amount equals incremental investment.	$PP <$ a predetermined number of years, determined by management
ARR	Average net income per dollar of investment	$$ARR = \frac{\text{avg. cash flows} - \text{avg. deprec.}}{\text{investment}}$$ (for both even and uneven cash flows).	$ARR > r$

CHAPTER SUMMARY

Capital budgeting is planning for the acquisition and financing of long-term investments—primarily in fixed assets. The capital budgeting methods used to evaluate investment proposals fall into two categories: *discounted cash-flow methods* and *nondiscounted cash-flow methods.* The former methods involve the use of present value analysis, while the latter methods do not.

The two discounted cash-flow methods are *net present value (NPV)* and *internal rate of return (IRR).* The net present value method finds the present value of all future cash flows and from this amount subtracts the *net incremental investment* for the project. If the excess (the NPV) is positive, the project is acceptable; if it is negative, it must be rejected.

The internal rate of return is the exact rate of return to be earned on the project. It represents that rate of interest for which the total present value of future cash flows equals the incremental investment. Expressed a little differently, it is the rate for which the NPV is zero. If the IRR is greater than the *cost of capital,* the project is acceptable; but if it is less than the cost of capital, it must be rejected.

The nondiscounted cash-flow methods include (1) the payback period method and (2) the accountant's rate of return method. The ***payback period*** is the number of years needed for a project to accumulate enough cash flows to pay for the initial cost of the investment. The weaknesses in this method are that (1) the time value of money is not considered and (2) the life of the project beyond the payback period is disregarded.

The ***accountant's rate of return*** is the percentage that the average expected annual net income is to the investment required to generate this income. The accountant's rate of return is the only method in which averages are employed and allowed. In all other methods the use of an average would distort the answer.

Sensitivity analysis evaluates the effect that a change in the value of an input variable in a decision model has on the results of using that model. It deals with "what if" situations. It can also be used to determine how much an input variable in a capital budgeting model would have to change in order to obtain a specific answer for a model.

IMPORTANT TERMS USED IN THIS CHAPTER

Accountant's rate of return The ratio of the average annual net income from a project to the investment required to generate this income (average net income divided by investment). (page 295)

Capital budgeting The planning for the acquisition and financing of long-term investments. (page 272)

Cost of capital The interest rate for determining the total present value of cash flows in a capital budgeting problem. Also called the ***minimum desired rate of return.*** (page 286)

Discounted cash-flow methods The category of capital budgeting methods that employs present value analysis. The two discounted cash-flow methods are net present value and internal rate of return. (page 275)

Incremental cash flows The cash generated by the incremental investment in capital budgeting. (page 273)

Internal rate of return That interest rate for which the net present value of an investment is zero. It is the exact rate of return to be earned on a project. (page 287)

Interpolation The process of finding an exact number when it falls between two other numbers. (page 287)

Minimum desired rate of return The interest rate used to determine the total present value of cash flows in a capital budgeting problem. Also called the ***cost of capital.*** (page 286)

Net incremental investment The required outlay of resources to obtain a fixed asset and prepare it for productive use. (page 273)

Net present value The difference between the total present value of future cash flows and the incremental investment of a project. (page 281)

Nondiscounted cash-flow methods The category of capital budgeting methods that does not use present value analysis. The category includes payback period and accountant's rate of return. (page 293)

Payback period The number of years needed for a project to accumulate enough cash flows to pay for the initial cost of the investment. (page 293)

Sensitivity analysis An evaluation tool that measures the effect that a change in the value of an input variable in a decision model has on the results of using that model. (page 299)

Trial and error The manner of determining the internal rate of return when the cash flows from a project are not the same each year. (page 289)

APPENDIX 7-1: INCREMENTAL ANALYSIS

Incremental analysis is best suited to keep-vs.-replace decisions

Throughout the chapter we have been applying the capital budgeting methods to different projects, using what we called a *total approach.* In the total approach we calculate the results for each project individually, keeping the information and analysis for one project separate from those for any other project. In some situations, however, we may want to use an *incremental approach,* in which we determine the differences between individual projects and calculate the results for the NPV, IRR, payback, and ARR on the basis of these incremental differences. The incremental approach can be used any time we are comparing two competing projects, but it becomes cumbersome when we are comparing more than two projects. A decision situation that is always suitable for incremental analysis is one we refer to as the *keep-vs.-replace decision.* In this situation a firm is considering replacing an old depreciable asset with a new one because the new asset is thought to be either more productive or more efficient than the original asset. There is no way that both projects can be undertaken at the same time—they are mutually exclusive.

A typical keep-vs.-replace decision is presented in Example 7-3 for the Dianawick Amusement Park. We will use this example to compare the total approach with the incremental approach.

Example 7-3

A keep-vs.-replace situation

DIANAWICK AMUSEMENT PARK

The Dianawick Amusement Park offers a variety of enjoyable things for children to do. One of its rides, the musical merry-go-round, needs to be completely overhauled to the tune of $10,000. The owner, Beth Mcguire, prefers not to spend this sort of money on an old merry-go-round when she can buy a new one for $37,000.

The useful life for both the old and the new merry-go-rounds is 4 years; for either, the cash receipts from operations will be $50,000 per year. The cash operating costs for the old merry-go-round are $30,000 and for the new will be $23,000, or $7,000 less per year. If Dianawick keeps the old merry-go-round, it will have a disposal (salvage) value of $3,000 in 4 years. However, if the new merry-go-round replaces the old one, the old one can be sold for $5,000 at the time of the replacement. Dianawick expects the new merry-go-round to have a disposal value of $10,000 in 4 years.

The firm's cost of capital is 15%.

Net Present Value

The keep-vs.-replace decision is evaluated in Exhibits 7-5 and 7-6 with the net present value method. In Exhibit 7-5 the total approach is employed, and in Exhibit 7-6 the incremental approach is used.

EXHIBIT 7-5 Analysis of Keep-vs.-Replace Decision: Total Approach

	15% PV Factor	15% Present Value	Sketch of Cash Flows					
			0	1	2	3	4	
Keep:								
Costs of overhaul	1.000	(10,000)	(10,000)					
Cash operating receipts	2.854	142,700		50,000	50,000	50,000	50,000	
Cash operating costs.	2.854	(85,620)		(30,000)	(30,000)	(30,000)	(30,000)	
Disposal	.571	1,713					3,000	*These are the*
Net cash per year			(10,000)	20,000	20,000	20,000	23,000	*totals each*
NPV		48,793						*year for keep*
Replace:								
Cost of new merry-go-round . . .	1.000	(37,000)	(37,000)					
Cash operating receipts	2.854	142,700		50,000	50,000	50,000	50,000	
Cash operating costs.	2.854	(65,642)		(23,000)	(23,000)	(23,000)	(23,000)	
Disposal of old	1.000	5,000	5,000					*These are the*
Disposal of new.	.571	5,710					10,000	*totals each*
Net cash per year			(32,000)	27,000	27,000	27,000	37,000	*year for*
NPV		50,768						*replace*
Difference in NPVs		1,975						

This is the difference between $48,793 and $50,768. Replace has an NPV $1,975 higher than keep

Total Approach

Irrelevant items can often be deleted from the total approach

In this approach, all the facts—the *total* facts—that relate to each alternative are included in the analysis whether they were relevant to the decision or not. For example, the annual cash inflows of $50,000 are the same for the keep analysis and the replace analysis, so this particular information is irrelevant. Nevertheless, the fact that the annual cash receipts are included in the analysis does not necessarily mean this information has to be included. If our only interest is in determining the difference in the NPVs for the two alternatives, it would be acceptable to omit the annual cash receipts, as well as any other irrelevant item. However, if we want to

EXHIBIT 7-6 Analysis of Keep-vs.-Replace Decision: Incremental Approach

	15% PV Factor	15% Present Value	Sketch of Cash Flows					
			0	1	2	3	4	
Replace:								
Incremental outlay	1.000	(27,000)	(27,000)					
Cash operating savings	2.854	19,978		7,000	7,000	7,000	7,000	
Disposal of old:								
Year 0	1.000	5,000	5,000					
Year 4	.571	3,997					7,000	
Net cash per year			(22,000)	7,000	7,000	7,000	14,000	
NPV		1,975						

This is the same difference found in the total approach in Exhibit 7-5. Since this NPV is not zero, 15% is not the IRR.

This row represents the differences in the relevant items (found in the total approach in Exhibit 7-5) for Dianawick

know the NPV for each alternative, then it would be necessary to include in the analysis the annual cash receipts even though this specific information has no impact on the ultimate decision.

The NPV for keep is $48,793, and for replace it is $50,768. The difference of $1,975 indicates that it is preferable for Dianawick to make the replacement.

Incremental Approach

Only differences appear in the incremental approach

The initial outlay in year 0 under the incremental approach is $27,000. This represents the difference between the cost of the $10,000 overhaul—if the old merry-go-round is kept—and the $37,000 purchase price—if a new one is bought. In year 0 the disposal value of the old merry-go-round represents a $5,000 inflow that is available only if the replacement is made. When the $5,000 is subtracted from the $27,000, the net of $22,000 represents the *net incremental investment.* Net incremental investment is especially important when you are using the IRR, payback, and ARR methods.

Net incremental investment = $22,000

The disposal value of $7,000 shown in year 4 is the net of the disposal values for keep and replace ($10,000 − $3,000) which were shown separately in the year-4 column of Exhibit 7-5. By making the replacement, Dianawick will have an incremental inflow of $7,000 cash from disposal.

Notice that the annual cash receipts from operations do not appear in the incremental analysis. This is because the difference in annual cash receipts for keep and replace is zero ($50,000 − $50,000). The annual cash operating costs do appear, however, because they are different for keep and replace. They are $30,000 for keep and $23,000 for replace, a cash savings of $7,000.

The difference in the NPVs with the incremental approach is $1,975, which is exactly the difference we got with the total approach.

Internal Rate of Return

In most keep-vs.-replace decisions the incremental approach is recommended for the IRR, payback, and ARR. Using the total approach may lead to results that are inconsistent with those determined incrementally.

If there were no disposal, determining IRR would be a lot simpler

If it weren't for the disposal values in year 4, determining IRR would be an easy matter. We'd merely find the present value factor that equates the present value of the cash inflows (the savings of $7,000 per year) to the net incremental investment, using the following calculation:

$$\text{Factor} = \frac{\text{net incremental investment}}{\text{cash flow per year}}$$

$$= \frac{\$22,000}{7,000} = 3.143$$

Then we'd look for this factor in the Present Value of an Ordinary Annuity table (Table 7-2 on page 280). Doing this, we'd find that it is situated between the factors for 10% and 12%. The interpolated value would be the exact IRR.

The cash flow in year 4 is different from years 1 to 3

Unfortunately this approach cannot be used for Dianawick. This is because the cash flows in each year are not the same. While the net cash flow is $7,000 in years 1 to 3, it increases to $14,000 in year 4, due to the $7,000 incremental disposal value. Unless the cash flows are exactly the same each year, the approach mentioned above for determining the IRR would be incorrect—the IRR would be understated because the positive cash flow from the disposal in year 4 would have been disregarded.

We use trial and error for IRR

The only way to calculate the IRR in this situation is by using trial and error, which you should remember is how we calculated the IRR for project B on pages 289–291. The use of trial and error requires that we find a specific interest rate at which the NPV of the cash flows, using that rate, will equal zero. Since it is highly unlikely that the exact answer will ever be a nice even number, what we realistically try to do is find two interest rates that are close to the exact IRR. For one rate the NPV should be positive, and for the other it should be negative. For Dianawick these two rates are 15% and 20%.

The IRR must be between 15% and 20%; at that point NPV = 0

| | Cash Flow | 15% | | 20% | |
		PV Factor	Present Value	PV Factor	Present Value
Net incremental investment, year 0 ($27,000 − $5,000)	$(22,000)	1.000	$(22,000)	1.000	$(22,000)
Net cash savings from operations, years 1–4	7,000	2.854	19,978	2.588	18,116
Difference in disposal values, year 4	7,000	.571	3,997	.482	3,374
			$ 1,975		$ (510)

At 15% the NPV is positive, and at 20% the NPV is negative. Therefore, the exact IRR must fall somewhere between these two rates. Using interpolation, we find the exact IRR to be 18.974%:

	NPV	NPV
15%	$1,975	$1,975
?	-0-	
20%		(510)
Difference	$1,975	$2,485

The point at which NPV = 0 is 79.48% of the way from 15% to 20%

$$\frac{\$1,975}{\$2,485} = 79.48\% \times (20\% - 15\%) = \quad 3.974\%$$

$$\underline{15.000\%}$$

$$\text{IRR} = 18.974\%$$

The Payback Period

Whenever a project's cash inflows are not the same each year, the general approach to determining payback is to accumulate the annual net cash inflows until the cumulative total reaches the net incremental investment.[3] Using this approach, the payback period for the merry-go-round is determined as follows.

First, we accumulate the cash inflows until they reach $22,000 — the initial incremental investment:

---

[3] Since the net cash inflows are the same amounts each year until the end of year 4 (when Dianawick will receive the $7,000 disposal value) and since the payback comes before the cash flows stop being equal, an easier way to determine the payback period is to use the following equation:

$$\text{PP} = \frac{\$22,000}{\$7,000} = 3.143 \text{ years}$$

	Cash Inflow Per Year	Cumulative Cash Flow
During year: 1	$7,000	$ 7,000
2	7,000	14,000
3	7,000	21,000
Payback period		22,000
End of year 4:		
Prior to disposal	7,000	28,000
After disposal.........................	7,000	35,000

The cumulative cash flow reaches $22,000 in the fourth year

As you can see, the initial incremental investment will be completely recovered sometime during year 4. The exact answer is found with interpolation:

		Cumulative Cash Flows
End of year 3	$21,000	$21,000
Needed to pay for investment........................	22,000	
End of year 4 (prior to disposal)		28,000
Difference	$ 1,000	$ 7,000

$$\text{Fraction of year} = \frac{\$1,000}{\$7,000} = .143 \text{ year}$$

The cumulative cash flow reaches $22,000 about 14.3% of the way into year 4

$$\text{Payback period} = 3 \text{ years} + .143 \text{ year} = 3.143 \text{ years}$$

Accountant's Rate of Return

Using the incremental investment, incremental cash flows, and incremental depreciation, the ARR for the merry-go-round is determined as follows:

The projected income should average 14.8% of the initial investment

$$\text{ARR} = \frac{\text{average incremental cash flows} - \text{incremental depreciation}}{\text{net incremental investment}}$$

$$= \frac{\$7,000 - \$3,750}{\$22,000} = \frac{\$3,250}{\$22,000} = 14.8\%$$

The incremental depreciation was determined in the following manner:

$$\text{Depreciation} = \frac{\text{net incremental investment} - \text{incremental disposal}}{\text{life}}$$

$$= \frac{\$22,000 - \$7,000}{4} = \frac{\$15,000}{4} = \$3,750$$

In determining the incremental depreciation, we assume that the major repair for the keep alternative was capitalized and would need to be depreciated. Therefore, the incremental investment of $22,000 ($37,000 − $10,000 − $5,000) all relates to depreciable assets, and the depreciation was appropriately based upon this amount.

QUESTIONS

1. Define *capital budgeting.*

2. Give several decision situations in which the capital budgeting planning models discussed in this chapter would be applicable.

3. What is the main difference between the capital budgeting methods that are classified as *discounted cash-flow methods* and those that are called *nondiscounted cash-flow methods?*

4. What are the two most important factors to be considered in the use of all capital budgeting methods? Name three other factors common to the use of most capital budgeting methods.

5. The cash flows from operations needed for all capital budgeting methods usually refer to cash generated from the continuing, repetitive use of a fixed asset. Name five types of cash flows that might appear in the capital budgeting problem which probably would be treated separately from the cash flows from operations.

6. Is it the amount or the timing of cash flows that affects the net present value of a project?

7. Explain why an understanding of the time value of money is important in capital budgeting analysis.

8. "The higher the cost of capital, the lower the net present value." Do you agree? Explain.

9. "The higher the cost of capital, the higher the internal rate of return." Do you agree? Explain.

10. "The net present value can be positive or zero, but never negative." Do you agree? Explain.

11. "As long as the present value of a project is greater than zero, the project should always be purchased by the firm." Comment.

12. Define the *internal rate of return.*

13. "The internal rate of return is another name for the cost of capital." Comment.

14. Proponents of ARR may argue that it is superior to IRR and NPV because ARR considers depreciation but NPV and IRR do not. How would you respond to this criticism?

15. Assume that a new project expects to earn an IRR of 12% over a 5-year life. How would you express the IRR in terms of what rate is going to be earned in each and every year of the project's life?

16. Explain how sensitivity analysis can be used to help management make a better decision in a capital budgeting situation.

17. What are the criteria for acceptance or rejection of a project when the internal rate of return method is used?

18. Explain what is meant by the *trial-and-error method.*

19. If the nondiscounted cash-flow methods are inferior to the discounted cash-flow methods, why do you have to learn them?

20. "When two projects are being compared, the one with the greater cash flows in the early years of life will always have the greater NPV." Discuss whether you agree or disagree.

21. Explain how a discounted cash-flow method and a nondiscounted cash-flow method might be used together to evaluate a capital project.

22. "Financial accounting and capital budgeting relate to different time periods and different segments within the organization." Explain what we mean by this observation.

23. The selection of a depreciation method will not affect the accountant's rate of return. Why?

24. "The accountant's rate of return will be higher if the cash flows from a project are heavier in the early years of life than they are in the later years." Do you agree? Explain.

EXERCISES

Exercise 7-1
Answering miscellaneous present value questions

Answer each of the present value questions below by using Tables 7-1 and 7-2:
a. What is the factor for the present value of $1 at 6% for 8 years?
b. What is the factor for $P_{\overline{10}|8\%}$?
c. How much must be invested today at 10% to accumulate to $1 in 5 years?
d. How much must be invested today at 4% in order to receive $1 per year for 4 years.
e. What is the maximum amount that you would invest today at 12% in exchange for eight annual receipts of $10,000?
f. If you invest $321 today which will accumulate to $1,000 in 10 years, at what interest rate is the money invested?
g. If an investment of $6,144 at 10% promises a return of $1,000 per year, for how many years would the $1,000 be expected?
h. What is the present value of $2,500 per year for 20 years if the interest rate is 8%?
i. If the payback period for a 5-year machine is 3.604 years, what is the internal rate of return?
j. If the internal rate of return for a 15-year project is 6%, what is its payback?
k. What is the present value of the following cash flows for an r of 4%.?

Year	Cash Flow
1	$8,000
2	6,000
3	7,000
4	4,000
5	3,000
	$28,000

l. If the NPV for a project is zero using a cost of capital of 11%, what is its internal rate of return?

Exercise 7-2
Determining the characteristics of different capital budgeting methods

For each description given below, place an X in the column(s) representing the method(s) to which the description applies:

	PP	ARR	NPV	IRR
a. **Example:** The answer is stated in number of years.	X			
b. The answer is given in dollars.				
c. The answer is stated as a percentage.				
d. Is acceptable whenever the answer is positive.				
e. Disregards the concept of time value of money.				
f. Is an averaging technique.				
g. The answer is influenced by life of project.				
h. Includes depreciation in the computation.				
i. Is not affected by timing of cash flows.				
j. Is dependent upon the value of r.				

Exercise 7-3
Computing all the
methods for even cash
flows

The Bellafonte Company is considering the acquisition of a new machine which will cost $10,000 and have an expected 5-year useful life. The new machine should generate $2,800 per year in cash savings. The cost of capital is 12%.

Compute the following:
a. The payback period
b. The net present value
c. The internal rate of return

(Check figure: 15.393%)

d. The accountant's rate of return (For this part, assume there is a $400 disposal value at the end of year 4.)

Exercise 7-4
Evaluating the NPV for
different costs of capital

One of the machines at the Burford License Plate Company has just broken down. Burford realizes that a new machine must be purchased immediately since the production of 1989 plates is about to begin. The most efficient machine available would cost $36,040, but it will generate additional cash flows of $10,000 per year over an estimated 5-year useful life. Burford has decided to employ the net present value method.
a. Would the machine be acceptable if the cost of capital for Burford was 10%?
b. Would the machine be acceptable if the cost of capital was 15%?

[Check figure: NPV = $(2,520)]

c. Is there any interest rate in the present value tables at which NPV = 0? If so, what is it? What is this rate called?

Exercise 7-5
Calculating the NPV and
IRR for uneven cash flows

The Phelps Company is about to spend $29,200 for a new machine which promises the following annual cash inflows:

Year	Cash Inflow
1	$20,000
2	10,000
3	4,000
	$34,000

a. If the cost of capital is 10%, compute the net present value.
b. Is the answer to part **a** the internal rate of return? Why or why not?
c. Compute the net present value using rates of 8% and 12%.

[Check figure: NPV = $(546) for 12%]

d. Where is the internal rate of return? Why?

Exercise 7-6
Comparing IRR to ARR

The R. J. West Secretarial Pool is considering the purchase of new Tangerine PC computers for the secretaries to use. The computers would replace several typewriters and one copying machine. The net incremental investment for the computers is $15,000 and for the word processing software, $1,000. West expects to save $4,000 annually in operating costs (labor, typing, and copying) over the 5-year useful lives. At the end of 5 years, West expects to sell the computers and software for $3,000. The firm's cost of capital is 10%.
a. Calculate the internal rate of return for this project.
b. Calculate the accountant's rate of return.

(Check figure: 8.75%)

c. Discuss whether or not the project is acceptable.

Exercise 7-7
Working backward to determine *r*

Kim Knight of Florida Fried Chicken has decided to invest in a new chicken fryer, costing $750, because the projected net present value is $237.40. The fryer has an estimated life of 6 years and should have a salvage value of $100 at the end of 6 years. It is expected to save $200 per year in operating costs.
a. What is Knight's cost of capital?
b. What is the project's expected internal rate of return?

(Check figure: 17.46%)

Exercise 7-8
Pointing out a weakness of payback

The Mangrove Gardens Ski Show is considering the purchase of two new boats. The first boat—the Streak—costs $14,400 and will generate net cash inflows of $2,400 per year. The second boat—the Typhoon—costs $15,000 and should generate net cash inflows of $3,000 per year.
a. Compute the payback period for each machine.
b. Entirely on the basis of the answer to part **a**, which machine should be acquired?
c. If the useful lives of Streak and Typhoon are 15 years and 6 years, respectively, determine the internal rate of return for each.

(Check figure: Typhoon = 5.47%)

d. Using IRR, would the decision to invest be the same as in part **b**?

Exercise 7-9
Determining payback from the ARR

The Fourth National Bank of Arcadia will probably invest $20,000 in several new, sophisticated money-counting machines. The life of the machines is 10 years.
 What is the payback period if the accountant's rate of return is 15%

(Check figure: 4 years)

Exercise 7-10
Filling in the blanks for capital budgeting methods

For each of the situations below, fill in the blanks concerning several capital budgeting methods:

	Situation		
	1	2	3
Initial investment	$60,000	$?	$50,000
Cash flow per year	$10,000	$4,000	$10,000
Life	10 years	8 years	9 years
Discount rate.	10%	10%	? %
Salvage value	$0	$2,000	$0
Net present value	$?	$2,268	$18,010
Internal rate of return	? %	? %	? %
Payback period	?	?	5 years
Accountant's rate of return.	? %	? %	? %

[Check figures: IRR for (1) = 10.58%; investment for (2) = $20,000; IRR for (2) = 12.97%]

Exercise 7-11
Computing the life based upon results of the ARR

Radio Station WJCS has purchased a new turntable which promises to reduce operating costs by $300 per year. The turntable, which cost $1,500, is expected to have an accountant's rate of return of 10%. At the end of its useful life, the turntable should be sold for $300.
 Determine the expected useful life of the turntable.

(Check figure: Depreciation = $150)

Exercise 7-12
Calculating the weighted average *r*

The Heavy Leveraged Company is interested in investing in a project that has a projected useful life of 20 years. Top management decides to finance the entire investment with long-term debt that currently has a cost of 12% per year. The costs of Heavy's other sources of financing for long-term investments are as follows:

Common stock 20%
Retained earnings. 18%

Although Heavy expects to finance this investment solely with debt, it expects to use the three sources of long-term financing in the following percentages during the next few years:

Long-term debt. 40%
Common stock 50%
Retained earnings. 10%

Determine the cost of capital that Heavy should use to calculate the project's NPV.

(Check figure: 16.6%)

Exercise 7-13
Determining the subtle elements associated with the IRR

Reckless Ricky's Bicycle Delivery Service purchases a new fleet of bicycles for $15,000. The estimated useful life of the fleet is 3 years; the expected cash receipts per year are $7,122; and the anticipated IRR is 20%.

For each of the 3 years of life, calculate the following:
a. The dollar return on investment
b. The recovery of investment

(Check figure: Year 1 = $4,122)

c. The unrecovered investment at the end of each year

Exercise 7-14
Including nondepreciable investment in capital budgeting

The Claudine Savage Ski Company is considering the purchase of a new machine that produces a new type of ski which is not only faster but also safer. The new machine costs $14,000 and will have a useful life of 5 years. The cash flows are expected to be $5,000 per year. In addition to the investment in machinery, Savage will have to increase its average investment in inventory by $2,000 during the 5-year life, all of which will be recovered at the end of the 5 years. The cost of capital is 20%.

Calculate the following for this new machine:
a. The net present value
b. The internal rate of return
c. The accountant's rate of return
d. The payback period

(Check figure: 3.2 years)

Exercise 7-15
Working backward from the NPV

The Abbott Medical Clinic is considering the purchase of a second dental chair for its office. The owner, Phil Milwauk, feels that his business is good enough to have a second chair and that it will be used continuously. The new chair will cost $50,000 and will have a salvage value of $5,000 at the end of its useful life. The payback is expected to be 2.5 years; the ARR, 31%; and the NPV, a quite acceptable $51,595.

On the basis of the facts given above, determine each of the following items related to the new dental chair:
a. The annual cash flows
b. The useful life

(Check figure: 10 years)

c. The cost of capital (*Hint:* You need to use trial and error.)

Exercise 7-16
Evaluating the sensitivity
of results to changes in
key variables

The oldies radio station, WGLD, is considering a new sound system that will be used for on-site broadcasts. The cost of the new system will be $25,000, but the anticipated increase in cash flows from the additional engagements is expected to be $9,000 per year for at least the next 4 years. The station's cost of capital is 12%.

For this exercise, you may need the following table in addition to Tables 7-1 and 7-2:

	Present Value of $1				Present Value of Annuity of $1			
n	24%	28%	30%	40%	24%	28%	30%	40%
1	.806	.781	.769	.714	.806	.781	.769	.714
2	.650	.610	.592	.510	1.457	1.392	1.361	1.224
3	.524	.477	.455	.364	1.981	1.816	1.816	1.589
4	.423	.373	.350	.260	2.404	2.241	2.166	1.879
5	.341	.291	.269	.186	2.745	2.532	2.436	2.035

a. On the basis of the projections given above, determine the IRR and NPV.

(Check figure: 16.43%)

b. Assume that the estimate of useful life may be overstated or understated by 1 year. Determine the new IRRs and NPVs based on the possible new lives of 3 and 5.

c. Now assume instead that the cash flows may be overstated or understated by 25%. Determine the new IRRs and NPVs based on the revised cash flow possibilities of $6,750 and $11,250.

d. Finally, assume instead that the cost of capital may have been misstated by 25%. Determine the new IRRs and NPVs based on the revised costs of capital of 9% and 15%.

e. Evaluate your results in light of the sensitivity that exists for the IRR and NPV because of the possible errors in the original estimates.

Exercise 7-17
Choosing the appropriate
PV factors

Hairaldo Riviera is a free-lance photographer who is losing numerous assignments because of the poor quality of his camera equipment. He is considering the purchase of new equipment costing $20,000. Additional facts related to the purchase are given below:

Additional cash receipts per year	$5,000
Useful life	5 years
Disposal value	$1,000
Cost of capital	.10

a. Using Tables 7-1 and 7-2, calculate the NPV.

b. Assume you now have the following additional information concerning the timing of the cash flows. The receipts expected for the first year are the result of an advance on a contract that should be signed in the middle of the year. The remaining cash receipts will flow evenly during each of the last 4 years. In addition, $5,000 of the equipment won't actually be purchased and paid for until the middle of the first year.

Using the additional present value table given below, calculate the NPV a second time. This time, however, try to match the present value factors more carefully with the exact timing of the cash flows.

	Present Value of Cash Received	
Year	At the Midpoint of the Year	Evenly during the Year
1	.952	.955
2	.866	.868
3	.787	.789
4	.715	.717
5	.650	.652

(Check figure: $990)

c. Discuss the significance of the difference in your answers to parts **a** and **b**.

PROBLEMS: SET A

Problem A7-1
Calculating the PP, ARR, and IRR for an uneven stream

Brenda's Isometric Gym is considering the purchase of an exercise machine which is expected to reduce operating costs over the next 4 years. If the machine is purchased for $2,000, the operating costs should be reduced by the following amounts:

Year	Reduced Labor Costs
1	$700
2	800
3	900
4	300

The gym's cost of capital is 11%.

Required

1. Determine the payback period.
2. Compute the internal rate of return. On the basis of this answer, should the machine be purchased?
3. Determine the accountant's rate of return.

(Check figure: 8.75%)

Problem A7-2
Determining whether an old machine should be kept or replaced

The Chapman Contracting Company is considering the replacement of an old steam shovel with a new one. The old steam shovel was purchased 3 years ago for $70,000. It currently can be sold for $54,000; but if kept until the end of its remaining 4-year useful life, it can be sold for only $6,000.

The new steam shovel will cost $216,000 and will have a 4-year useful life. At the end of that time it is expected that it can be sold for $36,000. The cash operating costs with the new steam shovel should be $650,000 per year, $80,000 lower than the operating costs will be if the old steam shovel is kept. The old steam shovel, if kept, will need a $6,000 major overhaul immediately and another costing $6,400 in 2 years.

The company's cost of capital is 10%.

Required

Using the present value method, determine whether the old steam shovel should be kept or replaced. Compute the present values for the keep-vs.-replace decisions separately. What is the difference in the present values?

[Check figure: Present value for replace = $(2,197,262)]

Problem A7-3
Finding the NPV for a new bus

Bubba Karras, an ex-football player, is now working for the county recreation department, and he is trying to convince the county commissioners to purchase a used bus to transport youngsters to the summer sports camps. Karras feels that the bus could substantially increase enrollment. The bus costs $3,500 and should last for 5 years. At the end of its useful life, the bus is expected to have a disposal value of $1,000. The additional enrollments are expected to increase cash receipts by $3,000 per year but will necessitate hiring another part-time coach for $1,500 per year. At the end of 2 years it is expected that the bus will need to undergo $500 of repairs in order to last the 3 remaining years.

Required

Using the net present value method, determine whether the bus should or should not be purchased. Assume a 12% cost of capital.

(Check figure: NPV = $2,074)

Problem A7-4
Expanding the analysis of Problem A7-3

$\boxed{\textit{Required}}$

Refer to the facts given in Problem A7-3. Calculate each of the following:
1. The internal rate of return

(Check figure: 31.728%)

2. The accountant's rate of return
3. The payback period

Problem A7-5
Deciding whether or not to buy a patent

The administrator of City Hospital has been approached by an inventor, Denise Jossi, who is trying to sell a new patent. If purchased, the patent would enable City Hospital to convert its semiautomatic x-ray machinery to automatic. Such a change would reduce the hospital's variable labor costs of operation. The patent would cost $175,000, and it would be necessary to spend an additional $50,000 to make the machinery conversions. The variable cost per x-ray with the semiautomatic machinery is $9 and the expected cost with the automatic machinery is $7 per x-ray.

Patients are billed $25 apiece for x-rays. If the machinery is converted to automatic, 12,000 x-rays can be processed, 3,000 more than the semiautomatic machinery can handle.

The machinery has a remaining 5-year life and will have a $2,000 higher salvage in 5 years if it is fully automated. The patent is expected to be sold for $5,000 in 5 years.

The cost of capital is 12%.

$\boxed{\textit{Required}}$

Using the net present value method, decide whether City Hospital should purchase the patent from Jossi. *(Check figure: PV for automatic = $557,433)*

Problem A7-6
Expanding the analysis of Problem A7-5

$\boxed{\textit{Required}}$

Refer to the facts given in Problem A7-5. Calculate each of the following:
1. The internal rate of return

(Check figure: 18.781%)

2. The payback period
3. The accountant's rate of return

Problem A7-7
Calculating the NPV for rearranging a plant

The president of the Instant Charge Battery Corporation has asked the management advisory department of its CPA firm to help it decide whether production efficiency can be improved by rearranging the plant layout. The consultant recommended that rearrangements should be undertaken and estimated that the costs of rearrangement would be $300,000. The consultant also estimated that such a change would substantially reduce direct labor during the next 5 years. In the first year, direct labor should decrease by $1.50 per unit produced. For years 2 to 5 the reduction should increase to $3 per unit. In addition, one less supervisor will be needed in each of the 5 years, a savings of $17,000 per year. The units to be produced in each year are expected to be 20,000 in year 1, 22,000 in year 2, and 30,000 per year for years 3 to 5.

$\boxed{\textit{Required}}$

Using the net present value method, determine whether or not the plant layout should be rearranged. The firm's cost of capital is 12%. *(Check figure: NPV = $12,800)*

Problem A7-8
Calculating the NPV for renovating a facility

Cheap Way is a discount store in Florida that has decided to upgrade the quality of its merchandise and hopefully appeal to a different group of customers. In order to accomplish this, Cheap Way plans to completely renovate its facility—which had originally been an abandoned airplane hanger—by changing its store front, lowering its ceiling, replacing the flooring and store fixtures, and upgrading its cash registers as well as everything else inside and out. This will require a capital outlay of $1,000,000 on Jan. 1, 1988. In addition, Cheap Way will change its name to Luxury for Less and will spend $50,000 in 1988 and 1989 promoting the changes to the public. Cheap Way expects to be able to sell its old fixtures for $25,000 at the beginning of 1988 if the renovation takes place.

Once the renovations have been made, Cheap Way anticipates a substantial increase in cash receipts—probably slow at first, but growing dramatically after the first or second year. Cheap Way's accountant, Robin West, has come up with the following projections for the 5-year useful life of the new project:

Year	Additional Operating Receipts
1988	$ 100,000
1989	150,000
1990	600,000
1991	600,000
1992	800,000
	$2,250,000

One significant increase in operating costs (not included in net operating receipts above) that Cheap Way expects is for salaries of sales personnel. Due to the change in emphasis from a discount store to a luxury outlet, many more employees will be needed. The additional salaries should be about $50,000 in 1988 and 1989 and $100,000 for the remaining 3 years.

Currently, Cheap Way is leasing some space to the Injuries Can Be Profitable law firm for $12,000 per year. Since Cheap Way plans to break the lease, it will no longer be receiving the annual rentals. In addition, it will be necessary for Cheap Way to compensate the law firm $7,500 on Jan. 1, 1988, for breaking the lease.

| **Required** |

Calculate the net present value for the planned renovation for Cheap Way. Use a cost of capital of 15%. *(Check figure: $23,024)*

Problem A7-9
Doing sensitivity analysis

The following information relates to a project that is being considered by Lucky Hunch, Inc.:

Initial outlay.................................. $65,000
Estimated annual cash receipts.................. $15,000
Estimated useful life .... 7 years
Estimated cost of capital .... .10
Estimated salvage $0

| **Required** |

1. Determine **(a)** the net present value, **(b)** the internal rate of return, **(c)** the payback period, and **(d)** the accountant's rate of return.

For each of the next five parts, assume that everything given in the original set of facts remains the same except the single item that is changed in that one part:

2. What would the cost of capital have to be in order to have an NPV of $15,835?
3. How much would the cash receipts have to increase in order for the payback period to be reduced by 1 year?
4. How much would the cash receipts have to be in order to have an IRR equal to the cost of capital?
5. Assume that you now think there might actually be salvage value at the end of the useful life of the project. What would it have to be in order to increase the ARR to 10%?

(Check figure: $5,500)

6. What will be the change in the NPV as a percentage of the original estimate of the NPV if the estimate of useful life is **(a)** increased by 1 year or **(b)** decreased by 1 year?

PROBLEMS: SET B

Problem B7-1
Calculating the payback,
IRR, and ARR

The National Vertigo Society is a little-publicized charity that uses a great number of workers to label, seal, and stamp envelopes. If a machine is purchased that will seal the envelopes, the society expects the labor costs to decrease substantially. The machine will cost $2,100 and is expected to last 5 years. During that time the reduced labor costs are predicted to be:

Year	Reduced Labor Costs
1	$300
2	450
3	750
4	750
5	900

At the end of 5 years, Vertigo expects to sell the machine for $100. The society's cost of capital is 14%.

| **Required** |

1. Determine the payback period.
2. Compute the internal rate of return. On the basis of this answer, should the machine be purchased?

(Check figure: 13.68%)

3. Determine the accountant's rate of return.

(Check figure: 10.95%)

Problem B7-2
Comparing keep with
replace for an old machine

The Hogan Construction Company is considering the replacement of an old crane with a new one. The old crane was purchased 3 years ago for $100,000 and has a remaining book value of $61,000. It can be sold for $48,000 if disposed of at the present time or for $9,000 if disposed of at the end of its 4-year remaining useful life.

   The new crane will cost $195,000 and is expected to have a $12,000 disposal value in 4 years. The cash operating costs for the old and new crane, will be $250,000 and $200,000 per year, respectively. If the old crane is kept, it will require a major repair costing $10,000 at the end of 2 years.

   The company's cost of capital is 8%.

| **Required** |

1. Using the present value method, determine whether the old crane should be kept or replaced. Compute the present values for the keep-vs.-replace decisions separately.
2. Using the incremental approach described in Appendix 7-1, determine each of the following:
   a. The net present value
   b. The internal rate of return
   c. The payback period
   d. The accountant's rate of return

(Check figure: Net present value = $29,375)

Problem B7-3
Calculating the NPV for an
equipment purchase

Billie Joe Everrett, a tennis star for 25 years, has just retired and opened a tennis complex. One thing that Everrett would like to purchase is a ball tossing machine—which automatically tosses balls to players every few seconds, at a variety of speeds, spins, and trajectories. The machine costs $1,800 and is expected to last for 6 years. At the end of its useful life it should have a disposal value of $300.

The machine is expected to generate additional cash receipts for the complex of $5,000 per year. It will necessitate the addition of one part-time employee at an annual salary of $4,000. Finally, an overhaul costing $400 will probably be required at the beginning of year 5.

| Required |

Using the net present value method (assuming a 12% cost of capital), determine whether or not the ball tossing machine should be purchased.

(Check figure: NPV = $2,209)

Problem B7-4
Expanding the analysis of
Problem B7-3

| Required |

Refer to the facts given in Problem B7-3. Calculate each of the following:
1. The internal rate of return (For this calculation it will be necessary to find present value tables that go as high as 50%.)

(Check figure: 49.157%)

2. The payback period
3. The accountant's rate of return

Problem B7-5
Computing the NPV of a
patent

The president of the Trim Lines Jeans Company is approached by an inventor, Mark Carnac, concerning a new patent. The patent would enable Trim Lines to convert its manual machinery to semiautomatic, thereby reducing the labor costs of production. The patent would cost $900,000, and an additional $300,000 would be required to make the machinery conversions. The variable costs per unit using the manual and semiautomatic machinery are $10 and $8, respectively.

If Trim Lines decides to acquire the patent, it will produce and sell 100,000 units per year for the next 5 years. If Trim Lines continues to use the manual equipment, production and sales will be only 70,000 units per year. The sales price will be $16 per unit, regardless of the decision made.

The patent will be worthless in 5 years, but the disposal value of the semiautomatic machinery will be $15,000 higher than that of the manual machinery.

If the patent is acquired, Trim Lines will have to increase its investment in inventory by $25,000 at the beginning of the patent's life—all of which will be recovered at the end of 5 years.

The cost of capital for Trim Lines is 10%.

| Required |

Using the net present value method, decide whether Trim Lines should purchase the patent from Carnac. First, calculate the NPV using the total approach; then redo the calculation using the incremental approach.

(Check figure: NPV with incremental approach = $240,000)

Problem B7-6
Expanding the analysis of
Problem B7-5

Using the information presented for Trim Lines Jeans Company in Problem B7-5:

| Required |

1. Determine the internal rate of return for the incremental investment.
2. Determine the payback period for the incremental investment.
3. Determine the accountant's rate of return for the incremental investment.

(Check figure: 11.673%)

Problem B7-7
Deciding whether a plant layout should be rearranged

A foreman on the assembly line at Mitsui Motorscooters took advantage of the company's suggestion box by recommending that the arrangement of machinery within the factory be changed. He felt that the efficiency of the production operation could be vastly improved by arranging machinery so that the flow of goods from one worker to another would be more orderly and less time consuming.

  The president of Mitsui hired a team of consultants to determine whether the foreman was correct. The final report of the consultants not only supported the foreman's claim but made suggestions on how the rearrangement should be done. The consulting team estimated that it would cost $375,000 to make the rearrangements, which would result in substantial reductions in the costs of production over the next 5 years. The direct labor costs would be reduced by $1 per unit in year 1. In years 2 through 5, after the laborers have become more familiar with the revised flow of production, the direct labor costs should be reduced by $2 per unit. In addition, one less foreman will be needed in years 2 through 5, a savings of $10,000 per year. The units to be produced during the next 5 years are predicted to be:

Year	Production
1	50,000
2	60,000
3	75,000
4	75,000
5	75,000

  The consultants charged the company $15,000 for the analysis and final report, and the foreman received $500 for his suggestion.

| *Required* |

Using the net present value method, determine whether or not the plant layout should be rearranged. The cost of capital is 15%.

(Check figure: NPV = $42,730)

Problem B7-8
Calculating the NPV for expansion of business

In 1985—3 years ago—Dr. Mel Practise opened a new chiropractic clinic in a building he built for $100,000. He uses one-half of the building for his practice and leases the remainder to a dentist for $5,000 per year (on a 5-year lease).

  Practise anticipates a great boom in business and is currently considering expanding his practice by adding an associate, whom he will pay a guaranteed annual salary. This means he must cancel the dentist's lease in order to use the entire building for his own practice. It will cost him $10,000 to break the lease on Jan. 1, 1988. If he does take over the entire building, he will have to furnish the additional space with cabinets, desks, chairs, rugs, and equipment—which should cost $75,000. In 5 years he plans to sell the furnishings for $13,000 and move to a new location. In addition, he will need to increase his investment in working capital (supplies and receivables) by $2,000 in order to accommodate the increase in business. All $2,000 will be recoverable at the end of 5 years.

  With the addition of a second doctor, Practise expects the cash receipts from his practice to increase substantially over the next 5 years, as shown below:

Year	Additional Cash Receipts
1988	$ 65,000
1989	85,000
1990	100,000
1991	175,000
1992	200,000
	$625,000

The main additional cash disbursement that Practise expects annually is the salary of the new doctor and one new nurse. These additional expenditures should be:

Year	Doctor	Nurse
1988	$ 30,000	$15,000
1989	30,000	15,000
1990	50,000	18,000
1991	50,000	18,000
1992	50,000	18,000
	$210,000	$84,000

In addition, he expects his malpractice insurance to increase by $5,000 per year because of the addition of the second doctor to his practice.

Due to the fact that Practise is in a bad part of town and gets little walk-in business, he feels that he'll need to advertise his expansion in order to reach new potential customers. He plans to spend $15,000 on promotions during 1988.

Required

Determine the net present value for Practise's expansion, using a cost of capital of 12%.

(Check figure: $87,346)

Problem B7-9
Doing sensitivity analysis

The Romero Dating Service is considering the purchase of several new VCRs, at a total cost of $4,000, and wants you to determine whether they would be a good buy. After some in-depth analysis, you have finally come up with the following estimates:

Net cash receipts .... $1,000 per year
Useful life .... 6 years
Cost of capital........................... .10
Salvage $0

Required

1. Determine (a) the net present value, (b) the internal rate of return, (c) the payback period, and (d) the accountant's rate of return.

For each of the next five parts, assume that everything given in the original set of facts remains the same except the single item that is changed in that one part:

2. What will be the effect on the NPV if the cost of capital is (a) overstated by 2 percentage points or (b) understated by 2 percentage points?
3. What would the net cash receipts have to be each year if the IRR is zero?
4. How much would the cash receipts have to decrease in order for the payback period to be increased by 1 year?
5. How long would the life have to be in order to have an ARR of 10%? Assume now that the salvage is $400.

(Check figure: 6 years)

6. If the VCRs are disposed of 1 year earlier, there will be a salvage value at that time. What would the salvage have to be at the end of 5 years in order for the NPV to be the same as we estimated it to be in part 1?

CHAPTER 8

Capital Budgeting: Tax Considerations

- Explain why it is necessary to consider income taxes when evaluating investment opportunities
- Understand how depreciation can increase the cash flows from an investment
- Select the depreciation method that maximizes the tax advantages from a depreciable investment
- Integrate the income tax considerations into the net present value and internal rate of return methods
- Explain what a nontaxable exchange is and why a new project may be acquired through an exchange rather than with cash
- Calculate the payback period and accountant's rate of return using net-of-tax cash flows

The title of this chapter confesses that in the capital budgeting methods we used to evaluate long-term investment proposals in the last chapter, we deliberately did not consider the effects of income taxes. We ignored the effects of income taxes on a project's cash flows to keep things simple as you began to build your understanding of capital budgeting methods. You are now prepared for the real life of capital budgeting. Enter taxes.

In this chapter we will expand our analysis for projects A and B, which we started in Chapter 7, to include those income tax considerations that seem to affect all capital budgeting decisions. We will show how each tax consideration affects the amount and timing of cash flows for a project, and we will point out why the results for projects A and B are different from what they were when taxes were ignored.

Taxes will now be considered

Although the consideration of income taxes may greatly complicate the analysis, the mechanics of each capital budgeting method are no different from the procedures you learned in the previous chapter. The calculation of NPV, for example, is still exactly the same as it was in Chapter 7. The only difference is that now we will use aftertax cash flows rather than before-tax cash flows. Everything you learned in the previous chapter is still applicable, but now you need to determine the aftertax cash flows for the analysis.

[322]

THE EFFECT OF INCOME TAXES ON CASH FLOWS

In Chapter 7 we evaluated two projects, A and B, both of which required an initial outlay of $10,000, had a useful life of 8 years, and promised to generate total cash flows over that life of $16,000. The only difference in the two projects was the timing of the cash flows. They were as follows:

	Incremental Cash Flows	
Year of Life	Project A	Project B
1	$ 2,000	$ 4,000
2	2,000	3,000
3	2,000	3,000
4	2,000	2,000
5	2,000	1,000
6	2,000	1,000
7	2,000	1,000
8	2,000	1,000
Total	$16,000	$16,000

Original set of facts from Chapter 7

The original NPV — no tax

The NPV for project A — ignoring income taxes — was:

$$\text{TPV} = P_{8|10\%} \times \$2,000 = 5.334 \times \$2,000 = \$10,668$$
$$\text{NPV} = \$10,668 - \$10,000 = \$668$$

Assumption 1: The Tax Rate Is 40% — But Depreciation Is Not Deductible

We will now assume that income taxes are paid at 40% of income before tax.[1] We will also pretend for the moment that the depreciation from project A is not deductible on the tax return. By ignoring depreciation in this section, it will be easier to see in the next section exactly how depreciation affects income taxes and, thus, the cash flow from a project. The income before tax for project A is shown below to be $2,000, and the net-of-tax cash flow is 40% lower — or $1,200:

Without depreciation we have to tax all the cash flow

Cash flow from operations (income before depreciation and taxes)............	$2,000
Depreciation (assumed not to be deductible)	-0-
Income before tax..	$2,000
Income tax (@ 40% of income before tax)	800
Cash flow from operations (net of related tax)	$1,200

Using the net-of-tax cash flow of only $1,200 instead of the pretax cash flow of $2,000, the NPV for the project falls from $668 to $(3,599).

Taxes cause NPV to drop substantially

$$\text{TPV} = 5.334 \times \$1,200 = \$6,401$$

and

$$\text{NPV} = \$6,401 - \$10,000 = \$(3,599)$$

---

[1] Throughout this chapter we are assuming there are no timing differences between financial accounting income and taxable income. Therefore, financial accounting income will be equal to taxable income, and there is no reason to be concerned with the deferred income tax issue.

Assumption 2: Depreciation Is Deductible

Depreciation is a "tax shield"

Fortunately, the Internal Revenue Code does allow depreciation to be deducted on the tax return in determining taxable income. Although depreciation itself is not a cash item—that is, it does not involve a cash inflow or outflow—it does have an indirect but very favorable effect on cash flows. Since depreciation is a deduction on the tax return, it shields, or protects, income from being taxed. This is why depreciation is often referred to as a **tax shield.** As a result, taxes do not have to be paid that would have to be paid if the income were not shielded by depreciation. The company thus reduces its taxes because of depreciation, and reduced taxes mean more cash. The reduction in taxes due to the depreciation tax shield is referred to as the **tax savings from depreciation.**

If Depreciation Equals Cash Flow

Tax shields save taxes

Let's assume for now that the depreciation each year for project A is $2,000 (which it is not, as we will find out in a moment). This means that depreciation equals the cash flow from operations and that the income before tax is zero ($2,000 − $2,000). The $2,000 deduction for depreciation shields $2,000 of income from being taxed. As a result, the taxes are zero instead of $800—a savings of $800. The net-of-tax cash flow is now $2,000 instead of $1,200. This represents an increase of $800, due entirely to the tax savings from the $2,000 depreciation tax shield.

For Depreciation of $1,250

You might recall from our discussion of the accountant's rate of return in Chapter 7 that the depreciation per year for project A is only $1,250 ($10,000 ÷ 8 years). Since the tax shield is not $2,000 per year, it will now be necessary to pay some income tax on the resulting taxable income. But the tax is not nearly as high as it would be without the $1,250 tax shield. Using the $1,250 for depreciation, the schedule below indicates that the net-of-tax cash flow for project A is now $1,700:

$1,250 of depreciation protects $1,250 of income from being taxed

	Income	Cash Flow
Cash flow from operations...............................	$2,000	$2,000
Depreciation...	1,250	-0-
Income before tax (and cash remaining before taxes, respectively)..	$ 750	$2,000
Income tax	300	300
Net income (and net-of-tax cash flow, respectively).........	$ 450	$1,700
	Net income	*Net-of-tax cash flow*

In the preceding schedule the income column includes all items that go on the income statement and tax return—whether or not they affect cash. The cash flow column includes only those items that are cash inflows or outflows.

Since depreciation is a deductible expense, it belongs in the income column. Because depreciation does not represent an outflow of cash, it does not appear as a deduction in the cash flow column. Even though depreciation reduces the income before tax by $1,250, to $750, there is still $2,000 of cash remaining before taxes are paid. Because of the $1,250 tax shield, taxes are only $300 and the net-of-tax cash flow is $1,700. The effect of depreciation saves the company $500 — the amount of tax that would have to be paid on $1,250 of income if it were not shielded from taxation.

A Second Way to Get Net-of-Tax Cash Flow

The $1,700 net-of-tax cash flow can also be determined another way, which is the approach we will use throughout the rest of this chapter. This approach separately calculates:

1. The net-of-tax cash flow for the $2,000 cash flow from operations

2. The tax savings from the $1,250 of depreciation

First, the cash flow from operations:

Cash flow from operations	$2,000
Tax effect (at 40%)	(800)
Cash flow from operations (net of tax)..................................	$1,200

$1,250 of depreciation saves $500 (.40 × $1,250) in taxes

And now the tax savings from depreciation:

Depreciation	$1,250
Tax rate	×.40
Tax savings from depreciation...	500
Net-of-tax cash flow..	$1,700

The $500 of tax savings from depreciation is the amount of tax that is saved because depreciation shields $1,250 of income from being taxed. This $500 represents the amount of taxes that would have to be paid on the $1,250 of income if it were not shielded by depreciation.

The tax savings improve the NPV

The NPV for project A can now be determined using the net-of-tax cash flow of $1,700:

$$TPV = 5.334 \times \$1,700 = \$9,068$$

and $$NPV = \$9,068 - \$10,000 = \$(932)$$

Even though the NPV is negative, which would probably result in rejection of the project, notice the impact that depreciation has on the NPV. Without the tax savings from depreciation the NPV is $(3,599), but with the tax savings from depreciation the NPV rises to $(932), an increase of $2,667.

Depreciation Accounting under the Tax Reform Act of 1986

In your financial accounting course you learned about the different depreciation methods that a company can use to report its income to stockholders and creditors. The methods you probably discussed the most were straight line (SL), sum-of-the-years' digits (SYD), and double declining balance (DDB). Unfortunately, when depreciation is being calculated for income tax purposes, the SYD method is not allowed and the SL and DDB methods are not employed in exactly the same manner as they are in financial accounting.

Depreciation is not based on useful life

Under the Tax Reform Act of 1986, a company can use one of two approaches—an *accelerated approach* or an *optional straight-line approach*. Under either approach the depreciable asset is to be written off over a period of time specified by the Internal Revenue Code—regardless of what the expected useful life of the asset is. In essence, the useful life of a depreciable asset has little relevance in calculating depreciation for tax purposes—and thus little relevance for determining the tax savings from depreciation in capital budgeting.

Depreciation is based on eight recovery periods

All depreciable assets fall into one of eight **recovery periods** specified by the Tax Reform Act. Each recovery period represents a different number of years over which assets may be depreciated. The recovery periods are 3, 5, 7, 10, 15, 20, 27.5, and 31.5 years. Each depreciable asset must be depreciated using one of these eight recovery periods, regardless of the actual useful life of the asset.

The recovery period is based on the ADR midpoint life

The appropriate recovery period depends upon something called the **asset depreciation range (ADR)** midpoint life for the particular asset to be depreciated. For the sake of simplicity, however, we won't worry about what midpoint lives are or how they are used in determining the appropriate recovery period. Instead, we'll skip a few steps and go directly to a list of typical assets that are included in the most commonly used recovery periods. The list, given in Exhibit 8-1, includes only the recovery periods of 5, 7, 10, and 31.5 years. The list is not intended to be all-inclusive for each recovery period; it simply offers you some good examples.

EXHIBIT 8-1
Assets Found in the Most Common Recovery Periods

These are some examples of assets that are depreciated using the most common recovery periods

Recovery Period	Types of Assets
5 years	Automobiles, taxis, all trucks, certain airplanes, typewriters, calculators, copying equipment, computers, etc.
7 years	Office furniture, fixtures, and equipment; most production machinery and equipment; etc.
10 years	Remaining production machinery and equipment
31.5 years	Most buildings used in a business

Once you know the appropriate recovery period for a specific asset, you can then determine the depreciation method (or methods) that can be used by examining Exhibit 8-2. For the most commonly used recovery periods (except 31.5 years) you have a choice of using either straight line or double declining balance. The 150% declining-balance method is allowed for most of the remaining recovery periods, but since it doesn't apply to the most common recovery periods, you don't need to be concerned with how to use it.

EXHIBIT 8-2
Required Depreciation Methods for Different Recovery Periods

The choice for 5, 7, and 10 years is DDB or SL

Recovery Period	Depreciation Method
5 years	DDB or SL
7 years	DDB or SL
10 years	DDB or SL
31.5 years	SL

Assume, for example, that you are going to depreciate a new computer. First of all, by looking at Exhibit 8-1, you can see that the appropriate recovery period is 5 years. Then, when you go to Exhibit 8-2, you see that you can use either the straight-line method or the double-declining-balance method to depreciate the computer over the 5-year period.

DDB and SL differ for taxes and book

As we said before, use of the DDB and SL methods for tax purposes differs somewhat from their use in financial accounting. For each method (except the SL method for 31.5-year assets), the following rules apply to calculating depreciation for tax purposes, but not for financial accounting (or book) purposes:

1. Salvage value is ignored in determining depreciation. This allows the depreciable asset to be depreciated to a zero book value.

2. The taxpayer must take a half year of depreciation in the year of acquisition. In addition, if the useful life of the depreciable asset is longer than the recovery period, the taxpayer must take a half year of depreciation in the last year of the recovery period. If the useful life of the asset is shorter than the recovery period, the taxpayer must take a half year of depreciation in the year of disposal. The half-year provision applies regardless of exactly when, during a year, an asset is acquired. (The rule does not apply, however, to the assets in the 31.5-year recovery period.)

3. For the double-declining-balance method, the taxpayer must switch to straight line in the first year that SL depreciation (based on the remaining book value at the time of the switch) is greater than DDB depreciation.

Depreciation with the DDB Method

The depreciation each year for projects A and B with the DDB method is calculated in Exhibit 8-3. The calculations are based upon the requirements listed in the previous section.

We will first determine the annual depreciation without worrying about the half year of depreciation in the first and last years. This is step 1, shown in Exhibit 8-3. After we have determined the full year of depreciation for each of the 7 years, we will then show you how to integrate the half-year provision into the annual depreciation calculations. This is step 2, given in Exhibit 8-4.

**EXHIBIT 8-3
DDB Depreciation
Ignoring the Half-Year
Provision**

For the moment, we're ignoring the half-year provision; the switch to SL is in year 5

Year	Book Value at Beginning of Year	×	Depreciation Percentage	=	DDB Depreciation with Switch in Year 5
1	$10,000	×	.2857	=	$ 2,857
2	7,143	×	.2857	=	2,041
3	5,102	×	.2857	=	1,458
4	3,644	×	.2857	=	1,041
5	2,603		na		868
6	1,735		na		868
7	867		na		867
8	-0-		na		-0-
					$10,000

SL rate = 1 ÷ recovery period, not 1 ÷ life

Although the useful life of the production machinery is 8 years, the recovery period (look back at Exhibit 8-1) is either 7 years or 10 years. Assuming the appropriate recovery period is 7 years, the straight-line rate for depreciation is:

$$1 \div \text{recovery period} = 1 \div 7 = .14285$$

And double the straight-line rate is:

$$.14285 \times 2 = .2857$$

The DDB rate is multiplied by the book value at the beginning of each year. The book value starts at $10,000—the initial investment—and is reduced each year by the depreciation taken in that year. As you can see in Exhibit 8-3, we switch to straight line in year 5 and continue using straight line until the asset is fully depreciated. (We will explain shortly why we switch to straight line and how we determine when to switch.) By the end of the seventh year the asset is 100% depreciated, so there is no depreciation to be taken in year 8.

Now we assume the half-year provision

In Exhibit 8-3 a full year of depreciation is shown for each year of the 7-year recovery period. Remember, however, that the taxpayer can take only a half year of depreciation in the first and last years. As a result, each year's depreciation is composed of two parts: (1) one-half of the previous year's depreciation and (2) one-half of the current year's depreciation. The annual depreciation for projects A and B—assuming the half-year provision—is shown in Exhibit 8-4.

EXHIBIT 8-4
Depreciation per Year Assuming a Half Year of Depreciation Is Taken in the First and Last Years of the Recovery Period

Year 2 is one-half of year 1 and one-half of year 2

The last half year of depreciation is in year 8

Year of Life	Depreciation	
1	$2,857 × .50 =	$ 1,428.50
2	$2,857 × .50 = $1,428.50 $2,041 × .50 = 1,020.50	2,449.00
3	$2,041 × .50 = $1,020.50 $1,458 × .50 = 729.00	1,749.50
4	$1,458 × .50 = $ 729.00 $1,041 × .50 = 520.50	1,249.50
5	$1,041 × .50 = $ 520.50 $ 868 × .50 = 434.00	954.50
6	$ 868 × .50 = $ 434.00 $ 868 × .50 = 434.00	868.00
7	$ 868 × .50 = $ 434.00 $ 867 × .50 = 433.50	867.50
8	$ 867 × .50 =	433.50
		$10,000.00

Although it may look like we're depreciating the machinery over 8 years, we really aren't. For when we add up 6 full years of depreciation and 2 half years, we get a total of 7 years—which is the recovery period for this machinery.

If life < recovery period, the last half is in the year of disposal

Remember: If we plan to keep the asset for a period of time shorter than the recovery period, we must take a half year of depreciation in the year of disposal. For example, if the useful life is only 5 years, then in year 5 the depreciation will be only $520.50—the last half of the depreciation from year 4. Since we won't fully depreciate the cost of the asset in this situation, a book value will remain at the time of disposal which will be equal to the depreciation not taken. This remaining book value will affect the gain or loss on disposal and the related tax effect on that gain or loss.[2]

---

[2] For an example of a situation in which the life is shorter than the recovery period, see the keep-vs.-replace decision in the appendix to this chapter.

Why and When to Switch

DDB by itself cannot depreciate 100% of cost

We switch from DDB depreciation to SL depreciation because DDB by itself will not depreciate a full 100% of the cost of the asset. In the case of projects A and B, $9,051 would be the total depreciation, based upon depreciation at a rate of .2857 times the remaining book value each year for 7 years. This leaves the difference between $10,000 and $9,051, or $949, as the book value at the end of 7 full years. By switching to straight line, we can depreciate the full 100% of the cost over the same period of time. Without switching to straight line, we would lose the tax savings from the $949 of depreciation that cannot be taken with DDB. Therefore, we switch to straight line to be able to fully depreciate the asset and thereby take advantage of the entire tax savings available.

A question related to "Why switch?" is "When do we switch?" The answer: We should switch in that year when the SL depreciation (based upon the remaining book value, or BV, at the beginning of each year divided by the remaining years from the beginning of the year to the end of the recovery period) is greater than the DDB depreciation for that same year.

Each year's SL = remaining BV at beginning of year ÷ remaining years of recovery

Look again at Exhibit 8-3. In year 4 the DDB depreciation is $1,041 and the book value at the beginning of that year is $3,644. The number of years remaining of the 7-year recovery period is four — years 4, 5, 6, and 7. If we switch to straight line at the beginning of year 4, depreciating the remaining book value over the remaining years, the SL depreciation each year would be $911:

$$\text{SL depreciation} = \$3,644 \div 4 = \$911$$

Since this is smaller than the DDB depreciation of $1,041, there is no reason to switch.

In year 5 the DDB depreciation is .2857 times the $2,603 book value at the beginning of that year — resulting in $744 of depreciation. If we switch to straight-line at the beginning of year 5, the remaining book value at that time, $2,603, will be depreciated evenly over the 3 remaining years of recovery — years 5, 6, and 7. The SL depreciation each year would be:

$$\text{SL depreciation} = \$2,603 \div 3 = \$868$$

Since the SL depreciation is now greater than the DDB depreciation, the switch to SL in year 5 is appropriate.

In order to save you some work, we have determined the year in which a switch to straight line is appropriate for each of the three recovery periods that use the DDB method. They are as follows:

For recovery periods of 5, 7, and 10, we switch in 4, 5, and 6, respectively

Recovery Period	Correct Year for Switch*
5 years	Year 4
7 years	Year 5
10 years	Year 6

* This is the year in which SL depreciation exceeds DDB depreciation for the first time.

The tax savings from depreciation each year are found by multiplying the annual depreciation times the tax rate. In a later section we'll present these calculations and discuss how the DDB method of depreciation affects the NPV for each project.

Depreciation with the Optional Straight-Line Method

SL is different for book and taxes

An alternative way of calculating depreciation for tax purposes is the optional straight-line method. Although this approach is similar to the straight-line method you used in financial accounting, there are three important differences. They are:

Ignore salvage

1. For financial accounting purposes the amount to be depreciated is the cost less salvage. For tax purposes the entire cost is depreciated.

Use recovery not life

2. For financial accounting purposes the asset is depreciated over its useful life. For tax purposes the asset is usually depreciated using the same recovery periods that were used with DDB.

3. For financial accounting purposes depreciation in the first and last years of a depreciable asset's life is based on the number of months the asset is used during those years. For example, for an asset bought on May 1, depreciation in the first year is for 8 months — two-thirds of a year — and depreciation in the last year is for 4 months (if the asset is kept for its entire life) — one-third of a year.

Take $\frac{1}{2}$ year of depreciation in first and last year of recovery; if disposal is before end of recovery, take $\frac{1}{2}$ in year of disposal

For tax purposes a half year of depreciation is taken in the first year regardless of when the asset is placed in service. Whether the asset is purchased on Jan. 1, May 1, or Dec. 31, a half year of depreciation is taken in the first year of the recovery period and the remaining half year is taken in the last year of the recovery period (or year of disposal if the life is shorter than the recovery period).

For projects A and B the optional straight-line depreciation for a full year is $1,428.57 ($10,000 ÷ 7 years). Using the half-year provision, the amount of depreciation in each of the 8 years is as shown in Exhibit 8-5.

EXHIBIT 8-5
Optional Straight-Line Depreciation Assuming the Half-Year Provision

Year of Life	Depreciation	
1	$ 714.29*	← $\frac{1}{2}$ year
2	1,428.57	
3	1,428.57	
4	1,428.57	
5	1,428.57	
6	1,428.57	
7	1,428.57	
8	714.29*	← $\frac{1}{2}$ year
	$10,000.00	

* $1,428.57 \times \frac{1}{2} = $714.29.

$(2 + \frac{1}{2}) + (6 \times 1) = 7$

As with the DDB method, a full year's depreciation is taken in years 2 to 7 but only a half year's depreciation is taken in years 1 and 8 of the recovery period. When we add up 6 full years and 2 half years, we get a total of 7 years — which is the recovery period for this machinery.

Selection of the Better Depreciation Method

Since the DDB and the optional straight-line methods both depreciate the same total cost over the same period of time, does it really make any difference which depreciation method we use in capital budgeting? After all, the tax savings from

*Which method is better—
SL or DDB?*

depreciation are the same under the two methods because the total depreciation is the same. So aren't the total benefits to the firm from these tax savings also the same? The answer to the first question is definitely yes, but the answer to the second question is definitely no. In most situations, as long as the company has taxable income, it is better to use DDB rather than optional straight line. Here's why.

*DDB maximizes the PV of
tax savings*

The first thing to remember is that our purpose in capital budgeting is to maximize present value. In order to do this, we need to maximize the present value of the tax savings from depreciation, which means we want to use the depreciation method with the highest present value of tax savings. Given the choice between DDB and optional straight line, the DDB method will—in almost all situations—maximize present value. The reason it does so can be explained this way:

Same total over same years

1. Both methods take the same total depreciation over basically the same period of time. Therefore, both methods generate the same total amount of tax savings.

Early vs. late tax savings

2. The tax savings with the DDB method are accelerated; that is, with the exception of year 1, a large portion of the total comes in the early years and a much smaller amount comes in the later years. For optional straight line—with the exception of the first and last years—the depreciation is the same from year to year. As a result, DDB has more depreciation than straight line in the early years of an asset's life and less depreciation than straight line in the later years.

*The PV is better in early
years*

3. The present value of a dollar received in early years is greater than the present value of a dollar received in later years.

The PV from DDB is better

4. Therefore, the present value of the tax savings from DDB is usually greater than that from straight line because the present value of tax savings that come primarily in the early years of an asset's life is higher than the present value of the same total tax savings if they come in later years.[3]

You can see proof of this in the following schedule. The present value of the tax savings at 10% is $2,888 with DDB depreciation but only $2,655 with SL depreciation.

*The total depreciation and
total tax savings are the
same, but the PVs of tax
savings are not*

Year	DDB Depreciation			SL Depreciation		
	Depreci-ation	Savings at 40% Rate	Present Value at 10%	Depreci-ation	Savings at 40% Rate	Present Value at 10%
1	$ 1,428	$ 571	$ 519	$ 714	$ 285	$ 259
2	2,449	980	809	1,428	571	472
3	1,750	700	526	1,428	571	429
4	1,249	500	342	1,429	572	391
5	954	382	237	1,429	572	355
6	868	347	196	1,429	572	323
7	868	347	178	1,429	572	293
8	434	173	81	714	285	133
	$10,000	$4,000	$2,888	$10,000	$4,000	$2,655

Here are the exceptions

[3] Straight line may be preferable (*a*) when tax rates are expected to rise, making the tax savings in later years higher than the tax savings on the same amount of depreciation taken in early years, and (*b*) when the company experiences losses in the early years of a project and the taxpayer takes the option of depreciating with straight line over longer recovery periods.

ADDITIONAL TAX CONSIDERATIONS IN CAPITAL BUDGETING

Additional tax considerations that can affect the present value of a project are the investment tax credit, capital gains rates, progressive tax rates, and nontaxable exchanges. Let's look first at the investment tax credit.

Investment Tax Credit

The ITC was used to reduce the cost of investing

Since 1961 the ***investment tax credit (ITC)*** has been an on-again, off-again government stimulus to investment spending. The ITC reduced the cost of any property that qualified for the credit by reducing the taxes paid by the investor in the year that a qualifying asset was acquired. The credit was usually found by multiplying 10% times the cost of the qualifying property. For projects A and B this would have amounted to $1,000, so the tax bill in the first year of the project's life would have been reduced by $1,000. In essence, the net cost of projects A and B would have been $9,000.

We have been referring to the ITC in the past tense because, unfortunately, this incentive was repealed by the Tax Reform Act of 1986. Since the ITC was extremely popular, however, many tax accountants feel that it won't be long before the ITC is reenacted. So it's quite possible that by the time you read this chapter, the ITC may have returned.

Capital Assets

Capital gains rates were lower

Many investments—such as stocks and bonds—are in a class of assets called ***capital assets.*** Prior to 1987, if a taxpayer held this type of investment long enough, the resulting gain when the investment was sold was considered to be a long-term capital gain. This meant that the gain would be taxed at ***capital gains rates,*** which were lower than the rates applied to ordinary income. For example, whereas tax rates for corporations were previously as high as 46%, the tax rate applicable to a long-term capital gain was no higher than 20%. Naturally, any time an organization sold an asset at a gain, it would prefer to pay tax on the gain at the lower rate if possible.

Unfortunately, the favorable capital gains tax rates were also a casualty of the Tax Reform Act of 1986. Starting in 1987, the capital gains for corporations will be taxed at the same rates as those applied to ordinary corporate income.

This change in the tax law greatly affects the taxes that corporations have to pay on the sale of such investments as stocks and bonds. Interestingly, however, the change does not have as much effect as you might expect on capital budgeting. Even before the Tax Reform Act, many assets were not defined as "capital assets"; consequently, most gains on the sale of business assets were not treated as capital gains. Gains on the sale of such assets were usually taxed at ordinary rates.

There is some good news, however. Starting in 1987, the maximum tax rate on ordinary income will no longer be 46%. Instead, for all income in excess of $335,000, the maximum tax rate will fall to 34%.

Progressive Tax Rates

In our previous examples we used a single tax rate to determine the net-of-tax cash flows for a project. Realistically, however, not all income for an organization is taxed at just one rate. Instead, corporations use a ***progressive tax rate*** schedule, in which the tax rates on income start out quite low but progressively increase as the amount of income increases. There are currently five different tax rates applicable to the income of a corporation. They are:

These are the progressive tax rates

Income before Tax	Tax Rate
$50,000 and below.................	15%
$50,001 –$75,000.................	25%
$75,001 –$100,000	34%
$100,001–$335,000	39%
$335,000 and above	34%

Multiple tax rates cause us problems

There are several potential problems in capital budgeting when we try to integrate multiple tax rates into the analysis. The first problem is knowing which tax rate to use. The obvious answer may seem to be to base the tax rate on the expected income from the project. The problem with the obvious, however, is that tax rates don't depend upon the income from a project. Instead, they depend upon the income of the firm as a whole. For example, let's assume that a company is expected to have an income — excluding the income from a proposed project — of, say, $49,000 and that the expected income from a new project in year 1 is $27,000. The expected income of the company as a whole — including the proposed project — totals $76,000. The tax rates and related tax applicable to the incremental $27,000 for the proposed project would be:

Income	Tax Rate	Tax
$1,000 ($50,000 − $49,000)	15%	$ 150
$25,000 ($75,000 − $50,000)	25%	6,250
$1,000 ($76,000 − $75,000)	34%	340
		$6,740

Now imagine how much more troublesome it would be to determine a proposed project's taxes if there are many proposed projects that are not mutually exclusive — that is, the acceptance of one does not preclude the acceptance of any others. In such a situation the problem is deciding which project's income to tax at the lower rates and which one (or ones) to tax at the higher rates. Since the tax rate used certainly affects the NPV for a project, it seems inappropriate for one project to benefit from a low tax rate while another suffers from a high tax rate. To eliminate any prejudicial effect on the NPVs of different projects due to the use of different tax rates, it would be necessary to use a single *average* tax rate with all projects. Getting this average, however, would probably be difficult.

We need to use a single tax rate

What is ideal, of course — for capital budgeting purposes — is to be able to use a single tax rate for all income on all projects that are being considered. In order to justify using a single rate, one of three situations must exist:

1. There are multiple tax brackets, and an average tax rate has been determined.

2. There is only one tax rate applicable to all income of the corporation.

3. The company's income — without considering any projected income from new projects — is expected to be far in excess of $335,000. Therefore, all income from proposed projects will be taxed at the single tax rate in the highest tax bracket — which currently is 34%. Likewise, no loss is expected to be great enough to take the income of the corporation as a whole below the $335,000 level — thus the only tax rate applicable to any loss will also be 34%.

We assume we're in the highest tax bracket

For the sake of simplicity, when we use a single rate in this chapter — and we always will — we will justify it on the basis of the third situation presented above. The income of the corporation as a whole — exclusive of the project being considered — will be far above $335,000. Therefore, no matter how much a project is expected to earn or lose, there will be only one tax bracket applicable to the project — the highest one, 34%.

Also for the sake of simplicity (especially for those of you who are still doing the calculations manually) we will often use a more manageable tax rate than 34% — rates such as 20%, 30%, or 40%.

Nontaxable Exchanges

In most capital budgeting situations there is no mention made of the exact resources that are going to be used to make the investment in the new project. This is because it usually doesn't matter in the analysis whether we finance the investment with cash, marketable securities, receivables, debt, or capital stock. It is the market value (or cash equivalent) of the consideration given that goes in year 0 as the net incremental investment, and this amount is also the basis for calculating depreciation. For example, in order to finance project A or B, we would use $10,000 in cash, or we could use receivables worth $10,000 or marketable securities valued at $10,000. We could even sign a note payable having a present value of $10,000. For each one of these possibilities, the initial investment in year 0 would be $10,000, and the depreciation to be taken would be based on $10,000.

Trades of similar productive assets are nontaxable exchanges

On the other hand, if a project is financed by trading similar productive assets (i.e., land for land, building for building, equipment for equipment, etc.), then this transaction qualifies as a ***nontaxable exchange*** and is subject to special tax implications that affect the capital budgeting analysis.

With a nontaxable exchange, any difference between the book value of the asset being traded and its fair market value may appear to be a gain or a loss. This apparent gain or loss, however, is not recognized as a gain or loss for tax purposes. Thus, there is no tax to be paid on the apparent gain, and there are no tax savings to be recognized on the apparent loss.

No gain, no pain

Let's assume that we are considering trading an old machine as the means of acquiring the new machine needed for project A or B. The old machine has a fair market value (FMV) of $10,000 and a book value of $6,000; the difference between them is an apparent gain of $4,000 ($10,000 − $6,000). If the old machine is sold for $10,000, and the new machine is bought for $10,000 in an independent transaction, the gain of $4,000 on the sale of the old machine will have to be recognized for tax purposes and taxes on the $4,000 gain will have to be paid. By trading the old machine for the new machine, however, the gain will not have to be recognized and no taxes will have to be paid.

Should we trade?

Should we sell the old machine, pay tax on the gain, and then buy a new machine, in two independent transactions? Or should we trade the old machine for the new one?

Logically, it seems that we should trade the old machine for the new one so that we can avoid paying the tax. Conversely, if the sale were expected to result in a loss, logic would say that we should sell the old machine in order to take the loss as a deduction. But is the logical answer the correct answer?

Depreciable Base in Nontaxable Exchange

According to the tax laws, if you avoid paying tax on a gain by trading, then you can't take as much depreciation on the new asset as you could by selling the old and buying the new. Conversely, if you give up the tax reduction that results from a loss by trading, then you can take more depreciation on the new asset than you could by selling the old and buying the new.

If there is an apparent gain when assets are traded (and assuming it might also be necessary to give some cash in addition to the old asset), the basis for depreciation is:

When we have an unrecognized gain, we can't depreciate as much

$$\text{Depreciable base} = \frac{\text{book value of}}{\text{old asset traded}} + \frac{\text{cash}}{\text{paid}^4}$$

For project A or B the depreciable base would be:

$$\text{Depreciable base} = \$6,000 + \$0 = \$6,000$$

The depreciable base, if there is an apparent gain, can also be determined in the following manner:

$$\text{Depreciable base} = \frac{\text{market value of}}{\text{old asset traded}} + \frac{\text{cash}}{\text{paid}} - \frac{\text{gain not}}{\text{recognized}}$$

$$= \quad \$10,000 \quad + \ \$0 \ - \$4,000 \quad = \$6,000$$

The basis for depreciation has to be reduced by the gain that isn't recognized. In our example the depreciable base would be $6,000 ($10,000 − $4,000). Since we don't have to pay tax on the $4,000 gain—a savings of $1,600 ($4,000 × .40)—the depreciable base is lowered by the amount of gain. By lowering the base by $4,000, our tax savings are based on a total of $6,000 of depreciation instead of $10,000. As a result, our tax savings from depreciation are lower by $1,600 ($4,000 × .40) than they would have been if we hadn't traded the assets.

It's better to save the tax on the gain and have lower tax savings from depreciation

The tax we save on the $4,000 gain comes at the beginning of the project, so it has a present value equal to total savings, $1,600. The $1,600 of tax savings we lose by the reduced depreciation is spread out over the recovery period of the project, so the present value of the lost tax savings from depreciation is less than $1,600. Since the present value of the $1,600 saved in year 0 is greater than the present value of the $1,600 of lost tax savings from depreciation, we would benefit by trading when there is an apparent gain.

By not recognizing the loss, we can get more tax savings from depreciation

If there is an apparent loss when assets are traded (and assuming it might also be necessary to give some cash in addition to the old asset), the basis for depreciation is:

$$\text{Depreciable base} = \frac{\text{book value of}}{\text{old asset traded}} + \frac{\text{cash}}{\text{paid}}$$

Or it can be determined in the following manner:

$$\text{Depreciable base} = \frac{\text{market value of}}{\text{old asset traded}} + \frac{\text{cash}}{\text{paid}} + \frac{\text{loss not}}{\text{recognized}}$$

The basis for depreciation is increased by the loss that isn't recognized. In this situation the tax savings we lose by not recognizing the loss are equal to the additional tax savings from the additional depreciation. Since the tax savings for the loss are immediate, the present value of these tax savings is greater than the present value of the tax savings from the additional depreciation. This is because the tax savings from the additional depreciation are spread out over the recovery period of the project.

Don't trade when there is a loss

We are better off selling the asset.

---

[4] Technically, any monetary consideration (not just cash) that is given in an exchange should be added to the book value of the old asset. In tax terms this monetary consideration is called "boot," and it includes cash, receivables, and payables.

Initial Outlay for Nontaxable Exchange

The outlay in year 0 is the FMV

The amount of initial outlay in year 0 of the sketch of cash flows is unaffected by the manner of acquiring the new asset. Whether the company is giving up $10,000 of cash, marketable securities, inventories, or similar productive assets, the simple fact is that it is committing $10,000 of the firm's resources to the new project—the initial outlay is $10,000. It is unaffected by the tax law.

COMPLETE ANALYSIS OF NPV WITH TAX CONSIDERATIONS

Now we are ready to do a complete analysis of projects A and B, integrating into the analysis most of the tax considerations that we have just discussed. In this section we'll do NPV. In later sections we'll do the analysis for IRR and then for the nondiscounted cash-flow approaches. The NPV is determined first for project A in Exhibit 8-6 and then for project B in Exhibit 8-7.

Additional Facts

Disposal values for projects A and B

We will also add one additional bit of information for the two projects. Each one will have a disposal value at the end of its useful life. Project A's disposal value is expected to be $1,500, while project B's disposal value is expected to be $500. In addition, the firm plans on selling the asset for its expected disposal at the end of the ⌐seful life. Also, for comparative purposes, we still use the SL method for project A and the DDB method for project B.

Outlay-Related Items for Projects A and B

The initial outlays in year 0 are exactly the same, $10,000, for project A (Exhibit 8-6) and project B (Exhibit 8-7). The depreciable base for both projects is $10,000. The recovery period is 7 years, but as you can see, it actually takes 8 years to completely depreciate the assets. Remember, the tax law stipulates that no matter

---

THE CHANGING COURSE OF INCOME TAXES

The historic rewrite of the tax code . . . does a lot more than determine how much in taxes individuals and businesses will have to pay the tax collector in years to come. By fundamentally changing the rules by which Americans spend, save, borrow and invest, it will affect the course of the entire economy. Whether that influence ultimately is positive or negative continues to be the $4 trillion question. . . .

Underpinning the legislation—which drops individual tax rates to the lowest levels since Calvin Coolidge was president 60 years ago while sharply reducing the number of breaks—is a major philosophical shift away from using federal taxes to encourage certain types of economic activity

toward a more laissez-faire approach to economic life.

The rules have changed. . . . People will have to look to the market for signals in order to make decisions rather than to Washington for subsidies. Economist A. Gary Shilling, head of the New York consulting firm that bears his name, agrees: "the bill's overarching attitude is very much in line with the recent trend toward deregulation. Rather than using the tax code to push certain social and economic goals, the new law lets people decide what to do with their money." . . .

Proponents of the new tax system predict it will produce a more efficient and productive economy. Because investments will

no longer be steered by artificial tax incentives, there shouldn't be a repetition of the current glut of half-filled office towers or underutilized factories. "By allowing the market to operate more freely, tax reform permits capital to flow to the most productive uses," says attorney Robert Lubick, a former assistant secretary for tax policy in the Carter administration. Harvard economist Dale Jorgenson expects "significant benefits from the allocation of capital," but adds that it could be "decades before they're fully in place."

Source: "Changing Course," *U.S. News & World Report,* Oct. 6, 1986, pp. 46–47.

EXHIBIT 8-6   NPV for Project A

Description		10% PV Factor	Present Value	0	1	2	3	4	5	6	7	8
Initial outlay:		1.000	(10,000)	(10,000)								

Tax Savings
Year	Deprec.	@ 40%											
1	714	285	.909	259		285							
2	1,428	571	.826	472			571						
3	1,428	571	.751	429				571					
4	1,429	572	.683	391					572				
5	1,429	572	.620	355						572			
6	1,429	572	.564	323							572		
7	1,429	572	.513	293								572	
8	714	285	.466	133									285
	10,000	4,000											

Sale of machinery:													
Book value	-0-												
Sales price	1,500	1,500											
Gain (loss)	1,500												
Tax	.40	600											
Net-of-tax cash flow		900	.466	419									900

Cash flow from operations	2,000												
Tax on income @ 40%	800												
Net-of-tax cash flow from operations	1,200	5.334	6,401		1,200	1,200	1,200	1,200	1,200	1,200	1,200	1,200	
				(10,000)	1,485	1,771	1,771	1,772	1,772	1,772	1,772	2,385

| Net present value | | | (525) | | | | | | | | | | |

Project A has a negative NPV

which depreciation method is used, only a half year's depreciation may be taken in the year of purchase, regardless of the time during the year that the purchase takes place. During the next 6 years a full year of depreciation is allowed. And in the last year—year 8—the last half year of depreciation is taken.

For each year the tax savings from depreciation are found by multiplying the depreciation deduction by the tax rate of 40%. The present value (at 10%) of each tax savings is determined individually with the Present Value of $1 table.

Sale of Machinery

For both projects A and B the book value of the equipment at the end of 8 years is zero because 100% of the depreciable base will have been depreciated. Since the book value is zero, the gain is equal to the proceeds of $1,500 for project A and $500 for project B. The tax on each gain—$600 and $200, respectively—is found by multi-

Tax the gain—not the proceeds

EXHIBIT 8-7 NPV for Project B

Description			10% PV Factor	Present Value	Sketch of Cash Flows								
					0	1	2	3	4	5	6	7	8
Initial outlay:			1.000	(10,000)	(10,000)								

Year	Deprec.	Tax Savings											
1	1,428	571	.909	519		571							
2	2,449	980	.826	809			980						
3	1,750	700	.751	526				700					
4	1,249	500	.683	342					500				
5	954	382	.620	237						382			
6	868	347	.564	196							347		
7	868	347	.513	178								347	
8	434	173	.466	81									173
	10,000	4,000											

Sale of machinery:													
Book value		-0-											
Sales price		500	500										
Gain (loss)		500											
Tax		.40	200										
Net-of-tax cash flow			300	.466	140									300

Cash flow from operations (net of tax):

	10% PV Factor	Present Value	0	1	2	3	4	5	6	7	8
1. 4,000 − 1,600 = 2,400	.909	2,182		2,400							
2. 3,000 − 1,200 = 1,800	.826	1,487			1,800						
3. 3,000 − 1,200 = 1,800	.751	1,352				1,800					
4. 2,000 − 800 = 1,200	.683	820					1,200				
5. 1,000 − 400 = 600	.620	372						600			
6. 1,000 − 400 = 600	.564	338							600		
7. 1,000 − 400 = 600	.513	308								600	
8. 1,000 − 400 = 600	.466	280									600
			(10,000)	2,971	2,780	2,500	1,700	982	947	947	1,073
Net present value		167									

Project B has a positive NPV

plying the tax rate times the gain. *The tax is* not *found by multiplying the tax rate times the proceeds from the sale.* For projects A and B, because the book value is zero in both cases, it may seem to make little difference whether you multiply the tax rate times the proceeds or the gain. But if the book value is not zero, and the proceeds are not equal to the gain, it makes a big difference. So be careful, because it's very easy to make this kind of mistake when handling the sale of an asset.

The two parts to the net-of-tax proceeds

    As you can see in Exhibits 8-6 and 8-7, the net-of-tax cash flow for the sale of an asset consists of two parts (except when there is no gain or loss). The first part is the proceeds from the sale, and the second part is the tax on the gain (or tax savings on the loss, when applicable). For project A the proceeds are expected to be $1,500, and the tax on the $1,500 gain is $600. The net of these two parts—$900—represents the net-of-tax cash proceeds from the sale. For project B the proceeds are expected to be $500 and the tax on the gain, $200. The net-of-tax cash flow from this sale will be $300.

The net-of-tax proceeds are then placed in the last year of the project's life ($900 in year 8 for project A) and are discounted back to the present ($419 for project A) using the appropriate present value factor for that year.

If a sale results in a loss, the tax savings from the loss are added to the proceeds to arrive at the net-of-tax cash flow from the sale.

Cash Flow from Operations

The net-of-tax cash flow from operations is the cash flow less the tax effect at 40% of the cash flow. The present values of the cash flows for project A ($1,200 per year) are determined with the Present Value of an Annuity table because the cash flows in each of the 8 years are the same. The present values of the cash flows for project B are determined with the Present Value of $1 table, since the cash flows are different each year.

The Final NPV for Projects A and B

NPV for B is better—
better timing of tax savings
from depreciation is the key

Finally, we can see from the bottom line in Exhibits 8-6 and 8-7 that the NPV of $(525) for project A is $692 less than the NPV of $167 for project B. The main advantage of project B, other than the preferable timing of its cash flows from operations, is its use of DDB depreciation rather than straight line. The only advantage of project A is that it has the higher salvage value in year 8 ($1,500 vs. $500). However, what starts out as a $1,000 advantage for project A (because of its higher sales price) turns out to be much less after taxes are paid and the net-of-tax cash flow is discounted back to the present from year 8. The before-tax cash advantage of $1,000 is only a $279 ($419 − $140) advantage in terms of the present value of net-of-tax cash flows.

INTERNAL RATE OF RETURN

IRR with trial and error

We learned in the previous chapter (1) that the internal rate of return (IRR) represents the actual rate of return earned by a project, and (2) that at this rate the present value of all future cash flows will equal the incremental outlay, leaving an NPV of zero. We also found out (3) that when the cash flows for a project are not exactly the same each year, the only way to calculate the IRR is by using trial and error. Since both projects A and B have uneven cash flows, it is necessary to determine the IRR for both of them with trial and error. In fact, whenever tax effects are being considered in capital budgeting, the IRR must be determined with trial and error. This is because the tax savings from depreciation will never be the same in every year of the life of an asset. This is true even for straight line, since the tax savings in the first and last years of the recovery period will always be different from the tax savings for the in-between years.

In some of the homework
problems, you can ignore
the half-year provision

Project A

Choose any r and calculate
NPV

We will now repeat the steps listed in Chapter 7 for determining IRR with trial and error:

STEP 1: Select any reasonable interest rate and compute the NPV of the cash flows, using the PV of $1 table. We already did this for project A in Exhibit 8-6, when we calculated the NPV at 10%. Remember, the NPV was $(525).

If NPV ≠ 0, try again

STEP 2: If the NPV calculated in step 1 is greater than zero, repeat the calculation using a higher interest rate. If the NPV is less than zero, repeat using a lower interest rate.

Since the NPV was a negative $525 at 10%, we will now repeat the calculation at a lower rate. Let's try 8%. As you can see below, the NPV is now a positive $243. For the sake of space we have not repeated the sketch of cash flows, we have merely listed the items by year and shown their present values.

IRR (where NPV = 0) is between 10% (where NPV < 0) and 8% (where NPV > 0)

			Present Value	
Description	Year	Net-of-Tax Cash Flows	10%	8%
Initial outlay..............................	0	(10,000)	(10,000)	(10,000)
Tax savings from depreciation	1	285	259	264
	2	571	472	489
	3	571	429	453
	4	572	391	420
	5	572	355	389
	6	572	323	360
	7	572	293	333
	8	285	133	154
Sale of machinery	8	900	419	486
Cash flow from operations	1–8	1,200	6,401	6,895
NPV..			(525)	243

STEP 3: Continue repeating step 2 until you have an NPV > 0 and an NPV < 0. We have already accomplished this. At 10% the NPV is negative and at 8% the NPV is positive.

STEP 4: Interpolate to get the exact IRR. The process of interpolation for project A is shown below. (If you forgot how to do interpolation, you might need to go back to the detailed discussion in Chapter 7.)

Zero is between 243 and (525)

	NPV	NPV
8%	243	243
?	-0-	
10%		(525)
Difference	243	768

IRR is 31.6% of the way from 8% to 10%

$$\frac{243}{768} = 31.6\% \times (10\% - 8\%) = \quad .632\%$$
$$\underline{ 8.000\%}$$
$$IRR = 8.632\%$$

Project B

Since the process of determining the IRR for project B is exactly the same as it is for project A, we will not repeat all the steps. Instead, we will show all calculations at one time. As you can see, the IRR for project B is 12.612%. Notice that the IRR for project B is higher than the IRR for project A. This should come as no surprise because project B had the higher NPV.

		Present Value	

Description	Year	Net-of-Tax Cash Flows	10%	12%
Initial outlay............................	0	(10,000)	(10,000)	(10,000)
Tax savings from depreciation	1	571	519	509
	2	980	809	781
	3	700	526	498
	4	500	342	318
	5	382	237	217
	6	347	196	176
	7	347	178	157
	8	173	81	70
Sale of machinery	8	300	140	121
Cash flow from operations	1	2,400	2,182	2,141
	2	1,800	1,487	1,435
	3	1,800	1,352	1,280
	4	1,200	820	762
	5	600	372	340
	6	600	338	304
	7	600	308	271
	8	600	280	242
NPV...			167	(378)

IRR is between 10% and 12%, since 0 is between 167 and (378)

The IRR must be between 10% and 12%. The exact IRR is determined by the following interpolation:

	NPV	NPV
10%	167	167
?	-0-	
12%		(378)
Difference	167	545

IRR is 30.6% of the way from 10% to 12%

$$\frac{167}{545} = 30.6\% \times (12\% - 10\%) = \quad .612\%$$

$$\underline{10.000\%}$$

$$IRR = 12.612\%$$

NONDISCOUNTED CASH-FLOW METHODS

The two nondiscounted cash-flow techniques we introduced in Chapter 7 were the payback method and the accountant's (or accounting) rate of return. Let's first consider the payback method.

Payback Method

The payback period represents the number of years it takes for the cash flows from a project to recover its original investment. The easiest and quickest way to calculate the payback period for projects A and B is to begin by adding a line at the bottom of the sketch of cash flows, as we did in Exhibits 8-6 and 8-7, listing the cash flows for each year. Normally, we think of using the sketch of cash flows only when calculating the NPV or IRR. However, as you will see, in determining payback (and also the accounting rate of return), a sketch of cash flows is also helpful.

The lines we are referring to are shown below as they appeared in Exhibits 8-6 and 8-7:

Sketch of Cash Flows — Exhibit 8-6 and 8-7									
	0	1	2	3	4	5	6	7	8
Project A	(10,000)	1,485	1,771	1,771	1,772	1,772	1,772	1,772	2,385
Project B	(10,000)	2,971	2,780	2,500	1,700	982	947	947	1,073

These are the summations of each column in the sketch of cash flows

When the cash flows are not exactly the same each year, the payback must be determined by accumulating the cash flows 1 year at a time until the cumulative cash flow equals the incremental investment. The cash flows to be accumulated are the ones listed above that were taken from the sketch of cash flows in Exhibits 8-6 and 8-7. The incremental investment continues to be $10,000.

Project A

The payback period for project A is determined in the following manner:

Year	Net-of-Tax Cash Flow	Cumulative Cash Flow
1	1,485	1,485
2	1,771	3,256
3	1,771	5,027
4	1,772	6,799
5	1,772	8,571
Payback period	?	10,000
6	1,772	10,343
7	1,772	12,115
8	2,385	14,500

The project's cumulative cash flow reaches $10,000 in the sixth year

At some point in the sixth year, the incremental investment of $10,000 will be fully recovered. The exact point, found through interpolation, is 5.81 years. (If you have any trouble as you look over the interpolation process below, refer to the interpolation explanation for payback on page 343 of Chapter 7.)

It takes $1,429 of year-6's cash of $1,772 to reach $10,000

		Cumulative Cash Flows	
End of year 5		$ 8,571	$ 8,571
Needed to recover incremental investment		10,000	
End of year 6			10,343
Difference		$ 1,429	$ 1,772

$$\text{Fraction of year} = \frac{\text{cash flow needed in year to pay for investment}}{\text{cash flow for full year}}$$

$$= \frac{\$1,429}{\$1,772} = .81 \text{ year}$$

$$\text{Payback period} = 5 \text{ years} + .81 \text{ year} = 5.81 \text{ years}$$

Project B

For project B the payback period is calculated in a similar manner:

Year	Net-of-Tax Cash Flow	Cumulative Cash Flow	
1	2,971	2,971	
2	2,780	5,751	
3	2,500	8,251	
4	1,700	9,951	
Payback period	?	10,000 ⟵	*Project B recovers the 10,000th dollar in year 5*
5	982	10,933	
6	947	11,880	
7	947	12,827	
8	1,073	13,900	

At some point in the fifth year, the incremental investment of $10,000 will be fully recovered. The exact point, found through interpolation, is shown below to be 4.05 years:

It only takes $49 of year 5's cash to reach $10,000

	Cumulative Cash Flows	
End of year 4	$ 9,951	$ 9,951
Needed to recover incremental investment	10,000	
End of year 5		10,933
Difference	$ 49	$ 982

$$\text{Fraction of year} = \frac{\text{cash flow needed in year to pay for investment}}{\text{cash flow for full year}}$$

$$= \frac{\$49}{\$982} = .05 \text{ year}$$

$$\text{Payback period} = 4 \text{ years} + .05 \text{ year} = 4.05 \text{ years}$$

Accountant's Rate of Return

The accountant's rate of return can be calculated using one of two closely related equations. The first one, which emphasizes the income generated by a project, is:

$$\text{ARR} = \frac{\textbf{average net income}}{\textbf{incremental investment}}$$

The second equation, which is merely a variation of the first, emphasizes the cash flows generated by a project. It is:

ACF − average depreciation = average NI

$$ARR = \frac{\text{average cash flows} - \text{average depreciation}}{\text{incremental investment}}$$

The approach we used in Chapter 7 employed the latter of these two equations. We will continue to use this approach as long as there is no salvage value expected at the end of the project's useful life. When there is no salvage, the only difference from the equation we used in Chapter 7 is that now the cash flows referred to in the numerator of the equation are net of tax:

It's income after tax

$$ARR = \frac{\dfrac{\text{average cash flows from}}{\text{operations (net of tax)}} - \text{average depreciation}}{\text{incremental investment}}$$

When the project is expected to have a salvage value at the end of the useful life, an adjustment is needed in the numerator for any gain or loss on the sale of the asset. The adjusted ARR becomes:

Now we add the gain or subtract the loss

$$ARR = \frac{\dfrac{\text{average cash flows from}}{\text{operations (net of tax)}} - \dfrac{\text{average}}{\text{depreciation}} \pm \dfrac{\text{average gain}}{\text{or loss (net of tax)}}}{\text{incremental investment}}$$

There are several important points related to this equation that you need to be aware of:

1. The average cash flows from operations in the numerator exclude the proceeds from the sale of the asset.

What our gain or loss is depends on the salvage value, the life, and the recovery period

2. In calculating the average depreciation, the salvage value is ignored (which is required by law in determining depreciation for tax purposes). In addition, as long as the life of the project is longer than the recovery period, the average depreciation can be found by simply dividing the cost of the project by the life of the project. It doesn't matter how much depreciation is actually taken in each year. Since we are calculating an average rate of return over the life of the project, the life—*not* the recovery period—is used in the depreciation calculation.

Average depreciation

On the other hand, if the recovery period is greater than or equal to the life of the project, the average depreciation is calculated by adding the depreciation taken in each year of useful life and then dividing the sum by the life. The book value that has not been depreciated by the end of the life will affect the gain or loss at the time the asset is sold.

3. Total income over the life of an asset includes any gain or loss on the disposal of the asset at the end of its useful life. In the year of disposal, the gain or loss on the income statement has the following related tax effect:

Net-of-tax gain (or loss) = gain (or loss) × (1 − tax rate)

The average gain (or loss) over the life of the project is then determined as:

Average gain (loss) is net of tax

$$\text{Net effect of gain (or loss) on average income} = \frac{\text{gain (or loss)} \times (1 - \text{tax rate})}{\text{life of asset}}$$

The resulting amount is added to (or subtracted from) the numerator in the ARR calculation.

Projects A and B

Before we can calculate the ARR, we need to determine the average cash flows from operations. To do this, we merely add up the cash flows for the life of the project, given in the next-to-last line of Exhibits 8-6 and 8-7, and divide the total by the life. Be sure, however, to exclude the proceeds from the sale of the asset in year 8 when you do this. Remember: Those proceeds are not part of normal operations.

The average cash flows exclude sale of the asset

$$\text{Average cash flows for project A} = \frac{\begin{array}{c}1{,}485 + 1{,}771 + 1{,}771 + 1{,}772 + 1{,}772 + \\ 1{,}772 + 1{,}772 + 1{,}485\end{array}}{8 \text{ years}}$$

$$= \frac{13{,}600}{8} = 1{,}700$$

$$\text{Average cash flows for project B} = \frac{\begin{array}{c}2{,}971 + 2{,}780 + 2{,}500 + 1{,}700 + 982 + \\ 947 + 947 + 773\end{array}}{8 \text{ years}} = \frac{13{,}600}{8} = 1{,}700$$

As you can see, the average cash flows are the same for projects A and B. Remember, the total cash from operations (before tax) over the life of the project is $16,000 for both projects. When taxes are paid, the net-of-tax cash flow from operations will still be the same—in total. In addition, the total depreciation over the 8-year life is $10,000 for each project. Therefore, the total tax savings over the 8-year life will be the same for each project. The only difference between the cash flows for projects A and B is the timing of the cash flows—not their totals. Since the ARR ignores the timing of cash flows and uses an average, the average cash flows from operations (net of tax) are the same for projects A and B.

The average cash flows for A and B are the same

The ARR for each project can now be calculated. For project A it is:

$$\text{ARR} = \frac{\$1{,}700 - (\$10{,}000 \div 8) + [(1 - .40)(\$1{,}500) \div 8]}{\$10{,}000}$$

$$= \frac{\$1{,}700 - \$1{,}250 + (\$900 \div 8)}{\$10{,}000}$$

$$= \frac{\$1{,}700 - \$1{,}250 + \$112.50}{\$10{,}000} = \frac{\$562.50}{\$10{,}000} = 5.625\%$$

And the ARR for project B is as follows:

$$\text{ARR} = \frac{\$1{,}700 - \$1{,}250 + [(1 - .40)(\$500) \div 8]}{\$10{,}000}$$

$$= \frac{\$1{,}700 - \$1{,}250 + \$37.50}{\$10{,}000} = \frac{\$487.50}{\$10{,}000} = 4.875\%$$

The ARR for project A is 5.625% and for project B is 4.875%. The only reason they differ at all is because project A has the higher salvage value at the end of the useful life and therefore has a greater gain on the sale.

CHAPTER SUMMARY

We expanded the analysis of Chapter 7 to include the income tax considerations that affect all capital budgeting decisions. We showed you how each tax consideration affects the amount and timing of cash flows for a project. And we pointed out why the results for projects when taxes are considered are different from the results when taxes are ignored.

Although depreciation is not a cash item — that is, it does not involve a cash inflow or outflow — it does have a very favorable indirect effect on cash flows. Since depreciation is a deduction on the tax return, it shields, or protects, income from being taxed. This is why depreciation is often referred to as a *tax shield.* As a result, taxes that would otherwise have to be paid on income do not have to be paid. The company thus reduces its taxes because of depreciation — and reduced taxes mean more cash. The reduction in taxes due to the tax shield from depreciation is referred to as the *tax savings from depreciation.*

Under the Tax Reform Act of 1986, companies must depreciate their assets over one of eight possible *recovery periods.* Which recovery period to use in depreciating an asset for tax purposes depends upon the ADR midpoint life of the asset (which is probably not the same as its useful life). On the basis of the midpoint life, the asset is depreciated over 3, 5, 7, 10, 15, 20, 27.5, or 31.5 years. The most common assets fit into one of four recovery periods — 5, 7, 10, and 31.5 years. For all assets with recovery periods of 5, 7, or 10 years, companies can choose between the double-declining-balance (DDB) method and the straight-line (SL) method. For either method:

1. Salvage is ignored.

2. A half year of depreciation is taken in the first and last years of the recovery period.

In addition, for DDB the taxpayer must switch from DDB to SL in the first year that SL depreciation exceeds DDB depreciation. In this way the taxpayer is able to depreciate 100% of the cost of the asset.

Assets (primarily buildings) that are in the 31.5-year recovery period must use SL depreciation.

The decision of whether to use the DDB or the SL method should be based on which method maximizes the present value of the tax savings from the depreciation. In most situations use of the DDB method of depreciation will accomplish that purpose. Although both methods provide the same total tax savings over the life of the asset, most of the tax savings from DDB are in the early years when the present value of $1 is greatest. Much of the tax savings from SL depreciation is in the later years when the present value of $1 is lower. Therefore, DDB is usually better because the present value of tax savings that come primarily in the early years of an asset's life is higher than the present value of the same total tax savings if they come in later years.

Several tax items that were quite popular in the past were unfortunately repealed by the Tax Reform Act of 1986. One of these was the *investment tax credit (ITC).* The ITC was a credit — usually 10% of the cost of any new asset that qualified for this credit — that could be used to reduce income taxes in the year the asset was acquired. Since the ITC effectively reduced the cost of the asset, it was therefore expected to provide a stimulus to investment spending.

The other popular tax item that was repealed by the Tax Reform Act was the favorable system of *capital gains tax rates.* The tax rates on long-term capital gains had been much lower than the tax rates on ordinary income, but the Tax Reform Act revised them so that the capital gains tax rates are currently the same as the rates on ordinary income.

In most capital budgeting situations it makes little difference what type of resources are used by a firm to make an initial investment. This is because it is the market value (or cash equivalent) of the resources paid that usually goes in year 0 as the initial outlay, and this amount is also the basis for depreciation. On the other hand, if an asset is acquired by trading similar productive assets, the transaction qualifies as a ***nontaxable exchange.*** In a nontaxable exchange any apparent gain or loss is not recognized as a gain or loss for tax purposes. Thus, there is no tax to be paid on the apparent gain, and there are no tax savings to be derived from the apparent loss.

If an old asset is traded for a new one, the basis for computing depreciation is:

$$\textbf{Depreciable base} = \frac{\textbf{market value of}}{\textbf{old asset traded}} + \frac{\textbf{cash}}{\textbf{paid}} \pm \frac{\textbf{loss or gain not}}{\textbf{recognized}}$$

Or it is:

$$\textbf{Depreciable base} = \frac{\textbf{book value of}}{\textbf{old asset traded}} + \frac{\textbf{cash}}{\textbf{paid}}$$

In all our examples we used a single tax rate to determine the net-of-tax cash flows for a project. Realistically, however, not all income for a corporation is taxed at just one rate. Instead, corporations use a ***progressive tax rate*** schedule, in which the tax rates on income start out quite low but increase as the amount increases.

The use of multiple tax rates in capital budgeting would make the analysis much more complicated; therefore, for the sake of simplicity, we use a single tax rate. We justify its use by assuming that the company's income is so great that, no matter what a project is expected to earn or lose, there will be only one tax bracket applicable to the project—the highest one.

The capital budgeting methods are more complicated when tax considerations are integrated into the analysis. One reason for the added complications is that the aftertax cash flows have to be determined. Another reason is that the net-of-tax cash flows will never be the same for all years of the asset's useful life. When the DDB method is used, the tax savings are different in every year, except for the years after the switch to straight line. Even when the straight-line method is used, the tax savings are not the same in each and every year. Although the tax savings may be the same in every year in which there is a full year of depreciation, nevertheless, because of the half-year provision, the first and last years of the recovery period are different from all other years. Since the cash flows will never be the same in all years, the NPV cannot be calculated by using only the Present Value of an Annuity table. The IRR must be calculated by trial and error. The payback must be determined by accumulating each year's cash flows until the initial investment is recovered. And the ARR will often have an average gain or loss to add to the numerator of the calculation.

IMPORTANT TERMS USED IN THIS CHAPTER

Capital gains rates Tax rates applicable to the gains on the sale of capital assets. Prior to the Tax Reform Act of 1986, the rates were much lower than the rates on ordinary income. They are now the same as ordinary tax rates. (page 332)

Investment tax credit A reduction of taxes in the year of acquisition of qualifying assets, usually based on 10% of the cost of the asset. The ITC was repealed by the Tax Reform Act of 1986. (page 332)

Nontaxable exchange An exchange of similar productive assets. No gains or losses are recognized for tax purposes. (page 334)

Progressive tax rates Tax rates that start out quite low but increase as the amount of taxable income increases. (page 332)

Recovery period The number of years over which assets must be depreciated for tax purposes. The recovery period depends on the ADR midpoint life. (page 326)

Tax savings from depreciation The taxes that are saved by the depreciation tax shield. The savings represent the taxes that would have been paid on income if the depreciation had not shielded that income from taxation. (page 324)

Tax shield The effect that depreciation has on taxable income. It "shields" or protects income from being taxed. (page 324)

APPENDIX 8-1: TAX CONSIDERATIONS AND THE KEEP-VS.-REPLACE DECISION

Go back to Appendix 7-1 for Dianawick

We will now show you how to evaluate the keep-vs.-replace decision when all the tax considerations are integrated into the analysis. Because of the many similarities in the preceding analyses for projects A and B, this decision can be explained in less detail than the other projects.

First, turn back to Example 7-3 and Exhibits 7-5 and 7-6, and refresh yourself with the facts concerning the Dianawick Amusement Park. Then proceed to the additional facts given in Example 8-1.

Example 8-1

ADDITIONAL FACTS FOR THE DIANAWICK AMUSEMENT PARK

Additional facts — tax considerations

The Dianawick Amusement Park purchased the old merry-go-round 4 years ago for $30,000 and decided to use the straight-line method of depreciation over the 5-year write-off period. In its first year of operation Dianawick took only a half year of depreciation, which was required at the time by tax regulations, and it took a full year's depreciation in each of the following 3 years. The book value of the old merrry-go-round at the present time is $9,000, but it will be increased by $10,000, the cost of a complete overhaul. The total book value of $19,000 will be depreciated over the remaining write-off period of $1\frac{1}{2}$ years.

Depreciation on the new merry-go-round will be based on the provisions of the Tax Reform Act of 1986. The DDB method will be used, and it has been determined that the appropriate recovery period is 7 years, even though the useful life is only 4 years.

The cash operating receipts have been offset by the cash operating costs to reduce the number of calculations. The net cash inflows (receipts less disbursements) will be:

	Old Merry-Go-Round	New Merry-Go-Round
Cash operating receipts............................	$50,000	$50,000
Cash operating costs	30,000	23,000
Net cash inflows................................	$20,000	$27,000

NPV for Keep vs. Replace

Look at Exhibits 8-8 and 8-9

The present value calculations using the total approach are given in Exhibit 8-8; the calculations using the incremental approach are given in Exhibit 8-9.

EXHIBIT 8-8 Analysis of Keep vs. Replace: Total Approach

			15% PV Factor	Present Value	Sketch of Cash Flows				
					0	1	2	3	4
Keep:									
Cost of overhaul			1.000	(10,000)	(10,000)				
Net cash inflows	20,000								
Less tax @ 40%	8,000	12,000	2.854	34,248		12,000	12,000	12,000	12,000
Depreciation (deprec. base = 9,000 + 10,000):									
Yr.	Deprec. ×	Tax Rate =	Tax Savings						
1	12,667 ×	.40 =	5,067	.869	4,403		5,067			
2	6,333 ×	.40 =	2,533	.756	1,915			2,533		
	19,000									
Disposal:									
Book value	-0-								
Sales price	3,000	3,000							
Gain on disposal	3,000								
Tax effect	× .40	1,200	1,800	.571	1,028					1,800
						(10,000)	17,067	14,533	12,000	13,800
NPV — keep				31,594					
Replace:									
Cost of new merry-go-round			1.000	(37,000)	(37,000)				
Disposal of old merry-go-round:									
Book value	9,000								
Sales price	5,000	5,000							
Loss on disposal	4,000								
Tax effect	× .40	1,600	6,600	1.000	6,600	6,600			
Net cash inflows	27,000								
Less tax @ 40%	10,800	16,200	2.854	46,235		16,200	16,200	16,200	16,200
Depreciation (deprec. base = 37,000):									
Yr.	Deprec. ×	Tax Rate =	Tax Savings						
1	5,285 ×	.40 =	2,114	.869	1,837		2,114			
2	9,061 ×	.40 =	3,624	.756	2,740			3,624		
3	6,472 ×	.40 =	2,589	.657	1,701				2,589	
4	2,697 ×	.40 =	1,079	.571	616					1,079
	23,515									

(continued)

Disposal of new merry-go-round:
Book value

(37,000 − 23,515)	13,485								
Sales price	10,000	10,000							
Loss on disposal	3,485								
Tax effect	× .40	1,394							
		11,394	.571	6,506					11,394
					(30,400)	18,314	19,824	18,789	28,673
NPV — Replace				29,235					

**Difference in NPVs
if merry-go-round is replaced**   (2,359)

EXHIBIT 8-9   Analysis of Keep vs. Replace: Incremental Approach

			15% PV Factor	Present Value	Sketch of Cash Flows				
					0	1	2	3	4
Incremental outlay (37,000 − 10,000)			1.000	(27,000)	(27,000)				

Disposal of old merry-go-round:

Book value	9,000								
Sales price	5,000	5,000							
Loss on disposal	4,000								
Tax effect	× .40	1,600	6,600	1.000	6,600	6,600			

Net incremental receipts	7,000								
Less tax @ 40%	2,800	4,200	2.854	11,987		4,200	4,200	4,200	4,200

Depreciation:

	Keep: SL	Replace: DDB						Sketch of Cash Flows			
Yr.	Deprec.	Deprec.	Diff.	× Rate	=	Tax Savings	15% PV	PV	1	2	3	4
1	12,667	5,285	(7,382) ×	.40	=	(2,953)	.869	(2,566)	(2,953)			
2	6,333	9,061	2,728 ×	.40	=	1,091	.756	825		1,091		
3	-0-	6,472	6,472 ×	.40	=	2,589	.657	1,701			2,589	
4	-0-	2,697	2,697 ×	.40	=	1,079	.571	616				1,079
	19,000	23,515	4,515									

Difference in disposals of merry-go-rounds:

Book value	(13,485 − 0)	13,485							
Disposal	(10,000 − 3,000)	7,000	7,000						
Net loss on disposal		6,485							
Tax effect	× .40	2,594							
		9,594	.571	5,478					9,594
					(20,400)	1,247	5,291	6,789	14,873
NPV if merry-go-round is replaced				(2,359)					

This represents the incremental cash outlay that is needed for ARR and payback

The column summations for years 1–4 are also needed for ARR and payback

Depreciation

The depreciation for the keep alternative is somewhat different from what we've seen so far. Remember: The asset has already been depreciated for 4 years of its life. But because the straight-line depreciation method allows only a half year of depreciation in the first year, only $3\frac{1}{2}$ years of depreciation have been taken. This means $1\frac{1}{2}$ years of depreciation are still left—a full year in year 1 and a half year in year 2. The

The book value of the old is increased by the overhaul

depreciation cannot, however, be based upon the original cost of $30,000 or the remaining book value of $9,000, because the $10,000 overhaul is to be added to the depreciable base. This means that the book value will increase to $19,000, all of which should be depreciated over the next 2 years. Since there will be a full year of depreciation in year 1 and half that in year 2, two thirds of the $19,000 will be depreciated in year 1 ($\frac{2}{3} \times \$19,000 = \$12,667$) and the remaining one-third will be depreciated in year 2 ($\frac{1}{3} \times \$19,000 = \$6,333$).

Use the 7-year recovery period even though the life = 4

For the replace alternative the 7-year recovery period should be used to depreciate the new merry-go-round despite the fact that the firm's intention is to keep it for only 4 of the 7 years. The depreciation for each of the 4 years is calculated below. Notice that the depreciation in year 4—the year of disposal—is for only a half year.

Depreciable Base	×	Depreciation %	=	Depreciation	×	.5	=	Depreciation per Year	Year of Depreciation
$37,000	×	.2857*	=	$10,571	×	.5	=		$5,285	1
$26,429	×	.2857	=	$10,571 $ 7,551	× ×	.5 .5	= =	$5,285 3,776	$9,061	2
$18,878	×	.2857	=	$ 7,551 $ 5,393	× ×	.5 .5	= =	$3,775 2,697	$6,472	3
				$ 5,393	×	.5	=		$2,697	4

* $\frac{1}{7}$ years = .2857/year

At the end of 4 years some of the depreciation will not have been taken, so the resulting book value will not be zero. In this situation, the book value for the new merry-go-round will be $13,485 ($37,000 − $23,515), which is needed in the calculation of the loss on the sale.

All items in the incremental approach represent the differences between keep and replace

For the incremental approach shown in Exhibit 8-9, you can see that in year 1 the SL depreciation (the keep alternative) exceeds the DDB depreciation (the replace alternative) but in years 2 through 4 the SL depreciation is less than the DDB depreciation. Therefore, the tax savings are greater for keep in year 1 (as indicated by the parentheses in Exhibit 8-9), but they are greater for replace in years 2 through 4 (as indicated by the lack of parentheses in Exhibit 8-9).

(Within the incremental analysis, the use of parentheses around a number means that the cash flow and related present value of the keep alternative are preferable to those of the replace alternative. The lack of parentheses indicates that the cash flow and related present value of the replace alternative are preferable to those of the keep alternative.)

Disposals in Year 1

In year 4 the old asset will be sold for $3,000 in the keep alternative, and the new asset will be sold for $10,000 in the replace alternative. For each separate calculation the gain or loss and the tax effect of that gain or loss must be determined. Then the tax effect is added to or subtracted from the proceeds of the sale.

The difference in disposals

For the incremental approach the first thing we do is find the difference in the book values for keep and replace ($13,485 − $0 = $13,485). Then we find the difference in the proceeds for keep and replace ($10,000 − $3,000 = $7,000). Next, we subtract the difference in the proceeds from the difference in the book values to get the net gain or loss ($13,485 − $7,000 = $6,485). Finally, we add the tax savings on the net loss to the proceeds to get the net-of-tax incremental proceeds of $9,594.

The Incremental NPV

As Exhibits 8-8 and 8-9 both show, the NPV will be higher for the Dianawick Amusement Park if the old merry-go-round is kept. In Exhibit 8-8 the NPV for keep is $31,594, while the NPV for replace is only $29,235; the difference is $2,359. In Exhibit 8-9 the bottom line also indicates that the keep alternative is $2,359 higher than the replace alternative.

Internal Rate of Return

In the calculations for the IRR, trial and error is used with the incremental numbers given in the sketch of cash flows in Exhibit 8-9. All the tax calculations are left out; the net-of-tax cash flows are the only items listed. In addition, the sketch of cash flows is left out simply to allow us enough room for the calculations:

			Present Value		
	Year	Cash Flow	15%	12%	6%
Incremental outlay........	0	(27,000)	(27,000)	(27,000)	(27,000)
Disposal of old merry-go-round..................	0	6,600	6,600	6,600	6,600
Net incremental receipts ...	1–4	4,200	11,987	12,755	14,553
Depreciation tax savings ...	1	(2,953)	(2,566)	(2,634)	(2,785)
	2	1,091	825	870	970
	3	2,589	1,701	1,841	2,172
	4	1,079	616	685	855
Difference in disposals of merry-go-rounds.........	4	9,594	5,478	6,092	7,598
NPV......................................			(2,359)	(791)	2,963

The sketch of cash flows is deleted to save space

IRR falls between 6% and 12%

The NPV is negative at costs of capital of 15% and 12%—(2,359) and (791), respectively—but positive at 6%—2,963. Therefore, the IRR—the interest rate that gives us an NPV of zero—must be between 12% and 6%. With interpolation the exact IRR is determined to be 10.73%:

	NPV	NPV
6%	2,963	2,963
?	-0-	
12%		(791)
Difference	2,963	3,754

A zero NPV lies 78.9% of the way from 2,963 to (791), so the IRR is 78.9% of the way from 6% to 12%

$$\frac{2,963}{3,754} = 78.9\% \times (12\% - 6\%) = \quad 4.73\%$$

$$6.00\%$$

$$\text{IRR} = \underline{10.73\%}$$

Payback Period

Using the total cash flows for each year, listed on the last line of the sketch of cash flows in Exhibit 8-9, the payback period is determined to be 4 years:

	Net-of-Tax Cash Flow	Cumulative Cash Flow	
During year: 1	$1,247	$ 1,247	
2	5,291	6,538	
3	6,789	13,327	
4	5,279	18,606	*This is the*
Payback period...............	?	20,400	← *incremental outlay*
End of year 4	9,594	28,200	*($27,000) less the*

This is the incremental outlay ($27,000) less the disposal of the old asset ($6,600)

The incremental cash outlay (look at the bottom of the zero column in the sketch of cash flows in Exhibit 8-9) for the merry-go-round is the difference between the $27,000 outflow and the $6,600 inflow—a difference of $20,400. The payback for the replace decision is achieved when the cumulative cash flow reaches this amount.

The cumulative cash doesn't reach $20,400 until the end of year 4

During the fourth year the cash flows from operations amounted to $5,279. This includes the $4,200 net-of-tax cash savings and the $1,079 tax savings from depreciation (see column 4 in the sketch of cash flows in Exhibit 8-9)—both of which occurred during the year. It excludes, however, the net-of-tax proceeds from the disposal, because the disposal occurred at the end of the year. The cumulative cash receipts by the end of the fourth year, but prior to the disposal, were $18,606, which was short of the $20,400 incremental cash outlay in year 0. It's not until the disposal is made at the end of the fourth year that the cumulative cash flow exceeds $20,400. Therefore, since the payback depends upon receipts from the disposal at the end of the fourth year, the payback period is 4 years.

Accountant's Rate of Return

We use the equation we developed earlier in the text for project B:

$$ARR = \frac{\text{average cash flows from operations} - \text{average depreciation} \pm \text{average gain or loss (net-of-tax effect)}}{\text{incremental investment}}$$

The ARR is determined to be 12.5% for the Dianawick Amusement Park:

Avg. Income = 12.5% of I

$$ARR = \frac{\$4,652 - \$1,129 - \$973}{\$20,400} = \frac{\$2,550}{\$20,400} = 12.5\%$$

The amounts in the numerator were calculated as follows:

1. The incremental average cash flows from operations are:

$$\frac{\$1,247 + \$5,291 + \$6,789 + \$5,279}{4 \text{ years}} = \frac{\$18,606}{4} = \$4,652$$

Notice that the fourth year's cash flow excluded the $9,594 net-of-tax disposal and included only the $4,200 net-of-tax savings and the $1,079 tax savings from depreciation. The disposal is excluded because it's not a cash flow from the operations of the merry-go-round.

2. The incremental average depreciation is:

$$\frac{\$23,515 - \$19,000}{4 \text{ years}} = \frac{\$4,515}{4} = \$1,129$$

The $23,515 is the total depreciation taken under the replace alternative, and the $19,000 is the total depreciation taken under the keep alternative (see the depreciation section of Exhibit 8-9).

3. The average incremental gain or loss (net of tax) is:

$$\text{Incremental loss (net of tax)} = \$6,485 \times .60 = \$3,891$$
$$\text{Average} = \$3,891 \div 4 \text{ years} = \$973$$

QUESTIONS

1. Explain the difference between *tax evasion* and *tax avoidance.*

2. Why is depreciation referred to as a *tax shield?* Are there any other tax shields besides depreciation?

3. How can depreciation have a significant impact on the present value of cash flows even though depreciation itself is not a cash inflow or cash outflow?

4. How does tax depreciation under the Tax Reform Act of 1986 differ from the depreciation methods we use for financial accounting?

5. "The useful life of a project has no effect on the tax savings from depreciation." Do you agree? Explain.

6. What are the two most important determinants of the present value of cash flows?

7. The methods of depreciation under the Tax Reform Act of 1986 are probably not acceptable methods for financial accounting. They are not considered to be GAAP. What type of accounting problem does this inconsistency cause in the preparation of financial statements?

8. Why are accelerated methods of depreciation typically preferable to straight line?

9. When an asset is sold for an amount other than its book value, what are the two cash flows that must be considered in the capital budgeting model?

10. How might an anticipated change in tax rates affect the decision to use straight line for tax purposes?

11. Decide whether each of the following statements is true or false. If a statement is false, explain why it is false.

    a. "The total depreciation for accelerated and straight-line depreciation methods is exactly the same."
    b. "The total tax savings from an accelerated depreciation method are greater than the tax savings from straight line."
    c. "The present value of tax savings is greater for an accelerated depreciation method than it is for straight line."

12. What is an *investment tax credit?* How does it affect the present value of a project?

13. What is a *nontaxable exchange?* How do we account for it in a capital budgeting situation?

EXERCISES

**Exercise 8-1
Calculating all methods
with simplifying
assumptions**

The Dr. Jay Tennis Shoes Company is considering an investment in a machine that costs $20,000 and has a 7-year useful life. The cash receipts per year are expected to be $6,000; the tax rate is 40%; and the cost of capital is 10%. The machine is to be depreciated using a recovery period of 7 years.

a. Assume that the company is using the SL method and that the half-year provision can be ignored. Determine:
  1. The net present value

(Check figure: $3,087)

  2. The internal rate of return
  3. The payback period
  4. The accountant's rate of return
b. Now assume that the DDB method is being used and that the half-year provision and the switch to straight line can be ignored. Calculate each of the four methods that were required in part **a**.

(Check figure: IRR = 15.6%)

**Exercise 8-2
Redoing Exercise 8-1
without simplifying
assumptions**

Redo parts **a** and **b** of Exercise 8-1, but now assume the following:
1. The half-year provision is used with both the SL and DDB methods.
2. For DDB the switch to straight line is required.

*(Check figure: Part **a**, NPV = $2,861)*

**Exercise 8-3
Determining NPV with
simplifying assumptions
for depreciation**

The owner of Sutton Appliance Rental is considering expanding his operations to include car rentals. He is looking at a fleet of factory recalls that would cost $35,000. He expects to be able to rent the cars continuously during their useful lives. The net cash inflows from operations are estimated to be $20,000 per year. The cost of capital is 20%; the tax rate is 40%; and the DDB method of depreciation will be used.

Determine the NPV for the new investment opportunity on the basis of each of the two different assumptions listed below concerning the useful life of the fleet. (In this exercise, assume for simplicity that a full year's depreciation can be taken in the year of purchase and that there is no switch to straight line and that the recovery period is 5 years.)

(Check figure: $182)

b. Assume the useful life is 6 years.

**Exercise 8-4
Repeating Exercise 8-3
with no simplifying
assumptions**

Redo the two parts that are required in Exercise 8-3, but now assume the following:
1. One-half year of depreciation must be taken in the first and last years.
2. There will be a switch from DDB to SL depreciation at the appropriate point during the recovery period.

*[Check figure: Part **a**, NPV = $(209)]*

**Exercise 8-5
Determining the PV of
proceeds from the sale of
an asset**

The 6-12 Convenience Market just purchased a meat-cutting machine for $1,500. During the next 4 years 6-12 expects to take $1,200 of depreciation and then sell the machine at the end of the fourth year. The cost of capital for 6-12 is 15%, and the tax rate is 30%.
a. Assume that the machine is sold for $200. Determine the present value of the net cash flows from the sale.
b. Assume that the machine is sold for $650. Determine the present value of the net cash flows from the sale.

(Check figure: $311)

Exercise 8-6
Evaluating the effect of cost of capital on the PV of tax savings from depreciation

The Darling Linda Company has decided to purchase an asset costing $5,000, but hasn't decided whether to use the DDB or the SL method of depreciation. Darling's tax accountant, Jonnie Dee, recommends that the company use the method that maximizes the present value of the tax savings. The recovery period for depreciating the asset is 3 years; the life of the asset is 6 years; the tax rate is 30%; and the cost of capital is 12%.

a. Determine the present value of the tax savings for each of the two methods.

(Check figure: DDB present value = $1,208)

b. Repeat part **a**, but assume that the cost of capital is 20%.
c. Repeat part **a**, but assume that the recovery period is 5 years.
d. For which set of assumptions is the advantage of using the DDB method the greatest?

Exercise 8-7
Evaluating a nontaxable exchange

Artistic Flowers has an old truck that it is considering either selling outright or trading for a new delivery truck. The book value of the old truck is $2,000, and it can be sold today for $1,400. If the old truck is traded for the new truck, Artistic will have to give $8,600 in cash plus the old truck in exchange. The market value of the new truck is $10,000. The transaction does qualify as a nontaxable exchange.

You are to provide an analysis that shows whether the present value for the new truck will be higher if Artistic sells the old truck and then buys the new one or trades the old truck for the new one. Use a discount rate of 12%, a tax rate of 40%, and a useful life of 6 years. Assume that Artistic expects to use the straight-line depreciation method, and that the half-year provision can be ignored.

(Check figure: For trade = $3,056)

Exercise 8-8
Determining the depreciable base and initial outlay for a nontaxable exchange

Reread the facts that are given in the first paragraph of Exercise 8-7 for Artistic Flowers. Assume that Artistic has decided to trade the old delivery truck for the new one. Answer each of the following questions:

a. What will be the depreciable base?
b. What amount will go in year 0 of the sketch of cash flows as the initial investment?

Exercise 8-9
Comparing NPVs with DDB and SL depreciation

Johnson Myers Pharmaceutical is considering purchasing a new machine that seals bottles of aspirin in an improved tamperproof manner. The seal is not only childproof but also impossible for adults to open on the first try. It costs $85,000 and is expected to be used for 7 years. At the end of 7 years the machine will have a zero disposal value. The recovery period for this type of machinery is 10 years. For simplicity the half-year rule can be ignored.

The cost of capital is 10%, and the tax rate is currently 30%. The accountant expects the tax rate to remain unchanged in the first 2 years of life, but to increase to 45% in the last 5 years, when a different political party is expected to be in the White House.

The market research department feels that the new safety-seal bottle will increase the firm's cash receipts per year by $40,000.

a. Calculate the NPV for the project using the SL method of depreciation.

(Check figure: $54,793)

b. Calculate the NPV using the DDB method, assuming a switch to straight line in year 6.

Exercise 8-10
Calculating the ARR and payback

The Lake State Bank is trying to decide whether or not to install an automatic teller machine (ATM) in its new branch office. The ATM, called Easy Money, has a cost of $20,000. If the machine is purchased, Lake State expects to use it for 4 years and then sell it for $4,500. In addition, if the machine is acquired, it will be necessary to have an extra $5,000 in cash on hand at all times.

The tax rate in all years is expected to be 40%, and the additional cash flow for the bank should be $9,000.

Assume that the recovery period is 7 years, that one-half year of depreciation is taken in the year of purchase, and that a switch to straight line will be taken, if appropriate.

If the DDB method is used to depreciate the machine, what will be the payback period and the accountant's rate of return?

(Check figure: Payback = 3,719; ARR = 12.30%)

PROBLEMS: SET A

Problem A8-1
Determining the NPV for a
new patent

Laurie Cobb is the friend of an inventor who claims to have developed "a better mousetrap." The inventor is in dire need of cash and is willing to sell the rights to the invention to Cobb for $74,000 plus 10% of any fees earned from the patent. Cobb engages a patent attorney to assist her in deciding whether or not to make the purchase. The patent attorney tells Cobb that he will be glad to handle her case and quotes her the following fee schedule:

Cost of registering patent......................	$ 5,000
Costs of incorporating	1,000
Cost of research and consultations..............	25,000

The attorney's fees for research and consultations will be charged to Cobb regardless of the decision concerning the purchase of the patent. The costs of incorporation and registering the patent will be paid only if Cobb decides to make the purchase. The costs of the patent will be amortized over 5 years using the straight-line method.

The inventor claims that he has been approached by a firm that is interested in manufacturing the mousetrap and that is willing to pay the owner of the patent $0.50 for each mousetrap it produces. Projected production for the manufacturer during the next 5 years is as follows:

Year	Production
1	50,000 units
2	60,000 units
3	75,000 units
4	100,000 units
5	100,000 units

In addition, the manufacturer is willing to sign an agreement that binds the firm to buying the patent rights from Cobb for $15,000 in 5 years, regardless of how valuable or worthless the patent may be at that time. If Cobb signs the contract, it will also be binding on her, regardless of the patent's value in 5 years.

The tax rates are expected to be 35% in years 1 and 2 and 40% in years 3 through 5. The cost of capital for Cobb is 12%.

Required

Determine the net present value of the patent. (Note: The guidelines of the Tax Reform Act of 1986 do not apply to intangible assets.)

(Check figure: $20,689)

Problem A8-2
Determining the IRR, ARR,
and payback for Problem
A8-1

Refer to the facts for Laurie Cobb in Problem A8-1, and calculate each of the following:

Required

(Check figure: 20.80%)

1. The internal rate of return
2. The payback period
3. The accountant's rate of return

Problem A8-3
Determining the NPV for a
nontaxable exchange
using DDB depreciation

Land O' Lakes Airlines is considering trading in its fleet of WW II planes (book value: $750,000; market value: $450,000) for a fleet of new planes. The new planes cost $1,500,000, have a useful life of 5 years, and should be sold for $500,000 at the end of their useful lives. If the trade is made, it will be necessary for Land O' Lakes to give $1,050,000 in cash in addition to the old planes.

Land O' Lakes plans to depreciate the planes using a 5-year recovery period with the DDB method.

The additional cash receipts and cash operating costs over the next 5 years are expected to be:

Year	Additional Cash Receipts	Additional Operating Costs
1	$ 280,000	$300,000
2	450,000	325,000
3	650,000	375,000
4	900,000	450,000
5	$1,350,000	600,000

At the beginning of the first and third years, Land O' Lakes expects to conduct extensive advertising campaigns—costing $75,000 and $90,000, respectively. The costs will be deducted in the year they are incurred.

The cost of capital for Land O' Lakes is 10% and the tax rates are expected to be 30% in all 5 years.

Required

Determine the NPV for the new fleet of airplanes.

(Check figure: $37,101)

Problem A8-4
Evaluating the keep-vs.-replace decision in Problem A7-2 (after tax) with NPV, using SL depreciation for both alternatives

This is basically the same as Problem A7-2, except for the additional facts related to tax considerations.

Should We Keep?

The Chapman Contracting Company is considering the replacement of an old steam shovel with a new one. The old steam shovel was purchased 3 years ago for $70,000. It has a remaining book value of $35,000, which will be depreciated over the next $2\frac{1}{2}$ years with the straight-line method. It currently can be sold for $54,000; but if kept until the end of its remaining 4-year useful life, it can be sold for only $6,000.

The new steam shovel will cost $216,000 and will have a 4-year useful life. It will be depreciated with the straight-line method, using the half-year provision and a recovery period of 7 years. At the end of 4 years Chapman expects to be able to sell it for $36,000. The cash operating costs with the new steam shovel should be $650,000 per year, $80,000 lower than the operating costs will be if the old steam shovel is kept. If the old steam shovel is kept, it will need a $6,000 major overhaul immediately and another costing $6,400 in 2 years.

The company's cost of capital is 10%, and the tax rate is 40%.

Required

1. Using the present value method, determine whether the old steam shovel should be kept or replaced. Compute the present values for the keep and replace decisions separately. What is the difference in present values?

[Check figure: Present value for replace = $(1,327,748)]

2. Determine the NPV of the keep-vs.-replace decision using the incremental approach.

Problem A8-5
Expanding the analysis of Problem A8-4 to include the IRR, payback, and ARR

Required

Calculate (1) the IRR, (2) the payback period, and (3) the accountant's rate of return for the Chapman Contracting Company in Problem A8-4.

(Check figure: ARR = 17.724%)

**Problem A8-6
Determining the NPV
using DDB depreciation**

Bubba Karras, an ex-football player is now working for a summer recreation program that is privately funded, and he is trying to convince the board of directors to purchase a used bus to transport youngsters to the summer sports camps. Karras feels that the bus could substantially increase enrollment. The bus costs $3,500 and should last for 5 years. At the end of its useful life, the bus is expected to have a disposal value of $1,000. The additional enrollments are expected to increase cash receipts by $3,000 per year but will necessitate hiring another part-time coach for $1,500 per year. At the end of 2 years it is expected that the bus will need to undergo $500 of repairs in order to last the 3 remaining years.

The bus will be depreciated with the DDB method, based on a 5-year recovery period. One-half year of depreciation will be taken in year 1, and the switch to straight line will take place in year 4.

Assume a 12% cost of capital and a 30% tax rate.

| **Required** |

Using the net present value method, determine whether the bus should or should not be purchased.

(Check figure: NPV = $1,180)

**Problem A8-7
Computing the IRR, ARR,
and payback for Problem
A8-6**

| **Required** |

Refer to the facts given in Problem A8-6. Calculate each of the following:
1. The internal rate of return
2. The accountant's rate of return

(Check figure: 18.00%)

3. The payback period

**Problem A8-8
Calculating the NPV with
SL depreciation**

Tricky Dicky has just been released from jail after serving time for counterfeiting, but unfortunately he has not learned his lesson. As soon as he was released, he dug up his ill-gotten gains from his last venture and went looking for some new action. He was able to find an engraver who was willing to sell him plates for one-dollar bills for $50,000. He also found a high-quality printing press that could be had for another $25,000.

Since he had been convicted on a previous occasion for income tax evasion, he decided it would be best to pay income taxes (at 45%) on whatever he earned. He feels that the printing press and plates should be depreciated with the straight-line method, using the half-year provision. The recovery period is 7 years.

Tricky figures he won't be greedy this time: He will print the bills for only 3 years. At the end of that time he'll sell the printing press and plates for $35,000 and retire until he runs out of money.

In addition to the investment in fixed assets, Tricky realizes it will also be necessary to invest in current assets (paper, ink, etc.) of about $3,000, which will remain outstanding for the full 3 years. His operating costs will be $8 per stack of 100 one-dollar bills, and he expects to fence the money at about 35% of face value. He expects to print 30,000, 40,000, and 50,000 stacks of bills in each of the 3 years, respectively.

Tricky's cost of capital is 20% (higher than you might expect, because of the high-risk factor).

| **Required** |

Determine the NPV for Tricky's proposed operation.

(Check figure: $1,886,564)

PROBLEMS: SET B

Problem B8-1
Calculating the NPV for a copyright

The McGraw McGraw Publishing Company is considering purchasing the rights to "The Jimmy Hoffa Story—I Know Where He Is" from Hoffa's former secretary. The cost of the copyright is a staggering $2,200,000. In addition, McGraw McGraw's attorneys estimate it will cost an additional $500,000 to get a local family to drop its claim to the manuscript.

McGraw McGraw is certain of the public's continuing interest in the story and is willing to take a chance. Conservatively, estimates of future sales are quite encouraging. With the proper promotion in years 1 and 2 ($100,000 in each year, which is fully deductible), net cash receipts from the sale of the book are expected to be the following in the next 5 years:

Year	Net Receipts from Book
1	$200,000
2	350,000
3	900,000
4	450,000
5	100,000

In addition, McGraw McGraw feels that the screen rights can be sold for $2,000,000 at the end of 2 years, all of which will be recognized as income in year 2. Once the television movie is completed, McGraw McGraw expects to receive a royalty on the film's domestic and foreign showings of $1.5 million in year 4 and $0.75 million in year 5.

For tax purposes all costs associated with the copyright will be written off over the next 5 years, using the straight-line method. At the end of 5 years McGraw McGraw expects to sell the copyright for $200,000 to a foreign publisher of paperback novels.

The tax rate is 45% in each year, and the cost of capital is 15%.

| **Required** |

Determine the net present value of the copyright. (Note: The guidelines of the Tax Reform Act of 1986 do not apply to intangibles, such as copyrights.)

(Check figure: $322,026)

Problem B8-2
Calculating the IRR, ARR, and payback for the copyright in Problem B8-1

| **Required** |

Reread the information presented in Problem B8-1. Calculate for the copyright:
1. The internal rate of return

(Check figure: 19.50%)

2. The payback period
3. The accountant's rate of return

(Check figure: 14.46%)

Problem B8-3
Evaluating a nontaxable exchange with NPV, using SL depreciation

Plaid Cabs is planning to buy 15 new cabs by trading in the same number of old ones. The total cost of the new cabs is $150,000, and the old cabs are currently worth $30,000 (with a book value of $35,000). Plaid will sign a promissory note for the difference in the cost of the new cabs and the fair market value of the old ones. The new cabs have a useful life of 3 years, and they can be sold for $35,000 at the end of that time. Plaid expects to depreciate the cabs with the straight-line method. The recovery period is 5 years.

The additional net cash receipts from operating the cabs during the next 3 years are expected to be:

Year	Additional Cash Receipts
1	$100,000
2	80,000
3	60,000

Plaid expects to have major overhauls costing $10,000 at the beginning of the second year, and it plans to spend $1,500 at the end of year 3 to get the cabs in shape before they are sold. The cost of capital for Plaid is 12%, and the tax rates are expected to be 30% in each year.

Required

Determine the NPV for the 15 new cabs.

(Check figure: $32,065)

Problem B8-4
Calculating the aftertax NPV for the keep-vs.- replace decision in Problem B7-2, using both DDB and SL

This is basically the same as Problem B7-2, but there are a few additional facts related to income tax considerations.

The Hogan Construction Company is considering the replacement of an old crane with a new one. The old crane was purchased 5 years ago for $100,000 and has a remaining book value of $50,000 (using the SL method of depreciation). It can be sold for $48,000 if disposed of at the present time or for $9,000 if disposed of at the end of its 5-year remaining useful life.

The new crane will cost $200,000 and is expected to have a $12,000 disposal value in 5 years. Hogan will use the DDB method for the new crane. (For simplicity, however, the half-year provision and the switch to straight line will not be used.) Assume that the recovery period is 7 years.

The cash operating costs for the old and new crane will be $250,000 and $200,000 per year, respectively. If the old crane is kept, it will require a major repair costing $10,000 at the end of 2 years.

The company's cost of capital is 8%. The income tax rates should be 30% for all 5 years.

Required

1. Using the present value method, determine whether the old crane should be kept or replaced. Compute the present values for the keep and replace decisions separately.
2. Using the incremental approach, calculate the NPV for the keep-vs.-replace decision.

(Check figure: Net present value = $32,276)

Problem B8-5
Calculating the IRR, payback, and ARR for Problem B8-4

Required

Calculate (1) the IRR, (2) the payback period, and (3) the accountant's rate of return for the Hogan Company in Problem B8-4.

(Check figure: IRR = 16.0%)

Problem B8-6
Determining the NPV using DDB depreciation

Billie Joe Everrett, a tennis star for 25 years, has just retired and opened a tennis complex. One thing that Everrett would like to purchase is a pitching machine—which automatically tosses balls to players every few seconds, at a variety of speeds, spins, and trajectories. The machine costs $3,000 and is expected to last for 6 years. At the end of its useful life it should have a disposal value of $300. In addition to the investment in the machine, it will also be necessary to invest about $500 in tennis balls each year, all of which will be thrown away when they lose their bounce.

The machine is expected to generate additional cash receipts for the complex of $5,750 per year. It will necessitate the addition of one part-time employee at an annual salary of $4,000. Finally, an overhaul costing $400 will probably be required at the beginning of year 5.

Everrett will use the straight-line method of depreciation. The recovery period is 7 years, and the half-year provision will be used.

The cost of capital is 12%, and the tax rate is 40%.

| Required |

Using the net present value method, determine whether or not the pitching machine should be purchased.

(Check figure: NPV = $780)

Problem B8-7
Calculating the IRR,
payback, and ARR for the
facts given in Problem B8-6

| Required |

Determine: (1) the internal rate of return, (2) the payback period, and (3) the accountant's rate of return for Billie Joe Everrett in Problem B8-6.

(Check figure: IRR = 14.6%)

Problem B8-8
Calculating the NPV using
DDB depreciation

The Death Valley Motel operates in a small suburb outside of Las Vegas. The owner has decided to place a slot machine in each room. Currently, there are 100 rooms; but in 2 years, when a new wing is built, the room capacity will double. Each slot machine costs $750 at the present time, will have a 5-year life, and will have a $50 disposal value in 5 years when the owner hopes to sell the motel and all its furnishings to a conglomerate such as MBM Pictures. The owner feels that by that time the conglomerate will be interested in opening a branch motel in the suburbs and that the Death Valley Motel will be an ideal purchase. The slot machines that will be purchased in 2 years will cost 10% more than the ones purchased today; but when they are sold 5 years from now (after only 3 years of use), their disposal value will be $450 per slot machine.

In addition to the investment in depreciable assets, it will also be necessary for the motel to invest $250 in quarters in each machine and to maintain that balance throughout the next 5 years.

The Death Valley Motel plans to depreciate the original purchase of slot machines with the DDB method, over 5 years; and the second purchase for 3 years; the recovery period is 7 years; the half-year provision will be used; and the switch to straight line will be made at the appropriate time.

The slot machines are expected to generate the following cash receipts in each of the five years:

1. $50,000 **4.** $125,000
2. $60,000 **5.** $150,000
3. $125,000

The tax rates are expected to remain at 30% during the next 5 years, and the motel's cost of capital will be 15%.

| Required |

Determine the net present value for the investment in slot machines.

(Check figure: $110,735)

The Planning and Control of Operations in the Short Run

Part Four begins with a discussion of the master budget in Chapter 9. The *master budget* is a comprehensive budget that recognizes the relationships among the interacting activities of different departments within an organization and combines the individual budgets of the departments into a harmonious composite for the firm as a whole. It is prepared before a period begins and is based upon the most likely level of activity within the near future. It is the quantitative expression of management's plans.

Once the plan for an organization is implemented and monitored by management, it is up to the accountant to gather feedback about the results of operations during the period just completed. This feedback is reported to management in a *performance report*. The report spotlights the major differences between actual and budgeted results that it would be cost-effective to investigate.

The foundation of a good control system is the assignment of responsibility to individuals within units of activity called *responsibility centers*. There are three types of responsibility centers—cost centers, profit centers, and investment centers. In Chapter 10 we'll be concerned only with cost centers, looking primarily at the producing departments within a manufacturing concern. We'll show you how to prepare flexible budgets (rather than the master budget) that are compared to actual results within the performance report. Then we'll discuss how to use standard costs in conjunction with flexible budgets to evaluate the efficiency of each department.

In Chapter 11 we'll discuss profit centers and investment centers. You'll see how the contribution margin format for an income statement—which we discussed in Chapters 4 through 6 as a planning tool—can also be used as part of the control process to evaluate the performance of profit centers. In addition, you'll learn how to use ROI—return on investment—to evaluate the performance of investment centers.

CHAPTER 9

The Master Budget

When you have finished studying this chapter, you should have learned:

- What a master budget is and how it is used to assist management in the planning function
- Who the participants are in the budgetary process
- How important the sales forecast is in preparing the master budget
- What the different types of operating budgets and financial budgets are
- How the historical cost balance sheet relates to the master budget
- How to prepare a master budget for both a manufacturer and a retailer

In almost every business organization there are a number of different activities going on at the same time, such as selling, producing, purchasing, distributing, and financing. All these activities are interrelated in such a way that together they affect the attainment of the organization's objectives. Thus, planning for an entire organization means planning for each of the specific activities within it. Further, it means planning the individual activities to achieve goals that lead smoothly to the attainment of overall organization goals as well.

REASONS TO USE BUDGETS

There are more reasons to use budgets than not to use budgets

People who don't understand the purposes of budgets and how to use them often object to them on these grounds:

> "Budgets are too costly."

> "My firm is small and uncomplicated. I can do all my planning in my head."

> "The employees don't respond well to the pressure imposed on them by budgets."

Although there may be some basis for these objections, budgets do offer advantages and benefits that should far outweigh any costs or disadvantages, regardless of the type and size of firm.

[365]

Four benefits that budgets can provide for all firms are (1) better planning, (2) control of performance, (3) communication and coordination, and (4) employee motivation.

Better Planning

Budgets help managers plan

Budgets indicate to management (1) the amount of profit the firm is expected to have and (2) the resources that are expected to be generated or used during the forthcoming budget periods. When changes from normal operating activities are being considered, a budget can also inform management of the consequences of alternative courses of action, providing a basis for deciding which will be the best alternative. Without a budget management can only hope that it is going in the best direction; it has little idea of what the ultimate results will be.

Managers who prepare a budget for the first time usually are surprised by what they learn about the group they manage and its activities. For example, the sales manager may learn that the average collection period for sales to customers is 120 days for items sold with credit terms of 2/10, n/30. A production manager may find out that the new machine which is so badly needed may not generate enough cash flows over the useful life to pay for itself. Both of these managers may realize that they couldn't plan as well in their heads as they could with a written budget. As the president of the Soso Toy Company finds out in Example 9-1, there are many complications to keep track of when planning and the best way to anticipate potential pitfalls is through a budget.

Example 9-1

THE SOSO TOY COMPANY

Molly McGuire, the president of the Soso Toy Company, plans to modify one of the company's machines during March in order to produce playing boards for a new game, Oligopoly. She expects sales to be high in March and April and assumes the cash balance will be adequate to pay for the March modifications.

The controller, Budd Jett, is not as confident of the availability of cash during March and April and decides to prepare a budget for the first 6 months of the year. The budget indicates that although revenues and profits will be high, just as Molly assumes, the cash flow does not look good. Past collection experience indicates a long lag between sales and collections. In addition, Soso pays for all its purchases and acquisitions immediately. As a result, much more cash will be going out in March and April than will be coming in.

Control of Performance

Budgets help managers control

In many organizations, control systems are developed to evaluate the actual performance of employees on the basis of some predetermined measure of what their performance is expected to accomplish. The budget is an integral part of such a system since it represents the standard against which actual performance is compared. The performance report, prepared by the accountant, shows the actual results, the budgeted results, and any differences (referred to as *variances*) between actual and budget. Any significant variances are noted and analyzed in an attempt to identify what caused them. Once the cause is identified, the appropriate remedy can be determined and set into action in an attempt to shrink these differences between actual and budget during the next performance report period.

If the expectations in the budget are communicated to all concerned at the beginning of a period, the employees will know exactly what is expected of them and will understand the basis for their evaluation at the end of the period.

The type of budget used in a performance report for *controlling operations* is called a *flexible budget,* which we will cover in detail in the next chapter. For now, we will continue to be concerned with the master budget, a tool used by accountants to assist in the *planning of operations.*

Communication and Coordination

Budgets provide communication and coordination

The overall goals of the organization must be communicated to the manager of each department within the organization. The overall goals must be understood by the middle- and lower-level managers and accepted by them as consistent with their own goals.

If the managers of different departments believe that by helping to attain the company's goals they also accomplish their own goals, the chances are good that the efforts, activities, and goals of all managers will be coordinated toward achieving the goals of the organization. If each department is interested only in its own performance, all the departments may become competitive rather than cooperative, and the organization as a whole may suffer.

Once the organization's overall goals have been communicated to all departments, the manager of each department is responsible for the budget of that department and for coordinating that budget with the budgets of the other departments. Each individual budget becomes an integral part of the budget for the organization as a whole.

If the organization does not prepare a budget, the manager of each department might not consider the effects of implementing the plans for the department's goals on the attainment of the goals of other departments and on the goals of the organization as a whole.

Employee Motivation

Budgets motivate— hopefully in a constructive manner

Some common doubts about whether a budget motivates employees toward an organization's goals are:

1. Budgets only pinpoint failures and trouble spots.

2. Budgets express the unrealistic expectations of management.

3. Budgets disregard the human factors within an organization.

4. Budgets cause accountants to find too much enjoyment in detecting the mistakes of others.

Where budgets can truly be characterized by these things and little else, surely there will be unnecessary pressure on managers, and they, as well as their personnel, will suffer poor morale and inefficiency. However, where these problems do exist, they are caused by the people implementing the budget—not by the budget itself. With the right atmosphere the budget can be a positive influence in motivating employees toward achieving company goals. For this positive atmosphere to exist, the budget must first have the complete support of top-level management. Next, top-level managers must convince middle- and lower-level managers that (1) the budgetary process is essential to the attainment of company goals; (2) the goals of each unit within the organization are an integral part of the overall goals; and (3) the goals are realistic and attainable.[1]

---

[1] Robert N. Anthony and Glenn A. Welsch, *Fundamentals of Management Accounting.* (Homewood, Ill.: Richard D. Irwin, Inc., 1977), p. 491.

PLAN? WHAT PLAN?

Although there are quite a few good reasons for most organizations to participate in the planning process and to be supportive of the budgetary process, not everyone seems to agree. There are numerous good examples of hot companies that had a good idea that later turned out successful, but never had a plan—such companies as David's Cookies, Banana Republic and Cuisinart. Another firm without a plan is one of the most devoutly antiplan companies around. The company is Newman's Own—which was co-founded by actor Paul Newman and author A. E. Hotchner.

"The company, which makes spaghetti sauce, salad dressing and popcorn, didn't have a plan when it was founded in 1982; it doesn't have a formal plan now, despite the fact that 1985 sales were $24 million, up from $15 million the year before. The founders share an almost philosophical aversion to planning," says Hotchner.

"That's really the nature of the lives that we have led," he says. "There's been no plan. . . . When you begin to work things out with a slide rule, you take the fun out of it. You just fly by the seat of your pants and hope you don't crash." . . .

The founders, however, have a more casual outlook than most entrepreneurs can afford. "We don't care whether the market growth is 25%, or 12%, as long as we stay on the black side of the ledger," says Hotchner.

When asked what Newman's Own future holds, Hotchner replied that, "We have no idea what we're going to do next, or whether we'll ever have another product."

Source: Erik Larson, "The Best-Laid Plans," *INC.,* February 1987, p. 62. Reprinted with permission. Copyright © 1987 by INC. Publishing Company, 38 Commercial Wharf, Boston, Mass., 02110.

Just because some companies, however, are able to manage by the seat of their pants, have no need to plan, and wouldn't use a budget if they did plan, does not mean it's a good idea to use their experiences as a role model. The reasons we discussed in the text for using budgets apply to most organizations and it would be foolish to take the same attitude as someone whose main hope is that he doesn't crash.

THE MASTER BUDGET

The master budget is a comprehensive budget for the entire firm

The **master budget** is a comprehensive budget that expresses the overall business plan for the whole organization for a period covering 1 year or less. The master budget:

1. Recognizes the relationships among the interacting activities of the departments within the organization

2. Summarizes the individual budgets of these departments

3. Combines the individual budgets into a harmonious composite for the firm as a whole

The master budget actually consists of two types of budgets: (1) operating budgets and (2) financial budgets.

Operating budgets

Operating budgets express the expected results of the firm's operations during the budget period. Operating budgets contain expectations of "when" and "how much" with respect to such things as revenues, expenses, and net income. The typical schedules and statements included in the operating budget are:

Operating Budget

■ The sales forecast

■ The production budget (only for a manufacturer)

■ The selling and administrative expenses budget

■ The budgeted income statement

■ The budgeted retained earnings statement

Financial budgets

Financial budgets include statements that report on the projected sources of cash and other resources used in operations, the uses of that cash and other resources, and, of course, the ending balances in cash and other resources. This category is composed of:

- The budgeted statement of cash receipts and disbursements
- The budgeted balance sheet

PARTICIPANTS IN THE BUDGETARY PROCESS

All areas of an organization participate in budget preparation

Managers at all levels in an organization must actively participate in preparing the master budget if it is to be a truly useful tool. The major source of information in the budget is supplied by the departments to which the budgets apply. Thus, sales managers, production supervisors, and purchasing agents are as involved in the budgetary process as are the accounting department personnel and top-level company executives.

Most larger organizations have a **budget committee,** composed of top executives of the different divisions or departments of the company. A budget director and the budget committee provide guidance and coordination as the budget is prepared. Also, the budget committee makes sure:

1. There are guidelines for preparing the budget.
2. These guidelines are communicated to and followed by the people who prepare the budget.
3. Any conflicts among departments regarding their own goals or those of the organization are resolved.
4. The budget package is completed and promptly submitted to the president.

The accountant's role in the budget process

The **budget director** is the member of the budget committee responsible for much of the mechanical compilation of the budget; that is, he or she develops the many schedules and statements that make up the master budget. The budget director — who is probably an accountant serving on the controller's staff — deals directly with the managers of different departments by:

1. Providing them with useful historical data to assist in their estimates for the coming period
2. Making computations based on their estimates
3. Combining the budgets of the individual subunits into a complete and integrated package — the budget package[2]

PREPARING THE MASTER BUDGET

Preparing a master budget is a sequence of many steps, each subsequent step built on the preceding steps. We will take you through a detailed illustration for a typical company, step by step, from beginning to end, explaining the process as we move along and pointing out the specific things for you to learn about preparing any master budget.

[2] *Ibid.*

The illustration for the Underhill Company (see Example 9-2) begins with:

1. The company's balance sheet on the day before the master budget period begins (which becomes the beginning balance sheet for the budget period)
2. Predictions of activity for the forthcoming budget period
3. Other relevant information describing the company's policies and expectations — such as sales terms, collection experience, desired ending inventories, and minimum cash balances

The illustration then continues with the preparation of the following supporting schedules in the sequence listed:

1. The sales forecast
2. The schedule of cash collections
3. The production budget
4. Costs of production
5. Purchases
6. Cost of goods sold expense
7. Selling and administrative expenses

Finally, based on the information in these schedules, the illustration concludes with the budgets for:

- The statement of cash receipts and disbursements
- The income statement and retained earnings statement
- The balance sheet

The master budget process begins with a balance sheet for the first day of the budget period. It then proceeds through numerous budgeted schedules and statements until it finishes with a budgeted balance sheet for the last day of the budget period.

The illustration we will discuss is for a manufacturing firm rather than a service firm or a merchandising firm. Once you know how to develop the budgetary process for a manufacturer, it is not difficult to adapt what you have learned to other types of organizations. As we proceed through the example, we will specify and explain the steps that are different for an organization that doesn't produce the product it sells. At the end of the chapter we have a self-study problem for a retailer that you will want to work through.

The underlying principles of financial accounting that you learned in your financial accounting course apply just as well to the preparation of budgeted financial statements as they do to the preparation of historical financial statements. The only difference is that budgeted statements portray what we expect in the future, whereas historical statements show what actually happened in the past. Budgeted statements involve a great deal of subjectivity and uncertainty; historical statements deal with more factual and objective evidence.

The Underhill Company

*Read the facts carefully
before you look at the
schedules that follow*

The remainder of this chapter involves the preparation of a master budget for the Underhill Company. Read carefully the facts about Underhill that we give you in Example 9-2. Then proceed carefully through each of the schedules and statements that follow. It is important for you to understand each step before you proceed to the next.

Example 9-2

THE UNDERHILL COMPANY

The Underhill Company produces a good luck charm requiring a single raw material. Its controller, Kelly Hernandez, has decided to prepare a master budget for the first quarter of 1988. She starts with the balance sheet for Dec. 31, 1987, shown in Exhibit 9-1.

EXHIBIT 9-1
This is the balance sheet on Dec. 31, 1987 — at the end of the year preceding the master budget period. The last step in the master budget will be another balance sheet — the budgeted balance sheet for Mar. 31, 1988.

UNDERHILL COMPANY Balance Sheet December 31, 1987			
Assets		**Liabilities**	
Cash	$ 102,250	Accounts Payable..........	$ 46,000
Accounts Receivable	75,000	Dividends Payable	80,000
Inventories:		Total Liabilities	$126,000
Raw Materials..........	8,000		
Finished Goods	75,000*	**Stockholders' Equity**	
Machinery...............	420,000	Capital Stock..............	$200,000
Accumulated Depreciation .	(126,000)	Retained Earnings	228,250
		Total Stockholders' Equity..	$428,250
		Total Liabilities and	
Total Assets...............	$ 554,250	Stockholders' Equity	$554,250

* 5,000 units at $15/unit.

Next, the vice president of sales provides Hernandez with his best prediction of sales for the first 4 months of 1988, as shown below:

	Unit Sales	Dollar Sales
January	10,000	$250,000
February	20,000	500,000
March	24,000	600,000
April..	18,000	450,000

*Sales predictions and
collection experience*

Sales for December 1987 were 8,000 units, totaling $200,000. During the past year cash sales averaged 25% of total sales. In addition, one-half of the credit sales were typically collected in the month of sale, and the remaining one-half in the month following the sale. These past averages are expected to pertain to Quarter I, 1988, as well. No discounts are offered by the company, and bad debts are not expected to occur.

Minimum inventories

Hernandez feels it is necessary to maintain ending inventories of both finished goods and raw materials as a safety measure against a sudden surge in demand for the charms. The desired month-end inventory of finished goods will be equal to 50% of the following month's unit sales. Starting in January the desired ending inventory for raw materials will be $10,000 each month.

Hernandez estimates the costs of production to be:

Costs of production

Direct Materials	$5 per unit
Direct Labor	$6 per unit
Variable Overhead	$3 per unit
Fixed Overhead	$15,000 per month

All units started in production each month will be completed during that period, and the beginning and ending balances in work-in-process inventory are assumed to be zero. All labor and overhead costs for the production department (other than depreciation on production machinery—totaling $2,000 per month) will be paid when incurred.

All purchases are on account

All purchases will be made on account and will be paid in full in the month following purchase.

S & A

The selling and administrative expenses are expected to be $2 per unit variable and $8,000 per month fixed. These expenses (other than the depreciation of office equipment in the selling and administrative departments—totaling $1,500 per month) will be paid in the month incurred.

Dividends

Dividends of $80,000 are paid during the first month of each quarter, after being declared in the previous month.

Machine purchase

In January the company plans to purchase a new machine costing $30,000. The $2,000 of depreciation given previously for the production overhead includes expected depreciation on this machine.

Cash balance and loans

The treasurer, Gus LaBretta, recommends that a minimum cash balance of $50,000 be maintained during each month. Whenever the company anticipates falling below that amount, a short-term loan will be taken out at the beginning of that month. The loan will be repaid when cash becomes available. Interest will accrue at 14% of the unpaid balance and will be paid when the principal is repaid (based on the amount of principal repaid). All repayments take place at the end of the month.

Relationship of the Dec. 31, 1987, Balance Sheet to the 1988 Budgets

Every item in the Dec. 31, 1987, balance sheet is needed in preparing the master budget

The balance sheet (Exhibit 9-1) on Dec. 31, 1987, serves as the starting point for the anticipated activities of 1988. Each account balance given in the Dec. 31, 1987, balance sheet is in some way employed in the budgeted schedules and statements for 1988.

For example, the cash balance of $102,250 on Dec. 31, 1987, becomes the Jan. 1, 1988, cash balance to start off the cash receipts and disbursements budget for the forthcoming quarter. (Take a peek at Exhibit 9-12, beginning cash balance for January—line 1.) Similarly, the $8,000 balance on Dec. 31, 1987, for raw materials inventory becomes the starting point, or the beginning inventory, in the schedule of purchases budgeted for January 1988 (see Exhibit 9-8 on page 382—line 4). All the balances in the accounts on the Dec. 31, 1987, balance sheet are used in a similar way in preparing the schedules and statements that eventually form the master budget.

With this brief introduction, we will now help you to become more familiar with each of the schedules and statements that make up the master budget.

The Operating Budgets

The Sales Forecast

The cornerstone of all budgeting: the sales forecast

The first step in the budget process is the *sales forecast*—a prediction of expected sales throughout the budget period. The responsibility for developing the sales forecast is assigned to a top-level marketing officer. The sales forecast is considered the starting point for all budgeting (whether it be for a manufacturer or a nonmanufacturer) because all the other budgets—that is, nearly all the elements of the master budget—depend on it.

Figure 9-1 shows the relationships among the schedules and statements comprising the master budget and the sequence in which each is developed. Notice that none

FIGURE 9-1   The Master Budget: The Relationship of the Parts That Make Up the Whole
Every step we take in preparing the master budget depends on the sales forecast (step 1). Each step we take leads toward the final product—the budgeted financial statements (steps 8 to 11).

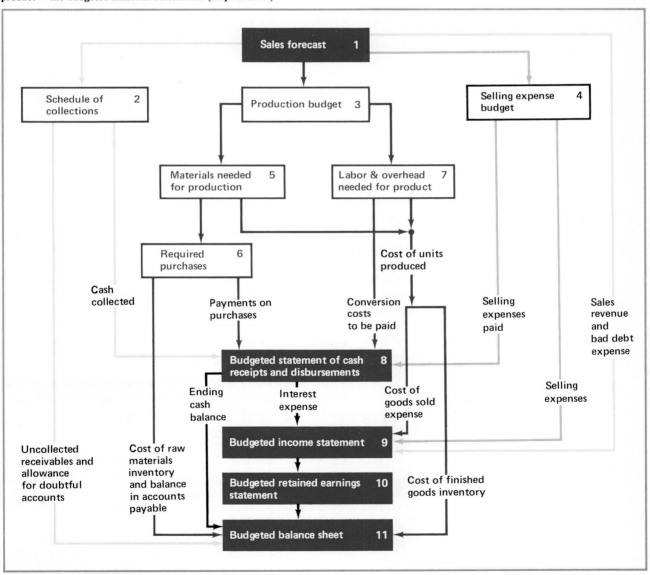

THE CORNERSTONE OF ALL BUDGETING MAY BE A LITTLE SHAKY

The sales forecast is considered the cornerstone — the starting point for all budgeting. As a result the entire master budget depends upon it. Unfortunately the cornerstone itself depends upon a future which is uncertain at best. Many feel that sales forecasts are the weakest feature of most business plans. A fortune teller with tea leaves and a copy of Lotus 1-2-3 could do better. Well maybe scratch the 1-2-3. Lotus Development Corp. which makes 1-2-3, the software tool of choice among entrepreneurs working up their five-year forecasts, had perhaps the most wildly wrong forecast in modern business history. Mitchell D. Kapor, the founder, wrote in his initial plan that he

expected first year sales of about $6 million. Ben Rosen, who invested in the Cambridge, Mass., company, expected the business would take in $3 million. Lotus went right ahead and ignored the plan, posting first-year sales of $53 million.

In 1982, Rosen and partner L. J. Sevin, a couple of lucky guys, invested in a company, then called Gateway Technology Inc. Gateway's plan said the company would make a portable computer compatible with IBM's personal computer and would sell 20,000 machines for $35 million in its first year — "which we didn't believe for a moment," says Rosen. The sales projection for the second year was even more outra-

geous: $198 million. "Can you imagine seeing a business plan like this for a company going head-on against IBM, and projecting $198 million?" he asks. He and Sevin told the fledgling company to scale down its projections.

Gateway later changed its name to Compaq Computer Company. In its first year, sales were actually $111 million. And in its second year sales were a whopping $329 million. So much for sales forecasts.

Source: Erik Larson, "The Best-Laid Plans," *INC.,* February 1987, p. 61. Reprinted with permission. Copyright © 1987 by INC. Publishing Company, 38 Commercial Wharf, Boston, Mass., 02110.

of the steps in the figure can be determined until after the sales forecast (step 1) is developed.[3]

For example, not until the sales are forecast is it possible to determine the number of units that have to be produced (step 3). Then, only after the production budget is prepared, can we estimate the materials needed (step 5), the required purchases (step 6), and the conversion costs (step 7) needed for production.

The schedule of collections (step 2) depends on the sales forecast and so does the selling expense budget (step 4).

The four budgeted financial statements (steps 8 through 11) depend on the estimates in all the preceding budgeted schedules (steps 2 through 7), which, of course, depend on the sales forecast. So everything in a master budget depends on the sales forecast. That's the main thing you should understand from Figure 9-1. As we proceed, we will show you in detail exactly how each of the budgeted schedules and statements develops from the budgets that precede it.

Sales Forecast and Reliability   The accuracy of the sales forecast will determine the reliability of all the other budgeted schedules and statements. As a result, the sales forecast is the most important as well as the most difficult step. It is difficult because future sales are influenced by such diverse factors as:[4]

---

[3] Certain items that are found within the schedules and statements making up the master budget (e.g., depreciation, accumulated depreciation, long-term investments, long-term notes payable, capital stock) are not actually dependent upon the sales forecast, but the completion of the schedules and statements in which they appear is highly dependent upon the sales forecast.

[4] Charles T. Horngren, *Cost Accounting: A Managerial Emphasis,* 5th ed. (Englewood Cliffs, N.J.: Prentice-Hall, 1982), p. 141.

Factors to consider in the sales forecast

- Past sales (last year's, last month's, the same month last year)
- Industry conditions
- Advertising
- GNP and disposable income
- Changing consumer preferences

- Population
- Quality of sales personnel
- Production capacity
- Prediction of sales force
- Government regulations

Not only are these factors often uncontrollable, but it is also difficult to determine which factors will have an influence on sales and to what extent. The sales executive, with the help of others, is expected to consider all these factors and derive, either subjectively or statistically, an accurate prediction of (or one that closely approximates) the sales for each period. This is not an easy task.

Sales are the basis for cash collections

The sales forecast for Quarter I, 1988, for the Underhill Company is shown in Exhibit 9-2 (page 376). The total sales are broken down into cash sales (25%) and credit sales (75%). In addition, Exhibit 9-2 includes the sales for the month of December — because only one-half of the credit sales of that month were collected in 1987, the other one-half will be collected in January 1988. We need to show where the cash collections (shown in Exhibit 9-3) in January come from — some will come from January's sales and some will come from December's sales.

The arrows from the sales forecast (Exhibit 9-2) to the ***cash collections budget*** (Exhibit 9-3) point out the month in which each month's sales are expected to be collected. For example, in January the sales of $250,000 are $62,500 cash and $187,500 credit. The cash sales are obviously collected in the month of sale (shown by the dark blue arrow). Based on the facts given in Example 9-2, 50% of the credit sales are collected in the month of sale, with the balance collected in the following month. Therefore, $93,750 (50% of the credit sales in January) is collected in January (the black arrow). The remaining $93,750 is collected in February (the light gray arrow).

The cash collections for each month are composed of three parts. For January they are:

1. The cash sales of the month, $62,500

2. The collection of 50% of December's credit sales, $75,000

3. The collection of 50% of January's credit sales, $93,750

The total of these three specific cash collections is $231,250 for January. The total of these categories of collections is $406,250 for February and $562,500 for March. These totals, representing expected cash receipts each month during the first quarter, are transferred to the second line of the budgeted statement of cash receipts and disbursements (Exhibit 9-12). When the cash receipts are added to the beginning cash balance ($102,250 for January), the sum of the two is the total cash available before current financing (line 3 in Exhibit 9-12). Hopefully, this total cash available is large enough to cover the cash needs for the month. If not, financing will need to be arranged.

Budgeted statement of cash receipts and disbursements

The budgeted statement of cash receipts and disbursements provides a formal listing of the different types of budgeted cash receipts and disbursements for each month of the quarter and the expected balance in cash at the end of each month. In essence, it shows how the T-account for cash is expected to change in the coming

EXHIBIT 9-2
Past and Future Sales

The sales are 25% cash and 75% credit. Total forecasted sales for Quarter I are $1,350,000.

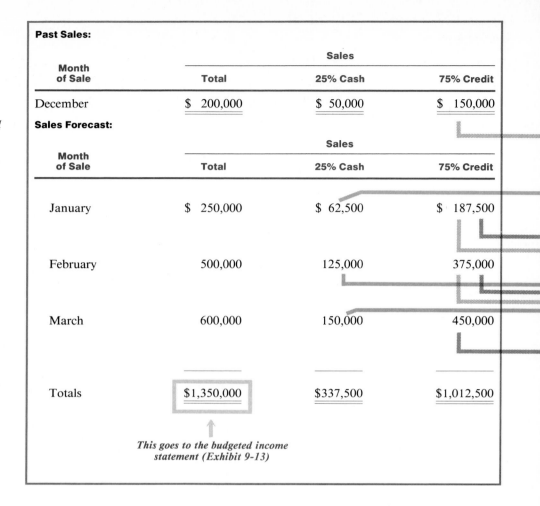

Past Sales:

Month of Sale	Total	25% Cash	75% Credit
		Sales	
December	$ 200,000	$ 50,000	$ 150,000

Sales Forecast:

Month of Sale	Total	25% Cash	75% Credit
		Sales	
January	$ 250,000	$ 62,500	$ 187,500
February	500,000	125,000	375,000
March	600,000	150,000	450,000
Totals	$1,350,000	$337,500	$1,012,500

This goes to the budgeted income statement (Exhibit 9-13)

months. The expected debits to the Cash account are represented by the budgeted cash receipts, and the expected credits are represented by the budgeted cash disbursements:

The budgeted statement of cash receipts and disbursements represents the changes expected to take place in the Cash T-account

Cash	
Beginning balance Plus budgeted: Cash collections Issuance of stock Sale of assets Financing with debt Etc.	Less budgeted: Payments for purchases Payments for manufacturing costs Payments for selling and administrative expenses Purchase of fixed assets Repayments of financing Cash dividends Etc.
Equals: ending balance	

EXHIBIT 9-3
Budgeted Schedule of Cash Collections: Quarter I, 1988

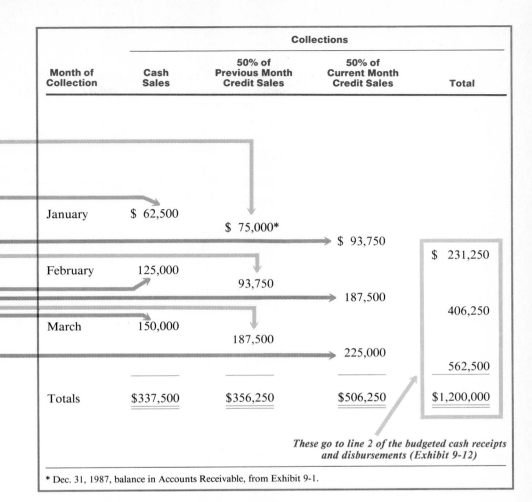

Month of Collection	Cash Sales	50% of Previous Month Credit Sales	50% of Current Month Credit Sales	Total
January	$ 62,500	$ 75,000*		
			$ 93,750	$ 231,250
February	125,000	93,750		
			187,500	406,250
March	150,000	187,500		
			225,000	562,500
Totals	$337,500	$356,250	$506,250	$1,200,000

These go to line 2 of the budgeted cash receipts and disbursements (Exhibit 9-12)

* Dec. 31, 1987, balance in Accounts Receivable, from Exhibit 9-1.

Although budgeted income statements and budgeted balance sheets can be prepared monthly, *for simplicity these statements are being prepared only on a quarterly basis* in this illustration.

The total forecasted sales for the quarter, $1,350,000, is transferred to the first line in the budgeted income statement (Exhibit 9-13).

The balance in Accounts Receivable represents the uncollected credit sales on Mar. 31, 1988. For Underhill this is simply the 50% of March's credit sales that are expected to be collected in April. A useful general format for obtaining a balance in Accounts Receivable is shown in Exhibit 9-4.

EXHIBIT 9-4
Expected Balance in Accounts Receivable: March 31, 1988

Month	Total Sales	× % Credit	= Credit Sales	× % of Credit Sales Uncollected by End of Quarter	= Uncollected Amount at End of Quarter
March	$600,000	.75	$450,000	.50	$225,000

This goes to the budgeted balance sheet (Exhibit 9-15)

The uncollected receivables go on the balance sheet

One-half of the budgeted credit sales of March, $225,000—the uncollected portion—is the budgeted balance in Accounts Receivable on Mar. 31. This amount is transferred to the budgeted balance sheet (line 2 in Exhibit 9-15).

In this example we have assumed that all credit sales would eventually be collected—no bad debts expense was expected. More realistically, we probably should have assumed that some of the accounts are going to go bad. If Underhill had expected some bad debts and had been using an estimation method for bad debts—such as percentage of sales—a few things would be different. First, there would have been an Allowance for Uncollectibles account on the Dec. 31, 1987, balance sheet. Next, we would have some bad debts expense in the budgeted income statement— Exhibit 9-13. Finally, the Allowance for Uncollectibles account would have to be adjusted for the additional estimated bad debts in Quarter I. When you go through the self-study problem at the end of the chapter, you'll get a chance to see just how the schedules and statements would be affected by the complication of having bad debts.

The sales forecast, the cash collections budget, and the schedule for calculating the expected balance in Accounts Receivable are represented by steps 1 and 2 in the flow chart in Figure 9-1. And as you just saw, these budgets are eventually reflected (with light blue lines in Figure 9-1) in the budgeted statement of cash receipts and disbursements (for the cash collections), the budgeted income statement (for the sales revenue), and the budgeted balance sheet (for the ending balance in Accounts Receivable).

The Production Budget

If we were preparing a master budget for a retailer or a wholesaler instead of a manufacturer, we would skip the next few sections and go right to the calculation of purchases on page 382. If the organization were a service company, we would jump directly to the discussion of selling and administrative expenses on page 385. But our example is a manufacturer, so we will now continue on with the next logical step for the manufacturer—the production budget.

The **production budget** indicates the units that need to be produced in each future period to meet the expected sales. In this budget the production department must decide the amount of finished goods inventory that must be on hand at the end of each month during the budget period. Every manufacturer should maintain some minimum level of finished goods inventory to help stabilize production from month to month and to avoid the possibility of losing sales when demand exceeds the available finished goods. Once the required—the *desired*—minimum ending inventory in finished goods has been determined, the production required during each month of the budget period can be calculated by finding the unknown value in the T-account for finished goods inventory:

Finished Goods Inventory	
Beginning balance Plus: Units to be produced	Less: Units to be sold
Equals: Desired ending balance	

Units to be produced is the unknown quantity in the finished goods inventory.

The quantity to be produced (highlighted in blue in the T-account) is the unknown; all other variables are assumed to be known. The required production is determined by figuring out the number of units that must be added to the beginning balance in order to have the desired ending inventory after the expected sales are subtracted. In a more direct manner, the units to be produced can be determined with the following schedule, which is simply a list of the items in the T-account in reverse order:

Determining the units to be produced

Desired minimum ending inventory of finished goods
plus
Unit sales expected for the forthcoming period
equals
Total inventory needs for the forthcoming period
less
Beginning inventory of finished goods
equals
Units to be produced

The minimum ending inventory balance determined to be needed each period may be expressed:

1. In absolute terms, which would be the same amount, regardless of the level of future inventory needs. For example, Underhill may desire an ending inventory of 10,000 units, whether the following month's sales are expected to be 50,000 units or 1,000 units.

2. In relative terms, which would probably be determined as a percentage of sales expected in future months. For example, Underhill may prefer its ending inventory of finished goods always to be at least 50% of the next month's expected unit sales.

Assuming that Underhill decides to use the second policy mentioned above, then on Jan. 31, the company will want its inventory to be at least 50% of unit sales for February. Since the sales for February are expected to be 20,000 units, the inventory of finished goods on Jan. 31 should be at least 10,000 units. The required ending inventories for February and March are determined in a similar manner.

Starting with the figures for the required ending inventory of finished goods each month, the number of units to be produced is determined in Exhibit 9-5 — 15,000 units in January, 22,000 units in February, and 21,000 units in March.

EXHIBIT 9-5   Budgeted Unit Production Report: Quarter I, 1988
On the basis of the forecasted sales and desired minimum ending inventories of finished goods, the units to be produced are determined for each month of Quarter I.

	January	February	March
Desired Minimum Ending Inventory, Finished Goods*	10,000	12,000	9,000
Sales for Month	10,000	20,000	24,000
Total Needs for Month	20,000	32,000	33,000
Beginning Inventory, Finished Goods	5,000†	10,000‡	12,000‡
Units to Be Produced	15,000	22,000	21,000

* 50% of sales (in units) for February, March, and April, respectively.
† Given in the footnote to the Dec. 31, 1987, balance sheet (Exhibit 9-1).
‡ The desired ending inventory of each previous month.

These units are needed in Exhibit 9-6

Budgeted Costs of Production Report

On the basis of the units to be produced each month, as shown in the production report, the budgeted costs of producing the units are determined as shown in Exhibit 9-6.

EXHIBIT 9-6 Budgeted Costs of Production Report: Quarter I, 1988

Starting with the units to be produced (Exhibit 9-5), the budgeted costs of production are calculated for each month. The average cost per unit for the quarter is $14.78.

	January	February	March	Total for the Quarter
Units to Be Produced	15,000	22,000	21,000	58,000
Direct Materials ($5 per unit)	$ 75,000	$110,000	$105,000	$290,000
Direct Labor ($6 per unit)	90,000	132,000	126,000	348,000
Variable Overhead ($3 per unit)	45,000	66,000	63,000	174,000
Fixed Overhead*	15,000	15,000	15,000	45,000
Total Production Costs...........................	$225,000	$323,000	309,000	$857,000
				÷58,000 units
				$ 14.78 /unit

* The $15,000 includes $2,000 of depreciation on production machinery.

The variable production costs are based on the following rates per unit:

Direct Materials...............................	$5
Direct Labor	6
Variable Overhead	3

These per-unit rates are assigned to the budgeted units of production, 15,000, 22,000, and 21,000 for the 3 months of the quarter. The fixed factory overhead assigned to production is expected to be $15,000 per month regardless of activity. For the 3 months combined, the total production costs ($857,000) divided by the total budgeted units of production (58,000) results in an expected average cost per unit produced at $14.78. (In the next section this cost per unit will be assigned to the ending inventory of finished goods to determine the budgeted cost of goods sold expense.)

Budgeted Schedule of Cost of Goods Sold Expense

The cost of goods sold expense predicted for Quarter I is calculated in Exhibit 9-7. The beginning inventory of finished goods, $75,000, was given in the Dec. 31, 1987, balance sheet (Exhibit 9-1). The total costs of production for the quarter come from Exhibit 9-6, and the ending inventory, $133,020, is calculated by applying the FIFO method to the desired ending inventory of 9,000 units from Exhibit 9-5 at the end of March. Under the FIFO method the ending inventory comes from current production, which should have an average cost of $14.78 per unit (Exhibit 9-6). For simplicity a single average for the quarter was determined rather than a different one for each month's production. The cost of the ending inventory is:

$$9,000 \text{ units} \times \$14.78 \text{ per unit} = \$133,020$$

Subtracting the cost of the ending inventory from the total available for sale leaves $798,980, which is the cost of goods sold expense.

Jan. 1 Finished Goods Inventory......................................	$ 75,000
Cost of Production: Quarter I (Exhibit 9-6).........................	857,000
Total Available for Sale	$932,000
Mar. 31 Finished Goods Inventory	133,020
Cost of Goods Sold Expense..	$798,980

This goes on the budgeted balance sheet (Exhibit 9-15)

This goes on line 2 of the budgeted income statement (Exhibit 9-13)

The budgeted cost of goods sold goes on the budgeted income statement

The cost of goods sold expense is subtracted from the sales revenue in the budgeted income statement (Exhibit 9-13), yielding a budgeted gross profit of $551,020. And the ending inventory of finished goods of $133,020 is an asset in the Mar. 31, 1988, budgeted balance sheet (Exhibit 9-15).

Purchases and Payments

A major item included in the budgeted costs of production report (Exhibit 9-6) is the budgeted amount of direct materials needed for each month's production. These estimates enable us to calculate the raw materials that have to be purchased in each period as well as the cash needed to pay for them.

What raw materials we purchase depends on what we need in production

Just as a firm sets a policy regarding the minimum quantity of finished goods inventory it likes to have at the end of each accounting period, so also may that firm decide on a policy about the minimum quantity of raw materials inventory at the end of a period. Knowing what the required—or desired—minimum raw materials balance must be makes it possible to calculate the purchases of raw materials needed to fulfill that balance. Some minimum quantity of raw materials must be kept on hand at all times so that production is not disrupted when the demand to produce finished goods is greater than anticipated.

Once the required ending inventory for raw materials has been determined, the amount of raw materials to be purchased each period can be calculated by finding the unknown value in the T-account for raw materials inventory:

Raw Materials Inventory	
Beginning balance Plus: Units to be purchased	Less: Units used in production
Equals: Desired ending balance	

Purchases is the unknown quantity in raw materials inventory

The quantity to be purchased (highlighted in blue in the T-account) is determined by figuring out the number of units that must be added to the beginning balance in order to have the desired ending inventory after the units expected to be used in production are subtracted. In a more direct manner, the units to be purchased can be determined with the following schedule:

*Determining purchases for
a manufacturer*

> Desired ending inventory of raw materials
> plus
> Raw materials needed for production
> equals
> Total needs for the period
> less
> Beginning inventory of raw materials
> equals
> Required purchases of raw materials

EXHIBIT 9-8   Budgeted Schedule of Purchases: Quarter I, 1988

Notice that the desired ending inventory of one month becomes the beginning inventory of the next month. Also, the desired ending inventory of March goes on the budgeted balance sheet.

	January	February	March
Desired Ending Inventory, raw materials (given in Example 9-2)........	$10,000	$ 10,000	$ 10,000
Materials Needed for Production of Month (Exhibit 9-6)...............	75,000	110,000	105,000
Total Needs.......................................	$85,000	$120,000	$115,000
Beginning Inventory, Raw Materials	8,000	10,000	10,000
Purchases for Month.......................................	$77,000	$110,000	$105,000

*March's ending inventory
goes on the budgeted balance
sheet (Exhibit 9-15)*

*The purchases are needed to
get cash payments (Exhibit 9-9)*

The **budgeted schedule of purchases** for the Underhill Company is provided in Exhibit 9-8. The minimum required ending inventory of raw materials of $10,000 each month was given in Example 9-2. The beginning inventory for January was taken from the Dec. 31, 1987, balance sheet (Exhibit 9-1). Finally, the beginning raw materials inventory for February is the ending inventory for January; and the beginning inventory for March is the ending inventory for February. The expected ending inventory for March of $10,000 is classified as an asset in the budgeted balance sheet on Mar. 31, 1988 (Exhibit 9-15).

The purchases shown in the budgeted schedule of purchases (Exhibit 9-8) are not paid for in the month of purchase. Instead, Underhill typically pays for its purchases in the month following the purchase. The schedule of purchase payments (Exhibit 9-9) indicates what the cash payments will be in each month.

The payments in January, $46,000, are for the purchases of December. Since these purchases were not paid for before Dec. 31, 1987, they appeared as the balance in Accounts Payable on the Dec. 31, 1987, balance sheet (Exhibit 9-1). The cash payments in February and March are for the purchases of January and February. The purchases of March ($105,000) will not be paid for until April, so this $105,000 of unpaid bills represents the balance in Accounts Payable in the Mar. 31, 1988, budgeted balance sheet (Exhibit 9-15).

The cash payments from Exhibit 9-9 are listed on the first line under cash disbursements in the budgeted statement of cash receipts and disbursements (Exhibit 9-12).

EXHIBIT 9-9   Schedule of Purchase Payments: Quarter I, 1988
The purchases are paid for in the following month. The March purchase will be paid for in April—it is an account payable on Mar. 31.

	December	January	February	March	April
		Quarter I			
Purchases	$46,000	$77,000	$110,000	$105,000*	
Payments—in Month Following Purchase		$46,000	$ 77,000	$110,000	$105,000

* On Mar. 31 the unpaid purchases represent the balance in Accounts Payable.

Trace these to line 4 of the budgeted cash receipts and disbursements (Exhibit 9-12)

Determining purchases for a nonmanufacturer

If the Underhill Company were a retailer or wholesaler instead of a manufacturer, the purchases would be for merchandise inventory rather than raw materials inventory. The schedule of purchases for a retailer and a wholesaler is slightly different than for a manufacturer, as shown below:

> Desired ending inventory of merchandise
> plus
> Merchandise needed for current sales
> equals
> Total needs for the period
> less
> Beginning inventory of merchandise
> equals
> Required purchases

Once again, the T-account approach—this time using raw materials inventory—could be employed, just as it was with finished goods and raw materials for the manufacturer.

If the company were a service firm, there would be no purchases because service firms don't have inventories.

In the situation we've been examining for the Underhill Company in Example 9-2, we found that the purchases were dependent on the company policy concerning a desired ending inventory of raw materials. Sometimes the company policy concerning purchases is stated more directly. Instead of specifying a desired ending inventory and calculating purchases as we did in Exhibit 9-8, the company may come up with a policy that specifies that purchases will be based entirely on future sales. For example, the policy may be to purchase in each month enough units to cover the sales of the following month. This situation would actually be a lot easier to deal with than the one we've been examining; all you'd have to do is figure out what the sales are for the period covered by the policy, and then buy that amount 1 month earlier. If you want to see how this works, take a look at the self-study problem for a retailer at the end of this chapter.

Cash Disbursements for Conversion Costs

Depreciation is a noncash item

The conversion costs (direct labor plus fixed and variable factory overhead) listed in the budgeted costs of production report (Exhibit 9-6), with the exception of depreciation, are to be paid for when incurred. Exhibit 9-6 shows $15,000 of fixed factory overhead. This amount includes $2,000 in depreciation costs. But depreciation does not involve a cash outlay. Therefore, the actual cash outlay for fixed factory overhead each month is $13,000, or $2,000 less than the $15,000 shown in the budgeted costs of production report. Exhibit 9-10 lists the monthly budgeted cash payments for conversion costs, which are also listed on the second line under cash disbursements in the budgeted statement of cash receipts and disbursements (Exhibit 9-12).

EXHIBIT 9-10
Budgeted Schedule of Disbursements for Conversion Costs: Quarter I, 1988

	January	February	March
Direct Labor	$ 90,000	$132,000	$126,000
Variable Overhead	45,000	66,000	63,000
Fixed Overhead........................	13,000	13,000	13,000
Total Disbursements	$148,000	$211,000	$202,000

Trace these to line 5 of the budgeted cash receipts and disbursements (Exhibit 9-12)

The budgeted production reports (Exhibits 9-5 and 9-6), the budgeted cost of goods sold expense (Exhibit 9-7), the budgeted schedules of purchases and payments of purchases (Exhibits 9-8 and 9-9), and the budgeted schedule of disbursements for conversion costs (Exhibit 9-10) are represented by steps 1, 3, 5, 6, and 7 in the flow chart for the master budget (Figure 9-1).

As you saw, the budgets in Exhibits 9-5 through 9-10 are also reflected in the budgeted financial statements (shown in Figure 9-1 with dark blue lines). For the budgeted income statement (Exhibit 9-13) we got the budgeted cost of goods sold expense from Exhibit 9-7. For the budgeted statement of cash receipts and disbursements (Exhibit 9-12) we got the budgeted purchase payments from Exhibit 9-9 and the budgeted disbursements for conversion costs from Exhibit 9-10. Finally, for the budgeted balance sheet (Exhibit 9-15) we got the finished goods inventory balance from Exhibit 9-7, the raw materials inventory balance from Exhibit 9-8, and the accounts payable balance from Exhibit 9-9.

Selling and Administrative Expenses

Selling expenses are the costs of promoting, selling, and shipping the product to customers. These costs include a variety of items that can be divided into variable and fixed costs.

Variable selling costs, such as commissions and shipping costs, can be estimated by taking a percentage of the estimated total sales dollars or by multiplying a cost per unit by the number of units sold.

Fixed selling costs include salaries, advertising, rent, and depreciation. They are budgeted at an unchanging amount per month.

Administrative costs are associated with such activities as giving overall direction to the company and providing services for personnel. Although most administrative costs are fixed, some items such as supplies and telephone costs are variable costs.

Both manufacturers and nonmanufacturers have S & A costs

The selling and administrative (S & A) expenses for Underhill are estimated to be $2 per unit variable and $8,000 per month fixed. On the basis of the budgeted sales of

10,000, 20,000, and 24,000 units for the first 3 months of 1988, a budget is prepared for the selling and administrative expenses.

As shown in Exhibit 9-11, the total budgeted expenses for the quarter, $132,000, are transferred to the budgeted income statement (Exhibit 9-13).

Cash disbursements for selling and administrative items, with the exception of depreciation, are made when the expense is incurred. Thus the total expenses for each month, less the $1,500 of depreciation, represent the selling and administrative cash disbursements for each month. These monthly disbursements are also listed on the

EXHIBIT 9-11   Budgeted Schedule of Selling and Administrative Items — Expenses and Disbursements: Quarter I, 1988
Total expenses less $1,500 of depreciation equals total disbursements. Remember, depreciation is a noncash item.

	January	February	March	Total	
Variable*....................	$20,000	$40,000	$48,000	$108,000	*The total expenses go to the budgeted income statement (Exhibit 9-13)*
Fixed	8,000	8,000	8,000	24,000	
Total Expenses..............	$28,000	$48,000	$56,000	$132,000	
Total Disbursements†	$26,500	$46,500	$54,500	$127,500	*The disbursements are found on line 6 of the budgeted cash receipts and disbursements (Exhibit 9-12)*

* $2/unit sold × the number of units sold in each month.
† Total expenses less the $1,500/month for depreciation of office equipment — a noncash item.

third line under cash disbursements in the budgeted statement of cash receipts and disbursements (Exhibit 9-12).

The schedule for selling and administrative items (Exhibit 9-11) is represented by step 4 in the master budget flow chart (Figure 9-1). The gray arrows from step 4 lead to (1) step 9 for the selling and administrative *expenses* that go on the budgeted income statement (Exhibit 9-13) and (2) step 8 for the selling and administrative *disbursements* that go on the budgeted statement of cash receipts and disbursements (Exhibit 9-12).

A Financial Budget: The Statement of Cash Receipts and Disbursements

We have not yet completed all the operating budgets — the budgeted income statement lacks one step and the budgeted retained earnings statement hasn't been started. We cannot complete these operating budgets until we have finished the budgeted cash receipts and disbursements statement — the first of two financial budgets.

The only item missing from the budgeted income statement is interest expense. And we cannot calculate interest expense until we know if any financing is needed during the forthcoming quarter. We find out what financing is necessary in the budgeted statement of cash receipts and disbursements — and only then can we determine interest expense.

The purpose of the **budgeted statement of cash receipts and disbursements** is to show the amount and source of cash inflows and cash outflows expected throughout the budget period and the resulting anticipated cash balances at key times during the budget period. This budget indicates to management when cash receipts will be far in excess of cash disbursements, resulting in large cash balances. In this situation management knows how long the excess cash will be available and must decide how it should be invested to earn maximum returns. The budgeted statement also points out when cash outflows are expected to be much larger than cash receipts, which could lead to seriously low cash balances. This information allows management enough time to arrange financing so that when the day comes to meet payrolls, distribute dividends, and pay creditors, the cash will be available.

The many items to be included in the budgeted statement of cash receipts and disbursements can be arranged in a variety of ways. The general format given below will be employed in this text:

This is the form of the budgeted cash receipts and disbursements statement

---

Beginning cash balance
plus
Cash receipts
equals
Total cash available before current financing
less
Cash needs — cash disbursements plus minimum cash balance
equals
Excess or deficiency of cash
plus
Financing of deficiency
less
Repayments of financing from excess
less
Investment of excess
equals
Ending cash balance

You might want to envision this statement in terms of Figure 9-2. Try to imagine the beginning cash balance as a water level within a bucket. During the budget period this level is increased by cash receipts and decreased by cash disbursements. If the cash receipts during the budget period are greater than the cash disbursements, the water (or cash) level will go up. But if the cash receipts are less than the cash disbursements, the water (or cash) level will go down. When there is a decrease, the level of cash will be somewhere below the beginning level but never below the minimum level.

The budgeted statement of cash receipts and disbursements for the Underhill Company is presented in Exhibit 9-12.

The cash receipts and the first three types of cash disbursements for purchases, conversion costs, and selling and administrative costs have already been discussed. The cash disbursement for the dividends paid in January follows from the December 1987 declaration. If you refer to the balance sheet on Dec. 31, 1987, in Exhibit 9-1, you'll see the $80,000 liability for dividends payable.

The $80,000 of dividends declared in March will be paid in April and therefore do not affect the budgeted statement of cash receipts and disbursements during Quarter I. However, the dividends declared in March do reduce retained earnings (Exhibit 9-14) at that time, and the related liability for the April payment must be included in the Mar. 31, 1988, budgeted balance sheet (Exhibit 9-15).

The cash disbursement of $30,000 is for the January cash purchase of machinery. The depreciation of machinery is not included in this budgeted statement because it is a noncash item. It is included in the budgeted income statement, however, as a part of the cost of goods sold expense and as a part of the selling and administrative expenses.

FIGURE 9-2 The Budgeted Statement of Cash Receipts and Disbursements, Viewed as a Changing Water Level in a Bucket of Cash

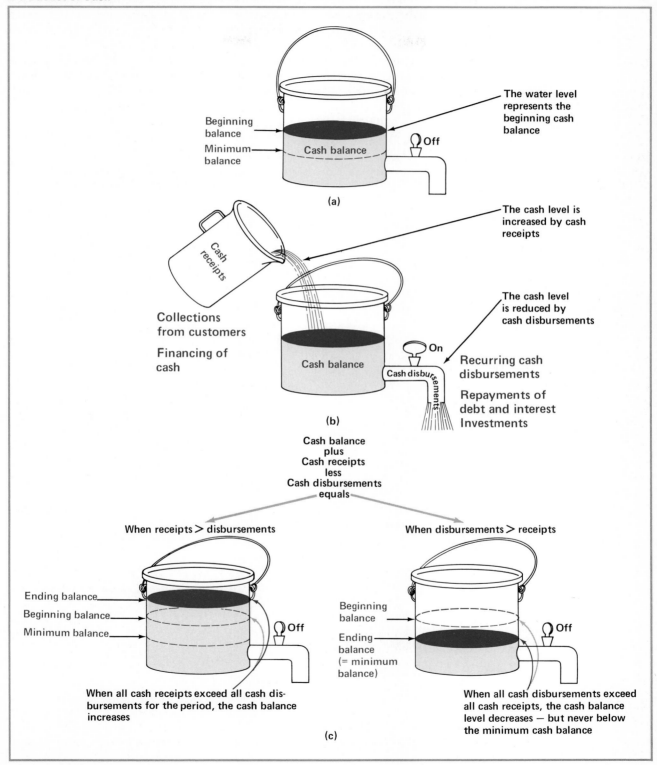

Minimum cash balance is a cash need also

A $47,000 deficiency needs to be financed

Notice in Exhibit 9-12 that the total cash needs are not represented entirely by the cash disbursements. In addition, the minimum desired cash balance is also a cash need. To avoid the possible consequences of being out of cash, it is common to set a minimum cash balance to be maintained throughout each month. If the combination of total cash disbursements plus minimum cash balance exceeds the cash available before financing, then a deficiency arises. In January for Underhill the total cash needs are expected to be $380,500 ($330,500 + $50,000) and the total cash available before financing is expected to be $333,500. The difference of $47,000 is the anticipated deficiency, and financing needs to be arranged well in advance of the occurrence of the actual deficiency.

EXHIBIT 9-12 Budgeted Statement of Cash Receipts and Disbursements: Quarter I, 1988

There is excess cash in February and March but a deficiency in January. Therefore, financing is required in January which should be repaid in February. The interest expense of $1,097 goes on the budgeted income statement, and the Mar. 31 cash balance, $269,653, goes on the budgeted balance sheet.

	January	February	March
Beginning Cash Balance (Exhibit 9-1 for Jan.)	$102,250	$ 50,000	$ 73,653
Cash Receipts (Exhibit 9-3)	231,250	406,250	562,500
Total Cash Available before Current Financing........................	$333,500	$456,250	$636,153
Total Cash Needs:			
Cash Disbursements:			
Purchase Payments (Exhibit 9-9)	$ 46,000	$ 77,000	$110,000
Conversion Costs (Exhibit 9-10).	148,000	211,000	202,000
Selling and Administrative (Exhibit 9-11)	26,500	46,500	54,500
Dividends Paid	80,000	-0-	-0-
Purchase of Machinery	30,000	-0-	-0-
Total Cash Disbursements	$330,500	$334,500	$366,500
Minimum Cash Balance..........	50,000	50,000	50,000
Total Cash Needs............	$380,500	$384,500	$416,500
Excess (Deficiency) of Cash	$ (47,000)	$ 71,750	$219,653
Financing and Repayments:			
Financing of Deficiency	$ 47,000	$ -0-	$ -0-
Repayment of Excess:			
Principal.....................	-0-	(47,000)	-0-
Interest.....................	-0-	(1,097)*	-0-
Total Effects of Financing and Repayments	$ 47,000	$ (48,097)	$ -0-
Ending Cash Balance†..............	$ 50,000	$ 73,653	$269,653

This goes to the budgeted income statement (Exhibit 9-13)

This goes to the budgeted balance sheet (Exhibit 9-15)

* $47,000 × .14 = $6,580/year × $\frac{2}{12}$
           = $1,097 for 2 months

† Minimum cash balance + excess cash − total effects of repayments, or minimum cash balance − deficiency + total effects of financing.

Ending cash for January

If financing of exactly $47,000 is arranged, the actual cash balance at the end of the month should be equal to the minimum cash balance. If the financing is in excess of the deficiency, then the ending cash balance will be the minimum cash balance plus the amount of financing in excess of the deficiency. For example, if Underhill borrows $50,000 instead of $47,000, then the cash balance will be the minimum cash balance of $50,000 plus the $3,000 of financing which is in excess of the deficiency ($50,000 − $47,000).

For February

The expected ending cash balance for January of $50,000 becomes the beginning cash balance for February. During February the cash available before financing is $456,250 ($50,000 + $406,250) and the total cash needs are $384,500 ($334,500 + $50,000) — the difference represents excess cash of $71,750. Of the excess, $47,000 will be used to repay the entire principal of the loan made in January, and $1,097 will be used to pay the interest on the loan. The interest is for 2 months, since the principal was borrowed at the beginning of January and will not be repaid until the end of February. The Feb. 28 cash balance is $73,653. This ending cash balance is found by adding the excess cash that was not used to repay the loan and interest to the minimum cash balance. Remember: When we have excess cash, it means that we have more than the minimum needed. Therefore, if we use only $48,097 of the excess to repay the loan, then we still have $23,653 ($71,750 − $48,097) of the excess remaining — $23,653 in excess of the $50,000 minimum.

For March

In March the excess cash is expected to be $219,653. None of this is needed to repay a loan, so all the excess will be on hand at the end of the month in addition to the $50,000 minimum. Therefore, the ending cash balance will be $269,653 ($219,653 + $50,000).

It would be prudent to invest the excess in March, $219,653 ($269,653 − $50,000), in short-term securities if the firm wants to use all its resources in the most profitable manner.

The Mar. 31 cash balance of $269,653 is transferred to the asset section of the Mar. 31 budgeted balance sheet (Exhibit 9-15). In Figure 9-1 this transfer is shown by the black line going from step 8 to step 11.

The Budgeted Statements of Income and Retained Earnings

Only now can we complete the ***budgeted income statement.*** We see from Exhibit 9-12 that the interest expense is $1,097. (In Figure 9-1 this is represented by the black line going from step 8 to step 9.) When we subtract this amount from the operating income in Exhibit 9-13, we get the net income — $417,923.

EXHIBIT 9-13   Budgeted Income Statement: Quarter I, 1988

The budgeted net income will be transferred to the budgeted statement of retained earnings.

Sales (Exhibit 9-2)..	$1,350,000
Cost of Goods Sold Expense (Exhibit 9-7)................................	798,980
Gross Profit	$ 551,020
Selling and Administrative Expenses (Exhibit 9-11)	132,000
Operating Income...	$ 419,020
Interest Expense (Exhibit 9-12)	1,097
Net Income	$ 417,923 ← *This goes to Exhibit 9-14*

What if we have an unpaid note on Mar. 31?

For a moment let's assume instead that on Mar. 1, 1988, we need to borrow an additional $20,000, which we will not repay until Quarter II. In this situation, is there any additional interest in either the budgeted statement of cash receipts and disbursements or the budgeted income statement?

Since we will not pay the interest on the $20,000 loan until we repay the loan, there won't be any additional interest in the budgeted statement of cash receipts and disbursements. However, since the $20,000 loan will be outstanding for the month of March, there will be 1 month of interest expense. It will be

$$\$20,000 \times .14 \times \tfrac{1}{12} = \$233$$

which we would add to the $1,097 of interest expense already shown on the budgeted income statement. In addition, the Mar. 31 budgeted balance sheet would include a current liability for Notes Payable—$20,000—and a current liability for Interest Payable—$233.

Underhill expects stockholders' equity to increase by $337,923 ($417,923 − $80,000) in Quarter I

From the Dec. 31, 1987, balance sheet (Exhibit 9-1) you can see that the Jan. 1, 1988, balance in Retained Earnings is $228,250. We can now add the budgeted net income for Quarter I, $417,923, to this beginning balance—the total being $646,173, as shown in Exhibit 9-14. From this amount the dividends of $80,000—declared in March—are subtracted. The remainder of $566,173—the Mar. 31 **budgeted balance in retained earnings**—is transferred to the budgeted balance sheet (Exhibit 9-15).

EXHIBIT 9-14 Budgeted Retained Earnings Statement: Quarter I, 1988
The budgeted balance in retained earnings, $566,173, now goes on the budgeted balance sheet.

Retained Earnings, Jan. 1, 1988 (Exhibit 9-1)	$228,250	*This goes to Exhibit 9-15*
Net Income (Exhibit 9-13)	417,923	
	$646,173	
Dividends Declared	80,000	
Retained Earnings, Mar. 31, 1988	$566,173	

The Budgeted Balance Sheet

The **budgeted balance sheet** is shown in Exhibit 9-15. It represents the culmination of the budgeted schedules and statements that we discussed in previous sections. It is the final step (step 11) in the master budget flow chart of Figure 9-1. We have already discussed all the items in the balance sheet with the exception of Capital Stock, Machinery, and Accumulated Depreciation.

Since there are no capital stock transactions expected during Quarter I, the budgeted balance of $200,000 in Capital Stock shown in Exhibit 9-15 is exactly what it is on Dec. 31, 1987 (Exhibit 9-1).

The Dec. 31, 1987, balance in the Machinery account (Exhibit 9-1) is $420,000. With the $30,000 purchase of machinery during January, the balance on Mar. 31 should be $450,000. The balance in Accumulated Depreciation is $126,000 in the Dec. 31, 1987, balance sheet, and during Quarter I the depreciation is:

Production machinery (3 × $2,000/month)	$ 6,000
Selling and administrative machinery (3 × $1,500/month)	4,500
	$10,500

EXHIBIT 9-15
Budgeted Balance Sheet:
March 31, 1988
**This is what Underhill expects
its assets, liabilities, and
stockholders' equity accounts
to look like on Mar. 31, 1988.**

Assets		Liabilities	
Cash (Exhibit 9-12).........	$ 269,653	Accounts Payable (Exhibit 9-9).....................	$105,000
Accounts Receivable (Exhibit 9-4).....................	225,000	Dividends Payable	80,000
Inventories:		Total Liabilities.............	$185,000
Raw Materials (Exhibit 9-8)	10,000		
Finished Goods (Exhibit 9-7)....................	133,020	**Stockholders' Equity**	
		Capital Stock	$200,000
Machinery	450,000	Retained Earnings (Exhibit 9-14)	566,173
Accumulated Depreciation ...	(136,500)	Total Stockholders' Equity ...	$766,173
		Total Liabilities and	
Total Assets	$ 951,173	Stockholders' Equity........	$951,173

When we add the $10,500 of depreciation to the Dec. 31, 1987, balance in Accumulated Depreciation, we get $136,500 — the amount shown in the budgeted balance sheet of Exhibit 9-15.

Notice in Exhibit 9-15 that the total assets, liabilities, and stockholders' equity result in the proper balance of the accounting equation:

$$\textbf{Assets} = \textbf{Liabilities} + \textbf{Stockholders' Equity}$$

$$\$951,173 = \$185,000 + \$766,173$$

$$\$951,173 = \$951,173$$

The process of preparing the master budget started with the balance sheet on Dec. 31, 1987; continued on with numerous budgeted schedules and statements; and finally, now, ends with the preparation of the budgeted balance sheet for Mar. 31, 1988.

The Budget's Use — After the Fact

The budget has been employed thus far to predict the consequences of future expectations. After the budget period has passed, the actual results are collected and compared to the estimates in a budget to decide if the firm operated according to plan. This comparison is made in the performance report. What type of budget to include in the performance report — the master budget or a flexible budget — is discussed in the next chapter.

PROBLEM FOR SELF-STUDY

Throughout this chapter we have discussed the steps in the preparation of a master budget for a manufacturer. Although we did discuss a few differences that you would experience if you were doing the work for a retailer or a wholesaler instead, we thought it might be a good idea for you to have a separate problem for a retailer. This is what you'll now find in the problem for self-study. The fact that the problem is for a different type of organization is not the only difference from Example 9-2 on the Underhill Company. You'll find a few other differences in Example 9-3 on the Elia Sangria Company. So as you go through this problem, you might want to give special attention to the following items:

1. Purchases are calculated differently. Instead of having a policy of maintaining some desired ending inventory, the inventory policy now will simply be to

purchase enough inventory each month to cover the following month's sales.

2. In order to simplify the mechanics, we are going to prepare the master budget for only 2 months instead of for an entire quarter.

3. The company in our example expects to have some bad accounts. Therefore, you'll see Bad Debts Expense on the income statement and Allowance for Bad Debts on the balance sheet.

4. The amount that we have to borrow in the budgeted statement of cash receipts and disbursements is not fully repaid by the end of the budget period. As a result, you'll see Notes Payable and Interest Payable on the budgeted balance sheet; and more interest expense on the income statement than you'll have in the budgeted statement of cash receipts and disbursements.

Let's look now at the master budget for the Elia Sangria Company.

Example 9-3

MASTER BUDGET FOR A RETAILER

The Elia Sangria Company began operation in December of last year, and it expected to have the following balance sheet at year-end:

ELIA SANGRIA COMPANY
Balance Sheet
December 31, 1987

Assets			Liabilities		
Cash		$ 50,000	Accounts Payable		$160,000
Accounts Receivable	$80,000				
Less: Allowance for Bad Debts	(8,000)	72,000	**Stockholders' Equity**		
Merchandise			Capital Stock	$50,000	
Inventory		100,000	Retained Earnings	12,000	62,000
			Total Liabilities and		
Total Assets		$222,000	Stockholders' Equity		$222,000

Elia had sales in December of $100,000, and expects the sales of the first quarter of 1988 to be:

January $150,000
February 200,000
March 225,000

Elia expects that 20% of all sales will be cash sales; of the credit sales 90% will be collected in the month following sale, and the remaining 10% will go uncollected. No bad accounts have been *written off* in December, nor are any expected to be during the first few months of 1988.

The cost of merchandise averages about 60% of retail prices. The company's policy, starting in January, concerning merchandise purchases is to buy enough each month to cover the following month's sales — at cost. December's purchases — since it was the first month in the company's life — were substantially higher than what the new policy requires. All purchases are on credit and will be paid for 1 month after purchase.

The variable operating costs should average 10% of sales, and the fixed operating costs will be $10,000 in January and $6,000 in February. Disbursements for these expenses will be made in the month incurred.

Elia hopes to maintain a minimum cash balance of $20,000. If the cash balance falls below this amount, Elia plans to borrow money to meet its needs, at a rate of 15% per annum. All borrowings and repayments will be made at the beginning and end of the month, respectively. Interest will be paid based on the amount of principal repaid. All borrowings and repayments will be made in multiples of $1,000. The controller for Elia now prepares the following master budget for the first 2 months of 1988:

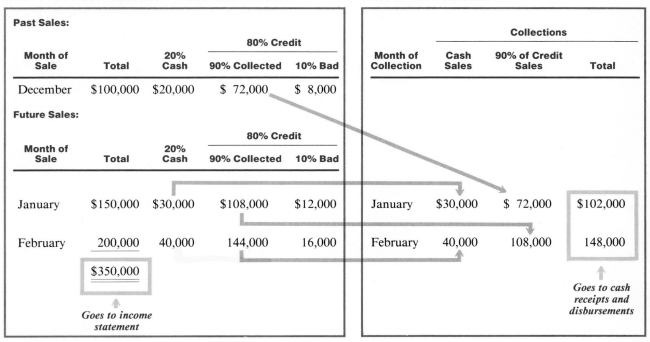

STEP 1 Past and Future Sales — The Sales Forecast

Past Sales:

Month of Sale	Total	20% Cash	80% Credit 90% Collected	80% Credit 10% Bad
December	$100,000	$20,000	$ 72,000	$ 8,000

Future Sales:

Month of Sale	Total	20% Cash	80% Credit 90% Collected	80% Credit 10% Bad
January	$150,000	$30,000	$108,000	$12,000
February	200,000	40,000	144,000	16,000
	$350,000			

Goes to income statement

STEP 2 Cash Collections

Month of Collection	Cash Sales	Collections 90% of Credit Sales	Total
January	$30,000	$ 72,000	$102,000
February	40,000	108,000	148,000

Goes to cash receipts and disbursements

STEP 3 Uncollected Balance in Accounts Receivable, Bad Debts Expense, and Allowance for Uncollectibles

Month	Total Sales	× % Credit =	Credit Sales ×	% of Credit Sales Uncollected by End of February =	Uncollected Amount at End of February	10% Estimated Uncollectible
December	$100,000 ×	.80 =	$ 80,000 ×	.10	=	$ 8,000	$ 8,000
January	$150,000 ×	.80 =	$120,000 ×	.10	=	12,000	12,000
February	$200,000 ×	.80 =	$160,000 ×	1.00	=	160,000	16,000
						$180,000	$36,000

$28,000 goes to income statement — bad debts expense

Goes to balance sheet — accounts receivable

Goes to balance sheet — allowance for uncollectibles

STEP 4   Schedule of Purchases and Payments, and Ending Balance in Inventory

	Month of Sale		
	January	February	March
Sales	$150,000	$200,000	$225,000
Cost of Sales %	×.60	×.60	×.60
Cost of Goods Sold	$ 90,000	$120,000	$135,000

	December	January	February	March
Purchases........................	$160,000*	$120,000	$135,000	← *Accounts payable, Feb. 28, 1988*
Payments.....................................		$160,000	$120,000	$135,000

* Shown as Dec. 31, 1987, balance in Accounts Payable.

Feb. 28 Balance in Merchandise Inventory

Balance, Jan. 1.................................		$100,000
Purchases:		
January...........................	$120,000	
February...........................	135,000	255,000
Total Available		$355,000
Less: Cost of Sales:		
January...........................	$ 90,000	
February...........................	120,000	210,000
Ending Inventory		$145,000

Goes to balance sheet

**STEP 5
Schedule of Variable
Operating Costs —
Expenses and
Disbursements**

	Month of Sale		
	January	February	Total
Sales	$150,000	$200,000	$350,000
Variable Costs %	×.10	×.10	×.10
Variable Operating Costs	$ 15,000	$ 20,000	$ 35,000

*Goes to cash
receipts and
disbursements*   *Goes to
income
statement*

STEP 6 Budgeted Statement of Cash Receipts and Disbursements

	January	February	
Beginning Cash Balance	$50,000	$ 20,000	
Cash Receipts	102,000	148,000	
Total Cash Available Before Current Financing	$152,000	$168,000	
Total Cash Needs:			
Cash Disbursements:			
Purchase Payments	$160,000	$120,000	
Variable Operating Costs	15,000	20,000	
Fixed Operating Costs	10,000	6,000	
Total Cash Disbursements	$185,000	$146,000	
Minimum Cash Balance	20,000	20,000	
Total Cash Needs	$205,000	$166,000	
Excess (Deficiency) of Cash	$ (53,000)	$ 2,000	
Financing and Repayments:			
Financing of Deficiency	$ 53,000	$ -0-	*Net of these two — $52,000 — is in Notes Payable*
Repayment of Excess:			
Principal	-0-	(1,000)	
Interest	-0-	(25)	*Part of interest expense (additional interest associated with $52,000 note payable)*
Total Effects of Financing and Repayments	$ 53,000	$ (1,025)	
Ending Cash Balance	$ 20,000	$ 20,975	*Goes to balance sheet*

* $1,000 \times .15 \times \frac{2}{12} = \$25$

STEP 7
Income Statement

Sales		$350,000	
Cost of Goods Sold		210,000	
Gross Profit		$140,000	
Operating Costs:			
Variable	$35,000		
Fixed	16,000		
Bad Debts Expense	28,000	79,000	
Operating Income		$ 61,000	
Interest Expense		1,325*	
Net Income		$ 59,675	*This amount is added to the beginning balance in Retained Earnings to get the Feb. 28, 1988, balance on the balance sheet*

* See the footnote to the balance sheet.

STEP 8 Balance Sheet

Assets			Liabilities and Stockholders' Equity		
Cash..		$ 20,975	Accounts Payable...............	$135,000	
Accounts Receivable............	$180,000		Notes Payable..................	52,000	
Less: Allowance for Bad Debts....	(36,000)	144,000	Interest Payable.................	1,300*	$188,300
Merchandise Inventory.....................		145,000	Capital Stock...................	$ 50,000	
			Retained Earnings..............	71,675	121,675
Total Assets.............................		$309,975	Total Liabilities and Stockholders' Equity.....		$309,975

* The $1,300 is interest that has accrued on the $52,000 note, at 15%, for 2 months. When added to the amount of interest paid on the payment of $1,000 in principal—$25—we get total interest expense of $1,325, which we find on the income statement.

CHAPTER SUMMARY

The *master budget* provides an overall view of the short-term effects that a forecasted level of sales should have on operating results and financial position. The master budget is made up of *operating budgets* and *financial budgets.*

Operating budgets include schedules and statements associated with the estimated revenues, expenses, and resulting income.

Financial budgets report on the sources, uses, and ending balances of cash and other resources used in operations.

Four benefits that budgets can provide for all firms are (1) better planning, (2) control of performance, (3) communication and coordination, and (4) employee motivation.

All departments in an organization should actively participate in preparing the master budget. Most large companies have a *budget committee* which provides guidance and coordination in preparing the budget.

The starting point in the budgetary process is the preparation of the *sales forecast.* All other elements of the budget depend on the sales forecast.

For a manufacturer the next most important forecast is determined in the *production budget,* which calculates the units that need to be produced in each future period on the basis of the sales forecast. Once the production budget is completed, it is then possible to determine the costs of production, the estimated costs of goods sold, and the required purchases of raw materials.

Once the following four budgeted financial statements are prepared, the master budget is completed:

1. The budgeted income statement
2. The budgeted retained earnings statement
3. The budgeted statement of cash receipts and disbursements
4. The budgeted balance sheet

IMPORTANT TERMS USED IN THIS CHAPTER

Budget committee A committee composed of a budget director and top-level executives from departments within the organization. The budget committee provides guidance and coordination in the preparation of the budget. (page 369)

Budget director   The member of the budget committee responsible for putting together the many schedules and statements that make up the master budget. (page 369)

Budgeted balance sheet   A statement depicting the estimated assets, liabilities, and stockholders' equity at the end of a budget period. (page 390)

Budgeted income statement   A statement listing the predicted revenues, expenses, and resulting income for a budget period. (page 389)

Budgeted retained earnings statement   A statement showing the estimated change in the retained earnings balance during a budget period. (page 390)

Budgeted schedule of cash collections   A monthly schedule listing the estimated collection from cash and credit sales. (page 375)

Budgeted schedule of purchases   A schedule determining the raw materials that must be purchased for production needs (for a manufacturer) or the merchandise that must be purchased to meet sales demand (for a retailer or wholesaler). (page 382)

Budgeted statement of cash receipts and disbursements   A statement listing the different types of anticipated cash receipts and disbursements for a budget period, as well as the estimated ending cash balance. It helps management to know when extra cash may be available for investment or when potential cash shortages may require additional short-term financing. (page 385)

Financial budgets   A category of the master budget that includes statements reporting on the projected sources, uses, and ending balances for cash and other resources used in company operations. (page 369)

Master budget   A comprehensive budget that expresses the overall business plan of the organization for a period covering 1 year or less. (page 368)

Operating budgets   A category of the master budget that includes schedules and statements related to budgeted revenues, expenses, and income. (page 368)

Production budget   A schedule indicating the units that have to be produced during a budget period. (page 378)

Sales forecast   The starting point for all budgeting — the projection of sales for the budget period. (page 373)

QUESTIONS

1. Why is the sales forecast often referred to as the starting point in all budgeting?

2. Discuss four purposes or benefits of budgeting.

3. "The master budget includes all budgets prepared by accountants to assist in both long-range and short-range planning." Do you agree? Explain.

4. List several factors that affect the sales forecast.

5. "The accountant bears sole responsibility for the preparation of all aspects of the master budget." Comment.

6. If the sales forecast is considered the starting point for all budgeting, why is it that the forecast cannot be made until the selling expense budget has been at least partially completed?

7. Explain the differences between *historical financial statements* and *budgeted financial statements*.

8. Why should human problems be considered in the preparation of a master budget?

9. "For control purposes actual results for the current period should be compared to actual results for the previous period." Do you agree? Explain.

10. Why does a firm maintain minimum balances in the finished goods inventory?

11. "In order to avoid the consequences of running out of cash, a firm should maintain as much cash on hand as possible." Comment.

12. Discuss the purpose of preparing a budgeted statement of cash receipts and disbursements.

13. Why isn't depreciation expense included in the budgeted statement of cash receipts and disbursements?

14. "When a firm expects high sales volume and significant profits for a period, the existence of an adequate inflow of cash is guaranteed." Comment.

15. "The budgeted cost of goods sold equals the combined costs of materials, labor, and overhead assigned to production during a period." Do you agree? Explain.

16. Explain why dividends to be declared during a budget period might not be included in the budgeted statement of cash receipts and disbursements.

EXERCISES

Exercise 9-1
Tracing the balance sheet items to the budgeted statements and schedules

On Mar. 31, 1988, the Navritalova Company prepared the following balance sheet at the end of Quarter I, prior to preparing a master budget for Quarter II:

NAVRITALOVA COMPANY
Balance Sheet
March 31, 1988

Assets		Liabilities	
Cash......................	$ 4,000	Accounts Payable	$ 32,000
Accounts Receivable	48,000	Notes Payable, due June 1,	
Allowance for Uncollectibles	(2,000)	1988....................	30,000
Merchandise Inventory	70,000	Interest Payable on Note....	1,000
Prepaid Insurance..........	1,600	Total Liabilities............	$ 63,000
Equipment	20,000	**Stockholders' Equity**	
Accumulated Depreciation..	(4,000)	Capital Stock	$ 40,000
Patent	2,400	Retained Earnings..........	37,000
		Total Stockholders' Equity ..	$ 77,000
		Total Liabilities and	
Total Assets	$140,000	Stockholders' Equity.......	$140,000

Indicate how each account on the Mar. 31, 1988, balance sheet will affect the Quarter II master budget. For example, the cash balance of $4,000 is added to the cash receipts in the statement of cash receipts and disbursements.

Exercise 9-2
Distinguishing income statement items from cash receipts and disbursements

There are several items described below that affect the budgeted income statement and budgeted statement of cash receipts and disbursements for July 1988. For each item you are to determine (1) the amount of revenue (or expenses) to be shown in the budgeted income statement and (2) the amount of cash receipts (or disbursements) included in the budgeted statement of cash receipts and disbursements.

a. Uncollected sales from June are $48,000. Sales for July should be $300,000, 30% of which are for cash. Credit sales are collected 60% in the month of sale and 40% in the following month. No bad debts are expected.

b. The cost of goods sold averages 65% of sales. The beginning and desired ending inventories for February are $24,000 and $36,000, respectively. All purchases are paid for in the month of purchase.

c. A 3-year insurance policy, costing $1,350, will be purchased in the middle of the month.

d. Machinery costing $45,000 was purchased on June 1. The estimated useful life is 10 years.

e. Dividends of $300,000 will be declared in July to be paid in August.

f. Wages earned during the first 2 weeks of each month are paid 3 days into the third week. Wages earned during the last 2 weeks of each month are paid on the third day of the next month. Wages are earned by workers as follows:

June:		July:	
First 2 weeks..............	$13,200	First 2 weeks...............	$14,400
Last 2 weeks..............	14,100	Last 2 weeks	15,300

Exercise 9-3
Calculating purchases after the desired ending inventory is determined

The Solid Binding Textbook Company sells its only book, *Principles of Macramé,* in many university bookstores throughout the country. One of these bookstores—at the University of Cripp—buys copies of the book from Solid Binding for $12 per text and marks them to sell at 50% over cost. On Sept. 1, 1988, the bookstore has 1,500 texts on hand. Student enrollment in the beginning macramé courses is expected to be 1,200, 1,000, 900, and 300 in Quarters I through IV, respectively, of the 1988–1989 academic year. In addition, the sales are expected to be 1,300 texts in Quarter I of the 1989–1990 school year. The bookstore plans to maintain at the end of each upcoming quarter enough texts to cover 150% of the following quarter's forecasted sales.

Purchases will be made at the end of each quarter and paid for within 30 days of purchase. Accounts Payable on Aug. 31, 1988, has a balance of $17,400.

Determine the unit purchases and cash payments for each quarter of the 1988–1989 academic year.

(Check figure: Purchases for Quarter I = 1,200 books)

Exercise 9-4
Determining purchases when desired ending inventory is given

The Carny Medication Company produces a product called Snake-Eye Elixir which is sold at circus and carnival sideshows. Each 12-ounce bottle, which contains 3 ounces of alcohol, is to be used for purely medicinal purposes. During September and October of 1988 Carny expects to produce 30,000 and 40,000 bottles of elixir. Also, Carny hopes to maintain on hand at least 5,000 ounces of alcohol at all times—beginning in September.

On Sept. 1, 1988, Carny has 4,800 ounces of alcohol in the raw materials inventory. The cost per ounce of alcohol is $0.12.

Determine the cost of purchases for September and October.

(Check figure: October purchases = $14,400)

Exercise 9-5
Preparing a budgeted statement of cash receipts and disbursements

During the last 2 months of 1988, the Muncies Candy Bar Company expects the following items concerning its cash flow:

	November	December
Cash Receipts	$100,000	$130,000
Cash Disbursements...............................	112,000	125,000

The Nov. 1 cash balance was $18,000, and the company requires a minimum cash balance each month of $12,000. If a cash deficiency is expected during a month, a loan is arranged at the beginning of that month, at 12% interest. Any repayments of principal plus interest based upon the principal repaid are made at the end of the month when cash becomes available. All borrowing and repayments of principal are made in multiples of $1,000.

Prepare a statement of cash receipts and disbursements for November and December.

(Check figure: Ending cash balance for December = $12,920)

Exercise 9-6
Preparing a budgeted statement of cash receipts and disbursements

Due to financial setbacks during 1988 the Lutz Butter Corporation was severely short of cash at the end of the year. The company treasurer found it necessary to take out an $80,000 loan on Dec. 31, at 16%, to be repaid in the next month or two from cash generated from operations. During January the cash receipts and disbursements from operations are expected to be $400,000 and $240,000, respectively.

Lutz plans to maintain a minimum cash balance of $10,000, which is the actual balance on Jan. 1. Any cash (in $1,000 multiples) in excess of the minimum will be invested at the end of the month to earn 10% interest. Dividends of $50,000 will be paid in January, and a 2-year insurance policy costing $4,000 will be taken out in the same month.

Prepare a statement of cash receipts and disbursements for January 1988.

(Check figure: Ending cash balance = $10,933)

PROBLEMS: SET A

Problem A9-1
Preparing a sales forecast and schedule of cash collections

John Stanton, the budget director for the Crete Corporation, is in the midst of preparing the master budget for the third quarter of 1989. The sales vice president has supplied John with the following sales projections for July through September:

July $150,000
August..................................... 180,000
September.................................. 240,000

Cash sales are expected to be 30% of total sales. Credit sales are expected to be collected in the following manner:

- 40% collected in the month of sale
- 50% collected in the month following sale
- 10% uncollectible

On July 1, 1987, the Accounts Receivable balance is $60,000, of which $18,000 is expected to be uncollectible.

| **Required** |

1. Prepare a sales forecast for the 3 months of Quarter III, 1989.
2. Prepare a schedule of collections for the 3 months of Quarter III, 1989.

(Check figure: Total cash collections, July = $129,000)

3. Determine what the Sept. 30, 1989, balance in Accounts Receivable is expected to be assuming that uncollectible accounts have still not been written off by that time.

(Check figure: $141,900)

Problem A9-2
Calculating monthly cash collections

In the months of November and December 1989, the Davidson Company had sales revenues of $33,000 and $40,000, respectively. The sales predictions for the first quarter of 1990 are as follows:

January $25,000
February 35,000
March 20,000

Cash sales are 60% of total sales, and no credit sales are expected to be uncollectible. Davidson offers a 5% cash discount on credit sales paid off in the month of sale. Collection experience for the company is expected to be:

- 70% collected in the month of sale (with discount)
- 30% collected in the month following sale (without discount)

The Accounts Receivable balance (recorded at the gross amount of sales) on Dec. 31, 1989, was $4,800.

Required	Prepare a schedule of cash collections for the months of January, February, and March, 1990.

(Check figure: Cash collections, February = $33,310)

Problem A9-3
Determining the month's
ending cash balance

Mina Pawpaw is about to prepare a cash budget for the first time for her shop, Mina's Wickery. On July 1, 1988, the shop's balance in Accounts Receivable was $4,932. From this balance only $1,868 is expected to be collectible, and this amount should all be collected in July. Pawpaw projects the sales for July and August to be $32,000 and $30,000, respectively. Typically, 80% of the sales are cash sales. Of the credit sales, one-third is expected to be collected in July and the same amount in August. The remaining one-third will probably go uncollected.

Pawpaw purchases wicker materials 1 month in advance of their expected sales. The cost of the wicker materials averages 60% of their retail value. All purchases are paid for in the month of purchase. The following operating expenses are expected for the month of July:

Utilities	$1,000
Salaries	4,800
Property Taxes	200
Advertising	3,000
	$9,000

Utility bills are received at the end of each month and paid for at the beginning of the following month (the June utility bill was $900). Salaries are paid at the end of the month. Property taxes for the year of $2,400 ($200 × 12 months) are paid to the county on July 1. A $3,000 payment to WYRN-TV for four commercials to be aired in July was made on June 30.

Required	Prepare a budgeted statement of cash receipts and disbursements for July. Assume that the cash balance on July 1 is $4,000 and that no minimum cash balance is desired.

(Check figure: Ending cash balance = $7,501)

Problem A9-4
Determining net income
and cash receipts and
disbursements

Sandy Grinnell has been working for a large national CPA firm for about 1 year. However, in August 1988, when she learned that she had passed the CPA exam, she decided to open her own practice. After 2 months of preparation she finally opened her doors on Oct. 15. One of the first things she decided to do was to prepare a cash budget for November.

Her client fees in October were $1,000, none of which were collected in that month. Grinnell expects to collect $800 of this amount in November. The remaining amount relates to a client that skipped town after Grinnell prepared a tax return that indicated a massive liability to the IRS. The fees for November are expected to be $2,000, and Grinnell anticipates collecting nearly the entire amount in that month, since she will not turn over her finished reports to her clients until the cash is received. Only 10% will remain to be collected in December.

Grinnell expects the following cash disbursements in November:

Salaries of $400 for a part-time college student and a full-time secretary.
Payment of $120 for her professional licenses for the year (November 1988–October 1989).
Purchase of office furniture for $3,600. The useful life of the furniture is 6 years.
Utilities for October of $150. The November bill, to be paid in December, will be $175.

In addition, on Oct. 15, 1988, Grinnell signed a 3-month lease and made a prepayment of $1,200 at that time.

Required	**1.** Prepare a budgeted income statement for the month of November.

(Check figure: Net income = $965)

2. Assume that Grinnell had a Nov. 1, 1988, cash balance of $4,000. Prepare a budgeted statement of cash receipts and disbursements for November.

(Check figure: Ending cash balance = $2,330)

Problem A9-5
Preparing a budgeted statement of cash receipts and disbursements

Gales Metalworks, which manufactures steel lawn furniture, had sales in December 1988, of $3,750,000. Each piece of furniture was priced to sell at $150 and is expected to remain at the same price for the next 4 to 6 months. The projected sales for the first 4 months of 1989 are the following:

January...................	20,000 units	March....................	35,000 units
February.................	40,000 units	April	30,000 units

Cash sales average 25% of total sales, and credit sales are typically collected in full in the month following sale.

Starting in January the company wants to maintain the following ending inventories to ensure that it never runs out of stock:

Raw Materials .... 180,000 pounds
Finished Goods .... 75,000 units

The Jan. 1 balances in raw materials and finished goods were 210,000 pounds and 60,000 units, respectively. The Jan. 1 and Jan. 31 balances in work-in-process are and will be zero.

Six pounds of raw materials (at $2.50 per pound) are required for each finished unit. Purchases of raw materials are all for cash. Additional costs for Gales Metalworks during January are:

Direct Labor $1,800,000
Factory Overhead (including $100,000 of
  depreciation)............................ 1,000,000
Selling Department Costs.................. 400,000

All payments are made when the costs are incurred.

The Jan. 1 cash balance for Gales is $75,000, but the company hopes to maintain at least a $100,000 ending cash balance beginning in January. All financing, if necessary, is made at the beginning of the month. Repayments will include interest at 12% of the principal repaid.

Required

Prepare a budgeted statement of cash receipts and disbursements for January.

(Check figure: Payments for purchases = $450,000)

Problem A9-6
Preparing a complete master budget

The Pinacina Company, which sells a hair dye called Natural, has just completed operations for 1988 and has prepared the balance sheet shown below.

PINACINA COMPANY
Balance Sheet
December 31, 1988

Assets		Liabilities	
Cash.......................	$ 11,000	Accounts Payable	$ 48,000
Accounts Receivable	94,000	Notes Payable	40,000
Merchandise Inventory	80,000	Interest Payable............	666
Building....................	50,000	Total Liabilities...........	$ 88,666
Accumulated Depreciation ..	(2,400)		
Prepaid Insurance..........	9,000	**Stockholders' Equity**	
		Capital Stock	$ 80,000
		Retained Earnings..........	72,934
		Total Stockholders' Equity ..	$152,934
		Total Liabilities and	
Total Assets	$241,600	Stockholders' Equity.......	$241,600

All sales are credit sales. Collections are expected to be made in the following manner:

- 50% collected in the month of sale
- 30% collected in the first month after sale
- 20% collected in the second month after sale

The actual sales for November and December 1988, were $120,000 and $140,000, respectively. The projected sales for upcoming months are as follows:

January 1989	$160,000	March 1989.................	$130,000
February 1989	160,000	April 1989..................	100,000

The sale price for all months is $10 per bottle.

Sixty percent of the purchases are made on account, and all credit purchases are to be paid in the month following purchase. Pinacina desires to maintain the following ending inventories of Natural (at $5 per bottle) each month:

November 1988..........	14,000 bottles	February 1989	12,000 bottles
December 1988	16,000 bottles	March 1989	8,800 bottles
January 1989	16,000 bottles		

In the Dec. 31, 1988, balance sheet, the only transactions recorded in Accounts Payable are for purchases of merchandise. The prepayment of insurance was made on Oct. 1, 1988, for a 1-year policy. The monthly cash operating expenses of $20,000 are paid when incurred. Depreciation expense is $200 per month.

Pinacina plans to declare and pay dividends during March 1989, amounting to $50,000. In addition, a new building, costing $150,000, will be purchased at the end of March 1989, for cash.

The note payable shown in the Dec. 31, 1988, balance sheet was signed on Nov. 1, 1988, and is due to be repaid plus 10% interest on Jan. 31, 1989. If any future monthly cash balance is expected to fall below a minimum of $10,000, additional financing will have to be arranged, at 12% interest, at the beginning of that month.

| **Required** | Prepare the following for Quarter I, 1989: |

1. Budgeted income statement

(Check figure: Net income = $160,460)

2. Budgeted retained earnings statement
3. Budgeted statement of cash receipts and disbursements

(Check figure: Cash balance, January 31 = $16,000)

4. Budgeted balance sheet

(Check figure: Total assets = $354,000; total liabilities = $90,606)

Be sure to include all supporting schedules.

PROBLEMS: SET B

Problem B9-1
Preparing a sales forecast
and schedule of cash
receipts

Bob Cox, the sales vice president of Video View, has just given the budget director the sales forecast for the first quarter of 1988. Sales are projected to be 22,500 units in January, 12,000 units in February, and 13,500 units in March. Video View sells its cassette tapes for $8 each and expects to collect its sales in the following manner:

Cash sales......................................	15%
Credit Sales	85%
Collected in month of sale	30%
Collected in month following sale..........	60%
Uncollectible.............................	10%

On Jan. 1, 1988, Video View had a balance in Accounts Receivable of $97,500. Of this amount $11,820 is expected to be uncollectible.

<table>
<tr><td>**Required**</td><td></td></tr>
</table>

1. Prepare a sales forecast for the first 3 months of 1988.

2. Prepare a schedule of cash collections for the same months.

(Check figure: Total cash collections, January = $158,580)

3. Determine the predicted Mar. 31, 1988, balances in Accounts Receivable and Allowance for Doubtful Accounts (assume no accounts were written off during the quarter).

(Check figure: Accounts Receivable = $99,540)

Problem B9-2
Determining the cash
collections from sales —
discount offered

During May and June 1989, Center's Wholesale had sales of $400,000 and $600,000, respectively. During the next 3 months sales are forecasted to be:

July	$ 500,000
August	1,000,000
September	750,000

In the past credit sales were 80% of total sales, and this experience is expected in the future months as well. All credit sales are considered collectible. The firm offers a 3% cash discount on credit sales, and it is expected that many customers will take advantage of the discount within the allowed payment period. The collection of credit sales typically occurs in the following manner:

- 40% collected in the month of sale (with discount)
- 40% collected in the first month following sale (without discount)
- 20% collected in the second month following sale (without discount)

The June 30 balance in Accounts Receivable (recorded at the gross amount of sales) is $330,000.

Required

Prepare a schedule of cash collections for July, August, and September.

(Check figure: Total cash collections, September = $782,800)

Problem B9-3
Determining the month's
ending cash balance

Gary Smiley runs a chain of florist shops called Gary's Garden, and he is about to prepare his first cash budget. On Aug. 1 customers owe the shops $350 for sales made in June and $3,150 for sales made in July. Gary expects all of the June receivables and $1,050 of the July receivables to go uncollected. He predicts sales for August and September of $35,000 and $28,000, respectively. Typically, 70% of the sales are for cash. The credit sales should be collected as follows:

- 70% collected in the first month
- 20% collected in the second month
- 10% uncollectible

Gary had decided to purchase enough flowers each month to cover that month's sales. Flowers are purchased to sell at a markup of 100% of cost, and they are paid for within 10 days of purchase. This means that approximately one-third of each month's purchases are paid for in the subsequent month. The purchases for July were $13,125.

The following expenses will be incurred in August:

Salaries	$ 2,800
Utilities	875
Rent	5,250
Gasoline	350
Advertising	875
Total	$10,150

Salaries and gasoline are paid for when the expense is incurred. Utilities are paid for in the following month (the July utility bill was $787). Three months' rent was prepaid on July 1. On Aug. 1 an advance of $1,750 was given to an advertising agency for 2 months of promotion.

The cash balance for Gary's Garden on Aug. 1 was $2,625. No minimum balance has been set for the month-end.

| **Required** | Prepare a budgeted statement of cash receipts and disbursements for August. |

(Check figure: Ending cash balance = $14,846)

Problem B9-4
Preparing statements of income and cash receipts and disbursements

Robert Knealson recently passed his bar examination and has opened a law office. September was his first month of business, and Knealson has decided to prepare budgets starting in October.

All client fees in September were billed on account. At the end of September fees amounting to $2,000 were uncollected. Half of that amount is expected to be collected in October. The remaining half is not expected to be collected since the client, destitute at the time, died when hearing the guilty verdict. In addition, Knealson has a 30-day note receivable, dated Sept. 15, from Ann Kirstin for $3,000, which he expects to collect on Oct. 15 (plus 10% annual interest), when the life insurance of Ann's late husband is paid.

During October Knealson expects the law fees to be $8,000, 20% of which will be cash fees for wills and quickie divorces. Of the credit fees, one-half are expected to be collected in each of the following 2 months.

Knealson expects the following cash disbursements during October:

Purchase of law books for $3,000 on Oct. 1. The books are expected to have a 10-year useful life.
Prepayment of $1,000 for 2 months' rent on Oct. 1.
Salary of $200 for a full-time law student.
Birthday presents costing $1,600 for the children of three judges.
Advertising costing $2,000 in the *Florida Enquirer Newspaper.*

On Oct. 1 Knealson had a cash balance of $75.

| **Required** | **1.** Prepare a budgeted income statement for October. |

(Check figure: Net income = $3687.50)

2. Determine how much cash Knealson would have to borrow during October (if any) in order to attain an Oct. 31 ending cash balance of $200.

(Check figure: $2,300)

Problem B9-5
Preparing a budgeted statement of cash receipts and disbursements

Rube's Tubes is a manufacturer that produces a product using a single raw material. The controller, Dave Knight, prepares a master budget each month and is currently in the process of preparing the November budget. The actual sales for October (at a $150 sales price) and the forecasted sales for the next 4 months are provided below by the sales vice president, Tom Kinsey:

October	25,000 units	January...................	35,000 units
November	20,000 units	February.................	30,000 units
December	40,000 units		

The sales are broken down as follows:

- 20% for cash
- 80% for credit, to be collected in the first month after the sale

The desired ending inventories are determined to be:

- Finished goods — the next 2 months' sales (in units)
- Raw materials — the next month's production requirements

The beginning and ending inventories of work-in-process are immaterial in amount. The Nov. 1 inventories for finished goods and raw materials are 60,000 units and 105,000 pounds, respectively. It takes 3 pounds of raw materials for each finished unit, each pound costing $5. All purchases are for cash.

Other costs for Rube's Tubes during November are predicted to be as follows:

Direct Labor	$1,800,000
Factory Overhead	1,000,000
Selling and Administration	400,000

Included in the factory overhead is $100,000 of depreciation. All cash payments are made for the items above when the cost is incurred.

The cash balance on Nov. 1 is $75,000, and the company hopes to maintain, starting in November, a minimum cash balance each month of $150,000. If financing is required, loans will be taken out at the beginning of the month at 10% interest.

Required	Prepare a budgeted statement of cash receipts and disbursements for November.

(Check figure: Payments for purchases = $450,000)

**Problem B9-6
Preparing complete
master budget**

The Quickie Wipes Company sells disposable moist wipes for babies at $2.50 per package (500 wipes per package). Although the company will begin its fourth month of operation on Jan. 1, 1989, the controller is about to prepare the company's first master budget for the first quarter of 1989. The balance sheet for Quickie on Dec. 31, 1988, is given below.

QUICKIE WIPES COMPANY
Balance Sheet
December 31, 1988

Assets		Liabilities	
Cash	$ 11,000	Accounts Payable	$ 48,000
Accounts Receivable	99,000	Notes Payable	40,000
Allowance for Doubtful		Interest Payable	666
Accounts	(18,000)	Total Liabilities	$ 88,666
Merchandise Inventory	80,000	**Stockholders' Equity**	
Prepaid Rent	9,000	Capital Stock	$ 80,000
		Retained Earnings	12,334
		Total Stockholders' Equity	$ 92,334
		Total Liabilities and	
Total Assets	$181,000	Stockholders' Equity	$181,000

The note was signed on Nov. 1, 1988, and is due to be repaid on Jan. 31, 1989, at 10% annual interest. If any future monthly cash balance is expected to fall below a minimum of $8,000, additional financing will have to be arranged at the beginning of that month.

Sales are all on credit. Collections are expected to be 50% in the month of sale, 30% in the first month after sale, and 15% in the second month after sale; 5% will be uncollectible (estimated and recorded at the end of each quarter). No accounts considered as bad have been written off the books. The actual sales for the last quarter and the predicted sales for the next 4 months (assuming a $2.50 sales price) are as follows:

October 1988	$100,000	February 1989	$160,000
November 1988	120,000	March 1989	130,000
December 1988	140,000	April 1989	100,000
January 1989	160,000		

Purchases for cash are 40% of all purchases, and all credit purchases will be paid in the month after purchase. Quickie desires the following monthly ending inventories for its wipes:

November 1988........	56,000 packages	February 1989	48,000 packages
December 1988	64,000 packages	March 1989	35,200 packages
January 1989	64,000 packages		

The cost of the inventory is $1.25 per package.

In the Dec. 31, 1988, balance sheet, the only transactions recorded in Accounts Payable are for purchases of merchandise. The prepayment for rent was made on Oct. 1 for a 1-year lease. A $200,000 cash purchase of land is planned for March. The operating expenses are paid when incurred. They amount to $20,000 per month.

Required

Prepare the following statements for Quarter I, 1989:

1. Budgeted income statement

(Check figure: Net income = $138,504)

2. Budgeted statement of retained earnings

3. Budgeted statement of cash receipts and disbursements (month by momth)

(Check figure: Cash balance, February 28 = $67,000)

4. Budgeted balance sheet

(Check figure: Total assets = $340,500; total liabilities = $109,622)

Be sure to include all necessary supporting schedules.

CHAPTER 10

The Flexible Budget, Standard Costs, and Variance Analysis

After you finish reading this chapter, you will have learned:

- What a performance report is used for
- What a responsibility center is and how it relates to responsibility accounting
- The distinction between *static budgets* and *flexible budgets,* and why flexible budgets should be used in performance reports
- What standard costs are and the different ways they are used
- How the standard costs for direct materials, direct labor, and factory overhead are determined
- How to prepare a performance report and calculate the price variance, quantity variance, and flexible budget variance for each product cost
- Why and how we calculate a predetermined rate for fixed factory overhead; what fixed factory overhead applied is; and how to calculate a volume variance for fixed factory overhead
- How to determine which variances need to be investigated

In the previous chapter you learned that the master budget is a tool that looks into the future, characterizing in a quantitative way the things that should happen during the budget period if sales occur as forecasted. Here, we are going to look back over the budget period, after it is completed, to compare what should have happened with what did indeed happen. We will calculate the differences between "budgeted" and "actual" results in order to help managers control their current operations.

When we look back on what we have done, the budget we must compare to the actual results is the flexible budget, not the master budget. The master budget tells us what we expect — before a period begins — for the level of activity expected in the forthcoming period. *The flexible budget tells us — after the fact — what we expect to have happened for the level of activity that has actually taken place.*

In this chapter we will explain exactly what a flexible budget is and why we use it instead of the master budget in the performance report. In addition, we will show you how to prepare a performance report, and we will explain how it is used by accoun-

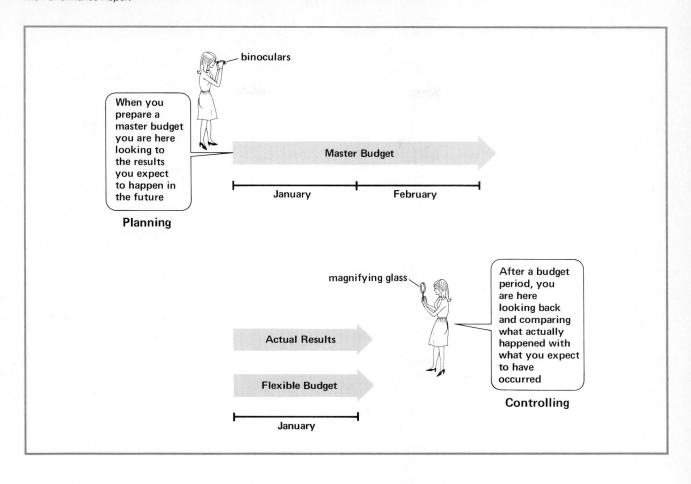

tants to help management control current operations. We will also explain what standard costs are and what their role is in flexible budgets and performance reports. And we will discuss the different types of *variances,* which are the *differences* between the actual results and the flexible budget.

THE PERFORMANCE REPORT

From Example 9-2, recall that Underhill Company budgeted 15,000 units to be produced in January (see page 379) and that production costs were budgeted for that month based on the following estimates:

Direct Materials...............	$5 per unit
Direct Labor..................	6 per unit
Variable Overhead.............	3 per unit
Fixed Overhead	15,000 per month

The total budgeted production costs for January were given in Exhibit 9-6. They were:

	Budgeted Costs of Production (for 15,000 Units) in January
Direct Materials (15,000 × $5/unit).............................	$ 75,000
Direct Labor (15,000 × $6/unit)................................	90,000
Variable Overhead (15,000 × $3/unit)	45,000
Fixed Overhead	15,000
	$225,000

Let us assume for now that on Jan. 31 we learn that 15,000 units were actually produced — exactly the number Underhill predicted on Jan. 1 — and that the actual costs of producing these units were as follows:

	Actual Costs of Producing 15,000 Units in January
Direct Materials...	$ 76,000
Direct Labor..	93,000
Variable Overhead...	44,000
Fixed Overhead	14,900
	$227,900

We can now compare the budgeted results to the actual results for January in a performance report, shown in Exhibit 10-1. *Remember: We have assumed that 15,000 units were budgeted to be produced and that exactly 15,000 units were actually produced.* (When the units budgeted are equal to what is actually produced, the master budget and the flexible budget are exactly the same, so there is no reason to be concerned with which budget we should use. We will discuss this issue in more detail later.)

EXHIBIT 10-1
Performance Report—
Underhill Company
(In this case units produced equal units budgeted)
A comparison of actual and budgeted results when units produced equal units budgeted.

	Actual Costs of Producing 15,000 Units	Budgeted Costs of Producing 15,000 Units	Total Differences*
Direct Materials......................	$ 76,000	$ 75,000	$1,000 U
Direct Labor.........................	93,000	90,000	3,000 U
Variable Overhead	44,000	45,000	1,000 F
Fixed Overhead	14,900	15,000	100 F
	$227,900	$225,000	$2,900 U

* Differences shown with the letter U are unfavorable, meaning that the actual costs are over budget, and those shown with the letter F are favorable, indicating that the actual costs are under budget.

To begin to control operations for the period, management, with the accountant's help, looks at the performance report, examines the information in the differences column, and asks several questions that require immediate answers. Management asks questions such as:

Important questions to ask about the performance report

1. Who is responsible for the differences—the variances—that appear in the performance report?
2. Which differences should be investigated?
3. What is the cause of each difference that is to be investigated?
4. What (if any) corrective actions need to be taken?

As we progress through this chapter, you should begin to understand why these questions are so important and how the accountant can help management answer each of them to management's satisfaction.

RESPONSIBILITY ACCOUNTING

Before the first question can be answered, it is necessary to understand what we mean by two very important terms: responsibility centers and responsibility accounting.

Responsibility center: unit of activity, authority, and responsibility

A ***responsibility center*** is an area of activity within an organization for which an individual has been delegated authority to plan activities and assigned responsibility for those activities for a period of time. Within the Underhill Company there are responsibility centers for at least each of the production, selling, and administrative departments. In Exhibit 10-1 the activities of the production department were reported in the performance report; therefore, the responsibility center in that report is the production department. Within each department there can be numerous smaller responsibility centers as well. For example, the production department could have responsibility centers for individual workers, for a foreman supervising a group of workers, or for a superintendent over several foremen (each of whom supervises a group of workers). A responsibility center can be very small or quite large.

Responsibility accounting is based on responsibility centers

Responsibility accounting is the process of:

1. Designating the responsibility centers
2. Delegating authority to individuals within the responsibility centers
3. Preparing budgets, accumulating actual results, and preparing performance reports for the responsibility centers
4. Holding the individuals with authority responsible or accountable for their actions

So you see, responsibility centers are the heart of a responsibility accounting system. For once we know what the responsibility centers are and who is in charge, then budgets can be formulated and put into action; actual costs can be accumulated after the fact; and performance reports can be prepared and evaluated. Then the process starts all over again—for each responsibility center.

Responsibility accounting is the backbone of all planning and control systems.

Controllable and Uncontrollable Costs

Controllable costs: significant influence during a period of time

Within each responsibility center the costs that a manager is held responsible for are those that are controllable by him or her. ***Controllable costs*** are costs within a responsibility center that can be significantly influenced by the manager of that center during a given period of time. If a manager has no influence over a cost during a given period of time, then the cost is an ***uncontrollable cost*** (a noncontrollable cost). If costs are uncontrollable, it doesn't make sense to hold a manager accountable when the actual costs are not what they should be.

To determine if a cost is controllable or uncontrollable, you must consider two things: (1) the responsibility center and manager to which the cost relates and (2) the period of time covered by the performance report.

Significant influence

First, you do not classify a cost as controllable just because there is someone, somewhere, who exerts influence over the cost. Instead, you specify that a cost is controllable or uncontrollable because there is or is not influence by a manager at a specific level of responsibility within the organization. For example, when classifying the cost of direct materials in the assembly department as controllable or uncontrollable, you first need to know: "For whom am I considering it controllable or uncontrollable?" If the answer is the production foreman in assembly, then the cost is probably controllable. If the answer is the vice president of sales, then the cost is definitely uncontrollable.

Time period

Second, whether or not a cost is controllable depends on the period of time covered by the performance report. In the extreme long run, such as 50 years, every cost within an organization is controllable by someone. On the other hand, in the extreme short run, such as 1 second, there are probably no costs that are controllable by anyone. Which period of time we are using to classify costs as controllable or uncontrollable can make a big difference.

The performance of a responsibility center and the manager of that center might be evaluated as frequently as daily, weekly, or monthly. Or performance might be evaluated for longer periods of time—such as quarterly or annually. If a manager's performance is evaluated only once a year, then controllable costs are any costs that he or she can influence during a full 365-day period. On the other hand, if performance is evaluated each and every day, then a controllable cost is one that can be influenced on a day-to-day basis.

For our purposes we will classify any cost as controllable if a manager has a significant amount of influence over it during a period of 1 year or less.

The concept of controllability is simple to define and easy to understand, but it may be quite difficult to apply in a real-world situation. This is because some costs are influenced by many people, with no single individual exerting an obviously significant amount of influence.

For example, assume that a maintenance department takes far more time to repair a machine than it should have taken. Who has the most influence on the cost of this repair? Is it the maintenance foreman who didn't keep track of the work being performed by the mechanic? Or could it be the production foreman who postponed normal maintenance during the busy periods and allowed workers to misuse the machinery?

There is no simple answer, but a useful guideline might be that the individual to be assigned responsibility for controlling a cost is the one having the greatest day-to-day continuing influence over that cost.

Once a cost has been determined as controllable at one level of responsibility, it is also considered controllable at all higher levels of responsibility in the chain of command. To understand this, refer to page 14 which shows a simple organization chart for a typical manufacturer. If a cost is classified as controllable by a foreman in production department no. 1, it would also be considered controllable by the production superintendent, the vice president of manufacturing, and the president. If a cost is controllable by sales manager no. 1, it is also controllable by the vice president of sales and the president.

Behavior of Costs vs. Controllability

Are all controllable costs variable?

A common misconception is that variable costs are synonymous with controllable costs and that fixed costs are synonymous with uncontrollable costs.

All variable costs, however, are not necessarily controllable, and all fixed costs are not categorically uncontrollable. Remember, *controllability* deals with a manager's ability to influence the amount of a cost during a period. *Behavior of costs* refers to the relationship between total costs and activity.

There are variable and fixed costs that are clearly controllable, and variable and fixed costs that are clearly uncontrollable. For example, the direct material costs (variable) and salaries of production foremen (fixed) are controllable by the vice president of manufacturing, but the sales commissions (variable) and the president's salary (fixed) are uncontrollable by the vice president of manufacturing.

Distinguishing Responsibility from Blame

Responsibility isn't the same as blame

Another common misunderstanding concerns the difference between *responsibility* and *blame.* They are not synonymous. Assigning someone the responsibility is not the same as placing the blame.

For example, looking at the performance report in Exhibit 10-1, you can see that the direct labor costs were $3,000 higher than they were expected to be. The fact that production foremen are assigned responsibility to control the performance of workers does not, however, automatically mean that they are blamed for the $3,000 difference. First of all, it is possible that the unfavorable difference was beyond anyone's control. A plausible explanation could be that a damaging storm caused a shutdown for several days during which time the laborers were still paid. Or the unfavorable difference might have been due to lack of foresight in the budget, which did not anticipate the higher wage rates that went into effect during the period. Still another likely cause for the difference might be the actions of another department. The sales manager may have accepted a large unexpected rush order that forced costly overtime work; or the purchasing agent may not have acquired the materials in time for production, causing lengthy idle time.

In each situation, the production foreman assumes initial responsibility for the unfavorable difference, but the blame was placed on someone else, or on no one at all. This is not to say that the foreman could not have been blamed, for indeed the differences could have been due to the workers' inadequate supervision. *The point is simply that responsibility and blame are not synonymous.*

A way to distinguish the two terms might be as follows: Responsibility is assigned before a cause is determined. Blame is assigned only after a cause has been determined. Setting responsibilities ensures that someone can be asked, "What went wrong?" Only after this question is answered can the second question be asked: "Who's to blame?"

USE OF A STATIC BUDGET

The performance report in Exhibit 10-1 compared the actual results to a budget based on 15,000 units. We assumed that the number of units actually produced was the same as the number of units budgeted for production.

Let us now assume that only 12,500 units were actually produced, whereas 15,000 units had been budgeted for production. The performance report comparing the actual costs to make 12,500 units to the master budget for the 15,000 budgeted units is shown in Exhibit 10-2. The actual costs are much less than they were in Exhibit

**EXHIBIT 10-2
Performance Report—
Master Budget Employed
(Units produced differ
from units budgeted)**
The actual costs are compared
to the master budget, but the
units produced aren't equal to
the units budgeted.

	Actual Costs (12,500 Units)	Master Budget (15,000 Units)	Difference
Direct Materials	$ 65,000	$ 75,000	$10,000 F
Direct Labor	78,000	90,000	12,000 F
Variable Overhead	39,000	45,000	6,000 F
Fixed Overhead	14,900	15,000	100 F
	$196,900	$225,000	$28,100 F

10-1 (when we assumed that 15,000 units were actually produced), which is to be expected since we have now produced 2,500 fewer units. The master budget, however, is the same as it was in Exhibit 10-1 because the master budget is based on the prediction that we made at the beginning of the month. Since the master budget remains the same regardless of the number of units actually produced, it is often referred to as a *static (or unchanging) budget.*

Each actual cost in Exhibit 10-2 is less than the budgeted cost—designated as favorable by the letter F beside each difference. The total of the individual differences, $28,100 F, is significant and might result in the responsible parties being praised for their efficient performance during January.

It would be a mistake, however, to conclude from this favorable difference that production was conducted in an efficient manner. Efficiency had nothing to do with it. Remember, the actual costs of production were based on 2,500 fewer units than were the budgeted costs. Even if the workers were grossly inefficient, doesn't it seem reasonable to expect them to incur less actual variable costs in the production of only 12,500 units than they were expected to incur for the production of 15,000 units? The only thing we know for sure from Exhibit 10-2 is that the production department was unable to reach the 15,000-unit production goal set by management, and as a result, the actual costs were less than predicted. Whether or not the 12,500 units were produced for more or less costs than they should have been has yet to be determined.

Just in case you're not yet convinced of the irrelevance of the differences in the performance report when the master budget is compared to the actual results, we will now take the situation to an extreme. We will now assume that there was zero actual production for the month even though we had expected 15,000 units to be produced. The actual variable costs would, of course, be zero, as you can see in the performance report of Exhibit 10-3. The comparison of these zero actual costs to the unchanging master budget amounts now results in fantastically favorable variances. Do the $210,100 of favorable variances in Exhibit 10-3 have any meaning or relevance? Of course not!

Rule: don't use the master budget in the performance report

Although Exhibit 10-3 represents an extreme and silly situation, it should help to plant an important generalization in your mind: *When the master budget is included in the performance report, irrelevant and meaningless variances result.* This is because the master budget is a static, unchanging prediction of what the costs might be in the upcoming period, rather than an indication of what the costs are expected to be to produce the actual units worked on. When the master budget is used in the performance report, as it was in Exhibits 10-2 and 10-3, it is not possible to determine if the organization was operated effectively or efficiently.

EXHIBIT 10-3
Performance Report for Zero Production
If you use the master budget in your performance report, you'll have terrific variances when production is zero. But does it make sense?

	Actual Costs (0 Units)	Master Budget (15,000 Units)	Difference
Direct Materials	-0-	$ 75,000	$ 75,000 F
Direct Labor	-0-	90,000	90,000 F
Variable Overhead	-0-	45,000	45,000 F
Fixed Overhead	$14,900	15,000	100 F
	$14,900	$225,000	$210,100 F

Effectiveness and Efficiency

Effectiveness refers to the attainment of objectives. It is measured by comparing the actual output (the finished units produced by the organization) to the original goals. *Efficiency* refers to the relationship of inputs to outputs, that is, how well the company controls the use of its inputs (materials, labor, and overhead) in generating the outputs (the finished units).[1]

You can be effective but not efficient, and vice versa

For example, let's assume that you have a mouse in your kitchen, and you want to kill it. If you decide to solve your problem by having an exterminator's tent put on your house (at a cost of $300), your approach would be quite effective — a dead mouse. However, it wouldn't be very efficient — $300 for one little mouse? Assume instead that you borrow the ferocious cat from next door and she kills your mouse in exchange for a box of catnip treats (costing $0.49). Now you have been both effective — a dead mouse — and efficient — a cost of only $0.49.

Let's now look back at the performance report in Exhibit 10-2 for the Underhill Company. Unfortunately, the differences that are shown give us no indication of whether the production department was run effectively, efficiently, or both. Each difference is actually a combination of effectiveness and efficiency. Part of each difference exists because the department produced 2,500 fewer units than were hoped for — this means that it was not effective. The other part of each difference exists because the 12,500 units were produced for either more or less than they might have been — this is where efficiency comes in.

From now on our main concern is efficiency

Although management naturally has to be concerned with both the effectiveness and the efficiency of its operation, within this chapter we are concerned primarily with management's interest in efficiency. Performance reports must provide variances that isolate efficiency rather than a confusing combination of efficiency and effectiveness. The only way to do this is to compare the actual costs to a budget that indicates what the costs are expected to be for the units actually produced. Such a budget is a flexible budget.

THE FLEXIBLE BUDGET

Flexible budgets are predictions of costs at different levels of activity

The master budget is based on the single most likely level of activity to take place, and it is prepared before any activity at all occurs. A *flexible budget* is a prediction of costs at various levels of activity, based on a knowledge of how costs are expected to behave in response to activity. A flexible budget can be prepared before a period begins, indicating what the predicted costs might be for many possible levels of future activity — one of which will probably be the master budget level. Or a flexible budget

[1] Robert N. Anthony, *Planning and Control Systems: A Framework for Analysis* (Boston: Harvard Business School, 1965), pp. 27–28.

can be prepared after the period is completed and the actual activity is known; in this case a flexible budget indicates the costs that you would expect for the actual production that has just taken place.

For example, the best estimate of production activity for the Underhill Company during January 1988 (Exhibit 9-5 in the previous chapter) was 15,000 units. However, budgets for activity above and below that level of production might have also been useful.

EXHIBIT 10-4   Flexible Budgets for January

Here flexible budgets are prepared for three levels of possible future activity. One of these is the master budget level.

			Flexible Budgets	
	Budgeted Cost per Unit	14,000 Units	Master Budget, 15,000 Units	16,000 Units
Direct Materials...............................	$5	$ 70,000	$ 75,000	$ 80,000
Direct Labor....................................	6	84,000	90,000	96,000
Variable Overhead	3	42,000	45,000	48,000
Fixed Overhead.................................	na	15,000	15,000	15,000
Total Production Costs.......................		$211,000	$225,000	$239,000

Underhill may have wanted to know the possible effect on the company's financial statements if the results were different from its best estimate. Flexible budgets help to provide this kind of information. Exhibit 10-4 portrays flexible budgets for the production department for January at several possible levels of production—the master budget level, as well as above and below that level. If production is anywhere between 14,000 and 16,000 units, the company will have a good idea of what the costs will be for the month.

Flexible budgets, such as the one in Exhibit 10-4, are prepared before the period begins, to assist management in planning for that period. When January's production of 12,500 units is completed and the actual costs of producing that quantity are determined, another flexible budget must be prepared, this one to be used in the performance report for control purposes. This flexible budget is based on the actual units—12,500—produced during January.

The performance report based on the flexible budget for 12,500 units is provided in Exhibit 10-5. The budgeted variable costs are based on the budgeted per-unit costs

**EXHIBIT 10-5
Performance Report:
Flexible Budget Based on
Units Produced**
Now a flexible budget is prepared based on the units that were actually produced. When subtracted from the actual results, we have the flexible budget variance.

	Actual Costs (12,500 Units)	*Cost/unit × 12,500* Flexible Budget: Based on Units Produced (12,500 Units)	Total Flexible Budget Variance
Direct Materials....................$	65,000	$ 62,500	$2,500 U
Direct Labor........................	78,000	75,000	3,000 U
Variable Overhead..................	39,000	37,500	1,500 U
Fixed Overhead....................	14,900	15,000	100 F
Total Production Costs	$196,900	$190,000	$6,900 U

[column (1) in Exhibit 10-4] multiplied by 12,500 units; the budgeted fixed costs are the same amount, $15,000.

The difference between actual costs and the flexible budget based on the units produced is referred to as the ***flexible budget variance*** (which some people call the controllable variance). Notice that we are now using the term *variance* rather than *difference* in column (3). *Difference* is a general term meaning that two numbers are not the same amount; when this difference occurs in a performance report, it is referred to as a *variance,* a more specific term.

From the flexible budget variances we can determine whether or not the units were produced efficiently. In Exhibit 10-5 you can see that each of the actual variable costs is higher than the corresponding costs in the flexible budget, resulting in unfavorable flexible budget variances. On the basis of these unfavorable variances we can now say that the 12,500 units were not made very efficiently—the company spent more to make the 12,500 units than it expected to spend.

We can determine if Underhill is *effective* or not by comparing the actual units produced to the number of units originally estimated in the master budget. Since 2,500 fewer units were produced than anticipated, the company was not as effective as it could have been. In order to convert the unit measure of effectiveness—2,500 below the master budget level—into dollars, we have to assume that if the units were produced they could have been sold. If this assumption is correct, then the effect of producing *and* selling 2,500 units fewer than expected is a reduction in the firm's net income, due to a lower contribution margin from a smaller sales volume.

We can determine the dollar measure of effectiveness—also called the ***sales volume variance***—by:

The master budget can be used to measure effectiveness

1. Preparing a budgeted income statement for Underhill based on production and sales of 12,500 units.

2. Comparing this statement to the budgeted income statement based on the master budget level of activity, 15,000 units.

3. Finding the difference in the budgeted net incomes on the two statements. This is the dollar measure of effectiveness—the sales volume variance.

If the budgeted net income is higher at the master budget level of activity, there will be less income than originally expected because of producing and selling fewer units. This is the situation for Underhill, which produced and sold 2,500 fewer units than originally estimated.

If the budgeted net income is lower for the master budget level of activity, the net income will be higher than expected because of producing and selling more units than originally estimated.

We can determine the sales volume variance in an easier manner—it will not be necessary to prepare complete comparative statements of budgeted net income. We can do this with the following equation:

Effectiveness is measured in terms of profits lost by not reaching our original goal

$$\begin{matrix} \text{Sales} \\ \text{volume} \\ \text{variance} \end{matrix} = \begin{matrix} \text{difference} \\ \text{in profits} \end{matrix} = \begin{matrix} \text{difference in units} \\ \text{budgeted and units} \\ \text{actually produced} \end{matrix} \times \begin{matrix} \text{contribution} \\ \text{margin per} \\ \text{unit} \end{matrix}$$

For Underhill the contribution margin per unit was $9.

Sales Price		$25
Variable Costs per Unit:		
Direct Materials	$5	
Direct Labor	6	
Variable Overhead	3	
Variable Selling	2	16
Contribution Margin per Unit		$ 9

Based on the difference between the units actually produced, 12,500, and the units originally budgeted, 15,000, the amount of profit lost by Underhill due to ineffectiveness was:

$$\text{Sales volume variance} = (15{,}000 \text{ units} - 12{,}500 \text{ units}) \times \$9 \text{ per unit}$$
$$= 2{,}500 \text{ units} \times \$9 \text{ per unit}$$
$$= \$22{,}500$$

Since Underhill produced and sold 2,500 fewer units than it planned to, its net income will be $22,500 less than it was originally estimated to be.

In the example above we assumed that if the number of units produced was lower than originally planned, then the sales were also lower, resulting in reduced net income. It's quite possible, however, that the unit measure of effectiveness cannot be completely or simply explained in dollars. For example, let's assume that Underhill had originally anticipated selling 2,500 units fewer than it produced in order to increase the inventory level in this period to meet significantly increased demand in the following period. In this situation the reduced production in this period may have only led to higher production in the next period. As a result, Underhill really didn't lose any income this period by producing below the master budget level of activity. In those situations in which the unit measure of effectiveness does not actually affect the sales for the firm, we may have to be satisfied with measuring effectiveness in terms of units of output. In this chapter, however, whenever production is below (or above) the master budget level, we will assume that the result is a decrease (or increase) in sales and resulting income — making the sales volume variance the appropriate dollar measure of activity.

Sales volume variance may not always measure effectiveness

STANDARD COSTS

The budgets so far expressed expectations in terms of actual costs

Thus far, we have been concerned with predictions of what actual costs "will be" or "would have been" rather than what the costs "should be" or "should have been." For example, suppose we know that a worker can make a unit for $10, as long as the worker shows a reasonable amount of care and concentration. We expect to produce 1,000 units next month and are preparing the master budget. We learn from the worker's supervisor that the worker has not been performing as well as expected because of personal problems. So instead of budgeting $10,000 (1,000 units × $10), we budget the costs to be 10% higher — $11,000 (1,000 × $11). The $11,000 is a prediction of what the actual costs "will be"; it does not indicate what the costs "should be" — 1,000 units × $10 = $10,000.

Now let's assume that the month is over, that 1,200 units have actually been produced, and that we are now preparing the flexible budget for the performance report. Remembering what the supervisor told us about the worker's personal problems, we budget the costs at $13,200 (1,200 × $11). This amount is an estimate of what we think the actual costs "would have been" to make 1,200 units; it does not indicate what the costs "should have been" to make the 1200 units—1,200 × $10 = $12,000.

We're now interested in what costs should be or should have been

When we estimate what costs should be instead of will be (when we look into the future), and what costs shoud have been instead of would have been (when we look back at the past), we are dealing with a type of costs we call "standard costs." **Standard costs,** which are carefully predetermined estimates of what costs should be or should have been, are target costs to aim for rather than merely anticipated actual results. Standard costs are determined in an extremely careful manner rather than on the basis of rough estimates. They may be used for several purposes, including:

1. Building master budgets

2. Evaluating performance with flexible budgets

3. Facilitating product costing

4. Reducing bookkeeping costs

Uses of Standard Costs

Building Master Budgets

The master budget will now be an estimate of what costs should be in the future

We can use standard costs in the preparation of the master budget, in which case the budget represents *what we think the costs should be in the forthcoming period, instead of what we think the actual costs will be.* For our worker mentioned above, who had personal problems, we would budget $10,000 for the period instead of $11,000. Now during the period control will be exerted to reach the $10,000 goal. If we set out to attain a $10,000 goal we have a better chance of reaching it than if we set our goal at $11,000 and hope to spend only $10,000. If we aim at $11,000, we will probably have a self-fulfilling prophecy.

Evaluating Performance with Flexible Budgets

The flexible budget can now be an estimate of what costs should have been in the past

The flexible budget shown in Exhibit 10-5 provided a rough estimate of what the actual costs were expected to be in producing 12,500 units. If the company were using a standard cost system, and if the per-unit costs were standard costs per unit, the *same flexible budget would represent what the costs should have been in producing 12,500 units.*

If managers are to determine the causes of variances and take the necessary corrective action to reduce variances to an acceptable amount in the next period, it is better that the variances represent the deviations of costs from what they should have been than from what they were expected to be. If costs are exactly as we expect them to be, we might not realize that what we expect is based on an inefficiently run operation and that a zero difference between actual and expected does not necessarily mean that adequate control is being exerted. The use of standards gives better assurance to managers that (1) the operation is being properly controlled when variances are zero or insignificant, and (2) a significant variance means that the operation is out of control, warranting the time and costs of an investigation.

Before we go on to the third reason for using standard costs, remember one important point: The master budget and the flexible budget are merely mechanical tools used by accountants to predict costs at different levels of activity and at different points in time; *standard costs represent the type of costs* being predicted in the master budget and the flexible budget.

Facilitating Product Costing

Standard costs make good inventory costs

Product costs are those that are associated with and assigned to units in inventory. The costs are classified as assets until the units are sold, at which time they become an expense—cost of goods sold. The costs assigned to units in inventory can be actual costs or standard costs.

Proponents of standard costing contend that for units in inventory, the definition of an asset—a resource having a future economic benefit—is better met by assigning standard costs rather than actual costs to inventory. They argue that standard costs, not actual costs, provide future economic benefits in terms of revenues generated from the sale of units. What they mean is this.

Let's suppose that after all the production is said and done, and all the units are on the shelves in inventory waiting for sale, and all the costs are determined, it turns out that the actual costs are higher than the standard costs. The difference—the excess costs—at this point cannot be passed on to buyers in terms of higher prices. (Remember: The selling price was set much earlier, when the costs were budgeted; more than likely, that price has been advertised or a commitment to it made in some way to customers.) Therefore, that part of the actual costs above the standard costs, which we tend to think of as "the excess costs" and which we refer to as *unfavorable variances,* provides no future benefits and, as a result, should not be considered a cost of this particular asset, the units in inventory.

How, then, do we account for the part of the actual costs in excess of standard costs, that is, the unfavorable variances? These costs are considered by proponents of standard costing to be losses for the period which should be deducted on the income statement when they occur.

We "apply" costs for product costing

When we employ standard costs for product costing, we use the word *applied* to represent the amount assigned to the units using a predetermined standard rate for each unit. Although the term *applied* is often used only when dealing with overhead, it certainly has a general enough meaning to be used with direct labor and direct materials as well. So from now on, whenever you see the word *applied,* whether we're talking about direct materials, direct labor, or factory overhead, you'll know exactly what it means. It is the amount assigned—for product costing purposes—to the units being produced in work-in-process, using a standard rate for each unit.

Reducing Bookkeeping Costs

Bookkeeping costs are less with standard costs

It is less expensive to keep records when standard costs are used in determining the cost of a product than it is when actual costs are used. Fewer calculations are required for a product costing system using standard costs.

For example, assume that a company produces 10 units during a month and that the standard cost of making each unit is $16. That is all there is to the recordkeeping of costs, whereas a product costing system using actual costs must keep track of the exact materials, labor, and overhead costs to assign to each unit or group of units as they progress from one production department to another. A standard cost system merely keeps track of the number of units produced during the month, and then at month-end assigns $16 to each unit. When the units are sold, using actual costs to determine the actual cost of goods sold requires one of the inventory methods (FIFO, LIFO, etc.) because each batch of units must be distinguished from the others. Under a standard cost system all like units bear the same cost. Therefore, the assignment of costs to the units sold is simply $16 multiplied by the number of units sold.

Remember, what we are referring to here is that the *bookkeeping costs* for an actual cost system are greater than for a standard cost system. However, there are costs other than bookkeeping costs for a standard cost system that don't exist for an actual cost system. These include the costs of developing and implementing the standard cost system, the costs of determining and evaluating variances, and the costs of implementing corrective actions.

Proponents of standard costing argue, however, that these costs are outweighed by the benefits of better information and the elimination of inefficiencies.

Types of Standards — A Matter of Tightness

A standard cost represents the amount it should cost to produce a unit of output. But is the amount it should cost based on extremely tight or lax conditions? Is a standard cost the least amount it can ever cost to make a unit, or is it the cost to make a unit when workers are merely doing a pretty good job? Is a standard virtually impossible or relatively easy to attain? The answers to these questions depend on the types of standards that we use — ideal standards or currently attainable standards.

Ideal Standards

Ideal standards are usually impossible to attain for a sustained period of time

Ideal standards represent what it should cost to produce a unit if production conditions are perfect. This assumes that workers can perform at peak efficiency 100% of the time, that all units are 100% perfect, that there are no spoiled or defective units, that machines never break down, and that overtime is never necessary. Of course, exceptions to all these assumptions do occur; they are expected and are even accepted, within reasonable limits, as part of the process of production. Thus we realize that it is impossible for workers and machinery to attain these standards of perfection, resulting in variances that are always unfavorable.

One possible consequence of using ideal standards is that there may be a negative response on the part of employees to improve. If they can never attain the goal, they might develop an attitude of "why try?" Instead of standards helping to find and eliminate inefficiencies, they might cause greater inefficiencies.

Currently Attainable Standards

Currently attainable standards are realistic expectations

Currently attainable standards provide allowances for normal and acceptable imperfections in the production process. Currently attainable standards are realistic expectations of what should be accomplished under continuing efficient operating conditions.

They are not easy to attain, but they are possible to attain.

Currently attainable standards are recommended over ideal standards for several reasons:

1. The master budget will be a more useful planning device if it offers a realistic approximation of future expectations.

2. Since currently attainable standards give a realistic indication of what workers should have accomplished, any variances that result will provide a better clue to areas that need to be investigated.

3. Currently attainable standards are more likely to be recognized by workers as reasonable expectations of management, and are thereby more likely to motivate workers in a positive manner.

Categories of Standards and Variances

Standard costs are set for each type of production cost—direct materials, direct labor, and factory overhead. Each of these standards has two components: (1) a price standard and (2) a quantity standard. A *price standard* measures the dollar cost that should be paid for each of the inputs needed for production. For direct materials the inputs can be measured in gallons, pounds, bottles, packages, etc. For direct labor and variable overhead, inputs are usually measured in hours.

A *quantity standard* represents the quantity of each input that should be used for each unit completed.

Price variance plus quantity variance equals the total flexible budget variance

Variances occur whenever actual results are different from the standard. Because there are two components of a standard cost, there are also two corresponding variances—the *price variance (PV)* and the *quantity variance (QV)*. The addition of the price variance and quantity variance is the *total flexible budget variance (FBV)*—or just flexible budget variance. There is a price variance, a quantity variance, and a flexible budget variance for each variable production cost (direct materials, direct labor, and variable overhead). For fixed overhead there is a price variance, but there is no quantity variance (this will be explained later).

In addition, there is a different type of variance just for fixed factory overhead—the volume variance. We will postpone discussion of this variance until the end of the chapter.

Standard Costs and Flexible Budgets

The flexible budget is a tool for predicting costs; standard costs are the type of cost being predicted

The terms *standard cost* and *flexible budget* are often used interchangeably, which is acceptable, even though they do mean different things. As we mentioned earlier, the flexible budget is the tool for predicting costs, and standard costs are the type of costs being predicted. Since the only costs that we will now be predicting in the flexible budgets are standard costs, we will refer to the flexible budgets and to the standard costs within the flexible budgets as if they were the same. A second way that these two terms differ relates to whether we are referring to total dollars or per-unit dollars. The term *standard cost* technically refers to a cost per unit, or per pound, or per hour, rather than to the total costs for some level of activity. Conversely, the term *flexible budget* technically is a measure of total dollars, rather than dollars per unit or per hour. For example, if a standard cost is $5 per unit, then the flexible budget for 1,000 units is $5,000. Once again there is a conceptual difference in the two terms, but the difference has tended to blur through indiscriminate usage. So the $5-per-unit standard cost might be referred to as the flexible budget per unit and the $5,000 flexible budget might be called the total standard costs. This will be perfectly acceptable.

AN ILLUSTRATION OF STANDARD COSTING

For the purpose of this illustration, additional details concerning the production costs of the Underhill Company are provided in Example 10-1.

We will use these details to calculate the standard costs and the variances. The standard costs per unit are the same as the budgeted costs per unit shown in Exhibit 10-4.

In Exhibit 10-4 we assumed that the per-unit amounts represented what we *expected the actual costs to be* during production. Now we are assuming—by using standards—that the per-unit amounts are what *it should cost* to produce each unit. In addition, each per-unit standard cost is broken down into a price standard and a

Example 10-1

ADDITIONAL FACTS FOR THE UNDERHILL COMPANY

The Underhill Company has recently developed a standard cost system for the control of its production operations. According to the controller, Kelly Hernandez, the following standards for variable costs have been set for the production of each unit (a good luck charm):

Direct Materials ($\frac{1}{2}$ lb/unit @ $10/lb) $5

Direct Labor (2 hr/unit @ $3/hr).   6

Variable Overhead (2 hr/unit @ $1.50/hr).   3

Fixed overhead is budgeted at $15,000 per month.

At the beginning of January 1988, 15,000 units were budgeted for production. There were only 12,500 units actually produced during the month. The actual results for the month's production were as follows:

6500 Purchase

6,404 pounds ~~purchased and~~ used, at a cost of $10.15 per pound

26,621 hours worked

$78,000 of direct labor costs ($2.93 per hour)

$39,000 of variable overhead costs ($1.465 per hour)

$14,900 of fixed overhead

quantity standard, which will allow us to determine individually the price and quantity variances as well as the total flexible budget variance. In Exhibit 10-5 we were only able to calculate the total flexible budget variance.

Direct Materials

The purchasing agent is responsible for direct materials price variances

The purchasing agent is usually the person responsible for determining the standard price for materials. He or she is also responsible for acquiring the proper quantity and quality of materials required for production at the standard price. Determining the standard price can be a difficult task because it often is no more than a guess of what price the suppliers will be charging in the future rather than a carefully determined calculation of the price the company "ought" to be charged.

The purchasing agent shops around to find the best price, being sure to take into consideration cash and quantity discounts and different means and costs of transportation. Having set the standard price, purchases in the future at any other price result in a price variance.

Quantity standards are set by the engineering department in companies that have one. Otherwise, the quantity standard will probably be determined by production superintendents and foremen based on their working knowledge of the materials needed for each unit, as well as the ability of laborers and the quality of machinery to be used.

The quantity standard is converted into dollars by the accounting department. For example, the Underhill Company has a standard quantity for direct materials of $\frac{1}{2}$ pound per unit. In dollars this standard converts to $5 per unit ($\frac{1}{2}$ pound per unit × $10 per pound). And the flexible budget for the 12,500 units produced is $62,500 (12,500 units × $5 per unit).

Production foremen are responsible for seeing that workers in their departments use the correct amount of materials. If the actual usage is different from the standard allowed for the units produced, there will be a quantity variance.

Calculating the Variances

The purchasing agent has a responsibility to pay the established standard price (the "price" charged by the supplier becomes the "cost" for the buyer) for whatever he or she purchases in the current period. If a purchase is made at a price other than the standard price, then the resulting price variance should be based on the quantity purchased currently, even if some of the purchase is not used in production until a later period. The price variance is not based on the quantity used (unless the quantity used happens to be the same as the quantity purchased) because the event causing the variance is the purchase of materials at a price different from standard—not the usage of materials. Furthermore, a price variance must be recognized at the time of purchase, not later when the material is used. If recognition is postponed to a time later than the event that caused the price variance, the explanation for paying the excessive price would no longer be very useful information.

The ***materials price variance*** (direct materials) can be computed using the following equation:

You use the standard price to get the quantity variance

$$\text{Materials price variance} = \begin{matrix}\textit{actual} \\ \textbf{quantity} \\ \textbf{purchased}\end{matrix} \times \begin{matrix}\textit{difference} \textbf{ between} \\ \textit{actual} \text{ and } \textit{standard} \textbf{ costs} \\ \textbf{per unit of input purchased}\end{matrix}$$

Based upon the information in Example 10-1, the price variance for Underhill, where the materials price standard is $10 per pound, is:

$$\text{Materials price variance} = 6{,}404 \text{ lb} \times (\$10.15 - \$10.00)$$
$$= 6{,}404 \text{ lb} \times \$0.15/\text{lb} = \$960 \text{ U}$$

The $960 materials price variance is considered to be unfavorable because the actual price paid for each pound purchased ($10.15) was higher than it should have been ($10.00).

The ***materials quantity variance*** (direct materials) is based on the difference between the actual quantity used and the standard quantity allowed. The ***standard quantity allowed*** represents the quantity of direct materials that should have been used to make the units produced during the period. If this quantity is different from the actual quantity used, there is a quantity variance.

The dollar amount of the materials quantity variance can be calculated with the following equation:

The materials price variance is based on the quantity purchased

$$\text{Materials quantity variance} = \begin{matrix}\textit{difference} \textbf{ between} \\ \textit{actual} \textbf{ quantity used} \\ \textbf{and } \textit{standard} \textbf{ quantity} \\ \textbf{allowed}\end{matrix} \times \begin{matrix}\textit{standard} \textbf{ cost per} \\ \textbf{unit of input}\end{matrix}$$

The materials quantity variance for Underhill, where the materials quantity standard is $\frac{1}{2}$ pound per unit, is:

$$\text{Materials quantity variance} = [6{,}404 \text{ lb} - (\tfrac{1}{2} \text{ lb} \times 12{,}500 \text{ units})] \times \$10/\text{lb}$$
$$= (6{,}404 \text{ lb} - 6{,}250 \text{ lb}) \times \$10/\text{lb}$$
$$= 154 \text{ lb} \times \$10/\text{lb} = \$1{,}540 \text{ U}$$

The materials quantity variance (also known as the ***materials usage variance***) of $1,540 is unfavorable: Instead of using 6,250 pounds to produce 12,500 units, 6,404 pounds were used, or 154 pounds too many.

Why use the standard cost per pound?

The 154 pounds is multiplied by the standard cost per pound—not the actual cost per pound—to get the quantity variance in dollars. One reason we use the standard rate to calculate the direct materials quantity variance (as well as the direct labor and variable overhead quantity variances) is to avoid double counting of the price variance. The $0.15 variance has already been fully accounted for in the price variance of $960. If the $10.15 actual rate is used to calculate the quantity variance, instead of the $10.00 standard rate, then the $0.15 variance affects the quantity variance as well as the price variance—it is being double-counted.

Double counting

A second reason—which is related to the first—for using the standard rate in the calculation of the quantity variance has to do with the fact that responsibility center managers should be assigned responsibility for only those things they can control. In most situations the purchasing agent has more control over the price paid for the raw materials than any other person in the organization, while the production foreman usually has little, if any, control over the price paid. For this reason the responsibility for the price variance is usually assigned to the purchasing agent and not to the production foreman. If we determine the quantity variance using the actual rate of $10.15, then we are assigning the price variance of $0.15 not only to the purchasing agent but also to the production foreman. In this situation the production foreman's quantity variance is $0.15 higher for each pound of variance because the price paid by the purchasing agent was too high. Since the quantity variance should be unaffected by the excessive cost, we use the $10 standard rate instead.

The foreman shouldn't be assigned the price variance

The total flexible budget variance for direct materials is then:

FBV = PV + QV

Total flexible budget variance = price variance + quantity variance
$$= \$960 \text{ U} + \$1,540 \text{ U} = \$2,500 \text{ U}$$

Another approach to calculating variances makes use of an analysis that is quite similar in appearance to a performance report. This approach, called a ***three-column analysis,*** is presented in Exhibit 10-6. Notice that in columns (2) and (3) of Exhibit 10-6 we are once again using the term *flexible budget.* We started with a standard cost per unit or per pound, and now we are converting these unit standards into total dollars with the flexible budget. Remember: When we have a standard cost system, the flexible budget indicates what the costs "should have been" for a specified level of activity. Column (2)—the flexible budget based on the actual quantity—indicates that we should have spent $10 per pound for each of the 6,404 pounds that were purchased—we should have spent $64,040 to acquire the direct materials. Column (3)—the flexible budget based on the standard quantity allowed—indicates that we should have used 6,250 pounds at a price of $10 per pound to make 12,500 units—we should have spent $62,500 to make 12,500 units.

Refer to Exhibit 10-5 (on page 416), and compare the first line across, direct materials, to this expanded three-column analysis in Exhibit 10-6. In both figures the actual costs are $65,000; the flexible budget costs [column (3) in Exhibit 10-6] are $62,500; and the total flexible budget variance is $2,500. Exhibit 10-6 shows that with the addition of the flexible budget based on actual quantity [column (2) in Exhibit 10-6] the $2,500 can be broken down into price and quantity variances. The flexible budget in column (3) is based on the standard quantity allowed to produce 12,500 units (6,250 pounds); the flexible budget in column (2) is based on the actual quantity used to produce 12,500 units (6,404 pounds). Column (2), the flexible budget based

**EXHIBIT 10-6 Three-Column Analysis for Direct Materials
(Quantity used equals quantity purchased)**

We have a price variance because we paid too much for what we bought. We have a quantity variance because we used too many pounds.

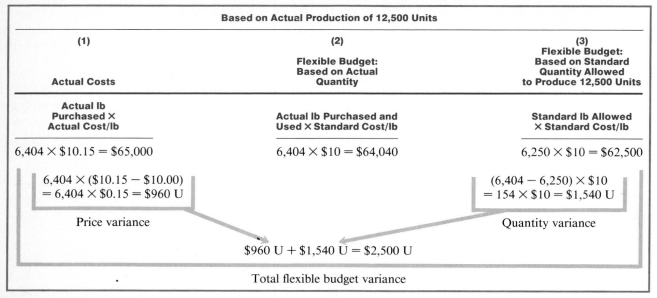

Remember, we are now assuming that we purchase and use the same number of pounds — 6,404

on the quantity purchased and used (6,404 pounds × $10 = $64,040), is compared to the actual costs for what was purchased to get the price variance, and it is compared to the flexible budget in column (3) to get the quantity variance.

In Exhibit 10-6 we found the flexible budget variance ($2,500 U) by adding together the price variance ($960 U) and the quantity variance ($1,540 U). We could also have calculated the flexible budget variance by subtracting column (3), $62,500, from column (1), $65,000. *A warning, though, if you use this second approach: It doesn't work for direct materials if the quantities purchased and used are different amounts (see Exhibit 10-7).*

Example 10-1 specified that 6,404 pounds were purchased and all of it was used. If the quantity used were different from the quantity purchased, the formula for calculating the price variance would be the same. However, the three-column analysis for direct materials would need some minor adjustments. Assume that 6,404 pounds were used in production but that 6,500 pounds were purchased. The three-column analysis would be as shown in Exhibit 10-7.

The price variance is $975 because 6,500 pounds were purchased. When we assumed that 6,404 were purchased, the price variance was $960. *The fact that 6,404 pounds were actually used in production has no bearing on the price variance and how we calculate it. The actual quantity used only enters into the quantity variance calculation.*

The flexible budget variance is now $2,515 U, found by adding together the price variance ($975 U) and the quantity variance ($1,540 U). Notice now, however, that the alternative way of determining the flexible budget variance no longer works for direct materials. When we subtract column (3), $62,500, from column (1), $65,975, we get $3,475 U — which is not the same as $2,515 U.

The Cause of Each Variance

Now find out what went wrong

Once the variances are calculated, the next step for a manager is to find out what caused them.

Was the price variance due to a change in the price? Buying in too small a quantity? Buying better-quality materials than are required?

Was the quantity variance due to improper standards? Machine breakdowns? Poor workmanship? Poor-quality materials?

Only after the causes have been determined can corrective action be taken. The standard may need to be revised; the laborers may need additional training; the purchasing agent may need to shop around for better deals. If the information revealed by the variances is not put to good use in making these kinds of corrections, then the costs of devising, implementing, and applying a standard cost system will be wasted.

Standard Costs and Product Costing

The product costs were the standard costs in column (3)

Thus far, all our attention in this section has been directed to using standards and flexible budgets to control operations. Remember, standard costs can also be used for product costing. If we do decide to assign standard costs instead of actual costs to the units produced, what amount of standard costs do we assign to the 12,500 units? If you look back to Exhibit 10-6, you'll see the answer. Column (3) is standard pounds multiplied by the standard cost per pound:

$$6{,}250 \text{ lb} \times \$10/\text{lb} = \$62{,}500$$

The flexible budget of $62,500 represents how much we should have spent to make 12,500 units. This is the amount to assign to the units produced. This is the amount applied.

**EXHIBIT 10-7   Three-Column Analysis for Direct Materials
(Quantity purchased differs from quantity used)**

When the quantities purchased and used aren't the same, the middle column is split into two parts: the actual quantity purchased and the actual quantity used.

Based on Actual Production of 12,500 Units			
(1)	**(2)**		**(3)**
	Flexible Budget: Based on Actual Quantity		**Flexible Budget: Based on Standard Quantity Allowed to Produce 12,500 Units**
Actual Costs			
Actual lb × Actual Cost/lb	**Actual lb × Standard Cost/lb**		**Standard lb Allowed × Standard Cost/lb**
	Quantity purchased	Quantity used	
$6{,}500 \times \$10.15 = \$65{,}975$	$6{,}500 \times \$10 = \$65{,}000$	$6{,}404 \times \$10 = \$64{,}040$	$6{,}250 \times \$10 = \$62{,}500$
$6{,}500 \times (\$10.15 - \$10.00)$ $= 6{,}500 \times \$0.15 = \$975 \text{ U}$			$(6{,}404 - 6{,}250) \times \$10$ $= 154 \times \$10 = \$1{,}540 \text{ U}$
Price variance			Quantity variance
	$\$975 \text{ U} + \$1{,}540 \text{ U} = \$2{,}515 \text{ U}$		
	Total flexible budget variance		

Remember, we are using the term *applied* to mean the amount that is assigned to the units produced—for product costing purposes—on the basis of a predetermined rate. For direct materials, as it will be for direct labor and variable factory overhead, the amount applied is equal to the flexible budget based upon the standard quantity allowed. Thus we are using the same amount—$62,500—for two purposes. Not only is it the flexible budget that is used to determine the quantity variance in the performance report—for control purposes—but it is also the amount applied to production—for product costing purposes.

The flexible budget in column (2) does not represent the standard costs of producing 12,500 units because it is based on the actual pounds used (6,404), not the standard pounds allowed (6,250).

Graphic Approach to Direct Materials

Before you go on to the discussion of direct labor, you may want to look at the first section of Appendix 10-1, which shows the graphic approach to variance analysis for direct materials. The graphic approach is compatible with the three-column variance analysis we've just completed. It should be helpful in obtaining a more complete understanding of flexible budgets, performance reports, and variances.

Direct Labor

Price standard

The labor price (or rate) standard is not usually set by management and imposed upon workers. Instead, labor rates are typically determined either by labor contracts negotiated between management and labor or by local conditions of supply and demand for labor. The exact rates may also depend on conditions within the company, since different rates apply based on a worker's position, seniority, and the difficulty or skill of tasks performed. All these factors affect the direct labor price standard.

Quantity standard

Labor quantity standards (also called labor efficiency standards) are often difficult to establish. Given a variety of workers, each with different skills and abilities, the idea behind a labor quantity standard is to determine what an average worker under continuing normal conditions can accomplish. The method of making such a determination is called a **time and motion study** and is conducted by the engineering department. A time and motion study is a scientific analysis of an entire labor operation and its component parts, determining the best way to make each part and the amount of time needed to do each part, so that the entire operation can be performed most efficiently.

Another means of setting labor quantity standards is the test run. Test runs of the labor operation are conducted under controlled conditions for a short period of time; the results are observed, documented, and analyzed. On the basis of these results, labor quantity standards are set.

Foremen are usually held responsible for both the labor price (or rate) variance and the labor quantity (or efficiency) variance. Labor price variances should be quite small, since the rates are not usually subject to sudden change. However, they will probably not be zero, because there will be cases where a worker earning one rate is substituted for another earning a different rate, and also because of overtime premiums.

Calculating the Variances

Direct materials variances are calculated for two distinct events—the purchase of materials and the subsequent use of those materials.

For direct labor these two events occur simultaneously—the labor hours are purchased and used at exactly the same time. Therefore, the labor price variance and

The labor price variance is based on the actual hours worked

The actual hours are purchased and used

Notice the similarity of variances

labor quantity variance are both calculated based on the actual hours that are used (or worked).

The ***labor price variance*** is calculated using the following equation:

$$\text{Labor price variance} = \text{actual hours worked} \times \text{difference between actual wage rate and standard wage rate}$$

Compare this equation with the one for the materials price variance; note the similarities. Although labor deals with hours worked rather than quantity purchased, and the price for labor is a wage rate rather than a cost per pound, the equation for the price variance for materials and the one for labor have exactly the same form. Notice the colored words in the equation for the labor price variance and compare them to the colored words in the equation for the materials price variance; then compare them to the equation for the variable overhead price variance that comes later. All three price variances involve an actual quantity multiplied by the difference between actual and standard prices.

For Underhill, where the labor price standard is $3 per hour, the labor price variance is:

$$\text{Labor price variance} = 26{,}621 \text{ hr} \times (\$2.93 - \$3.00)$$
$$= 26{,}621 \text{ hr} \times \$0.07/\text{hr} = \$1{,}863 \text{ F}$$

The labor price variance of $1,863 is favorable because the actual wage rate paid to workers ($2.93) was less than the standard rate ($3.00) set for the operation.

The ***labor quantity variance*** is calculated with the following equation:

Use the standard rate per hour for the quantity variance

$$\text{Labor quantity variance} = \text{difference between actual hours worked and standard hours allowed} \times \text{standard rate per hour}$$

The term ***standard hours allowed*** represents the direct labor-hours that should have been worked to produce the units completed during the period.

The equation for a direct labor quantity variance can be shown as having the same form as the equations for the direct materials quantity variance and the variable overhead quantity variance. Each quantity variance involves a difference between actual quantity used and standard quantity allowed, the difference multiplied by a standard price. Recognizing the similarities in variances for materials, labor, and variable overhead can be helpful in learning, understanding, and remembering them. It is easier to learn two basic variances—price variance and quantity variance—and to adapt them to the three production costs than it is to learn six variances as if they were completely dissimilar.

The labor quantity variance for Underhill, where the labor quantity standard is 2 hours per unit, is:

$$\text{Labor quantity variance} = [26{,}621 \text{ hr} - (2 \text{ hr} \times 12{,}500 \text{ units})] \times \$3/\text{hr}$$
$$= (26{,}621 \text{ hr} - 25{,}000 \text{ hr}) \times \$3/\text{hr}$$
$$= 1{,}621 \text{ hr} \times \$3/\text{hr} = \$4{,}863 \text{ U}$$

The labor quantity variance is unfavorable, since 1,621 actual hours were used in excess of the standard allowed (26,621 − 25,000 = 1,621 hours).

EXHIBIT 10-8 Three-Column Analysis for Direct Labor
For direct labor the hours purchased and used are always the same. So column (2) never has to be split into two parts as it does for direct materials.

Based on Actual Production of 12,500 Units		
(1)	**(2)**	**(3)**
	Flexible Budget: Based on Actual Quantity Worked	**Flexible Budget: Based on Standard Quantity Allowed to Produce 12,500 Units**
Actual Costs		
Actual hr × Actual Rate/hr	**Actual hr × Standard Rate/hr**	**Standard hr Allowed × Standard Rate/hr**
$26,621 \times \$2.93 = \$78,000$	$26,621 \times \$3 = \$79,863$	$25,000 \times \$3 = \$75,000$

$26,621 \times (\$2.93 - \$3.00)$
$= 26,621 \times \$0.07 = \$1,863 \text{ F}$

Price variance

$(26,621 - 25,000) \times \$3$
$= 1,621 \times \$3 = \$4,863 \text{ U}$

Quantity variance

$\$1,863 \text{ F} + \$4,863 \text{ U} = \$3,000 \text{ U}$

Total flexible budget variance

The total flexible budget variance for direct labor is the sum of the labor price variance and the labor quantity variance.

FBV = PV + QV

Total flexible budget variance = $1,863 F + $4,863 U = $3,000 U

The three-column approach to calculating the direct labor variances is shown in Exhibit 10-8 above, and the graphic approach is discussed in Appendix 10-1.

Notice in Exhibit 10-8 that the total flexible budget variance can be found in two ways. In addition to the way shown in the exhibit ($1,863 F + $4,863 U = $3,000 U), you can also find it by subtracting column (3) from column (1)—$78,000 − $75,000 = $3,000 U.

The Cause of Each Variance

What is the cause of each variance?

Once we have calculated the variances, it is then necessary to determine their causes and to take corrective action when warranted. A price variance can occur when different workers are used on a job rather than the ones that we expected. For example, we may use a worker with less seniority and therefore pay a lower wage rate than we had planned on.

Labor quantity variances can occur for a variety of reasons. It could be that the worker mentioned above is paid a lower wage rate because of inexperience; as a result, the worker might take longer to finish the job than the worker we planned on using would have taken. Other causes include machine breakdowns, defective materials, poor workmanship, and inadequate supervision.

Standard Costs and Product Costing

The product costs are the standard costs

If we are using standard costs for product costing as well as for control—that is, we are assigning standard costs to the units produced instead of assigning actual costs—then the amount we would assign is $75,000. This is the standard hours allowed multiplied by the standard rate per hour (25,000 hours × $3 per hour) that we find in column (3) of Exhibit 10-8. The $75,000 represents how much Underhill should have spent to produce 12,500 units.

Therefore, just as we saw for direct materials, column (3) serves two purposes:

Column (3) is used for both control and product costing

1. It is the flexible budget based on standard hours allowed, which we use to calculate the quantity variance and the flexible budget variance. We use it in this manner to help managers *control*.

2. It is also the dollar amount that we assign to the units produced when we are using a standard cost system for *product costing*. It is the amount of direct labor applied to production.

Variable Factory Overhead

Direct materials and direct labor are direct costs because they either are physically related to or become an integral part of the units produced. It is possible to determine the exact amount of direct materials and direct labor going into each unit. To set standards for direct materials and direct labor, engineers figure the exact quantity of materials and hours of direct labor that should go into each unit. From these quantities the standard costs per unit are calculated, representing the costs that should be incurred to produce each and every unit.

Variable overhead is indirectly related to production

Variable overhead costs are indirectly related to production. This means that although the costs are necessary, they cannot be closely, or directly, associated with specific units of production. For this reason setting standards for variable overhead costs is somewhat different from setting standards for direct materials and direct labor. Rather than determining an exact amount of variable overhead that should be incurred every time a unit is completed, an average is determined. The average represents how much overhead should be incurred per unit in a batch of units produced over an extended period of time.

For example, assume that the standard costs per unit for the production of Formica-top tables include $2.00 for Formica (a direct material) and $0.50 for utilities (an indirect item of variable overhead).

Each table would require one Formica table top and thus $2.00 of materials cost, whether it was the first, tenth, or one-thousandth table produced.

The $0.50 per table for utilities has a different explanation. It would not be reasonable to expect the utility bill to increase by exactly $0.50 every time a table was finished. However, over a longer period of time, say, a month, we might expect the total utility bill to average $0.50 per table.

In order to develop standards for variable overhead, it is necessary to deal with averages rather than exact costs per unit. We can determine these averages with the aid of statistical tools for evaluating the behavior of costs. These tools are beyond the scope of this text, however, and will be covered in your upper-level statistics and cost accounting courses. For our purposes we'll merely accept the fact that Underhill has evaluated the behavior of its total overhead costs and has determined that the variable overhead costs should average $1.50 per hour. And since we already know (from the discussion of direct labor) that the standard hours allowed per unit are 2, the standard variable overhead rate per unit is $3.00, determined as follows:

$$\text{Variable overhead cost per unit} = \text{standard hours per unit} \times \frac{\text{variable overhead cost}}{\text{per hour}}$$

$$= 2 \text{ hr/unit} \times \$1.50/\text{hr} = \$3/\text{unit}$$

Calculating the Variances

The price variance is just like direct labor's

The calculations of price and quantity variances for variable overhead are nearly the same as those for direct labor. The **variable overhead price** (or **spending**) **variance** is:

$$\frac{\text{Variable overhead}}{\text{price variance}} = \frac{\text{actual}}{\text{hours worked}} \times \frac{\text{\textit{difference} between \textit{actual}}}{\text{cost per hour and \textit{standard}}} \atop \text{cost per hour}$$

For Underhill it would be:

$$\text{Variable overhead price variance} = 26{,}621 \text{ hr} \times (\$1.465 - \$1.50)$$

$$= 26{,}621 \text{ hr} \times \$0.035/\text{hr} = \$932\text{F}$$

The price variance is favorable because the average variable overhead cost incurred per hour ($1.465) was $0.035 less than it was expected to be ($1.50) for the 26,621 actual hours employed in production.

The formula for the **variable overhead quantity variance** is:

So is the quantity variance

$$\frac{\text{Variable overhead}}{\text{quantity variance}} = \frac{\text{\textit{difference} between \textit{actual}}}{\text{hours worked and \textit{standard}}} \atop \text{hours allowed} \times \frac{\text{\textit{standard} cost}}{\text{per hour}}$$

The quantity variance for Underhill is:

$$\frac{\text{Variable overhead}}{\text{quantity variance}} = (26{,}621 \text{ hr} - 25{,}000 \text{ hr}) \times \$1.50/\text{hr}$$

$$= 1{,}621 \text{ hr} \times \$1.50/\text{hr} = \$2{,}432 \text{ U}$$

The quantity variance for variable overhead is based on the difference in actual hours (26,621 hours) and standard hours (25,000 hours) of direct labor. Once these two quantities are determined, the dollar amount of quantity variance is derived by multiplying the quantity difference by the standard cost per hour.

The **total flexible budget variance** for variable overhead is the sum of the price variance and the quantity variance:

FBV = PV + QV

$$\frac{\text{Total flexible}}{\text{budget variance}} \atop \frac{\text{for variable}}{\text{overhead}} = \text{price variance} + \text{quantity variance}$$

The flexible budget variance of $1,500 U in Exhibit 10-9 can also be found by subtracting column (3) from column (1)—$39,000 − $37,500 = $1,500 U.

The three-column approach for determining the variable overhead variances is shown in Exhibit 10-9, and the graphic approach is discussed in Appendix 10-1.

The Cause of Each Variance

The VO quantity variance is closely related to direct labor

Since variable factory overhead is closely related to the number of direct labor-hours used in production, anything that causes a quantity variance for direct labor also results in a quantity variance for variable overhead. So once we have determined the hours of variance for direct labor and the causes of the variance, then we have also determined the hourly variance and causes for variable overhead. The only difference between the quantity variances for direct labor and variable overhead is the standard rate that is multiplied by the difference in actual and standard hours.

EXHIBIT 10-9   Three-Column Analysis for Variable Overhead
The total flexible budget variance for variable overhead is the amount over- or underapplied.

Based on Actual Production of 12,500 Units		
(1)	**(2)**	**(3)**
	Flexible Budget:	**Flexible Budget:**
	Based on Actual	**Based on Standard**
	Quantity Worked	**Quantity Allowed**
Actual Costs		**to Produce 12,500 Units**
Actual hr		**Standard hr**
× Actual Cost/hr	**Actual hr × Standard Cost/hr**	**Allowed × Standard**
		Cost/hr
26,621 × \$1.465 = \$39,000	26,621 × \$1.50 = \$39,932	25,000 × \$1.50 = \$37,500

26,621 × (\$1.465 − \$1.50)
= 26,621 × \$0.035 = \$932 F

(26,621 − 25,000) × \$1.50
= 1,621 × \$1.50 = \$2,432 U

Price variance   Quantity variance

\$932 F + \$2,432 U = \$1,500 U

Total flexible budget variance = underapplied variable overhead

The VO price variance is a residual

The variable overhead price (or spending) variance represents the remainder of the flexible budget variance—the portion that is not explained by the quantity variance. It may arise for a variety of reasons, the exact cause depending on the specific overhead cost being evaluated. It could be that the best measure of activity for some of the overhead costs may not be hours of labor, but that for convenience the same measure of activity is being used for all overhead costs. As a result, the standard rate per hour may not result in as precise an estimate of costs in the flexible budget as we would like—resulting in a price variance. On the other hand, a price variance could be explained by paying a higher average hourly rate than we should have for the indirect laborers. Or it could even be due to the inefficient use of supplies that wasn't already explained by the quantity variance (i.e., wasn't due to the use of too many direct labor-hours).

Standard Costs and Product Costing

The product costs come from column (3)— standard times standard

We have used column (3) in Exhibit 10-9 as the flexible budget based on standard hours allowed to get the quantity variance and the flexible budget variance. We're sure you remember that column (3) can also be used for a second purpose—for product costing. If we are using the standard cost system for product costing, then the dollar amount we assign to the 12,500 units produced is \$37,500—the standard hours allowed multiplied by the standard rate per hour. The \$37,500 is the amount of variable overhead costs that should have been incurred to produce 12,500 units. The \$37,500 is the amount applied to production for the period.

When we compare the amount of overhead applied to what was actually incurred, the difference is commonly referred to as the over- (or under-) applied overhead. If the amount applied is less than the actual, the difference is called *underapplied overhead;* if the amount applied is greater than the actual, the difference is called *overapplied overhead.*

As you look at Exhibit 10-9, you may also notice that the underapplied overhead of $1,500 is the same as the total flexible budget variance. The over- (or under-) applied overhead and the flexible budget variance will always be the same for variable factory overhead. However, they will never be the same for fixed factory overhead, as you will see in the next section. For fixed factory overhead the over- (or under-) applied overhead will be the sum of the flexible budget variance plus the volume variance. There is no such variance as a volume variance for any of the variable manufacturing costs—only for the fixed factory overhead.

More Detail for Variable Overhead

Variable overhead should actually be evaluated on an item-by-item basis

Actually, the variable overhead costs and variances shown in Exhibit 10-9 would probably be broken down into many specific variable overhead costs. An analysis of the variances would be performed for each cost item so that management would have the information needed to take corrective actions. For example, the $932 F price variance and the $2,432 U quantity variance from Exhibit 10-9 might comprise the following items:

	Price Variance	Quantity Variance
Supplies	$1,800 U	$ 811 U
Utilities	600 U	405 U
Indirect Labor	3,332 F	1,216 U
	$ 932 F	$2,432 U

Each variance might have its own cause, its own person bearing responsibility for that item, and its own necessary corrective action.

If the variable overhead cost items have to be treated individually rather than collectively, separate variance calculations must be made for each item. Assume that the total variable overhead rate ($1.50 per hour) and the actual costs ($39,000) used in Exhibit 10-9 are broken down into separate variable overhead cost items as follows:

	Standard Rate	Actual Costs
Supplies	2 hr @ $0.50/hr = $1.00/unit	$15,111
Utilities	2 hr @ $0.25/hr = 0.50/unit	7,255
Indirect Labor	2 hr @ $0.75/hr = 1.50/unit	16,634
Total Variable Overhead	2 hr @ $1.50/hr = $3.00/unit	$39,000

Using the three-column approach for supplies, you can see that the analysis for any of the variable overhead cost items (Exhibit 10-10) is the same as the analysis for the three costs combined (Exhibit 10-9).

Instead of having to do a three-column variance analysis for each different overhead cost item, there is an alternative six-column format that is more compact and treats all items together.

The analysis for supplies is shown in this slightly modified format in Exhibit 10-11. The first three columns do not show the calculations used to determine each number; otherwise, they are the same as in Exhibit 10-10. The other difference relates to the positioning of the variances. Each variance is listed in its own column [columns (4)

EXHIBIT 10-10   Three-Column Analysis for Supplies

	Based on Actual Production of 12,500 Units	
(1)	**(2)** Flexible Budget: Based on Actual Quantity Employed	**(3)** Flexible Budget: Based on Standard Quantity Allowed
Actual Costs		
Actual hr × Actual Cost/hr	**Actual hr × Standard Cost/hr**	**Standard hr Allowed × Standard Cost/hr**
26,621 × $0.5676* = $15,111	26,621 × $0.50 = $13,311	25,000 × $0.50 = $12,500

26,621 × ($0.5676 − $0.50)
= 26,621 × $0.0676 = $1,800 U

(26,621 − 25,000) × $0.50
= 1,621 × $0.50 = $811 U

Price variance   Quantity variance

$1,800 U + $811 U = $2,611 U

Total flexible budget variance, supplies

*$15,111 ÷ 26,621 = $0.5676.

This illustration is only for supplies. But the analysis would be identical for utilities and indirect labor

through (6)] in Exhibit 10-11, whereas each one is positioned in between the columns in Exhibits 10-9 and 10-10.

EXHIBIT 10-11   Six-Column Analysis for Supplies

	Based on Actual Production of 12,500 Units					
(1) Actual Costs	**(2)** Flexible Budget: Based on Actual Quantity Employed	**(3)** Flexible Budget: Based on Standard Quantity Allowed	**(4)**	**(5)**	**(6)**	
Actual hr × Actual Average Cost/hr	**Actual hr × Standard Cost/hr**	**Standard hr Allowed × Standard Cost/hr**	**Price Variance**	**Quantity Variance**	**Total Flexible Budget Variance**
Supplies	$15,111	$13,311	$12,500	$1,800 U	$811 U	$2,611 U
Utilities	—	—	—	—	—	—
Indirect Labor	—	—	—	—	—	—

A Choice in Terminology

Throughout our discussion of the variable production costs (direct materials, direct labor, and variable overhead), we have referred to price and quantity standards and price and quantity variances. Because other texts use different terms, we usually gave you an alternative name that you could use. For example, the term *usage variance* is an acceptable alternative to quantity variance for direct materials.

We use only one set of terms in this text—price and quantity—to emphasize the similarity in form of each type of variance whether we calculate it for direct materials, direct labor, or variable overhead. We feel that you should have no trouble learning two types of variances—and then applying each type to a different variable production cost.

If you'd prefer a choice instead, take a look at Exhibit 10-12. It gives a list of commonly used terms for our price and quantity variances, and it also gives a summary of the equations used in calculating each variance.

EXHIBIT 10-12
Summary of Variances for Variable Production Costs
This exhibit gives commonly used alternative terms for our price and quantity variances. It also shows how to calculate each price and quantity variance.

Variances: Terminology Employed in Text	Commonly Used Alternatives	Equation
Direct materials:		
Price variance	None	Difference in actual and standard price × actual quantity purchased
Quantity variance	Usage variance	Difference in actual quantity used and standard quantity allowed × standard price
Direct labor:		
Price variance	Rate variance	Difference in actual and standard rate per hour × actual hours worked
Quantity variance	Efficiency, time, or usage variance	Difference in actual hours worked and standard hours allowed × standard rate per hour
Variable overhead:		
Price variance	Spending variance	Difference in actual and standard cost per hour × actual hours worked
Quantity variance	Efficiency variance	Difference in actual hours worked and standard hours allowed × standard cost per hour

Fixed Factory Overhead

Our analysis of fixed factory overhead is somewhat different than it is for direct materials, direct labor, and variable overhead. Although we can use a similar multi-column format as we used for the variable cost items, there will be several differences:

The analysis of fixed overhead differs from the analysis of the variable costs

1. We do not have a quantity variance for fixed factory overhead.

2. Although there is a price variance for fixed factory overhead, we do not calculate it in the same manner.

3. We will have to expand the three-column format to four columns when we introduce a new variance—the volume variance.

The fixed factory overhead for the Underhill Company is expected to be $15,000 per month. Since total fixed costs are not expected to change in response to changes in activity, this $15,000 is the amount we budget, regardless of activity. Therefore, the flexible budget based on actual hours of 26,621 and the flexible budget based on the standard hours allowed of 25,000 are both the same amount—$15,000. You can see this when you look at columns (2) and (3) in Exhibit 10-13.

**EXHIBIT 10-13
Three-Column Analysis for
Fixed Overhead**

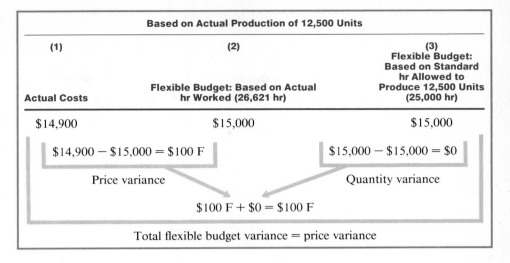

Based on Actual Production of 12,500 Units		
(1)	(2)	(3) Flexible Budget: Based on Standard hr Allowed to Produce 12,500 Units (25,000 hr)
Actual Costs	Flexible Budget: Based on Actual hr Worked (26,621 hr)	
$14,900	$15,000	$15,000

$14,900 − $15,000 = $100 F

Price variance

$15,000 − $15,000 = $0

Quantity variance

$100 F + $0 = $100 F

Total flexible budget variance = price variance

Graphically, the flexible budget for fixed overhead looks like this:

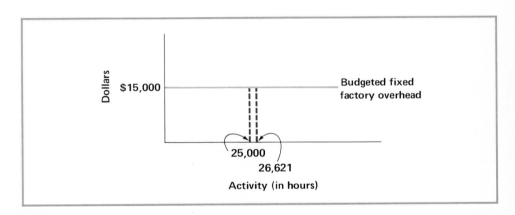

*Budgeted fixed factory
overhead is the same at all
levels of activity*

If the hours in the performance report were 15,000 or 21,000 or 28,000 instead, the flexible budget for fixed factory overhead would still be $15,000.

Calculating the Price Variance

When we subtract the budgeted fixed factory overhead — column (2) — in Exhibit 10-13 from the actual costs incurred — column (1) — we get a favorable *fixed overhead price* (or *spending*) *variance* of $100:

*Price variance for fixed =
actual − budgeted*

$$\begin{array}{c}\textbf{Fixed factory}\\ \textbf{overhead price}\\ \textbf{variance}\end{array} = \begin{array}{c}\textbf{actual}\\ \textbf{costs}\end{array} - \begin{array}{c}\textbf{flexible budget}\\ \textbf{for fixed}\\ \textbf{factory overhead}\end{array}$$

$$= \$14,900 - \$15,000 = \$100 \text{ F}$$

Notice that we did not calculate the fixed overhead price variance in the same way as we did for the variable overhead price variance (difference in the actual and the standard rate per hour × actual hours). Not only didn't we do it that way in Exhibit 10-13 but we will *never* do it that way — because the price variance for fixed factory overhead is not affected by the number of actual hours that we use.

The quantity variance is always zero

Now look at columns (2) and (3) in Exhibit 10-13. Since the amount of fixed factory overhead that we budget for the actual hours and for the standard hours are the same (and will *always* be the same), there is *never* a quantity variance for fixed factory overhead. And since the quantity variance is zero, the total flexible budget variance for fixed factory overhead will always equal its price variance:

The price variance always equals the total flexible budget variance for the total fixed overhead

$$\begin{array}{c} \textbf{Total flexible budget} \\ \textbf{variance for fixed factory} \\ \textbf{overhead} \end{array} = \begin{array}{c} \textbf{price} \\ \textbf{variance} \end{array} + \begin{array}{c} \textbf{quantity} \\ \textbf{variance} \end{array}$$

$$= \frac{\text{price}}{\text{variance}} + \$0$$

$$= \frac{\text{price}}{\text{variance}}$$

Most likely, the total fixed costs shown in Exhibit 10-13 are not represented by merely one item. Instead, there are probably numerous fixed costs (depreciation, part of the utilities, salaries, property taxes, etc.) making up the total. For control purposes it would be necessary to calculate price variances for each of the different fixed costs prior to determining their causes.

The reasons for the fixed overhead price variance

The reason a firm has price variances is simply that it spent more or less than it expected to. It could be that top management decided to reward a department manager with a bonus, in addition to fixed salary, for outstanding performance during the current period. It could be that depreciation was not as predicted because of an unexpected sale of depreciable assets or because of a change in the method of depreciation. Or it might be that the county decreased property tax rates or began to assess property taxes on an amount closer to market value.

The product costs for fixed overhead do not come from column (3)

In our discussion of direct materials, direct labor, and variable overhead, we pointed out that the third column in the performance report served two purposes:

1. For control purposes it is the flexible budget, based on the standard quantity (or hours) allowed, that we use to determine the quantity variance and the flexible budget variance.

2. For product costing purposes it is the amount of standard costs assigned to units produced.

Does column (3) also serve these same two purposes for fixed factory overhead? No, it does not — although we do use it to help control operations by getting a flexible budget variance, we do not use it for product costing.

Fixed Factory Overhead and Product Costing

If budgeted costs were product costs then the per-unit cost would fluctuate dramatically

Let's assume for a moment that we do use column (3) in Exhibit 10-13 — the budgeted fixed factory overhead — for product costing. This means that we will assign the $15,000 to the 12,500 units produced, resulting in a cost per unit of $1.20:

$$\$15,000 \div 12,500 \text{ units} = \$1.20 \text{ per unit}$$

Now let's see what the cost per unit would be if only 1,000 units were produced or if as many as 25,000 units were produced:

$$\$15,000 \div 1,000 \ = \$15 \text{ per unit}$$
$$\$15,000 \div 25,000 = \$0.60 \text{ per unit}$$

Fixed overhead rates could fluctuate greatly with wide swings in activity

Depending upon the number of units produced, the fixed factory overhead per unit can fluctuate quite a bit from month to month. And when you add the fixed overhead costs per unit to the unchanging costs per unit for direct materials, direct labor, and variable factory overhead, you can see that the total costs per unit fluctuate as dramatically:

Units Produced	12,500	1,000	25,000
Costs per Unit:			
Direct Materials..............................	$ 5.00	$ 5.00	$ 5.00
Direct Labor...................................	6.00	6.00	6.00
Variable Overhead...........................	3.00	3.00	3.00
Fixed Overhead	1.20	15.00	0.60
Total Cost per Unit..........................	$15.20	$29.00	$14.60

Now let's assume that the selling price is $25 per unit and that the costs above are for the months of January, July, and November, respectively. Because of the wide swings in the unit costs, look what happens to the monthly gross profits, assuming the units produced are also sold:

	January	July	November
Units Produced and Sold	12,500	1,000	25,000
Sales Price	$25.00	$25.00	$25.00
Total Cost per Unit	15.20	29.00	14.60
Gross Profit per Unit........................	$ 9.80	$(4.00)	$10.40

Looking at the gross profit figures above, one might mistakenly get the impression that the production department was run inefficiently in July but efficiently in January and November. It might even be tempting to consider dropping the product line during the low-volume months because of the negative gross profit per unit.

Neither of these two thoughts would be correct, however. The much higher cost per unit in July was due entirely to the fact that the unchanging fixed overhead of $15,000 was spread over far fewer units than it was in January or November. It has nothing to do with how efficiently the units were produced in July or November or January. As to whether the product line should be dropped, we learned in Chapter 6 that the fixed factory overhead is usually irrelevant to the decision of dropping a product line, since it will probably remain the same in total. What is relevant is whether there is a positive contribution margin — not whether there is a positive gross margin.

Meaningful interim statements require a predetermined fixed overhead rate

If we are going to prepare meaningful monthly income statements, more than likely we'd prefer that the results are not distorted by a fluctuating fixed overhead cost per unit. In order to have meaningful results, we need to find a way to smooth out the wide swings in the per-unit cost during the year, even when production fluctuates significantly from month to month.

We use fixed overhead rates only for product costing

A Predetermined Rate for Fixed Factory Overhead So what do we do? How do we apply fixed factory overhead to production? Well, what we need to do first is to get a predetermined overhead rate for fixed factory overhead, which will remain the same throughout the year. Then we assign this unchanging rate to the units produced (or to the hours needed to produce these units) in each month. We calculate this rate at the beginning of the year, and we use it only for product costing—we do not use it to calculate flexible budgets or to determine the price and quantity variances.

The predetermined fixed factory overhead rate is calculated in the following manner:

$$\text{Predetermined fixed factory overhead rate} = \frac{\textbf{budgeted fixed factory overhead for the year}}{\textbf{normal activity}}$$

We use normal activity in the denominator

The budgeted fixed overhead is the amount that we feel should be spent in the upcoming year. *Normal activity* may be a prediction of activity for a single year, or it may be a prediction of average activity over a period of 4 or 5 years.

Assume that the budgeted fixed overhead for the year for Underhill is $180,000; the normal activity in units is 180,000; and the standard hours allowed are 2 hours per unit.

In most standard cost systems, normal activity is measured in terms of "standard hours." Therefore, the first thing we need to do is to convert normal activity measured in units to normal activity measured in standard hours:

$$180{,}000 \text{ units} \times 2 \text{ hr/unit} = 360{,}000 \text{ standard hr of normal activity}$$

Next, we calculate the fixed overhead rate per standard hour:

The rate: using annual costs and activity

$$\text{Predetermined fixed overhead rate per standard hr} = \frac{\$180{,}000}{360{,}000 \text{ standard hr of normal activity}}$$
$$= \$0.50/\text{standard hr}$$

We have gotten the fixed overhead rate of $0.50 per standard hour using the budgeted fixed overhead for the *year* and normal activity for the *year*. We can also determine this rate using the budgeted fixed overhead for the *month* and the normal activity for the *month*. To calculate the rate this way, we first divide the annual amounts by 12:

$$\text{Monthly budgeted fixed overhead} = \frac{\$180{,}000}{12 \text{ months}} = \$15{,}000$$

and

$$\text{Monthly normal activity} = \frac{360{,}000 \text{ hr}}{12 \text{ months}} = 30{,}000 \text{ hr}$$

We then calculate the rate as follows:

The same rate: using monthly costs and activity

$$\text{Predetermined fixed overhead rate per standard hour} = \frac{\textbf{budgeted fixed overhead per month}}{\textbf{normal activity per month}}$$

$$= \frac{\$15{,}000}{30{,}000 \text{ standard hr of normal activity}}$$
$$= \$0.50/\text{standard hr}$$

The applied is standard hours × standard rate

Fixed Factory Overhead Applied Now that we have a fixed overhead rate per standard hour of $0.50, we can assign fixed factory overhead to the 12,500 units produced in January. We do this by multiplying $0.50 per standard hour times the standard hours allowed to produce these units. For 12,500 units the standard hours allowed are 25,000 (12,500 × 2 hours per unit)—just as they were for direct labor and variable overhead—and the fixed overhead assigned to production (called *fixed overhead applied*) is:

$$\frac{25{,}000 \text{ standard}}{\text{hr allowed}} \times \frac{\$0.50/}{\text{standard hr}} = \$12{,}500 \text{ fixed overhead applied}$$

In order to integrate the fixed overhead applied into the multi-column analysis, we need to use four columns instead of the three that we have been using. Look now at Exhibit 10-14, which has four columns, and notice how it is exactly the same as Exhibit 10-13, except that column (4)—the fixed overhead applied—has been added.

Volume Variances

The volume variance is the difference between columns (3) and (4)

We are introducing a new variance in Exhibit 10-14—the *fixed overhead volume variance.* It is the difference between:

1. The fixed overhead budgeted of $15,000 in column (3)—which is the amount that *should* be incurred during January's production—and

2. The fixed overhead applied $12,500 in column (4)—which is the amount we assign (apply) to the units produced, based on a predetermined fixed overhead rate

Why do we have a volume variance?

The volume variance (also called the *idle capacity variance*) of $2,500 means that we have *applied* fewer dollars to the units that were produced than we were *budgeted* to spend during the month. The reason that we have a volume variance has to do with the fact that we applied the fixed overhead rate to 25,000 standard hours allowed for the 12,500 units produced but the normal activity is 5,000 hours higher—or 30,000 hours. Let us now explain what we mean.

EXHIBIT 10-14
Four-Column Analysis for Fixed Factory Overhead
Column (4) is the fixed overhead applied, which we need only for product costing. We still use the first three columns to aid in control. The difference in the budget and the applied is the volume variance.

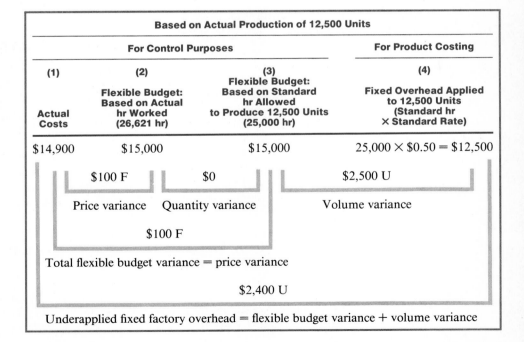

		Based on Actual Production of 12,500 Units		
		For Control Purposes		**For Product Costing**
(1)	**(2)**	**(3)**		**(4)**
	Flexible Budget: Based on Actual hr Worked (26,621 hr)	**Flexible Budget: Based on Standard hr Allowed to Produce 12,500 Units (25,000 hr)**		**Fixed Overhead Applied to 12,500 Units (Standard hr × Standard Rate)**
Actual Costs				
$14,900	$15,000	$15,000		25,000 × $0.50 = $12,500
	$100 F	$0		$2,500 U
	Price variance	Quantity variance		Volume variance
		$100 F		
	Total flexible budget variance = price variance			
		$2,400 U		
	Underapplied fixed factory overhead = flexible budget variance + volume variance			

We found the $0.50 per hour rate with the following calculation:

$$\text{Fixed overhead rate per standard hour} = \frac{\text{budgeted fixed overhead}}{\text{normal activity}}$$

$$= \frac{\$15,000}{30,000 \text{ standard hr of normal activity}} = \$0.50$$

If the standard hours allowed during January had been exactly 30,000 — equal to normal activity — then we would have applied $15,000 of fixed factory overhead:

$$30,000 \text{ standard hr allowed} \times \frac{\$0.50/}{\text{standard hr}} = \$15,000 \text{ fixed overhead applied}$$

The fixed overhead budgeted and the fixed overhead applied would both have been $15,000, and there would have been no volume variance.

However, the standard hours allowed to produce 12,500 units are only 25,000 — or 5,000 hours below normal activity. When we multiply $0.50 times 5,000 hours below normal activity, we get

$$25,000 \text{ standard hr allowed} \times \$0.50/\text{standard hr} = \$12,500 \text{ fixed overhead applied}$$

which is $2,500 less than the $15,000 budgeted.

Therefore, whenever the standard hours allowed for the actual units produced are different from the normal activity, we will have a volume variance. And it can be calculated in the following manner:

Another way to calculate the volume variance

$$\text{Fixed overhead volume variance} = \frac{\text{standard hours allowed} - \text{normal activity in hours}}{} \times \text{fixed overhead rate per hour}$$

For Underhill it is:

$$\text{Fixed overhead volume variance} = (25,000 \text{ hr} - 30,000 \text{ hr}) \times \$0.50/\text{hr} = \$2,500 \text{ U}$$

Why is the volume variance unfavorable?

We've indicated that the volume variance is unfavorable. The easiest way to understand why it is unfavorable is to know what we do with the variance at the end of the year. Throughout the year we keep track of each month's volume variance. In some months the standard hours allowed will be less than normal activity (just like what happened in January) and in other months the standard hours allowed will be greater than normal activity.

The cumulative volume variances for the year are added to or subtracted from cost of goods sold expense on the income statement. If the cumulative effect after 12 months of activity is that the standard hours allowed (for the units produced) were less than the normal activity and that the fixed overhead applied was less than the fixed overhead budgeted, then the cumulative volume variances would be added to cost of goods sold expense. When you increase cost of goods sold expense, you decrease net income. And that is why the $2,500 volume variance is unfavorable — it reduces net income.

Over- or underapplied fixed overhead = total flexible budget variance + volume variance

Let's now look at Exhibit 10-14 one last time. Since the fixed overhead applied of $12,500 is less than the actual costs of $14,900, the difference of $2,400 is the amount of underapplied fixed factory overhead. This is made up of two parts: the $100 F flexible budget variance and the $2,500 U volume variance.

Graphic Approach to Fixed Factory Overhead

The budget is: ⌞

The graph for fixed factory overhead displayed in Figure 10-1 shows separate lines for the amount budgeted and for the amount applied. The budget line is the horizontal line representing an unchanging $15,000 at all levels of activity; the applied line starts at the origin and slopes upward and to the right. Each point on the applied line is

The applied is: ⌐

determined by multiplying the fixed factory overhead rate of $0.50 per hour times the number of standard hours allowed. For the current month the standard hours allowed were 25,000, so the amount applied for fixed factory overhead is $12,500 (25,000 hours × $0.50 per hour). The vertical distance from this point on the applied line to the horizontal budget line is the volume variance—$2,500 U ($12,500 − $15,000).

No VV when activity is at "normal" level

Notice in Figure 10-1 that if the standard hours allowed had been 30,000, then the fixed factory overhead applied would have been $15,000 (30,000 hours × $0.50 per hour)—exactly equal to the fixed overhead budgeted. For this situation—and for this situation alone—the volume variance would be zero.

The actual costs incurred for fixed overhead, $14,900, are represented by the point directly above the actual hours of 26,621. The vertical distance from this point to the budget line represents the fixed overhead spending variance. In Figure 10-1 you can see it is $100 F ($14,900 − $15,000).

Direct Labor, Factory Overhead, and Automation

In our examples we have assumed that direct labor costs have been a significant portion of the total production costs of a manufacturer and that the total overhead costs fluctuate in proportion to the number of direct labor-hours. As more and more processes are being automated, however, the significance of direct labor costs have been diminishing as a percentage of total manufacturing costs for many organizations. At the same time total overhead costs have been increasing as a percentage of total manufacturing costs; a much bigger portion of total overhead is becoming fixed; and the variable portion of total overhead has become more closely related to the number of machine-hours than to the number of direct labor-hours. Consequently,

FIGURE 10-1
Graphic Analysis for Fixed Factory Overhead

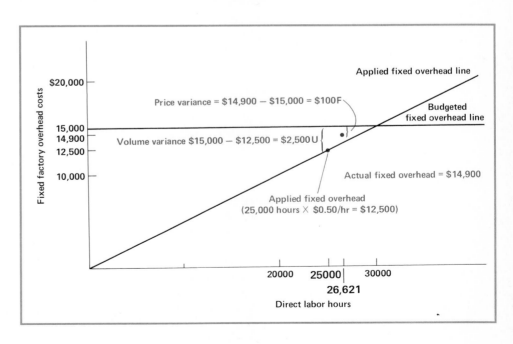

AS THE JOBS DWINDLE DOWN
TO A PRECIOUS FEW

At the big Vought Aero Products plant rising from the plain here, an automated wonder known as a flexible manufacturing system, or FMS, is drilling, grinding, and polishing parts for the aft fuselage of an Air Force B-1B bomber with startling efficiency. Except for a computer operator who sits in a glass-enclosed control booth high above the plant floor and two workers who load and unload parts at the beginning and end of the process, the place practically runs itself. . . .

Labor requirements for the FMS are dramatically different from those of conventional systems. At the Vought plant here, only 19 workers, including those who do maintenance, are needed to run the firm's $10.1 million, eight-machine FMS through three shifts. Gene Swift, manager of flexible-machining production, says he would need 24 machines and 72 workers to get the same output with a conventional system. The plant makes 568 parts for the B-1B bomber in 40,000 square feet of floor

space, in contrast with 120,000 that a conventional system would require. And the most highly skilled person in the FMS is the computer operator.

Source: "Factories That Turn Nuts into Bolts," *U.S. News & World Report,* July 14, 1986, pp. 44–45.

for these organizations the effort exerted to control direct labor costs cannot be as easily justified from a cost-benefit standpoint. Instead, emphasis is being shifted somewhat to the development of better ways to control overhead costs. No longer are direct labor-hours an appropriate way to measure activity in the control of variable overhead costs. Nor is direct labor appropriate as the basis for applying variable and fixed overhead costs for product costing purposes.

Absorption Costing vs. Direct Costing

Throughout our discussion in the previous sections we have been treating fixed factory overhead as a product cost. The fixed factory overhead rate, the fixed factory overhead applied, and the fixed factory overhead volume variance exist only because fixed overhead is assumed to be a product cost. In Chapter 5 you learned that the product costing method that treats fixed factory overhead as a product cost is called *absorption costing.* You also learned, however, that there is an alternative method that treats fixed factory overhead as a period cost instead of as a product cost. This method is called *direct costing.*

We calculate only volume variances with absorption costing

If the Underhill Company had been using direct costing rather than absorption costing, the analysis of variance for fixed factory overhead would have been much simpler. Since fixed factory overhead is treated as a period cost for direct costing, there would be no need to determine the fixed overhead rate, there would be no fixed overhead applied, and there would be no volume variance. The only variance for fixed overhead would be the price variance, which is the simplest of all variances in standard costing to calculate.

Frequency of Variance Investigation

The formal performance reports and spotlighted variances displayed in this chapter are prepared each month in summary form. For these reports to be meaningful and helpful, significant variances must be investigated promptly and corrective actions put into effect as soon as possible. For direct materials and direct labor this means tracing variances to responsibility centers as they occur on an hourly or daily

The more timely the better

basis. For factory overhead it would be both impractical and impossible to attempt to exert control so frequently. First of all, the individual overhead cost items are not significant enough in amount to justify the costs of such a control system. Second, as we discussed in an earlier section, the expected relationships between overhead costs and production activity may be valid for long periods of time but not for periods as short as a day—much less an hour. Therefore, control of overhead will likely be performed over no shorter period of time than a month.

Materiality and Variance Investigation

It makes sense to evaluate only significant variances

Although we discussed the concept of **management by exception** in Chapter 1, we need to mention it again at this time. The term means that all material ("material" in the sense of "significant" or "meaningful") variances are to be spotlighted on the performance report, so only those variances warranting evaluation will be investigated. The emphasis is placed on the word *material,* for if the variances are insignificant in amount, not only might the causes never be determined but the benefits to the firm of eliminating the variances could not outweigh the costs of investigation and corrective action.

Just how do we determine whether a variance is material? There is no perfect answer, but there are several approaches that we might be able to take:

1. *Hunch*   Managers may feel that they can intuitively detect when a process is out of control and requires investigation. This approach is not considered theoretically valid.

2. *Absolute amounts*   A fixed dollar amount is set. If the variance exceeds that amount, it is investigated.

3. *Percentage of standard*   A percentage, such as 10%, is decided upon. If the variance is greater than this percentage of the standard, it is investigated.

4. *Statistical control limits*   Boundaries can be set above and below the standard representing an allowable number of standard deviations away from the standard. This approach is based on a belief that results that fall within the control limits are caused by random influences for which no cause can be determined. Results falling outside the limits are considered to be due to systematic and determinable causes and should be investigated.

DO STANDARD COSTS FUEL INFLATION?

The "ratchett effect" is a term economists use to describe the tendency of prices to climb higher and higher, resisting the downward pressures of the market place (even in times of low demand) and refusing to return to former levels even if the cost elements that apparently cause the rise . . . have done so.

What causes the ratchett effect? The budgetary process and the financial control systems of American business must take a share of the blame. . . .

How can a financial control system encourage higher costs? It does so by allowing cost increases to generate favorable variances. Here is how this comes about.

In their planning, companies project expected rates of increases in costs. Then they budget the expected increases.

In 1974, as a plant manager for Rockwell International, I was told by my division headquarters to budget an 8% increase in mate-

rials prices for 1975. I did so and the new budget, once approved, was used to establish our plant's standard costs for 1975.

As a result I got gold stars all year for a favorable purchase price variance because I was able to buy raw materials at only 6% above the previous year's costs. I was motivated by the variance reports not so much to force suppliers to hold their price level as to prevent them from increasing them beyond 8%.

We got increases, perhaps because we planned them. At any rate, we no doubt resisted them less because our variance reports showed as favorable any cost increases less than those planned. Spread this experience to the entire private sector and the result is an appalling effect on inflation. Bigger budgeted increases lead to higher toleration of cost increases which lead to more inflation and still larger budgeted cost increases. . . .

Nowadays, when the standard cost line takes a quantum leap ahead every year, many managers are "achieving" favorable cost variances every year. Are they better managers than those of the 1960s? No, their grading scale is inflating faster than their costs.

The cure for this industrial gradeflation is fairly simple: let standard costs stand for at least three years. I will argue with those that insist that this cure will lead to unrealistic standards. Standard costs are what management feels costs should be, not what management fears they may become.

CHAPTER SUMMARY

Accountants prepare performance reports to help managers control their operations. Within a *performance report* actual results are compared to budgeted results and the differences are spotlighted for investigation. A performance report should use a *flexible budget* rather than the master budget.

The master budget is a *static budget;* that is, it is an "inflexible budget" prepared before a period begins for a single unchanging level of expected activity. The flexible budget can be prepared for various levels of activity, one of which is the activity that actually takes place during a period. Comparing actual results to a static budget does not help a manager tell if production was operated efficiently or not. Since a flexible budget is prepared for the level of activity that has just taken place, it provides more meaningful information in the performance report; that is, the manager can tell if the activities were or were not performed efficiently.

In the performance report a flexible budget can either be an estimate of what the actual costs were expected to be or an estimate of what the costs should have been. *Standard costs* are carefully predetermined estimates of what costs should be or should have been. When standard costs are used with flexible budgets, the performance report provides an even better measure of comparison. Rather than merely comparing actual costs to what costs were expected to be, standards provide a comparison to what the costs should have been. Standard costs are used not only for controlling performance; they can also be used for (1) building better master budgets and (2) product costing.

For each variable production cost there is a *price standard* and *quantity standard.* If actual costs differ from standard costs, there will be a *price variance* and a *quantity variance.* The sum of the price variance and the quantity variance is the *total flexible budget variance.* The price variance is calculated for direct materials, direct labor, and variable overhead in the following manner:

$$\text{Price variance} = \text{actual quantity} \times \begin{array}{c}\text{difference between}\\ \text{actual and standard}\\ \text{costs per unit of}\\ \text{input}\end{array}$$

And the quantity variance is calculated as follows:

$$\text{Quantity variance} = \begin{array}{c}\text{difference between}\\ \text{actual quantity used}\\ \text{and standard}\\ \text{quantity allowed}\end{array} \times \begin{array}{c}\text{standard}\\ \text{cost per}\\ \text{unit of}\\ \text{input}\end{array}$$

The price variance for fixed overhead is simply the difference between the actual costs and the budgeted costs. There will never be a quantity variance for fixed overhead.

There will be a variance for fixed factory overhead that we do not have for any other cost; this is the *fixed overhead volume variance.* The volume variance is the difference between the budgeted fixed overhead and the fixed overhead applied. The fixed overhead applied is found by multiplying the predetermined fixed overhead rate (budgeted fixed overhead ÷ normal activity) times the standard hours allowed.

Management by exception means that we should only investigate significant variances. We can use several approaches to determine if a variance is significant. These approaches include: (1) hunch, (2) an absolute amount, (3) a percentage of standard, and (4) statistical control limits.

IMPORTANT TERMS USED IN THIS CHAPTER

Controllable cost A cost that can be significantly influenced by a manager of a responsibility center during a given period of time. (page 411)

Currently attainable standards Standards that allow for realistic amounts of normal inefficiencies. (page 421)

Effectiveness A measure of whether or not objectives were attained; determined by comparing actual output to the original goals. (page 415)

Efficiency A measure of the relationship of inputs to outputs; a determination of how well a company controls its inputs to generate outputs. We compare the actual inputs (direct materials, direct labor, and factory overhead) to what we expected them to be based on the actual output (the finished unit). (page 415)

Fixed overhead price variance The difference between the actual fixed overhead cost and the budgeted fixed overhead cost. Also called the *controllable variance* or the *spending variance.* (page 437)

Fixed overhead volume variance The difference between the budgeted fixed overhead and the applied fixed overhead (where the applied is the standard hours allowed $\times$ standard fixed overhead rate per hour). (page 441)

Flexible budget A prediction of costs at various levels of activity, based on a knowledge of how costs relate to changes in activity. Once we know what activity might be in the future or was in the past, we can estimate the costs at that level of activity. (page 415)

Ideal standards Standards representing what it should cost to produce a unit under perfect conditions. (page 421)

Labor price variance The actual hours worked multiplied by the difference between the actual wage rate paid and the standard wage rate. Also known as a *labor rate variance.* (page 429)

Labor quantity variance The difference between the actual hours worked and the standard hours allowed, multiplied by the standard wage rate. Also called the *labor efficiency variance.* (page 429)

Learning curve A quantitative model that is used to predict the labor time in a production operation in which workers perform their tasks in less and less time because the tasks are continuously repeated. (page 452)

Materials price variance For a particular direct material, the actual quantity purchased multiplied by the difference between the actual cost per unit of input and the standard cost per unit of input. (page 424)

Materials quantity variance For a particular direct material, the difference between the actual quantity used and the standard quantity allowed, multiplied by the standard cost per input used. Sometimes called the *materials usage variance.* (page 424)

Normal activity The level of activity used in the denominator of the calculation for the predetermined fixed overhead rate. (page 440)

Price standard The dollar amount that should be paid for each of the inputs needed for production (e.g., a cost per pound or a rate per hour). (page 422)

Price variance A variance that results whenever the actual price paid and the standard price allowed for a unit of input differ. (page 422)

Quantity standard The amount of each input that should be used to produce a unit (such as the required number of pounds per unit or hours per unit). (page 422)

Quantity variance A variance that results when the actual quantity of inputs used differs from the standard quantity allowed for the units actually produced. (page 422)

Responsibility accounting The process within an organization of: (1) designating the responsibility centers; (2) delegating authority to individuals within each responsibility center; (3) preparing budgets, accumulating actual results, and preparing performance reports for responsibility centers; and (4) holding the individuals with authority responsible for their actions. (page 411)

Responsibility center An area of activity for which an individual has been delegated the authority to plan and control activities and has been assigned responsibility for those activities. (page 411)

Sales volume variance The dollar measure of effectiveness. Units budgeted less units produced X cm per unit. (page 417)

Standard costs Carefully predetermined estimates of what costs should be or should have been. (page 419)

Standard hours allowed The labor-hours that should have been worked to make the units that were produced during the period. (page 429)

Standard quantity allowed The quantity of direct materials that should have been used to make the units produced during the period. (page 424)

Static budget A budget that is based on a single and unchanging level of predicted activity. Master budgets are static budgets. (page 414)

Time and motion study A method used by engineers to determine labor quantity standards. (page 428)

Total flexible budget variance The sum of the price variance and the quantity variance for any predicted cost item. (page 422)

Variable overhead price variance The actual hours worked multiplied by the difference between the actual and standard costs per hour. Sometimes referred to as the *variable overhead spending variance.* (page 432)

Variable overhead quantity variance The difference between the actual hours worked and the standard hours allowed, multiplied by the standard variable overhead cost per hour. Also known as the *variable overhead efficiency variance.* (page 432)

APPENDIX 10-1: GRAPHIC APPROACH TO VARIANCE ANALYSIS

The graphic approach to analyzing variances is similar to the three-column approach. By comparing actual results to flexible budgets based on actual and standard quantities, we can determine the price and quantity variances. The key to understanding the graphic approach is knowing how to prepare the flexible budget line.

Flexible budget line

Remember: A flexible budget is simply a prediction of what costs should be at different levels of activity. A flexible budget line is a visual representation of the flexible budgets for all possible levels of activity for the responsibility center. Each point on the line represents a different quantity multiplied by the standard rate. There are typically two flexible budgets (three for direct materials) found in a performance report. These are based on the actual quantities used and the standard

FIGURE 10-2
Flexible Budget Line for
Underhill

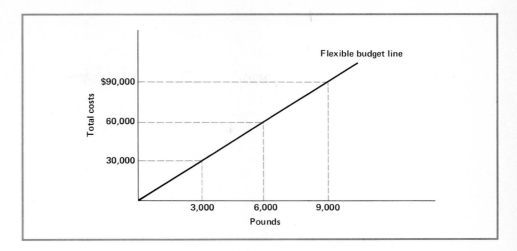

quantities allowed for the units produced during the period. These flexible budgets are two of the many possible points on the flexible budget line.

Graphic Approach for Direct Materials

The flexible budget line for direct materials for the Underhill Company is shown in Figure 10-2. Each point on the line is simply the number of pounds of direct materials multiplied by the standard rate of $10 per pound.

The same line is repeated in Figure 10-3, in which the representation of what's going on from 6,000 to 6,500 pounds is graphically enlarged. This particular range of activity includes the flexible budgets for Underhill that are in the performance report in Exhibit 10-7.

FIGURE 10-3
Graphic Variance Analysis
for Direct Materials

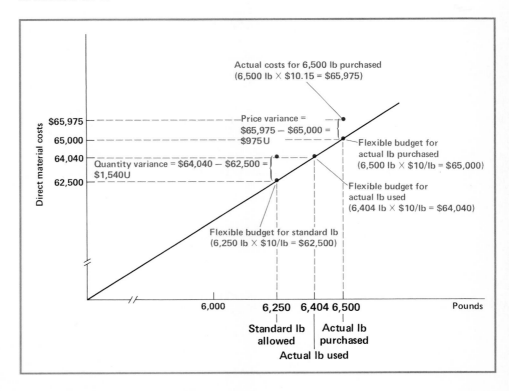

PART FOUR The Planning and Control of Operations in the Short Run
Appendix 10-1: Graphic Approach to Variance Analysis

450

There are three flexible budgets highlighted on the line in Figure 10-3. These are based on (1) the 6,500 pounds that were actually purchased [left side of column (2), Exhibit 10-7], (2) the 6,404 pounds that were actually used [right side of column (2), Exhibit 10-7], and (3) the 6,250 standard pounds allowed [column (3), Exhibit 10-7].

The actual costs are not on the flexible budget line

There is one point on the graph in Figure 10-3 that does not fall on the flexible budget line. This point represents the actual costs incurred—$65,975—to pay for the 6,500 pounds actually purchased. This point is directly above the quantity of 6,500 pounds on the horizontal axis and just a little bit above the $65,000 (on the flexible budget line) representing the flexible budget for 6,500 pounds. The vertical distance between $65,975 and $65,000 represents $975, the direct materials price variance (DMPV).

DMPV

DMQV

The direct materials quantity variance (DMQV) is represented in Figure 10-3 by the difference between the flexible budget for the actual pounds used (6,404 × $10 = $64,040) and the flexible budget for the standard pounds allowed (6,250 × $10 = $62,500). The difference of $1,540 is represented by the vertical distance between the points for these two flexible budgets.

Graphic Approach for Direct Labor

The graphic determination of the price and quantity variances for direct labor for Underhill is shown in Figure 10-4. Each point on the flexible budget line is found by multiplying the direct labor-hours times the standard rate per hour of $3. The two flexible budgets shown in the graph—based upon the actual hours worked and the standard hours allowed—are the same as those used in Exhibit 10-8.

The point that lies directly over the 26,621 direct labor-hours and just below the flexible budget line represents the actual wages paid, $78,000, for the actual hours worked, 26,621. When this is compared to the flexible budget of $79,863 for the actual hours worked, the vertical distance between these two points represents the direct labor price variance (DLPV)—$1,863 F.

DLPV

DLQV

The direct labor quantity variance (DLQV) is the difference between the flexible

FIGURE 10-4
Graphic Variance Analysis for Direct Labor

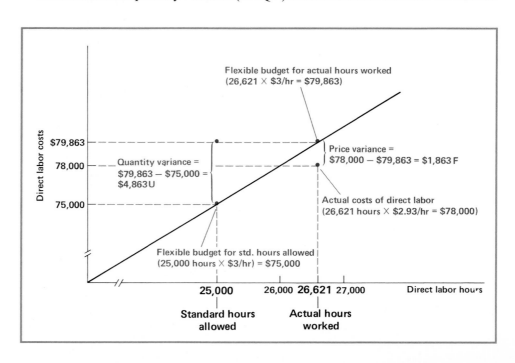

Flexible budget for actual hours worked
(26,621 × $3/hr = $79,863)

Price variance =
$78,000 − $79,863 = $1,863 F

Quantity variance =
$79,863 − $75,000 =
$4,863 U

Actual costs of direct labor
(26,621 hours × $2.93/hr = $78,000)

Flexible budget for std. hours allowed
(25,000 hours × $3/hr) = $75,000

Direct labor costs

$79,863
78,000
75,000

25,000   26,000 **26,621** 27,000   Direct labor hours

Standard hours allowed   Actual hours worked

FIGURE 10-5
Graphic Analysis for
Variable Overhead

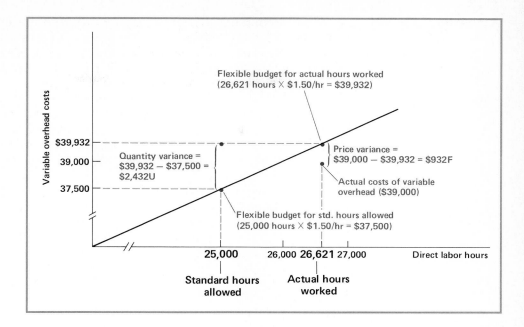

budgets for the actual hours ($79,863 for 26,621 hours) and the standard hours allowed ($75,000 for 25,000). This amount, $4,863 U, is shown on the graph as the vertical distance between the points representing the two flexible budgets.

Graphic Approach for Variable Factory Overhead

The graphic method of determining the price and quantity variances for variable overhead for Underhill is shown in Figure 10-5. Each point on the flexible budget line is found by multiplying the direct labor-hours times the standard rate of $1.50 per hour. The two flexible budgets shown in the graph—based upon the actual hours worked and the standard hours allowed—are the same as those used in Exhibit 10-9.

The point that lies directly above 26,621 hours worked and below the flexible budget line represents the actual variable overhead costs, $39,000. When this cost is compared to the flexible budget for the actual hours worked, the result is the variable *VOPV* overhead price variance (VOPV) of $932 F, represented by the vertical distance between these two points.

VOQV The variable overhead quantity variance (VOQV) is the difference between the flexible budgets for the actual hours worked ($39,932 for 26,621 hours) and the standard hours allowed ($37,500 for 25,000 hours). The quantity variance, $2,432 U, is shown on the graph as the vertical distance between the points representing the two flexible budgets.

APPENDIX 10-2: LEARNING CURVES

At some point, each of you has done a task for the very first time. Like many tasks, it probably involved a detailed series of interrelated steps. The first time you performed the task, you very carefully followed specific directions to do it correctly. As you *Learning through repetition* repeated it, you realized that you were doing it more quickly and efficiently. You were learning how to perform the task, and as a result, you were doing it in increasingly less time.

This learning phenomenon also occurs in many business environments, especially in manufacturing. What is especially important about it is that the rate at which people learn in business and manufacturing situations can often be determined and integrated into an organization's planning and control models.

Cumulative doubling— average falls by constant %

The relationship between repetition of performance and learning was first documented in the 1930s, when it was appropriately dubbed the *learning curve theory.* According to this theory, as cumulative output doubles (e.g., x, $2x$, $4x$, etc.), the average labor time for the cumulative output falls by a constant percentage. An 80% learning curve, for instance, means that as cumulative output doubles, the average labor time falls by 20%. Stated another way, as cumulative output doubles, the average labor time falls to 80% of what it was before the output doubled. Let's now look at an example to see how it works.

Example 10-2

THE DIGITAL MANUFACTURING COMPANY

The Digital Manufacturing Company produces exercise equipment and utilizes a significant amount of labor in its operation. During January of the first year of operation 500 machines were produced, requiring 5,000 hours of labor—an average of 10 hours per machine. The controller of Digital used to work at a competing firm and knew that this sort of production process would probably benefit from an 80% learning curve over an extended period of time. The controller then prepared the following schedule showing the output that cumulatively doubled, the average time needed to produce different amounts of cumulative output, and the total time expected for the different cumulative outputs:

Cumulative Output	×	Average Time (hr/Unit)	=	Total Labor-Hours
500	×	10	=	5,000
1,000	×	8 (10 × .8)	=	8,000
2,000	×	6.4 (8 × .8)	=	12,800
4,000	×	5.12 (6.4 × .8)	=	20,480

Cumulative doubles

The first column in the schedule in Example 10-2 is cumulative output. It starts with the initial batch of 500 units that had already been produced in January. Then, the 500 doubles to become 1,000 units; the 1,000 doubles to 2,000 units; and so on. Remember: The learning curve theory states that as *cumulative* output *doubles,* the average labor time for the cumulative output falls by a constant percentage. It is extremely important to realize that in the first column we are concerned with *cumulative* output. There are not four independent batches of 500, 1,000, 2,000, and 4,000, totaling 7,500. Rather, there is an initial batch of 500, which is increased by another 500, giving us a cumulative total of 1,000 units. When another 1,000 units are added to this 1,000, the cumulative total increases to 2,000 units. Each cumulative total is twice the previous cumulative total.

Average falls by constant %

The middle column in the schedule is the average labor time for the cumulative production. The average time of 10 hours per unit for the first 500 units was determined by dividing the initial 5,000 total hours by the initial batch of 500 units. The learning curve theory states that the average time needed to produce the cumulative output will be a *constant percentage* of what the average time was before the output doubled. The easiest way to calculate the average time is simply to multiply 80% by the average production time—before output doubles. Thus, when output doubles from 500 to 1,000 units, the average production time for 1,000 units is simply 80% of the average production time for 500 units:

$$10 \text{ hr} \times 80\% = 8 \text{ hr/unit}$$

When output doubles again, from 1,000 to 2,000 units, the average production time falls to 6.4 hours per unit:

$$8 \text{ hr} \times 80\% = 6.4 \text{ hr/unit}$$

And it works exactly the same way when production doubles to 4,000 units:

$$6.4 \text{ hr} \times 80\% = 5.12 \text{ hr/unit}$$

Total hours depend on the average—cumulative units × average time

The third column in the schedule is the total hours expected for the cumulative production. The total time is found by multiplying the cumulative units (first column) by the average time for those cumulative units (second column). For example, the total time to produce the first 4,000 units should be 20,480 hours (4,000 units × 5.12 hours per unit).

Notice that the 20,480 hours is the total time expected to produce the *first* 4,000 units—that is, from the first to the 4,000th unit. It is not, however, the total production time to produce any 4,000 units. Since learning is constantly taking place, the total labor time required to produce the next 4,000 units, or any other 4,000 units, will be less than 20,480 hours.

Incremental Analysis

In the schedule in Example 10-2 we showed you how to determine the average and total times for different levels of cumulative output. Once that schedule has been prepared, we can determine the average and total times on an incremental basis as well as on a cumulative basis. For example: We expect it will take 8,000 hours to produce the first 1,000 units. However, we know it took 5,000 hours to produce the first 500 units (which are included in the cumulative 1,000 units). Therefore, on an incremental basis it should take an additional 3,000 hours (8,000 hours − 5,000 hours) to produce the second batch of 500 units. And the average time to produce these incremental 500 units should be 6 hours (3,000 hours ÷ 500 units). In the following schedule you can see the total and average production times for the other incremental batches of production:

Incremental output generates incremental hours

Cumulative Production	Incremental Production	Total Time (in hr) for Incremental Production	Average Time (hr/Unit) for Incremental Production	
500	500	5,000	10	(5,000/500)
1,000	500	3,000 (8,000 − 5,000)	6	(3,000/500)
2,000	1,000	4,800 (12,800 − 8,000)	4.8	(4,800/1,000)
4,000	2,000	7,680 (20,480 − 12,800)	3.84	(7,680/2,000)

In-Between Numbers

What about output in between doubling points

Notice in both preceding schedules how everything works out well as long as the cumulative production is constantly doubling. But what if production doesn't double? Can we still use the learning curve theory to determine the average and total times? For example, if Digital plans to produce 150 units in February, how long will it take to produce them? Don't forget that Digital has already produced 500 units in January, so the first time cumulative production doubles, the total will accumulate to

1,000 units. Since Digital plans to produce only 150 units in February, the projected cumulative total reaches only 650 units—somewhere between the cumulative totals of 500 and 1,000 units.

Can we still determine the average and total times when cumulative production doesn't fall exactly on a doubling point? Yes.

We cannot interpolate

Do we simply interpolate to find the average for 650 units at some proportionate distance between the averages for 500 and 1,000 units? No.

To understand why interpolation is unacceptable, look at the graphic representation of the learning curve. As you can see, as cumulative production (represented on the horizontal axis) is increasing, average labor time (represented on the vertical axis) is constantly falling. The problem is that the average is falling in a curvilinear rather than a linear manner.

Average time falls in a curvilinear manner

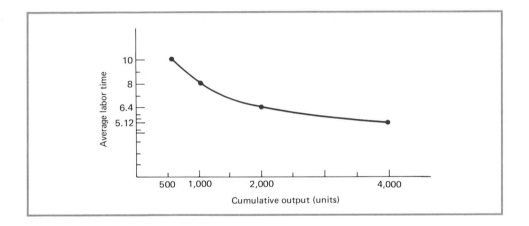

Since the distance from one point to another on a curve is not linear, the use of interpolation can lead to quite significant errors and is to be discouraged.

The process of using learning curves to predict labor time when the cumulative production does not fall on a doubling point is much more difficult than what we have shown you so far. It requires an understanding of the use of logarithms. Since you may not have a complete familiarity with logarithms, we will defer their discussion to an upper-level course in accounting or quantitative methods. All homework at the end of this chapter will require an understanding of what we've presented in the previous sections only.

Solutions for in-between numbers require logarithms

Assuming No Learning

In the Digital Manufacturing example we assumed an 80% learning curve and pointed out that the production times for Digital are much lower than they would be if learning were not taking place. Now let's see how much lower the production times will actually be for Digital when compared to the possibility that no learning is occurring.

For no learning LC% = 100%

When there is no learning taking place in a production setting, the learning curve percentage (LC%) is 100%. This means that as cumulative output doubles, the new average is 100% of the average before the doubling occurred. Stated differently, as cumulative output doubles, the average falls by 0% (100% − 100%). Regardless of which way we express it, the significance of a 100% learning curve is that the average labor time stays the same as cumulative output increases.

If you now look at the diagram below for Digital, you can see what the average and total labor times are for the same four levels of cumulative output, this time assuming a 100% learning curve. As you can see, the total time to produce 4,000 units would be 40,000 hours, 19,520 (40,000 − 20,480) more than with an 80% learning curve.

With no learning total hours are proportionate to units

Cumulative Output	×	Average Time (hr/Unit)	=	Total Labor-Hours
500	×	10	=	5,000
1,000	×	10 (10 × 1.00)	=	10,000
2,000	×	10 (10 × 1.00)	=	20,000
4,000	×	10 (10 × 1.00)	=	40,000

Costs Affected by Learning

The costs that are most obviously affected by the learning curve phenomenon are direct labor costs. Since the number of labor-hours per unit falls as cumulative output increases, the direct labor costs associated with the units of output will also fall. As a result, the total direct labor costs to be paid to workers for a given amount of production will be budgeted at a lower amount when workers are learning than when they are fully experienced.

Direct labor costs benefit from learning

Any other costs that are strongly influenced by direct labor, such as variable factory overhead costs, are similarly affected by learning. As the average labor time per unit and direct labor costs fall, so too will the average variable overhead costs. And as the average for variable overhead falls, the total variable factory overhead budgeted for any given level of production will also be less than it would be if there was no learning.

So does variable overhead

The production cost that is least likely to be affected by learning is fixed factory overhead. Although the time needed to produce units may be continuously decreasing, and the total hours and labor costs needed for a given level of production may be less because learning is taking place, nevertheless the total fixed factory overhead budgeted for a period remains the same as it would be if there were no learning at all. Just as we discussed earlier in this chapter, the fixed overhead budgeted for the period is the same regardless of the level of activity. No matter how many units we produce, no matter how many hours we take to produce those units, the total budgeted fixed overhead will be unchanged.

Budgeted fixed overhead is unaffected

Whereas the amount of *fixed overhead budgeted* is unaffected by learning, the amount of *fixed overhead applied* for *product costing* purposes is affected by learning. Since fixed factory overhead is applied to production at a predetermined rate based upon direct labor-hours, the fixed overhead applied to each unit will fall during the learning stages of production. It falls because the number of hours needed to produce each unit is constantly falling.

Applied fixed is affected by the decline in average labor time

To make quite clear whether learning does or does not affect fixed factory overhead, let's return to the Digital Manufacturing Company, which produced 500 units in January. Let's assume that near the end of the month, the company was considering accepting a special order for 500 units, which would double its cumulative total for January from 500 to 1,000 units. Let's also assume that Digital budgets its fixed overhead at $240,000 per year, or $20,000 per month; its normal activity for the year is 60,000 hours; and its fixed overhead rate is $4 per hour ($240,000 ÷ 60,000 hours). What will be the budgeted and applied fixed overhead for January if the order is accepted?

The fixed overhead budgeted for January is $20,000, whether Digital produces 500 units or 1,000 units. The special order for an additional 500 units will have no effect on the total fixed overhead—the incremental fixed overhead is zero.

On the other hand, the amount of fixed overhead applied depends upon the number of direct labor-hours worked. As you will recall from our original learning curve schedules, it took 5,000 hours to produce the initial batch of 500 units. At the $4-per-hour rate the fixed overhead applied will be $20,000 if the special order is rejected (5,000 hours × $4 per hour). However, if the 500-unit order is accepted, the cumulative production will be 1,000 units; the cumulative time will be 8,000 hours; and the fixed overhead applied will be a total of $32,000 (8,000 hours × $4 per hour). The first 500 units were applied $20,000, and the additional 500 units will be applied the remaining $12,000 (3,000 hours × $4 per hour).

We'll assume the cost of direct materials is unaffected

The last production cost to consider is direct materials. Is it or is it not affected by learning? Usually, it's assumed that learning does not affect the cost of direct materials. However, some research has documented situations in which the impact of learning does reduce the amount of wasted direct materials. The better the workers know the process, the fewer materials they waste in the process. The same research, however, indicates that the learning rate for direct materials—when applicable—is never the same as what it is for direct labor. So, for our purposes, if we give a single learning rate for a process, it will be applicable only to direct labor and related costs, not to direct materials.

Applications of Learning Curves

The earliest applications of learning curves were found during the 1930s in the airframe industry in the area of competitive bidding on government contracts. Following World War II the use of learning curves caught on in most industrial environments. Whenever cost information needed to be accumulated for a production setting that was benefiting from the effects of learning, the application of learning curve theory was found to be appropriate.

During the last 40 years the accounting literature has provided examples of learning curves being used in cash budgeting, operational budgeting, capital budgeting, cost-volume-profit analysis, human resources planning, special-order decisions, development of standards, flexible budgeting, and analysis of variance. These are only a few of the many potential applications of learning curve theory.

Although each of these applications should be of interest to us, because they relate to topics we've already studied in this text, the only ones we will now discuss further are those that relate specifically to this chapter. These applications relate to the development of standards and the subsequent analysis of variance.

During learning the quantity standard is a sliding scale

In the early stages of a new process, in which learning is still taking place and a standard cost system is being used to help control operations, there is no single measure of the quantity standard for direct labor. Since workers in this phase of production are able to perform their tasks in less and less time, management expects constant improvements in the workers' performance. In order to determine the quantity variance during this learning phase, it is necessary for the accountant to develop a quantity standard that uses a sliding scale—that is, with greater cumulative production the quantity standard will be smaller and smaller. This need for a changing quantity standard is naturally suited to the use of the learning curve model. By substituting the amount of cumulative production into the learning curve model, the accountant can determine what the total number of hours should have been for the units that were recently produced—this total number of hours represents the standard quantity allowed. Then, when we compare this standard quantity allowed to the actual hours used, we get the quantity variance (in hours).

Once learning ceases, the quantity standard is set where it stops

Naturally, we use this approach only for determining the quantity variance as long as the workers continue to learn. Once learning ceases, the quantity standard will be an unchanging number of hours per unit from that point on. With the learning curve the accountant can anticipate the level in production at which learning stops. If the average labor time is plotted on a graph, there is going to be some point, or range, after which the average seems to level off. At this level the average labor time either stops falling or continues to fall at an insignificant rate. The level at which the average labor time stops falling is the long-run quantity standard. This level is shown in the following graph.

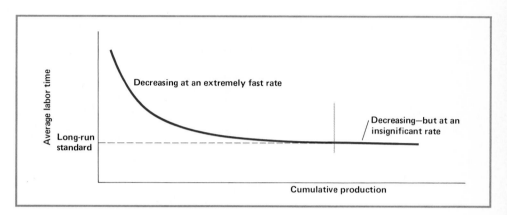

Extremes of Learning

The learning curve % can take on different values

The last thing we'll discuss relates to the percentage that is used in the learning curve model. Thus far, we've used in our example 80%, a learning curve percentage that is quite common both in practice and in the accounting literature. However, the exact percentage for a particular firm depends upon several factors, the most important of which is the ratio of labor time to machine time in a production operation. The larger the number of hours of direct labor in a process relative to the number of hours of machine time, the greater the potential for learning—since workers, and not machines, are the ones learning. For example, when a production process is nearly all labor time with very little machine time, the learning curve percentage may be as low as 70% or less. On the other hand, when the number of machine-hours used in production is large relative to the number of direct labor-hours, there is very little potential for learning and the learning curve percentage will be high—such as 90% or above.[2]

100% is a practical upper limit

The practical upper limit for a learning curve percentage is 100%, which, as we discussed earlier, means that no learning is taking place at all. It may be theoretically possible to have a learning curve higher than 100%, indicating that it takes longer to perform a task each time it is repeated, but we will assume that this possibility is not realistic in most learning environments.

50% is a mathematical lower limit

At the other extreme is a mathematical lower limit. This represents a learning curve percentage that can be approached but never reached or exceeded. This lower limit is 50%. With a 50% learning curve percentage, the average falls by 50% as cumulative production doubles, resulting in a *total time* for cumulative production that remains the same. In this situation, additional units could be produced for zero

---

[2] With the current shift in much U.S. industry to a higher ratio of capital to labor, 90% may become a more common learning rate than it was in the past.

additional time—an impossibility. For a learning curve percentage smaller than 50%, the incremental time needed to produce additional units would be negative—again, an impossibility. To be sure you understand the significance of a 50% learning curve, look at the table below, which shows the average, total, and incremental times for Digital, assuming a 50% learning rate:

With a 50% learning curve all incremental hours after the first batch are zero

Cumulative Output	×	Average Time (hr/Unit)	=	Total Labor-Hours	Incremental Hours
500	×	10	=	5,000	5,000
1,000	×	5 (10 × .5)	=	5,000	-0-
2,000	×	2.5 (5 × .5)	=	5,000	-0-
4,000	×	1.25 (2.5 × .5)	=	5,000	-0-

QUESTIONS

1. What is the difference between a *static budget* and a *flexible budget?*

2. Distinguish *flexible budgets* from *standard costs.*

3. Why shouldn't the master budget be compared to actual results in the performance report when the efficiency of a responsibility center is being evaluated?

4. Define *responsibility accounting.*

5. Distinguish *responsibility* from *blame.*

6. Discuss how to determine if costs are controllable or noncontrollable.

7. "All variable costs are controllable and all fixed costs are noncontrollable." Do you agree? Explain.

8. Discuss why it would be preferable to compare the actual results for the current period to standard costs rather than to the actual costs of the previous period.

9. Define the term *standard costs,* and list three uses for standard costs.

10. How can a manager determine if a variance is material enough to warrant investigation?

11. What is the difference between the concepts of *effectiveness* and *efficiency?*

12. Is it possible for a responsibility center to be effective but not efficient? Explain.

13. Which type of standards do you feel will better motivate employees toward company goals—ideal or currently attainable? Explain.

14. Define *ideal* and *currently attainable standards.*

15. Define what is meant by a *price variance.* A *quantity variance.*

16. "The purchasing agent should be blamed for all price variances." Do you agree? Explain.

17. Who should be held responsible for the extra production costs caused by a rush sales order? Explain.

18. Why is there no quantity variance for fixed overhead?

19. "The accountant is solely responsible for the development of standards used in a standard cost system." Discuss why you feel this statement is correct or incorrect.

20. "Fixed overhead applied represents the amount of fixed overhead that should have been incurred during a period of time." Comment.

21. Explain why a department might have a fixed overhead volume variance.

22. What do we mean when we say that costs have been "applied"?

23. Distinguish between *fixed overhead budgeted* and *fixed overhead applied.*

24. Why do we calculate a predetermined fixed overhead rate? Why don't we simply assign the fixed overhead budgeted each month to the units produced that month?

25. There is no fixed overhead volume variance when the standard hours allowed equal the normal hours. Explain why this is true.

26. "The only way to adequately control a production process is to investigate all variances in every reporting period." Do you agree? Explain.

27. For each of the learning curve applications below, explain how the analysis would be in error if the effects of learning were ignored:

 a. Cost-volume-profit analysis
 b. Cash budgeting
 c. Analysis of variance

28. The relationship between labor time and repetition is explained by the learning curve theory as follows: "As production increases, total time falls in a continuous manner." Are there any corrections or improvements that can be made to this statement? Explain what they are. Restate the relationship after making any necessary revisions.

29. What would it mean if we had a 105% learning curve? A 40% learning curve?

EXERCISES

Exercise 10-1
Calculating variances for direct materials

On Jan. 1, 2,000 units were budgeted for production. During the month 3,800 gallons of direct materials were purchased for $6.25 per gallon, and 3,500 gallons were used in the production of 2,400 units. The standards for direct materials were $1\frac{1}{2}$ gallons per unit at $6 per gallon.

 Compute the price, quantity, and total flexible budget variances for direct materials. Indicate with a U or an F whether the variance is unfavorable or favorable.

(Check figure: Price variance = $950 U)

Exercise 10-2
Calculating variances for direct labor and variable overhead

The Howsman Hose Company makes a product expected to require 6 hours to produce. The standard direct labor and variable overhead rates per hour are $2.50 and $1.25, respectively. During January 600 units were produced, although 500 units had been budgeted. The actual conversion costs were:

Direct Labor (3,200 hr) $7,840
Variable Overhead............................. 4,160

 Determine the price, quantity, and total flexible budget variances for each of the conversion costs. Indicate with a U or an F whether the variances are unfavorable or favorable.

(Check figure: Labor quantity variance = $1,000 F)

Exercise 10-3
Calculating variances for direct materials and direct labor

The Spartacus Company produces vitamins and uses standards to help control its operations. During January the 10,000 cases budgeted for production were actually produced. Purchases and usage of direct materials were 3,200,000 ounces at a cost of $0.14 per ounce. The direct labor incurred for January was 4,850 hours at $10.25 per hour. The standards per case are as follows:

Direct Materials (300 oz @ $0.15/oz)................ $45
Direct Labor ($\frac{1}{2}$ hr @ $10/hr) 5

 Determine the price, quantity, and total flexible budget variances for direct materials and direct labor. Indicate whether each variance is favorable (F) or unfavorable (U).

(Check figure: Direct materials flexible budget variance = $2,000 F)

Exercise 10-4
Determining unknowns from a performance report

During August 1988 the Skibinski Corporation produced 10,500 units, which was the number of units budgeted for the month. The standards that Skibinski uses to help control production are as follows:

Direct Materials .... 2 pounds per unit @ $1.75 per pound
Direct Labor .... $4\frac{1}{2}$ hours per unit @ $4.50 per hour

During August Skibinski purchased and used the same quantity of raw materials. The performance report for August spotlighted the following variances:

Direct Materials:		Direct Labor:	
Price Variance	$5,000 F	Price Variance	$25,000 U
Quantity Variance	1,750 F	Quantity Variance	12,375 U

Determine the following:
a. The actual pounds purchased and used

(Check figure: 20,000)

b. The actual price paid per pound
c. The actual hours worked
d. The actual rate paid per hour

(Check figure: $5)

e. The total flexible budget variances for direct materials and direct labor

Exercise 10-5
Distinguishing effectiveness from efficiency

The Watson Company produces a hair product called Greasy Adult Stuff and uses a standard cost system. The predetermined standards per case for direct labor are $\frac{1}{2}$ hour at $7.00 per hour. The number of cases produced during January was 100, which was 20 less than the number budgeted. The actual costs for January were $420 (56 hours). The product is sold at a price that contributes $5 per case.

Determine dollar measures of the company's (a) effectiveness and (b) efficiency for January.

(Check figure: Part a = $100)

Exercise 10-6
Determining the budgeted units for an ineffective month

The Waikiki Hula Skirt Company produced 5,000 boxes during the month, spending $151,000 of variable production costs. The sales price and standard variable costs per box were:

Sales Price	$60	Variable Overhead	$8
Direct Materials	10	Variable Selling....................	4
Direct Labor	12		

Waikiki earned $5,200 less profit than originally predicted, due to producing and selling fewer units than budgeted.

How many units were budgeted for the month?

(Check figure: 5,200 units)

Exercise 10-7
Determining the volume variance

Schleman Faucets, which produces washerless faucets, determined that the standard time to produce a faucet is 30 minutes. During March Schleman produced 80,000 faucets, which was 40,000 faucets below the average monthly normal activity. Schleman budgeted its fixed costs to be $60,000 per month but actually incurred $56,000 during March.

Determine the price variance, quantity variance, and volume variance for fixed overhead.

(Check figure: Volume variance = $20,000 U)

Exercise 10-8
Analyzing fixed overhead

At the beginning of the year Harvey Electrical Products budgeted its annual fixed costs to be $360,000 ($30,000 per month). During the first month of the year the actual fixed costs were $33,000. In addition, Harvey's standard cost system specified that 2 hours be used per unit. During January 6,600 hours were employed to produce 3,000 units. The normal activity for Harvey is 30,000 units per year.

Calculate the following variances for Harvey Electrical:

a. Fixed overhead price variance
b. Fixed overhead quantity variance
c. Fixed overhead flexible budget variance
d. Fixed overhead volume variance

(Check figure: $6,000 F)

e. Fixed overhead over- (or under-) applied

For each variance specify whether it is unfavorable (U) or favorable (F).

Exercise 10-9
Working backward to get
unknowns

The Willjack Company produces pennants for all the teams in the SASL (South American Soccer League). Willjack budgeted $400,000 of fixed overhead for 1988, but it had the following actual results for the year:

Fixed Overhead Incurred...................... $425,000
Standard Fixed Overhead Applied (based on
 105,000 standard hr allowed)   420,000

The standard time allowed per case of pennants was 4 hours; the actual hours incurred in 1988 were 111,000.

Determine each of the following on the basis of the facts given above:

a. What was the standard fixed overhead rate for Willjack?
b. How many units were produced during 1988?
c. What is Willjack's normal activity (in hours)?

(Check figure: 100,000 hours)

Exercise 10-10
Evaluating variable and
fixed factory overhead

The Lindsay Company uses standard costs and flexible budgets for control and product costing. Its standards for conversion costs are as follows:

Direct Labor............ 3 hours per unit @ $4 per hour
Variable Overhead....... 3 hours per unit @ $2 per hour
Fixed Overhead:
 Budgeted $150,000
 Applied .... 3 hours per unit @ $1 per hour

During December 40,000 units were produced and the actual results were:

Actual Hours Worked 125,000
Actual Overhead Costs:
 Variable.................................... $255,000
 Fixed $156,000

Calculate the price variance, quantity variance, and flexible budget variance for variable overhead. In addition, calculate the price variance, flexible budget variance, and volume variance for fixed overhead.

(Check figure: Volume variance = $30,000 U)

Exercise 10-11
Doing graphic analysis for
direct labor

The following facts relate to the operations of a production department for last month:

Units produced 15,000
Standard direct labor-hours allowed per unit 4
Standard direct labor rate per hour $10
Actual direct labor-hours worked.............. 65,000
Actual direct labor costs incurred $700,000

On the basis of this information, draw a graph, as close to scale as possible, that shows **(a)** the price variance and **(b)** the quantity variance.

Exercise 10-12
Doing graphic analysis for fixed factory overhead

The budgeted fixed factory overhead for the mixing department of the Low Calorie Cookie Company is $50,000 per month, and the normal level of activity is 10,000 bags (2,500 hours). During the past month 15,000 bags were produced, taking 3,500 hours. The actual fixed overhead for the month was $55,000.

Draw a graph, as close to scale as possible, that shows each of the following variances for fixed factory overhead:
a. The price variance
b. The quantity variance
c. The volume variance

Exercise 10-13
Doing learning curve analysis

Waterfront Docktor, a new company in the bayou country of Louisiana, specializes in building and repairing docks for waterfront homes. Recently, a hurricane swept through Jumbalaya Parish and washed away all the docks in the Riverside housing development. The president of the local civic association has asked Waterfront to bid on a contract for 15 docks.

Waterfront has just finished a similar dock for Kingfish Long that took 25 hours to complete. On the basis of its experience with other dock work, Waterfront expects to benefit from an 80% learning curve.

Using this information, estimate the answers to the following questions for Waterfront:
a. What would be the average time for building 16 docks?
b. What would be the total time for building 16 docks?
c. How many hours should it take to build the 15 docks that Waterfront is bidding on?
d. What would be the average time for the contract for 15 additional docks?

(Check figure: 9.26 hours)

e. How long would it take Waterfront to build the 15 docks if no learning took place?
f. Assuming, again, that learning is taking place, how long would it take to build 25 docks?

Exercise 10-14
Filling in the blanks for a learning curve situation

Fill in the blanks in the table below related to a government contract for the production of toilet seats for the U.S. Army. The company does benefit from learning, but it is not sure of the learning curve percentage.

Cumulative Production	Average Time (in min)	Total Time (in min)
10 seats	?	30
? seats	2.1	?
40 seats	?	?
? seats	?	?

(Check figure: Total time for 40 seats = 59 minutes)

PROBLEMS: SET A

Problem A10-1
Preparing flexible budgets before and after production is completed

The Talavera Company manufactures track shoes and utilizes flexible budgets and standard costs to control its operations. The master budget for October's expected production of 60,000 units is shown below. All the costs are variable.

	Master Budget
Direct Labor.........	$120,000
Supplies.............	6,000
Utilities.............	3,000
	$129,000

| Required |

1. Prepare flexible budgets for 45,000, 54,000, and 66,000 units of production.

(Check figure: Total costs for 45,000 units = $96,750)

2. The actual units produced were 75,000. Prepare a performance report if the actual costs were:

Direct Labor	$147,000
Supplies	9,000
Utilities..............................	3,900
	$159,900

The report should include the following three cost columns: (1) actual costs, (2) flexible budget, and (3) total flexible budget variance.

Problem A10-2
Preparing flexible budgets

| Required |

Referring to Problem A10-1, assume that the standard hours allowed per unit are 2.

1. List the standard costs per unit from the previous problem.
2. List the standard costs per hour.

(Check figure: Direct labor = $1)

3. Prepare flexible budgets for 105,000, 120,000, and 135,000 hours.

(Check figure: Total costs at 105,000 hours = $112,875)

4. Assume that the standard and actual hours for the month were 150,000 and 156,000 hours, respectively. Prepare a performance report having the following six cost columns: (1) actual costs, (2 and 3) two flexible budgets, (4) price variance, (5) quantity variance, and (6) total flexible budget variance.
5. Compare the results from part 4 in this problem to those from part 2 in the previous problem.

Problem A10-3
Determining variances for all production costs

Standard costs for the Flying High Flagpole Company have recently been developed by the company controller with the help of a management consulting firm. The standards are the following:

Direct Materials (100 lb/flagpole @	
$0.05/lb)	$5 per flagpole
Direct Labor (1 hr/flagpole @ $2/hr) ..	2 per flagpole
Variable Overhead (1 hr/flagpole @	
$1/hr).............................	1 per flagpole
Fixed Overhead	12,000 per month

During December 1,200 flagpoles were budgeted for production (1,200 is also the normal activity for the month), but only 1,000 were produced. The actual results related to this production were as follows:

Direct Material	104,000 pounds purchased @
	$0.045 per pound
	110,000 pounds used
Direct Labor...............	1,120 hours @ $2.075 per
	hour
Variable Overhead	$1,140
Fixed Overhead	$12,850

| Required |

Compute the individual and total flexible budget variances for each production cost. Indicate whether each variance is favorable or unfavorable. Also determine the volume variance for fixed factory overhead.

(Check figure: Materials price variance = $520 F)

Problem A10-4
Calculating variances for the prime costs: two materials and two labor operations

The Barge Corporation brews a beer from nuclear-power-plant river water that glows in the dark. Production requires the use of two materials and two labor operations. The standards for these prime costs are the following:

	Quantity	Price
Material A..............	3 lb/barrel	$2/lb
Material B..............	10 gal/barrel	$3/gal

	Operation	
Direct Labor	**1**	**2**
Hours per barrel................	2	1
Rate per hour	$4	$6

During the period 25,000 barrels were finished. Purchases totaled 100,000 pounds ($2.15 per pound) for material A and 200,000 gallons ($2.95 per gallon) for material B. The pounds and gallons used in production were 78,000 and 240,000, respectively.

The direct labor costs for the period were:

	Operation	
	1	**2**
Total hours	51,000	26,500
Rate per hour	$3.75	$6.10

Required

Compute all individual and total variances for (1) each direct material and (2) each direct labor operation.

(Check figure: Direct labor price variance, operation 1 = $12,750 F; operation 2 = $2,650 U)

Problem A10-5
Figuring out the unknowns on the basis of a partial performance report

Frazier Pool Supplies produces pumps for pool filtering systems, and it uses standard costs and flexible budgets to help control its operations. At the end of August the chief cost accountant, Clara Williams, prepared the following production report. Read it carefully and then answer the four questions that follow.

	Actual Costs	Flexible Budgets	
		Based on Actual Quantity	Based on Standard Quantity
Direct Materials	$ 28,000	$ 28,800* 25,200†	$ 24,000
Direct Labor	144,000	152,000	160,000
Variable Overhead	30,800	30,400	32,000
Fixed Overhead......................	32,000	30,000	30,000

* Based on the amount purchased.
† Based on the amount used in production.

Required

1. Determine the price variance, quantity variance, and total flexible budget variance for each of the four production costs included in the performance report.
2. If the standard costs for direct labor are $40 per unit (8 hours per unit @ $5 per hour), how many units were produced? What were the actual hours used and actual rate paid?

(Check figure: Actual rate paid = $4.737)

3. If the direct materials required are 4 pounds per unit what were the standard pounds allowed for production and the actual pounds used? What is the standard price per pound and the actual price paid?

(Check figure: Actual pounds used = 16,800)

4. What was the standard rate per hour for variable overhead? What was the average actual rate per hour paid for variable overhead?

(Check figure: Actual rate = $1.013)

Problem A10-6
Evaluating variances for all production reports

The Nettles Corporation manufactures the bases used by the Greengrass Valley Baseball League. Controller Luci Van Pelt prepared the following master budget for May 1988:

	Master Budget (2,000 Bases)*
Direct Materials.	$ 8,000
Direct Labor	16,000
Variable Overhead.	6,000
Fixed Overhead	12,000
	$42,000

* The normal activity per month is also 2,000 bases.

Quantity standards for these production costs were 4 pounds and 2 hours per unit.

During May 9,800 pounds of direct materials were purchased and 10,400 pounds were used in the production of 2,500 units. The price paid per pound was $0.95. In addition, 5,500 hours were worked and actual conversion costs were:

Direct Labor	$19,000
Variable Overhead	7,800
Fixed Overhead	11,800
	$38,600

Required

Determine the price, quantity, and total flexible budget variances for each of the production costs. Also compute the volume variance for fixed overhead. Indicate whether each variance is favorable (F) or unfavorable (U).

(Check figure: Materials quantity variance = $400 U)

Problem A10-7
Preparing income statements at the actual and budgeted levels of activity

The Melva Parachute Company budgeted 5,000 parachutes for production for August 1988. Each parachute is expected to be sold for $150. The controller expects the following costs for the month:

Variable Production Costs.	$60 per parachute
Variable Selling Costs.	40 per parachute
Fixed Production Costs	200,000 per month
Fixed Selling Costs	40,000 per month

The company managed to produce and sell only 4,000 parachutes in August, and each parachute was sold for $148. The actual costs for the month were as follows:

Variable Production Costs.....	$275,000	Fixed Production Costs	$210,000
Variable Selling Costs.........	190,000	Fixed Selling Costs...........	39,000

Required

1. Prepare income statements using the contribution margin format with the following five column headings:

(1)	(2)	(3)	(4)	(5)
Actual Results	Difference	Flexible Budget for Units Produced	Difference	Master Budget

[Check figure: Net income for flexible budget = $(40,000)]

2. Analyze what the difference columns [(2) and (4)] represent.

Problem A10-8
Preparing a performance report for the entire company

The Religious Medallions Company produces and sells gold crosses. Each month a performance report is prepared for the entire company rather than just for the production department. In it the actual results are compared to both a flexible budget and the master budget for that month. The only two variances that are calculated are the flexible budget variance and the sales volume variance. After the controller had prepared the October report at the office, he brought it home and left it on the kitchen table. At dinner his little girl spilled grape juice on the report, and very little of the report was still readable afterward. The controller knew the president wanted him to call that night to discuss the report, but he didn't want to go back to the office to look up all the facts he based the report on. Luckily, however, his wife was able to read the following facts through the grape stains:

Master Budget:
    Units 10,000
    Income $28,000
Actual Results:
    Income $15,500
    Units Produced 8,000
    Sales..................................... $78,000
Variances:
    Flexible Budget Variance for Variable Costs.. $1,000 U
Budgeted Variable Cost per Unit............. $6
Budgeted Fixed Costs....................... $12,000

From these bits and pieces the controller was able to reconstruct the report. And now it's up to you to do the same thing.

Required

Working with the limited facts that the controller's wife could read through the grape stains, fill in all the blanks in the performance report that is given below:

	Actual Results	Flexible Budget Variance	Flexible Budget for Units Produced	Sales Volume Variance	Master Budget
Units	_____	_____	_____	_____	_____
Sales Revenue	_____	_____	_____	_____	_____
Total Variable Costs	_____	_____	_____	_____	_____
Total Contribution Margin	_____	_____	_____	_____	_____
Total Fixed Costs	_____	_____	_____	_____	_____
Net Income	_____	_____	_____	_____	_____

(Check figure: Net income for middle column = $20,000)

Problem A10-9
Doing overhead analysis
with mixed costs

On the first day of January Coby Stephens, the chief cost accountant with the Cincinnati Automotive Parts Company, gave a 1-month notice and said that he'd be willing to train his replacement before he left. His boss, Margo Shot, was so angry at Coby that she fired him on the spot. It took a month before Margo was able to hire a replacement, Bernie Dawg, to take Coby's place. One of the first things that Margo wanted from Bernie was a performance report for the overhead costs within the machining department for January. Bernie looked through the files that Coby had not thrown away and found the following flexible budgets, which Coby had prepared for January before he had left:

Levels of activity:		
Units.....	1,000	1,500
Machine-Hours	4,000	6,000
Overhead Costs:		
Salaries.....	$40,000	$50,000
Utilities	1,000	1,400
Supplies	300	400
Indirect Materials.....	4,000	6,000
Depreciation	5,000	5,000
Payroll Taxes	6,000	7,500
	$56,300	$70,300

Next, Bernie learned that 1,200 units were actually produced during the month and that the actual overhead costs totaled $64,000. In addition, he found out that there were 5,000 machine-hours used in January. The normal level of activity is 1,250 units.

Required

Prepare a performance report for January that includes the following variances:

    Price variance
    Quantity variance
    Flexible budget variance
    Volume variance

(Check figure: $1,132 U)

    Total variance

Problem A10-10
Setting a price based on
learning curve analysis

During June 1989 Skinny Dip Pools started building a new style of pool, called Midnight Delight. The prototype for the pool, which was built on the lot behind the company's office, took 160 hours to complete. The second pool, however, which was built for a customer, took only 80 hours to complete. The costs incurred in the production of the first two pools were as follows:

Direct Materials	$10,480
Direct Labor	1,680
Variable Overhead (based on direct labor-hours)	720
Fixed Overhead Applied (based on direct labor-hours)	360
	$13,240

The owner of Skinny Dip expects to sell 63 pools (not including the first one, which is being used for promotional purposes) during the first year of building the Midnight Delight, and she plans to sell them at a price that will provide a 50% contribution based on the average cost of building all 64 pools in the first year.

Required

1. Determine the price per pool that Skinny Dip will charge during the first year.

(Check figure: $8,287.16)

2. On the basis of this price, determine the total contribution margin for the first pool sold in 1989 (which was the second pool built).
3. Determine the total contribution margin for the year. (Assume that costs of the first pool have not been expensed.)

PROBLEMS: SET B

Problem B10-1
Preparing flexible budgets before production and after production is finished

The Duda Company manufactures tape measures and uses flexible budgets and standard costs to control its operations. Given below is the master budget for December's expected production:

	Master Budget (20,000 Units)
Direct Labor..................	$60,000
Supplies......................	4,000
Utilities	2,000
Rent	1,200
	$67,200

Required

1. Prepare flexible budgets for 17,000, 21,000, and 25,000 units of production. (All costs except rent are variable.)

(Check figure: Total costs for 17,000 units = $57,300)

2. The actual units produced during December were 19,000, and the actual costs incurred were:

Direct Labor	$55,100
Supplies..................................	3,840
Utilities..................................	1,920
Rent.....................................	1,400
	$62,260

Prepare a performance report. The report should include the following three cost columns: (1) actual costs, (2) flexible budget, and (3) flexible budget variance.

Problem B10-2
Preparing flexible budgets for the actual hours and for the standard hours allowed

Required

Referring to the previous problem, assume that the standard hours allowed per unit are 6.
1. List the standard costs per unit from the previous problem.
2. Compute and list the standard costs per hour.

(Check figure: Direct labor = $0.50/hr)

3. Prepare flexible budgets for 100,000, 120,000, and 130,000 hours.

(Check figure: Total for 100,000 hours = $56,200)

4. Assume that the standard and actual hours for the month were 114,000 and 117,000 hours, respectively. Prepare a performance report having the following six cost columns: (1) actual costs, (2 and 3) two flexible budgets, (4) price variance, (5) quantity variance, and (6) flexible budget variance.

Problem B10-3
Determining variances for all production costs

The Sirrock Company manufactures leather belts and uses standard costs to assist in the control and product costing of its operations. The standard costs of producing a leather belt are:

Direct Materials (3 lb/belt @ $2/lb) .... $6 per belt
Direct Labor (2 hr/belt @ $5/hr) .... 10 per belt
Variable Overhead (2 hr/belt @
  $0.50/hr) .... 1 per belt
Fixed Overhead .... 5,000 per month

During February 1,250 belts were budgeted for production (1,250 is also the average monthly normal activity), but only 1,000 belts were actually produced. The actual results for February were as follows:

Direct Materials (3,500 lb purchased;
  3,300 lb used) $7,350
Direct Labor (1,900 hr worked) 9,405
Variable Overhead .... 1,140 ÷ 1900
Fixed Overhead 5,200

Required

Compute the individual and total variances for each production cost. Indicate whether each variance is favorable (F) or unfavorable (U).

(Check figure: Direct labor quantity variance = $500 F; fixed overhead volume variance = $1,000 U)

Problem B10-4
Analyzing two direct materials and two labor operations

The Carter Bottling Company produces a product that tastes exactly like beer, but it has no alcohol or caffeine and very few calories. The key difference in Carter's beer is the substitution of soybeans for barley. Information concerning its raw materials during May 1989 is as follows:

	Hops	**Soybeans**
Standards	2 lb/case @ $0.50/lb	1 lb/case @ $3/lb
Actual results:		
Purchased.................	18,000 lb @ $0.60/lb	10,500 lb @ $2.70/lb
Used	19,500 lb	10,333 lb

Information concerning the labor operations is given below:

	Operation 1	**Operation 2**
Standards	½ hr/case @ $7.00/hr	1 hr/case @ $4.00/hr
Actual results................	4,950 hr @ $7.50/hr	10,500 hr @ $3.90/hr

The cases produced during February numbered 10,000.

Required

Determine all individual and total variances for (1) each raw material and (2) each labor operation.

(Check figure: Direct materials price variances: Hops = $1,800 U and soybeans = $3,150 U)

**Problem B10-5
Calculating the unknown
from a partial performance
report**

An incomplete performance report is given below for the Reflecto Wall Mirror Company:

	Actual Costs	Flexible Budget	
		Based on Actual Quantity	Based on Standard Quantity
Direct Materials	$25,000	$30,000*	
		27,600†	$27,000
Direct Labor	40,375	38,000	36,000
Variable Overhead	7,125	7,600	7,200
Fixed Overhead....................	2,000	2,300	2,300

* Based on the quantity purchased.
† Based on the quantity used.

Required

1. Determine the price variance, the quantity variance, and the total flexible budget variance for each of the four production costs shown above.
2. If the standard costs for direct labor are $24 per mirror (3 hours per mirror @ $8.00 per hour), how many mirrors were produced? What were the actual hours used and the actual labor rate paid per hour?

(Check figure: Mirrors produced = 1,500)

3. If the direct materials required are 30 pounds per mirror, what were the standard pounds allowed for production and the actual pounds used? What is the standard price per pound and the actual price paid?

(Check figure: Pounds purchased = 50,000)

4. What was the standard rate per hour for variable overhead? What was the average actual rate per hour paid for variable overhead?

(Check figure: Standard rate = $1.60)

**Problem B10-6
Evaluating variances for
all production costs**

The Xenon Corporation manufactures the kicking tees used by the American Football League. Its controller, Danny Trivillon, prepared the following master budget for August 1988 based on anticipated production of 2,000 kicking tees (which is also the normal level of activity):

	Master Budget
Direct Materials	$4,000
Direct Labor	3,000
Variable Overhead...............	1,000
Fixed Overhead	500
	$8,500

Quantity standards are 2 gallons and ½ hour per unit.
During August 2,400 kicking tees were produced and the actual costs incurred were:

Direct Materials..................	$6,450*
Direct Labor.....................	4,500
Variable Overhead	1,200
Fixed Overhead	525

* Based on gallons purchased.

In addition, 6,000 gallons were purchased during August and 5,200 gallons were used. The actual hours needed for production were 1,400.

Required	Determine the price, quantity, and total flexible budget variances for each of the production costs. In addition, calculate the fixed overhead volume variance. Indicate whether each variance is favorable (F) or unfavorable (U).

(Check figure: Materials quantity variance = $400 U)

Problem B10-7
Preparing income statements at the actual and budgeted levels of activity

The Repass Company sells lightning surge protectors for television sets at $18 per unit. Although Repass expected to produce and sell only 3,000 units during August, it was able to produce and sell 4,000 units as a result of a substantial increase in lightning storms in several areas of the country. The standard and actual results for the month are as follows:

	Standard	Actual
Variable Manufacturing Costs............	$ 6/unit	$ 6.50/unit
Variable Selling Costs	3/unit	2.80/unit
Fixed Manufacturing Costs	20,000/month	20,600/month
Fixed Selling Costs.....................	3,000/month	3,500/month

Repass's actual revenues for August were $75,000.

Required	1. Prepare income statements using the contribution margin format with the following five column headings:

(1)	(2)	(3) Flexible Budget for Units Produced	(4)	(5)
Actual Results	Difference		Difference	Master Budget

(Check figure: Net income for flexible budget = $13,000)

2. Analyze the results for each of the difference columns.

Problem B10-8
Determining various items in a performance report based on limited information

During December 1989 a staff accountant for Carget Company was told to go to the plant cost accountant and get the performance report for the factory overhead in the assembly department. The cost accountant's secretary reluctantly admitted that her boss had left early and could probably be found at the Cheers Bar and Mud Wrestling Emporium, which was having an amateur night. When the staff accountant found the cost accountant, he learned that the cost accountant had dropped the report in the mud ring and was able to find only the parts of the report that gave the following information about the combined overhead costs:

Actual Factory Overhead...................	$235,000
Flexible Budget Variance...................	$15,000 U
Volume Variance.........................	$20,000 U
Normal Activity..........................	25,000 units
Combined Overhead Rate.................	$10 per unit

With a little bit of work, and two matches later, the two accountants were able to reconstruct most of the performance report.

Required	1. Determine the variable and fixed overhead rates per unit. 2. Determine the amount of budgeted fixed costs.

(Check figure: $100,000)

Problem B10-9
Doing overhead analysis with mixed costs

Soni Lookalike Electronics is a small manufacturer of television sets. The production process has been fine-tuned to produce TVs that break down just after the warranty date expires. Since the sets can be repaired only at authorized Soni Repair Stores, the sets can be sold at a very low price, with the expectation of making a large profit when the sets are returned for repairs. One of Soni's departments, testing and adjustments, spends a great deal of time ensuring that all the company's sets are good enough to make it past the warranty date—but not much further.

The overhead costs within this department are assigned to the product at a predetermined rate per machine-hour. During the last 2 months the total overhead applied to the product, the number of sets tested, and the related machine-hours (actual and standard) were the following:

	June	July
Sets tested	23,000	27,000
Machine-hours:		
Actual	35,000	39,600
Standard	34,500	40,500
Total overhead applied.............................	$86,250	$101,250

During the same 2 months the flexible budgets for total overhead were $87,750 and $96,750, respectively.

In August 30,000 sets were tested; the actual machine-hours used in the testing were 47,000; and the total overhead costs incurred were $108,900.

Required

1. Calculate each of the following variances for August:

Price variance   Volume variance
Quantity variance   Total variance
Flexible budget variance

2. Determine the normal activity in units and in hours.

(Check figure: 36,000 hours)

**Problem B10-10
Determining incremental
results from learning
curves**

Seymore Rubit invented a new toy in 1987, and he introduced it to the game-hungry public during the Christmas season of that year. It's called "Rubit's Octagon," a much more difficult variation of a similar game introduced several years earlier. By the middle of 1989 several million Rubit's Octagons had been sold. The main problem with the octagon was that nobody could ever get the eight sides back to their original colors. One of the few people to truly master the octagon, I. N. Stine, realized there could be a market for a new service he could provide to purchasers of Rubit's Octagon. He could, for a charge, arrange the octagon so that the eight colors were back in their original places. In addition, he would send each customer a copy of his guide to solving the octagon themselves.

Stine had already rearranged the octagon for 20 of his friends, averaging 40 minutes per octagon. He was sure that he could cut the average time to 32 minutes by the time he had rearranged 40 octagons. And who knows how fast he could do it by the time he had done 5,000 or 10,000 of them.

Stine decided to advertise his service each week on a new game channel on his cable system. The ad, costing $250 per week, gave an address to which the octagon (and a check for $5) could be sent.

Stine figured he would incur the following costs:

The cost of the guide—$1 per copy
The cost of mailing each octagon back to the customer—$0.75
The cost of running his air conditioner while he was working—$0.50 per hour (Stine ran his air conditioner only when he worked.)

During the first week of operation business was a little slow. Only 300 customers sent their octagons for rearrangement.

Required

1. How long should it take Stine to rearrange the 300 octagons, assuming he can continue to learn at the same pace?

(Check figure: 71.05 hours)

2. What will be the net income for Stine for his first week of operation?

CHAPTER 11

Responsibility Centers, Service Department Cost Allocations, Transfer Pricing, and Return on Investment

After reading this chapter, you should have learned:

- The different types of responsibility centers — cost centers, profit centers, and investment centers — within an organization
- What *service departments* are, and why and how their costs should be allocated to operating departments
- The difference between a *centralized* and a *decentralized* organization
- How to use the contribution margin income statement to evaluate the operations of different profit centers within an organization
- What we mean by *transfer pricing,* and how it relates to the evaluation of profit centers within an organization
- How to determine the return on investment (ROI) for an organization, and how to use it to evaluate the performance of investment centers

In Chapter 10 we discussed flexible budgets and standard costs and showed how they were used to evaluate the performance of production departments for a manufacturer. We pointed out that each different production department was a *responsibility center* — an area of activity for which an individual has been delegated authority to plan and control activities and assigned responsibility for those activities during some period of time. We also pointed out how important it was to distinguish between costs that were controllable and those that were uncontrollable.

What we did not point out in Chapter 10 is that there are different types of responsibility centers and that a production department represents a type of responsibility center that we call a *cost center.* In addition to cost centers there are also *profit centers* and *investment centers.* The first part of this chapter will look at some different aspects of cost centers that were not discussed in Chapter 10. The remainder of the chapter will cover profit centers and investment centers.

We will try to help you understand why an organization may have different types of responsibility centers; what the different types of cost centers, profit centers, and investment centers are within an organization; and how the performance of each of these centers, as well as the manager of each center, can be evaluated periodically.

COST CENTERS

Cost center managers influence costs but not revenues or investments

A *cost center* is a responsibility center in which the responsible parties can exert an influence over its costs but have little, if any, influence over its revenues or its investment in fixed assets that generate revenues. Within the single production department we evaluated in Chapter 10, we assumed that production foremen had the primary responsibility for controlling the center's costs—direct materials, direct labor, variable factory overhead, and fixed factory overhead costs (although it is questionable that a production foreman would have much influence over the fixed factory overhead costs). On page 416 we showed you the condensed performance report (reproduced here in Exhibit 11-1) that we used to evaluate the performance of that cost center.

EXHIBIT 11-1
Performance Report—
Underhill Company

A cost center performance report from Chapter 10

	Actual Costs	Flexible Budget	Flexible Budget Variances
Direct Materials	$ 65,000	$ 62,500	$2,500 U
Direct Labor	78,000	75,000	3,000 U
Variable Overhead	39,000	37,500	1,500 U
Fixed Overhead...........................	14,900	15,000	100 F
Total	$196,900	$190,000	$6,900 U

We certainly can have a more detailed performance report if we need one. As we did in Chapter 10, we can separate the flexible budget variance for the variable costs into its component parts—the quantity variance and the price variance. In a performance report we also can calculate the actual costs, budgeted costs, and variances for the year to date (all the months combined from the beginning of the year up through the current month), as well as for individual months. Furthermore, we can indicate what percentage each variance is of the budget as a quick way to measure materiality of the variances. There can be a great deal of flexibility in how we present a report that evaluates performance. The approach we use will always be acceptable, but it certainly will not be the only approach allowable.

Multiple Cost Centers

We assumed in Chapter 10 that there was only one production department for the Underhill Company. We will now assume that there are three departments—an assembly department, a machining department, and a finishing department—each department a cost center whose center manager reports to the vice president of manufacturing. The relevant section of Underhill's organization chart appears in Figure 11-1.

An expanded set of performance reports for Underhill is shown in Exhibit 11-2. At the bottom of the exhibit is the performance report for the assembly department. Notice how the summarized report (bottom-line totals) for the assembly department is combined with the summarized reports for the machining and finishing departments in the report to the vice president of manufacturing. The summarized report for the vice president of manufacturing is combined with the summarized reports for sales and finance in the report to the president.

Cost center performance reports at all levels within the organization

You also may have noticed that we left the fixed factory overhead in the assembly department report in Exhibit 11-2 (as well as in other reports not shown), even though it probably wasn't controllable at the department manager's level. We left it in

FIGURE 11-1
Expanded Organization
Chart for the Underhill
Company
Each production department is
a cost center.

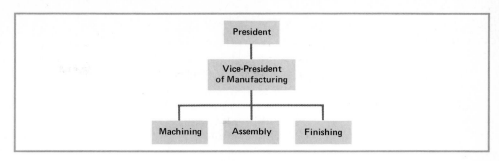

because it may be controllable at the vice president's level of responsibility. Since we did include it, however, we probably should have separated it from the costs that were controllable, identifying which costs were controllable and which were not.

Service Department Costs

So far in this text we have ignored a very important group of departments for most manufacturers. These departments are not directly involved in the production process, although they are closely related to the producing departments because of the services they provide. These are the *service departments.* The service or assistance

EXHIBIT 11-2 Progression of Performance Reports

President	Actual Costs	Flexible Budget	Flexible Budget Variances
President's Department	$ 18,000	$ 18,200	$ 200 F
Vice Pres., Manufacturing	557,400	560,750	3,350 F
Vice Pres., Sales	270,000	265,000	5,000 U
Vice Pres., Finance	65,000	64,000	1,000 U
Total	$910,400	$907,950	$ 2,450 U

Company performance report
(responsible manager — president)

Vice President, Manufacturing	Actual Costs	Flexible Budget	Flexible Budget Variances
Vice President's Dept.	$ 15,500	$ 15,750	$ 250 F
Machining Department	225,000	240,000	15,000 F
Assembly Department	196,900	190,000	6,900 U
Finishing Department	120,000	115,000	5,000 U
Total	$557,400	$560,750	$ 3,350 F

Manufacturing departments
performance report (responsible
manager — vice president,
manufacturing)

Assembly Department	Actual Costs	Flexible Budget	Flexible Budget Variances
Direct Materials	$ 65,000	$ 62,500	$ 2,500 U
Direct Labor	78,000	75,000	3,000 U
Variable Overhead	39,000	37,500	1,500 U
Fixed Overhead	14,900	15,000	100 F
Total	$196,900	$190,000	$ 6,900 U

Assembly department performance
report (responsible manager — assembly
supervisor)

Service departments provide services to manufacturing (and other) departments

they provide to the producing, or operating, departments is often so valuable that the producing departments would have difficulty operating efficiently without them. For example, a machine maintenance department is a service department responsible for keeping the machinery in all operating departments in good condition. This department is usually not directly involved in producing units, but without its services the operating departments wouldn't be able to continue production for very long.

Examples of service departments

Other examples of service departments include the factory storeroom, a factory cafeteria, a janitorial service, personnel, purchasing, quality control and inspection, factory administration, and a medical clinic. Some of these service departments—such as the cafeteria or personnel—may actually service both producing and non-producing departments. We, however, are primarily concerned here with the services provided to the producing departments.

The Need for Allocation

Since service departments are needed to operate production departments efficiently, it seems reasonable that a portion of the costs of providing the services should be assigned to the operating departments that benefit from them. The accounting procedure used to assign the service department costs to the operating departments is called *cost allocation.* The final result of cost allocation is that each operating department ends up with a portion of the costs of each service department.

We need to allocate service department costs to the departments serviced—for three reasons

The costs that are allocated can be useful to the operating departments in three areas: (1) product costing, (2) evaluation of performance, and (3) special decisions.

Reason 1: product costing within a manufacturing department

1. Product Costing After the costs of the service departments have been allocated to an operating department, they become a part of the cost of the finished product, just like the direct materials, direct labor, and factory overhead costs that relate to the specific operating departments themselves. Since the allocated costs are not directly associated with the units produced, they are treated as indirect product costs—which, as we know quite well by now, are the factory overhead costs. Previously, whenever we talked about factory overhead costs, we assumed that these costs were all incurred right there within the operating department itself. Now we are going to assume that the factory overhead costs of each operating department include some of the costs of each service department that provides it service. What happens is that the allocated service department costs are added to the overhead costs of the operating department, and this combined total for overhead is assigned to the units produced in that department. Remember how we assigned the overhead costs to the units in Chapter 10. The overhead was applied to production—using a predetermined rate that was established at the beginning of the year. For the service department costs to be a part of these product costs for overhead, they must be a part of the overhead rate. This means that for product costing purposes service department costs must be allocated at the beginning of the year before the departmental overhead rate is determined. In order to perform this allocation at the beginning of the year, it is necessary to use the service department costs that are budgeted at the beginning of the year and the expected allocation bases for the upcoming year. (More on allocation bases a little later.)

Reason 2: evaluating performance of departments serviced

2. Evaluation of Performance The allocated service department costs will be an integral part of the factory overhead cost which is evaluated in a monthly performance report for an operating department. Some of the costs of the service departments are indeed influenced by production managers—and are therefore considered controllable by them. A manager is held accountable not only for those costs that he or she influences within his or her own department but also for the costs that can be influenced within other departments. For example, let's assume that the costs of the machine maintenance department are excessive because of an operating manager's reluctance to have department machinery undergo regular maintenance checks. The result will be machine breakdowns and extensive repairs at large costs. The manager of the operating department should be held accountable for these excessive costs.

The service department costs that are found in the performance report of the operating department represent allocations that are made after a month of operations has been completed. The performance report includes an allocated portion of the service department costs that actually occurred during the month—in the actual costs column—and an allocated portion of budgeted service department costs—in the flexible budget column.

Reason 3: helping managers make special decisions with relevant information

3. Special Decisions The allocation of service department costs may also provide the operating departments with relevant information that is needed in a variety of special decisions but may have been overlooked if the costs had not been allocated. For example, assume that a company is considering replacing a manual operation with fully automated machines. The manual operation most likely has had little impact on the total costs of the machinery maintenance department. On the other hand, the purchase of new automated machinery would definitely affect the costs of maintenance. If the costs of this service department were not identified as being associated with specific operating departments, the decision maker might ignore the impact of the automated machines on maintenance costs—costs that are relevant to the decision that will be made.

The Three Steps in Cost Allocation

Assume that we know that the costs of the machinery maintenance department were $12,000 and that 50% of its service was to the machining department, 25% was to assembly, and the remaining 25% was to finishing. In this situation the allocation of service department costs to the operating departments would be quite simple. The amounts allocated to each operating department would be:

A simple allocation

	Total to Be Allocated		Percentage Applied to Each Department		Amount Allocated to Each Department
Machining	$12,000	×	.50	=	$ 6,000
Assembly	$12,000	×	.25	=	3,000
Finishing	$12,000	×	.25	=	3,000
					$12,000

Unfortunately, the process is never quite this simple. It involves a number of different decisions at each step in gathering the information that will affect the percentage of service applied to each operating department.

Three steps in the allocation process

There are three steps in allocating service department costs: (1) accumulating the costs to be allocated, (2) identifying the operating departments that receive service from each service department and determining the measure of activity to use as an allocation base, and (3) selecting the appropriate method of allocation.

*Step 1: determine the costs
to be allocated*

STEP 1: *Accumulating the Costs to Be Allocated* This first step may seem easy enough, but it isn't quite as obvious as it first appears. For example, do we allocate the total costs of all service departments combined, in one step? Do we allocate the total costs of each service department separately? Do we allocate the individual costs of each service department separately? The answer is somewhere in the middle. We combine the costs of each service department into *cost pools* and then we allocate each of the cost pools individually. A cost pool is simply a group of costs that have a common characteristic. The most common cost pool characteristic is based upon the behavior of costs (variable and fixed) within the service department. The reason for separating costs into different cost pools is that there are usually different allocation bases that are applicable to different types of costs.

*Step 2: determine the
departments to allocate to
and select the best basis for
allocation*

STEP 2: *Identifying the Departments Serviced and Determining the Allocation Base* It shouldn't be too difficult to identify the operating departments that have received service from each service department. However, we do have a problem with the mechanics of allocation when some of the service departments are servicing each other as well as the operating departments — a situation involving something called *reciprocal services.* We will talk more about this situation in step 3 when we select a method of allocation.

Once we have identified the departments that have received service, we allocate the costs of the service department to the recipients using an appropriate allocation base. An *allocation base* is the link between the service department and the operating department. It helps measure the amount of service that a service department provides to an operating department and, therefore, provides the basis for determining the portion of costs to be allocated to each operating department.

For example, the number of hours the machine maintenance department spends working on an operating department's machinery would be an excellent allocation base for the service department. Here's why: We expect the costs of the machinery maintenance department to be significantly influenced by the number of hours it spends working on machinery. The greater the hours of maintenance, the greater the costs of the maintenance department. For every hour worked in machine maintenance, some operating department is receiving the benefit of this service. Since the hours spent on the machinery of specific operating departments can be identified, the percentage of total service given to each department can be based on the number of hours needed to service each department. And the percentage of total costs to be allocated to each operating department will be based on the hours used to service each department. If 25% of the time is spent working on the machinery of the assembly department, then the assembly department will receive 25% of the allocated costs.

Possible allocation bases for each of the other service departments we mentioned earlier are shown in Exhibit 11-3.

*Allocating variable and
fixed costs separately*

Different Allocation Bases for Variable Costs and Fixed Costs

When the costs of a service department can be separated into their variable and fixed components, it is better to allocate each cost pool separately rather than to allocate them in combination. As a rule, variable costs are usually allocated on the basis of the amount of actual, or expected, activity for a single operating period. On the other hand, fixed costs are allocated on the basis of the capacity needed to provide service over the long run — this is the amount of capacity that is *available* rather than the portion that is actually used or expected to be used within a single period.

Variable costs

Variable costs change in direct proportion to changes in activity within a given period of time. The greater the service provided to a particular department and,

**EXHIBIT 11-3
Allocation Bases for
Different Service
Departments**

Service Department	Possible Allocation Base
Machinery maintenance	Hours of maintenance time; hours of machine time worked in operating departments
Storeroom	Number of requisitions issued to each department
Cafeteria	Number of employees served
Janitorial	Square feet of space cleaned
Personnel	Number of employees; direct labor-hours; number of employees hired
Purchasing	Number of purchase orders processed
Inspection	Number of units inspected
Factory administration	Total labor-hours
Medical clinic	Number of employees; number of patients

Use activity for the current period

therefore, the greater the activity, the greater the variable costs incurred in the service department and, therefore, the greater the costs that should be allocated to the department serviced. The amount of activity that actually takes place, or is expected to take place, should provide the basis for allocating these costs — the level of activity for a single period is what affects the amount of the variable costs during that period. If the allocation base for the machinery maintenance department is the number of hours worked repairing machinery, then the variable costs for a period will be directly influenced by the number of labor-hours worked during that period. For example, assume that the machinery maintenance department worked 760 hours this month repairing machines in other departments. Of this total, 380 hours were for service to the machining department, 190 hours were used to service the assembly department, and the remaining 190 were used to service the finishing department. If the variable costs of the maintenance department were $4,000, then this amount would be allocated in the following manner:

Operating Department	Hours of Service	Percentage of Total	×	Variable Costs to Be Allocated	=	Amount Allocated
Machining	380	380/760 = 50%	×	$4,000	=	$2,000
Assembly	190	190/760 = 25%	×	$4,000	=	1,000
Finishing.	190	190/760 = 25%	×	$4,000	=	1,000
	760	100%				$4,000

An example of allocating variable costs

Fixed costs

Allocate on the basis of capacity available

Fixed costs are costs that are not expected to be influenced by the level of activity during a given period of time. For a service department the fixed costs are not affected by the amount of capacity used by that service department during a single period of time. Instead, the amount of fixed costs is based upon the amount of capacity for the service department that is available for an extended period of time — such as the life of the service department's fixed assets. The greater the capacity to provide a service each year, the greater the fixed costs for the service department, and vice versa. The amount of fixed costs that relates to each operating department depends upon the expected amount of capacity needed to service that department. Furthermore, the expected capacity is determined when the fixed costs were incurred originally. For example, assume that the costs of the machinery maintenance department for the month are $12,000 (of which $8,000 is fixed) and that the total time that can be spent repairing machinery is 800 hours per month. Also assume that the fixed costs were incurred with the expectation of providing the following hours of service to each operating department each month:

An example of allocating fixed costs

Service to:	Expected Hours per Month	Expected % of Total
Machining..	480	480/800 = 60%
Assembly..	160	160/800 = 20%
Finishing..	160	160/800 = 20%
	800	100%

Based upon these percentages, the fixed costs of the machinery maintenance department would be allocated to the operating departments as follows:

Operating Department	Total to Be Allocated	×	Allocation Percentage	=	Amount Allocated
Machining	$8,000	×	60%	=	$4,800
Assembly	$8,000	×	20%	=	1,600
Finishing	$8,000	×	20%	=	1,600
					$8,000

Step 3: use either the direct method or the step method

STEP 3: *Selecting the Allocation Method* There are two methods of allocating service department costs to operating departments. They are the *direct method* and the *step method.* Which method to use depends upon whether or not service departments provide service to each other as well as to operating departments. Theoretically, whenever service departments also provide services to other service departments, the step method should be used. However, for practical purposes the most commonly used method is the direct method, whether or not there are reciprocal services. Therefore, the direct method will be used in this chapter. (We will, however, briefly compare the direct method with the step method after we have completed the discussion of the mechanics of the direct method.)

The direct method

The ***direct method,*** as its names implies, allocates all its costs in a single direct step to the operating departments. The services that one service department provides another are completely ignored—no service department costs are ever allocated to other service departments.

Variable and fixed costs are combined

An illustration of the direct method For the sake of simplicity, we will assume in Example 11-1 that the total costs cannot be broken into their variable and fixed components. (In fact, when you work the problems for this chapter, you should be concerned with allocating the variable and fixed costs separately only when the problem tells you specifically to do so.)

As you can see from the use of the direct method in Exhibit 11-4, the total service department costs allocated to machining are $226,050. When this amount is added to the $810,000 of overhead budgeted for the machining department, the total overhead budget for machining is $1,036,050. The total budgeted overhead costs for assembly and finishing — after the allocated service department costs have been added — are $1,018,410 and $719,940, respectively. These budgeted amounts of overhead are needed to determine the departmental overhead rates.

Example 11-1

In this example there are three production departments and three service departments

Total costs

Allocation bases

Information related to allocation bases

COST ALLOCATION FOR UNDERHILL

The Underhill Company has three operating departments — machining, assembly, and finishing — and three service departments — cafeteria, personnel, and machinery maintenance. The overhead costs budgeted for each department at the beginning of the year are as follows:

Machining	$810,000	Cafeteria..............	$540,000
Assembly	630,000	Personnel	264,000
Finishing	386,400	Machinery maintenance .	144,000

These costs represent the combination of variable and fixed costs budgeted for the entire year. (All costs in previous examples were for a single month.) The cafeteria and personnel departments service the employees of all six departments, but machinery maintenance services only the operating departments. The allocation base for the cafeteria is the total number of workers to be employed during the year; for personnel it is the expected number of employees to be hired during the year; and for machinery maintenance it is the expected number of hours to be worked repairing machines during the year. The following is a summary of other budgeted data that is necessary in order to use the direct method of allocation in this example:

	Service Departments				Operating Departments				
Budgeted	Cafe-teria	Per-sonnel	Machine Maint.	Total	Machining	Assembly	Finishing	Total	Total for All Depts.
Number of repair-hours.....	—	—	9,120*	9,120	—	—	—	—	9,120
Number of employees	10	15	5	30	75	175	150	400	430
Number of employees hired .	2	1	—	3	5	11	9	25	28
Direct labor-hours	—	—	—	—	144,000	312,000	264,000	720,000	720,000

* This total is distributed to the operating departments as follows: 4,560 hr to machining, 2,280 to assembly, and 2,280 to finishing.

For *product costing* purposes the predetermined factory overhead rate for each department (for variable and fixed costs combined) is found by dividing the budgeted overhead costs (which include the allocated service department costs) by the direct labor-hours budgeted for the year. The predetermined rates are:

The overhead rates = total budgeted overhead ÷ by direct labor-hours

$$\text{Machining} = \$1,036,050 \div 144,000 \text{ direct labor-hours}$$
$$= \$7.19 \text{ per direct labor-hour}$$
$$\text{Assembly} = \$1,018,410 \div 312,000 \text{ direct labor-hours}$$
$$= \$3.26 \text{ per direct labor-hour}$$
$$\text{Finishing} = \$719,940 \div 264,000 \text{ direct labor-hours}$$
$$= \$2.73 \text{ per direct labor-hour}$$

EXHIBIT 11-4
Direct Method of Service Department Cost Allocation

	Service Departments			Operating Departments		
	Cafeteria	Personnel	Mach. Maint.	Machining	Assembly	Finishing
Overhead costs before allocation	$540,000	$264,000	$144,000	$ 810,000	$ 630,000	$386,400
Allocation of cafeteria to:						
Machining (75/400 = 18.75%).	(101,250)			101,250		
Assembly (175/400 = 43.75%).	(236,250)				236,250	
Finishing (150/400 = 37.5%)	(202,500)					202,500
Remaining to be allocated.	$ -0-					
Allocation of personnel to:						
Machining (5/25 = 20%).		(52,800)		52,800		
Assembly (11/25 = 44%).		(116,160)			116,160	
Finishing (9/25 = 36%)		(95,040)				95,040
Remaining to be allocated.		$ -0-				
Allocation of machine maint. to:						
Machining (4,560/9,120 = 50%)			(72,000)	72,000		
Assembly (2,280/9,120 = 25%)			(36,000)		36,000	
Finishing (2,280/9,120 = 25%).			(36,000)			36,000
Remaining to be allocated.			$ -0-			
Total costs allocated to each operating department.				$ 226,050	$ 388,410	$333,540
Total overhead costs of operating departments.				$1,036,050	$1,018,410	$719,940

The costs of cafeteria, personnel, and maintenance are allocated directly to machining, assembly, and finishing

These rates are used in the following manner. Assume we have a standard cost system (which we discussed in the previous chapter) which we are using for product costing purposes. The standard overhead cost per unit is found in each different department by multiplying the appropriate standard cost rate per hour times the standard hours allowed for each unit. The standard costs for all the units produced within each department are simply the standard cost rate per hour times the total standard hours allowed for all the units produced. The amount assigned to the units produced is called the *factory overhead applied.* For example, if the standard hours allowed for January's production in the machining department were 12,000, the total factory overhead applied to that production would be $86,280 (12,000 hours × $7.19 per hour). These product costs (along with direct materials and direct labor) start out in work-in-process, go on to finished goods when the units are completed, and continue on to cost of goods sold expense when the units are sold.

The overhead rates are applied to production for product costing

The overhead rate is part of the performance report

To *evaluate performance,* we must wait until the end of each month. At that time we prepare a performance report, comparing actual costs to the flexible budget. The actual costs for overhead should include the actual costs of the operating department plus an allocated portion of the actual costs of the service departments. The flexible budget for overhead should include an amount budgeted for the month just for the operating department, plus an allocated portion of the monthly flexible budget for the service departments. For this purpose it would be necessary to separate the variable and fixed costs to get accurate flexible budgets.

A comparison of the direct method and the step method Even though the cafeteria and personnel departments provided service to all three service departments (each service department services itself as well) in addition to the operating departments, the direct method of allocation ignored these reciprocal services. The costs of these two other service departments were allocated directly to each of the operating departments. None of the service department costs were allocated to any of the service departments. The diagram below shows how the costs of all three service departments were allocated:

With the direct method nothing is allocated to other service departments

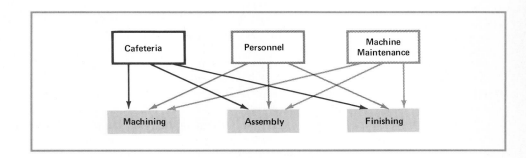

The step method recognizes services rendered to other service departments

The ***step method*** of cost allocation recognizes services that one service department provides another service department. This method allocates the service department costs to all departments that receive service. Eventually, however, even with the step method, all costs end up (via a less direct route) being assigned to the operating departments. Sometimes service departments provide services to each other reciprocally. That is, one service department not only provides service to another service department but also receives service from another service department. Reciprocal service costs can be properly recognized only with a variation of the step method, called the ***reciprocal services method.*** The diagram below shows the allocations that would be necessary to recognize the reciprocal services for Underhill:

The reciprocal services method allocates to production departments and to other service departments

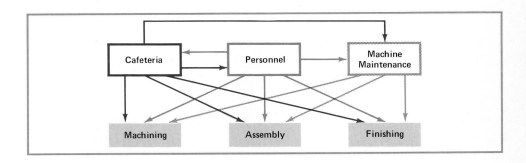

For simplicity we'll use only the direct method

As you can see, it's not that difficult to follow, but it can get pretty complicated to implement. For this reason, it may not be cost-effective for a company to use the step method of allocation. Unless its use somehow leads to more tangible benefits (such as better decisions) to the organization than does the direct method, the additional costs of implementation would probably not be justified.

PROFIT CENTERS

A profit center manager influences revenues and costs

So far we have looked at only one type of responsibility center—the cost center. In cost centers managers are given responsibility over the amount of costs that are incurred within their centers, but they have little, if any, responsibility for the revenues. The second type of responsibility center is the ***profit center,*** in which the manager is given responsibility for not only the costs but also the revenues. This means that the manager is responsible for most aspects of profit. It becomes the manager's responsibility to generate a desirable profit for his or her center during a specific period of time. If, for example, the Underhill Company was a single division of a multi-division organization, and if each division president, or manager, was responsible for generating an acceptable profit for the parent organization, then each of these divisions would be considered a profit center.

Different types of profit centers

We have assumed that Underhill makes a single product, and we will continue to do so. We will also assume that there are several other divisions that each make a single major product. This is a popular way to differentiate between different profit centers, each profit center representing a different major product line. For an organization that manufactures appliances, the different divisions might produce washing machines and dryers, refrigerators, stoves, and trash compactors.

On the other hand, different profit centers could be designated according to geographic location. For example, each section of the country, such as the north, south, east, and west, might represent a profit center responsible for the production and sale of many different product lines.

In addition, an organization might be separated into different geographic regions, with each region further divided according to the type of product produced and sold within that region. For example, the organization chart in Figure 11-2 shows four regions reporting to the corporate headquarters. Within each region there are three different product lines, and within each product line there are sales and production activities. Each of the four regional divisions would probably be a profit center, and each of the three product-line divisions within each region would probably also be a profit center. The individual sales and production departments of each product-line

FIGURE 11-2 Profit Centers—Regions and Products

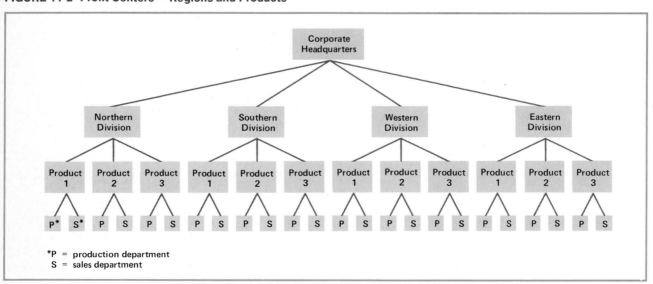

*P = production department
S = sales department

division, however, would probably be cost centers rather than profit centers (although the sales department might also be a profit center), because each department manager would bear responsibility for the control of costs within his or her center only.

Centralized and Decentralized Organizations

Usually, top management allows its profit center managers to have more responsibility than its cost center managers. Top management delegates some of its own decision-making authority to lower-level managers. After all, it is not possible for one person, or even a select few, to make all the day-to-day decisions in a large and complicated organization. While it is always necessary to give people some freedom to make decisions at lower levels, the critical question is how much responsibility to delegate.

In highly decentralized organizations much authority is delegated to lower-level managers

At one extreme, each and every division within our four-region firm in Figure 11-2 could be treated as a completely separate, independent, and autonomous operating unit in which the manager is given the responsibility of making nearly all decisions that affect the success or failure of the division. Top management would agree not to meddle in the day-to-day decisions. In this situation the organization would be considered highly *decentralized.*

The reverse is true in centralized organizations

At the other extreme, if top management decides to maintain most of the decision-making authority at the corporate headquarters level, then the division managers end up having little responsibility to make decisions that affect their own divisions. Nearly every decision of any significance would have to be approved through corporate headquarters first. The division manager would have very little freedom. In this situation the organization would be considered highly *centralized.*

Most organizations are somewhere in between the two extremes. Top-level managers realize that they cannot make all the decisions, but they also do not want to give complete freedom to middle- and lower-level managers. While there are many arguments for and against centralization or decentralization, there is no one best answer for every organization. It is up to the top-level management at the corporate headquarters level to decide the level of decentralization that is best for its situation.

Decentralization and Profit Centers

Decentralization and profit centers — do they always go together?

It may seem to make sense that a highly decentralized organization will have a large number of profit centers, while a highly centralized organization would have primarily cost centers. Indeed, that conclusion is intuitively appealing, but is not necessarily a reflection of reality. Some highly decentralized organizations use only cost centers, even though their managers are responsible for far more than merely controlling the costs of their responsibility centers. On the other hand, there are numerous examples of highly centralized organizations that have many profit centers, even though their managers are not given the responsibility — or the authority — for all the variables that enter into profit.

For our purposes we will assume that in an organization with profit centers, the managers are held accountable for both revenues and costs — that is, the organization is highly decentralized. For an organization that has only cost centers, we'll assume that managers are held accountable for only the costs, not the revenues, of their responsibility centers — that is, the organization is highly centralized.

In some decentralized organizations managers of responsibility centers also have a significant influence over the amount of investment that they are using to generate their profit. In this situation the so-called profit center is actually what's called an *investment center.* More on this later.

DECENTRALIZATION AT NCR

In 1972 NCR's situation was desperate. For decades it had coasted on the market domination in cash registers and related equipment established by its forceful founder, John H. Patterson, who died in 1922. His successors built a bloated bureaucracy and stayed with electromechanical cash registers even as retailers began clamoring for electronic machines. Competitors from Singer to the Japanese began winning NCR customers.

NCR was losing money—a frightening thing for a company that had long been a star in the industrial firmament. A major problem identified by Charles Exley, a newly

hired executive, related to the perceived inability of NCR's marketing organization to adjust to the times. But the marketing staff wasn't the only bureaucracy that was attacked. In 1980 NCR switched its centralized R&D operations into 12 indvidual profit-and-loss centers. Says Exley of his R&D decentralization: "Letting individuals make key product decisions has increased our agility as a company enormously."

NCR also gave plant managers discretion to spend up to tens of millions on development projects without asking Dayton's [i.e., corporate headquarters] permission.

The radical decentralization has pro-

duced its flops. But the flops have been outweighed by the successes. One such is the new NCR 9800 general purpose, fault-tolerant mainframe; this came from NCR's Rancho Bernardo, Calif. lab and plant.

Another example is NCR's Tower, conceived and created in the Columbia, S.C. plant. The tower is a series of microcomputers that can run software written for machines made by others.

Source: Gary Slutsker, "Playing for the Long Haul," *Forbes*, Nov. 3, 1986, pp. 43–44. Excerpted by permission of *Forbes* magazine. Copyright © 1986 by Forbes, Inc.

Evaluating the Performance of Profit Centers

We evaluate profit centers with segment income statements

The performance of a profit center and the manager of that profit center is evaluated by the information reported in *segment income statements.* A segment is simply any part of an organization for which both costs and revenues can be identified as relating to that part. For each segment it is possible to both identify and measure operating performance, usually on the basis of profitability. The segment income statement is simply the income statement that we prepare for each segment, or profit center.[1] The format recommended for segment income statements is the contribution margin approach you learned about in Chapter 4. Here, the format will be more elaborate—it will not only distinguish variable costs from fixed costs, but it will also distinguish direct costs from indirect costs and controllable costs from uncontrollable costs.

Look at Exhibit 11-5 for Underhill's segment income statement

The segment income statements for Underhill and the other two divisions are shown in Exhibit 11-5. (All numbers are assumed in this exhibit. Do not try to figure out where they came from by referring to previous exhibits.)

Remember: We are assuming that Underhill is one division of a multi-division organization and that the different divisions represent different product lines. We will refer to the three divisions as Division A (Underhill), Division B, and Division C. Since each division will be evaluated on the basis of the profit it generates, each division is a profit center and the income statement for each division will be a segment income statement. Although we saw in Figure 11-2 that we could have both geographic regions and product lines as profit centers within the same division, we will assume for simplicity that there are no regional profit centers. And we are assuming that all three division managers report directly to corporate headquarters. (See Figure 11-3.)

Although we are assuming in our Underhill example that each of the profit centers (the segments) is a division of the same company, this does not mean that all profit

---

[1] Some managers prefer to treat a segment as any part of an organization for which cost information is collected and reported. This definition would treat both cost centers and profit centers as segments. We will limit the use of the term *segment* to profit centers.

EXHIBIT 11-5 Segment Income Statements
This exhibit distinguishes between variable and fixed costs and between controllable and noncontrollable costs.

	Segments			Total for All Segments
	Division A (Underhill)	Division B	Division C	
Sales...	$1,252,000	$500,000	$435,000	$2,187,000
Less: Variable Costs:				
Variable Manufacturing*..................................	$1,034,000	$345,000	$240,000	$1,619,000
Variable Selling and Administrative of Segment..............	96,000	34,000	44,000	174,000
	$1,130,000	$379,000	$284,000	$1,793,000
(1) Total Contribution Margin...................................	$ 122,000	$121,000	$151,000	$ 394,000
Less: Direct Fixed Costs Controllable by Segment Manager*.....	80,000	30,000	55,000	165,000
(2) Contribution Controllable by Segment Manager................	$ 42,000	$ 91,000	$ 96,000	$ 229,000
Less: Fixed Costs of Segment Not Controllable by Segment Manager*..	13,200	14,000	17,500	44,700
(3) Contribution of Segment to Common Costs...................	$ 28,800	$ 77,000	$ 78,500	$ 184,300
Common Costs for All Segments	82,000	28,000	25,000	135,000
(4) Net Income	$ (53,200)	$ 49,000	$ 53,500	$ 49,300

* Including the allocated service department costs.

centers are divisions. It's also probable that subsidiaries of a consolidated company are treated as profit centers. In addition, individual departments, regions, or branches of a division might also be treated as profit centers.

TCM = total sales − total variable costs

Total Contribution Margin

The first significant line [identified as line (1) in Exhibit 11-5] within the segment income statement is the total contribution margin for each division — total sales less total variable costs. This is the amount that each division contributes to the coverage of its own fixed costs. This would most likely be controllable by the division manager.

Contribution Controllable by Segment Manager

TCM less fixed costs controllable by segment manager

Fixed costs that are controllable by the division manager are subtracted from the total contribution margin. The net is the ***contribution controllable by segment manager*** [identified as line (2) in Exhibit 11-5]. The fixed costs that are subtracted here include many discretionary fixed costs and some committed fixed costs. For exam-

**FIGURE 11-3
Underhill as a Product-Line Division**

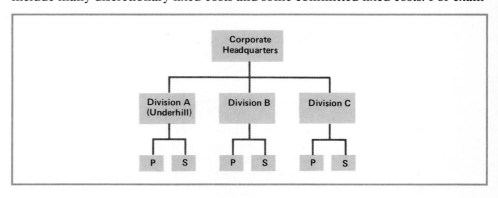

*Examples of controllable
fixed costs — committed
and discretionary*

ple, quite possibly such discretionary expenditures as division advertising, sales promotion, recruiting, training programs, contributions, and bonuses would be controllable by the division manager. In addition, committed fixed costs such as the salaries
of key personnel (other than those of the division manager) would probably be
controllable by the division manager.

On the other hand, discretionary expenditures such as research and development
and national advertising may be the responsibility of someone at the corporate
headquarters level, even though the costs are a part of the division to which they
relate. In addition, many of the committed fixed costs of the division are probably the
ultimate responsibility of someone higher than the division manager; these are costs
such as salaries of the division manager, depreciation, property taxes, rent, insurance,
etc. In situations in which a division manager can control these costs, it is probably
because the manager has been given the authority and responsibility to make decisions that affect the productive capacity — the investment — of the division. When
the division manager makes the decisions affecting the investment in fixed assets for
the division, then that manager has some control over the costs that relate to this
capacity — the committed fixed costs. In this situation the division would probably
no longer be considered a profit center, but instead would be treated as an investment
center. But once again, more on investment centers later.

*Contribution controllable
by segment manager is a
good measure of the
manager's performance*

The contribution controllable by segment manager usually represents the best
measure of performance for managers of profit centers (which in our situation are
divisions). Any income figures that come later in the statement are considered less
appropriate for this purpose, because the manager will probably have little influence
over the items that are subtracted in determining that income.

Contribution of Segment to Common Costs

*Now we subtract the
noncontrollable costs of the
segment*

The next costs to be subtracted are the fixed costs of the division that the division
manager has no control over. We identified these discretionary and committed fixed
costs in the previous section. When these uncontrollable fixed costs are subtracted,
the remainder is called the **contribution of segment to common costs** [line (3) in
Exhibit 11-5]. Basically, this represents the income that each division would earn on
its own if it were an independent company rather than one division of a multi-division company.

*Contribution to common
costs is a good measure of
segment performance*

The contribution of segment to common costs is the best measure of the profitability of the division because all the costs do indeed relate directly to that division.
However, this figure is not the best measure for evaluating the performance of the
division manager. Remember: The manager does not control all the costs that were
subtracted in determining the contribution of the division to common costs. As you
will recall, we evaluate the manager with the income referred to as *contribution
controllable by segment manager.*

When the incomes for all the divisions are added together, the total is the income
for the entire company ($184,300 in Exhibit 11-5) before the costs of running the
corporate headquarters are subtracted.

Direct vs. Indirect Costs

*The distinction between
direct and indirect costs
depends on the point of view*

Up to this point we have used the terms *direct costs* and *indirect costs* primarily
from a product costing standpoint. The direct costs were the direct materials and
direct labor incurred in the production department, and the indirect costs were the
overhead costs incurred in the production department. The terms *direct* and *indirect*
can also relate to an entire department or division, as well as to the product. For
example, although factory overhead incurred in a production department is an

indirect cost of the product, it would be considered a "direct cost" from the standpoint of the production department. Because it can be easily traced to a department, it is a direct cost associated with that department. On the other hand, service department costs which are necessary for the efficient and effective running of the production departments are not actually incurred within the production departments. They are related to production—but only indirectly—so they are indirect costs of the production department. When you look at service department costs from the standpoint of an entire division, however, because they can be easily traced to a specific division, they are direct costs of that division.

Common costs are indirect costs of a segment

So you see, whether we define a cost as direct or indirect depends upon the center of activity we are relating it to. Right now we are looking at income statements for entire divisions. Therefore, any costs incurred within a division are considered direct costs of that division. Any costs incurred outside a division but assigned to the division as if they are somehow related to, or associated with, that division are indirect costs, or ***common costs.*** The costs that are considered common costs in our situation are the costs of corporate headquarters. Although they are not incurred by any one division, they are thought of as being incurred for the benefit of all divisions and are therefore considered to be indirectly related to each division.

Should we allocate common costs to segments?

An important issue concerns the treatment of common costs when the segment income statements are being prepared. Should common costs be fully allocated to the different divisions (as we did with the $135,000 in Exhibit 11-5), or should no attempt be made to associate common costs with specific divisions? Many accountants contend that the profitability of a division is best measured by the contribution of segment to common costs rather than by net income. They feel that by fully allocating common costs, the evaluation of a division may be based upon the wrong performance measure—namely, net income instead of contribution of segment to common costs. This might easily happen because of the almighty concern for the "bottom line"—which, when common costs are allocated, is the net income for each division. For example, if we are evaluating Underhill (Division A) and comparing it to Divisions B and C, we should look at the contribution of segment to common costs, $28,800, rather than at the net loss, $53,200, as the measure of Underhill's profitability. This is because many of the common costs (such as national advertising and administrative costs of the corporate headquarters) allocated to Underhill would not be incurred by Underhill if it were an independent company.

Arguments against allocation

Opponents of allocation prefer to see the common costs deleted from the segment statements and included only in the total income column for the company as a whole.

Arguments for allocation

Despite these objections, many companies do allocate their common costs to their divisions, just as we have done in Exhibit 11-5. These companies feel it is important for each division to realize that it is responsible for contributing enough to the company as a whole to cover all costs, including the common costs. It is not enough for each division merely to show a satisfactory profit—that is, a profit that would be considered acceptable for an independent company. Instead, the combined profit for all the divisions must be great enough to cover the common costs and still leave a satisfactory profit for the company as a whole. Only by letting each division know its fair allocated share of common costs will each division fully realize its responsibility.

Assessment of Income Statements

How to evaluate the performance of profit centers

Now that we have prepared segment income statements, just how do we use this information to evaluate the performance of each division manager and/or division? Using the contribution controllable by segment manager to evaluate the division manager and using the contribution of segment to common costs to evaluate the division, how do we know from these numbers whether the manager and the division were as profitable as they should have been? One way to evaluate the profitability of the division manager or the division is to compare the actual income earned for the period to the income that was budgeted for the period in the master budget. In addition, we can also determine measures of efficiency and effectiveness (discussed in Chapter 10) by comparing the results to a flexible budget for income based upon the level of activity actually achieved for the period. The general format of such a performance report would look something like Exhibit 11-6.

With flexible budgets

EXHIBIT 11-6   Performance Report for Segment Incomes

	(1) Actual Results	(2) Flexible Budget	(3) Master Budget	(4) (Col. 1 − 2) Flexible Budget Variance	(5) (Col. 2 − 3) Sales Volume Variance	(6) (Col. 1 − 3) Master Budget Variance
Sales						
Less: Variable Costs						
Total Contribution Margin						
Less: Direct Fixed Costs Controllable by Segment Manager						
Contribution Controllable by Segment Manager						
Less: Fixed Costs of Segment Not Controllable by Segment Manager						
Contribution of Segment to Common Costs						

Here we compare the actual income to the income expected at the beginning of the period and to the income we should have had based on the activity actually achieved.

As you learned in the previous chapter, we measure **efficiency** with the flexible budget variance [column (4)]—the difference between the actual results [column (1)] and the flexible budget [column (2)] based on the actual units produced and sold. If we have a standard cost system and we want to evaluate the individual components of the flexible budget variance, it's simple to calculate the price and quantity variances for each variable item in the statement.

Sales volume variance

Effectiveness is measured by the sales volume variance [column (5)]—the difference between the flexible budget [column (2)] and the master budget [column (3)]. (The sales volume variance can be found more quickly by multiplying the contribution margin per unit times the difference between the actual units sold and the master budget level of unit sales.)

We can compare division profits to each other

Another way to evaluate the profitability of the division or division manager is to compare, within the same company, the results of one division with the results of other divisions that are somewhat similar in the nature of operations. The divisions or division managers that generate the most profit are assessed as having done the best job. In addition, the division results can be compared with the results of comparable entities outside the company.

It may be inappropriate to compare the profits of one division with those of another if the divisions are not similar in size. Take, for example, two divisions that both show a profit of $100,000. With that information alone, would you consider them to be equally profitable? Would you still feel the same way if you knew that one division had assets totaling $400,000 and that the other division had assets totaling $4,000,000? Of course not. The one with more assets should certainly be able to generate more income. To compare divisions, we need to consider the amount of investment as well as the amount of profit. The profitability measure that considers both profit and investment is called the *return on investment (ROI)*. We will cover the ROI later in the chapter when we discuss investment centers.

Problems in Determining Profit for Profit Centers

In addition to the problem of comparing the profits of different-sized divisions, there are two other problems in evaluating the performance of all profit centers:

1. If we do decide to allocate common costs to the divisions, how do we do it?

2. When divisions conduct business with each other and products transfer from one division to another, how do we determine the amount of revenue to be credited to the division that transfers its product to another division?

Allocation of Common Costs

How do we allocate common costs?

When a company decides to allocate its common costs to the individual divisions, how does it determine the amount to assign to each division? Theoretically, we should attempt to determine an allocation base that creates a close link between the common costs and the activities of each division, as we did when allocating the service department costs to operating departments. For example, it would be ideal if we knew that the amount spent on advertising at the national level was directly related to the level of sales in each division. Then we could allocate the common costs on the basis of the total sales of each division. The problem, however, is that there is hardly ever a close relationship between the common costs and any measure of activity that we might consider. Therefore, any allocation base that we use is purely arbitrary, and consequently, so too will be the resulting allocation of costs.

For the company that insists on allocating its common costs, all that can be hoped for is that each division manager accepts that the amount allocated to his or her division is fair and that the division is not being allocated a disproportionate share relative to other divisions. This is especially important when the division is being evaluated (inappropriately) on the basis of the bottom-line net income rather than on the basis of the contribution of segment to common costs. Of course, if division managers know that their own performance and their divisions' performance are to be evaluated on the basis of controllable measures, then they won't be overly concerned with the method of allocation or with the amount that is allocated.

One common way of allocating common costs is on the basis of the sales of each division. Other possibilities might include the total assets of each division or even the total costs of each division.

Transfer Pricing

How do we value goods transferred from one division to another?

It is not uncommon for different divisions within the same organization to buy and sell from each other. For example, a large conglomerate like General Motors will have a division that manufactures tires and another that manufactures batteries. The producers of the batteries and tires will naturally sell to the different car divisions within General Motors, such as Pontiac and Chevrolet, as well as to the general public. When the tire division or battery division sells its product to another division within the company, naturally the selling division has revenue from the sale that becomes a part of its segment income statement. At the same time the purchasing division incurs the cost of buying each battery or set of tires, which ultimately becomes a part of the cost of the cars that are produced. When the cars are sold, these costs become part of the costs of goods sold expense on the segment income statement of the division that bought the batteries or tires.

We value the goods using a transfer price

The value that is assigned to the goods or services that are transferred from one segment to another is called the *transfer price.* The value designated as the transfer price will obviously have an impact on the profits and subsequent evaluation of performance of both the buying and selling divisions and the division managers. Therefore, the determination of the transfer price is critical to each division manager.

*The transfer price affects
the profits of both divisions*

As we shall see, there are several different transfer prices that might be used. Each different transfer price leads to a different profit for both the buying and selling divisions. Worse yet, the choice of which transfer price to employ is normally not made by either division manager; it is usually made at the corporate headquarters level. This means that someone else's choice of a transfer price will affect the amount of profits reported for each division.

If each division were an independent business, then the buyer and seller would have to agree upon a price that was acceptable to them both. This would be the market price for the product—the result of an arm's length transaction. In a *completely* decentralized organization, corporate management allows its divisions to act as independent businesses by permitting them to determine a mutually agreeable price through the bargaining process. If an agreeable price between divisions cannot be reached, there will be no internal deal. Instead, the buying division will buy from the outside at an acceptable price. When a buying and selling division agree upon a

*Market price as the
transfer price*

price, this price, called the ***market transfer price,*** will be basically the same as the price that would be charged on regular sales by the selling division to outside customers.

For several reasons, however, the transfer price is typically not a market price. It could be that there is no outside market for the product in its present form, and therefore there is no market price. Or it might be that top-level management does not want to let the two divisions negotiate a price. You see, when two divisions bargain, there is always the chance that they won't agree upon a price; as a result, both divisions may go to outside buyers and sellers to try to get the price that each wants. This may defeat the very purpose of having one division that can serve as the supplier to another division. It may be much more economical for the organization as a whole to have the two divisions deal with each other, and thus it may be necessary to force this interaction by imposing a transfer price that each party must accept.

For whatever reason, what usually occurs—especially in a centralized organization—is that top-level corporate management specifies how the transfer price will be determined. The resulting "value" assigned to the transfer becomes the sales revenue to the seller and the cost to the buyer. The most commonly used values for the transfer price, other than a market price, are the following:

*Other ways to determine
the transfer price*

1. ***Variable costs*** For the selling division these are either the actual or standard variable costs of producing the product and distributing it to the buying division. There is no profit for the seller. The buyer will show all the profit for both divisions when the final product is sold to an outside customer.

2. ***Full costs*** These are the absorption costs that we discussed in Chapter 5. Full costs include the actual or standard variable manufacturing costs plus the fixed manufacturing costs. Once again, there will be no profit for the seller, because its revenues will equal its costs. All profit will be recorded by the buyer when the completed product is later sold.

3. ***Costs plus a markup*** Using either of the two preceding costing approaches, a desired profit margin is added to the costs to arrive at the transfer price. For variable costing the profit margin is the contribution margin. For full (absorption) costing the profit margin is the gross margin. With a cost-plus approach the selling division is able to recognize some profit, which in turn makes the cost to the buyer higher. As a consequence, the profits of the buying division (when the product is later sold to an outside customer) are lower than under either of the preceding approaches.

Although it's quite possible that the three divisions shown in Exhibit 11-5 were buying from and selling to one another, there really isn't any way to tell for sure whether any transfers were taking place or which transfer pricing methods were used for any transfers that did occur.

INVESTMENT CENTERS

Investment center managers influence costs, revenues, and investments

We are now ready to go on to the third type of responsibility center—*investment centers.* Before we begin, we want to make an important point. Nearly everything we discussed about profit centers—the need for and component parts of the segment income statements, as well as the problems associated with their preparation (common cost allocations and transfer pricing)—applies equally well to the discussion of investment centers. We merely take the concept of profit centers one step further by relating the profit to the investment that generated the profit.

Investment centers are more likely to exist in highly decentralized organizations

An organization that is highly decentralized lets its division managers make all decisions that relate to their own divisions. In these cases the division manager has control over not only the revenues and costs but also over the investment available to generate the profit. The division manager makes decisions that affect the amount of productive, marketing, and administrative facilities and, as a result, is able to control both the discretionary and committed fixed costs—if not in the short run then at least in the long run.

In the case of Underhill (Division A), if it had been an independent company before it became a division of a larger company, it would have definitely been an investment center prior to its acquisition. After it was aquired, it could be considered an investment center only if corporate management continued to let the division manager make all, or most, of the decisions related to sales, costs, and the investment in productive capacity. There's a good chance, however, that the division manager would not be given this much authority and that most investment decisions would be made at the corporate level. Although the division manager may still have a significant input into the investment decision, the ultimate decision would most likely no longer be his or hers to make.

Although the divisions might not be investment centers, the company as a whole —which is made up of the three divisions—would certainly be an investment center.

Return on Investment

Investment centers are evaluated with the ROI

The performance of an investment center is evaluated by its *return on investment (ROI).* The ROI indicates the income of the investment center as a percentage of investment. The investment can be either the stockholders' equity (the net assets) or the total assets of the investment center. For our purposes we will use only total assets, and we will assume that the three divisions in Exhibit 11-5 are now investment centers.

ROI = income ÷ assets

The calculation of the ROI is:

$$\text{ROI} = \frac{\text{division income}}{\text{division assets}}$$

Since the best measure of the profitability of a division is the contribution of segment to common costs, this will be the measure of income that we use in the numerator of the ROI equation. In the denominator we will use the value of only the division's assets plus an allocated portion of the value of any assets shared with other divisions. We will normally not include any allocated assets of the corporate headquarters (although there are certain exceptions that we won't worry about here). We exclude these allocated assets in order to be consistent with the income measure we are using in the numerator. Since we exclude the allocated common costs from the income in the numerator, we must also exclude the assets that generate the allocated common costs from the denominator.

The income comes from line (3) of Exhibit 11-5

To calculate the ROIs for the three divisions shown in Exhibit 11-5, we need to know how large the investment is for each division. So let's assume that the total assets of each division are as follows:

The assets are assumed to be:

Division A (Underhill) $2,000,000
Division B 550,000
Division C .... ' 314,000

The resulting ROI (using the contribution of segment to common costs found in Exhibit 11-5) for each division is as follows:

Division C has the best ROI — it is 25%

$$\text{ROI (Underhill)} = \$28,800 \div \$2,000,000 = 1.4\%$$
$$\text{ROI (Division B)} = \$77,000 \div \quad \$550,000 = 14\%$$
$$\text{ROI (Division C)} = \$78,500 \div \quad \$314,000 = 25\%$$

The income for Underhill was the smallest not only in dollar value but also as a percentage of investment. The income of $28,800 was only 1.4% of Underhill's total assets, meaning that for every dollar of assets, the division was only able to generate an additional $0.014 from operations — not very good no matter how you look at it. The 14% ROI for Division B is much better than Underhill's ROI, but not nearly as good as the 25% ROI for Division C. When you compare the results for Divisions B and C, you will realize why it is so important to use the ROI, rather than merely dollar profits, to evaluate investment centers. Divisions B and C had almost the same dollar amounts of profit, which may have prompted an initial impression that they were equally profitable. However, when you realize that Division C was able to earn roughly the same amount of profit as Division B but with a much smaller investment in assets, you can see that the manager of Division C did a much better job of using the division's investment than did the manager of Division B. Only with the ROI are we able to properly assess the relative profitability of the three divisions.

Assessing Performance with ROI

How do we decide if the ROI is good enough?

Once we have the ROI percentages for each division, what do we do with this information? What do we compare it to? Well, the obvious thing we can do is to compare the ROIs of the different divisions to see which division is most profitable. The manager of the most profitable division would be a likely candidate for a possible promotion, raise, or year-end bonus.

Use a minimum ROI?

Instead of comparing one division with another, it may be better to compare the division ROI with a minimum ROI that was specified before the period began. For example, different divisions may be involved in industries in which the risk of failure is very different — an ROI that is acceptable for one industry may be quite unacceptable for another industry. In this case an acceptable ROI would be geared to the specific risk associated with each industry — high risk requires a greater return than does low risk. Here is another situation in which it might be better to compare the division ROI with a predetermined standard: A new manager is assigned to turn around a previously unsuccessful division. Is the new manager going to feel comfortable having his or her division compared with divisions that have a long history of success? Probably not. The new manager might reject the assignment, or accept it only if promised that rewards will be based upon an improvement in the division's ROI rather than a comparison with other divisions.

Compare to previous years or to an industry average?

It might also be informative to top management to compare ROIs in the current year with ROIs in the previous years, as well as with ROIs of independent companies in the same industry and also with an industry average ROI. Management must be careful, however, not to assume that past results, the results for another firm, or an average for the industry necessarily provide a good indication of what the division's performance should have been in the current year. The fact that the division may have done much better than the year before, much better than a competitor, and much better than the average firm in the industry doesn't necessarily mean that it did as well as it could or should have done.

A Breakdown of ROI into Key Factors

To properly evaluate the ROI for an investment center, it is a good idea to separate it into its component parts. It is easier to see how to improve the ROI or to evaluate the reasons for a change in the ROI if we realize that it is actually made up of asset turnover and return on sales. The calculation of the ROI begins with:

$$\text{ROI} = \frac{\text{division income}}{\text{division assets}}$$

This can be divided into:

$$\text{ROI} = \frac{\text{sales}}{\text{assets}} \times \frac{\text{income}^2}{\text{sales}} = \frac{\text{income}}{\text{assets}}$$

The component parts of ROI are asset turnover and return on sales

And since

$$\frac{\textbf{Sales}}{\textbf{Assets}} = \textbf{asset turnover} \quad \textbf{and} \quad \frac{\textbf{Income}}{\textbf{Sales}} = \textbf{return on sales}$$

the ROI becomes:

$$\textbf{ROI} = \textbf{asset turnover} \times \textbf{return on sales}$$

Using the facts from Exhibit 11-5 and the assets listed on page 494, the 1.4% ROI for Underhill (Division A) is composed of the following two parts:

$$\text{ROI (Underhill)} = \frac{\$1,252,000}{\$2,000,000} \times \frac{\$28,800}{\$1,252,000}$$

$$= .626 \times .023 = .014 = 1.4\%$$

Asset turnover = .626

The asset turnover indicates the dollars of revenue that each dollar of assets was able to generate in the current period. In this example each dollar of assets was able to generate only $0.626 of sales.

Return on sales = .023

The return on sales indicates the percentage of every sales dollar that remains after all costs have been covered. Underhill was able to generate only $0.023 of profit for each dollar of sales.

When the manager of Underhill gets the results of her ROI, she will likely be disappointed, whether she is comparing her division's results with other divisions'

---

[2] Remember, we are still using the contribution of segment to common costs as the best income measure for the segment.

results, industry averages, or predetermined standards of performance. Let's face it, an ROI of 1.4% is pathetic, especially when you realize that the value of the assets could instead be invested in risk-free government bonds and earn at least 7%. Improvements are needed, and this is where the two components of the ROI come into play.

How to improve the ROI

To improve the ROI for Underhill, or for any other investment center, management can do one of two things. It can either increase the asset turnover without reducing the return on sales or increase the return on sales without reducing the asset turnover. It can accomplish these goals in the following manner:

There are three ways

1. Increasing sales

2. Reducing costs

3. Reducing total assets

Increase sales

By increasing sales, the asset turnover improves (assuming the total assets don't also increase), but at the same time the return on sales is reduced (assuming no increase in income). If nothing changes but sales dollars, then the offsetting effects on asset turnover and return on assets nullify each other. Hopefully, an increase in sales will also increase income, because an increase in income has a favorable effect on the return on sales. As long as income increases, the ROI will be improved.

Reduce costs

A reduction in costs (without an equivalent reduction in sales) will increase the profits of the division and, therefore, the return on sales. A larger return on sales with no change in asset turnover will increase the ROI.

Reduce total assets

Finally, a reduction in the asset base without a reduction in sales will also improve the ROI. First of all, the asset turnover will improve. Second, the return on sales might also improve if there is a reduction of committed fixed costs that may be associated with the assets that have been reduced. For example, if we retire a productive asset that is still being depreciated, and the work can be done with other assets that we currently own, then the sales remain the same, the depreciation expense goes down, the profit goes up, and the return on sales improves.

Look now at Example 11-2 for Underhill (Division A) and see how the division manager plans to improve Underhill's ROI for next year.

Example 11-2

IMPROVING THE ROI FOR UNDERHILL

The division manager feels that by slightly increasing Underhill's sales price, the division can increase total sales by 5% without increasing any of its variable costs. In addition, an old machine which has served as a backup and is still being depreciated will be retired at its book value. The book value of the machine is $200,000, and the annual depreciation has been $40,000. All other fixed costs will remain the same.

The results of the changes mentioned in the example will be as follows:

The changes from Example 11-2

1. Total assets will decrease from $2,000,000 to $1,800,000.

2. Sales should increase to $1,314,600 ($1,252,000 $\times$ 1.05), an increase of $62,600.

3. Costs will decrease by $40,000.

4. Income will increase by $102,600 ($62,600 + $40,000) to $131,400 ($28,800 + $102,600).

The new ROI will be 7.3%:

The result of the changes on ROI

$$\text{ROI} = \frac{\$1,314,600}{\$1,800,000} \times \frac{\$131,400}{\$1,314,600} = .73 \times .0999 = .073 = 7.3\%$$

By increasing the asset turnover from .626 to .73 and the return on sales from .023 to .0999, the ROI will increase from 1.4% to 7.3%—still not outstanding, but a significant improvement.

CHAPTER SUMMARY

There are three types of responsibility centers—cost centers, profit centers, and investment centers. In a ***cost center*** the responsible manager exerts influence over the costs incurred within that center and is held accountable for keeping those costs within acceptable limits. The cost center manager has little, if any, influence over revenues or the investment in fixed assets that generate revenues.

Many production departments receive assistance from other departments that are not actually involved in the production process but are considered necessary for the efficient operation of the production departments. These are ***service departments.*** Examples of service departments are machinery maintenance, the storeroom, the cafeteria, the janitorial service, personnel, purchasing, and factory administration. Since service departments are needed to enable production departments to operate efficiently, their costs are assigned to the production departments through a procedure referred to as ***cost allocation.*** The service department costs that are allocated to each production department are treated as factory overhead costs of the production department. The allocated costs can be useful to the production department for product costing, evaluation of performance, and special decisions.

The three steps in cost allocation are (1) accumulating the costs to be allocated; (2) determining the departments that were serviced and the allocation base to be employed, and (3) selecting the appropriate allocation method. The allocation method described in this chapter is the ***direct method,*** which allocates the costs of each service department directly to the producing departments. With the direct method the services that one service department provides to another (called ***reciprocal services***) are ignored—that is, no service department costs are ever allocated to other service departments. The direct method may be less theoretically sound than other methods that do recognize reciprocal services, but for practical purposes it is usually considered to be acceptable.

The second type of responsibility center is the ***profit center.*** Within a profit center the manager is responsible for both the costs and the revenues generated by that center and is held accountable for most aspects of profit. Examples of profit centers include divisions, regions, subsidiaries, and branches of a company. We usually equate profit centers with organizations that are somewhat ***decentralized,*** organizations in which the profit centers are treated as separate, independent, and autonomous operating units and the managers are given the responsibility of making nearly all decisions that affect the success or failure of the division.

Within some organizations managers of divisions or branches that we normally think of as profit centers are given only the responsibility of controlling costs and have little influence over the revenue aspects of profit. Within these organizations most of the decision-making authority resides at the corporate headquarters. This type of organization is considered to be highly *centralized.* The managers of these responsibility centers are actually no more than cost center managers, regardless of what the center is called.

The performance of a profit center and the profit center manager is evaluated by the information reported in a *segment income statement.* The segment income statement uses a contribution margin approach — it distinguishes not only variable costs from fixed costs but also controllable costs from uncontrollable costs. The profitability of a profit center manager is measured by the contribution margin controllable by segment manager, and the best measure of profitability for the entire profit center is the contribution of segment to common costs.

When different profit centers within the same organization buy from and sell to one another, the value assigned to the goods that are transferred is extremely important to both the buyer and the seller. The value, which is called the *transfer price,* is revenue to the seller and the cost of the inventory purchased to the buyer. The transfer price obviously has an impact on the profits of both the buyer's and the seller's profit centers. Sometimes profit centers employ the market value of the goods as the transfer price. More frequently, a cost or cost-plus-a-markup approach is used.

The third type of responsibility center is the *investment center.* Within an investment center the manager is allowed to make all decisions that relate to that center. The manager has control over the costs incurred and the revenues generated, as well as influence over the amount of investment that is available to generate the profit of the center. A manager who has a significant influence over the costs, revenues, *and* investment is considered responsible for an investment center rather than a profit center. (Some writers prefer not to distinguish between profit centers and investment centers. They refer to both categories simply as profit centers.)

The performance of an investment center is evaluated by its *return on investment (ROI).* The ROI is calculated by dividing the investment center's income by its assets. The component parts that make up the ROI are the asset turnover and return on sales:

$$\textbf{ROI} = \textbf{asset turnover} \times \textbf{return on sales}$$

$$= \frac{\textbf{sales}}{\textbf{assets}} \times \frac{\textbf{income}}{\textbf{sales}} = \frac{\textbf{income}}{\textbf{assets}}$$

IMPORTANT TERMS USED IN THIS CHAPTER

Centralized organizations Organizations in which top management maintains all decision-making authority at the corporate level; management does not allow responsibility centers to operate as separate, independent, and autonomous operating units. (page 485)

Common costs The costs of running a corporate headquarters which are only indirectly related to the different segments of the organization. (page 489)

Cost allocation The procedure used to assign the costs of service departments to production departments. (page 476)

Cost center A responsibility center whose manager exerts influence over the costs but not over the revenues that may be generated by the center or the investment that generates the revenues. (page 474)

Decentralized organizations Organizations in which top management permits and encourages responsibility centers to operate as separate, independent, and autonomous operating units. The responsibility center manager makes nearly all decisions that affect the success or failure of that center. Profit centers and investment centers are typically found in a decentralized organization. (page 485)

Direct method The method of allocating service department costs in a single direct step to each of the production departments that was serviced; the direct method ignores reciprocal services. (page 480)

Investment center A responsibility center whose manager makes all decisions that relate to that center. The manager is given the authority to control the costs and revenues as well as the investment that generates the profit. (page 493)

Profit center A responsibility center whose manager is given the responsibility of controlling not only the center's costs but also its revenues. (page 484)

Reciprocal services A situation in which one service department not only provides service to another service department but also receives service from another service department. (page 483)

Return on investment (ROI) The measure of performance for an investment center. It is determined by dividing the investment center's assets into its income. (page 493)

Segment income statement The evaluation tool for measuring the performance of profit centers and profit center managers. (page 486)

Service departments Departments that provide assistance, or service, to production departments. They are not directly involved in the production process but are needed to enable the producing departments to operate as efficiently as possible. (page 475)

Step method A method of allocating service department costs to other service departments; this method recognizes reciprocal services. All service department costs are ultimately assigned to the production departments, but in an indirect manner involving several steps. (page 483)

Transfer pricing The process of determining a value to assign to the goods that are sold by one segment to another within the same organization. (page 491)

QUESTIONS

1. What are the three types of responsibility centers? Explain each type.

2. What are *service departments?* Give several examples.

3. The costs of service departments become a part of the cost of a manufactured good. Explain why this is so, since service department costs are not incurred within the producing departments.

4. "All service department costs are product costs." Do you agree? Explain.

5. When service department costs are allocated to production departments, are the allocated costs treated as direct materials, direct labor, factory overhead, or all three? Explain your answer.

6. The allocation of service department costs helps the managers of the producing departments in three ways. What are they?

7. Factory overhead costs are often assigned to units as product costs using a predetermined rate. How do service department costs get assigned to the units produced in the production departments?

8. Since producing departments and service departments are separate departments, how can the manager of a producing department influence the costs of a service department?

9. What are the three steps in allocating service department costs?

10. What are *cost pools?* How do they relate to the allocation of service department costs?

11. Why is the selection of an activity base so important to the proper allocation of service department costs?

12. Explain the difference between the direct method and the step method of allocating service department costs.

13. Explain what a *profit center* is. How does it differ from a *cost center?*

14. Distinguish between *centralized* and *decentralized* organizations.

15. If an organization has numerous profit centers, would you expect that organization to be highly centralized or decentralized? Explain.

16. When a segment income statement is prepared, which measure of income should be used to evaluate the profit center manager? The profit center?

17. What is a *segment income statement?*

18. How would you evaluate the performance of a profit center manager once you have determined the contribution controllable by segment manager?

19. What is an *investment center?* How does it differ from a *profit center?*

20. If a division manager has a significant amount of influence over the committed fixed costs of his or her division, what type of responsibility center would you expect the division to be? Explain.

21. Explain what *direct costs* and *indirect costs* are. What does the classification of direct costs and indirect costs depend upon?

22. What are *common costs?* Do you think they should be allocated to the different profit centers?

23. How do we measure the performance of an investment center?

24. What is an *ROI?* What are its component parts?

25. Discuss several ways that the ROI for an investment center can be improved.

26. Why may it be inappropriate to base bonuses or promotions for profit center managers on the amount of profit earned by each profit center? (That is, the manager earning the most profit gets the biggest bonus or is the first manager to be promoted.)

27. What is a *transfer price?*

28. List several different ways that a transfer price might be determined.

EXERCISES

Exercise 11-1
Selecting an allocation base for service department costs

For each type of service department listed below in column A, select an allocation base from column B that would be the best basis for allocating the costs of that service department. Place the number from column B in the space provided in column A:

Service Department	Allocation Base

_____ **a.** Maintenance

_____ **b.** Medical clinic

_____ **c.** Storeroom

_____ **d.** Day care

_____ **e.** Personnel

_____ **f.** Factory administration

_____ **g.** Employees lounge

_____ **h.** Janitorial service

_____ **i.** Computer services

_____ **j.** Exercise room

1. Number of units produced

2. Direct labor-hours worked

3. Number of employees serviced

4. Total employees

5. Machine-hours used in production

6. Square feet of space

7. Number of requisitions

8. Hours of computer time

Exercise 11-2
Identifying key items on a segment income statement

Shown below is the format for a segment income statement. You are to identify which line is being described in the list that follows the statement by placing the number of the line in the space provided.

(1) Sales
(2) Less: Variable Costs:
      Variable Manufacturing
      Variable Selling and Administrative of Segment
(3) Total Contribution Margin
(4) Less: Direct Fixed Costs Controllable by Segment Manager
(5) Contribution Controllable by Segment Manager
(6) Less: Fixed Costs of Segment Not Controllable by Segment Manager
(7) Contribution of Segment to Common Costs
(8) Common Costs for All Segments
(9) Net Income

_____ **a.** The best measure of the performance of the segment manager

_____ **b.** The income that the segment would have if it were an independent company

_____ **c.** The sum of these for all segments represents the income for the entire firm

_____ **d.** Advertising costs, determined for the segment by the segment manager

_____ **e.** The amount by which the total income for the firm would decrease if a segment is eliminated

_____ **f.** An example of this cost is depreciation on the building which houses this segment's operations

_____ **g.** An example of this cost is national advertising for the firm as a whole

_____ **h.** The most controllable measure of income in the short run

Exercise 11-3
Classifying direct and indirect costs

The Adirondack Company has several divisions, each of which is run as an independent company. The costs listed at the top of the next page were taken from the segment income statement of one of the divisions. You are to classify each cost as a direct or indirect cost of the product, of the production department, of the service department, and of the division as a whole. Use D for direct, I for indirect, and N for not applicable.

	Direct or Indirect Cost of:			
	Product	**Production Department**	**Service Department**	**Division**
1. Materials that are an integral part of the finished product	_____	_____	_____	_____
2. Laborers working on the machines that make the product	_____	_____	_____	_____
3. Supplies of the selling department	_____	_____	_____	_____
4. Salary of the division president	_____	_____	_____	_____
5. National advertising allocated to the division	_____	_____	_____	_____
6. Insurance on the assets used in the service department	_____	_____	_____	_____
7. Depreciation of equipment used in production	_____	_____	_____	_____
8. Salaries of production foremen	_____	_____	_____	_____
9. Common costs from corporate offices	_____	_____	_____	_____

Exercise 11-4
Allocating service department costs

The Chow Chow Dog Food Company has two service departments and two operating departments. The two service departments are machine maintenance and the storeroom—each one services only the two operating departments. The operating departments are machining and assembly. The costs of machine maintenance ($30,000) are allocated to the operating departments on the basis of the number of hours worked on the machines of the two operating departments. The costs of the storeroom ($60,000) are allocated on the basis of the number of requisitions processed for each operating department. In addition, the following information relates to the two allocation bases:

Allocation Base	Machining	Assembly
Hours of maintenance on machines.	2,500	1,500
Requisitions processed	500	300

Determine the amount of costs of each service department that would be allocated to machining and assembly.

(Check figure: Allocated to assembly by storeroom $22,500)

Exercise 11-5
Determining overhead rates after service department costs are allocated

The Foxy Lady Lingerie Company has two operating departments, cutting and sewing, and is currently trying to determine their factory overhead rates for the upcoming year. The factory overhead rates will be used to assign factory overhead to the units being produced. Listed below are the factory overhead costs budgeted for each production department for the upcoming year, as well as the budgeted costs for two service departments. In addition, you are shown the allocation base needed to allocate the costs of each service department.

Department	Budgeted Costs	Allocation Base
Cutting	$65,000	na
Sewing............................	98,000	na
Stores.............................	12,000	Time spent processing requests
Janitorial.........................	15,000	Square feet of department cleaned

Factory overhead is applied to production on the basis of the number of direct labor-hours worked. The expected labor-hours for the year and information related to the allocation bases are:

	Cutting	Sewing	Total
Expected direct labor-hours.............................	10,000	9,000	19,000
Expected time needed to process orders (in hr).............	1,200	800	2,000
Square feet of department...............................	2,000	3,000	5,000

Determine the factory overhead rates for the cutting and sewing departments.

(Check figure: Overhead rate for cutting = $7.82)

**Exercise 11-6
Allocating variable and
fixed service department
costs separately**

The High Tech Machine Shop has several service departments, one of which is a medical clinic. The costs of running the clinic are expected to be $125,000 for 1989, of which $75,000 is expected to be fixed and the remainder variable. The clinic was built to accommodate a work force much larger than is presently employed by High Tech. The company is expected to grow significantly in the future, so it seemed logical to invest more at the beginning instead of having to increase the capacity of the clinic at a later date.

Relevant information concerning the clinic and the two operating departments is given below:

		Operating Departments	
	Clinic	1	2
Budgeted costs for year:			
Variable......................................	$ 50,000	$500,000	$ 700,000
Fixed	75,000	200,000	340,000
	$125,000	$700,000	$1,040,000
Employees to be serviced:			
Maximum work force.........................	10	200	700
In coming year...............................	5	150	450

a. Allocate the combined costs of running the clinic to the two operating departments, using (1) the maximum work force as the allocation base and (2) the employees expected to be serviced in the coming year as the allocation base.

b. Allocate the variable and fixed costs separately using (1) the maximum work force as the allocation base for the fixed costs and (2) the employees expected to be serviced in the coming year as the allocation base for the variable costs.

c. Allocate the variable and fixed costs separately using (1) the maximum work force as the allocation base for the variable costs and (2) the employees expected to be serviced in the coming year as the allocation base for the fixed costs.

(Check figure: Variable costs allocated to department 1 = $11,111)

d. Which approach do you prefer? Why?

Exercise 11-7
Using several approaches
to determine a transfer
price

The Okidokie Electronics Company has several divisions. One division makes nothing but printers for computers. The printer division sells to both the computer division and other computer companies. During 1989 the printer division expects to sell 4,000 printers to other companies for $575 apiece. In addition, it expects to sell 6,000 printers to the computer division, which will then sell them as part of a package with the computers.

    The costs associated with the production and sale of the printers by Okidokie (based on the expected production and sale of 10,000 printers) are as follows:

Variable manufacturing	$100
Fixed manufacturing	50
Variable selling	55
Fixed selling	25
	$230

a. Listed below you will find several different approaches to determining the transfer price for the 6,000 printers. For each one determine the revenue that would be reported by Okidokie for the sale of 10,000 printers (6,000 to the computer division and 4,000 to the outside companies).

    1. Variable cost
    2. Variable cost plus a 40% markup
    3. Absorption cost
    4. Absorption cost plus a 50% markup

(Check figure: Transfer price = $225 per unit)

    5. Market price
b. Which approach would Okidokie prefer? Which approach would the computer division prefer?

Exercise 11-8
Comparing results with
different transfer prices

On Jan. 1, 1988, the Panasony Television Company acquired Sharp Image, a picture-tube manufacturer. Starting immediately, Sharp Image must sell all its picture tubes to Panasony at a price that will ensure Sharp Image a contribution margin percentage of 20% of sales (the same as 25% of variable costs).

    Prior to 1988 Sharp sold only to American television manufacturers, and Panasony purchased its picture tubes from a company in Taiwan. The income statements for both companies for 1987 are given below:

	Sharp Image	Panasony Television
Unit Sales	10,000	10,000
Sales Revenue	$1,500,000	$7,500,000
Total Variable Costs:		
Manufacturing	$ 600,000	$4,000,000
Selling	150,000	750,000
	$ 750,000	$4,750,000
Total Contribution Margin	$ 750,000	$2,750,000
Total Fixed Costs:		
Manufacturing	$ 500,000	$1,000,000
Selling	150,000	200,000
	$ 650,000	$1,200,000
Operating Income	$ 100,000	$1,550,000

The cost of each picture tube for Panasony was $125 in 1987.

a. If Panasony had owned Sharp Image in 1987, what would have been the operating income of each company and of the two combined?

[Check figure: Sharp Image income = $(462,500)]

b. Compare the answers in part **a** to the incomes shown in the statement above. If you were the president of Panasony, how would you feel about the new transfer price? What if you were the president of Sharp Image?

Exercise 11-9
Evaluating the ROI and its component parts

The income statement below was prepared by the accounting department of the College Division of the Irvin Book Company:

Sales..		$52,000,000
Less: Variable Costs:		
Variable Manufacturing	$15,000,000	
Variable Selling and Administrative of Segment	10,000,000	25,000,000
Total Contribution Margin..........................		$27,000,000
Less: Direct Fixed Costs Controllable by Segment Manager		10,000,000
Contribution Controllable by Segment Manager		$17,000,000
Less: Fixed Costs of Segment Not Controllable by Segment Manager.....		5,000,000
Contribution of Segment to Common Costs.........................		$12,000,000
Common Costs for All Segments..................................		3,000,000
Net Income		$ 9,000,000

The total assets of the College Division are $30,000,000.

a. Calculate the ROI that would be the best measure of the performance of the division manager. Also determine the component parts (asset turnover and return on sales) of the ROI.

(Check figure: ROI = .5667)

b. Repeat the requirements of part **a**, but this time let the answer represent the best measure of the performance of the division as a whole.

Exercise 11-10
Filling in the unknowns for the ROI

The Acrossamerica Company is a multi-division organization that uses the ROI to determine each division's profitability. Partial information concerning three of its divisions is shown below. Fill in all the missing blanks.

	Division A	Division B	Division C
Sales	$500,000	$2,100,000	?
Total Assets.................................	$250,000	?	?
Income......................................	$ 25,000	?	$30,000
Return on Sales	?	15%	1%
Asset Turnover..............................	?	3.00	?
ROI...	?	?	4%

(Check figure: ROI for B = .45)

Exercise 11-11
Comparing the ROI to a minimum acceptable return

Given below is information related to three territories of the J. R. Dallas Oil Company:

	American	Canadian	Mideast
Sales.....................................	$87,000,000	$42,000,000	$96,000,000
Total Contribution Margin...............	$23,000,000	$10,000,000	$58,000,000
Contribution Controllable by Segment Manager	$15,000,000	$ 4,000,000	$28,000,000
Contribution of Segment to Common Costs	$10,000,000	$ 1,500,000	$16,800,000
Net income............................	$ 7,000,000	$ (700,000)	$12,000,000

The total assets for each territory are $50,000,000 for the American territory, $30,000,000 for the Canadian territory, and $60,000,000 for the Mideast territory.

Each territory is expected to earn an ROI that is related closely to the level of risk involved as well as to past performances of that territory. The American territory is expected to earn at least the average ROI for the industry, 15%. The Canadian territory has been extremely unprofitable during the last 10 years, so not much is expected of it. The company will be satisfied if the new territory manager is able to show any profit at all in the current year. Finally, all American investments in the Mideast territory are considered to be extremely risky because of the threat of terrorist takeovers, so that territory is expected to generate an ROI of 30%.
a. Calculate the appropriate ROI for evaluating the performance of each territory.

(Check figure: ROI for American = .20)

b. Based upon the actual ROI and the minimum ROI for each division, which division seemed to be the most successful?

Exercise 11-12
Preparing an income statement that emphasizes controllability of costs

The income statements presented below are for the three divisions of Allied Automotive Parts:

	Division A	Division B	Division C
Sales	$6,250,000	$10,000,000	$30,000,000
Total Variable Costs......................	$3,750,000	$ 6,000,000	$18,000,000
Total Fixed Costs:			
Controllable by Segment Manager	900,000	1,000,000	4,000,000
Related to Segment but Not Controllable by Segment Manager....................	600,000	500,000	4,800,000
Allocated Common Costs...............	800,000	1,500,000	1,200,000
Total Costs..............................	$6,050,000	$ 9,000,000	$28,000,000
Net Income	$ 200,000	$ 1,000,000	$ 2,000,000
Total Assets	$5,000,000	$10,000,000	$40,000,000

a. Rearrange the segment income statement into one that emphasizes contribution margin and the controllability of costs.
b. Evaluate the performance of the three divisions. Which division is more profitable? Which division manager has been the most profitable with what he or she should control?

**Exercise 11-13
Rearranging an income
statement from a
territorial emphasis to a
product emphasis**

The Florida division of Wamway Products is divided into three territories, each of which is run by a territory manager. Within each territory there are three product-line managers. The territorial income statements are given below:

	Southern Territory	Northern Territory	Panhandle Territory
Sales.....................................	$5,000,000	$12,500,000	$7,000,000
Total Variable Costs......................	3,000,000	7,225,000	3,750,000
Total Contribution Margin.................	$2,000,000	$ 5,275,000	$3,250,000
Fixed Costs Controllable by Territory Manager..................................	800,000	1,000,000	900,000
Contribution Controllable by Territory Manager..................................	$1,200,000	$ 4,275,000	$2,350,000
Territorial Fixed Costs Not Controllable by Territory Manager.......................	600,000	800,000	700,000
Contribution of Territory to Common Costs ..	$ 600,000	$ 3,475,000	$1,650,000
Common Costs Allocated..................	500,000	600,000	550,000
Net Income	$ 100,000	$ 2,875,000	$1,100,000

The sales of the three product lines are represented by the fractions given below:

	Fraction of Total Sales
Southern territory:	
Product 1	$\frac{1}{5}$
Product 2	$\frac{2}{5}$
Product 3	$\frac{2}{5}$
Northern territory:	
Product 1	$\frac{40}{125}$
Product 2	$\frac{60}{125}$
Product 3	$\frac{25}{125}$
Panhandle territory:	
Product 1	$\frac{5}{7}$
Product 2	$\frac{1}{7}$
Product 3	$\frac{1}{7}$

The variable cost ratio of each product line is the same in all three territories. The ratios are:

	Variable Cost Ratio
Product 1	50%
Product 2	60%
Product 3	65%

None of the fixed costs that are controllable by the territory managers are controllable by the product-line managers. All the fixed costs and common costs are allocated evenly among the product lines in each territory.

Prepare new income statements based on product lines, instead of territories. The format should be:

	Product 1	Product 2	Product 3
Sales			
Total Variable Costs			
.			
.			
.			
Net Income			

(Check figure: Product 1 income = $2,850,000)

PROBLEMS: SET A

Problem A11-1
Allocating service department costs to aid in the control process

The R. Jackson Company produces baseballs for universities and colleges. There are two operating departments—cutting and sewing—and two service departments—stores and janitorial. At the beginning of 1989 the company controller determined the following budgeted amounts for the year:

Operating Departments	Factory Overhead	Direct Labor-Hours
Cutting	$480,000	20,000
Sewing...	420,000	16,000

Service Departments	Total Costs
Stores	$24,000
Janitorial	96,000

The budgeted costs of the storeroom are allocated to the operating departments on the basis of the number of orders to be filled. The costs of the janitorial department are allocated on the basis of the square feet of space that is cleaned each night. At the beginning of the year the allocation bases were expected to be:

Departments	Allocation Base	
	Orders to Be Filled	Square Feet to Be Cleaned
Cutting department............................	3,600	1,000
Sewing department	1,200	3,000
Stores	na	500
Janitorial department	na	200

Factory overhead is applied to the balls produced on the basis of the number of direct labor-hours worked.

At the end of each month, the actual costs of each service department are allocated to the operating departments using the actual results for each allocation base. Performance reports are then prepared which compare the actual costs to the costs applied.

	Required

1. Determine the amount of budgeted service department costs that would be assigned to each operating department in order to come up with the factory overhead rate for the year.
2. What is the factory overhead rate for each operating department?

(Check figure: Cutting = $26.10)

3. Assume that the actual results for January 1989 were as follows:

	Cutting	Sewing	Stores	Janitorial
Total costs.................................	$43,000	$30,000	$1,800	$7,000
Direct labor-hours..........................	1,550	1,450	na	na
Number of orders filled	320	90	na	na
Square feet cleaned	1,000	3,000	500	200

Prepare a performance report for factory overhead that shows the actual costs, the applied, and the difference.

**Problem A11-2
Preparing income
statements that
emphasize controllability**

Buffalo Chips Farm Supply has three different departments. They are the fertilizer department, the garden plants department, and the garden tools department. Relevant information about these three departments is given below for 1988:

	Ferti-lizer	Garden Plants	Garden Tools
Sales	$60,000	$40,000	$50,000
Variable Cost Percentage:			
Manufacturing......................................	40%	30%	35%
Selling	20%	20%	10%
Fixed Costs of Department:			
Controllable by Department Manager	$ 8,000	$ 7,000	$15,000
Not Controllable by Department Manager	$ 6,000	$ 7,000	$10,000
Allocated Common Costs	$ 3,000	$ 2,000	$ 6,000

	Required

1. Prepare detailed segment income statements. Have separate columns for each department and for the company as a whole.

(Check figure: Income for fertilizer department = $7,000)

2. Which income figure would be the best measure of the performance of the department manager?
3. Which income figure would be the best measure of the profitability of the department?

**Problem A11-3
Using segment income
statements to assist
management in making a
variety of decisions**

Refer to the information given in Problem A11-2, and answer each of the following questions.

	Required

1. Assume that the sales vice president proposes an advertising campaign during the next year, costing $10,000. She is confident that the result will be an increase of at least 30% in the sales in each department. The store president is willing to undertake the campaign only if it will increase the store's net income by at least $5,000. Should the campaign be undertaken by the store?
2. Disregard part 1. If the sales mix for the store remains unchanged, what do the total sales for the store have to be to have a net income of $10,000 for the store? What will the sales of each department be at this level of sales?

(Check figure: Total sales for store = $155,234)

3. Disregard parts 1 and 2, and assume that Buffalo is going to discontinue the garden tools department. This change will allow the garden plants department to double its capacity. The fixed costs that were controllable by the garden tools manager will now be controllable by the garden plants department. The remaining fixed costs of the garden tools department will be distributed evenly between the remaining two departments. Prepare new segment income statements.

Problem A11-4
Evaluating the effect of various changes on the ROI for a firm

Recap Tires is a wholly owned subsidiary of the Zusuki Motors Corporation. Its condensed income statement for 1988 showed an income of $2,000,000:

Sales.	$18,000,000
Total Variable Costs.	(9,000,000)
Total Fixed Costs:	
Directly Related to Recap Tires.	(4,000,000)
Allocated Common Costs.	(3,000,000)
Net Income	$ 2,000,000

The condensed balance sheet for Recap on Dec. 31, 1988, had the following items:

Current Assets.	$ 3,000,000	Current Liabilities	$ 1,000,000
Fixed Assets (Net)	7,000,000	Long-Term Liabilities	3,000,000
		Stockholders' Equity	6,000,000
	$10,000,000		$10,000,000

Required

1. Calculate the ROI for Recap using the contribution of segment to common costs as the income measure. Also determine the component parts that make up the ROI—asset turnover and return on sales.
2. Recap is considering several ways to improve its ROI. For each change listed below, calculate the new asset turnover, return on sales, and ROI:

Change 1 Increasing advertising by $500,000 should increase sales by $2,000,000.
Change 2 Disposing of backup fixed assets that have a book value of $500,000 will reduce depreciation expense by $50,000. The proceeds from the sale will equal the book value of the fixed assets being sold, and will be distributed as dividends.
Change 3 Decreasing the sales price by 10% (with no change in the variable cost per unit) is expected to increase dollar sales by 30%.

(Check figure: ROI for change 3 = .64)

Problem A11-5
Comparing the effect of different transfer prices on the ROI

Comfort Products is a company that has been in existence just over a year. It manufactures a cordless phone that doubles as a walkman radio. During the first year Comfort was quite profitable, as the income statement below indicates:

Sales (50,000 units).		$4,000,000
Variable Costs:		
Manufacturing.	$1,500,000	
Selling	600,000	2,100,000
Total Contribution Margin.		$1,900,000
Fixed costs:		
Manufacturing.	$ 600,000	
Selling	100,000	700,000
		$1,200,000

At the beginning of Comfort's second year, the National Telephone & Telegraph Company (NT&T) acquired a controlling interest in Comfort in a hostile takeover. The president of Comfort was allowed to keep his job, but his performance was to be evaluated annually based on the ROI of his company.

One thing that NT&T insists upon is that Comfort sell its entire production of radiophones to one of NT&T's other subsidiaries—Home Products, Inc.—at a price agreed upon by the presidents of Comfort and Home. Once Comfort starts selling to Home, Comfort's costs will be substantially reduced. Since there will be no reason for Comfort to continue to have any salespeople, the sales commissions (15%) will no longer be paid. Also, since the fixed selling costs had been entirely for advertising, they too will be eliminated.

Prior to NT&T's acquisition of Comfort, Home sold a variety of home appliances and had hoped to begin selling telephones as well. Home's income statement for the previous year looked like this:

Sales	$8,000,000
Total Variable Costs	5,500,000
Total Contribution Margin	$2,500,000
Total Fixed Costs	2,250,000
Net Income	$ 250,000

The addition of the walkman radiophones to Home's product mix should have no effect on the sales of any of its other products. The fixed costs for Home will not increase, but $500,000 of the total will be allocated to this new product line. In addition, Home pays a 5% commission to its salespeople for all items that it sells.

The president of Comfort felt that the price of the radiophones should be the same as it was when Comfort was an independent company. The president of Home argued that the price had to be much lower than that, since that was the price at which Home planned to sell the product to the public. If Home had to buy the product at the same price as it would later sell it for, there would be no profit at all. Home's president felt that a price equal to the total manufacturing costs (variable plus fixed) per unit was appropriate, since that is roughly what it would cost Home to produce the units.

The total assets for Comfort are $10,000,000 and for Home are $20,000,000.

Required

1. Calculate the ROIs for Comfort and for Home for the year prior to NT&T's acquisition of Comfort.
2. Assume that the transfer price is the one that the president of Comfort wants. Also assume that the number of units produced and sold by Comfort in the second year is the same as it was in the first. Prepare the income statements and calculate the ROIs for both Comfort and Home in the second year. Determine the combined income for Comfort and Home.

(Check figure: Home Products income = $1,950,000)

3. Repeat the requirements of part 2. This time assume that the transfer price is the one wanted by the president of Home.
4. Assume now that the two presidents agreed upon a price midway between the other two prices. Repeat the requirements of part 2.

Problem A11-6
Evaluating the results of a profit center, using standard costs

At the beginning of the year, Masterdisk prepared the following budget for the upcoming 12 months (based upon expected production and sales of 10,000 boxes of floppy disks):

Sales		$200,000
Total Variable Costs:		
Direct Materials.....	$30,000	
Direct Labor.....	40,000	
Variable Overhead	10,000	
	$80,000	
Variable Selling	20,000	100,000
Total Contribution Margin		$100,000
Fixed Costs:		
Manufacturing.....	$60,000	
Selling	30,000	90,000
Net Income.....		$ 10,000

Masterdisk uses a standard cost system to assist in the planning and controlling of manufacturing operations. The standards for the variable production costs are:

Direct Materials...........   2 pounds @ $1.50 per pound   3
Direct Labor.............   ½ hour @ $8 per hour   4
Variable Overhead ....   ½ hour @ $2 per hour

The standard cost per unit for the selling costs is not broken down into price and quantity standards.

During the year Masterdisk produced and sold 8,000 units, and the actual costs incurred were as follows:

Direct Materials (17,000 lb purchased and used) .. $28,000
Direct Labor (3,900 hr used)...................   31,005
Variable Overhead   8,500
Variable Selling   15,200
Fixed Factory Overhead.......................   62,000
Fixed Selling................................   31,000

In addition, the average selling price for the year was $1 less than expected. 19

Required

1. Prepare a performance report for the entire income statement. Use the following format:

	Actual Results	Flexible Budget Variance	Flexible Budget for 8,000 Units	Sales Volume Variance	Master Budget
Sales					
Total Variable Costs					
.					
.					
.					
Net Income					

2. Determine the price and quantity variances for each of the variable production costs.

(Check figure: Price variance for direct materials = $5,500 U)

3. What does the sales volume variance represent?

Problem A11-7
Allocating service department costs, determining a transfer price, and calculating the ROI

Beach Blanket Bingo, which is a wholly owned subsidiary of Burling Industries, sells all it produces to another subdsidiary, Blanket Wholesalers. Blanket Wholesalers sells its product to a great number of independent retail establishments.

Beach Blanket Bingo — or BBB, for short — has one service department, two producing departments (A and B), and one operating department (shipping and administrative). The service department allocates its costs to the three other departments in the following proportions:

	Department A	Department B	Operating
Variable costs	.45	.45	.10
Fixed costs.	.35	.35	.30

Units produced in Department A are transferred to Department B, where they are completed and shipped to Blanket Wholesalers at a markup of 100% of variable costs. The costs budgeted for 1988 for BBB are as follows, based upon expected production of 100,000 units for departments A and B and based upon the shipment of 80,000 units to Blanket Wholesalers for the operating department:

	Variable Costs	Fixed Costs
Production:		
Department A	$150,000	$45,000
Department B	80,000	15,000
Service	10,000	6,000
Operating	25,000	10,000

During the year Blanket Wholesalers expects to sell all the blankets that are received from BBB at $15 apiece. Its budgeted costs, excluding the costs of the inventory bought from BBB, are $3.50 per unit variable and $280,000 fixed.

The total assets are expected to be $1,800,000 for BBB and $1,500,000 for Blanket Wholesalers, respectively. Both companies use the direct costing method for product costing purposes.

Required

1. Allocate the service department costs to each of the other departments. Then determine the total variable costs and total fixed costs (including the allocated amounts) for each of the three departments to which the costs are allocated.
2. What is the transfer price for each unit?
3. Prepare budgeted income statements for each company, using the contribution margin format. Be sure to separate the manufacturing costs and the operating costs within the statements.
4. Determine the ROI for each company.

(Check figure: BBB = .0784)

PROBLEMS: SET B

Problem B11-1
Including allocated service department costs in the evaluation of a production department

Orville Poppenbocker uses two operating departments, A and B, to produce a popcorn that tastes like chewing tobacco. In addition, there is a machine maintenance department that services the machinery used in the operating departments. The variable costs of the maintenance department are allocated between departments A and B on the basis of the number of labor-hours used by the maintenance department to keep the machines of each operating department in good condition. The fixed costs of the maintenance department are allocated evenly between the two operating departments.

The costs of each operating department (based upon production of 100,000 cases of popcorn) that were budgeted for 1988 are as follows:

	Department A	Department B
Variable Costs:		
Direct Materials.....................................	$ 600,000	$ 200,000
Direct Labor..	300,000	300,000
Variable Factory Overhead.........................	400,000	150,000
Fixed Factory Overhead.............................	700,000	350,000
	$2,000,000	$1,000,000

The budgeted costs of the maintenance department for 1988 are $180,000 variable and $60,000 fixed. In addition, Orville expected the maintenance department to spend 16,000 hours during the year doing maintenance on the operating machinery—12,000 for Department A and 4,000 for Department B.

Required

1. Determine for each department the combined factory overhead rate (variable plus fixed) per case of popcorn.
2. Determine the total costs that would be assigned to production for product costing purposes if 110,000 cases were actually produced.
3. Assume again in this part that 110,000 cases were produced. The actual overhead costs for the operating departments were $1,150,000 (of which $450,000 was variable) and $510,000 (of which $163,000 was variable) for departments A and B, respectively. The actual costs of the maintenance department were $251,000 (of which $190,000 was variable). The variable costs of maintenance were allocated to departments A and B in a 75:25 ratio, and the fixed costs were allocated evenly. Prepare a performance report for factory overhead. Have columns for the actual costs, the flexible budget for 110,000 cases, the applied overhead, the flexible budget variance, and the production volume variance.

(Check figure: Department A volume variance = $73,000 F)

4. What would have been the combined factory overhead rate for each department for 1988 if at the beginning of 1988 Orville had expected to produce 125,000 cases instead of 100,000?

Problem B11-2
Preparing segment
income statements

Potluck Garden produces lawn equipment and has three different divisions. They are the lawn-mower division, the edger division, and the weed-eater division. Relevant information about these three divisions is given below for 1988:

	Lawn Mower	Edger	Weed Eater
Units Sold...	1,000	1,500	2,800
Sales Price...	$ 450	$ 125	$ 60
Variable Costs:			
Manufacturing.....................................	$ 150	$ 40	$ 18
Selling and Administrative	$ 45	$ 10	$ 5
Fixed Costs of Division:			
Controllable by Division Manager.................	$ 80,000	$40,000	$15,000
Not Controllable by Division Manager.............	$100,000	$55,000	$15,000
Allocated Common Costs	$ 50,000	$50,000	$50,000

| Required |

1. Prepare detailed segment income statements. Have separate columns for each division and for the company as a whole.

(Check figure: Total income = $16,100)

2. Which income measure would be the best indicator of the performance of the division manager? Of the division?

Problem B11-3
Making a variety of decisions based upon results within segment income statements

Refer to the facts presented in Problem B11-2, and answer the following questions.

| Required |

1. Which, if any, division should Potluck close down if it wants to increase the income for the firm? Assume that the sales of each division cannot be increased beyond its current demand.
2. Disregard the information in part 1. Assume now that the common costs are going to be increased by $60,000 for a national advertising campaign. Assume also that the new unit sales for each division will be in the same proportion to total sales as they are currently (that is, the sales mix will be unchanged). What will be the breakeven point for the firm as a whole? What will be the unit sales of each division, based upon these total sales?
3. Calculate the ROI for each division if the total assets are as follows:

Lawn-mower division $225,000
Edger division 60,000
Weed-eater division 70,000

Assume that the income measure to be used in the ROI is the final net income after subtracting common costs.
4. If each division manager is expected to show a profit of at least 10% of the division's own sales, what would the minimum unit sales of each division have to be? Assume now that the income measure to be used is the income controllable by the division manager.

(Check figure: Weed-eater division sales = 484 units)

Problem B11-4
Evaluating the effect of several changes on a firm's ROI

Columbian Records is a division of Spielberg Enterprises. During 1988 the division turned a profit of $450,000:

Sales (200,000 records)		$1,400,000
Total Variable Costs...		600,000
Total Contribution Margin......................................		$ 800,000
Total Fixed Costs:		
Directly Related to Columbian...................	$200,000	
Allocated Common Costs	150,000	350,000
Net Income		$ 450,000

During 1988 Columbian's total assets average $2,000,000.

| Required |

1. Calculate the ROI for Columbian using the contribution of segment to common costs. Also determine the component parts that make up the ROI — asset turnover and return on sales.
2. Columbian is considering several independent ways to improve its ROI. For each change listed below, calculate the new asset turnover, return on sales, and ROI:

Change 1 Reducing the sales price by $1 should increase unit sales by 80,000 records.
Change 2 Reducing the average balance maintained in inventory by $200,000 is not expected to affect total sales but should reduce the costs of carrying inventory (insurance and interest) by $30,000.
Change 3 Decreasing the variable costs per unit by $0.50 and reducing under-the-table kickbacks by $25,000 is not expected to have any effect on the number of records sold.

(Check figure: ROI = .3625)

Problem B11-5
Determining the best
transfer price for related
divisions

Poured Plastics, Inc., and Spa Heaven are two divisions of Luxury World. Poured Plastics produces nothing but plastic shells for spas and hot tubs. Its entire output is sold to Spa Heaven, which adds the necessary equipment, siding, and decking and then sells the spas and hot tubs as portable units. Currently, the transfer price that has been imposed on both Poured Plastics and Spa Heaven is the variable costs plus a 50% markup. The income statements for the two divisions for 1988 are shown below. Poured Plastics produced and sold 5,000 shells to Spa Heaven, all of which were completed by Spa Heaven and sold as complete packages.

	Poured Plastics	Spa Heaven
Sales Revenue	$2,250,000	$10,000,000
Total Variable Costs:		
Manufacturing	$1,500,000	$ 5,000,000
Selling	-0-	1,000,000
	$1,500,000	$ 6,000,000
Total Contribution Margin	$ 750,000	$ 4,000,000
Total Fixed Costs:		
Manufacturing	$ 600,000	$ 2,100,000
Selling	-0-	300,000
	$ 600,000	$ 2,400,000
Net Income	$ 150,000	$ 1,600,000

Poured Plastics is dissatisfied with the transfer price. Its division manager argues that it could sell all its shells to outside companies at $600 per shell and that it should be allowed to either sell the shells to outsiders or sell the shells to Spa Heaven at the $600 price. The manager also realizes that if the division began selling to outsiders, it would be necessary to incur variable and fixed selling costs. There would probably be at least a 10% commission and $50,000 for advertising.

If Poured Plastics stopped selling directly to Spa Heaven, Spa Heaven would have to purchase the shells from other suppliers for $600 per shell, which naturally would reduce its profit margin and ROI. Since the organization is highly decentralized, the manager of Spa Heaven realizes that Poured Plastics has the right to sell to other customers, and he is concerned that it will do so. He appeals to the company president to convince the manager of the plastics division that continuing to supply Spa Heaven would be best for everyone concerned and, if this fails, to force Poured Plastics to do so.

The company president tells both managers to sit down and discuss the issue and to come up with something agreeable to both parties. They are not to leave their meeting until they have come to an agreement.

Required

1. Assume that the total assets for Poured Plastics and Spa Heaven are $1,250,000 and $10,000,000, respectively. Calculate the ROI for each company for 1988.
2. Assume that in 1988 the transfer price had been the $600 market price and that the assets assumed in part 1 are unchanged. Determine the incomes and ROIs for each division. In addition, determine the combined income and ROI for the two divisions and compare this amount to the combined results given in the original set of facts for 1988.
3. Now assume that Poured Plastics sells to outside customers and that Spa Heaven is forced to purchase the shells from other suppliers. Determine the incomes and ROIs for each division and for the two combined.

(Check figure: Combined income = $1,400,000)

4. Assume now that the two managers agree upon a price that should allow each division to have the same ROI. Assume also that this price had been used in 1988 for the 5,000 shells

transferred between divisions. Prepare the income statements and ROI for each division, and determine the transfer price agreed upon by the managers.

Problem B11-6
Evaluating a profit center
with standard costs

The Dryup Humidifier Company uses standard costs and flexible budgets in the planning and control of operations. The standards per unit for the variable costs are:

Direct Materials (1 lb @ $3/lb) $3.00
Direct Labor ($\frac{1}{3}$ hr @ $6/hr). 2.00
Variable Overhead ($\frac{1}{3}$ hr @ $3/hr) 1.00
Selling. 0.50
$6.50

The budgeted fixed costs are the following:

Factory Overhead $250,000
Selling. 100,000
$350,000

In addition, Dryup expects to sell the humidifiers for $20 each.

At the beginning of the year Dryup felt that it would produce and sell 35,000 units; but when the year was over, it had produced and sold 5,000 units fewer than it had expected. The actual costs incurred for the year were as follows:

Direct Materials (33,000 lb purchased and
   used) . . . . $ 98,000
Direct Labor (9,800 hr) 57,500
Variable Overhead 28,500
Variable Selling 14,700
Fixed Factory Overhead. 255,000
Fixed Selling. 99,500

In addition, the average selling price for the year was $22.

Required

1. Prepare a performance report for the entire income statement. Use the income statement format shown on page 490. In addition, include the following headings:

Actual Results	Flexible Budget Variance	Flexible Budget for 30,000 Units	Sales Volume Variance	Master Budget for 35,000 Units

2. Determine the price and quantity variances for each of the three variable production costs.

(Check figure: Price variance for direct materials = $1,000 F)

3. What would be an alternative way to calculate the sales volume variance?

Problem B11-7
Allocating service
department costs,
determining a transfer
price, and calculating the
ROI

Computer Paper, Inc., and Simple Computer Products are both divisions of the NBM Corporation. Computer Paper, Inc., produces boxes of computer paper which it sells to Simple Computer Products, a chain of retail outlets.

Computer Paper has two service departments—stores and cafeteria, one producing department, and an administrative department. Stores allocates its total costs to the three other departments on the basis of the number of orders processed for each department. The total costs of the cafeteria are allocated on the basis of the number of employees working in each department. The relevant amounts for each allocation base are expected to be:

Allocation Base	Producing Department	Administrative Department	Stores	Cafeteria
Number of orders processed	1,000	200	na	100
Number of employees.	200	20	3	5

The units that are sold to Simple Computer have a transfer price that allows a gross profit of 100% of cost. The costs budgeted for the upcoming year for Computer Paper are as follows (the projections are based upon expected production and sale of 200,000 boxes):

	Variable Costs	Fixed Costs
Production	$600,000	$250,000
Service:		
Stores..	-0-	40,000
Cafeteria	-0-	60,000
Administrative......................................	-0-	100,000

Simple Computer expects to be able to sell all 200,000 boxes of computer paper at a markup of 80% above cost. In addition, sales from other computer supplies are expected to be $20,000,000 (with the same 80% gross profit) for the year. Its variable operating costs average 20% of all sales and its fixed costs $4,000,000.

The total assets for Computer Paper will average $6,500,000 in the upcoming year. The total assets for Simple Computer will average $10,600,000.

Required

1. Determine the amount of costs of each service department to be allocated to the administrative department and to the production department.
2. Determine the transfer price for the paper sold by Computer Paper to Simple Computer. Also, determine the sales price for the paper when it is sold to the final customer.
3. Prepare budgeted income statements for Computer Paper and Simple Computer on the basis of the information given above. In addition, prepare an income statement for the two divisions combined.
4. Calculate the ROI for each division and for the two divisions combined.

(Check figure: Combined ROI = .1485)

PART FIVE

The Extremes of Product Costing: Job Order Costing and Process Costing

Way back in Chapters 1 and 2 we explained what the term *product costing* means. At that time we talked about the different types of product costs and then showed you how the product costs progress through the inventory accounts to cost of goods sold expense. We discussed only briefly the two extremely different approaches—job order costing and process costing—to assigning product costs to each unit produced. Now, in Part 5, we are going to discuss these two methods in great detail.

In Chapter 12 we tell you about job order costing. We explain how this method is used to assign product costs to units that are few in number, large in cost, and easily distinguished from one another. You'll see how the information is accumulated in the general ledger, and in subsidiary ledgers, and you'll also see where all this information comes from—the source documents. In addition, you'll learn how to make the journal entries that record the transfer of costs from one production account to another.

In Chapter 13 we explain how to use the process costing method—which is as different from job order costing as day from night. This method is used in production processes to account for units that are large in number, small in cost, and indistinguishable from one another. Rather than carefully tracing the exact costs to each different unit (or job), as we do in job order costing, we periodically calculate a single average cost for all units produced during that period. In the process costing method we measure units of activity in terms of *equivalent whole units*. An initial understanding of the meaning and significance of this term is essential to a good understanding of the method as a whole.

There are two different process costing methods—FIFO and weighted average. Since there is a significant difference of opinion as to which method is preferable, we explain both methods in detail. And due to the fact that your instructor may want to cover one method or the other, but not both, it will not be necessary for you to first read about one method in order to understand the other. Each discussion can stand completely on its own.

CHAPTER 12

Product Costing Methods
Part I: Job Order Costing

When you have finished studying this chapter, you should be able to:

- Explain the difference between *job order costing* and *process costing*
- *Determine the flow of costs through the production accounts and integrate this flow into the accounting records with journal entries and general ledger accounts*
- *Understand the purpose of subsidiary ledgers and the types of subsidiary ledgers needed for job order costing*
- *Relate the different types of source documents to the events or transactions they represent*
- *Discuss the interrelationships of the journal entry, the general ledger accounts, the subsidiary ledger accounts, and the source documents*
- *Understand why the overhead that becomes part of the cost of the product is not the actual factory overhead incurred but rather the factory overhead applied*
- *Calculate the factory overhead rate and the factory overhead applied*
- *Explain the meaning of over- or underapplied overhead, why each comes about, and how each is accounted for at year-end*

Product costing

In Chapter 2 we explained what we mean by the term ***product costing***—the accumulation of costs associated with inventory and the assignment of these costs to the units in inventory. We stressed how important it is to properly determine the product costs for an organization in order to have correct amounts in cost of goods sold expense (on the income statement) and in inventory at year-end (on the balance sheet). We also defined the three types of product costs for a manufacturer (direct materials, direct labor, and factory overhead) and described the flow of product costs through the production accounts (from raw materials inventory to work-in process inventory to finished goods inventory to cost of goods sold expense).

The costs we talked about accumulating and assigning to the units back in Chapter 2 were the actual production costs incurred during the period. In Chapter 10 we introduced the concept of ***standard costs*** and pointed out that many organizations feel that the standard costs associated with producing a product are better product

Actual, normal, and standard costing

costs than are the actual costs incurred. We showed you how to apply the costs of direct materials, direct labor, variable factory overhead, and fixed factory overhead to the product using predetermined rates for each product cost.[1] In this chapter we will look at somewhat of a compromise between actual costing and standard costing, called normal costing. With ***normal costing*** the product costs are the actual costs of direct material and direct labor but the applied costs of variable and fixed overhead. More about this system later.

What we have not yet explained is exactly how the product costs—whether they be actual, standard, or normal costs—are assigned to individual units; i.e., how do we determine the cost of each and every unit that is produced?

How to get a cost per unit

Do we spread the total production costs evenly over the many units being worked on—ending up with one unit costing exactly the same as any other—even when there may be obvious differences in the physical appearance, materials used, and attention given to different units? Or do we painstakingly keep track of the exact amount of materials, labor, and overhead used for each unit? Will each unit have a different cost—even when all units appear to be identical?

To answer these questions, we first need to know which cost accounting method—job order costing or process costing—is the more appropriate way to account for the product costs.

JOB ORDER COSTING AND PROCESS COSTING: AN INTRODUCTION

To begin to get an idea of what we mean by job order costing and process costing, consider the case of Bill Wiley.

Wiley has recently inherited a great deal of money and has acquired a controlling interest in two quite different companies—the Bubbly Champagne Company and the Heritage Construction Company. Wiley has spent the entire afternoon completing a contract to build a custom home for a new client. All the details have been clearly laid out in the contract that was signed by both parties. On his way home, Wiley stops off at the Bubbly warehouse to pick up a bottle of champagne, to celebrate the deal with his wife (after all, this will be the first house that he has ever undertaken to build for someone).

Cost accountants tend to think of the house as being produced according to a specific job order—one unit, different from any other unit—produced over an extended period of time. The champagne company would be producing bottles of champagne according to what cost accountants tend to regard as a process— thousands of units, each unit identical to the next. In both cases the product will have to be "costed." But in each case, the product costing method will be quite different. For the house, accountants use a ***job order costing method.*** For the champagne, accountants use a ***process costing method.***

The difference has to do with how to calculate the cost of each unit

The basic difference between job order costing and process costing is in the method of keeping track of the costs of each unit or batch of units being produced. As you might well imagine, and as we'll show in this and the next chapter, the cost accountant for Heritage Construction accounts for the costs of the house in a very different way than the cost accountant for Bubbly Champagne accounts for the cost of each bottle of champagne.

Standard costing

[1] If you would like to know how to account for job order costing with standard costs, read each of the footnotes that accompanies the entries for the Historical Replicas Company example that starts on page 526.

In the next section we'll begin the explanation of the job order costing method of accounting. We'll explain all about the process costing method in Chapter 13.

JOB ORDER COSTING

In manufacturing situations that can be described by the following characteristics, job order costing is used to account for the cost of a finished product:

Characteristics of job order costing

1. Only a small number of units or a few batches of units are produced.
2. Each unit or batch is clearly identifiable and distinguishable from others produced within the same production environment.
3. There is a very discernible beginning and end to the production of each unit or batch.
4. Each unit or batch is produced according to customer specifications.
5. Considerable costs are represented in each unit produced.

Who uses job order costing?

The name of this method describes what it is all about: The manufacturer produces a specific product according to a customer's *order;* the manufacturer refers to the product while in production as a *job* and assigns it a job number as a way of keeping track of it and its *costs* as it progresses toward completion. Industries that typically employ job order costing include furniture, heavy machinery, construction, printing, and shipbuilding—and any other industry, such as public accounting, advertising, or auto repairs, in which it is necessary and possible to distinguish among costs of different items being produced.

The key to accumulating product costs in a job order costing situation is to make sure that the costs of a specific job are carefully separated from the costs of any other job. The accountant cannot allow the costs of different jobs to be commingled. For example, assume that Bill Wiley has just signed a contract with a second customer to build another house. When you look at the situation from the standpoint of either Wiley or his customers, you should understand why it is so important *to keep the costs of one job separate from the costs of the other.* Naturally, neither customer wants to pay Wiley for costs that may relate to the construction of the other's house. And, from Wiley's viewpoint, when his accountant reports the revenues from the construction of one house on the income statement, Wiley naturally assumes that the accountant matches the appropriate costs with those revenues. For these reasons the customers and Wiley all agree that a method of accounting is needed that clearly separates the costs of the different projects—this method is job order costing.

You should understand that job order costing is used not only by manufacturers; it can be adapted to other types of organizations as well. For example, each of the clients audited by the CPA firm of Deloitte Haskins & Sells represents a different job, having distinctly different costs. Each car repair by a Toyota Service Center and each client's advertising campaign by the J. Walter Thompson Agency are also types of jobs.

Although we give all our attention to job order costing for a manufacturer, many of the concepts we will introduce apply to any type of organization that finds it necessary to distinguish among the costs of different projects that are being worked on.

Accounting Records in Job Order Costing

In Chapter 2 we used *T-accounts* to show you how the product costs for a manufacturer flowed from one inventory account to another, finally ending up in cost of goods sold. This basic progression was from raw materials to work-in-process to finished goods to cost of goods sold expense:

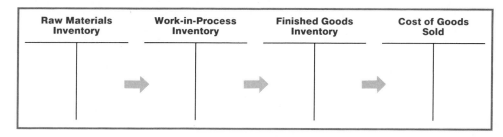

Raw Materials Inventory	Work-in-Process Inventory	Finished Goods Inventory	Cost of Goods Sold

General ledger and journal entries are the same for job order and process costing

In this chapter we will not only look at the T-accounts for a manufacturer (which represent in a simple form the **general ledger accounts** for an organization), but we will also be concerned with the formal **journal entries** that record the flow of costs from one T-account to the next. And after you have studied this chapter and the one on process costing, you'll realize that the T-accounts and the journal entries are exactly the same for these two extreme methods.

Subsidiary Ledgers

The job order costing method requires that a great deal of detail be maintained concerning the cost of its inventories. It is not enough merely to have general ledger accounts for raw materials, work-in-process, and finished goods; we also need a subsidiary ledger for each of these general ledger accounts.

Subsidiary ledgers provide a detailed breakdown of a general ledger account. In your financial accounting course you learned about the accounts receivable subsidiary ledger—a ledger that includes a different account for each different customer, detailing the transactions with that customer and the organization. The sum of the individual account balances in the subsidiary ledger for accounts receivable equals the balance in the general ledger account.

Manufacturers also maintain subsidiary ledgers for their inventories. The subsidiary ledger for work-in-process contains the basic document used in job order costing —the **job cost sheet.** For each job order there is a job cost sheet, on which are recorded the product costs (direct materials, direct labor, and factory overhead) associated with that job order.

When the job cost sheets for all unfinished jobs are combined, this makes up the subsidiary ledger for work-in-process. At the end of each reporting period the balance in the subsidiary ledger for work-in-process (the sum of the balances in the individual job cost sheets) should equal the balance in the general ledger account.

As soon as a job is completed, the job cost sheet is removed from the subsidiary ledger for work-in-process and becomes part of the subsidiary ledger for finished goods inventory. There are several additional subsidiary ledgers which will also be discussed in the example that begins on page 526, the Historical Replicas Company.

Source Documents

Where does the information come from?

The information concerning each event or transaction in the production operation that is recorded in subsidiary ledgers and general ledger accounts must come from some source that provides evidence of the event and its cost. This evidence is the **source document.** Examples of source documents are (1) a purchase invoice, which indicates that a purchase took place, the quantity purchased, and from whom the purchase was made, and (2) a work ticket, which indicates the hours worked by an employee on each different job during a pay period. These and other source documents (stores requisition, clock card, utility bill, depreciation schedule, etc.) will be discussed as the chapter progresses.

Job Order Costing: A More Complete View

Now we want to show you, with Figure 12-1, a more complete view of a job order costing system — one that combines the three basic elements we have just discussed:

1. The flow of costs through the three general ledger inventory accounts

2. The subsidiary ledgers for each general ledger inventory account

3. Selected source documents providing evidence concerning the flow of costs

The explanation of Figure 12-1

Across the top of Figure 12-1, running from left to right, you can see the T-accounts that record the progression of production costs through the general ledger of a manufacturer. Immediately below each general ledger account is the subsidiary

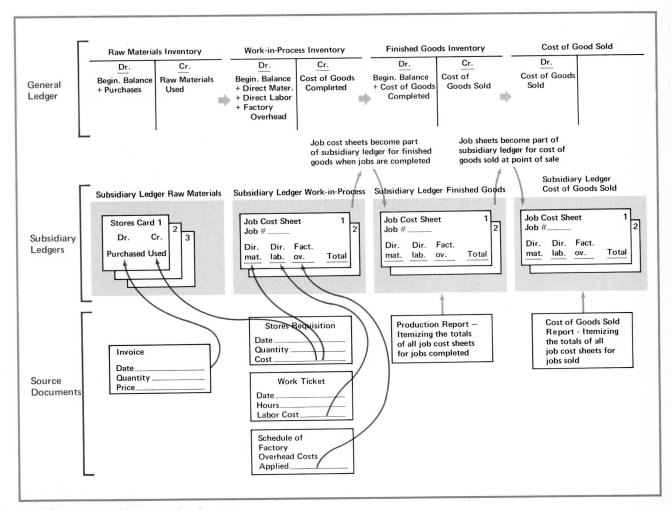

FIGURE 12-1 Job Order Costing System
The complete view of job order costing shows (1) the T-accounts from left to right across the top, (2) the subsidiary ledger below each T-account, and (3) the source documents.

ledger for that account. The subsidiary ledger for raw materials includes a different
stores card for each different type of raw material; the subsidiary ledger for work-in-
process keeps on file a different ***job cost sheet*** for each job. Notice that the job cost
sheets make up the subsidiary ledgers for finished goods and cost of goods sold
expense, as well as for work-in-process. As units are being produced, the job cost
sheets accumulate the costs that are assigned to work-in-process. When the units are
completed, the job cost sheets become the subsidiary ledger for finished goods — now
showing the detail of different jobs awaiting sale. Once the jobs are sold, the job cost
sheets provide the detail for cost of goods sold expense.

Below the subsidiary ledgers in Figure 12-1 are source documents. For instance,
the invoice provides evidence of the purchase of raw materials; the stores requisition
tells us about the raw materials transferred to work-in-process; and the work ticket
indicates the amount of labor employed on each job.

Now we should be ready to go on to the detailed illustration for job order costing,
which begins with the example below.

THE HISTORICAL REPLICAS COMPANY

The Historical Replicas Company produces, to customer specifications, metal art
of historical significance — such as Custer's Last Stand and *Star Trek's* Starship
Enterprise. The company uses a single direct material, bulk metal, which is
melted, cast, sculpted, and polished, all within one operating department.

At the end of January 1988 Historical Replicas was working on two unfinished
jobs, no. 788 and no. 789, and had a finished job, no. 787, awaiting delivery. The
general ledger accounts for each inventory show the following balances on Jan. 31,
1988:

Raw Materials Inventory		Work-in-Process Inventory		Finished Goods Inventory	
Bal. Jan. 31 8,000		Bal. Jan. 31 37,000 (Jobs 788 and 789)		Bal. Jan. 31 24,000 (Job 787)	

Subsidiary Ledger Details

The balances shown in the general ledger inventory accounts for Historical Replicas are supported by the subsidiary ledger accounts in Exhibits 12-1, 12-2, and 12-3
(pages 527 to 530). Two stores cards are presented first in Exhibit 12-1, one card for
bulk metal, the direct material, and the other card for metal polish, an indirect
material. The balance in the stores card for bulk metal on Jan. 31 is $7,800 (shown in
the gray shaded area). When this amount is added to the $200 balance (shown in the
gray shaded area) for the metal polish, the sum is $8,000, which is the balance in the
general ledger for raw materials inventory.

Also notice in Exhibit 12-1 that the perpetual inventory system is being utilized. As you may recall from financial accounting, when a ***perpetual inventory system*** is being maintained, the inventory accounts are continually updated as transactions take place. Each increase or decrease is recorded in the account as soon as it occurs, and a new balance is determined. For simplicity, in Exhibit 12-1 we have shown all the issues of bulk metal for January recorded as a single amount—$12,000 (see the eighth column in the first stores card)—and have done the same for metal polish—$160 (see the eighth column in the second stores card). In actuality, each issue would be listed separately, with a new balance determined after each issue.

EXHIBIT 12-1 Subsidiary Ledger for Raw Materials: The Stores Cards
The balances on Jan. 31 are shown in the gray shaded area, and the balances on Feb. 28 are shown in the blue shaded area.

Stores Card

Stock No. ___1___

Item ___Bulk metal___

	Received			Issued				Balance		
Date	Pounds	Unit Cost	Total Cost	Requisi-tion No.	Pounds	Unit Cost	Total Cost	Pounds	Unit Cost	Total Cost
Bal. 1/1								-0-		-0-
1/10	19,800	$1.00	$19,800					19,800	$1.00	$19,800
1/14–1/31				1110–1121	12,000	$1.00	$12,000	7,800	$1.00	$ 7,800
2/3	30,200	$1.00	$30,200					38,000	$1.00	$38,000
2/4				1123	5,000	$1.00	$ 5,000	33,000	1.00	33,000
2/7				1124	7,000	1.00	7,000	26,000	1.00	26,000
2/28				1125	21,000	$1.00	$21,000	5,000	$1.00	$ 5,000

Stores Card

Stock No. ___2___

Item ___Metal polish___

	Received			Issued				Balance		
Date	Cans	Unit Cost	Total Cost	Requisi-tion No.	Cans	Unit Cost	Total Cost	Cans	Unit Cost	Total Cost
Bal. 1/1								9	$40	$360
1/20–1/31				1109	4	$40	$160	5	$40	$200
2/1–2/28				1122	5	$40	$200	0	$40	-0-

The perpetual inventory method is also employed for work-in-process and finished goods, as you can see in the *job cost sheets* in Exhibits 12-2 and 12-3.

The Jan. 31 balance in the general ledger account for work-in-process, $37,000, represents the combined costs for the two unfinished jobs, 788 and 789. The subsidiary ledger accounts for these two jobs (the job cost sheets) are shown in Exhibit 12-2; the sum of the ending balances of $19,000 and $18,000 (shown in the gray shaded areas) equals the $37,000 balance in work-in-process. You probably also observed that there was a job cost sheet in Exhibit 12-2 for job 790. This job was started in February, so naturally it didn't have a balance on Jan. 31.

Finally, the balance of $24,000 in the finished goods general ledger account is represented by job 787, shown in Exhibit 12-3.

Don't be concerned for now with the factory overhead rate of $2 per hour

As you were examining the job cost sheets in Exhibits 12-2 and 12-3, you may have wondered what the factory overhead rate of $2 was (how it was determined and why we need to use it). This is an element of factory overhead that we explained in Chapter 10 and will also explain later in this chapter. So for now, do not be concerned with it.

EXHIBIT 12-2   Job Cost Sheets for Jobs 788, 789, and 790
The job cost sheets show the Jan. 31 balances (in the gray shaded areas), the transactions for February, and the Feb. 28 balances (in the blue shaded areas).

Job Cost Sheet

Job No. ___788___

Customer ___L. Hooper___   Date Completed ___2/17___

Date Started ___1/28___   Date Delivered ___2/21___

Date	Direct Materials Requisition No.	Amount	Direct Labor Work Ticket No.	Hours	Amount	Factory Overhead Rate	Amount	Total
1/28	1120	$7,000						
1/28–1/31			22111–22114	2,000	$8,000			
1/31						$2 per direct labor-hour	$4,000	
Bal. 1/31		$7,000			$8,000		$4,000	$19,000
2/4	1123	$5,000						
2/1–2/17			22121–22130	1,500	$6,000			
2/17						$2 per direct labor-hour	$3,000	
Completed costs		$12,000			$14,000		$7,000	$33,000

(continued)

EXHIBIT 12-2 *(continued)*

Job Cost Sheet

Job No. 789

Customer T. Pennachio   **Date Completed** 2/21

Date Started 1/29   **Date Delivered**

Date	Direct Materials Requisition No.	Amount	Direct Labor Work Ticket No.	Hours	Amount	Factory Overhead Rate	Amount	Total
1/29	1121	$3,000						
1/29–1/31			22115–22120	2,500	$10,000			
1/31						$2 per direct labor-hour	$5,000	
Bal. 1/31		$3,000			$10,000		$5,000	$18,000
2/7	1124	$7,000						
2/1–2/21			22131–22134	5,000	$20,000			
2/21						$2 per direct labor-hour	$10,000	
Completed costs		$10,000			$30,000		$15,000	$55,000

Job Cost Sheet

Job No. 790

Customer A. Robertson   **Date Completed**

Date Started 2/22   **Date Delivered**

Date	Direct Materials Requisition No.	Amount	Direct Labor Work Ticket No.	Hours	Amount	Factory Overhead Rate	Amount	Total
2/22	1125	$21,000						
2/22–2/28			22135–22140	2,500	$10,000			
2/28						$2 per direct labor-hour	$5,000	
Bal. 2/28		$21,000			$10,000		$5,000	$36,000

EXHIBIT 12-3   Subsidiary Ledger for Finished Goods
This job cost sheet represents the Jan. 31 balance in finished goods inventory.

<table>
<tr><td colspan="11" align="center">Job Cost Sheet</td></tr>
<tr><td colspan="11">Job No. <u>787</u></td></tr>
<tr><td colspan="5">Customer <u>G. Nichols</u></td><td colspan="6">Date Completed <u>1/25</u></td></tr>
<tr><td colspan="5">Date Started <u>1/11</u></td><td colspan="6">Date Delivered <u>2/3</u></td></tr>
<tr><td></td><td colspan="2" align="center">Direct Materials</td><td colspan="3" align="center">Direct Labor</td><td colspan="2" align="center">Factory Overhead</td><td></td></tr>
<tr><td align="center">Date</td><td align="center">Requisition No.</td><td align="center">Amount</td><td align="center">Work Ticket No.</td><td align="center">Hours</td><td align="center">Amount</td><td align="center">Rate</td><td align="center">Amount</td><td align="center">Total</td></tr>
<tr><td>1/11
1/11–1/25
1/25</td><td align="center">1119</td><td>$6,000</td><td align="center">22100–22110</td><td align="center">3,000</td><td>$12,000</td><td align="center">$2 per direct labor-hour</td><td>$6,000</td><td></td></tr>
<tr><td>Bal. 1/31</td><td></td><td>$6,000</td><td></td><td></td><td>$12,000</td><td></td><td>$6,000</td><td>$24,000</td></tr>
</table>

The Transactions for February

Each of the transactions related to production during February is now given, and as the transactions occur, they are numbered 1 through 9. For each transaction:

We'll discuss four things about each transaction

1. The source document providing the evidence of that transaction will be displayed.

2. The details of that transaction will be posted to subsidiary ledger accounts as soon as the transaction takes place.

3. The monthly summary general journal entry will be illustrated.

4. The journal entry will be posted to the general ledger accounts at month-end.

The Purchase of Raw Materials

Raw materials are bought

On Feb. 3 bulk metal in the amount of $30,200, purchased by the purchasing agent, was received and placed in the storeroom under the control of the storekeeper. As evidence of the purchase, Historical Replicas receives an *invoice* from its supplier, which is the *source document* for the purchase transaction. The invoice for the purchase of 30,200 pounds of bulk metal is shown in Exhibit 12-4. It indicates (1) the date, (2) the name of the supplier, (3) the terms of the purchase, (4) the quantity purchased, and (5) the total cost of the purchase.

As soon as the purchase of bulk metal is received, the subsidiary ledger for raw materials needs to be updated. You can see how this is done on the stores card for bulk metal in Exhibit 12-1.

EXHIBIT 12-4
The Invoice
The invoice is the source
document that gives evidence
of a purchase of raw materials.

	Invoice	

The Salvage 1 Junk Metal, Inc.   **No.** 12114
1969 Moon Drive
Canaveral, FL 32920   **Date** 2/1/88

Sold to: Historical Replicas Company
527 Southshore Boulevard
Land O'Ponds, FL 33539

Terms	FOB	Date Shipped
2/10, net 30	Shipping point	2/1/88

Description	Quantity	Unit Price	Amount
Bulk metal	30,200 lb	$1.00/lb	$30,200

At the end of the month a single journal entry is made that summarizes all the purchases made during the month. Although there could have been numerous purchases from different suppliers, we are assuming that the entire month's purchases were made on Feb. 3 from Salvage 1 Junk Metal, Inc. The following journal entry records this February purchase:[2]

The journal entry to record
a purchase of raw materials

1. Feb. 28 Raw Materials Inventory 30,200
           Accounts Payable (or Cash)   30,200
      Purchased raw materials on account (or for cash).

At the end of each month the debits and credits for each journal entry are posted to the general ledger. Exhibit 12-5 shows T-accounts for most of the general ledger accounts affected by entries 1 to 9 for Historical Replicas. Entry 1 for the purchase results in a debit to the T-account for Raw Materials Inventory and a credit to the T-account for Accounts Payable. The numbers in the T-accounts relate to the number of the entry being posted.

Standard costing: purchase
of raw materials

[2] The costs assigned to raw materials in entry 1 are the actual costs paid to the supplier of Historical Replicas. As we mentioned in the introduction to this chapter, we will be using a product costing system called *normal costing* within this chapter to account for the costs of the three inventories. Normal costing — like actual costing — assigns the actual costs incurred for direct materials and direct labor to the appropriate inventories but applies overhead at a predetermined rate. If we had been using a standard cost system — as discussed in Chapter 10 — we would have assigned the standard costs of the purchase to raw materials, rather than the actual costs. For example, if the standard cost per pound had been $0.95, then the amount recorded in entry 1 would have been $28,690 (30,200 pounds × $0.95) instead of $30,200, and a variance would be recorded for the difference between the actual and standard prices.

EXHIBIT 12-5 General Ledger Accounts for Historical Replicas Company
The journal entries (1–9) from our illustration are posted to these accounts.

Raw Materials Inventory				
Beg. Bal.	8,000	Transfer of Direct and Indirect Materials	33,000 (2)	
			200 (4)	
Purchases	(1) 30,200			
End. Bal.	5,000			

Work-in-Process Inventory				
Beg. Bal.	37,000			
Direct Materials	(2) 33,000			
Direct Labor	(3) 36,000	Completed Jobs Transferred to Finished Goods	88,000 (7)	
Overhead Applied	(5) 18,000			
End. Bal.	36,000			

Accounts Payable			
		Beg. Bal.	1,000
Payments	30,000	Purchases	30,200 (1)
		End. Bal.	1,200

Salaries Payable			
		Beg. Bal.	-0-
		Salaries Earned in February:	
		Direct	36,000 (3)
Salaries Paid in February	(6) 46,000	Indirect	10,000 (4)
		End. Bal.	-0-

Factory Overhead Incurred and Applied			
Incurred in February:		*Applied in February:*	
Ind. Mat.	(4) 200		
Ind. Labor	(4) 10,000		
Utilities	(4) 1,000		
Deprec.	(4) 2,800		18,000 (5)
	14,000		18,000

Each of the entries that follows will also be posted to T-accounts in Exhibit 12-5 above. Therefore, you will need to refer to this exhibit quite a few times before you are finished.

Use of Direct Materials

Direct materials are needed in production

During February $33,000 of *direct* materials was transferred from raw materials to work-in-process. These materials were needed to (1) continue the work on jobs 788 and 789, which were begun in January, and (2) start work on job 790. The $33,000 was distributed to the three jobs in the following manner:

Date	Job	Amount
Feb. 4	788	$ 5,000
7	789	7,000
22	790	21,000
Total direct materials used		$33,000

Finished Goods Inventory

Beg. Bal.	24,000		
Jobs Completed in February	(7) 88,000	Cost of Jobs Sold	57,000 (9)
End. Bal.	55,000		

Cost of Goods Sold Expense

Cost of Jobs Sold	(9) 57,000	

Sales Revenue

	Revenue from Jobs 787 and 788 85,500 (8)

To obtain the materials, a ***stores requisition,*** which is a source document representing a request for materials, is filled out by a supervisor or a designated individual in production and given to the storekeeper in exchange for the required materials. For example, the stores requisition for materials needed on Feb. 4 for job 788 is illustrated in Exhibit 12-6.

As you can see, stores requisition no. 1123 indicates that 5,000 pounds of bulk metal, having a cost of $5,000, is needed on Feb. 4 by M. Angelo for job 788.

Subsidiary ledgers affected by requisition: stores card and job cost sheets

Two subsidiary ledgers are affected by this transaction — the requisition of direct materials. First, the stores card is reduced by the $5,000 of direct materials issued to production. This is shown in Exhibit 12-1 as the first issue of raw materials in February; the second and third issues for February are for jobs 789 and 790.

The second subsidiary ledger affected by the use of direct materials is for work-in-process — the job cost sheets for jobs 788, 789, and 790. In Exhibit 12-2, $5,000 is entered in the direct materials column of the job cost sheet for job 788; $7,000 is assigned to the job cost sheet for job 789; and $21,000 is shown on the job cost sheet for job 790.

EXHIBIT 12-6
Stores Requisition
A source document
representing a request for
materials needed in production.

Stores Requisition

Date_____2/4_____   No. 1123

Job No._____788_____

Requested by_____M. Angelo_____

Stock No.	Item	Quantity	Unit Cost	Amount
1	Bulk metal	5,000 lb	$1.00/lb	$5,000

At the end of February a summarized journal entry is made for the total direct materials used during the month. The appropriate entry is:[3]

*The journal entry and
postings for direct materials*

2. Feb. 28   Work-in-Process Inventory 33,000
                      Raw Materials Inventory............................   33,000
                 Direct materials used during February, distributed to jobs as
                 follows:

> Job 788 $ 5,000
> Job 789   7,000
> Job 790 21,000
> $33,000

Following this journal entry, the debits and credits are posted to the general ledger accounts for raw materials and work-in-process. This posting is done in Exhibit 12-5, using the number 2 in the T-accounts to indicate the second entry.

Direct Labor

*Direct labor: labor costs
easily traceable to a
specific job*

The labor that is easily traceable to the manufacture of a specific product is called direct labor. To determine the exact amount of direct labor cost incurred for a particular job, it is necessary for each employee to fill out a source document called a *work ticket* for each job worked on. A work ticket for a single laborer who is working on job 788 on Feb. 6 might appear as shown in Exhibit 12-7; it shows the time involved on job 788, the hourly wage rate, and the total direct labor cost for the work performed.

*Standard costing: use of
direct materials*

[3] If Historical Replicas had been using a standard cost system, the debit to Work-in-Process would have been based upon the standard pounds allowed for the three jobs multiplied by the standard cost per pound, and the total would have been distributed to the three job cost sheets on the basis of the number of standard pounds required for each job. There might be a problem, however, in determining the standard quantity allowed if each of the jobs was significantly different in size—with each one requiring substantially different quantities of direct materials. You see, standard costing works best when there is some commonness—or standardization—among the products so that the standard applies to all units produced. If, for example, all historical replicas were a single size—or even several sizes—and each sized replica required the same amount of direct materials, then a standard quantity could be determined for each size and a standard cost system could be employed. The credit to Raw Materials would be for the actual pounds used multiplied by the standard price, and any quantity variance would be recorded to ensure equality of debits and credits.

EXHIBIT 12-7
Work Ticket
The source document that identifies labor costs with a department and a specific job.

Work Ticket	
	22124
Employee _____ O. B. Harris _____	
Department ___ Casting & Sculpting ___	Hours Worked _____ 8 _____
Job. No. _____ 788 _____	Rate _____ $4.00 _____
Date _____ 2/6 _____	Total _____ $32.00 _____

We will now assume that a summary of all work tickets used during February indicates that $36,000 was spent for labor, distributed as follows to the three jobs:

Job	Hours	×	Rate	=	Amount
788	1,500	×	$4/hr	=	$ 6,000
789	5,000	×	4/hr	=	20,000
790	2,500	×	4/hr	=	10,000
Total direct labor	9,000				$36,000

Check the postings in the job cost sheets

In actual practice we would post the direct labor costs to the job cost sheets on a daily basis. However, since the work occurred over quite a few days of the month, the job cost sheets would be quite lengthy and detailed if we posted all the daily entries separately. Therefore, for the purpose of *simplicity only,* we will make one posting of direct labor to each job cost sheet to represent the many postings that would actually take place.

So now if you look back to Exhibit 12-2, you will see that $6,000 of direct labor costs have been posted during February to job 788, $20,000 to job 789, and $10,000 to job 790.

The summarized journal entry made on Feb. 28 records a debit to Work-in-Process Inventory and a credit to Salaries Payable:[4]

The month-end entry and posting for direct labor

3. Feb. 28   Work-in-Process Inventory 36,000
            Salaries Payable   36,000
      Direct labor earned by laborers during February, distributed as follows:

         Job 788 $ 6,000
         Job 789   20,000
         Job 790   10,000
             $36,000

Standard costing: direct labor

[4] The costs assigned to Work-in-Process for direct labor in entry 3 are the actual costs incurred during the period—the appropriate amount to use under both the actual costing and the normal costing systems. Under standard costing the debit to Work-in-Process would be at standard costs instead; i.e., the standard hours allowed times the standard rate per hour. The use of standard hours (as with standard pounds for direct materials) would, of course, depend upon whether or not there were standard-size replicas requiring similar amounts of time to produce. The credit to Accrued Payroll would remain the same. In addition, any quantity and price variance would need to be recorded, since the debits and credits would not be equal without them.

The debits and credits in entry 3 are now posted, in total, to the general ledger accounts. Notice that the postings have been made by referring to Exhibit 12-5 and finding entry 3 in the Work-in-Process and Salaries Payable T-accounts.

Due to the fact that we will have an additional accrual of wages — for indirect labor — in the section on factory overhead that comes next, we will postpone the required entry for the payment of salaries until after we have finished the section on factory overhead.

Factory Overhead Incurred

Factory overhead costs are the indirect costs of production

All factory costs other than direct materials and direct labor are classified as factory overhead. During February the actual factory overhead incurred was as follows:

Indirect Materials	$ 200
Indirect Labor	10,000
Utilities	1,000
Depreciation	2,800
Total Factory Overhead Incurred	$14,000

The indirect materials are the raw materials that either (1) do not become an integral part of the finished good or (2) do become a physical part of the finished good but are immaterial in amount. For example, indirect materials might include glue, screws, polish, nails, varnish, maintenance supplies, and janitorial supplies. For Historical Replicas the indirect materials are the cans of metal polish.

The indirect labor relates to the production laborers who do not actually work on the jobs being produced. These laborers might be supervisors, maintenance people, material handlers, and janitors.

Source documents cannot identify specific jobs

There are a variety of source documents related to these miscellaneous overhead items. A stores requisition would once again be needed to obtain the indirect raw materials from the storeroom, and work tickets would be filled out by employees to indicate the amount of labor time indirectly related to production. As we will discuss shortly, there is no attempt to pinpoint the exact amount of indirect materials or indirect labor associated with specific jobs. The stores requisition and the work ticket will designate only the department in which the indirect materials and indirect labor are used — not a specific job. The bill from the power company is the source document for the utility charges, and a depreciation schedule is a source document that indicates the amount of depreciation associated with February's production.

Update the stores card for metal polish; it's now zero

When we use indirect materials (the metal polish) we must update the appropriate stores card — the subsidiary ledger account for raw materials. If you look back at the stores card for metal polish (Exhibit 12-1), you will see a balance of $200 on Jan. 31 (in the gray shaded area). If $200 of polish is used during February, the balance at the end of February would be reduced to zero (in the blue shaded area).

Factory overhead incurred goes to factory overhead cost sheets — not job cost sheets

All the factory overhead costs incurred — the actual factory overhead — are accumulated during the period on *factory overhead cost sheets* — a subsidiary ledger that is similar to a job cost sheet. The difference is that the factory overhead cost sheets trace costs only to the department where the costs are incurred — but not to any of the jobs being produced in the department. In our example, Historical Replicas has only one production department, so it will have only one factory overhead cost sheet. Firms with many production departments will have a different overhead cost sheet for each department.

Each factory overhead cost sheet will have enough columns to accommodate the

EXHIBIT 12-8
Factory Overhead Cost Sheet
The overhead cost sheet has a different column for each type of overhead incurred for a period. There is a different overhead cost sheet for each department.

\multicolumn{6}{c}{**Factory Overhead Cost Sheet**}					

Factory Overhead Cost Sheet

Department _____ Casting, Sculpting _____

Date	Indirect Materials	Indirect Labor	Utilities	Depreciation	Total
Jan.	. . .	. . .	. . .	. . .	. . .
Feb.	$200	$10,000	$1,000	$2,800	$14,000
Mar.	. . .	. . .	. . .	. . .	. . .
Apr.	. . .	. . .	. . .	. . .	. . .

different types of factory overhead costs incurred throughout the month. Exhibit 12-8 shows a factory overhead cost sheet for the casting and sculpting department for the month of February, listing the four individual overhead items from above as well as the total for the month, $14,000. There will be a similar posting in each month of the year, with the totals accumulating as the year progresses.

4. Feb. 28 Factory Overhead Incurred and Applied   14,000
                   Raw Materials Inventory.   200
                   Salaries Payable.   10,000
                   Accounts (or Utilities) Payable.   1,000
                   Accumulated Depreciation   2,800
             To record overhead incurred in February.

Notice in entry 4, for the factory overhead costs incurred, that the debit was not to the same account that we used in Chapter 2 — Factory Overhead Incurred — but to a similarly named account instead — Factory Overhead Incurred and Applied. Whereas the two account titles may sound the same, the presence of the new word — *applied* — in the title represents a major change in how we account for factory overhead as a product cost.

Note: If you've already studied Chapter 10, the following discussion will not be new to you. But it will still be a good idea for you to read it just in case you need to review or reinforce what you've already learned. On the other hand, if you're covering this chapter at an early stage in the course and have not yet read Chapter 10, then you'll need to read the next section extremely carefully and you may also want to read pages 438–441 in Chapter 10 as well.

Assigning Factory Overhead Costs to Jobs

Why not use actual costs as the product costs?

In Chapter 2 we first debited Factory Overhead Incurred. And then at the end of each period, after all the factory overhead costs had been accounted for, we closed the account with a credit and transferred the total to Work-in-Process with a debit. In this way, the actual overhead costs incurred ended up as product costs in Work-in-Process. In this chapter (as well as in Chapter 10), however, you'll find out that there are certain problems associated with the actual factory overhead costs being product costs, and that factory overhead *applied* will be the product costs instead. In order to keep track of two different types of factory overhead — the actual costs incurred and the costs applied — we need to use an account with an expanded title. The account is ***Factory Overhead Incurred and Applied.***

At this point you're probably thinking, "This certainly sounds confusing. Why don't we just continue using the same system that was introduced in Chapter 2 — first debiting Factory Overhead Incurred for the $14,000 and later transferring this total to Work-in-Process. Didn't we learn in Chapter 2 that factory overhead is a product cost just like direct materials and direct labor? And didn't we just assign the actual costs of direct materials and direct labor to Work-in-Process, in entries 2 and 3? So why don't we do the same thing for factory overhead; why don't we merely transfer the actual costs of $14,000 to Work-in-Process, just as we did in Chapter 2? Why aren't the actual factory overhead costs still the product costs?"

Factory overhead applied will be the product cost for two reasons

These are indeed extremely good questions. And the answers to these questions are vital if you are to understand the steps we are about to take for factory overhead.

Yes, factory overhead is definitely a product cost, just like direct materials and direct labor; and yes, factory overhead does need to be debited to Work-in-Process. However, for two very practical and important reasons, we are no longer going to use the actual factory overhead costs for product costing.

Reason 1: The Indirect Relationship   The first reason we don't debit Work-in-Process for the actual factory overhead incurred for a period is because of the relationship of overhead costs to the jobs in production. Direct materials and direct labor are costs that can be easily traced and assigned to the individual jobs to which they apply. This is why we refer to these costs as "direct." When these costs are debited to Work-in-Process, it is an easy task to distribute the total to the various job cost sheets, just as we did in Exhibit 12-2.

Reason 1: factory overhead can't be associated with specific jobs

Although factory overhead is also a product cost, it is indirectly rather than directly related to the jobs in production. Factory overhead is considered to be indirectly related to production because it is extremely difficult, if not impossible, to determine the exact amount of actual overhead to associate with each different job. For example, the salary paid to a foreman is part of factory overhead. The foreman may be supervising numerous workers, each of whom may be working on several different jobs. Not only is it very difficult to determine the exact amount of time spent by the foreman supervising each worker, but it is even more difficult to determine the amount of time associated with each particular job. If the actual overhead incurred is assigned to Work-in-Process, then we also have to distribute this amount incurred to the job cost sheets. Because of the indirect relationship between factory overhead and the jobs worked on, there is no way to know how much overhead cost we should assign to each job cost sheet. As a result, it normally isn't a good idea to debit Work-in-Process Inventory for the actual overhead incurred.

Reason 2: Fluctuating Activity   After reading the first reason, you may say to yourself, "But it doesn't seem necessary to find out the exact amount of overhead associated with each job. All we have to do is spread the overhead incurred each month evenly among all the jobs. Or better yet, we can spread the overhead evenly among the labor-hours worked, and then assign the actual overhead to each job based on the number of hours used on each job that month."

The problem with this line of reasoning relates to the effect that fluctuating production activity from month to month can have on the cost per finished unit and the resulting monthly income statements. This is especially true when a substantial portion of the overhead costs is fixed. The topic of fixed costs, along with variable costs, was discussed in detail in Chapter 3. But before we go on, we'll give you a basic refresher concerning the nature of variable and fixed costs—and then we'll explain the problem of fluctuating activity.

Variable costs are costs that fluctuate, in total, in proportion to changes in activity

EXHIBIT 12-9   Fluctuating Cost per Unit

Notice how the average cost per unit is very high in January when few units are produced and very low in July when many units are produced.

Month	Actual Overhead Costs	÷	Expected Units (or Jobs) to Be Produced	=	Overhead Cost per Unit	+	Direct Materials Plus Direct Labor per Unit	=	Total Cost per Unit
Jan.	$ 16,667		2		$8,334		$10,000		$18,334
Feb.	16,667		3		5,555		10,000		15,555
Mar.	16,667		4		4,167		10,000		14,167
July	16,667		12		1,389		10,000		11,389
Aug.	16,667		11		1,515		10,000		11,515
Nov.	16,667		3		5,555		10,000		15,555
Dec.	16,667		2		8,334		10,000		18,334
Year	$200,000		80		$2,500		$10,000		$12,500

—the more units you produce, the more variable costs you have. Fixed costs are those costs that, in total, are not expected to change as activity changes—no matter how many units you produce, the total fixed costs remain the same.

Reason 2: the cost per unit can fluctuate dramatically when production fluctuates from period to period

Since fixed costs in total will be the same no matter how many units are produced, the fixed costs per unit can be very large or very small depending on the number of units produced.

Suppose, for example, that an organization expects its factory overhead to be completely fixed, amounting to $200,000 for an entire year, and that the amount incurred each month is the same amount—$16,667 ($200,000 ÷ 12). Suppose also that activity throughout the year is expected to fluctuate dramatically. Exhibit 12-9 shows that the overhead cost and also the total cost per unit or per job can be quite a bit different from month to month due to these fluctuations in activity.

Because of fluctuations in production throughout the year, the monthly overhead cost per unit is expected to be as high as $8,334 in January and as low as $1,389 in July. Combining these amounts with the $10,000 per unit for the direct materials and direct labor (assumed for simplicity—however unrealistic—to be the same amount per unit worked on), we get a total cost per unit of $18,334 in January and $11,389 in July. Looking at overhead costs and total units produced on an annual basis (the bottom line of Exhibit 12-9), we get an overhead cost per unit of $2,500 ($200,000 ÷ 80), and a total cost per unit of $12,500 ($10,000 + $2,500).

Now let's assume that the selling price is $17,500 per unit—which will generate a gross profit of $5,000 per unit ($17,500 − $12,500) if we use the total cost per unit on an annual basis. Many organizations, however, want to prepare income statements for their own use more frequently than once a year. If monthly income statements are prepared using the monthly total cost per unit, the gross profit per unit would vary from month to month, as shown below for three of the months:

Month	Sales Price	Total Cost per Unit	Gross Profit per Unit
January	$17,500	$18,334	$(834)
July.................	17,500	11,389	6,111
November	17,500	15,555	1,945

Assigning actual overhead costs to jobs can result in meaningless interim income statements

The monthly gross profit is far below the $5,000 average of the year in January and November, but it is above the average in July. This might create the impression that the production department was run poorly in January and November but that it was run efficiently in July. The fact is, however, that the only reason the monthly results appear to be so dramatically different is that the number of units to which the $16,667 monthly overhead was assigned fluctuated quite a bit. As you can see, the assignment of monthly actual overhead to units produced each month can cause meaningless interim income statements.

To conclude, there are two reasons that it is better *not* to debit Work-in-Process for the actual overhead incurred:

1. Because of the indirect relationship between overhead costs and units produced, there is no practical way to determine the amount of actual overhead that is incurred for each individual job produced.

2. When an organization experiences fluctuating production activity, the average cost per finished unit can be very large or very small, often causing meaningless interim income statements.

Factory Overhead Applied

What is factory overhead applied?

The factory overhead that we will now assign to different jobs and debit to Work-in-Process is called ***factory overhead applied.*** To determine the factory overhead applied, we use a ***predetermined overhead rate.*** What that means is this: At the beginning of the year each production department makes an estimate of the total overhead costs and expected activity for the year. The estimated overhead costs are then divided by the estimated activity to get the predetermined overhead rate. During each month the actual activity for that month is multiplied by the predetermined overhead rate, resulting in an overhead cost we call factory overhead applied.

Actual vs. normal costing

This treatment of overhead is what distinguishes a ***normal costing system*** from an actual costing system. The overhead assigned to the product is the amount applied under the normal costing system, but it is the actual costs incurred under an actual costing system.

The controller looks for a good way to measure activity

Now let's get back to the Historical Replicas Company. Assume that on Jan. 1, 1988, the company controller, Steve Cobb, wanted to calculate the company's predetermined overhead rate for 1988 and estimated the factory overhead for the year to be $200,000. He initially thought he would (1) estimate the number of jobs (or units) to be worked on in 1988, (2) determine an average cost per job, and then (3) assign this average cost to each job produced as the year progressed. As a result, each job—no matter how long it took to produce—would have the same amount of factory overhead assigned to it.

Cobb figured that the company would work on only five jobs during 1988, four of them during the first 2 months (jobs 787–790) and only one during the remaining 10 months of the year. He realized that by spreading the $200,000 evenly among the five jobs, this would result in a cost per job of $40,000. The more he thought about this approach, however, the less sense it made. A job that takes 10 months to complete should be assigned a much bigger portion of the total overhead for the year than a job that takes only 1 or 2 months to complete. Cobb knew he needed to find a better measure of activity for the year than the number of jobs to be worked on.

It occurred to Cobb that direct labor-hours might be a more meaningful measure of activity, since overhead costs for the year are probably influenced more by the number of hours worked than by the number of jobs completed.

By using direct labor-hours, the overhead costs assigned to each job would better reflect the relative time, effort, and attention exerted on that job. A job taking 1,500 direct labor-hours does not require as much attention as one taking 5,000 hours or 50,000 hours. Therefore, by assigning overhead costs to jobs on the basis of the number of direct labor-hours needed for each job, far less overhead would be assigned to the 1,500-hour job than to the 50,000-hour job—a more equitable manner of distribution.

On Jan. 1, 1988, Cobb estimated that the total direct labor-hours for all jobs in 1988 would be 100,000 hours. He then determined an average overhead rate for 1988 using the following general equation:[5]

Getting a predetermined overhead rate for Historical Replicas

$$\text{Predetermined factory overhead rate} = \frac{\text{estimated factory overhead costs for the year}}{\text{estimated activity for the year}}$$

Using the specific data for Historical Replicas, the rate is determined in the following manner:

$$\text{Predetermined factory overhead per direct labor-hour} = \frac{\text{estimated factory overhead costs for the year}}{\text{estimated direct labor-hours for the year}}$$

$$= \frac{\$200,000}{100,000 \text{ hr}}$$

$$= \$2 \text{ per direct labor-hour}$$

For each direct labor-hour worked during a month, whether it be in February, July, or November, $2 of factory overhead is assigned (or applied) to Work-in-Process. The amount of overhead cost to be assigned to each specific job depends on the number of direct labor-hours used on each job.

If you'll now look back to the discussion preceding entry 3 for direct labor, you can see that the total hours of direct labor used in February were 9,000, broken down by job as follows:

Job	Direct Labor-Hours
788.	1,500
789.	5,000
790.	2,500
Total	9,000

Using the predetermined overhead rate of $2 per direct labor-hour, the total overhead assigned to production in February is:

Standard costing: determining the overhead rate

[5] In Chapter 10 we calculated the predetermined overhead rate in a similar manner. However, there were the following differences:

1. We used the equation to calculate the rate for fixed factory overhead only, since we handled the variable and fixed overhead separately.
2. The numerator of the equation related to what the overhead costs "should be" for the year—the amount budgeted—rather than to what the "actual costs are expected to be" for the year.
3. The denominator of the equation was represented by the standard hours of normal activity.

Job	Activity for Month (Direct Labor-Hours)	×	Overhead Rate per Hour	=	Overhead Cost Assigned to Production
788	1,500	×	$2.00	=	$ 3,000
789	5,000	×	2.00	=	10,000
790	2,500	×	2.00	=	5,000
					$18,000

The overhead applied in February is $18,000. How much goes to each job?

The $18,000 of overhead costs assigned to production must be posted to the appropriate job cost sheets. Exhibit 12-2 (on pages 528–529) shows that the amount posted to the job cost sheet for job 788 is $3,000; for job 789 it is $10,000; and for job 790 it is $5,000.

The journal entry needed on Feb. 28 to record the overhead costs applied is:[6]

Now you can debit Work-in-Process for overhead — the overhead applied

5. Feb. 28 Work-in-Process Inventory 18,000
               Factory Overhead Incurred and Applied   18,000
             Factory overhead applied to production, based on a $2 per hour predetermined rate for 9,000 hours of direct labor during February.

Be sure to notice in entry 5 the account that is being credited — Factory Overhead Incurred and Applied. This is the account that we debited for the factory overhead *incurred* in entry 4. Now we are crediting it for the overhead *applied*.

The amounts shown in entry 5 are now posted to general ledger accounts. If you look back to Exhibit 12-5, you'll notice that the Work-in-Process T-account has been debited for $18,000 and the Factory Overhead Incurred and Applied T-account has been credited for $18,000.

Can we measure activity in any other way? Dollars? Machine-hours?

Alternative Measures of Activity In the illustration for Historical Replicas, the controller decided to measure activity for the year in terms of *direct labor-hours.* An alternative measure of activity, which closely approximates the results of using direct labor-hours, is *direct labor-dollars.* Instead of the resulting rate being a cost per hour, it is a percentage of labor-dollars. For those production situations that involve a great deal of machine work, the number of *machine-hours* expected for the year could be a third possible measure of activity, and the overhead rate would be a cost per machine-hour.

The overhead incurred and overhead applied for February aren't the same amount

Overapplied and Underapplied Overhead Before we go on, let's look for a moment at what has been recorded during February for factory overhead. In entry 4 we debited the account Factory Overhead Incurred and Applied for $14,000 — the actual overhead incurred for the month. Now in entry 5, using an estimated average cost per direct labor-hour of $2, we credited the same account, Factory Overhead Incurred and Applied, for $18,000 — the overhead applied to production in February. The details of these entries are shown below in the T-account for Factory Overhead Incurred and Applied:

Standard costing: overhead incurred and applied

---

[6] If this were a standard cost system, the form of the journal entries for both the actual overhead incurred and the overhead applied (entries 4 and 5, respectively) would be basically the same. Since we evaluate fixed and variable overhead separately in a standard cost system, however, we normally prepare individual journal entries for the variable and fixed costs. Also, in a standard cost system, we multiply the overhead rates by the standard hours allowed rather than the actual hours worked to get the overhead applied.

Factory Overhead Incurred and Applied	
Incurred	**Applied**
Ind. Mat. (4) 200	
Ind. Labor (4) 10,000	
Utilities (4) 1,000	
Deprec. (4) 2,800	18,000 (5)
_____	_____
14,000	18,000

As you can see, the credits exceed the debits by $4,000 — the excess of what was applied during February over what was actually incurred. Factory overhead for February is said to be $4,000 "*overapplied.*" [7]

The difference is either overapplied or underapplied

The difference for each month between the debits and credits in the Factory Overhead Incurred and Applied account is called the overapplied or underapplied overhead. If the credits exceed the debits, as they do above, the overhead is **overapplied.** If the debits exceed the credits, the overhead is **underapplied.** Do not be surprised when the debits and credits are not equal — we do not expect the amount incurred in a month to equal the amount applied. In fact, for a firm with fluctuating activity, we fully expect to have overapplied overhead in some months and underapplied overhead in the other months. By year-end we hope that the debits will be fairly close to the credits, that is, that the incurred will equal the applied. If they are not equal by the end of the year, a special kind of entry will be made — one that is made only at the end of the year, not at the end of each month. We will discuss this problem later. For now, let's continue with the events of February for Historical Replicas.

Payment of Salaries

The labor costs accrued for the month of February were recorded in entry 3 (direct labor) and entry 4 (indirect labor — factory overhead). They totaled $46,000:

The payment of direct and indirect laborers

Direct Labor	$36,000
Indirect Labor	10,000
Total Labor Accrued	$46,000

If you look at the Salaries Payable T-account in Exhibit 12-5, you will see credits totaling to this amount.

At the time of these accruals, we pointed out that each laborer would have to fill out a work ticket to indicate which department he or she was working in (for both direct laborers and indirect laborers) and which job he or she was working on (for direct laborers only). In addition, each laborer needs to keep track of the total hours worked during the pay period — using a **clock card.** The clock card is a source document that informs the accounting department of the number of hours for which each laborer should be paid. The clock card does not specify which jobs the laborer

Standard costing: overapplied or underapplied

[7] In a standard cost system, there is a separate underapplied or overapplied overhead for each of the variable and fixed components. For the variable this difference (also called the *flexible budget variance*) is composed of two parts — the price variance and the quantity variance. For fixed overhead this difference is the sum of the price variance and the volume variance.

EXHIBIT 12-10
Clock Card

A source document that accumulates the total hours worked by an employee during a pay period. It is *not* the same as a work ticket.

			Hours	
Date	Time In	Time Out	Regular	Overtime
2/1	8:00	12:00	4	
	1:00	5:00	4	
2/2	8:01	11:55	4	
	1:00	5:02	4	
2/25	8:03	12:00	4	
	1:00	4:55	4	

Clock Card

Name_____Jerome Brown_____

Pay Period_____February 1988_____

has worked on; that is the purpose of the work ticket. A typical clock card for a single worker during February might appear as shown in Exhibit 12-10.

If we assume that the salaries are paid on the last day of each month and that the combined labor costs from clock cards for all employees is $46,000, then the appropriate entry to record the payment of salaries to laborers is shown below as entry 6:

6. Feb. 28 Salaries Payable 46,000
   Cash   46,000
   $36,000 was paid to direct laborers and $10,000 was paid to
   indirect laborers.

Entry 6 is posted to the appropriate general ledger accounts on Feb. 28, which we show in Exhibit 12-5.

Completion of Jobs

Jobs are completed and transferred to finished goods

During February two jobs were completed, jobs 788 and 789. As the job cost sheets in Exhibit 12-2 indicate, the total costs of producing these jobs were $33,000 and $55,000, respectively. The total of these two, $88,000, is transferred from Work-in-Process to Finished Goods as shown by the following entry:

7. Feb. 28 Finished Goods Inventory 88,000
      Work-in-Process Inventory   88,000
   Completion in February of jobs 788 and 789, and transfer of
   costs ($33,000 and $55,000, respectively) to finished goods.

The debits and credits in entry 7 are posted to the appropriate general ledger accounts, shown in Exhibit 12-5. When the jobs are completed during the month, the job cost sheets for the completed jobs are removed from the work-in-process inventory subsidiary ledger and become part of the subsidiary ledger for finished goods inventory.

Historical Replicas might prepare a cost of production report as a source document for entry 7, listing the costs of the jobs completed during the period and transferred to finished goods. The information presented on the report would be taken from the job cost sheets that are transferred from the subsidiary ledger for work-in-process to the one for finished goods.

Sale of Completed Jobs

Jobs 787 (the beginning inventory of finished goods) and 788 (completed during February) were the only jobs sold during February. Their respective costs (shown in Exhibits 12-3 and 12-2) were:

Job 787	$24,000
Job 788	33,000
	$57,000

If each job is sold at a markup of 50% over cost, the sales price for each job would have been:

Jobs 787 and 788 are sold at a markup of 50% over cost

Job No.	Cost	50% Markup	Sales Price
787	$24,000	$12,000	$36,000
788	33,000	16,500	49,500
	$57,000	$28,500	$85,500

The entries to record the sales and cost of goods sold are shown in entries 8 and 9, respectively. First, we record the revenue:[8]

You need two entries to record a sale: the revenue and the cost of goods sold

8. Feb. 28   Accounts Receivable (or Cash) 85,500
          Sales Revenue 85,500
          To record the sale of jobs 787 and 788 at prices of $36,000 and $49,500, respectively.

Next, we record the cost of goods sold:

9. Feb. 28   Cost of Goods Sold Expense 57,000
          Finished Goods Inventory 57,000
          To record the cost of goods sold for jobs 787 and 788. The costs were $24,000 and $33,000, respectively.

Entries 8 and 9 are posted to the general ledger accounts in Exhibit 12-5. At the time of sale the job cost sheets for jobs 787 and 788 would be removed from the subsidiary ledger for finished goods and placed in the subsidiary ledger for cost of goods sold. The source documents for entry 8 are copies of the sales invoices, and the source

Standard costing: completion and sale

---

[8] The accounts and amounts that are debited and credited in entries 6 and 8 are exactly as they would be for a standard costing system. Although the accounts are the same in entries 7 and 9, the amounts that would be debited and credited are not. Under a standard cost system the amounts assigned to the jobs that are in work-in-process and finished goods are completely at standard. Therefore, the amounts completed and transferred to Finished Goods (entry 7) and those that are transferred to Cost of Goods Sold (entry 9) would be assigned standard costs rather than the actual costs that have been used in the example above.

document for entry 9 is a cost of goods sold report. The cost of goods sold report itemizes the costs, from the job cost sheets of jobs 787 and 788, that are transferred to the subsidiary ledger for cost of goods sold.

An important reminder: The journal entries shown in entries 1 to 9 and the posting to the general ledger T-accounts displayed in Exhibit 12-5 are made in summarized form at month-end. The detailed records maintained in the subsidiary ledger accounts for each job would in most cases be maintained daily.

The Interim Statement

What you need for financial statements in February

Assume that monthly financial statements are prepared on Feb. 28. The income statement includes the sales of $85,500 and the cost of goods sold expense of $57,000 relating to the sales of jobs 787 and 788. In an actual situation there would also be operating expenses (selling and administrative), which were not included in this illustration. The balance sheet includes the following inventory balances taken from the T-accounts in Exhibit 12-5:

Raw Materials Inventory	$ 5,000
Work-in-Process Inventory	36,000
Finished Goods Inventory	55,000

The Raw Materials balance, $5,000, is supported by the blue shaded area of the stores card for bulk metal shown in Exhibit 12-1. The Work-in-Process balance, $36,000, represents the total in the blue shaded area of the job cost sheet for job 790 shown in Exhibit 12-2. Job 790 is still being worked on, on the last day of February. The balance in Finished Goods, $55,000, comes from the blue shaded area of the job cost sheet for job 789, which is also shown in Exhibit 12-2. Job 789 was finished in February and will probably be sold in March.

Year-End Handling of Over- or Underapplied Overhead

For the month of February the actual overhead incurred was $14,000 and the amount applied was $18,000. These represent the debits and credits to the Factory Overhead Incurred and Applied T-account shown in Exhibit 12-5. There were also debits and credits to this account for January (which we did not show), and there will be additional debits and credits for the next 10 months of 1988. At the end of the year, on the debit side of Factory Overhead Incurred and Applied there will be accumulated overhead incurred for the full 12 months of 1988. On the credit side will be accumulated 12 months of applied overhead. A question: By the end of the year, will the debits in this account equal the credits? Probably not.

In the ideal situation the applied overhead would exactly equal the overhead costs incurred; and to make matters even nicer, they would both equal the amount of overhead costs predicted for the year — the $200,000 — which was used in the calculation of the factory overhead rate (look back at this calculation on page 541). In the more realistic situation, however, the applied overhead will not equal the actual overhead for the year, and neither one will be exactly $200,000.

To see how we handle this, let's assume this set of facts for Historical Replicas at year-end:

What if the incurred doesn't equal the applied?

■ At the end of the year, all the bills for overhead add up to a total of $204,000 in factory overhead costs actually incurred.

■ The sum of the work tickets for the year shows that 98,000 labor-hours were worked in the manufacturing department. At the predetermined rate of $2 per direct labor-hour, this means that during the year, $196,000 in overhead costs was applied to all units produced.

The T-account for Factory Overhead Incurred and Applied might look like this for 1988:

Year-end balances of overhead for Historical Replicas

Factory Overhead Incurred and Applied			
Incurred		**Applied**	
Jan.	20,000	12,000	
Feb.	14,000	18,000	
.	.	.	
.	.	.	
.	.	.	
Dec.	16,000	18,000	
Totals for 1988	204,000	196,000	

In this more realistic case the debits do not equal the credits — the actual overhead incurred does not equal the applied. The difference in the actual costs of $204,000 and the applied costs of $196,000 indicates that the overhead costs were underapplied by $8,000. In this case the sum of the overhead costs applied to each unit produced does not add up to the total of overhead costs incurred. We don't find out until the end of the year that we didn't assign sufficient overhead costs to units produced to cover the actual overhead costs incurred. In this case we should have assigned $8,000 more in overhead costs than was assigned.

How do we account for this $8,000 in underapplied overhead costs at the end of the year? Let's see.

You need to close temporary accounts

The Factory Overhead Incurred and Applied account is a temporary, or nominal, account, which means that the balance must be closed — reduced to zero — at the end of the year. There are two ways to close this account. The first way is to close the Factory Overhead Incurred and Applied balance entirely to Cost of Goods Sold Expense:

Dec. 31   Cost of Goods Sold Expense   8,000
                Factory Overhead Incurred and Applied..................   8,000
            To close out the overhead account for the $8,000 of underapplied overhead.

The second way to close the Factory Overhead Incurred and Applied account is to allocate the over- or underapplied overhead among the Work-in-Process, Finished Goods, and Cost of Goods Sold accounts, based on the ending balances in these accounts prior to the closing entry.

We allocate to the accounts which have too much or too little overhead applied

We allocate to these three accounts for the following reason. During the year factory overhead was applied to quite a few jobs in the work-in-process inventory. When there is underapplied overhead for the year, we didn't apply enough overhead to the jobs worked on during the year. Each of the jobs has too little overhead included in its job cost sheet as its product cost. In essence, the cost of each job is understated. Some of the jobs which have too little overhead applied to them are still in process at the end of the year, so some of the underapplied overhead is allocated to

Work-in-Process in order to increase the costs assigned to these jobs. In addition, some of the jobs having too little overhead applied to them went on to finished goods during the year, but were not sold by the end of the year, so some of the underapplied overhead is allocated to Finished Goods. Finally, many of the jobs having too little overhead applied to them were finished and sold during the year. Therefore, much of the underapplied overhead is allocated to Cost of Goods Sold Expense.

For example, assume that the *year-end* balances for these accounts are as follows. (Caution: The balances shown in Exhibit 12-5 are only for the end of February, not for the end of the year.)

Work-in-Process Inventory	$ 40,000
Finished Goods Inventory	60,000
Cost of Goods Sold Expense	700,000

The $8,000 underapplied overhead is allocated to each account as follows:

	Ending Balance	Fraction of Total	×	Total Under-applied	=	Underapplied Overhead Allocated
Work-in-Process Inventory....	$ 40,000	$\frac{40}{800}$	×	$8,000	=	$ 400
Finished Goods Inventory.....	60,000	$\frac{60}{800}$	×	$8,000	=	600
Cost of Goods Sold Expense...	700,000	$\frac{700}{800}$	×	$8,000	=	7,000
	$800,000					$8,000

The closing entry using the second approach would be the following:[9]

Dec. 31	Work-in-Process Inventory	400	
	Finished Goods Inventory	600	
	Cost of Goods Sold Expense	7,000	
	Factory Overhead Incurred and Applied		8,000
	To close out the overhead account for the $8,000 of underapplied overhead.		

This second approach is usually required in order to be in accordance with generally accepted accounting principles (GAAP). However, if the over- or underapplied overhead is immaterial in amount, then it is acceptable to use either of the two approaches we have shown. When it is immaterial, it makes little difference whether we allocate or not, because the differences in the cost of goods sold and the resulting net income under the two approaches is also immaterial. However, if the over- or underapplied overhead is extremely large, then the amounts for cost of goods sold and net income could be quite a bit different under the two approaches, and the recommended approach is mandatory.

An Overview of Job Order Costing

Now that you have finished reading the chapter, you may feel that there were so many details over so many pages that you wish you could put them all into perspective on a single page. We did. In Exhibit 12-11 we have condensed the chapter into its

Standard costing: closing overhead

---

[9] The closing entries for factory overhead are basically the same under a standard costing system.

most basic elements. We offer you a summary of job order costing in matrix form. For each transaction, by reading from left to right, you can see the journal entry, subsidiary ledgers, and source documents affected.

EXHIBIT 12-11 Matrix Overview of Job Order Costing
For each transaction the entry, the subsidiary ledgers, and the source documents are listed.

Transaction	Journal Entry	Subsidiary Ledgers	Source Documents
1. Purchase of raw materials	Raw Materials Inventory (dr.) Accounts Payable (cr.)	Stores cards	Invoice
2. Use of direct materials	Work-in-Process Inventory (dr.) Raw Materials Inventory (cr.)	Job cost sheets Stores cards	Stores requisition
3. Accrual of direct labor	Work-in-Process Inventory (dr.) Salaries Payable (cr.)	Job cost sheets	Work tickets
4. Actual factory overhead incurred	Factory Overhead Incurred and Applied (dr.) Miscellaneous credits (cr.)	Factory overhead cost sheets Stores cards	Stores requisition, work tickets, utility bills, depreciation schedules
5. Factory overhead applied	Work-in-Process Inventory (dr.) Factory Overhead Incurred and Applied (cr.)	Job cost sheets	Schedule showing the determination of the predetermined factory overhead rate
6. Payment of salaries	Salaries Payable (dr.) Cash (cr.)		Clock cards
7. Completion of jobs	Finished Goods Inventory (dr.) Work-in-Process Inventory (cr.)	Job cost sheets	Cost of goods produced schedule
8. Sale of jobs: revenue	Accounts Receivable (dr.) Sales (cr.)	Accounts receivable subsidiary ledger	Invoice
9. Sale of jobs: costs	Cost of Goods Sold Expense (dr.) Finished Goods Inventory (cr.)	Job cost sheets	Cost of goods sold expense schedule

CHAPTER SUMMARY

Job order costing is used to account for the manufacture of identifiable units or batches, which are often produced to customer specifications. The costs of each unit or batch of units—the job—are carefully determined and kept separate from the costs of each other job.

The journal entries required in the job order costing method trace the flow of manufacturing costs from one production account to another:

Raw Materials Inventory	⟹	Work-in-Process Inventory	⟹	Finished Goods Inventory	⟹	Cost of Goods Sold Expense

The main subsidiary ledger account used in job order costing is the *job cost sheet,* which accumulates the product costs associated with each job. The total of all job cost sheets should be equal to the debit balance in Work-in-Process Inventory.

The costs of direct materials and direct labor are obviously related and easily traced to the different physical units of production. Therefore, the assignment of these costs to different jobs presents no difficulties. Factory overhead, however, is not related directly to units being produced throughout the year, and the actual overhead costs cannot be obviously or easily traced to the individual jobs. For this reason the factory overhead debited to Work-in-Process Inventory and assigned to the individual job cost sheets is the amount of *factory overhead applied* rather than the *actual* factory overhead incurred. The product costing system that applies overhead to the product using a predetermined rate, but includes the actual costs incurred for direct materials and direct labor, is called the *normal costing system.*

The overhead applied is debited to Work-in-Process Inventory and it is credited to *Factory Overhead Incurred and Applied.* The actual factory overhead costs incurred (rent, insurance, salaries, utilities, supplies, depreciation, repairs, etc.) are debited to Factory Overhead Incurred and Applied and are credited to a wide variety of miscellaneous accounts — such as Raw Materials Inventory, Accounts Payable, Unexpired Insurance, and Salaries Payable. The difference between the applied overhead and the actual overhead is called overapplied or underapplied overhead. If the applied exceeds the actual, it is *overapplied;* if the applied is less than the actual, it is *underapplied.* Overapplied overhead is represented by a credit balance in the account Factory Overhead Incurred and Applied; underapplied overhead is represented by a debit balance. The balance must be closed out at year-end, either entirely to Cost of Goods Sold Expense or allocated among Work-in-Process Inventory, Finished Goods Inventory, and Cost of Goods Sold Expense.

IMPORTANT TERMS USED IN THIS CHAPTER

Clock card   A source document that indicates the number of hours worked and salary earned by each employee during a pay period. (page 543)

Factory overhead applied (or assigned)   The overhead debited to Work-in-Process for product costing purposes. Applied overhead is determined by multiplying a predetermined factory overhead rate by the activity for the period. (page 540)

Factory overhead cost sheet   The subsidiary ledger for factory overhead incurred and applied. This sheet itemizes for each department the types of factory overhead costs incurred. (page 536)

Factory overhead incurred and applied   The general ledger account debited for factory overhead incurred and credited for factory overhead applied. (page 537)

Invoice   The source document for a purchase or sale. It indicates the quantity and cost of what is bought or sold. (page 530)

Job cost sheet   In job order costing, the basic document that accumulates the product costs associated with each job being worked on. The combination of all job cost sheets is the subsidiary ledger for work-in-process inventory. When units are completed and later sold, job cost sheets also provide the subsidiary ledgers for finished goods and cost of goods sold. (page 524)

Job order costing method   The method of accounting for the production of identifiable products, often to customer specifications. The costs of each job are carefully accumulated and kept separate from the costs of any other job. (page 522)

Normal costing A product costing system in which the product costs are the actual costs of direct materials and direct labor, plus the factory overhead applied using a predetermined rate. (page 522)

Overapplied overhead The difference between factory overhead applied and factory overhead incurred when factory overhead applied is the greater amount. (page 543)

Source document A document giving evidence of a transaction and the amount involved. (page 524)

Stores card A card indicating the receipts, withdrawals, and balance for each different type of raw material. The combination of all stores cards is the subsidiary ledger for raw materials inventory. (page 526)

Stores requisition A written request presented to the storekeeper by the operating department to acquire raw materials needed for production. (page 533)

Subsidiary ledger A file of accounts that provides the details of a general ledger account. The job cost sheets make up the subsidiary ledger for work-in-process inventory and the stores cards comprise the subsidiary ledger for raw materials inventory. (page 524)

Underapplied overhead The difference between factory overhead applied and factory overhead incurred when factory overhead incurred is greater. (page 543)

Work ticket A source document that indicates the time and salary a direct laborer spends on a specific job and the time and salary an indirect laborer spends in a particular department. (page 534)

QUESTIONS

1. Explain the differences between *job order costing* and *process costing.* Give several examples of industries in which each method would be used.

2. Name and describe the inventory subsidiary ledger accounts for a manufacturer.

3. Explain why actual factory overhead incurred is not debited to Work-in-Process as part of the product costing purpose of cost accounting.

4. What is *factory overhead applied?* How is it determined?

5. Why is a close approximation of the expected activity level so important for product costing?

6. What is *overapplied overhead? Underapplied overhead?*

7. What is the required accounting treatment for over- or underapplied overhead at year-end?

8. Explain several reasons why factory overhead might be overapplied at the end of the year.

9. "It makes little difference how a company measures activity when determining a predetermined factory overhead rate." Do you agree or disagree? Explain.

10. What is the purpose of the *job cost sheet?* What types of costs are recorded on job cost sheets?

11. Explain what we mean by the term *source document,* and describe at least three examples of source documents.

12. "Job order costing is the method used by most manufacturers of custom-made products to help control their operations." Discuss what is wrong with this statement.

13. If the Factory Overhead Incurred and Applied account has a debit balance at the end of a year, does this mean that the account received nothing but debits during the year? Is overhead overapplied or underapplied for the year? What adjustment do we make for the overapplied or underapplied balance at the end of each month? At the end of the year?

EXERCISES

Exercise 12-1
Calculating the
predetermined overhead
rate in different ways

On Jan. 1, 1989, the Walker Company estimates that the factory overhead for 1989 will be $500,000. It also estimates its direct labor-hours and direct labor costs for the year to be 100,000 hours and $250,000, respectively. During January 1989 Walker worked on two jobs, neither of which was completed on Jan. 31. The direct labor-hours worked in January were 7,000. The costs incurred in January were as follows:

Direct Labor:		
Job 1 (5,000 hr)	$ 12,500	
Job 2 (2,000 hr)	5,200	$ 17,700
Factory Overhead		50,000
Direct Materials:		
Job 1	$ 80,000	
Job 2	100,000	180,000

a. Determine the factory overhead assigned to each job if the actual overhead is split evenly between the jobs worked on.

b. Determine the factory overhead assigned to each job if the actual overhead is allocated to the jobs based upon the direct labor-hours used in January on each job.

(Check figure: Job 1 = $35,714)

c. Determine factory overhead assigned to each job if overhead is applied using a predetermined overhead rate, with the activity measured in terms of direct labor-hours.

(Check figure: Job 1 = $25,000)

d. Answer part **c** again, but assume that activity was measured in terms of direct labor-dollars.
e. Which approaches (**a** to **d**) would be recommended?
f. Was the factory overhead overapplied or underapplied in parts **c** and **d**? By what amounts?

Exercise 12-2
Determining product costs
for a job

The O'Drobinak Manufacturing Company uses the job order costing method. On Apr. 1 there were no incomplete jobs on hand. During April the following facts related to production:

Direct Materials	$50,000	Factory Overhead Incurred	$7,000
Direct Labor (1,000 hr)	20,000		

Factory overhead is applied using a predetermined rate of 40% of direct labor cost. None of the jobs worked on during April were finished at month-end.
a. Determine the Apr. 30 balance in Work-in-Process Inventory.   *(Check figure: $78,000)*
b. Determine the over- or underapplied overhead.

Exercise 12-3
Computing the over- or
underapplied overhead

During April 1988 Woody's Puppy Chow Company incurred the following manufacturing costs:

Direct Materials	$100,000	Factory Overhead	$275,000
Direct Labor (200,000 hr)	500,000		

Woody applies overhead to jobs at $1.50 per direct labor-hour.
   Determine the amount of over- or underapplied overhead for April.

(Check figure: $25,000)

Exercise 12-4
Evaluating the effect of
changing activity levels

On Jan. 1, 1988, Moonie Manufacturing accountant Jimmy James makes the following estimates for the year:

	Estimated Factory Overhead	Estimated Direct Labor-Hours
January...	$ 15,000	1,000
February..	20,000	2,000
March	30,000	4,000
.	.	.
.	.	.
July	85,000	15,000
.	.	.
.	.	.
.	.	.
December..	25,000	3,000
For the year	$375,000	50,000

During the months of February and July Moonie experiences the following:

	February	July
Actual factory overhead.......................................	$21,000	$81,000
Jobs worked on	2	4
Direct labor-hours:		
Job ·	.	.
.	.	.
.	.	.
6...	1,200	—
7...	600	—
.	.	.
.	.	.
21..	—	6,000
22..	—	4,000
23..	—	5,000
24..	—	1,000

Jobs 6 and 7 and 21 to 24 were the only jobs worked on during February and July, respectively.
a. Determine the overhead that would probably be assigned to job 6 in February and job 21 in July if Moonie was *not* using a predetermined factory overhead rate.
b. Answer part **a** again, this time assuming that Moonie does employ a predetermined factory overhead rate.
c. Determine the overapplied or underapplied factory overhead in February and in July.

(Check figure: July = $39,000)

Exercise 12-5
Working backward to
original estimate

The Wilkie Company employs a job order costing system and uses a predetermined factory overhead rate of 125% of direct labor-dollars. At the end of 1988 Wilkie's actual overhead incurred was $495,000, which resulted in $30,000 overapplied.
a. How much was spent by Wilkie in 1988 for direct labor?

(Check figure: $420,000)

b. If the *estimated* labor for the year had been $400,000, what would have been the estimated factory overhead costs for 1988, which were used to get the predetermined factory overhead rate on Jan. 1, 1988?

Exercise 12-6
Allocating product costs
between jobs

The Margie Wynn Advertising Agency uses a job order costing system for its different customer accounts. During January, the first month of operation, the agency accepted assignments from two customers, C. Huck and Melody Tune. The following costs were incurred:

Materials..	$ 6,000
Labor..	8,000
Overhead..	13,000

Wynn decided to employ a predetermined overhead rate of 200% of labor cost. The materials used were split evenly between the two jobs, but the labor was distributed two-thirds to the Huck job and one-third to the Melody Tune job.

Determine the costs assigned to each job for January.

(Check figure: Huck = $19,000)

Exercise 12-7
Analyzing factory
overhead incurred and
applied

The Talavera Company uses a predetermined overhead rate for product costing purposes of $2.50 per machine-hour. The following facts relate to 1988:

Direct labor-hours	$20,000	Factory overhead incurred......	$42,000
Machine-hours	18,000		

At year-end Talavera had the following balances in the production accounts:

Raw Materials Inventory	$20,000	Finished Goods Inventory	$50,000
Work-in-Process Inventory	30,000	Cost of Goods Sold Expense	70,000

a. Determine the over- or underapplied overhead for 1988.

(Check figure: $3,000)

b. Show the general ledger account for factory overhead incurred and applied.
c. Prepare the closing entry required if the over- or underapplied overhead is closed entirely to Cost of Goods Sold Expense.
d. Prepare the closing entry if the over- or underapplied overhead is allocated to the appropriate production accounts.

Exercise 12-8
Recognizing the
advantage of using
predetermined overhead
rates

Leonard Replicars uses the job order costing method to accumulate the product costs of its operation. At the beginning of 1989, when preparing a master budget for the year, the controller of Leonard, Dianna Donn, made the following projections for the year:

	Number of Jobs	Direct Labor-Hours	Total Factory Overhead
January	16	800	$ 7,500
February	16	850	8,050
March.......................................	17	1,000	8,500
April..	19	1,300	9,100
May	19	900	8,200
June	12	700	7,600
July...	12	600	7,300
August	11	600	7,000
September...................................	12	550	7,150
October	12	650	7,450
November....................................	13	700	7,600
December	12	750	7,750
	171	9,400	$93,200

At the end of the year Donn was quite surprised to learn that all the projections above came out exactly as planned.

a. Show numerically why it is preferable to apply factory overhead at a predetermined rate, rather than assigning the actual costs of each month to the jobs worked on.

b. Assume that jobs 60 and 125 were worked on during April and August, respectively, and that they were both replicas of the Ford Model T. Also assume the following information relates to these two jobs:

	Job 60	Job 125
Labor-hours worked	60	60
Direct-labor costs	$1,200	$1,200
Direct materials	$5,000	$5,000

In addition, assume that Leonard prices the "replicars" at a markup of 50% above cost. Determine the price of each car, assuming that the actual overhead costs of each month are assigned to the jobs on the basis of the number of labor-hours worked on each car.

c. Now repeat part **b** and determine the price of each car, assuming Leonard applies overhead costs based upon a predetermined annual rate (using labor-hours).

(Check figure = $10,192)

d. Explain why the prices determined in parts **b** and **c** are different.

**Exercise 12-9
Determining overhead
rates for several
departments**

Kinky Printers uses a job order costing system to account for the costs of each customer order. The costs of each order are the actual costs of materials and labor and the applied overhead. In the copying department overhead is applied on the basis of copy machine time; in the manual collating department overhead is applied on the basis of the number of pages collated; and in the stapling department overhead is applied on the basis of the number of items stapled. At the beginning of 1989 Kinky made the following projections for the year:

	Department		
	Copying	Manual Collating	Stapling
Copy machine time (hr)	8,320	na	na
Direct labor-hours	4,160	12,480	2,500
Number of pages to be processed	6,000,000	6,000,000	6,000,000
Number of items to be stapled	na	na	600,000
Shop overhead	$60,000	$15,000	$12,000

a. Determine the factory overhead rate for each department.

b. Job 45, for the Lake State Bank, went through each of the three departments, and the following results were determined:

Copy machine time	5 hours
Pages processed	3,500
Items stapled	1,100

What is the total cost of overhead applied to job 45?

c. The actual results for the year are given below. Determine the under- or overapplied overhead for each department for the year.

	Department		
	Copying	Manual Collating	Stapling
Copy machine time (hr)........................	8,500	na	na
Direct labor-hours..............................	4,400	12,000	2,300
Number of pages processed....................	5,800,000	5,800,000	5,800,000
Number of items stapled	na	na	500,000
Shop overhead	$61,000	$15,500	$11,000

(Check figure: Stapling = $1,000)

PROBLEMS: SET A

**Problem A12-1
Preparing journal entries
for job order costing**

The Stones Corporation is a manufacturer that uses the job order costing method of product costing. At the beginning of 1988 it had the following general ledger balances related to production:

Raw Materials Inventory		**Work-in-Process Inventory**	
1988		1988	
Jan. 1 200,000		Jan. 1 500,000	

Finished Goods Inventory	
1988	
Jan. 1 350,000	

The transactions for January 1988 are given below:
a. Raw materials purchased, $800,000
b. Indirect materials used in production, $25,000
c. Direct materials used in production, $750,000
d. Direct labor employed, $1,000,000 (200,000 hours)
e. Additional factory overhead incurred:

Indirect labor...............	$150,000	Property taxes	$10,000
Utilities....................	20,000	Prepaid insurance expired.....	5,000

f. Factory overhead applied, $1.25 per direct labor-hour
g. Cost of jobs completed, $2,100,000
h. Cost of jobs sold, $1,900,000
i. Sales revenue from jobs sold during January, $3,000,000

Required

1. Prepare the proper journal entry for each transaction given above.
2. Prepare a schedule determining the cost of goods sold for Stones.
3. Determine the Jan. 31 balance in each of the three inventory accounts.

(Check figure: Work-in-Process = $400,000)

Problem A12-2
Making journal entries
from T-account entries

Carson Comedy Shorts is a film production company that produces custom videotapes that are sold to businesses that are conducting seminars. At the more boring points in a seminar, when the lecturer sees people falling asleep and doodling on their desks, a short comedy routine is shown that pokes fun at the company management.

Carson uses a job order costing system to keep track of the orders from different companies. Its records for 1989 are shown below in T-account form:

Raw Materials Inventory

1989			
Jan. 1	27,000	Direct Mat.	105,000
Purchases	100,000	Ind. Mat.	16,000
Dec. 31	6,000		

Factory Overhead Incurred and Applied

Ind. Mat.	16,000	Fac. Over.	
Ind. Labor	20,000	Applied	75,000
Insurance	3,000		
Deprec.	8,000		
Closing Entry	28,000		
	75,000		75,000

Work-in-Process Inventory

1989			
Jan. 1	45,000	Cost of Goods	
Direct Mat.	105,000	Completed	340,000
Direct Labor	150,000	Allocated	
Fac. Over.		Overhead	1,985
Applied	75,000		
Dec. 31	33,015		

Salaries Payable

Salaries Paid	165,000	1989	
		Jan. 1	3,000
		Direct Labor	150,000
		Ind. Labor	20,000
		Dec. 31	8,000

Finished Goods Inventory

1989			
Jan. 1	55,000	Cost of Goods	
Cost of Goods		Sold	370,000
Completed	340,000	Allocated	
		Overhead	1,640
Dec. 31	23,360		

Prepaid Insurance

1989			
Jan. 1	12,000	Insurance Used	3,000
Dec. 31	9,000		

Cost of Goods Sold Expense

	370,000	Allocated	
		Overhead	24,375
	345,625		

Accumulated Depreciation

		1989	
		Jan. 1	45,000
		Deprec.	10,000
		Dec. 31	55,000

Required

From the information shown above in the T-accounts for Carson, prepare all the journal entries that were made during the year.

**Problem A12-3
Completing the
T-accounts for job order
costing**

The Banks Publishing Co. publishes yearbooks for high schools and universities, and it uses a job order costing system to keep track of the orders from different schools. It keeps its records in T-accounts, which are shown below in incomplete form for 1989:

Raw Materials Inventory					Factory Overhead Incurred and Applied			
1989								
Jan. 1	20,000	Direct Mat.	130,000		Ind. Mat.	?	Fac. Over.	
Purchases	?	Ind. Mat.	10,000		Ind. Labor	100,000	Applied	?
					Insurance	?		
Dec. 31	60,000				Deprec.	?		
					Other	30,000		
						?		?

Work-in-Process Inventory					Salaries Payable			
1989							1989	
Jan. 1	150,000	Cost of Goods			Salaries Paid	280,000	Jan. 1	16,000
Direct Mat.	?	Completed	?				Direct Labor	200,000
Direct Labor	?						Ind. Labor	?
Fac. Over.								
Applied	?						Dec. 31	?
Dec. 31	120,000							

Finished Goods Inventory					Prepaid Insurance			
1989					1989			
Jan. 1	120,000	Cost of Goods			Jan. 1	6,000	Insurance Used	2,000
Cost of Goods		Sold	360,000					
Completed	?				Dec. 31	4,000		
Dec. 31	?							

Cost of Goods Sold Expense			Accumulated Depreciation		
			1989		
?			Jan. 1		30,000
			Deprec.		?
			Dec. 31		34,000

Additional Information
a. All purchases are for cash.
b. Factory overhead is applied at a rate of 70% of direct labor cost.
c. No fixed assets are retired during 1989.

Required   Complete the T-accounts above by filling in the missing blanks.

(Check figure: Cost of goods completed = $500,000)

**Problem A12-4
Making journal entries and
posting to subsidiary
ledger**

At the end of 1987 the Wetden Publishing Company was working with potential authors on a single new project which is expected to be completed in 1988. Wetden makes use of the job costing method of accounting for its projects. The job cost sheet for the current project appears as follows on Dec. 31, 1987:

Job No. _____121_____

Author(s) _____Icerman_____

Date Started _____1987_____Date Completed _____

Date	Direct Materials	Direct Labor		Overhead		Total
		Hours	Cost	Rate	Amount	
1987	$5,000	100	$1,000	$2 per direct labor-hour	$200	$6,200

During 1988 (1) two additional projects were begun (jobs 122 and 123) for authors Black and Heck, respectively; (2) jobs 121 and 122 were finished; and (3) job 121 was sold. The following transactions took place during 1988:

```
Purchase of Raw Materials...........................................  $60,000
Usage of Direct Materials:
    Job 121.............................................  $25,000
    Job 122.............................................   20,000
    Job 123.............................................    6,000    51,000
Direct Labor:
    Job 121 (1,500 hr).................................  $15,000
    Job 122 (1,450 hr).................................   15,000
    Job 123 (220 hr)...................................    2,000    32,000
Factory Overhead Incurred:
    Indirect labor .....................................   $3,000
    Supplies ...........................................    1,500
    Rent ...............................................    1,000     5,500
```

Additional Information
a. Projects are priced to sell at 40% above their cost.
b. Overhead is assigned to jobs using a predetermined overhead rate, based upon the number of direct labor-hours worked.

Required

1. Prepare the journal entries to record the transactions for 1988.
b. Prepare job cost sheets for the three jobs.

(Check figure: Job 123 = $8,440)

3. Determine the over- or underapplied overhead for 1988.

(Check figure: $840)

Problem A12-5
Determining ending
balances in inventory

The Zvirblis Company produces customized farm equipment, and it uses the job order costing method to keep track of its different orders. Zvirblis applies factory overhead to each job (using direct labor-hours) on the basis of an overhead rate determined at the beginning of the year. At the end of January 1988 Zvirblis is working on two jobs. The cost information related to these two jobs is as follows:

	Job 105	Job 106
Direct Materials.	$ 4,000	$5,000
Direct Labor (at $5/hr)	10,000	9,500
Factory Overhead Applied	7,000	6,650

During February the following direct costs were incurred to continue work on jobs 105 and 106 and to start job 107:

	Job 105	Job 106	Job 107
Direct Materials	$3,000	$4,000	$3,000
Direct Labor (at $5/hr)	2,625	4,200	6,300

The factory overhead incurred in February was $10,000.

Jobs 105 and 106 were finished during February, and job 105 was sold for $35,000. There were no completed jobs in finished goods on Feb. 1.

Required

1. Determine the Feb. 28 balances in Work-in-Process and Finished Goods and the Cost of Goods Sold for February.
2. Calculate the over- or underapplied overhead for February.

(Check figure: $812)

Problem A12-6
Answering variety of
miscellaneous questions

The Ware Company uses a job order costing system and had one incomplete job (no. 21) on Jan. 1, 1988:

	Job 21
Direct Materials	$20,000
Direct Labor	16,000
Factory Overhead.	8,000
	$44,000

The Jan. 1, 1988, balances in Raw Materials and Supplies and in Finished Goods were $8,000 and $37,000, respectively.

On Jan. 1 Ware estimated direct labor and factory overhead for three possible levels of activity for 1988:

	Pessimistic	Most Likely	Optimistic
Expected labor:			
Hours	60,000	70,000	80,000
Dollars.	$1,020,000	$1,190,000	$1,360,000
Estimated overhead	$ 560,000	$ 630,000	$ 700,000

Overhead is applied on the basis of direct labor-hours.

During January the following costs were incurred:

Purchases:		
Raw Materials.	$28,000	
Supplies	5,000	$33,000
Requisitions:		
Raw Materials:		
Job 21.	$ 3,000	
Job 22.	16,000	
Supplies	7,000	26,000
Production Labor:		
Used on Job 21 (200 hr).	$ 3,500	
Used on Job 22 (800 hr).	13,000	
Foremen's Salaries (120 hr)	1,440	
Maintenance (200 hr)	1,500	
Security (80 hr).	800	20,240
Other Factory Costs:		
Insurance.	$ 800	
Property Taxes	900	
Utilities	450	2,150

Job 21 was finished in January and sold for $75,000. Job 22 was unfinished on Jan. 31, 1988.

Required

1. What was the Jan. 31 balance in Raw Materials and Supplies?
2. If the Jan. 31 balance in Finished Goods was zero, what was the cost of goods sold for January?

(Check figure: $89,300)

3. How much was debited to Work-in Process during January?
4. What was the under- or overapplied overhead for January 1988?

Problem A12-7
Allocating over- or
underapplied overhead

McMurtneys Used Car Lot purchases wrecked cars at a local auction and then does whatever is necessary to get them to run. McMurtneys then prices them at a 100% markup over cost. Shown below is information relating to five different cars that McMurtneys handled during its first month of operation. At month-end two were sold, two were in the process of being repaired, and one was on the lot awaiting sale.

	Edsel	Studabaker	Imperial	Rambler	Vega
Auction price.	$250	$250	$350	$250	$ 200
Materials needed for repairs	150	375	800	125	1,000
Labor repair costs	300	300	450	80	550
Overhead applied	150	150	225	40	275
Status.	Sold	In process	In process	Sold	Ready for sale

Factory overhead is applied on the basis of direct labor-dollars. The actual overhead incurred for the month was $1,000.

Required

1. Determine the over- or underapplied overhead for the month.
2. If over- or underapplied overhead is not allocated, what is the total cost of each job in the ending balance in Work-in-Process, Finished Goods, and Cost of Goods Sold?
3. Assume in this part that the over- or underapplied overhead is allocated on the basis of the total costs in Work-in-Process, Finished Goods, and Cost of Goods Sold. Determine the total cost (after allocation) of each job in the ending balance in Work-in-Process, Finished Goods, and Cost of Goods Sold.

(Check figure: Finished goods = $2,077)

4. Assume in this part that the over- or underapplied overhead is allocated on the basis of the overhead that was applied to the jobs in Work-in-Process, Finished Goods, and Cost of Goods Sold. Determine the total cost (after allocation) of each job in the ending balance in Work-in-Process, Finished Goods, and Cost of Goods Sold.

Problem A12-8
Determining standard
costs and variances with
job order costing

Graffiti, Inc., is a sign company that has been approached by a customer, Russell Adams Realty, to bid on a job for new signs for all the realty's branch offices. Graffiti uses a standard costing system for product costing, for job pricing, and for controlling its operations. Typically, Graffiti prices its work to ensure a markup of 100% of its standard cost of production.

After careful consideration, the controller of Graffiti came up with the following standards for each of the 10 signs:

Direct Materials:
 Plastic .... 150 square feet per sign @ $6 per square foot
 Steel Pole . 2,000 pounds per pole @ $0.70 per pound
Direct Labor 100 hours per sign @ $7 per hour
Overhead ... 100 hours per sign @ $3 per hour

Adams was satisfied with the price and ordered the 10 signs from Graffiti.

Six weeks later, when the signs were finished and delivered, the controller for Graffiti accumulated the following information concerning the actual costs of producing the 10 signs:

Plastic (1,650 sq ft) .... $10,000   Direct Labor (1,150 hr) $7,000
Steel (19,000 lb). 14,000   Overhead. 5,000

Required

1. What is the total standard cost of producing one sign?
2. How much was Adams charged for the 10 signs?

(Check figure: $66,000)

3. Determine the following variances for the 10 signs:

 ■ Direct materials price and quantity variances for each direct material
 ■ Direct labor price and quantity variances
 ■ Under- or overapplied overhead

4. Prepare a statement showing the gross profit for Graffiti for this order. Show all variances as an adjustment to Cost of Goods Sold.

PROBLEMS: SET B

Problem B12-1
Preparing journal entries
for job order costing

The Custom Couch Company produces luxury couches from customer specifications. On Jan. 1, 1988, the accountant, Jamie Lou, determined the following balances in the company's inventories:

Raw Materials Inventory $425,000
Work-in-Process Inventory. 820,000
Finished Goods Inventory 300,000

Required

For each transaction below, you are to do the following:
1. Make the required journal entry.
2. Indicate the subsidiary ledger(s) and source document(s) that would be affected by the transaction.
3. Determine the new inventory balances on Jan. 31.

Transactions
a. Materials were purchased in the amount of $1,000,000.
b. Materials used in production were direct materials, $700,000, and indirect materials, $100,000.

    c. Labor used in production amounted to $300,000 for direct labor and $175,000 for indirect labor.

    d. Miscellaneous items included:

Utilities	$18,000
Insurance	7,000
Depreciation	6,500

    e. Factory overhead is applied at a rate of 80% of direct labor cost.

    f. The jobs completed totaled $1,650,000.

    g. The sales revenue for January was $3,000,000, and the cost of jobs sold was $1,700,000.

Problem B12-2
Posting journal entries to T-accounts

The journal entries that were made during 1988 (actually the summation of 12 sets of entries for the year) for the Letterman Stage Props Company are given below. Letterman uses the job order costing method to keep track of its various projects.

	Debit	Credit
1. Raw Materials Inventory	104,000	
Accounts Payable		104,000
2. Work-in-Process	98,000	
Factory Overhead Incurred and Applied	7,000	
Raw Materials Inventory		105,000
3. Factory Overhead Incurred and Applied	84,100	
Utilities Payable		21,100
Accumulated Depreciation		18,000
Salaries Payable		20,000
Property Taxes Payable		25,000
4. Work-in-Process	120,000	
Salaries Payable		120,000
5. Work-in-Process	40,000	
Factory Overhead Incurred and Applied		40,000
6. Finished Goods	205,000	
Work-in-Process		205,000
7. Cost of Goods Sold	210,000	
Finished Goods		210,000
8. Accounts Receivable	300,000	
Sales Revenue		300,000
9. Work-in-Process	15,800	
Finished Goods	4,285	
Cost of Goods Sold	31,015	
Factory Overhead Incurred and Applied		51,100

In addition, the beginning balances for the year in the three inventory accounts were:

Raw Materials	$ 22,000
Work-in-Process	54,000
Finished Goods	34,000
	$110,000

Required

1. Post all the journal entries for Letterman in T-accounts.

2. Determine the ending balances in all three inventory accounts and for Cost of Goods Sold.

(Check figure: Work-in-process = $122,800

Problem B12-3
Completing T-accounts

The Bailey Company, which employs the job order costing method of accounting for its inventories, had the following incomplete general ledger accounts at the end of 1989:

Raw Materials Inventory

1989			
Jan. 1	60,000	Materials	
Purchases	210,000	Used	201,000
Dec. 31	?		

Work-in-Process Inventory

1989			
Jan. 1	96,000	Completed and	
Direct Mat.	?	Transferred	
Direct			?
Labor	264,000		
Fac. Over.			
Applied	?		
Dec. 31	?		

Finished Goods Inventory

1989			
Jan. 1	?	Sold	?
Completed	600,000		
Dec. 31	75,000		

Cost of Goods Sold Expense

Sold	645,000		

Accounts Payable

		1989		
Paid	216,000	Jan. 1	6,000	
		Purchases	210,000	
		Dec. 31	?	

Factory Overhead Incurred and Applied

Ind. Labor	?			
Insurance	90,000	Applied	?	
Deprec.	51,000			
Misc.	48,000			
	294,000		?	

Accrued Salaries Payable

		1989		
Paid	363,000	Jan. 1	3,000	
		Dir. Labor	?	
		Ind. Labor	105,000	
		Dec. 31	?	

Additional Information

a. All purchases are made on account, and no returns were made to the supplier.

b. All raw materials are used directly in production.

c. Factory overhead was predicted to be $300,000 for 1989. The predetermined overhead rate was computed using direct labor-hours for activity. The direct labor-hours were estimated as 60,000 for the year. The actual hours for 1989 were 66,000.

Required

Complete the T-accounts above by filling in the missing blanks.

(Check figure: Factory overhead applied = $330,000)

Problem B12-4
Preparing journal entries
and posting to subsidiary
ledger

The LeRoy Roswell Company accepts special orders from customers to acquire and renovate classic cars. January 1988 was the first month of operation, and at month-end one job (no. 1) was in Work-in-Process Inventory. Its job cost sheet appeared as follows:

Job No. ___1___

Customer ___Keith Watson___

Date Started ___1/13/88___   Date Completed _____

Date	Direct Materials	Direct Labor	Overhead Rate	Overhead Amount	Total
Jan.	$3,200	$2,100	60% of direct labor	$1,260	$6,560

During February materials costing $60,000 were bought on account, and on Feb. 7 two additional orders were accepted (jobs 2 and 3) from Mr. Watson. The following costs were incurred to renovate the three cars:

Direct Materials:		
Job 1..	$10,000	
Job 2..	18,000	
Job 3..	3,000	$31,000
Direct Labor:		
Job 1..	$12,000	
Job 2..	30,000	
Job 3..	4,500	46,500
Actual Factory Overhead:		
Indirect Labor..	$ 8,000	
Supplies..	3,000	
Utilities	3,000	
Insurance...	2,000	
Rent	6,000	22,000

Job 1 was completed and sold on Feb. 14; job 2 was completed on Feb. 18. Sales are made at a markup of 80% above cost.

Overhead is assigned to jobs with a predetermined overhead rate, using direct labor costs as the measure of activity.

Required

1. Prepare the journal entries to record the transactions for February.
2. Prepare job cost sheets for the three jobs.

(Check figure: Job 3 = $10,200)

3. Prepare a factory overhead cost sheet for the renovation department.
4. Determine the over- or underapplied overhead for February.

(Check figure: $5,900)

Problem B12-5
Determining the costs of
several jobs

Clyde Smith is in the home construction business and is usually working on several custom homes at one time. On July 1, 1989, Clyde was working on homes for Ray Moody and Ralph Trottier. The costs assigned to these homes on July 1 were as follows:

	Moody	Trottier
Direct Materials	$52,000	$61,000
Direct Labor:		
Hours......................................	2,000	4,200
Dollars.....................................	$16,000	$34,650
Factory Overhead Applied as % of Direct Labor Costs	$ 3,360	$ 7,277

During July Smith completed the Moody home and started work on a new home for Mark Pace. The costs incurred during July were:

	Client		
	Moody	Trottier	Pace
Direct Materials.....................................	$10,000	$25,000	$20,000
Direct Labor:			
Hours..	200	1,000	800
Dollars.......................................	$15,700	$ 8,200	$ 8,000

The factory overhead incurred during the month was $2,800.

Required

1. Determine the Cost of Goods Sold Expense for July (assume Smith is recognizing all revenues and expenses at completion). *(Check figure: $100,357)*

2. Determine the balances in Work-in-Process and in Finished Goods on July 31.

3. Calculate the over- or underapplied overhead for July.

Problem B12-6
Answering a variety of miscellaneous questions for job order costing

Tammy Haskins runs a small CPA firm and has several clients at any one time. She determines her fee for each client by taking a 25% markup, on top of the costs of materials, direct labor, and office overhead applied. Haskins applies overhead to jobs on the basis of direct labor-hours.

On Jan. 1, 1988, Haskins predicted that the office overhead would be $22,750 for the year. She also figured that the direct labor-hours would be 2,600 ($31,200).

On Dec. 1, 1988, Haskins's firm had only one client, Towne, and the costs associated with that client were as follows:

Materials...	$ 250
Direct Labor	1,900
Office Overhead Applied..	1,400
	$3,550

During January two new clients, Fonte and Christie, were found, and the following costs were incurred:

Materials Purchased..		$ 500
Materials Used:		
On Towne Job	$ 50	
On Fonte Job	150	
On Christie Job...	95	295
Labor:		
Secretary (160 hr)...	$ 400	
Accountants:		
Used on Towne Job (20 hr).................................	250	
Used on Fonte Job (120 hr).................................	1,450	
Used on Christie Job (85 hr)	1,000	
Clean-up Crew (40 hr).....................................	100	3,200

(continued)

Other Costs:		
Rent	$ 500	
Insurance	100	
Utilities...	150	750

The Towne job was completed and billed. The Fonte and Christie jobs were incomplete on Dec. 31. The direct labor and office overhead for the first 11 months of 1988 were $28,000 (2,300 hours) and $20,000, respectively.

Required

1. Determine how much was debited to Work-in-Process during December.
2. What was the balance in Work-in-Process on Dec. 31?   *(Check figure: $4,489)*
3. What was the over- or underapplied overhead for December? For the entire year?
4. What was the sales revenue for Haskins in December?

Problem B12-7
Allocating over- or
underapplied overhead in
different ways

Michaelangelo's Paint Shop, which specializes in new paint jobs for old sports cars, is in its second month of operation. Michaelangelo maintains records about the costs of each paint job on individual job cost sheets. On Dec. 1 (starting the second month of operation), Michaelangelo has two jobs that are finished and awaiting pickup by their owners. The job cost sheets for these two showed the following facts:

	Crockett's Ferrari	Magnum's Porsche
Materials	$3,000	$2,700
Direct Labor....................................	1,500 (60 hr)	1,800 (90 hr)
Overhead Applied (based on direct labor-hours).......	2,400	3,600
	$6,900	$8,100

The other cars painted by Michaelangelo in November had already been picked up by their owners during the month. The total cost associated with these jobs was $40,000 ($16,000 for materials, $9,000 for direct labor, and $15,000 for overhead).

During December four additional jobs were taken on by Michaelangelo, three of which were still being worked on at the end of the month. The fourth job (Steel's 300ZX) was finished, but had not been picked up or paid for by the customer by the end of December. This job was the only one remaining in finished goods on Dec. 31. Selected information from the job cost sheets for the four jobs worked on in December is given below:

	Rockford's Firebird	Milner's Corvette	Magnum's 75 T-Bird	Steel's 300ZX
Materials................................	$1,000	$1,600	$3,000	$2,200
Direct Labor:				
Hours..................................	40	50	75	65
Dollars................................	$ 900	$1,200	$1,800	$1,600
Overhead	$1,600	$2,000	$3,000	$2,600

The actual overhead incurred for the first 2 months of operation was $17,000.

Required

1. Determine the over- or underapplied overhead for the first 2 months of operation.
2. Assume that the year-end is Dec. 31 and that the over- or underapplied overhead is not allocated. **(a)** Make the closing entry for overhead; and **(b)** determine the total costs that are in the ending balance in Work-in-Process, Finished Goods, and Cost of Goods Sold.

3. Assume in this part that the over- or underapplied overhead is allocated on the basis of the total costs in Work-in-Process, Finished Goods, and Cost of Goods Sold. Determine the total costs (after allocation) that are in Work-in-Process, Finished Goods, and Cost of Goods Sold on Dec. 31.

(Check figure: Work-in-Process: $13,358)

4. Assume in this part that the over- or underapplied overhead is allocated on the basis of the overhead costs that were applied to jobs that are now in Work-in-Process, Finished Goods, and Cost of Goods Sold. Determine the total costs (after allocation) that are in Work-in-Process, Finished Goods, and Cost of Goods Sold on Dec. 31.

**Problem B12-8
Determining standard
costs and variances with
job order costing**

Fantasy Van Customizers specializes in customizing stripped-down vans into "rolling pleasure palaces." Fantasy uses standard costing to help price each different order. In addition, it finds that standard costs help to control its operations.

Fantasy agreed to customize 50 new vans during the next year for a local car dealer, Iapepsi Motors. Iapepsi was willing to pay for the job on a cost-plus-10% basis, and although Fantasy normally charges a 30% markup, it accepted this job at the lower markup. This was because Iapepsi promised to give Fantasy a lot of business next year at Fantasy's typical markup if this year's renovations are acceptable and if demand for the vans is great enough to make the venture profitable to Iapepsi.

Fantasy's accountant was able to come up with the following standards for each van:

Carpet............	5 square yards @ $25 per square yard
Velour............	6 square yards @ $10 per square yard
Captain's chairs	6 @ $300 per chair
Direct labor........	20 hours @ $15 per hour
Overhead applied...	20 hours @ $4 per hour

After the 50 vans had been completed, the owner of Fantasy, Ima Scuzzball, asked the accountant to tell her how much profit the company actually made on the deal. The accountant, Rock Farley, accumulated the following facts about the actual costs of the customizing that was done for Iapepsi:

Carpet..........	300 square yards @ $20 per square yard
Velour	285 square yards @ $11 per square yard
Captain's chairs ..	300 @ $325 per chair
Direct labor......	985 hours @ $15.50 per hour
Overhead........	$3,500

Required

1. What is the total standard cost of customizing one van?
2. How much was Iapepsi charged for the 50 vans?
3. Determine the following variances for the 50 vans:
   a. Direct materials price and quantity variances for each direct material
   b. Direct labor price and quantity variances
   c. Under- or overapplied overhead
4. Prepare a statement showing the gross profit for Fantasy for this order. Show all variances as an adjustment to cost of goods sold.

(Check figure: Gross profit = $4,672.50)

CHAPTER 13

Product Costing Methods Part II: Process Costing

After you have completed studying this chapter, you should be able to:

- Understand job order costing and process costing, and know the differences between them
- Explain what is meant by an *equivalent whole unit* and apply this concept to the different types of product costs
- Organize a process costing problem into its three basic steps, and understand the relationship of each step to the other
- Explain the difference between the *FIFO* and *weighted average* methods of product costing
- Prepare a production report and a summary of costs report using the FIFO method of product costing
- Prepare a production report and a summary of costs report with the weighted average method of product costing
- Prepare a production report and a summary of costs report using standard costing

In Chapter 12 we covered in detail *job order costing,* which is used to account for the costs of a manufactured product whenever:

1. There are only a small number of units or batches of units being produced.
2. Each unit or batch is probably being produced according to customer specifications.
3. Each unit or batch is easily distinguishable from any other unit or batch.

It was necessary for us to accumulate costs by job and to keep the costs of one job separate from the costs of each other job.

In this chapter we will look in detail at *process costing,* which you'll quickly realize is quite different from job order costing. In process costing it is not necessary for us to identify individual source documents (such as work tickets and materials requisitions) with specific jobs; nor will we need to maintain job cost sheets. In essence, it is not necessary to calculate exactly the cost of each unit individually — because all the units we're working on will be basically the same, and the cost of one unit will be identical to the cost of every other unit produced.

THE PROCESS COSTING METHOD

Process costing is used to determine the cost of units that:

1. Are produced continuously in large batches

2. Are indistinguishable from one another

Industries using process costing

The "process" of manufacturing units like these comprises a sequence of several manufacturing steps, each step discernible from the others. For instance, juice in a citrus processing plant first passes through a process in which the fruit is squeezed, the juice is strained for seeds and pulp, and the juice is chilled. In the next process the juice is bottled in presterilized containers, which are sealed or capped. Finally, the bottles are packaged in boxes or cartons and sent to finished goods to await sale. Process costing is also used to account for "processed" products such as cement, paint, oil products, chemicals, flour, and pharmaceuticals.

Through process costing, we can determine not only the costs to be assigned to finished units but also the costs to be assigned at each manufacturing step for partially completed units. But, as you may well imagine, we don't use job order costing to determine the cost to be assigned to 1 gallon of orange juice or to 1 bottle of champagne. We don't try to determine the exact cost of any one unit produced in a process. Because all units are identical in a process manufacturing situation, it would be pointless to even try to distinguish the cost of one unit from the cost of any other unit.

WHERE ELSE TO MAKE BATS BUT AT COOPERSTOWN

"Like peanuts and popcorn at a ballgame, a bat company in Cooperstown just seemed like a natural."

Thousands of baseball fans come to Cooperstown, New York, each year to see baseball's Hall of Fame. Naturally many of them hope to leave this exciting museum town with a souvenir, and what would be more appropriate than a baseball bat that was made right there in Cooperstown.

"The idea sort of evolved," said Don Oberriter from their rented garage on Chestnut Street where many of the bats are finished. "We're asked a lot of questions . . . especially by tourists and one of the questions was 'what do they make here in town I can bring back as a souvenir?' Some wanted to know where they could buy a bat because they promised someone they would bring back a bat from Cooperstown."

On the basis of this interest and two years of research, the Oberriters finally

opened the doors to Cooperstown Bat Company. Although the Oberriters were ready to make bats, unfortunately they had no idea how to make them. As a result there was very little success in the early stages of the production process. Only one bat in ten was good enough to be sold. Eventually however, with much more education, experience, and perseverance, the company improved its process to the point where it is now able to get 99 good bats out of a hundred. Once the company got the hang of it, the Oberriters have been able to double production each year and they have finally reached a point where they're showing a profit.

The Oberriters advertise their bats as being made from the finest northern ash. But what sets them apart from other bat companies is the creative touch they apply. The first bats had the bat company logo and a simple message:

Cooperstown

The Hall of Fame

Since then they have expanded their line of bats to include little league bats, softball bats, and commemorative bats. The commemorative bat line "started by doing a likeness of Abner Doubleday on it. Then one of Ebbett's Field in Brooklyn and Shibe Park in Philadelphia."

Next, the Oberriters realized that even though many of the people who buy their bats would end up playing with them, many more would want to hang them on their walls. This led to their latest complementary product line—bat racks. And who knows what else they might try.

Source: Ken Tingley, Sports Editor, "Cooperstown Bat Company Is a Natural," *The Daily Star,* August 1, 1986, p. 26.

What quantity should we use to get the cost per unit?

Instead, what we do in process costing is (1) determine the total production costs for an entire period, (2) determine the number of units produced during that period, and (3) divide the total costs by the units in production to get a cost per unit—which will be the same cost for each unit produced during that period. The key to understanding and using process costing is to realize exactly what we mean by the number of units produced.

Let's look first at an unrealistic but simple example of process costing. Then we will introduce some considerations that will make it more realistic, but less simple.

Example 13-1

A very simple example

THE TRUVILLION COMPANY

The Truvillion Company produces an item that is processed through only one manufacturing stage. At the end of that one process the units are complete and are transferred to finished goods. During August 80,000 units were started and completed, and $80,000 of production costs were incurred. There were no beginning or ending inventories of work-in process for the month. The cost per unit for Truvillion in August is simply:

$$\text{Cost per unit} = \$80,000 \div 80,000 \text{ units} = \$1$$

What made Example 13-1 so simple is that there were no beginning or ending inventories of work-in process. In other words, all the units that were started during the period were also completed by the end of the period. Now let's assume that not all the units are completed by the end of the period. That means there will be an ending inventory of work-in-process.

Example 13-2

A little tougher example

THE TRUVILLION COMPANY

Assume that for the Truvillion Company (1) there was no beginning inventory of work-in-process; (2) 80,000 units were started during August; (3) 76,000 units were completed by the end of the month; (4) the 4,000 incomplete units were left one-half completed; and (5) the production costs during the month were $78,000, and they were incurred evenly throughout the manufacturing process.

We don't use units started

Now, how do we calculate the cost per unit?

Do we divide the production costs of $78,000 by the 80,000 units started? No, because this would assign the same amount of cost to each of the units that are completed as would be assigned to each of the units that are only one-half completed.

We don't use units completed

Do we divide the $78,000 by the 76,000 units that were completed? No, because the $78,000 of production costs also helped to process the 4,000 units. Therefore, some of the costs should be assigned to the 4,000 units and not just to the 76,000 units.

We do use equivalent whole units

Here is the key: We have to give some consideration to the partially finished units—but not as much as to the completely finished units. We have to divide the $78,000 by the finished units plus some portion of the unfinished units. If the 4,000 units were exactly half-finished at the end of the period, then the work—and the costs—that went into them is equivalent to the work and costs that go into 2,000 finished units.

Thus, if we add together the finished units and the equivalent number of finished units that are still in process, we can spread the total costs over the "appropriate quantity" of units produced — the equivalent whole units. Here's how:

$$\underset{\text{units}}{76{,}000 \text{ completed}} + \left(\underset{\text{process}}{4{,}000 \text{ in}} \times \tfrac{1}{2} \text{ complete} \right) = \underset{\text{whole units}}{78{,}000 \text{ equivalent}}$$

$$\underset{\text{unit}}{\text{Cost per}} = \$78{,}000 \div \underset{\text{whole units}}{78{,}000 \text{ equivalent}} = \underset{\text{whole unit}}{\$1 \text{ per equivalent}}$$

Equivalent whole units is a new concept, which you must understand in order to learn the process costing method.

Equivalent Whole Units

The 80,000 units can be represented graphically, as shown:

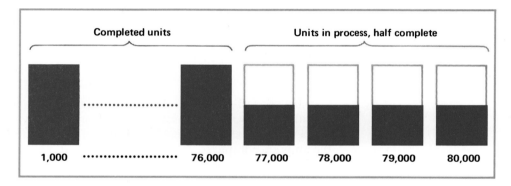

The first 76,000 units are completed and are represented as fully shaded boxes. The 4,000 half-complete units are represented by boxes that are half-shaded. The 4,000 half-shaded boxes are the equivalent of 2,000 fully shaded boxes. There is a total of 78,000 shaded boxes — 76,000 fully shaded and 4,000 half-shaded. The 78,000 boxes represent 78,000 equivalent whole units.

A Full Dosage of Costs

Equivalent units: a full dosage of costs

A good way to think of an equivalent whole unit is in terms of a "full dosage of costs." A completed unit requires 100% of all the costs needed to make it — saying it another way, a full dosage of cost must be added or incurred to make a whole unit. In the preceding example full dosages have been added to each of the 76,000 units to complete them. Each of the 4,000 half-completed units has only one-half of a full dosage of cost. If these 4,000 half-dosages of costs had been incurred instead to make only completed units, then the 4,000 half-dosages of costs would be equivalent to 2,000 full dosages of costs. The combination of 76,000 full dosages and 4,000 half-dosages produces 78,000 equivalent full dosages — or 78,000 equivalent whole units.

In Example 13-2 we assumed for simplicity that all production costs (direct materials, direct labor, and factory overhead) were incurred evenly throughout the production process. In the next example, and in most problems, this will be assumed for direct labor and factory overhead (conversion costs) but not for direct materials. Direct materials are usually assumed to be added in a lump sum rather than in a continuous manner throughout production.

Basic Steps in the Process Costing Method

With these simple examples we have presented some basic ideas about how to determine the cost of units produced in a process. Now we will look in much greater detail at the accounting procedures involved in process costing. The basic steps are:

Three basic steps to process costing

1. ***Tracing the physical flow***   In this step we determine two things: the number of units completed during the period and the number of incomplete units still in production at the end of the period (the ending inventory).

2. ***Preparing the production report***   On the basis of the completed units and the ending inventory of work-in-process, which we determined in step 1, we next calculate three things within the production report: the equivalent whole units, the total costs to account for, and the cost per equivalent whole unit.

3. ***Preparing the summary of costs report***   After the production report has been completed, we need to distribute the total costs to account for between these two groups of units: (1) the completed units and (2) the units in the ending inventory of work-in-process. We show this distribution in the ***summary of costs report.***

The Comprehensive Illustration

The following example will demonstrate the three steps we have just discussed.

Example 13-3

THE SPURRIER BALL COMPANY

The Spurrier Ball Company produces footballs that pass through two processing departments before they are completed. In the first department cowhide is cut and sewn into a football. In the second department the balls are pumped with air and boxed. The steps in this production process are represented by the following diagram:

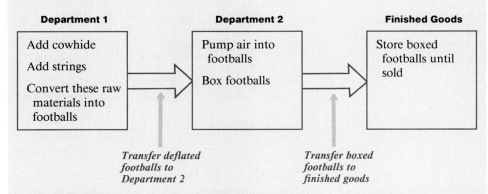

Information concerning Department 1 is presented at this point. Additional information concerning Department 2 will be provided after the discussion of Department 1 is completed.

Two different raw materials are needed in Department 1. Cowhide is added at the beginning, and the strings are added when the work required on the footballs is one-half complete. Conversion costs (direct labor plus factory overhead) are incurred evenly throughout production.

*There are no beginning
inventories in this example*

> On Aug. 1 there were no unfinished footballs in work-in-process. During August 40,000 footballs were started. On Aug. 31 there was an ending inventory of 20,000 footballs, each one exactly three-quarters complete.
>
> The costs incurred during the month of August were as follows:

Costs incurred during August:	
Cowhide	$120,000
Strings	20,000
Conversion costs	148,750
Total costs to account for	$288,750

As Example 13-3 indicates, there are no incomplete footballs in process in Department 1 on Aug. 1. For simplicity we are making this assumption for our initial set of exhibits. At a later point we will introduce a beginning inventory and point out just how it complicates matters.

Basic Steps for Department 1 — Assuming No Beginning Inventory

We will now go through the three basic steps for the Spurrier Ball Company. The first step is to trace the physical flow.

STEP 1: Tracing the Physical Flow

*We need the completed
units and the ending
inventory for the
production report*

In this step, remember, we determine two things: (1) the number of units completed during the period and (2) at the end of the period, the number of units remaining in the ending work-in-process inventory. This information is necessary for the production report. In many process costing problems only one of these two quantities is known, while the other must be determined. In most situations we know the beginning inventory and we know the number of units that were started. The addition of these two represents the *total units to account for* in production.

$$\text{Beginning inventory in work-in-process} + \text{units started} = \text{total units to account for}$$

If we also know the number of units in the ending work-in-process, we can calculate the number of units completed during the period, as follows:[1]

Finding the completed units

$$\text{Beginning inventory in work-in-process} + \text{units started} = \text{total units to account for} - \text{ending inventory in WIP} = \text{units completed}$$

Conversely, if we know the number of units completed we can determine the number of unfinished units in the ending work-in-process:

---

[1] We assume that the total units to account for always equal the ending inventory plus the units completed during the period and that all the units completed are good enough to sell in their present form at the normal sales price. More realistically, however, some of the units to account for will probably be defective or spoiled units, that is, units that fail to meet dimensional or qualitative standards. These units are removed from the production process as soon as they are detected. Spoiled units can either be junked or be sold as scrap in their present form; defective units might be reworked and sold at an amount much closer to their normal sales price. The existence of defective or spoiled units — which can greatly complicate process costing — will be completely ignored in our analysis.

Finding the number of incomplete units

$$\begin{array}{c}\text{Beginning inventory}\\\text{in work-in-process}\end{array} + \begin{array}{c}\text{units}\\\text{started}\end{array} = \begin{array}{c}\text{total}\\\text{units to}\\\text{account for}\end{array} - \begin{array}{c}\text{units}\\\text{completed}\end{array} = \begin{array}{c}\text{ending}\\\text{inventory}\\\text{in WIP}\end{array}$$

Tracing the physical flow for Spurrier will be easy because we have assumed—for now—a zero beginning inventory in work-in-process in Department 1. We have been given the ending inventory for work-in-process, so what we need to calculate is the number of units (footballs) that were completed during August. This is calculated as follows:

The completed footballs are 20,000

Beginning inventory, work-in-process (Dept. 1).	-0-
Add: Units started	40,000
Total to account for	40,000
Less: Ending inventory, work-in-process (Dept. 1)	20,000
Units completed and transferred to Dept. 2	20,000

The 20,000 footballs that are finished in Department 1 and the ending inventory of 20,000 unfinished footballs now become the basis for calculations in the production report, enabling us to determine the number of equivalent whole units and the cost per equivalent whole unit.

STEP 2: Preparing the Production Report

Once the completed units and the units in the ending inventory of work-in-process have been determined, then we prepare the ***production report.*** The production report is used to calculate a cost per equivalent whole unit for each different product cost—direct materials, direct labor, and factory overhead. In the first part of the production report we will calculate the equivalent whole units (also called *equivalent units*).

The production report — part 1

Part 2

In the second part of the production report we have to accumulate all the costs that are associated with the production of the period; this accumulation is referred to as the *total costs to account for.* In most situations the ***total costs to account for*** will be found by adding together the costs of the beginning inventory and the costs incurred during the period.

Part 3

In the third part of the production report we will divide the total costs to account for by the equivalent whole units; the result is the ***cost per equivalent whole unit (CPEWU).***

The production report for Department 1 is provided in Exhibit 13-1. The first column indicates the number of units that were completed during August (20,000). But a close look at this column shows that it represents units started and completed, and not merely units completed. Since there were no incomplete footballs in inventory on Aug. 1, all the units that were completed had to have been started during August. The reason we use the more specific term *units started and completed* will become clear when we discuss the FIFO and weighted average methods. For now don't be overly concerned.

All the units started were also completed

In the second column of Exhibit 13-1 we've placed the number of footballs that are still in process on Aug. 31 (20,000). The third column shows the fraction of a full dosage of cost that has been added to the 20,000 footballs by Aug. 31. To get column (4) we multiply column (2) by column (3) and add that result to column (1).

EXHIBIT 13-1 Production Report for Department 1: No Beginning Inventories
Department 1's production report calculates the CPEWU for each product cost. The total CPEWU — when there are no beginning inventories — is $7.75.

Product Cost	(1) Units Started and Completed	(2) Ending Inventory, WIP	(3) Fraction Completed	(4) Equivalent Whole Units*	(5) Total Costs to Account for	(6) Cost per Equivalent Whole Unit†
Cowhide...............	20,000	20,000	1	40,000	$120,000	$3.00
Strings	20,000	20,000	1	40,000	20,000	0.50
Conversion costs	20,000	20,000	¾	35,000	148,750	4.25
					$288,750	$7.75

* Col. (4) = col. (1) + [col. (2) × col. (3)].
† Col. (6) = col. (5)/col. (4).

Remember, 40,000 units were started; column (1) represents the 20,000 units from this batch that were completed during August. We can see and count every one of these footballs (and could even throw a few passes if they weren't still deflated). Column (2) represents the footballs we cannot yet throw or kick because they haven't been completely sewn together. Nevertheless, between columns (1) and (2) we're talking about 40,000 footballs, although some of them (one-half in this example) are unfinished.

Let's now discuss columns (3) and (4) in more detail.

Column (3) The ending inventory of work-in-process is the key to determining equivalent whole units. The fraction of work completed for each cost, shown in column (3), represents the percentage of a full dosage of cost that has been added to the unfinished units (20,000) by the end of a period. To calculate the fraction of completion for the unfinished units, it is necessary to know and compare the following items:

1. How far the unfinished units have progressed in the production process by period-end

2. How and when the product costs are added to the units as they are manufactured (lump sum? sporadically? uniformly?)

The balls are three-quarters complete

For item 1 the ending inventory for Spurrier of 20,000 footballs was said to be three-quarters complete — meaning that three-quarters of the total time and attention to be spent on each football has already occurred.

For item 2 we were told:

Materials are added in a lump sum

1. Cowhide is added in a lump sum (all at one time) at the very beginning of production.

2. Strings (or laces) are added to the footballs in a lump sum after the footballs have proceeded one-half of the way through the process.

Conversion costs are incurred evenly

3. Conversion costs are incurred uniformly (evenly) throughout the production process.

Let's take these in reverse order by looking first at the conversion costs — what should be its fraction in column (3)?

Treatment of each individual conversion cost

Conversion costs Conversion costs represent the addition of direct labor plus factory overhead. Although we certainly could treat these components individually, for simplicity conversion costs are usually handled in their combined form. And remember the distinction we made in Chapter 5: If the conversion costs include fixed factory overhead as a product cost, we are using absorption costing. If the fixed factory overhead is not included in the conversion costs as a product cost, but is treated as a period cost instead, we are using direct costing. Within this chapter, unless we tell you otherwise, assume we are employing an absorption costing system. Let's now see what the fraction is for the conversion costs.

The fraction for conversion costs is $\frac{3}{4}$

The ending inventory of 20,000 footballs is three-quarters complete. If it takes 4 hours to complete a football in Department 1, then at the end of the day on Aug. 31, 3 of the required 4 hours of work have already taken place on each of the 20,000 footballs—thus the footballs are three-quarters complete. Conversion costs are assumed to occur evenly over the 4 hours of production. Therefore, if the footballs are three-quarters complete, then three-quarters of a full dosage of conversion costs has been incurred.

Since three-quarters of a full dosage of conversion costs has been added, the fraction in column (3) in the production report is $\frac{3}{4}$.

We now have the rule for determining the fraction applicable to the ending inventory for conversion costs—it is:

The rule for conversion costs

■ *The fraction completed in the production report for conversion costs is always the same as the point in production reached by the units in the ending work-in-process.*

Materials Most of the time, direct materials are not added to the process in a uniform manner, as in the case of the conversion costs. Therefore, the rule for determining the fraction in column (3) has to be different for materials than it is for conversion costs.

Most of the time, we will assume that materials are added in a lump sum at a specific point in production. The fraction for column (3) depends on when the materials are added during the production process and how far along in this process the unfinished units are at month-end.

Notice that both materials are added before the three-quarter point Cowhide gets a full dosage

To get an idea of what we mean here, let's look at a time line diagram—which represents the production process going from beginning to end on a horizontal scale.

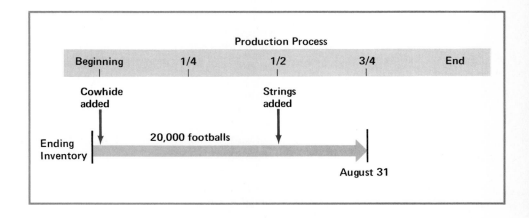

So do the strings

The cowhide is introduced in the process at the very beginning of production. Since the footballs have progressed to the three-quarter point in production, the cowhide had to have already been added. And the fraction must be 1—a full dosage.[2]

The strings are also added in a lump sum, but at the one-half point in production. The 20,000 footballs have already passed the one-half point, and there is no way to pass by without being strung. Each football, at the three-quarter point, has a full dosage of strings—the fraction is also 1.

Notice in the diagram that the downward arrows for cowhide and strings both intersect with the line representing the 20,000 footballs—where the lines intersect graphically represents that the materials have been added.

From this discussion we can now generalize about the rules for determining the fraction applicable to the ending inventory for direct materials:

The rule for materials

- *For any materials that are added in a lump sum at a point in production earlier than the point reached by the units in the ending inventory, the fraction is 1.*

- *For any materials that are added in a lump sum after the point in production reached by the units in ending inventory, the fraction is 0.*[3]

Column (1) + column (2) × column (3)

Column (4)   Column 4 in Exhibit 13-1—the equivalent whole units—is found by multiplying column (3) by column (2) and adding the result to column (1). (It may be a little more elaborate when there is a beginning inventory involved.) The equivalent whole units for cowhide, strings, and conversion costs were determined as follows:

	Column from Exhibit 13-1				
	(1)	+	[(2) × (3)]	=	(4)
Cowhide	20,000	+	(20,000 × 1)	=	40,000 equivalent whole units
Strings	20,000	+	(20,000 × 1)	=	40,000 equivalent whole units
Conversion costs	20,000	+	$(20,000 \times \frac{3}{4})$	=	35,000 equivalent whole units

Total costs to account for: beginning inventory plus incurred

Columns (5) and (6)   Column (5) lists the total costs to account for. The entries are calculated, for each production cost, by adding together the costs of the beginning work-in-process and the costs incurred during the entire month. For cowhide the cost of the beginning inventory given in Example 13-3 was zero (because there were no units in beginning inventory) and the costs incurred during August were $120,000. The total, $120,000 in cowhide costs, when divided by the equivalent whole units of 40,000 [column (4)], results in a cost per equivalent whole unit of $3 [column (6)]. For the strings the total costs to account for, $20,000, are incurred entirely in August. The resulting *cost per equivalent whole unit* for the strings is $0.50 ($20,000 ÷ 40,000).

CPEWU

Finally, the total conversion costs to account for are $148,750. Dividing that cost by the 35,000 equivalent whole units results in a conversion cost per equivalent whole unit of $4.25.

The total of all the total costs to account for in column (5) is the total of all the production costs represented in all the equivalent whole units worked on during the

---

[2] One is not actually a fraction, but it is the result of the fraction $\frac{1}{1}$.
[3] Zero is the result of the fraction $\frac{0}{1}$.

month. Thus, the total of all production costs to account for is $288,750 in our example. The total cost per equivalent whole unit in column (6) is $7.75.

Next, the total costs to account for, $288,750, are to be allocated between the 20,000 units completed and the 20,000 units remaining in work-in-process. We shall show you how to do that in the summary of costs report in step 3.

STEP 3: Summary of Costs Report

The purpose of the ***summary of costs report*** is to determine what part of the total costs to account for should be assigned to the units completed and transferred to Department 2 and what part of these costs should remain in Department 1 with the ending work-in-process. The number of completed units is multiplied by the combined costs per equivalent whole unit (this is simplified when there is no beginning inventory) for direct materials, direct labor, and factory overhead. We transfer this amount, with the units completed, to the next production department if there are several stages in production or to finished goods inventory if the units have no additional processing to be performed. The cost of the ending inventory of work-in-process is calculated by multiplying the equivalent whole units that are still in process by the appropriate cost per equivalent unit.

EXHIBIT 13-2
Summary of Costs Report for Department 1: No Beginning Inventories
Of the total costs to account for, $155,000 is transferred to Department 2 and the balance of $133,750 remains in work-in-process — Department 1.

Cost of units completed and transferred to Dept. 2 (20,000 × $7.75).......		$155,000*
Cost of ending inventory — work-in-process		
Cowhide (20,000 × 1 × $3).............................	$60,000†	
Strings (20,000 × 1 × $0.50)...........................	10,000†	
Con. costs (20,000 × ¾ × $4.25)........................	63,750†	133,750
		$288,750‡

* From Exhibit 13-1, col. (1) × the sum of col. (6).
† From Exhibit 13-1, col. (2) × col. (3) × col. (6).
‡ This total agrees with the total in col. (5) of Exhibit 13-1.

This report (Exhibit 13-2) indicates that $155,000 is assigned to the completed units, which, upon transfer to Department 2, requires the following journal entry:

The transfer to Department 2

Work-in-Process Inventory — Department 2........................	155,000	
Work-in-Process Inventory — Department 1....................		155,000
Cost of completed units transferred from Department 1 to Department 2.		

If Department 1 had been the only production department, then the 20,000 units would be transferred to finished goods and the debit in the entry above would be to Finished Goods Inventory rather than to Work-in-Process — Department 2.

Exhibit 13-2 also shows that the cost of the 20,000 unfinished footballs in Department 1 is $133,750 at the end of August. The $155,000 plus the $133,750 equals $288,750 — which agrees with the total costs to account for at the bottom of column (5) in the production report.

The Illustration Complicated — A Beginning Inventory for Department 1

Up to here we have simplified the analysis by assuming that there was no beginning inventory in work-in-process. Now we will introduce a beginning inventory and see how the analysis is affected. The new facts are given in Example 13-4.

Example 13-4

THE SPURRIER BALL COMPANY — DEPARTMENT 1: WITH A BEGINNING INVENTORY

Add to the basic facts given in Example 13-3 that the Spurrier Ball Company now has a beginning inventory of 10,000 footballs, one-fifth complete. The cost of this inventory on Aug. 1 is as follows:

Here's the beginning inventory

Cost of 10,000 footballs ($\frac{1}{5}$ complete), Aug. 1:	
Cowhide	$30,000
Strings	-0-
Conversion costs	7,570
	$37,570

One other way in which the facts in Example 13-4 are different from those in Example 13-3 is that the costs incurred during August for Department 1 are now assumed to be:

The costs incurred are a little different from those in Example 13-3

Costs incurred during August:	
Cowhide	$120,000
Strings	25,000
Conversion costs	172,430
	$317,430

The number of footballs started during August is still 40,000, and the inventory of work-in-process on Aug. 31 is still 20,000 footballs, three-fourths complete.

Once again we will go through the three basic steps for Department 1 in the Spurrier Ball Company. This time, however, some of the mechanics will be a little more complicated, due to the 10,000 footballs in beginning inventory.

STEP 1: Tracing the Physical Flow

In this example there are now 10,000 footballs in beginning inventory, in addition to the 40,000 footballs that were started. Because of these 10,000 additional footballs, the number completed is now 30,000, instead of the 20,000 calculated in the previous example:

Beginning inventory, Dept. 1	10,000 (10,000 additional footballs)
Add: Units started	40,000
Total to account for	50,000 (includes 10,000 additional footballs)
Less: Ending inventory, Dept. 1	20,000
Units completed and transferred to Dept. 2	30,000 (includes 10,000 additional footballs)

We logically assume that the beginning inventory is completed first

An important assumption that we make concerning the 10,000 footballs not yet finished in Department 1 on Aug. 1 is that these footballs are the first 10,000 (of the total of 30,000) to be completed in August. Only after we complete the beginning inventory do we complete those units that we start from scratch during August. The schedule above indicates that 30,000 footballs are completed in August. If 10,000 of this total came from the beginning inventory, where must the remaining 20,000 have come from? There can be only one possibility: They were part of the 40,000 units that were started during the month. Therefore, of the 40,000 units that were started, 20,000 were completed and the remaining 20,000 were incomplete at the end of the month. The diagram below should help to clarify these relationships:

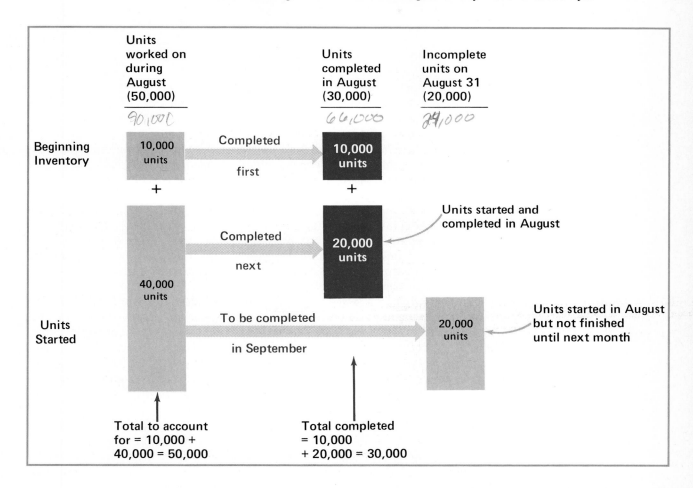

Whenever there is a beginning inventory in work-in-process that is completed in the current period, some of the total work needed to produce these units has already occurred — in the last period — and the remainder will occur in the current period. In our example part of the work (and costs related to this work) needed to produce the 10,000 units in the Aug. 1 inventory took place in July, and the remaining work (and related costs) to complete these units took place in August. In other words, some of the 10,000 equivalent units relate to July and some relate to August. The critical questions are:

The problem is how to account for the beginning inventory

How do we account for that part of the 10,000 equivalent units that was produced during July — in the August production report?

What do we do in this month's production report with the costs incurred last period to work on the beginning inventory?

Do we include or exclude the equivalent units and related costs of the beginning inventory in this month's production report?

FIFO and weighted average

FIFO vs. Weighted Average   Whether we include or exclude the equivalent units and related costs of the beginning inventory in the August production report depends on the process costing method we use to determine equivalent units. With the FIFO method we *exclude* them, but with the weighted average method we *include* them. Let's now see what the basic differences are in these two methods. Later we will look at each method in much greater detail.

First, FIFO

With the *FIFO method* we keep separate track of the work performed last period on the beginning inventory and the work performed during the current period. The equivalent units of the current period *include* the work performed to complete the beginning inventory plus any work that was performed on the units that were started this period and *exclude* the equivalent units that were in the beginning inventory. When the total number of equivalent units is divided into the total costs (which exclude the costs of the beginning inventory), the resulting cost per equivalent whole unit (CPEWU) relates only to the work performed in the current period. As suggested by the name of the method — FIFO — the first units assumed to be completed are the ones in beginning inventory. Their costs are composed of two parts: the cost of the beginning inventory (incurred last period) and the costs incurred this period to complete the beginning inventory. The next group of units to be completed are assumed to come from the units that were started in the current period; their cost is based entirely on the current CPEWU.

Now, weighted average

With the *weighted average method* we combine the units from the beginning inventory with the units that were worked on in the current period, and we treat the combination as if all the units were worked on entirely in the current period. We then combine the costs of the beginning inventory with the costs incurred currently and treat them as if they were all incurred in the current period. Therefore, when we calculate the equivalent units, they *include* the equivalent units from the beginning inventory. When this total number of units is divided into the total costs to account for — which *include* the costs of the beginning inventory — we come up with a weighted average cost per equivalent unit — which is the same for all units, whether they came from beginning inventory or from current production. The resulting cost of completed units that is transferred to the next department is found simply by multiplying the average cost per equivalent unit by all the units that were completed.

This is a different set of facts from those in Example 13-4; it is for purposes of comparing the two methods only

A graphic comparison of FIFO and weighted average is provided in Figure 13-1. We are assuming that there are 10,000 units, one-half complete in the beginning inventory, representing 5,000 equivalent whole units. In addition, we are assuming that the equivalent units of work performed in the current period were 31,000; that 30,000 equivalent units are completed during the period; and that there are 12,000 units, one-half complete at the end of the period, representing 6,000 equivalent whole units. All the related costs are shown in the blocks at the bottom of each diagram. Do not worry about how we got the 31,000 equivalent whole units that were worked on — your only concern for now should be how the units and costs are distributed differently under FIFO and weighted average.

Go back now three paragraphs, and reread the discussion concerning each method as you study the diagrams in Figure 13-1. The purpose of these diagrams is to give you a general understanding of the differences in the two methods before you study either of them in detail. Certain things have been simplified to facilitate the analysis; so if you later compare the diagrams to the production report or summary of costs report for either method, you may find some minor inconsistencies.

Selection of a Method   You now may be asking yourself: Which method is the better of the two? Which method am I going to have to learn? The answer to the first question depends on who you ask; the answer to the second depends on your teacher. Let's look first at some possible answers to the first question.

Arguments for using FIFO   Proponents of FIFO argue that it is preferable because:

1. It provides for a theoretically preferable matching of costs and revenues.

2. It is a better approximation of the physical flow of goods.

3. It's easier to learn the standard costing application to process costing if you first understand FIFO, since the calculations of equivalent whole units are the same for FIFO and standard costing.

On the other hand, proponents of the weighted average method counter with the following reasons for using weighted average:

Arguments for using weighted average

1. It is far easier to learn and to apply in practice.

2. Many more companies use weighted average than use FIFO in the real world.

As we said above, the method that you now learn will probably depend on the method your instructor prefers. *For this reason we are assuming that you will be using one method or the other, but not both. Therefore, we will cover each method in detail as if it is the only one you will learn.* This means that if you do cover both methods, there will be some redundancy within the two discussions. If you are covering only the FIFO method, read pages 583–595; but if you are covering only weighted average, you should skip to page 595 and read through to the end of the chapter.

Before you go on to either method, however, there is an important point we need to make. You see, the FIFO and weighted average methods represent two different ways to determine the *actual* costs of the units being produced. FIFO and weighted average are actual cost product costing methods. As you will recall, however, from our discussion in Chapters 10 and 12, some people feel that standard costs are better product costs than are actual costs. They contend that the standard costs of production are a better measure of the value of inventory. Whenever standard costs are used to cost the product in a process costing situation, the issue of FIFO vs. weighted average is irrelevant, because these methods are used only when actual costs are employed for product costing. As we will discuss at the end of this chapter, however, the FIFO method of process costing and the standard cost method of process costing do have some important similarities.

FIFO and weighted average are actual cost product costing methods

THE FIFO METHOD OF PROCESS COSTING

Step 1 in the preparation of a process costing solution — tracing the physical flow — was done in the previous section. Remember, there were 30,000 units completed, and 20,000 units were in the ending inventory, three-quarters complete. The remaining facts were given in Example 13-4. We can now go to step 2.

STEP 2: Preparing the Production Report

The first thing we need to do under the FIFO method is to distinguish between the units completed from the beginning inventory (they were started in July and finished

FLOW OF EWUs AND COSTS FOR FIFO

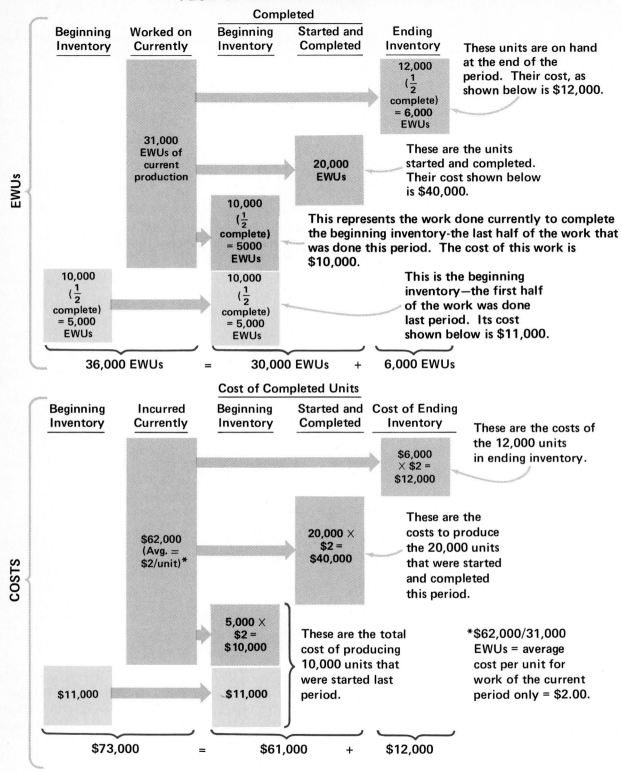

FIGURE 13-1 A Comparison of FIFO and Weighted Average.
The top part of each diagram shows, for each method, the equivalent units that were worked on during each period. Some of what was

FLOW OF EWUs AND COSTS FOR WEIGHTED AVERAGE

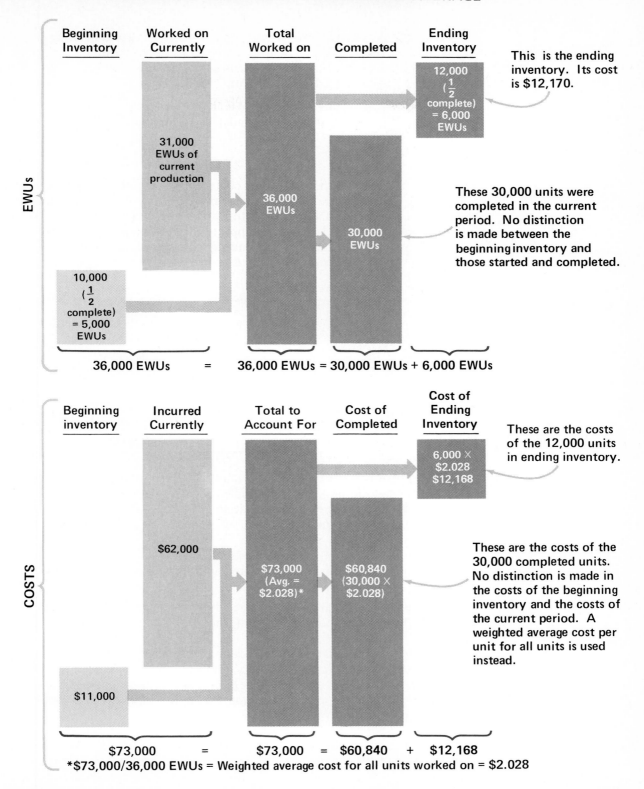

EWUs

Beginning Inventory	Worked on Currently	Total Worked on	Completed	Ending Inventory	

31,000 EWUs of current production

36,000 EWUs

30,000 EWUs

12,000 ($\frac{1}{2}$ complete) = 6,000 EWUs

This is the ending inventory. Its cost is $12,170.

These 30,000 units were completed in the current period. No distinction is made between the beginning inventory and those started and completed.

10,000 ($\frac{1}{2}$ complete) = 5,000 EWUs

36,000 EWUs = 36,000 EWUs = 30,000 EWUs + 6,000 EWUs

COSTS

Beginning inventory	Incurred Currently	Total to Account For	Cost of Completed	Cost of Ending Inventory	

$62,000

$73,000 (Avg. = $2.028)*

$60,840 (30,000 × $2.028)

6,000 × $2.028 $12,168

These are the costs of the 12,000 units in ending inventory.

These are the costs of the 30,000 completed units. No distinction is made in the costs of the beginning inventory and the costs of the current period. A weighted average cost per unit for all units is used instead.

$11,000

$73,000 = $73,000 = $60,840 + $12,168

*$73,000/36,000 EWUs = Weighted average cost for all units worked on = $2.028

worked on had already been started last period. The bottom part of each diagram shows the total costs to account for (beginning inventory costs plus costs incurred in the current period), and how they are assigned to the completed units and ending inventory.

in August) and the units that were started and completed in August. In most problems like the one we're doing for the Spurrier Ball Company, the beginning inventory is given but the units started and completed must be determined. We can calculate the units started and completed in the following manner:

Separation of completed units into two parts

$$\begin{aligned}\text{Units started} \atop \text{and completed} &= {\text{total units} \atop \text{completed}} - {\text{beginning} \atop \text{inventory}}\\ &= \quad 30,000 \quad - \quad 10,000\\ &= \quad 20,000\end{aligned}$$

Next we must show, in the first column of the production report (units completed), which units were completed from the beginning inventory and which units were started and completed. To make that distinction, we need three columns—(1a) the beginning inventory, (1b) a fraction to apply to the beginning inventory (which we will explain in a moment), and (1c) the units started and completed. For this example this section of the production report for Department 1 will now appear as shown below:

Notice that the sum of columns (1a) and (1c) always equals the total number of completed units

Product Cost	Completed		
	(1a) Beginning Inventory	(1b) Fraction	(1c) Started and Completed
Cowhide..........................	10,000	0	20,000
Strings...........................	10,000	1	20,000
Conversion costs..................	10,000	$\frac{4}{5}$	20,000
		30,000	

Column (1b) represents the fraction of a full dosage of costs incurred in the current period (in this case during August) to complete the units that were started last period. [The fraction can also be expressed in decimal form or as a percentage (e.g., $\frac{4}{5} = 0.80 = 80\%$).] To determine this fraction, we need to know the following two bits of information:

Determining the fraction to place in column (1b)

1. How far the beginning inventory progressed in the production process by the end of last period
2. How and when the product costs are added to the units as they are manufactured (lump sum? sporadically? uniformly?)

We know from the information given in Example 13-4 that the 10,000 footballs were only one-fifth complete on Aug. 1, so very little work had been done in July. We are also reminded that cowhide is added at the beginning of production; strings are added at the one-half point in production; and conversion costs are incurred evenly throughout production.

Four-fifths of the conversion process is left to complete the beginning inventory

Conversion Costs   During July one-fifth of the work had already been done to complete the 10,000 footballs. Since conversion costs are incurred evenly throughout production, one-fifth of a full dosage of costs must already have been added to these footballs by the end of July. Therefore, to complete the 10,000 footballs in August, the remaining four-fifths of a full dosage is needed—the fraction in column (1b).

Cowhide was added last period

Cowhide Since cowhide is added in a lump sum at the beginning of production, and since the 10,000 footballs were one-fifth complete in July, all the cowhide must have been added to these footballs when they were begun in July. This also means that none of the cowhide needs to be added to the 10,000 footballs in August to complete them. Therefore, none of the full dosage was added in August; thus the fraction in column (1b) is 0.

The strings were added this period

Strings If the strings are added only after the footballs get halfway through production, there is no way that the strings could have already been added to the 10,000 footballs in July. The process had not progressed far enough in July for the strings to have been added—the footballs got only one-fifth of the way through the process. Therefore, the full dosage of the cost of strings must have been added in August to complete the footballs; thus the fraction for strings in column (1b) is 1.

The Completed Production Report The completed production report for Department 1 is shown in Exhibit 13-3.

EXHIBIT 13-3 Production Report for Department 1: FIFO
Now that we have a beginning inventory, we have to use either FIFO or weighted average. The production report in this exhibit uses the FIFO method.

Product Cost	(1a) Beginning Inventory, WIP	(1b) Fraction Completed	(1c) Started and Completed	(2) Ending Inventory, WIP	(3) Fraction Completed	(4) Equivalent Whole Units*	(5) Total Costs to Account for	(6) Cost per Equivalent Whole Unit†
			Units Completed					
Cowhide	10,000	0	20,000	20,000	1	40,000	$120,000	$3.00
Strings	10,000	1	20,000	20,000	1	50,000	25,000	0.50
Conversion costs .	10,000	$\frac{4}{5}$	20,000	20,000	$\frac{3}{4}$	43,000	172,430	4.01
			30,000				$317,430	$7.51

Costs of beginning inventory ⟶ { $317,430 (30,000) *Costs incurred during August* 7,570 $355,000

* Col. (4) = [col. (1a) × col. (1b)] + col. (1c) + [col. (2) × col. (3)].
† Col. (6) = col. (5)/col. (4).

As you can see, columns (2) and (3) are exactly the same as they were in Exhibit 13-1; and since we discussed these columns in detail in an earlier section, we will not discuss them any further here. Column (4), however, deserves special attention because the calculation of the equivalent units shown in it is affected by the beginning inventory.

We calculate the equivalent units using FIFO in the following manner (using columns (1a) to (4) of Exhibit 13-3.

There are several parts to equivalent whole units for FIFO.

	(1a) Beginning Inventory	×	(1b) Fraction	+	(1c) Started and Completed	+	(2) Ending Inventory	×	(3) Fraction	=	(4) Equivalent Whole Units
Cowhide	(10,000	×	0	) +	20,000	+	(20,000	×	1	) =	40,000
Strings	(10,000	×	1	) +	20,000	+	(20,000	×	1	) =	50,000
Conversion Costs	(10,000	×	$\frac{4}{5}$	) +	20,000	+	(20,000	×	$\frac{3}{4}$	) =	43,000

Look now at column (5) in Exhibit 13-3—the total costs to account for. Remember, we mentioned earlier that these costs are represented by the addition of beginning inventory costs plus costs incurred during the current period. In Exhibit 13-1 there were no beginning inventory costs—because there were no units in beginning inventory. Now, however, we do have a beginning inventory, and its cost is $37,570 ($30,000 for cowhide plus $7,570 for conversion costs). This amount—shown in the lower portion of column (5)—is added to the $317,430 ($120,000 + $25,000 + $172,430) that was incurred during August. The total for column (5) is $355,000.

How to handle costs of beginning inventory

You may be wondering if it makes any difference just how we combine the costs of beginning inventory plus the costs incurred in the current period. In Exhibit 13-3 we added the beginning inventory costs, $37,570, to the sum of the three costs incurred during August, $317,430. Would it have been okay to individually add the corresponding components of the beginning inventory costs and the costs incurred currently? For example, couldn't we have added together the $30,000 and $120,000 for cowhide and merely placed the total of $150,000 on the first line in column (5), and then done the same thing for strings and conversion costs? Wouldn't the total for column (5) still be $355,000?

Although the total may still be $355,000, this alternative is not acceptable. Here's why.

For FIFO, CPEWU includes current costs only

The equivalent whole units in column (4) represent equivalent whole units of work performed *in the current period only.* These equivalent whole units exclude the work performed on the 10,000 units in the previous period. Remember, when we determined each fraction [column (1b)] to multiply by the beginning inventory of 10,000 footballs, we said that it represented the fraction of a full dosage of work that was incurred *in the current period.* That fraction of a full dosage representing work of *the previous period* was included in that period and therefore is not included in the current month's production report.

Because (1) the equivalent whole units represent the denominator of the cost per equivalent whole unit calculation (CPEWU) and (2) the equivalent whole units include only the work of the current period, for the sake of consistency the number of equivalent whole units must be divided into a numerator that represents costs incurred *in the current period only.* For FIFO we calculate the CPEWU using the following numerator and denominator:

CPEWU for FIFO

$$\text{CPEWU} = \frac{\text{costs incurred in current period}}{\text{equivalent units of work performed in current period}}$$

As you can tell from Exhibit 13-3, for cowhide the CPEWU is $3, which represents the costs incurred, $120,000, divided by the equivalent whole units, 40,000. In a like manner the respective CPEWUs for strings and conversion costs are $0.50 ($25,000 ÷ 50,000) and $4.01 ($172,430 ÷ 43,000).

STEP 3: Preparing the Summary of Costs Report

The last step we need to take is to allocate the total costs to account for—the $355,000—between the 30,000 completed units and the 20,000 units that are still in process on Aug. 31. We do this in the *summary of costs report.*

The costs that we assign to the 30,000 completed units—when we are using FIFO—are made up of three parts. They are:

Three parts to the cost of completed units

1. The costs assigned to the 20,000 units started and completed in August
2. The costs of the 10,000 units in beginning inventory (these costs were incurred last period)
3. The costs to complete the 10,000 units in beginning inventory (these costs are incurred in the current period)

The summary of costs report for Department 1 of Spurrier is shown in Exhibit 13-4. The cost of the units started and completed is $150,200 (20,000 × $7.51); the cost of the beginning inventory is $37,570 ($30,000 + $7,570); and the cost of completing the beginning inventory is $37,080 ($0 + $5,000 + $32,080). The total of these three parts is $224,850, which is the amount that is transferred with the 30,000 footballs to the second processing department, Department 2, where the footballs are pumped with air and boxed.

The cost assigned to the ending inventory is $130,150 ($60,000 + $10,000 + $60,150); when this amount is added to the $224,850, the total is $355,000, which agrees with the total in column (5) of the production report in Exhibit 13-3.

EXHIBIT 13-4 Summary of Costs Report for Department 1: FIFO
Because of the beginning inventory there are three parts to the calculation of the cost of the completed units—for FIFO.

Cost of units completed and transferred to Dept. 2:			
Started and completed (20,000 × $7.51)		$150,200	*Total costs of beginning inventory = $37,570 + $37,080 = $74,650*
Beginning inventory:			
Cost of beginning inv........................	$37,570		
Costs to complete:			*Total costs of units completed and transferred = $150,200 + $74,650 = $224,850*
Cowhide (10,000 × 0 × $3)........	$ -0-		
Strings (10,000 × 1 × $0.50).......	5,000		
Con. costs (10,000 × ⅘ × $4.01)....	32,080	37,080	
Total costs of producing beginning inv.................		74,650	*Total cost of ending inventory = $60,000 + $10,000 + $60,150 = $130,150*
Total costs of 30,000 completed units.........................		$224,850	
Cost of ending inventory—work-in-process:			
Cowhide (20,000 × 1 × $3)		$ 60,000	
Strings (20,000 × 1 × $0.50)		10,000	
Con. costs (20,000 × ¾ × $4.01)		60,150	
Total costs of ending inv......................................		130,150	
		$355,000	*Total costs to account for = $224,850 + $130,150 = $355,000*

Perhaps now would be a good time to stop and look at what we've been doing in Department 1 from a T-account approach. Exhibit 13-5 shows how the units and dollars flow through Department 1 on their way to Department 2. It shows that the $355,000 of total costs to account for—which we determined in the Exhibit 13-3 production report—is allocated between the completed units ($224,850) and the incomplete units ($130,150)—which we calculated in the Exhibit 13-4 summary of costs report. You can see the $224,850 going from Department 1 to Department 2 on the credit side of the Work-in-Process T-account, and the $130,150 remaining as the debit balance at the bottom of the Work-in-Process T-account.

EXHIBIT 13-5   T-Account Approach for Department 1: FIFO

		Work-in-Process — Department 1	
Beginning inv.: 10,000 units ($30,000 + $7,570)	$ 37,570		
PLUS			
Costs incurred in August to complete beg. inv. and start 40,000 more ($120,000 + $25,000 + $172,430)	317,430		
EQUALS			
Total costs to account for, associated with all 50,000 units	$355,000		
		LESS	
		Cost of 30,000 units that were completed in Dept. 1 ($37,570 + $37,080 + $150,200)	$224,850
EQUALS			
Ending inv.: 20,000 units ($60,000 + $10,000 + $60,150)	$130,150		

The combination of these three costs — $224,850 — is assigned to the 30,000 units that are transferred to Dept. 2 in August. Dept. 2 will call these costs "transferred-in costs."

To Work-in-Process — Dept. 2 ═══▶

The Illustration Continued

The 30,000 completed footballs are transferred from Department 1 to Department 2, where they are pumped with air and boxed. The costs of the 30,000 footballs transferred, $224,850, becomes a cost of Department 2. The costs transferred into Department 2 are referred to as *transferred-in costs* and will be treated like the costs of any other direct material. Example 13-5 provides the information we need to know about Department 2.

Example 13-5

Department 2 of the Spurrier Ball Company

THE SPURRIER BALL COMPANY — DEPARTMENT 2: FIFO

In Department 2 of the Spurrier Ball Company, footballs that are transferred in from Department 1 are pumped with air and boxed for shipment. On Aug. 1 there were 5,000 footballs (one-half complete) being processed in Department 2, and during August the 30,000 footballs completed in Department 1 were introduced into Department 2. Of the 35,000 footballs (5,000 + 30,000) worked on during August 29,000 were finished by Aug. 31, and the footballs in ending work-in-process are two-thirds complete.

The costs of the Aug. 1 beginning inventory of 5,000 unfinished balls and the costs incurred during August are as follows:

Cost of 5,000 footballs, Aug. 1:		
Transferred-in costs (costs transferred from Dept. 1 to		
Dept. 2 during July)	$ 34,000	
Conversion costs	2,400	$ 36,400
Costs incurred during August:		
Transferred-in costs (costs transferred from Dept. 1 to		
Dept. 2 in current period)	$224,850	
Conversion costs	30,600	
Boxes	7,250	262,700
Total costs to account for		$299,100

Basic Steps for Department 2

The cost per equivalent whole unit in Department 2 is found in the same way as it was in Department 1.

The footballs that are finally finished and boxed in Department 2 will be transferred directly to finished goods inventory to await sale to customers. Let's now do the three basic steps for Department 2.

STEP 1: Tracing the Physical Flow

We know that during the month of August 29,000 footballs were finished in Department 2. The footballs that were not finished in Department 2 at the end of August are determined as follows:

The ending inventory is 6,000 footballs

Beginning inventory, work-in-process (Dept. 2).............................	5,000
Add: Units started (transferred-in from Dept. 1 during August)..............	30,000
Total to account for	35,000
Less: Units completed and transferred to finished goods	29,000
Ending inventory, work-in-process (Dept. 2)	6,000

STEP 2: Preparing the Production Report

The production report for Department 2 (Exhibit 13-6) shows that three costs go into the final boxed product—the costs of making the football in the previous department (the transferred-in costs), the box in which the football is packaged, and the conversion costs of pumping air into the balls and packaging the balls.

Completed Units Columns (1a) and (1c) indicate that, in total, 29,000 footballs were completed in Department 2 during August. Of this total, 5,000 [column (1a)] were in process on Aug. 1; the remaining 24,000 [column (1c)] were started and completed during August. Column (1b)—fraction completed—indicates the fraction (or percentage) of a full dosage of costs incurred during August to complete the beginning inventory.

The beginning inventory had been worked on in July

Conversion costs are $\frac{1}{2}$

The 5,000 footballs had progressed halfway through the production process in July—therefore, one-half of the time and attention that these units will get was received during July, and the remaining one-half of the total time and attention takes place during August. Since the conversion costs are spread evenly over the production process, one-half of the full dosage of conversion costs takes place in August to do

EXHIBIT 13-6   Production Report for Department 2: FIFO
The second processing department will always have transferred-in costs—the costs that are transferred from one processing department to another.

Product Cost	(1a) Beginning Inventory, WIP	(1b) Fraction Completed	(1c) Started and Completed	(2) Ending Inventory, WIP	(3) Fraction Completed	(4) Equivalent Whole Units*	(5) Total Costs to Account for	(6) Cost per Equivalent Whole Unit†
Units Completed								
Transferred-in costs	5,000	0	24,000	6,000	1	30,000	$224,850	$7.495
Boxes	5,000	1	24,000	6,000	0	29,000	7,250	0.250
Conversion costs .	5,000	$\frac{1}{2}$	24,000	6,000	$\frac{2}{3}$	30,500	30,600	1.003
		29,000					$262,700	$8.748
						Costs of beginning inventory	34,000	*Costs incurred during August*
							2,400	
							$299,100	

* Col. (4) = [col. (1a) × col. (1b)] + col. (1c) + [col. (2) × col. (3)].
† Col. (6) = col. (5)/col. (4).

The boxes are added this period

These transferred-in costs came to Department 2 last month

The full dosage was added in July

the last one-half of the work on the incomplete units. The fraction for conversion costs in column (1b), therefore, is $\frac{1}{2}$.

The boxes are added at the end of processing—only a fully pumped football will be packaged in a box. Since the 5,000 footballs were only one-half complete in July, there was no way that boxes could already have been added to them. The boxes had to have been added during August—when the 5,000 footballs were completed. The fraction in column (1b) is 1.

Now we come to the transferred-in costs. Remember, these represent the costs assigned to units that are transferred from Department 1 to Department 2. Normally, we treat transferred-in costs just like the costs for a material that is added at the beginning of production. This is because the processing of units transferred into a new department usually begins as soon as the units are received, so the costs transferred with these units—the transferred-in costs—become the responsibility of the receiving department as soon as the work begins in the receiving department. This is just like the costs of raw materials that are transferred from a storeroom directly to the production department at the start of production. The only difference is in the name: Instead of being called direct materials (such as cowhide, strings, or package), they are called transferred-in costs.

If the transferred-in costs are treated the same as any raw material added at the beginning of production, then the fraction is just as easy to determine as it is for a direct material. Remember that the 5,000 units (as well as the transferred-in costs assigned to these units) in the beginning inventory on Aug. 1 would have been transferred from Department 1 to Department 2 during July. Therefore, the work (pumping and packaging) began on the 5,000 footballs in Department 2 sometime last month. Any costs—such as direct materials or, in this case, the transferred-in costs—that are added at the beginning of production would had to have been completely added to the 5,000 footballs last month, because that is when they were begun. Therefore, none of the full dosage of costs remains to be added in August, and the fraction must be 0.

Now we get the fractions for ending inventory

Ending Inventory In column (2) we see the 6,000 footballs (two-thirds complete) that were still in process at the end of August, and column (3) indicates the fraction of a full dosage of each cost that was added during August to these footballs. Since conversion costs are incurred evenly throughout production, and since two-thirds of the total time and attention took place during August in order to get the footballs to the two-thirds stage in production, two-thirds of a full dosage of conversion costs took place in August. The fraction in column (3) is $\frac{2}{3}$.

Conversion costs are $\frac{2}{3}$

The boxes will be added next period

Since the boxes are added at the end of production, and since the footballs are only two-thirds complete, there is no way that the boxes have yet been added to the ending inventory; therefore, the fraction in column (3) is 0.

And now for the transferred-in costs. The 6,000 footballs in ending inventory are from the batch of 30,000 that were transferred from Department 1 to Department 2 in August, which means that all 6,000 footballs were begun in August. Remember, we treat transferred-in costs just like a direct material added at the beginning of production. Since production on the 6,000 footballs has already begun — in fact, they are all two-thirds complete — the fraction for the transferred-in costs is 1, just as it would be for a direct material added at the beginning of production.

Transferred-in costs are 1

Costs per Equivalent Whole Unit (CPEWU) Once again we can calculate the equivalent units in column (4) rather simply. We merely add together the equivalent units from three sources: (1) beginning inventory, (2) units started and completed, and (3) units in ending inventory. This is shown in the following table:

EWU Calculation for Department 2: FIFO

	(1a) Beginning Inventory	×	(1b) Fraction	+	(1c) Started and Completed	+	(2) Ending Inventory	×	(3) Fraction	=	(4) Equivalent Whole Units
Transferred-in costs	(5,000	×	0	) +	24,000	+ (	6,000	×	1	) =	30,000
Package	(5,000	×	1	) +	24,000	+ (	6,000	×	0	) =	29,000
Conversion costs	(5,000	×	$\frac{1}{2}$	) +	24,000	+ (	6,000	×	$\frac{2}{3}$	) =	30,500

Remember: incurred at the top, beginning inventory at the bottom

Remember that the total costs to account for represent the sum of two groups of costs: the costs of beginning inventory plus the costs incurred during the current period. When we are using FIFO, however, we need to remember to place these two groups in two different sections of column (5) in Exhibit 13-6. The costs incurred ($224,850, $7,250, and $30,600) go at the top; these are the ones we divide by the equivalent units to get the CPEWU. The costs of the beginning inventory ($2,400 and $34,000) go at the bottom; these do not enter into the calculation of CPEWU.

CPEWU

For the transferred-in costs the costs of the current period (these were assigned to the 30,000 units transferred from Department 1 to Department 2 during August) were $224,850; when these were divided by the equivalent units of 30,000, we got the CPEWU of $7.495 — which you can see in column (6). The beginning inventory costs of $34,000 (these are costs that were assigned to the 5,000 units transferred from Department 1 to Department 2 last period but were incomplete in Department 2 at the end of last period) are shown in the bottom portion of column (5).

The costs incurred during the current period for the boxes were $7,250; when we divide them by the equivalent units of 29,000, we get the CPEWU of $0.25. There were no beginning inventory costs for the boxes in column (5) because the boxes had not been added to the units as of the beginning of August.

Finally, we come to the conversion costs. When the costs incurred during August —$30,600—are divided by the equivalent units of 30,500, we get a CPEWU of $1.003. The costs of beginning inventory, $2,400, are shown separately at the bottom of column (5).

STEP 3: Preparing the Summary of Costs Report

The final step is to allocate the total costs to account for in column (5) between the completed units and the ending inventory. We do this once again in the summary of costs report, shown in Exhibit 13-7.

EXHIBIT 13-7   Summary of Costs Report for Department 2: FIFO
The total cost of the 29,000 completed units transferred to finished goods inventory is $250,109.

Cost of units completed and transferred to finished goods:
Started and completed (24,000 × $8.748) $209,952
Beginning inventory:
   Cost of beginning inv. .... $36,400 ← *Total costs of beginning inventory = $34,000 + $2,400 = $36,400*
   Costs to complete:
     Trans.-in (5,000 × 0 × $7.495) ..... $ -0-
     Boxes (5,000 × 1 × $0.25) 1,250   *Total costs of units completed and transferred = $209,952 + $40,157 = $250,109*
     Con. costs (5,000 × ½ × $1.003) 2,507   3,757
   Total costs of producing beginning inv. 40,157
     Total costs of 29,000 completed units .... $250,109 ← *Total cost of ending inventory = $44,970 + $4,012 = $48,982*

Cost of ending inventory—work-in-process:
Trans.-in costs (6,000 × 1 × $7.495)..................... $ 44,970
Boxes (6,000 × 0 × $0.25)......................... -0-
Con. costs (6,000 × ⅔ × $1.003)......................... 4,012
   Total costs of ending inv....................................... 48,982

                                                     $299,091* ← *Total costs to account for = $250,109 + $48,982 = $299,091**

* $9 error due to rounding of $1.003 in production report.

The costs of the boxed footballs are made up of three parts

The costs assigned to the 29,000 footballs that were completed during August are composed of three parts:

1. The cost assigned to the units started and completed in August = 24,000 × the total CPEWU of $8.748.

2. The cost of the 5,000 footballs in beginning inventory = $36,400 ($34,000 + $2,400).

3. The costs incurred during August to complete the 5,000 footballs = $3,757 ($1,250 + $2,507). The $250,109 total is the amount that we transferred with the 29,000 footballs to finished goods inventory.

The ending inventory, $48,982 ($44,970 + $4,012), represents the balance in Work-in-Process—Department 2 on Aug. 31. When we add this amount to the cost of completed units, $250,109, we get a total of $299,091, which agrees (except for a $9 rounding error) with the total for column (5) in the production report.

Let's look now at the Work-in-Process T-account for Department 2. As you can see in Exhibit 13-8, the total costs to account for of $299,100—which we determined in the Exhibit 13-6 production report—are allocated between the 29,000 completed units and the 6,000 incomplete units—which we did in the Exhibit 13-7 summary of

EXHIBIT 13-8   T-Account Approach for Department 2: FIFO

Work-in-Process — Department 2		
Beginning inv.: 5,000 units ($34,000 + $2,400)	$ 36,400	
PLUS		
Costs incurred in August to complete beg. inv. and start 30,000 more ($224,850 + $7,250 + $30,600)	262,700	
EQUALS		
Total costs to account for, associated with all 35,000 units	$299,100	
	LESS	
	Cost of 29,000 units that were completed in Dept. 2 ($36,400 + $3,757 + $209,952)	$250,109
EQUALS		
Ending inv.: 6,000 units ($44,970 + $4,012)	$ 48,982*	

The combination of these three costs — $250,109 — is assigned to the 29,000 units that are transferred to finished goods in August

To Finished Goods Inventory

* $9 rounding error.

costs report. The costs that are transferred to Finished Goods with 29,000 units — the $250,109 — are shown as a credit in the Work-in-Process T-account, and the cost of the 6,000-unit ending inventory is shown as the debit balance at the bottom of the Work-in-Process T-account.

The journal entry required to transfer the costs from Work-in-Process — Department 2 to Finished Goods is as follows:

The final transfer

Finished Goods Inventory	250,109	
Work-in-Process — Department 2		250,109

Cost of completed units transferred from Department 2 to Finished Goods.

For some concluding remarks, go now to page 602, where we present a discussion of the multiple categories of product costs.

THE WEIGHTED AVERAGE METHOD OF PROCESS COSTING

Be sure you are familiar with Example 13-4

In Example 13-4 you were given an expanded set of facts for the Spurrier Ball Company. There were 10,000 units, one-fifth complete, in beginning inventory. The number of units that were started and the number that were in the ending work-in-process for Department 1 for August were still 40,000 and 20,000 footballs, respectively. By doing step 1 — tracing the physical flow — we learned that 30,000 footballs were completed in August, rather than the 20,000 that were completed in the original example for Spurrier (Example 13-3). We are now ready to go to step 2.

STEP 2: Preparing the Production Report

You already learned the basic format back in Exhibit 13-1

The production report that we use with the weighted average method has exactly the same format as the one used in Exhibit 13-1. As a matter of fact, all the procedures will be exactly the same—only the numbers will be different. The numbers are different because there are now 10,000 units (and related costs) in beginning inventory, which was assumed to be zero in the original example. This means that you have already basically learned the weighted average method, and now you need to see only how to include the beginning inventory in the production report. Remember, as we pointed out in the section comparing FIFO to weighted average, for weighted average we merge the beginning inventory (and costs) with the current production (and costs) and treat the combined totals as if there were one homogeneous group of units and one homogeneous group of costs. The resulting CPEWU is a weighted average—just as the name implies—found by dividing the combined units of last period and this period into the combined costs of last period and this period.

The reason for the name

The completed production report (which is combined with the summary of costs report) is shown in Exhibit 13-9. As you look it over, notice the following similarities and differences in Exhibit 13-9 and Exhibit 13-1.

The completed units are now 10,000 higher

Column (1) Column (1) in Exhibit 13-9 shows the number of units that were completed in August, 30,000. This is 10,000 higher than the number shown in

EXHIBIT 13-9 Combined Production Report and Summary of Costs Report for Department 1: Weighted Average
Weighted average is simpler because we do not keep the units in beginning inventory separate from those that were started and completed.

Product Cost	(1) Units Completed	(2) Ending Inventory, WIP	(3) Fraction Completed	(4) Equivalent Whole Units*	(5) Total Costs to Account for		(6) Cost per Equivalent Whole Unit†
Cowhide	30,000	20,000	1	50,000	$ 30,000 120,000	$150,000	$3.00
Strings	30,000	20,000	1	50,000	-0- $ 25,000	25,000	0.50
Conversion costs	30,000	20,000	$\frac{3}{4}$	45,000	$ 7,570 172,430	180,000	4.00
						$355,000	$7.50

Summary of Costs Report

Cost of units completed and transferred to Dept. 2:

$$30,000 \times \$7.50 \dots\dots\dots\dots\dots\dots\dots\dots\dots\dots\dots\dots \$225,000$$

Cost of ending inventory—work-in-process:

Cowhide (20,000 × 1 × $3.00)	$60,000	
Strings (20,000 × 1 × $0.50)	10,000	
Con. costs (20,000 × ¾ × $4.00)	60,000	130,000

Total costs to account for $355,000

* Col. (4) = col. (1) + [col. (2) × col. (3)].
† Col. (6) = col. (5)/col. (4).

column (1) of Exhibit 13-1 because of the additional 10,000 units in the beginning inventory. Also, column (1) is labeled "completed" in Exhibit 13-9, whereas it was called "started and completed" in Exhibit 13-1. This is because in Exhibit 13-1 we were assuming no beginning inventory. Therefore, all the units that were completed in August came from the units that were started during August.

Look back at pages 575–578 for explanation

Columns (2) and (3) The headings, numbers, and explanations of the numbers in columns (2) and (3) in Exhibit 13-9 are exactly what they were in the comparable columns of Exhibit 13-1. Since we discussed these columns in detail when we discussed Exhibit 13-1, we will not discuss them any further here.

Column (4) The equivalent whole units in column (4) of Exhibit 13-9 are calculated in exactly the same manner as they were in Exhibit 13-1. The results in Exhibit 13-9 for each product cost are 10,000 units higher than they were in Exhibit 13-1, since the completed units are now 10,000 higher. The calculation of equivalent whole units in Exhibit 13-9 is done as follows:

EWU Calculation for Department 1: Weighted Average

	Column in Exhibit 13-9							
	(1)	+	[(2)	×	(3)]	=	(4)	
Cowhide	30,000	+	(20,000	×	1)	=	50,000	equivalent whole units
Strings	30,000	+	(20,000	×	1)	=	50,000	equivalent whole units
Conversion costs	30,000	+	(20,000	×	$\frac{3}{4}$)	=	45,000	equivalent whole units

CPEWU for cowhide

Total costs to account for = beg. inv. + incurred

Columns (5) and (6) The costs that are included in column (5) of Exhibit 13-9 are higher than they were in Exhibit 13-1. Once again, the reason is the beginning inventory. Since there are now 10,000 footballs in the beginning inventory, there will also be costs associated with those footballs. For cowhide the beginning inventory costs were $30,000, which, when added to the $120,000 incurred, gives us a total to account for of $150,000. When this combination is divided by the equivalent whole units for cowhide of 50,000, we get a CPEWU of $3:

$$\text{CPEWU} = \frac{\text{total costs to account for}}{\text{equivalent whole units}} = \frac{\$150,000}{50,000} = \$3$$

CPEWU for strings

For the strings there were no beginning inventory costs, because the strings had not been added last period to the 10,000 footballs in beginning inventory. Remember, strings are added when the footballs are one-half complete. Since the footballs were only one-fifth complete at the beginning of August, there is no way they could have progressed far enough during July to have been strung. Therefore, the total costs to account for are represented entirely by the costs incurred during August, $25,000; and the resulting CPEWU is $0.50 ($25,000 ÷ 50,000).

CPEWU for conversion costs

Finally, the total conversion costs to account for are $180,000 ($7,570 in beginning inventory plus $172,430 incurred in August). Dividing that cost by the 45,000 equivalent whole units results in a conversion cost per equivalent whole unit of $4.

The total of all the total costs to account for in column (5) of Exhibit 13-9 is the total of all the production costs represented in all the equivalent whole units worked on during the month. The total of all the production costs to account for is $355,000 in our example. The total cost per equivalent whole unit in column (6) is $7.50.

Next, the total costs to account for will be allocated between the 30,000 completed units and the 20,000 units remaining in work-in-process. We will do this in step 3.

STEP 3: Preparing the Summary of Costs Report

As we mentioned before, the purpose of the summary of costs report is to determine what portion of the total costs to account for is to be assigned to the completed units and transferred with those units to the next department, and what part of these costs will remain in Department 1, assigned to the units in the ending inventory.

We're combining two reports into one

The summary of costs report for Department 1 is combined with the production report in Exhibit 13-9. We have combined these two reports in order to show you, with the use of arrows, (1) exactly where each number in the summary of costs report comes from and (2) how closely related the summary of costs report is to the production report.

Notice also that the summary of costs report in Exhibit 13-9 uses the same format as the one used in Exhibit 13-2, where there was no beginning inventory. The numbers will be different in the two reports, however, because of the additional 10,000 units in Exhibit 13-9.

Cost of completed units

Exhibit 13-9 indicates that $225,000 is assigned to the completed units (30,000 × $7.50), which, upon transfer to Department 2, requires the following journal entry:

Department 2 will refer to the $225,000 as transferred-in costs

Work-in-Process—Department 2 225,000
    Work-in-Process—Department 1   225,000
Cost of completed units transferred from Department 1 to Department 2.

Cost of ending inventory

Exhibit 13-9 also indicates that the cost of the 20,000 footballs on Aug. 31 in Department 1 is $130,000—representing $60,000 for cowhide, $10,000 for strings, and $60,000 for conversion costs. When the $130,000 is added to the costs assigned to completed units, $225,000, the total is $355,000, which agrees with the total at the bottom of the total costs to account for column [column (5)] of the production report.

Let's now look at what we've been doing in Department 1 from a T-account approach. Exhibit 13-10 shows how the units and dollars flow through Department 1 on their way to Department 2. It shows that the $355,000 of total costs to account for (which we determined in the Exhibit 13-9 production report) is allocated $225,000 to the completed units and $130,000 to the incomplete units (which we calculated in the Exhibit 13-9 summary of costs report). You can see the $225,000 going from Department 1 to Department 2 on the credit side of the T-account and the $130,000 remaining as the debit balance at the bottom of the Work-in-Process T-account.

Department 2: Weighted Average

The 30,000 completed footballs are transferred from Department 1 to Department 2, where they will be pumped with air and boxed. The costs assigned to these 30,000 footballs are $225,000, and they are transferred with the footballs to Department 2. When Department 2 receives these costs, it refers to them as "transferred-in costs" and treats them like the costs of any other direct material.

The facts related to Department 2 are provided in Example 13-6.

Example 13-6

THE SPURRIER BALL COMPANY—DEPARTMENT 2: WEIGHTED AVERAGE

In Department 2 of the Spurrier Ball Company, footballs that are transferred in from Department 1 are pumped with air and boxed for shipment. At the beginning of August there were 5,000 footballs (one-half complete) being processed in De-

EXHIBIT 13-10   T-Account Approach for Department 1: Weighted Average

Work-in-Process — Department 1		
Beginning inv.: 10,000 units ($30,000 + $7,570) **$ 37,570**		
PLUS		
Costs incurred in August to complete beg. inv. and start 40,000 more ($120,000 + $25,000 + $172,430) **317,430**		
EQUALS		
Total costs to account for, associated with all 50,000 units **$355,000**		
	LESS	
	Cost of 30,000 units that were completed in Dept. 1 ($30,000 × $7.50) **$225,000**	*$225,000 is assigned to the 30,000 units that are transferred to Dept. 2 in August. Dept. 2 will call these costs transferred-in costs.*
		To Work-in-Process — Dept. 2 ⟶
EQUALS		
Ending inv.: 20,000 units ($60,000 + $10,000 + $60,000) **$130,000**		

partment 2. During August the 30,000 footballs completed in Department 1 were introduced into Department 2. Of the 35,000 footballs (5,000 + 30,000) worked on during August, 29,000 were finished by Aug. 31, and the footballs in the ending work-in-process are two-thirds complete.

The costs of the Aug. 1 beginning inventory of 5,000 unfinished footballs and the costs incurred during August are as follows:

This is the same as Example 13-5 under FIFO except for the transferred-in costs of $225,000

Cost of 5,000 footballs, Aug. 1:		
Transferred-in costs (costs transferred from Dept. 1 to Dept. 2 during July)	$ 34,000	
Conversion costs	2,400	$ 36,400
Costs incurred during Aug.:		
Transferred-in costs (costs transferred from Dept. 1 to Dept. 2 in current period)	$225,000	
Conversion costs	30,600	
Boxes	7,250	262,850
Total costs to account for		$299,250

Basic Steps for Department 2

The cost per equivalent whole unit in Department 2 is found in the same way as it was in Department 1.

The footballs that are finally finished and boxed in Department 2 will be transferred directly to finished goods inventory to await sale to customers. Let's now do the three basic steps for Department 2.

STEP 1: Tracing the Physical Flow

We know that during the month of August 29,000 footballs were finished in Department 2. The footballs that were not finished in Department 2 at the end of August are determined as follows:

The ending inventory is 6,000 footballs

Beginning inventory, work-in-process (Dept. 2).............................	5,000
Add: Units started (transferred in from Dept. 1 during August)..............	30,000
Total to account for..	35,000
Less: Units completed and transferred to Finished Goods....................	29,000
Ending inventory, work-in-process (Dept. 2)	6,000

STEP 2: Preparing the Production Report

The production report for Department 2 (Exhibit 13-11) shows that three costs go into the final boxed product—the costs of making the football in the previous

EXHIBIT 13-11 Combined Production Report and Summary of Costs Report for Department 2: Weighted Average
Under weighted average the cost assigned to the 29,000 completed units is calculated in a single step in the summary of costs report.

Production Report

Product Cost	(1) Units Completed	(2) Ending Inventory, WIP	(3) Fraction Completed	(4) Equivalent Whole Units*	(5) Total Costs to Account for		(6) Cost per Equivalent Whole Unit†
Transferred-in costs	29,000	6,000	1	35,000	$ 34,000 225,000	$259,000	$7.40
Boxes	29,000	6,000	0	29,000	-0- $ 7,250	7,250	0.25
Conversion costs	29,000	6,000	$\frac{2}{3}$	33,000	$ 2,400 30,600	33,000 $299,250	1.00 $8.65

Summary of Costs Report

Cost of footballs completed and transferred to finished goods:

29,000 × $8.65....		$250,850

Cost of ending inventory—work-in-process (Dept. 2):

Transferred-in costs	(6,000 × 1 × $7.40)	$44,400	
Boxes	(6,000 × 0 × $0.25)	-0-	
Con. costs	(6,000 × $\frac{2}{3}$ × $1.00)............................	4,000	48,400
Total costs to account for..			$299,250

* Col. (4) = col. (1) + [col. (2) × col. (3)].
† Col. (6) = col. (5)/col. (4).

department (the transferred-in costs), the box in which the football is packaged, and the conversion costs of pumping air into the balls and packaging the balls.

Columns (1) and (2) indicate the number of complete and the number of incomplete footballs. The fraction of a full dosage of each production cost added to each of the 6,000 incomplete footballs is shown in column (3).

The fraction for conversion costs is $\frac{2}{3}$

The 6,000 footballs have progressed two-thirds of the way through the production process — therefore, two-thirds of the time and attention that these units will get has already been received during August. Since the conversion costs are spread evenly over the production process, two-thirds of a full dosage of conversion costs has been incurred to do two-thirds of the work on the incomplete units. The fraction for conversion costs in column (3), therefore, is $\frac{2}{3}$.

The box is a 0

The box is added at the end of processing — only a fully pumped football will be packaged. Since the 6,000 units are only two-thirds complete, there is no way that a box has been added to any of the 6,000 incomplete units. The fraction is a 0.

Finally, we come to the transferred-in costs (which are the dollars assigned to units transferred from Department 1 to Department 2). During August 30,000 units were completed in Department 1, at a cost of $225,000, and transferred to Department 2. Normally, the processing of units transferred into a new department begins as soon as the units are received, so transferred-in costs are just like the costs of a direct material added at the beginning of production. The only difference is in the name; instead of being called direct materials (such as cowhide, strings, or package), it is called transferred-in costs.

Transferred-in costs are a 1

If transferred-in costs are the same as any other direct material that is added in a lump sum at the beginning of production, then the fraction is just as easy to determine as it is for a direct material. Since the costs are added at the beginning, they had to have been added to the 6,000 units that are two-thirds complete — the fraction is a 1.

The equivalent whole units [column (4)] for each production cost are calculated as before, as follows:

	Column from Exhibit 13-11			
	(1)	+	[(2) × (3)] =	(4)
Transferred-in costs	29,000	+	(6,000 × 1) = 35,000 equivalent whole units	
Package	29,000	+	(6,000 × 0) = 29,000 equivalent whole units	
Conversion costs	29,000	+	(6,000 × $\frac{2}{3}$) = 33,000 equivalent whole units	

EWU for Department 2

The data in columns (5) and (6) for Department 2 are determined in the same manner as they were for Department 1.

The total costs to account for [column (5)] are determined by adding together the costs of beginning inventory and the costs incurred during the period. And the costs per equivalent whole unit [column (6)] are still determined by dividing the total costs to account for [column (5)] by the equivalent whole units [column (4)].

The total cost of producing an equivalent whole unit is $8.65 per unit, shown in column (6). The total costs to account for, for Department 2, are $299,250, shown at the bottom of column (5). This total of $299,250 will be allocated between the completed units (29,000) and the incomplete units (6,000) in the final step — the summary of costs report.

STEP 3: Preparing the Summary of Costs Report

The summary of costs report for Department 2 is shown below the production report in Exhibit 13-11. It shows that the cost of 29,000 footballs transferred to

EXHIBIT 13-12   T-Account Approach for Department 2: Weighted Average

Work-in-Process — Department 2		
Beginning inv.: 5,000 units ($34,000 + $2,400) $ 36,400		
PLUS		
Costs incurred in August to complete beg. inv. and start 30,000 more ($225,000 + $7,250 + $30,600) 262,850		
EQUALS		$250,850 is assigned to the 29,000 units that are transferred to finished goods in August
Total costs to account for, associated with all 35,000 units $299,250		
	LESS	
	Cost of 29,000 units that were completed in Dept. 2 (29,000 × $8.65) $250,850	To Finished Goods Inventory
EQUALS		
Ending inv.: 6,000 units ($44,400 + $4,000) $ 48,400		

finished goods is $250,850 and the cost assigned to the 6,000 unfinished footballs in Department 2 is $48,400. The total of these two ($250,850 + $48,400) equals $299,250, which corresponds to the total for column (5) in the production report.

The T-account for Department 2 is shown in Exhibit 13-12. The total costs to account for of $299,250 (which we determined in the production report part of Exhibit 13-11) are allocated between the 29,000 completed units and the 6,000 incomplete units (which we calculated in the summary of costs report part of Exhibit 13-11). The costs that are transferred to finished goods with the 29,000 units, the $250,850, are shown as a credit in the Work-in-Process T-account, and the cost of the 6,000-unit ending inventory, $48,400, is shown as the debit balance at the bottom of the Work-in-Process T-account.

The journal entry required to transfer the costs from Work-in-Process — Department 2 to Finished Goods Inventory is as follows:

The final entry

Finished Goods Inventory   250,850
    Work-in-Process Inventory — Department 2   250,850
Cost of completed units transferred from Department 2 to Finished Goods.

MULTIPLE CATEGORIES OF PRODUCT COSTS

Throughout this text you have been exposed to numerous terms that are related to the product costing function of cost accounting. In Chapter 2 you were told that the product costs were direct materials, direct labor, and factory overhead. In Chapter 5,

Many different types of
product costs

however, we told you that the fixed portion of factory overhead was a product cost only for absorption costing, not for direct costing. In Chapter 10 we told you that the product costs could be either actual costs or standard costs, and then in Chapter 12 we added normal costing as a compromise between actual costing and standard costing. Also in Chapter 12 we discussed job order costing, and then in this chapter we explained process costing. Have you kept all these terms straight in your mind?

As each term was initially explained in great detail, you probably had a good understanding of it—as long as you were still in the chapter in which it was first introduced. But as more and more terms were introduced, it was probably hard to keep track of them all, especially when several of them were being used within the same discussion. Understandably, you would no doubt be somewhat confused if a long list of them was now placed in front of you and you were asked to distinguish one term from another. Let's now try to put them in a comprehendible order.

Direct Costing vs. Absorption Costing

Direct vs. absorption
costing—how to handle
FFO

The first decision in product costing is determining which manufacturing costs should be treated as product costs. For absorption costing—which we used in Chapters 2, 10, 11, 12, and 13—all manufacturing costs are product costs, including fixed factory overhead. Absorption costing is usually considered the appropriate method to use in statements that are to be issued to the public. For direct costing only the variable manufacturing costs are product costs, and fixed factory overhead is a period cost. Direct costing—which is considered to be preferable for assisting management in decision making—was used in Chapters 4, 5, and 6.

The distinction between direct costing and absorption costing is the first level under the product cost heading in Figure 13-2.

FIGURE 13-2 Categories of Product Costs.

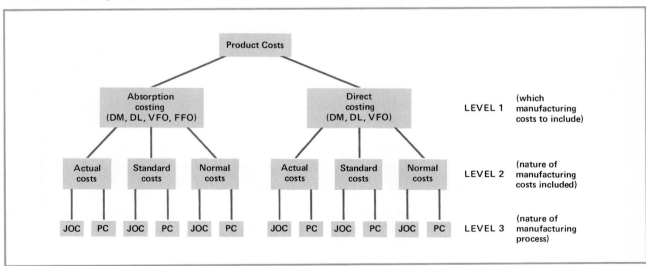

Actual Costing vs. Normal Costing vs. Standard Costing

Actual, normal, and
standard costing—
predetermined rates?

The second decision in product costing is deciding whether to assign the actual costs, the normal costs, or the standard costs to the product. This decision pertains to both the direct and the absorption costing methods. With the exception of Chapters 10 and 12, the actual costing method has been used throughout this text—sometimes with direct costing and sometimes with absorption costing. In Chapter 10 we employed a standard cost system with the absorption costing method, and in chapter 12 we used a normal costing system with the absorption costing method.

The distinction between actual, normal, and standard costing systems is shown in the second level under the product cost heading in Figure 13-2.

Job Order Costing vs. Process Costing

Job order vs. process — nature of production process

The third decision in product costing involves the nature of the production process itself. Are we producing a small number of identifiable units (or batches) to customer specifications, each of which has a different cost? Or are we producing a large number of indistinguishable units in a continuous process, each of which costs exactly the same? Do we go to a lot of trouble tracing different costs to different units, or do we merely spread the costs evenly over the many units being worked on? This choice is between the job order costing and process costing methods — whether we are assigning the actual costs, the normal costs, or the standard costs to these units and whether we are using the direct or absorption costing method.

Prior to Chapter 12 you were never told the nature of the production process, so it wasn't possible to determine whether the job order or process costing method was being employed. In the last chapter we discussed the job order costing method, primarily in conjunction with the normal costing approach to the absorption costing method. We could just as well have used direct costing instead of absorption costing, and we could have employed an actual or a standard cost system rather than a normal cost system. The choice was ours.

In this chapter, when we discussed the process costing method, we demonstrated it using actual absorption costs. However, as with job order costing, we do have choices — we could have used direct costing instead, and we could have used normal costing or standard costing instead.

The distinction between job order costing and process costing represents the third level under the product cost heading in Figure 13-2.

CHAPTER SUMMARY

The ***process costing method*** is used by companies that produce a large quantity of physically indistinguishable units in a continuous process. Since all units are identical, it is impractical and probably impossible to distinguish the exact cost of one unit from another. The cost per unit is determined by dividing the equivalent whole units produced during the period into the total costs to account for of that period.

In process costing the output is measured in ***equivalent whole units.*** This represents all fully completed units and the number of units that could be obtained if partially completed units could be somehow magically glued together to make whole ones. More realistically, equivalent whole units might be viewed as the number of units to which a full dosage of costs has been added.

There are three basic steps in all process costing situations:

1. Tracing the physical flow
2. Preparing the production report
3. Preparing a summary of costs report

The first step determines the units completed and the units in the ending work-in-process. Based on what was determined in the first step, the next step (1) determines the equivalent whole units for each product cost, (2) accumulates the total costs to account for, and (3) computes the costs per equivalent unit.

The third step allocates the total costs to account for between the units completed and the units in the ending work-in-process.

There are two different process costing methods for assigning actual costs to production: *FIFO* and *weighted average.* These methods differ in the way they handle the partially completed units in the beginning inventory, in both the production report and the summary of costs report. The steps associated with each method are summarized in the following chart:

Method	Trace the Physical Flow	Equivalent Whole Units	Total Costs to Account for	Cost per Equivalent Whole Unit	Cost of Completed Units	Cost of End. Inv.
FIFO	Beg. inv. + Units started = Total to account for − End. inv. (or completed units) = Units completed (or end. inv.)	Beg. inv. × fraction completed in current period + Units started and completed in current period + End. inv. × fraction completed in current period	Beg. inv. + Costs incurred in current period	Costs incurred in current period ÷ equivalent whole units	Cost of beg. inv. + Cost of completing beg. inv. + Cost of units started and completed	End. inv. × fraction complete × individual cost per equivalent whole unit
Weighted Average	Beg. inv. + Units started = Total to account for − End. inv. (or completed units) = Units completed (or ending inventory)	Units completed + End. inv. × fraction completed in current period	Beg. inv. + Costs incurred in current period	Beg. inv. costs + costs incurred ÷ equivalent whole units	Units completed × total cost per equivalent whole unit	End. inv. × fraction complete × individual cost per equivalent whole unit

With FIFO the completed units are first separated into two parts in the *production report* — the partially completed units in the beginning inventory and the units started and completed during the period. FIFO then assigns to the beginning inventory a fraction representing the fraction of a full dosage of costs added in the current period to complete these units. The number of equivalent whole units (EWU) in the production report for each different product cost is determined as follows:

$$\text{EWU} = \left[\begin{array}{cc} \text{beg.} & \text{fraction com-} \\ \text{inv. of} \times & \text{pleted (in} \\ \text{WIP} & \text{current period)} \end{array} \right] + \begin{array}{c} \text{started} \\ \text{and} \\ \text{completed} \end{array} + \left[\begin{array}{cc} \text{end.} & \text{fraction com-} \\ \text{inv. of} \times & \text{pleted (in} \\ \text{WIP} & \text{current period)} \end{array} \right]$$

The equivalent whole units in the production report represent work done in the current period only — the equivalent units of work done last period to the beginning inventory are excluded. In the total costs to account for column of the production report, FIFO separates the total costs into two groups: the costs incurred in the current period (these are the ones divided by the equivalent units to get the CPEWU) and the beginning inventory costs (these costs do not enter into the CPEWU calculation). Within the *summary of costs report* the costs assigned to the completed units are made up of three parts: (1) the costs of producing the units started and completed; (2) the costs of the partially completed units in the beginning inventory (incurred in the previous period); and (3) the costs of completing the beginning inventory (incurred in the current period).

When the weighted average method is used, no distinction is made within the production report between the units that were in the beginning inventory and the units that were worked on in the current period. The equivalent whole units for the current period include all of the beginning inventory even though some of the work may have been done in the previous period. The calculation is:

$$\text{EWU} = \begin{array}{c} \text{all} \\ \text{completed} \\ \text{units} \end{array} + \left[\begin{array}{c} \text{end.} \\ \text{inv. of} \\ \text{WIP} \end{array} \times \begin{array}{c} \text{fraction com-} \\ \text{pleted (in} \\ \text{current period)} \end{array} \right]$$

In the total costs to account for column no distinction is made between the costs of the beginning inventory and the costs incurred in the current period. They are simply added together and treated as if they all occurred in the current period. These combined costs are then divided by equivalent whole units to get a weighted average CPEWU. This CPEWU is the same for all units, whether they were worked on entirely in the current period or were worked on partially during the previous period and partially during the current period. Under weighted average, in the summary of costs report the cost of completed units is calculated in one simple step — the number of units completed multiplied by the total CPEWU.

With standard costing the equivalent whole units are determined in exactly the same manner as they are with FIFO. The equivalent whole units for each product cost are then multiplied by the respective standard unit costs to get the standard costs applied. The cost of the completed units is determined by multiplying the total completed units by the total standard cost per unit. The cost of the ending work-in-process is found in the same manner as it is with FIFO and weighted average.

IMPORTANT TERMS USED IN THIS CHAPTER

Cost per equivalent whole unit   The total costs to account for divided by the equivalent whole units. It represents the full dosage of each production cost assigned to each equivalent whole unit. (page 575)

Equivalent whole units   A measure of productive output in process costing manufacturing — measuring whole completed units as well as units not yet completed — which represents the number of units to which a full dosage of costs is added. It is computed by adding (1) the completed units and (2) the units in the ending inventory of work-in-process multiplied by the fraction completed. Also called *equivalent units.* (page 572)

FIFO method   The process costing method that distinguishes the work of the current period from that of the previous period. This method separates the units in beginning inventory from those that were started and completed; the CPEWU is calculated by dividing the costs of the current period by the equivalent units of work for the current period. (page 582)

Job order costing method The method of accounting for the production of identifiable products, often made to customer specifications. The costs of each job are carefully accumulated and kept separate from the costs of any other job. (page 569)

Process costing method The method of accounting for the production of a large volume of indistinguishable units in a continuous process. An average cost is determined by dividing the production costs by the equivalent whole units of production. (page 569)

Production report A basic step in the process costing method — a format for calculating the cost per equivalent whole unit. (page 575)

Summary of costs report The final step in the process costing method in which the total costs to account for are allocated between the completed units and the ending inventory of work-in-process. (page 579)

Total costs to account for The total of the costs of the beginning inventory of work-in-process and all the product costs incurred during the current period. (page 575)

Weighted average method The process costing method that makes no distinction between the units that were completed from the beginning inventory and those that were started and completed in the current period. The CPEWU is calculated by dividing the combination of beginning inventory costs plus costs incurred currently by the equivalent units for the period. The equivalent units include some work of the previous period. (page 582)

APPENDIX 13-1: PROCESS COSTING WITH STANDARD COSTS

In some ways standard costing is like FIFO

The discussion within this chapter dealt with the FIFO and weighted average methods of process costing. As we pointed out, these two methods represent two different approaches to assigning actual production costs to the units produced during a period. An alternative to assigning actual costs to the product is the assignment of standard costs using predetermined rates. When standard costs are used for product costing, there is no longer a need to argue about whether FIFO or weighted average is theoretically preferable, because we're no longer assigning actual costs to production. There is, however, a very practical reason to learn FIFO if you're going to learn only one actual costing method: It's a lot easier to learn how to do standard cost process costing if you already know FIFO.

Steps in Standard Cost Process Costing

The steps in the solution of a standard cost process costing problem are as follows:

Five keys to doing standard costing

1. Set up columns (1) to (4) of the production report as you did with FIFO, and determine the equivalent whole units. The equivalent whole units will always be the same for FIFO and standard costing.

2. Make column (5) the standard cost per unit for each different product cost.

3. Make column (6) the total standard costs applied to production. The standard costs applied in the current period are found by multiplying the equivalent whole units in column (4) times the standard costs per unit in column (5). The standard costs of the beginning inventory are added at the bottom of this column.

4. As long as the standard costs per unit are not different from what they were in the previous period (assume they have not changed unless you are specifically told otherwise), the cost of the units completed in the summary of costs report is easily found. You merely multiply the total units completed [column (1a) plus column (1c)] by the total standard costs per unit (summation of per-unit costs in the fifth column).

5. The cost of the ending work-in-process is found by using the procedure you've already learned.

Continuing with the Spurrier Ball Company

Standard costs for Spurrier Ball Company

Refer again to Example 13-4, and assume that Spurrier decides to use standard costs instead of actual costs in its production report and summary of costs report for Department 1. Also assume that Spurrier has determined the following standard costs per unit:

Cowhide...	$2.90
Strings..	0.50
Conversion costs..	4.00
Total...	$7.40

Finally, assume that the standard costs of the 10,000-unit beginning inventory of work-in-process were the following:

Cowhide...	$29,000
Strings..	-0-
Conversion costs	8,000
Total...	$37,000

EXHIBIT 13-13   Production Report for Department 1: Standard Costs

Product Cost	**Units Completed**			(2) Ending Inventory, WIP	(3) Fraction Completed	(4) Equivalent Whole Units	(5) Standard Cost per Unit	(6) Standard Costs Applied
	(1a) Beginning Inventory, WIP	(1b) Fraction Completed	(1c) Started and Completed					
Cowhide.............	10,000	0	20,000	20,000	1	40,000	$2.90	$116,000
Strings	10,000	1	20,000	20,000	1	50,000	0.50	25,000
Conversion costs	10,000	$\frac{4}{5}$	20,000	20,000	$\frac{3}{4}$	43,000	4.00	172,000
Col (4) is the same as it is in FIFO; columns (5) and (6) are different		30,000				*Costs of beginning inventory*	$7.40	$313,000 37,000 $350,000

The production report is shown in Exhibit 13-13, and the summary of costs report under standard costing is shown in Exhibit 13-14. Notice in Exhibit 13-14 how easily the cost of the completed units is determined. Even though the equivalent whole units were calculated in the same way as they were with FIFO, it is not necessary to determine the cost of the completed units in the same detail as with FIFO — as long as the standard costs per unit are the same as they were in the previous year. If the standard costs per unit are different from what they were in the previous year — for

A simplifying assumption for the summary of costs report

EXHIBIT 13-14
Summary of Costs Report:
Standard Costing

Cost of completed units (30,000 × $7.40).....................		$222,000
Cost of ending inventory—work-in-process:		
Cowhide (20,000 × 1 × $2.90)...................	$58,000	
Strings (20,000 × 1 × $0.50)...................	10,000	
Con. costs (20,000 × ¾ × $4.00)...............	60,000	128,000
		$350,000

example, if the standard cost for cowhide was $2.90 last year but is $2.95 this year—then the cost of the completed units would have to be calculated in the same detail as you use with FIFO.

Notice also in Exhibit 13-14 that the total costs figure in the summary of costs report—$350,000—agrees exactly with the total of column (6), the standard costs applied column, in the production report.

QUESTIONS

1. Explain the differences between *job order costing* and *process costing*. Give several examples of industries in which each method would be used.

2. The difference between job order costing and process costing has been described by some as "the breadth of the denominator." Explain what they might mean by this.

3. Job order costing and process costing are extremes of product costing. Describe a situation in which a combination of these two methods might be employed.

4. Explain the meaning of the term *equivalent whole unit.* How is it determined?

5. "The cost per equivalent whole unit is computed by dividing the costs incurred for the period by the number of units completed." Do you agree? Why or why not?

6. Explain how the fraction completed column in the production report is determined for materials added in a lump sum.

7. Will equivalent whole units be less than, equal to, or greater than the number of units completed?

8. In process costing what is the purpose of (1) the production report and (2) the summary of costs report?

9. Explain the differences in the *FIFO* and *weighted average* methods of process costing.

10. What are the three basic steps in the solution of any process costing problem?

11. Why is it so much easier to solve a process costing problem with FIFO when there is no beginning inventory in work-in-process?

12. "We ignore the beginning inventory in work-in-process whenever we use the FIFO method of process costing." Comment on this statement.

13. "As long as the totals in the summary of costs report agree with the total costs to account for column in the production report, the process costing problem was done correctly." Do you agree? Why or why not?

14. "When there is no beginning inventory in work-in-process, the equivalent whole units under FIFO and weighted average will always be identical." Discuss why you believe this statement to be true or false.

15. Explain what is meant by the term *transferred-in costs.*

16. How do the production reports and summary of cost reports differ for FIFO and standard costing?

17. Distinguish between *actual process costing* and *standard process costing.*

18. Within this text, you have studied the following costing methods:

> Direct and absorption costing
> Actual, normal, and standard costing
> Process costing and job order costing

For the two situations described below, identify which combination of product costing methods is being used:

a. Bair Aspirin produces 500 mg of aspirin in 250-tablet bottles. Bair agrees with the management accountants, who contend that fixed factory overhead is a period cost, and plans to assign all appropriate product costs using carefully predetermined rates.

b. Ester Gilliams Pools builds customized swimming pools for Hollywood movie stars (unfortunately it doesn't sell too many because the business is in Hollywood, Florida). Gilliams doesn't use any predetermined rates for determining the cost of each pool. In addition, all costs associated with the construction process are treated as product costs.

EXERCISES

Exercise 13-1
Filling in the fraction completed column for ending WIP

During December 1988 the NA (meaning "no alcohol") Beer Company completed 75,000 units; it had 15,000 units still in process on Dec. 31. NA uses four ingredients in its production process; they are:

Material A .. Added at the beginning of production
Material B .. Added when production is one-half complete
Material C .. Added at the end of production
Material D .. Incurred evenly throughout production

Three different situations are listed below. Each one represents a point in production to which the 15,000 units in inventory might have progressed by month-end. For each situation you are to fill in the blanks with the fraction that represents work completed for each product cost in determining equivalent whole units.

	Ending Inventory		
Product Cost	$\frac{2}{5}$ Complete	$\frac{3}{5}$ Complete	$\frac{3}{4}$ Complete
Material A	_____	_____	_____
Material B	_____	_____	_____
Material C	_____	_____	_____
Material D	_____	_____	_____
Conversion costs	_____	_____	_____

Exercise 13-2
Filling in the fraction completed column for beginning WIP (FIFO)

Refer to the facts presented in Exercise 13-1. Now assume that there is a beginning inventory on Dec. 1 of 10,000 units and that you are using the FIFO method. Once again, there are three situations below, but now they represent the beginning inventory rather than the ending inventory. This time you are to fill in the blanks with a fraction that represents the percentage of a full dosage needed to complete the beginning inventory during December.

Product Cost	Beginning Inventory		
	$\frac{2}{5}$ Complete	$\frac{3}{5}$ Complete	$\frac{3}{4}$ Complete
Material A	_____	_____	_____
Material B	_____	_____	_____
Material C	_____	_____	_____
Material D	_____	_____	_____
Conversion costs	_____	_____	_____

Exercise 13-3
Tracing the physical flow

The first step in the process costing method is tracing the physical flow. The items listed below are needed to make this computation. You are to fill in the blanks for the unknown quantities.

	Situations		
	1	2	3
Beginning inventory, work-in-process.................	20,000	?	44,000
Units started	60,000	120,000	?
Total to account for	?	190,000	200,000
Ending inventory, work-in-process....................	20,000	55,000	?
Units sold	?	?	180,000

Exercise 13-4
Preparing a summary of costs report — weighted average

The production report is shown below for the Montana Manufacturing Company. Assume in this exercise that there was a 40,000-unit beginning inventory in work-in-process, one-fourth complete. Montana is using the weighted average method.

Product Cost	Units Started and Completed	Ending Inventory, WIP	Fraction Completed	Equivalent Whole Units	Total Costs to Account for		Costs per Equivalent Whole Unit
Material A.................	240,000	50,000	1	290,000	$ 74,200 500,000 $ -0-	$574,200	$1.98
Package	240,000	50,000	0	240,000	96,000	96,000	0.40
Conversion costs	240,000	50,000	$\frac{3}{5}$	270,000	$ 10,000 260,000	270,000	1.00
						$940,200	$3.38

Using the information contained in the production report, prepare the summary of costs report.

(Check figure: Cost of ending work-in-process = $129,000)

Exercise 13-5
Preparing a summary of costs report — FIFO

Assume that the facts you used in Exercise 13-4 remain unchanged, except that now Montana is using the FIFO method. The production report is given below:

Product Cost	Beginning Inventory, WIP	Fraction Completed	Units Started and Completed	Ending Inventory, WIP	Fraction Completed	Equivalent Whole Units	Total Costs to Account for	Costs per Equivalent Whole Unit
			Units Completed					
Material A......	40,000	0	200,000	50,000	1	250,000	$500,000	$2.00
Package	40,000	1	200,000	50,000	0	240,000	96,000	0.40
Conversion costs	40,000	$\frac{3}{4}$	200,000	50,000	$\frac{3}{5}$	260,000	260,000	1.00
							$856,000	$3.40
							74,200	
							-0-	
							10,000	
							$940,200	

Prepare the summary of costs report for Montana.

(Check figure: Cost of completed goods = $810,200)

Exercise 13-6
Completing a production report — FIFO

Below is a partial production report for the Justin Tyme Stopwatch Company. You are to fill in the blanks that will complete the report. Justin is using the FIFO method.

Product Cost	Beginning Inventory, WIP	Fraction Completed	Started and Completed	Ending Inventory, WIP	Fraction Completed	Equivalent Whole Units	Total Costs to Account for	Costs per Equivalent Whole Unit
			Units Completed					
Material A......	2,000	0	6,000	1,000	1	?	$?	$2.50
Material B......	2,000	1	6,000	1,000	?	8,000	16,000	?
Conversion costs	2,000	$\frac{1}{5}$	6,000	1,000	?	?	28,600	4.00
							$?	$?
							4,800	
							-0-	
							6,240	
							$?	

Exercise 13-7
Completing a production report — weighted average

The incomplete production report for Tums Petroleum is shown below. You are to fill in the missing blanks, assuming Tums uses the weighted average method.

Product Cost	Units Completed	Ending Inventory	Fraction Completed	Equivalent Whole Units	Total Costs to Account for	Cost per Equivalent Whole Unit
Material A	50,000	10,000	?	60,000	$270,000	$?
Material B	50,000	10,000	-0-	?	?	5.00
Conversion costs....................	?	10,000	?	57,500	?	?
					$?	$11.00

Exercise 13-8
Preparing a production report and a summary of costs report for the second of two departments — FIFO

The Connors Company produces a product that goes through an assembly department and a finishing department prior to completion. During October 10,000 units were completed in the assembly department at $5 per unit and transferred to the finishing department. On Oct. 1 there was no beginning inventory in the finishing department, but on Oct. 31 there was an inventory of 2,000 units, one-half complete. The conversion costs incurred in October for the finishing department were $27,000.

Assume that there were 4,000 units on hand on Oct. 1, one-fourth complete. The costs of this beginning inventory were:

Conversion costs	$ 2,500
Transferred-in costs.	19,800
	$22,300

Prepare a production report and a summary of costs report for the finishing department, using the FIFO method.

(Check figure: Cost per equivalent whole unit for transferred-in costs = $5)

Exercise 13-9
Preparing a production report and a summary of costs report: weighted average

Now redo Exercise 13-8, but use weighted average instead of FIFO.

(Check figure: Cost of completed units = $87,060)

Exercise 13-10
Tracing the physical flow through two departments

The Arias Company produces a product that goes through two processing departments before it is completed and transferred to finished goods. You are to fill in the blanks for the two departments for two independent situations, A and B.

	Situation A		Situation B	
	Dept. 1	**Dept. 2**	**Dept. 1**	**Dept. 2**
Beginning inventory	3,000	4,500	11,000	14,000
Units started (or transferred in).	20,000	?	?	66,000
Total to account for.	?	?	?	80,000
Ending inventory	?	1,500	2,400	?
Units completed.	15,000	?	?	70,000

Exercise 13-11
Preparing a production report and a summary of costs report — standard costing

Mrs. Pawleys, Inc., manufactures frozen fish sticks and has decided to utilize its idle capacity to produce a complementary product — fish-stick cookies. The production will take place completely in one processing department. Fish sticks are added at the beginning of the process, cookie dough is added when the process is one-quarter complete, and a package (holding 1 pound of the frozen product) is added at the end. Conversion costs are incurred evenly.

On Jan. 1, 1989, Pawleys had 2,000 pounds of cookie dough in process, 20% complete. During the month 10,000 additional pounds were started and 9,000 1-pound packages were completed. The ending process was 80% complete on Jan. 31.

Pawleys uses predetermined standards for product costing. The standards per pound for each cost were determined to be as follows:

Fish sticks	$0.22
Cookie dough	0.25
Package	0.05
Direct labor.	0.15
Factory overhead	0.10
	$0.77

The cost of the 2,000 pounds of fish-stick cookie dough in the Jan. 1 inventory was $540.

Fish sticks......................................	$440
Direct labor	60
Factory overhead	40
	$540

Prepare the production report and the summary of costs report for Pawleys for January.

(Check figure: Cost of units completed = $6,930)

PROBLEMS: SET A

**Problem A13-1
Preparing a production
report and a summary of
costs report — FIFO**

The Wilson Manufacturing Company produces soccer balls for the Tampa Bay Rowdies in a continuous process. During the month of July 40,000 balls were started; at the end of the month 2,000 were still in process, one-tenth complete. There were no balls in process on July 1.

The only two product costs are direct materials (which are added in their entirety at the beginning of production) and conversion costs (which are incurred uniformly throughout production). The costs incurred during July were $160,000 for direct materials and $114,600 for conversion costs.

Required   Prepare a production report and a summary of costs report using the FIFO method.

(Check figure: Cost of balls completed = $266,000)

**Problem A13-2
Preparing a production
report and a summary of
costs report — FIFO**

The Rodney Corporation makes a citrus flavored drink called Pick Me Up, which is being used at more and more universities. It not only replaces the liquids lost through perspiration but also provides the daily requirements of all important nutrients needed by the human body (this allows coaches to practice straight through dinner, thereby saving the university the costs of one meal per day for the entire team).

During September 1988 Rodney started 50,000 gallons of Pick Me Up and completed 45,000. The inventory on Sept. 30 was 7,500 gallons, one-half complete. The production costs incurred during September were as follows:

Direct materials..............................	$50,000
Conversion costs	95,625

The inventory on Sept. 1 was three-fourths complete. The costs of this inventory were $2,500 for direct materials and $3,750 for conversion costs. Direct materials are added at the beginning of production.

Required   1. Prepare a production report. Use the FIFO method.
2. Prepare a summary of costs report.

(Check figure: Cost of units completed and transferred to finished goods = $136,725)

3. Prepare the journal entry to record the transfer of completed units to finished goods inventory.

**Problem A13-3
Preparing a production
report and a summary of
costs report — standard
costing**

Use the facts that were given in Problem A13-2 for the Rodney Corporation, but assume that Rodney is going to use standard costs for product costing. The standards are $0.90 per unit for direct materials and $2.00 for conversion costs. These standards are the same as they were in the previous period.

Required   1. Determine the cost of the beginning inventory on Sept. 1.
2. Prepare the production report for September.

(Check figure: Total standard costs applied to current production = $138,750)

3. Determine the cost of the units that were transferred to finished goods and the cost of the Sept. 30 ending inventory in work-in-process.

Problem A13-4
Preparing a production report and a summary of costs report—weighted average

Refer to the facts that were given in Problem A13-2, but this time assume that the Rodney Corporation uses the weighted average method.

Required

Repeat the three requirements of Problem A13-2.

(Check figure for part 2: Cost of goods completed = $136,733)

Problem A13-5
Using weighted average with several materials

On Dec. 1, 1988, the SKW Company had 8,000 units in work-in-process, one-fourth completed. The costs of this inventory were:

Material S	$14,000
Material K	8,000
Conversion costs	12,250

During December 32,000 units were started, of which 25,000 were completed by month-end. The costs incurred during December were:

Material S	$66,000
Material K	57,000
Material W	12,500
Conversion costs	74,000

Material S is added at the beginning of production. Material K is added evenly during the process until the units are one-half complete. Material W is added entirely at the end of production. The ending work-in-process is 25% complete, and SKW uses the weighted average method of process costing.

Required

1. Determine the cost assigned to the completed units transferred to finished goods in December. *(Check figure: $187,500)*

2. Determine the cost of the Dec. 31 inventory of work-in-process.

Problem A13-6
Using FIFO with several materials

Assume that the SKW Company in Problem A13-5 is using the FIFO method instead of weighted average.

Required

1. Determine the cost assigned to the completed units transferred to finished goods in December. *(Check figure: $187,439)*

2. Determine the cost of the Dec. 31 inventory of work-in-process.

Problem A13-7
Using FIFO with several materials and transferred-in costs

The Jetson Company produces a packaged fruit drink called Persimmon Punch. The persimmons are ground and blended in process 1; pink artificial coloring is added in process 2; and the concoction is chilled and packaged (at the end of processing) in process 3.

On Jan. 1, 1988, there were 30,000 pints of flavored punch in process 3, one-third complete. During January 100,000 pints were transferred from process 2 to process 3; at the end of January there were 25,000 pints of punch awaiting packaging, four-fifths complete.

The Jan. 1 costs of inventory were:

Conversion costs	$ 500
Transferred-in costs.	6,000

During December the average cost of producing a pint in process 2 was $0.20 per pint. In addition, the costs incurred for process 3 during January were:

Conversion costs	$5,750
Cartons	4,200

The Jetson Company uses the FIFO method for all three processes.

Required	Prepare a production report and a summary of costs report for process 3 for January.

(Check figure: Cost of completed units = $30,450)

**Problem A13-8
Using weighted average
with several materials and
transferred-in costs**

Assume that the Jetson Company in Problem A13-7 uses the weighted average method. All other facts remain the same.

Required	Prepare a production report and a summary of costs report for process 3 for January.

(Check figure: Cost of ending inventory = $6,000)

**Problem A13-9
Preparing a production
report and a summary of
costs report for two
departments — FIFO**

The Silver Trinkets Company makes sterling silver pacifiers in two production processes. In the first the metal is finely molded. In the second process the pacifiers are polished and boxed (100 pacifiers to a box). The silver metal is added entirely at the beginning of process 1, and the pacifiers are boxed at the end of process 2. The following additional facts relate to production for Silver Trinkets during November:

	Molding	Polishing
Beginning balance (Nov. 1), pacifiers.......................	10,000	3,000
Pacifiers started or transferred in...........................	50,000	-?-
Completed units:		
Pacifiers	55,000	na
Boxes	na	450
Completion percentage:		
Beginning inventory	75%	50%
Ending inventory	25%	75%
Costs of beginning inventory:		
Metal...	$1,000,000	na
Boxes	na	0
Conversion costs..	200,625	$ 12,000
Transferred-in costs	na	375,000
Costs incurred in November:		
Metal...	5,000,000	na
Conversion costs..	1,486,875	426,000
Boxes	na	90,000

Required	1. Using the FIFO method, prepare the production report and summary of costs report for the molding department for November.

(Check figure: Cost of pacifiers transferred to polishing = $7,149,375)

2. Using the FIFO method, prepare the production report and the summary of costs report for the polishing department for November.

(Check figure: Cost of ending inventory = $1,767,870)

**Problem A13-10
Preparing a production
report and a summary of
costs report for two
departments — weighted
average**

Refer to the facts presented in Problem A13-9 for the Silver Trinkets Company.

Required

Using the weighted average method, repeat both requirements of Problem A13-9.

*(Check figure: Cost of pacifiers transferred to polishing = $7,150,000;
cost of boxes transferred to finished goods = $6,288,300)*

Problem A13-11
Preparing a production report and a summary of costs report for two departments — standard costing

Assume that the Silver Trinkets Company in Problem A13-9 uses predetermined standards for product costing, rather than using FIFO or weighted average actual costs. In the molding department the standard costs per unit for metal and conversion costs are $98 and $30, respectively. In the polishing department the standards are $200 per box for the boxes and $750 per box for the conversion costs. These standards have remained the same during the entire year.

<u>**Required**</u>

1. Prepare a production report and a summary of costs report for the molding department for November.

(Check figure: Cost of units transferred to polishing = $7,040,000)

2. Prepare a production report and a summary of costs report for the polishing department for November.

Problem A13-12
Preparing all reports for two departments for 2 months — weighted average

On Jan. 1 the Warhawk Weapons Company began production of a new handgun, the "Saturday Night Extra-Special." All the materials are added at the beginning in the assembly department; completed guns are transferred to the inspection department, where each gun is inspected before it is transferred to finished goods. The following facts are given for each department, one month at a time:

January During the first month of operation production was started on 1,000 guns in the assembly department, of which 800 were completed. The costs incurred in January were $5,000 for direct materials and $2,125 for conversion costs. The ending inventory was one-fourth complete at the end of the month.

In the inspection department 700 guns were completely inspected and given the green light to be sold. They were transferred to finished goods. The remaining guns were one-half inspected on Jan. 31. The conversion costs incurred during January were $750.

February During February 1,400 guns were started, of which 400 (three-fourths complete) were unfinished on Feb. 28. The assembly department incurred $7,350 of costs for direct materials and $3,770 for conversion costs.

The costs incurred in the inspection department during February were $1,155 for conversion costs. There were 300 guns still on hand at the end of February, which had been only one-third inspected.

Warhawk uses the weighted average method to account for the production of handguns.

<u>**Required**</u>

1. Prepare the production report and the summary of costs report for the assembly department for January. Also make the appropriate journal entry for the transfer to the inspection department.
2. Prepare the production report and the summary of costs report for the inspection department for January. Also make the journal entry to record the transfer to finished goods.

(Check figure: Cost of guns completed = $5,950)

3. Prepare the production report and the summary of costs report for the assembly department for February. Once again, make the correct journal entry to record the transfer.

(Check figure: Cost of guns completed = $9,379)

4. Prepare the production report and the summary of costs report for the inspection department for February. One last time, make the correct journal entry to record the transfer.

Problem A13-13
Preparing all reports for two departments for 2 months — FIFO

The Warhawk Weapon Company discussed in Problem A13-12 is interested in using the FIFO method, rather than the weighted average method, to account for its two departments.

Required

1. Prepare the production report and the summary of costs report for the assembly department for January. Also make the appropriate journal entry for the transfer to the inspection department.
2. Prepare the production report and the summary of costs report for the inspection department for January. Also make the journal entry to record the transfer to finished goods.

(Check figure: Cost of guns completed = $5,950)

3. Prepare the production report and the summary of costs report for the assembly department for February. Once again, make the correct journal entry to record the transfer.

(Check figure: Cost of guns completed = $9,365)

4. Prepare the production report and the summary of costs report for the inspection department for February. One last time, make the correct journal entry to record the transfer.

PROBLEMS: SET B

Problem B13-1
Preparing a production report and a summary of costs report — FIFO

The Sweet-Tooth Candy Company produces a candy bar called Baby Brett in a single process. All ingredients (sugar, syrup, nuts, flour, etc.) are added at the beginning of production, and a package is added at the very end. At the beginning of 1988 there were no candy bars in process (the ones that would have been on hand were spoiled when the power went off during the night). During January 1,000,000 candy bars were begun, of which 300,000 were still in process (one-third complete) on Jan. 31.

The costs incurred during January were as follows:

Ingredients	$150,000
Conversion costs	80,000
Package	7,000

Sweet-Tooth uses the FIFO method of cost accounting.

Required

1. Prepare the production report for January.

(Check figure: Total CPEWU = $0.26)

2. Prepare the summary of costs report for January.
3. Make the journal entry that would be needed to record the transfer of the completed candy bars.

Problem B13-2
Preparing a production report and a summary of costs report — FIFO

On Mar. 1, 1989, the Henry Erin Bat Company, which produces metal baseball bats for Little League baseball teams, had 7,000 unfinished bats in process. Each one was about 25% complete. Its costs were:

Direct Materials	$10,400
Direct Labor	5,000
Factory Overhead	1,600

During March 23,000 bats were started; at the end of March there were 5,000 bats remaining in work-in-process, three-fifths complete. The costs incurred in March were $34,600 for direct materials, $80,000 for direct labor, and $26,400 for factory overhead. The direct materials are added at the beginning of the production process, and all conversion costs are incurred smoothly over the entire production process.

The FIFO method is being used by the company to account for the production process.

Required	Prepare each of the following:

$\frac{8}{10} = \frac{4}{5}$

1. The production report
2. The summary of costs report

(Check figure: Cost of ending work-in-process = $19,682)

Problem B13-3
Preparing a production report and a summary of costs report — standard costing

Use the facts that were given in Problem B13-1 for the Sweet-Tooth Candy Company, but this time Sweet-Tooth is going to use standard costs for product costing. The standards per unit are:

Ingredients.	$0.16
Conversion costs	0.11
Package	0.01
	$0.28

These standards are the same as they were in the previous period.

Required	1. Determine the cost of the beginning inventory on Jan. 1.

2. Prepare the production report for January.
3. Determine the cost of the units that were transferred to finished goods and the cost of the Jan. 31 ending inventory.

(Check figure: Cost of units transferred = $196,000)

4. Determine the under- or overapplied costs for each production cost for January.

Problem B13-4
Preparing a production report and a summary of costs report — weighted average

Assume that the Henry Erin Bat Company in Problem B13-2 would rather use the weighted average method than FIFO.

Required

Prepare each of the following:
1. The production report
2. The summary of costs report

(Check figure: Cost of ending work-in-process = $19,607)

Problem B13-5
Using weighted average with several materials

The Eric Orwell Manufacturing Company started 81,000 units during August 1989 and completed 66,000 during the month. Orwell uses three materials in production. Material A is added at the beginning of the process; material B is added evenly throughout production; and material C is added after production is 80% complete.
     On Aug. 1 Orwell had a 9,000-unit beginning inventory, 30% complete. Its costs were:

Material A.	$8,400
Material B.	4,020
Conversion costs	4,800

The costs incurred during August were:

Material A	$ 81,600
Material B.	103,980
Material C.	33,000
Conversion costs	120,300

The Aug. 31 inventory was 25% complete.

Required	Using the weighted average method, determine each of the following:

1. The costs assigned to finished goods inventory in August

(Check figure: $312,708)
Completed & Transferred

2. The cost of the Aug. 31 inventory in work-in-process

Problem B13-6
Using FIFO with several materials

Reread the facts above for the Eric Orwell Manufacturing Company, but assume that the FIFO method is being used instead of weighted average.

| **Required** |

Using the FIFO method, determine each of the following:
1. The costs assigned to finished goods inventory in August

(Check figure: $312,458)

2. The cost of the Aug. 31 inventory in work-in-process

Problem B13-7
Using FIFO with transferred-in costs

The Dr. Pibber Bottling Company produces a soft drink called Pepper Power. The ingredients for Pepper Power are mixed in Department 1, bottled in Department 2, and capped and packaged (six to a carton) in Department 3. During December 200,000 bottles (at $0.08 per bottle) were transferred from bottling to capping. On Dec. 1 there were 10,000 uncapped bottles in the capping department, one-fourth complete; during December 32,500 cartons were transferred to finished goods. The ending inventory of capped bottles was one-half complete.

The Dec. 1 inventory had the following costs:

Transferred-in costs..............................	$1,000
Conversion costs	175

The costs incurred during December in the capping department were as follows:

Conversion costs	$5,900
Caps (added at the one-third point in production)..	2,100
Cartons (added at the end of production).........	3,900

| **Required** |

Prepare the production report and the summary of costs report for the capping department. Use the FIFO method of costing the product. Calculate the equivalent units and the CPEWU in terms of the number of bottles.

(Check figure: Total CPEWU = $0.1395 per bottle)

Problem B13-8
Using weighted average with transferred-in costs

Refer to the facts presented in Problem B13-7 for the Dr. Pibber Company.

| **Required** |

Prepare the production report and the summary of costs report, but this time use the weighted average method to cost the product. Make all calculations in terms of the number of bottles produced.

(Check figure: Total CPEWU = $0.141 per bottle)

Problem B13-9
Preparing a production report and a summary of costs report for two departments — FIFO

The Swinging Door Company produces high-quality leaded glass doors that pass through an assembly department and a finishing department prior to completion. The wood is added at the beginning of assembly; the leaded glass is added at the 50% point in finishing; and a package is added at the very end of finishing. The following additional facts relate to production for Swinging Door during November:

	Assembly	Finishing
Beginning inventory, doors	2,500 ($\frac{1}{2}$ complete)	4,500 ($\frac{2}{3}$ complete)
Doors started or transferred in	12,500	-?-
Completed doors	8,000	10,500
Ending inventory, doors.	7,000 ($\frac{6}{7}$ complete)	2,000 ($\frac{1}{4}$ complete)
Cost of beginning inventory:		
Wood	$ 190,000	na
Transferred-in costs.	na	$434,000
Leaded glass	na	214,000
Package	na	0
Conversion costs	11,750	12,950
Costs incurred in November:		
Wood	1,025,000	na
Leaded glass	na	300,000
Package	na	21,000
Conversion costs	191,250	36,000
Method to be used.	FIFO	FIFO

Required

1. Prepare the production report and the summary of costs report for the assembly department.

(Check figure: Costs transferred to finishing = $754,000)

2. Prepare a production report and summary of costs report for the finishing department.

(Check figure: Costs transferred to finished goods = $1,581,200)

Problem B13-10
Preparing a production report and a summary of costs report for two departments — weighted average

Assume that the Swinging Door Company in Problem B13-9 uses the weighted average method. All other facts remain the same.

Required

Repeat both requirements of Problem B13-9.

(Check figure: Cost of doors transferred to finishing = $764,000)

Problem B13-11
Preparing a production report and a summary of costs report for two departments — standard costing

Assume that the Swinging Door Company in Problem B13-9 uses predetermined standards for product costing, rather than using FIFO or weighted average actual costs. The standard cost per unit for each product cost is listed below:

	Assembly	Finishing
Material:		
Wood	$80.00	na
Leaded glass	na	$ 50.00
Package	na	1.90
Conversion costs	16.00	4.00
Transferred in.	na	96.00
	$96.00	$151.90

These standards have remained the same during the entire year.

1. Prepare a production report and a summary of costs report for the assembly department for November. *(Check figure: Standard cost of beginning inventory = $220,000)*

2. Prepare a production report and a summary of costs report for the finishing department for November.

3. Prepare a performance report for each department for November. Show three columns in each performance report: actual, applied, and under- or overapplied. Do not include transferred-in costs in the report for the finishing department.

**Problem B13-12
Preparing all reports for two departments for 2 months — weighted average**

The Irving Eastern Book Company produces sleazy romance novels in two departments— binding and proofing. All materials are added at the beginning of production in the binding department. Bound books are transferred to proofing, where they are inspected to be sure that all the pages are included, the binding is secure, and the printing is legible. The following facts relate to Irving's production during January 1988:

Binding department On Jan. 1 there were 10,000 books in process (one-fifth complete). The costs incurred were $1,000 for direct materials and $2,500 for conversion costs. During the month 90,000 books were started and 80,000 were completed. The remaining books were three-fourths complete on Jan. 31. The costs incurred in January were $9,000 for direct materials and $83,700 for conversion costs.

Proofing department The beginning inventory was 2,000 books (one-fifth complete). The costs assigned to these books were $2,000 for transferred-in costs and $200 for conversion costs. The Jan. 31 balance in inventory was 4,000 books (one-half complete). The conversion costs for January in the proofing department were $39,800.

The facts given below relate to production during February:

Binding department In February 60,000 books were begun; there were 30,000 in process at the end of the month, two-thirds complete. The direct materials costs for February were $7,500, and the conversion costs were $57,750.

Proofing department The number of books transferred to finished goods during February was 45,000. The books that were still in process at the end of the month were one-third complete. The conversion costs for the month were $25,300.

Irving uses the weighted average method to account for its production costs in both the binding and the proofing departments.

Prepare the production report and the summary of costs report for:
1. The binding department for January *(Check figure: Cost of books transferred = $80,560)*

2. The proofing department for January
3. The binding department for February*(Check figure: Cost of books transferred = $56,910)*

4. The proofing department for February

**Problem B13-13
Preparing all reports for two departments for 2 months — FIFO**

Assume that the Irving Eastern Book Company discussed in Problem B13-12 is using the FIFO method rather than weighted average to account for its binding and proofing departments.

Prepare the production report and the summary of costs report for:
1. The binding department for January *(Check figure: Cost of books transferred = $80,700)*

2. The proofing department for January
3. The binding department for February*(Check figure: Cost of books transferred = $56,000)*

4. The proofing department for February

PART SIX

Using Financial Statements

In your financial accounting course you learned that there are four types of financial statements that most companies prepare each year. They are the balance sheet, the income statement, the statement of retained earnings, and the statement of cash flows. More than likely, you are well versed on the first three statements because each of the major topics in financial accounting—receivables, cash, inventories, bonds, common stock, tangible and intangible fixed assets, etc.—was probably evaluated in terms of its impact on one or more of these statements. The fourth statement—the statement of cash flows—is usually covered at the very end of financial accounting, if covered at all. Unfortunately, for the sake of time, the emphasis is often on the mechanics involved rather than the usefulness of the information to the user.

In Part Six of this book you will learn how to evaluate the three statements with the use of numerous financial ratios and how to prepare and use the fourth statement—the statement of cash flows. In Chapters 14 and 15 you'll see that there is a lot of valuable information related to the balance sheet, income statement, and statement of retained earnings that user groups might need in assessing a company's financial position —information which is not available by merely studying the first three statements alone.

Readers of a company's financial statements may want to know, "Will the company be able to pay its debts when they come due?" or "Does the company have more merchandise inventory than it can sell in a reasonable period of time?" or "Are selling expenses too high?" or "Is the company earning a satisfactory rate of return on my invested funds?" In Chapter 14 you will learn how to analyze the first three financial statements and calculate various ratios that will help answer these and many other questions.

There are other types of questions that can be answered only by evaluating the statement of cash flows— such questions as "Where did the company get the financial resources it needed to operate?" or "How did the business use these financial resources?" These and other similar questions will be discussed in Chapter 15 when we explain the statement of cash flows, which is intended to show the inflows and outflows of cash during a particular year.

CHAPTER 14

Financial Statement Analysis and Interpretation

The first course you took in accounting was about financial accounting. You learned how the accounting process works and how to prepare the financial statements that are the final product of this process. In this course you've learned about management accounting and how management accountants help managers plan and control for routine and nonroutine decisions. While we might have given you the impression that financial statements are an integral part of financial accounting only, in this chapter we're going to show you how financial statements can also be a management accounting tool. It all depends on your perspective.

You see, in both of your accounting courses so far, your only relationship to the financial statements was from the standpoint of a preparer. You pretended you were the accountant, and you worked your way through the accounting process just as an accountant would. Your main interest was to complete the statements as accurately as possible. As a result, it was extremely easy to lose sight of exactly how someone could use the information within the statements to make decisions. That's what this chapter is all about—management's use of financial statement information in its

[625]

decision-making process. The tool we will employ is referred to as *financial statement analysis.*

There are several situations in which financial statement analysis would be a useful tool for top management. The most obvious example occurs when management is considering an investment in, or loan to, another organization. The analysis of the financial statements of the other organization would provide a great deal of relevant information concerning the soundness of the investment. Top management might also employ financial statement analysis on its own financial statements in order to see how stockholders and creditors are going to evaluate them. For example, it is not all that uncommon for an organization to reject a capital project that has an acceptable net present value (NPV) because the resulting return on investment (ROI) for the organization will not be as good as that of another project with a much lower NPV. A third situation in which financial statement analysis might be employed by top management relates to a highly decentralized organization that has numerous divisions. Management will use the analytical tool to compare the performance of competing divisions and division managers.

ELEMENTS OF FINANCIAL STATEMENT ANALYSIS

Financial statement analysis involves the examination of a company's finished statements in order to learn about three key things. They are:

1. The company's earning performance

2. The company's financial structure

3. The company's long- and short-term debt-paying ability

Although much of what we learn about a company comes from the financial statements, a company's financial reporting goes way beyond the four financial statements. The auditor's report and the notes to the financial statements also provide valuable sources of information about the company's financial position and results of operations. The *auditor's report* contains the auditor's opinion about whether the presentations on the financial statements are fair within the boundaries of generally accepted accounting principles. Any significant departures from generally accepted accounting principles are noted in the audit report and their effect on the financial statements is quantified wherever possible. The auditor, an independent outside party, gives an opinion on the financial statements only after carefully reviewing and analyzing the statements and the supporting documents. A careful reading of the audit report provides important background information for the analysis of financial statements.

The auditor's report contains an opinion about whether the financial statement presentations are fair

The notes to the financial statements should not be viewed as an extra bit of data tacked on to the end of the annual report. These notes are an integral part of the statements. They provide significant information found nowhere else in the statements. We will examine the content of some typical notes after we show you how to analyze the financial statements themselves.

COMPARATIVE FINANCIAL STATEMENTS AND TREND ANALYSIS

Horizontal analysis compares financial data of a company for several years

One approach to financial statement analysis is to compare the financial data of a single company for 2 or more years. This **horizontal analysis** makes it possible to focus attention on items that have changed significantly during the period you are reviewing. Comparison of an item over several periods with a base year may show a trend developing. A **base year** is a year chosen as a beginning point.

Comparative Financial Statements

Comparative financial statements compare financial data for 2 or more years

Comparative financial statements usually show financial statement data for 2 or more years, the increase or decrease in each item on the statement, and the percentage change as compared with the earliest year reported. Exhibits 14-1 and 14-2 show such comparative balance sheets and income statements for Most, Inc.

On comparative statements the most current year's information is normally presented in the first column. Successive columns show amounts for progressively earlier and earlier years. The Most, Inc., 2-year comparative statements show the amount of change in each statement item. These increases and decreases are calculated simply by subtracting 1988 amounts from 1989 amounts, e.g., Cash: $5,368 − $6,574 = −$1,206. The percentage increase or decrease in each statement amount is also disclosed in the final column. These percentages are calculated by dividing the amount of change by the earliest year amount, e.g., Cash: −$1,206 ÷ $6,574 = −18.3%. The analyst will give most attention to material comparative statement items that show a significant percentage change during the year. Merchandise inventory is an illustration of a material item showing a significant percentage change (24.1%). Marketable securities also had a large percentage increase (96.8%), but this item would be viewed as much less important because of its relatively small dollar amount.

Material items showing significant changes should be given careful attention

Generally speaking there were no dramatic shifts in the asset, liability, or stockholders' equity structure of Most. The following observations are among those that may be made:

1. The decrease in cash is accompanied by an increase in marketable securities, indicating that Most may be managing its idle cash better in 1989 by investing a larger part of it.

2. While merchandise inventory has increased significantly (24.1%), there appears to be no cause for alarm because sales have also experienced a large boost (28.1%). It is necessary to have more inventory on hand to meet the growing customer demand.

3. There seems to be a slight shift from using debt to using equity to finance the company. Total liabilities increased only .2% while total stockholders' equity increased 18.1%. These changes occurred while total liabilities and stockholders' equity increased by 10.2%

Comparative statements provide a means for alerting the analyst to significant shifts that require further attention. He or she will then employ the various techniques we will discuss later in this chapter to analyze those shifts.

EXHIBIT 14-1

MOST, INC.
Comparative Balance Sheets
(000s Omitted)

	Dec. 31 1989	Dec. 31 1988	Amount Increase (Decrease)	Percent Increase (Decrease)
Assets				
Current Assets:				
Cash......	$ 5,368	$ 6,574	$(1,206)	(18.3)%
Marketable Securities......	3,090	1,570	1,520	96.8
Accounts Receivable (less allowance for uncollectibles of $710 in 1989 and $814 in 1988)......	35,382	32,936	2,446	7.4
Merchandise Inventory	62,582	50,434	12,148	24.1
Prepaid Expenses......	2,870	2,590	280	10.8
Total Current Assets......	$ 109,292	$ 94,104	$ 15,188	16.1
Investments:				
Investment in Common Stock	$ 6,000	$ 6,000	—	—
Property, Plant, and Equipment:				
Land	$ 4,520	$ 4,300	$ 220	5.1
Building......	72,540	72,540	—	—
Less: Accumulated Depreciation	(30,696)	(29,196)	1,500*	5.1
Equipment	18,907	16,717	2,190	13.1
Less: Accumulated Depreciation	(7,980)	(7,840)	140*	1.8
Total Property, Plant, and Equipment	$ 57,291	$ 56,521	$ 770	1.4
Total Assets	$ 172,583	$ 156,625	$ 15,958	10.2 %
Liabilities & Stockholders' Equity				
Current Liabilities:				
Accounts Payable	$ 24,235	$ 30,353	$(6,118)	(20.2)%
Accrued Payables	9,758	6,137	3,621	59.0
Income Tax Payable......	2,040	1,425	615	43.2
Current Portion of Long-Term Debt......	3,000	3,000	—	—
Total Current Liabilities	$ 39,033	$ 40,915	$(1,882)	(4.6)
Long-Term Liabilities:				
8% Mortgage Bonds Payable......	$ 25,000	$ 28,000	$(3,000)	(10.7)
10% Unsecured Note Payable......	5,000	—	5,000	†
Total Long-Term Liabilities......	$ 30,000	$ 28,000	$ 2,000	7.1
Total Liabilities......	$ 69,033	$ 68,915	$ 118	.2
Stockholders' Equity:				
5% Preferred Stock ($10 par)	$ 500	$ 500	—	—
Common Stock ($1 par)	10,000	9,500	$ 500	5.3
Paid-In Capital in Excess of Par—Common Stock	35,843	30,053	5,790	19.3
Retained Earnings......	57,207	47,657	9,550	20.0
Total Stockholders' Equity	$ 103,550	$ 87,710	$ 15,840	18.1
Total Liabilities and Stockholders' Equity......	$ 172,583	$ 156,625	$ 15,958	10.2 %

* The Accumulated Depreciation amounts increased. The effect of these increases is a decrease in assets. Remember, Accumulated Depreciation is a contra asset.

† When an amount increases or decreases from zero to another number, the percentage change is infinitely large and therefore meaningless ($\frac{5,000}{0} = \infty$).

EXHIBIT 14-2

<table>
<thead>
<tr><th colspan="7">MOST, INC.
Comparative Income Statements
(000s Omitted)</th></tr>
<tr><th></th><th colspan="2">Year Ended
Dec. 31</th><th>Amount
Increase
(Decrease)</th><th>Percent
Increase
(Decrease)</th></tr>
<tr><th></th><th>1989</th><th>1988</th><th></th><th></th></tr>
</thead>
<tbody>
<tr><td>Net Sales . . . . .</td><td>$ 862,915</td><td>$ 673,488</td><td>$189,427</td><td>28.1%</td></tr>
<tr><td>Cost of Goods Sold . . . . . .</td><td>(564,346)</td><td>(454,335)</td><td>110,011</td><td>24.2</td></tr>
<tr><td>Gross Profit on Sales . . . . .</td><td>$ 298,569</td><td>$ 219,153</td><td>$ 79,416</td><td>36.2</td></tr>
<tr><td>Operating Expenses:</td><td></td><td></td><td></td><td></td></tr>
<tr><td> Selling Expenses. . . . . . .</td><td>$(212,062)</td><td>$(162,571)</td><td>$ 49,491</td><td>30.4</td></tr>
<tr><td> General and Administrative Expenses. . . . . .</td><td>(58,771)</td><td>(35,928)</td><td>22,843</td><td>63.6</td></tr>
<tr><td>   Total Operating Expenses . . . . .</td><td>$(270,833)</td><td>$(198,499)</td><td>$ 72,334</td><td>36.4</td></tr>
<tr><td>Other Income and Expense:</td><td></td><td></td><td></td><td></td></tr>
<tr><td> Dividend Income. . . . . .</td><td>$ 516</td><td>$ 430</td><td>$ 86</td><td>20.0</td></tr>
<tr><td> Interest Expense. . . . .</td><td>(3,120)</td><td>(3,016)</td><td>104</td><td>3.5</td></tr>
<tr><td>   Net Other Income (Expense). . . . .</td><td>$(2,604)</td><td>$(2,586)</td><td>$ 18</td><td>.7</td></tr>
<tr><td>Income before Income Taxes . . . . .</td><td>$ 25,132</td><td>$ 18,068</td><td>$ 7,064</td><td>39.1</td></tr>
<tr><td>Income Tax Expense. . . . .</td><td>(7,557)</td><td>(5,693)</td><td>1,864</td><td>32.7</td></tr>
<tr><td>Net Income. . . . .</td><td>$ 17,575</td><td>$ 12,375</td><td>$ 5,200</td><td>42.0%</td></tr>
<tr><td>Earnings per Common Share . . . . .</td><td>$1.80</td><td>$1.30</td><td></td><td></td></tr>
</tbody>
</table>

Trend Analysis

Trend analysis is another type of horizontal examination that compares proportionate changes in selected financial statement information over time. The time period selected for comparisons is usually at least 5 years and may be as long as 10 or 20 years.

Trend percentages state selected financial data as a percentage of the same data in a base year

Trend percentages are calculated by selecting a year as a base year and calculating amounts of selected items in following years as percentages of the amount of the same item in the base year. (All amounts in the base year are set equal to 100%.) To illustrate, selected income statement amounts for Most, Inc., for the years 1985 through 1989 follow:

MOST, INC. Selected Income Statement Amounts Years Ended December 31 (000s Omitted)					
	1989	1988	1987	1986	1985
Net Sales	$862,915	$673,488	$562,104	$401,982	$388,500
Gross Profit................	298,569	219,153	218,181	213,986	209,790
Net Income................	17,575	12,375	11,088	10,666	10,560

These amounts are converted into trend percentages by dividing the amount in a given year by the 1985 base year amount, e.g., Sales—1986: $401,982 ÷ $388,500 = 103%; 1987: $562,104 ÷ $388,500 = 145%; etc. The Most, Inc., trend percentages are tabulated below:

MOST, INC. Selected Income Statement Data Shown as Percentages of 1985 Base Year Years Ended December 31					
	1989	1988	1987	1986	1985
Net Sales	222%	173%	145%	103%	100%
Gross Profit.................................	142	105	104	102	100
Net Income.................................	166	117	105	101	100

Comparisons of dollar amounts over the years indicate that sales, gross profit, and net income are increasing. Comparisons of the trend percentages reveal that gross profit has not increased nearly as rapidly as sales, indicating possibly that the cost of inventory has been increasing more quickly than the sales price. The percentage increase in net income is not nearly as great as the percentage increase in sales, but it generally exceeds the percentage increase in gross profit. One possible explanation for these trend relationships is that management is doing a good job of controlling either selling or general and administrative expenses, or both.

Trend percentages and comparative statements are used to get an overview of a company's performance

Trend percentages, like comparative financial statements, are used to get an overview of an entity's performance. This overview will highlight particular areas where further, more detailed analysis is needed. The analyst of Most, Inc.'s trend percentages, for example, would probably want to look into other ratios and comparisons relating to cost of goods sold and operating expenses.

COMMON-SIZE FINANCIAL STATEMENTS

Vertical analysis compares financial data within a single year

Common-size financial statements show each item on a statement as a percentage of a key item on that statement

Relating financial statement items to each other within a single time period is referred to as *vertical analysis.* Common-size financial statements and financial ratios are two tools employed in vertical analysis. Common-size statements will be discussed in this section and financial ratios in the next.

Common-size financial statements show each item on a statement as a percentage of one key item on that statement. No dollar amounts appear. Each item on an income statement is usually stated as a percentage of net sales. Common-size balance sheets often state all amounts as a percentage of total assets or total equities.

The Most, Inc., common-size income statements are shown in Exhibit 14-3. The computational technique is to take each item and divide by Sales of that year, e.g., Cost of Goods Sold 1989: $564,346 ÷ $862,915 = 65.40%; 1988: $454,335 ÷ $673,488 = 67.46%.

Common-size statements are useful for seeing how significant the components of a statement are. Dividend income and interest expense have a very minor effect on Most's net income (they are only .06% and .36% of 1989 sales), while cost of goods sold and selling expenses are of great significance (they are 65.4% and 24.58% of 1989 sales).

EXHIBIT 14-3

MOST, INC. **Common-Size Income Statements** **Years Ended December 31**		
	1989	**1988**
Net Sales	100.00%*	100.00%
Cost of Goods Sold	(65.40)	(67.46)
Gross Profit on Sales	34.60	32.54
Operating Expenses:		
Selling Expenses	(24.58)	(24.14)
General and Administrative Expenses	(6.81)	(5.33)
Total Operating Expenses	(31.39)	(29.47)
Other Income and Expense:		
Dividend Income	.06	.06
Interest Expense	(.36)	(.45)
Net Other Income (Expense)	(.30)	(.39)
Income before Income Taxes	2.91	2.68
Income Tax Expense	(.88)	(.85)
Net Income	2.03%	1.83%

* Percentages have been rounded.

The vertical analysis of a single year's statements—common-size statements—may be combined with horizontal analysis—comparative statements—to detect significant changes in financial statement components from year to year. Exhibit 14-3 shows such comparative common-size statements. Perhaps the most notable change occurred in cost of goods sold (which went down from 67.46% to 65.40% of sales) and in operating expenses (which increased from 29.47% to 31.39% of sales). While these changes are not substantial, they bear watching in future periods to see whether these trends continue.

Common-size statements can be used to compare companies of differing size

Common-size statements are especially helpful in comparing two companies that differ in size. Imagine comparing the Most, Inc., income statement with that of the Blaque Company shown below:

BLAQUE COMPANY
Income Statement
Year Ended December 31, 1989
(000s Omitted)

Net Sales	$ 4,535,600
Cost of Goods Sold	(2,585,292)
Gross Profit on Sales	$ 1,950,308
Operating Expenses:	
Selling	$ (689,411)
General and Administrative	(317,492)
Total Operating Expenses	$(1,006,903)
Income before Income Tax	$ 943,405
Income Tax Expense	(452,834)
Net Income	$ 490,571

Blaque is so much larger that a comparison of any number on the two income statements seems meaningless. When Blaque's statement is converted to a common size, comparisons are possible:

BLAQUE COMPANY
Common-Size Income Statement
Year Ended December 31, 1989

Sales	100.0%
Cost of Goods Sold	(57.0)
Gross Profit on Sales	43.0
Operating Expenses:	
Selling	(15.2)
General and Administrative	(7.0)
Total Operating Expenses	(22.2)
Income before Income Tax	20.8
Income Tax Expense	(10.0)
Net Income	10.8%

Most, Inc.'s cost of goods sold (see Exhibit 14-3) is a much higher percentage of sales (65.4%) than is Blaque's (57.0%). If the companies are in the same industry, we may question whether the difference is due to volume buying, better inventory management, or possibly just a difference in the inventory costing method (Most may be using LIFO and Blaque FIFO). Blaque's selling expenses are a much lower percentage (15.2%) than Most's (24.58%). The analyst may question what possible efficiencies Blaque has discovered that have eluded Most. Differences in advertising policies, policies on commissions paid to sales representatives, or economies of scale could account for the differences.

Many industry trade associations gather statistics from member firms and produce common-size financial statements based on averages for businesses falling within a predetermined size category. For example, sporting goods stores with annual retail sales under $3 million might submit their income statements in a standardized format to a trade association, which would then compute the average cost of goods sold and the other percentages for stores in this size range. These common-size statistics would provide one standard basis for comparisons that could be used to evaluate the relative performance of a company, in much the same way that Most was evaluated in comparison with Blaque.

FINANCIAL RATIO ANALYSIS

A *ratio* is the relationship between two amounts that results from dividing one by the other. The ratio of 1,000 to 500 would be $1,000 \div 500 = 2$, sometimes expressed as $2:1$. This means that the first number is twice as large as the second. The ratio of 25 to 50 would be expressed as .5 $(25 \div 50)$ or $.5:1$, signifying that the first number is half as large as the second. Ratio analysis can provide additional insights into the operating performance and financial position of Most, Inc.

Analysis of Earnings Performance

Stockholders and potential stockholders employ several ratios to help them evaluate management performance in using the resources of the entity to earn profits. Rate of return on total assets and rate of return on stockholders' equity are two such ratios.

Rate of return on total assets indicates management's efficiency in using all the firm's resources

The *rate of return (ROR) on total assets* is a measure of management's efficiency in using all resources at its disposal. The equation for computing this ratio is as follows:

$$\text{ROR on total assets} = \frac{\text{income before interest expense}}{\text{average total assets}}$$

Income before interest expense is used so that earnings will not be influenced by the manner in which the assets are financed. Interest is a cost of financing the business, not a cost of operating it. Average total assets reflect resources employed throughout the year, not those on hand at the beginning or at the end. This average could be computed by weighting the dollars of assets used by the number of days they are employed and dividing by 365. An approximation of this average may be obtained by adding the beginning and ending asset amounts and dividing by 2. This simplified technique will be used throughout the chapter wherever an average is required.

Most, Inc.'s return on total assets for 1989 is calculated as follows:

$$\text{ROR on total assets} = \frac{\text{net income} + \text{interest expense}}{(\text{total assets, beg. of year} + \text{total assets, end of year}) \div 2}$$

$$\text{ROR on total assets} = \frac{\$17,575,000 + \$3,120,000}{(\$156,625,000 + \$172,583,000) \div 2}$$

$$= \frac{\$20,695,000}{\$164,604,000} = .1257, \text{ or } 12.57\%$$

Most's management earned an average of 12.57% on each dollar of assets invested in the company.

Rate of return on common stockholders' equity indicates management's efficiency in using resources invested by common stockholders

The **rate of return (ROR) on common stockholders' equity** is a measure of management's effectiveness in using the resources invested by the common stockholders. This rate may be higher or lower than the return on total assets, depending on how judiciously management has combined debt and preferred stock with common stock in financing the company's resources. The equation for computing this ratio is as follows:

$$\text{ROR on common stockholders' equity} = \frac{\text{net income} - \text{preferred dividends}}{\text{average common stockholders' equity}}$$

The earnings amount in the numerator excludes both payments to holders of debt (interest expense) and holders of preferred stock (preferred dividends). Thus the net income less preferred dividends is the net amount earned on the equity of the common stockholders. Average common stockholders' equity is an approximation of the amount invested by this group of owners throughout the year.

The following preliminary computations are made for Most, Inc.:

Preferred dividends:	
Par value of preferred stock (at the time dividends are declared).........	$500,000
Dividend rate paid.......................................	5%
Amount of preferred dividends.......................................	$ 25,000

Average common stockholders' equity:

	Total stockholders' equity	− preferred stockholders' equity	= common stockholders' equity
Jan. 1, 1989	$87,710,000	− $500,000	= $ 87,210,000
+ Dec. 31, 1989	$103,550,000	− $500,000	= 103,050,000
Total			$190,260,000
			÷ 2
Average common stockholders' equity for 1989			$ 95,130,000

The rate of return on Most's common stockholders' equity for 1989 is as follows:

$$\text{ROR on common stockholders' equity} = \frac{\$17,575,000 - \$25,000}{\$95,130,000}$$

$$= .1845, \text{ or } 18.45\%$$

*Favorable leverage exists
when the company uses
assets provided by creditors
to earn a higher return for
common stockholders*

Since the 18.45% return on common stockholders' equity exceeds the 12.57% return on total assets, management has made effective use of *leverage,* or *trading on the equity.* Leverage or trading on the equity involves using the assets invested by common stockholders as collateral for debt financing (borrowing on notes or bonds) and limited-return equity financing (selling preferred stock) in an attempt to earn a higher return for the common stockholder. A simple example will help clarify this concept.

JOHN AND MABEL'S FRUIT STAND

John and Mabel Jones run a fruit and vegetable stand. They have $100 of their own money invested and earn a $5 profit (or 5% return). An additional $100 is borrowed from a friend at 6% interest. In order for John and Mabel to come out ahead on this loan, they must use the borrowed money to earn more than the $6 interest they will have to pay. Assuming that the net income on the $200 of assets is $7, the Joneses have used someone else's money to increase their return from 5% ($5 ÷ $100) to 7% ($7 ÷ $100). Remember, the $7 net income is *after* the interest expense deduction.

Rate of return on John and Mabel's total assets:

$$\frac{\text{Net income} + \text{interest expense}}{\text{Average total assets}} = \frac{\$7 + \$6}{(\$200 + \$200) \div 2} = \frac{\$13}{\$200}$$

$$= .065, \text{ or } 6.5\%$$

Rate of return on John and Mabel's stockholders' equity:

$$\frac{\text{Net income} - \text{preferred dividends}}{\text{Average common stockholders' equity}} = \frac{\$7 - \$0}{(\$100 + \$100) \div 2}$$

$$= \frac{\$7}{\$100} = .07, \text{ or } 7\%$$

Leverage, then, is simply an *attempt* to use funds supplied by nonowners to increase the return to owners. Any time the rate of return on common stockholders' equity exceeds the rate of return on total assets, leverage has been used to the stockholders' advantage.

Leverage may also work to the detriment of common stockholders. If the return on the borrowed and preferred stock capital is not sufficient to pay the interest and preferred dividends on that capital, some of the earnings that would normally be available to common stockholders is absorbed in making up the difference. Any time the rate of return on total assets is more than the rate of return on common stockholders' equity, leverage has been used to the detriment of the stockholders.

*Earnings per share of
common stock shows the
average dollars of income
for each share of common
stock*

Earnings per share of common stock (EPS) is a measure of the income earned on each share of common stock. Calculation of this ratio was discussed in Financial Accounting. The equation for a simple capital structure and the calculation of the

1989 EPS for Most, Inc., are presented below.

$$\text{EPS (simple capital structure)} = \frac{\textbf{net income} - \textbf{preferred dividends}}{\textbf{average number of common shares outstanding}}$$

$$= \frac{\$17,575,000 - \$25,000}{(9,500,000 \text{ shs} + 10,000,000 \text{ shs}) \div 2}$$

$$= \frac{\$17,550,000}{9,750,000 \text{ shs}} = \$1.80$$

Earnings per share amounts must appear on the face of the income statements of public companies. Nonpublic (closely held, or nonpublicly traded) companies are not required to disclose earnings per share amounts. If you review Most, Inc.'s income statement in Exhibit 14-2, you will see that the EPS is properly shown for 1989 and 1988.

Price-earnings ratio statistics are one more indicator of the earnings performance of common stock. The equation for calculating the price-earnings ratio is:

$$\text{Price-earnings ratio} = \frac{\textbf{market price per share of common stock}}{\textbf{earnings per share of common stock}}$$

Assuming a current market price of $27 for Most, Inc.'s stock, the price-earnings ratio would be as follows:

$$\text{Price-earnings ratio} = \frac{\$27}{\$1.80} = 15, \text{ or } 15:1$$

This simply means that Most's stock is currently selling for 15 times the amount that each share earned. Price-earnings ratios of 15 are not at all uncommon. A few range as high as 20 or more. The price-earnings ratio is the reflection of the stock market's assessment about the future earnings of the company. Investors have been willing to buy a share of stock for as many as 15 to 20 times the current per-share earnings because they feel that the future income growth of the firm will be sufficient to provide an adequate return on this investment. This return is normally received through a combination of dividends and an increased market value of the stock.

The price-earnings ratio reflects the stock market's assessment about the future earnings of the company

The *dividend yield rate* shows the current year's dividends as a percentage of the current market price of the stock. This indication of the cash payout rate on an investment allows stockholders and potential stockholders to compare interest rates on certificates of deposit, corporate bonds, and other securities with this measure of return on common stock. The investor should be aware that dividend yield rates ignore the potential increase in the market value of common stock. For this reason, the dividend yield rate should be combined with other statistics in making investment decisions.

The dividend yield rate indicates the cash payout rate on the common stockholders' investment

The equation for calculating dividend yield rates and the 1989 dividend yield rate for Most, Inc., assuming that $8,000,000 in dividends was paid to common stockholders, follows:

$$\text{Dividend yield rate} = \frac{\textbf{dividends per share of common stock}}{\textbf{current market price per share of common stock}}$$

$$\begin{array}{l} \text{1989 dividend yield} \\ \text{rate for Most, Inc.} \end{array} = \frac{\$8,000,000 \div 10,000,000 \text{ shs}}{\$27} = \frac{\$0.80}{\$27} = .0296, \text{ or } 2.96\%$$

This relatively low dividend yield rate of 3% on Most, Inc.'s common stock would not be attractive to investors who count on cash flow from dividends to pay their living expenses. A potential Most, Inc., stockholder would probably be an individual who is more interested in speculating on the growth in the market value of the stock. This type of investor would rely more heavily on growth in earnings per share and recent trends in the market price of the stock than on the dividend yield rate.

Analysis of Debt-Paying Ability

Creditors and potential creditors are interested in continuously monitoring a company's ability to pay interest as it comes due and to repay the principal of the debt at maturity. Times interest earned, debt to total assets ratio, and equity to total assets ratio are three statistics that provide information about this debt-paying ability. Later we will discuss several liquid position measures that indicate the ability to meet short-term debt responsibilities.

Times interest earned tells how many times a company could pay its interest expense with income derived from assets

Times interest earned is a ratio that indicates the margin of safety provided by current earnings in meeting the company's interest responsibilities. The equation for calculating this ratio is as follows:

$$\text{Times interest earned} = \frac{\text{income before interest expense and income taxes}}{\text{annual interest expense}}$$

Income before interest expense and income taxes is used because this is the amount that could be used to pay interest — provided it were available in the form of cash. Income taxes are excluded because interest is deductible in calculating income tax.

The 1989 times interest earned for Most, Inc., is as follows:

$$\text{Times interest earned} = \frac{\$17,575,000 + \$3,120,000 + \$7,557,000}{\$3,120,000}$$

$$= \frac{\$28,252,000}{\$3,120,000} = 9.1 \text{ times}$$

The amount of Most's income available to meet its interest responsibilities was about 9 times the amount of its interest expense. Usually, if interest is covered several times, long-term creditors consider this an acceptable margin of safety. Most's times interest earned ratio should be quite satisfactory to its creditors.

The debt to total assets ratio indicates the percentage of a company's assets provided by creditors

The ***debt to total assets ratio*** shows the percentage of the firm's assets financed by debt. The higher this percentage, the greater the risk that the company will be unable to meet its obligations when due. The debt to total assets ratio equation and the 1989 calculation for Most, Inc., follow:

$$\text{Debt to total assets ratio} = \frac{\text{total liabilities}}{\text{total assets}}$$

$$\text{1989 debt to total assets ratio for Most, Inc.} = \frac{\$69,033,000}{\$172,583,000} = .399 \text{ or } .40, \text{ or } 40\%$$

Forty percent of Most's total assets were financed by debt.

The stockholders' equity to total assets ratio shows the percentage of a company's assets provided by stockholders

The ***stockholders' equity to total assets ratio,*** sometimes called the ***equity ratio,*** shows the percentage of the firm's assets financed by stockholders. The higher this ratio, the smaller the risk that the company will be unable to meet its obligations when due. After a moment's reflection you should see that the debt to total assets ratio and the stockholders' equity to total assets ratio are complementary; that is, the two percentages should always add to 100%. This is true because all assets are financed by either debt or equity funds. The stockholders' equity to total assets ratio may be found by subtracting the debt to total assets ratio from 100%:

$$\text{Stockholders' equity to total assets ratio} = 100\% - \text{debt to total assets ratio}$$

1989 stockholders'
equity to total assets ratio $= 100\% - 40\% = 60\%$
for Most, Inc.

This ratio may also be calculated with the following equation:

$$\text{Stockholders' equity to total assets ratio} = \frac{\text{total stockholders' equity}}{\text{total assets}}$$

1989 stockholders'
equity to total assets ratio $= \dfrac{\$103,550,000}{\$172,583,000} = .60,\text{ or } 60\%$
for Most, Inc.

Sixty percent of Most's assets come from stockholders (including reinvested earnings) and 40% from creditors. This fact, coupled with the favorable leverage and times interest earned statistics, should be satisfactory to long-term creditors. Of course, each analyst will have standards in mind when financial analysis is begun. These standards may vary from analyst to analyst. Statistics satisfactory to one analyst may cause concern to another.

Analysis of Liquid Position

An analysis of a firm's liquid position provides indicators of its short-term debt-paying ability and of management's current operating efficiency. For this reason, *both* investors and creditors are particularly interested in these statistics.

Working capital is a measure of the liquid resources management has to use

Working capital is total current assets minus total current liabilities. A strong working capital position can be an advantage to a company attempting to obtain short-term credit at favorable interest rates. Investors and long-term creditors view a strong working capital position as indicating an ability to make expected dividend and interest payments in a timely manner. Most, Inc.'s working capital for 1989 is shown below:

Current Assets..	$109,292,000
− Current Liabilities...	39,033,000
= Working Capital	$ 70,259,000

The current ratio is one measure of a company's ability to pay its short-term debts

The **current ratio** is current assets divided by current liabilities. This statistic is often assigned great importance by creditors in making credit-granting decisions. The general equation and 1989 current ratio for Most, Inc., appear below:

$$\text{Current ratio} = \frac{\text{current assets}}{\text{current liabilities}}$$

1989 current ratio $= \dfrac{\$109,292,000}{\$39,033,000} = 2.80,\text{ or } 2.8:1$
for Most, Inc.

This means that for every dollar of current liabilities, Most has $2.80 of current assets. Many creditors feel that a current ratio of 2.0 is satisfactory. Relying too heavily on the current ratio may not be desirable, as the following illustration demonstrates. The current ratios for Company A and B are calculated as follows:

	Company A	Company B
Current Assets:		
Cash	$ 40,000	$175,000
Accounts Receivable....	60,000	125,000
Merchandise Inventory..	180,000	95,000
Prepaid Expenses.......	20,000	5,000
Total Current Assets	$300,000	$400,000
Current Liabilities	$100,000	$200,000
Current ratio............	$300,000 ÷ $100,000 = 3	$400,000 ÷ $200,000 = 2

Company A's current ratio of 3 : 1 is much better than Company B's 2 : 1. If we inspect the composition of the current assets, we see that A's cash and accounts receivable are only one-third of total current assets, whereas three-fourths of B's current assets are composed of these two particular liquid resources. In reality, B may be in a position to meet its current obligations as well as, if not better than, A.

Company A could further improve its current ratio by merely paying off $40,000 of current liabilities with the $40,000 cash on hand. If this were done, the new current ratio would be:

$$\text{Company A current ratio (revised)} = \frac{\$300,000 - \$40,000}{\$100,000 - \$40,000} = \frac{\$260,000}{\$60,000} = 4.33$$

This act of manipulating current assets close to the end of the time period can produce a ratio that may satisfy creditors while actually weakening the immediate liquid position of the company.

Limiting your analysis to too few statistics, relying on arbitrary rules of thumb, and not understanding the limitations behind the calculation of a ratio are pitfalls that you must carefully avoid.

The quick ratio is a measure of a company's immediate liquid position

The **quick ratio,** also known as the **acid-test ratio,** shows the relationship between highly liquid (quick) assets and current liabilities. *Quick assets* are those that may be converted directly into cash within a short period of time. These include cash, marketable securities, and receivables. Merchandise inventory is omitted because merchandise is normally sold on credit (converted into a receivable) and then the receivable must be collected before cash is realized. Thus inventory is two steps away from cash rather than just one. Prepaid expenses are also omitted because they are usually relatively small in amount and because they are used up in operations rather than converted into cash.

$$\text{Quick ratio} = \frac{\text{quick assets}}{\text{current liabilities}}$$

Most, Inc.'s quick assets ratio on Dec. 31, 1989, is as follows:

Cash...	$ 5,368,000
Marketable Securities.......................................	3,090,000
Accounts Receivable (net)...................................	35,382,000
Total Quick Assets	$43,840,000

$$\text{1989 quick ratio for Most, Inc.} = \frac{\$43,840,000}{\$39,033,000} = 1.12, \text{ or } 1.12 : 1$$

Creditors generally use the rule of thumb that a quick ratio of 1 : 1 is satisfactory. Most's quick ratio appears to be acceptable.

The quick ratio, when viewed with the current ratio, gives an idea of the influence of merchandise inventory and prepaid expenses. Looking at the Company A– Company B illustration again, one can see that the quick ratio is a tipoff that Company A's current ratio may be misleading as a sole indicator of debt-paying ability:

	Company A	Company B
Quick Assets:		
Cash..............	$ 40,000	$175,000
Accounts Receivable ..	60,000	125,000
Total Current Assets.....	$100,000	$300,000
Quick Ratio...........	$100,000 ÷ $100,000 = 1	$300,000 ÷ $200,000 = 1.5

Company B has the stronger quick ratio and the weaker current ratio, indicating that merchandise inventory and prepaid expenses play a less important role in its current position than these assets do in Company A's.

Inventory turnover indicates how quickly a company sells its average investment in inventory

Inventory turnover shows how many times the average dollars invested in merchandise inventory were sold (turned over) during the year. This statistic, when compared with the year-end merchandise inventory, provides the analyst with a basis for judging whether the company has an excessive investment in merchandise at the end of the year. A too-large ending inventory may indicate that sales volume was not as high as expected near year-end or possibly that management was inefficient in allowing too many unsold goods to accumulate. On the other hand, a large inventory may be present because of an unusually high sales volume expected near the beginning of the next period. In any case the analyst will be wise to attempt to discover the reasons for low turnover and excessive ending inventory.

Inventory turnover is calculated by dividing cost of goods sold by average merchandise inventory. Cost of goods sold is used instead of sales because sales includes gross profit, while cost of goods sold, like merchandise inventory, does not. The general equation and the 1989 Most, Inc., inventory turnover follow:

$$\text{Inventory turnover} = \frac{\text{cost of goods sold}}{\text{average merchandise inventory}}$$

$$\text{1989 inventory turnover for Most, Inc.} = \frac{\$564,346,000}{(\$50,434,000 + \$62,582,000) \div 2}$$

$$= \frac{\$564,346,000}{\$56,508,000} = 9.99 \text{ times}$$

Since Most's inventory turns over about 10 times per year, the year-end inventory should be about 10% of cost of goods sold. Most's inventory of $62,582,000 is a little above this amount (10% × $564,346,000 = $56,434,600). This excess is probably explained by Most's increasing sales volume.

Accounts receivable turnover indicates how quickly a company collects its average Accounts Receivable balance

Accounts receivable turnover indicates the number of times per year that the average balance of Accounts Receivable is collected. This ratio of sales on credit to average accounts receivable is calculated as follows:

$$\text{Accounts receivable turnover} = \frac{\text{credit sales}}{\text{average accounts receivable}}$$

Assuming that substantially all of Most, Inc.'s sales are on credit, the firm's 1989 receivables turnover is as follows:

$$\text{Accounts receivable turnover} = \frac{\$862,915,000}{(\$32,936,000 + \$35,382,000) \div 2}$$

$$= \frac{\$862,915,000}{\$34,159,000} = 25.3 \text{ times}$$

This ratio takes on more meaning when used in the calculation of the statistic discussed next.

Average age of receivables is another measure of how quickly a company collects its accounts receivable

The ***average age of receivables*** provides a rough approximation of the average time that it takes to collect receivables. The average age of receivables is determined as follows:

$$\text{Average age of receivables} = \frac{365 \text{ days}}{\text{accounts receivable turnover}}$$

$$\text{1989 average age receivables} \atop \text{for Most, Inc.} = \frac{365 \text{ days}}{25.3 \text{ times}} = 14.4 \text{ days}$$

Most, Inc., takes an average of 14 days to collect its receivables. If Most's credit terms are net 10 days, its collection efforts could be improved. If the credit terms are 15 or 30 days, Most's collection efforts appear to be excellent.

Creditors are interested in receivables turnover and the average age of receivables as indicators of how quickly the company's receivables are converted into the cash required for operations and debt repayment. Investors and creditors use receivables turnover as one more index of management efficiency.

INTERPRETATION OF FINANCIAL RATIOS

Ratios must be compared with some standard to be meaningful

A quick ratio of 1.12, an inventory turnover of 9.99, or a price-earnings ratio of 15 mean very little when considered in a vacuum. Financial ratios become relevant for decision making only when compared with some standards. Each analyst must decide on a set of standards for each ratio that he or she relies on to gauge the performance of the company being analyzed. Some common bases for establishing standards are considered below.

Company History

The company's ratios for past years may be used as a standard

Horizontal analysis has been defined as comparing financial data of a single company for 2 or more years. Comparative financial statements and trend analysis were presented as applications of horizontal analysis. Each of the financial ratios may be computed for a number of years and then compared to form an opinion about whether the company's performance is getting better or worse. If Most's inventory turnover has been 10, 12, and 16 during 1989, 1988, and 1987, respectively, the analyst should be concerned enough to attempt to discover the reason for the deterioration in this ratio. If management inefficiency seems to be the only plausible explanation, the analyst may expect continued problems that could lead to a decision of rejecting a credit application or not investing in stock of the corporation.

A major limitation of comparing amounts and ratios for a single company is that there is no basis for a decision about the significance of these statistics. Some external standard is needed against which to measure the company's ratios. For example, if the average inventory turnover in Most's industry is 4, the turnover of 10 may appear excellent. If the industry average is 12, a turnover of 10 may be a cause for concern.

External Standards

Average ratios of other firms in the industry may be used as a standard

Ratio information about other companies is often used as a yardstick against which to compare the statistics of the firm being analyzed. These external data may be obtained by analyzing the financial statements of the other firms; by obtaining copies of industry averages from the publications of trade associations; by examining data on industry norms, average ratios, and credit ratings from credit agencies such as Dun & Bradstreet; or by consulting statistics available in investment service publications such as *Annual Statement Studies* published by Robert Morris Associates.

Care must be taken in deciding which ratios are to be used as standards of comparison. Many companies are so diversified that it is difficult to identify one particular industry in which they operate. A current ratio or inventory turnover ratio for such a conglomerate would be meaningless if compared with those statistics of another firm operating in only one industry.

In most industries comparability will be affected by size. Larger firms will be able to avail themselves of economies of scale and certain sophisticated quantitative management techniques that may not be practical for smaller ones. Smaller companies may be able to maintain closer client relations and better customer relations than larger ones. These differences in operating techniques may influence different ratios in different ways. The larger firm, for example, may be expected to have a higher gross profit percentage and inventory turnover, while the smaller one may have a quicker receivables turnover and a lower percentage spent on advertising. Comparisons of similar-size entities in the same industry are desirable whenever possible.

The differences in accounting methods employed in generating financial information may also influence the comparability of ratios and other statistics. Among the different principles that firms may employ are different inventory techniques, depreciation methods, estimates of useful lives, methods of accounting for income taxes, and revenue recognition procedures. It is a fairly easy matter to discover which methods a particular company is using. Adjusting the financial information to compensate for differences in accounting methods may prove to be a difficult, if not impossible, task.

NOTES TO FINANCIAL STATEMENTS

Footnotes provide valuable information about financial statements

Notes to the financial statements, commonly called **footnotes,** provide additional information that may greatly influence your overall judgment about the future potential of the company. Some of the more important footnotes are discussed in this section.

Accounting Policies

When a company selects from several acceptable methods, the accounting policies note tells which method was chosen

Authoritative generally accepted accounting principles require that all financial statements contain a note outlining the various accounting methods that the company has elected to use. The accounting policies note explains which accounting method was selected from among several acceptable ones, for example, FIFO or LIFO inventory methods, straight-line or double-declining-balance depreciation. The **accounting policies note,** usually the first note to the financial statements, is helpful in deciding how comparable the financial statistics for two different companies are. The following illustration shows a typical accounting policies note:

SUMMARY OF ACCOUNTING POLICIES

Inventories   Inventories are stated generally at cost, which is not in excess of market. The cost of substantially all inventories is determined by the last-in, first-out (LIFO) method.

Depreciation and Depletion   The cost of most manufacturing plant and equipment is depreciated using an accelerated method based primarily on a sum-of-the-years'-digits formula. The cost of mining properties is depreciated or depleted mainly by the units-of-production method.

Consolidation   The financial statements include the consolidation of all wholly and majority-owned subsidiaries except the finance subsidiary. The finance company is so different from the other companies that, even though wholly owned, it is accounted for by the equity method. It appears as an investment on the balance sheet and as other income on the income statement.

Methods of accounting for research and development costs, recognition of warranty expenses, and translation of foreign subsidiary statements into U.S. currency are not appropriate accounting policy disclosures because only one acceptable method can be used for each of these.

Contingencies

Financial statements are analyzed in order to form an opinion about how well a company has performed in the past and to make an estimate about how well it is expected to do in the future. A large potential lawsuit loss could significantly change your forecast about the future of the company. This vital information can be obtained by reading the contingencies note.

A *contingency* is a future event that may occur but whose occurrence is not certain. The *contingencies note* must include a description of all future losses that are probable, reasonably possible, and in some cases even remote. If an estimate or a range of estimates of the amount of loss can be made, these must also be disclosed.

The contingencies note provides information about future events that may occur

The following contingencies note is a sample of the typical disclosures that may be made:

NOTE 7 CONTINGENCIES

Early in fiscal 1988, the Federal Trade Commission filed a formal complaint against the Company and two other manufacturers of gudgeon twisters, charging them with sharing an unlawful monopoly in violation of the Federal Trade Commission Act. The Commission seeks, among other things, divestiture of certain assets and royalty-free licensing of certain trademarks. The Company denies that it has violated the Act and is vigorously defending its position. Trial is continuing before an Administration Law Judge of the Federal Trade Commission, and it is expected that the litigation will continue for some time at considerable expense.

A lawsuit has been filed against the Company claiming damages from alleged environmental contamination by our Beaver Falls plant. The suit, filed on March 30, 1989, in the federal court in Pennsylvania, alleges damages of $1,000,000. The State of Pennsylvania has moved to intervene as plaintiff in this case, seeking $25,000,000 in compensatory and $1,000,000 in punitive damages. The Company will vigorously defend against this lawsuit.

As you learned in financial accounting, contingencies that are probable in nature and subject to reasonable estimation must be recognized as current period losses. The loss (or expense) must be shown on the income statement and the corresponding liability (or allowance account) must appear on the balance sheet. Bad debts and warranty expenses are illustrations of contingencies considered probable and subject to estimation.

Other Descriptive Notes

Other notes provide descriptive information about balance sheet and income statement items

Some information vital to the understanding of the financial statements is simply too long and detailed to be shown on the statements themselves. This information is usually shown in a descriptive note referenced to a particular item on the income statement or balance sheet. Typical are those providing supplementary information about the following:

Subject of Note	Information Included
Property, plant, and equipment	The types of assets included in this category, their estimated useful lives, and whether they are pledged as collateral for loans
Long-term liabilities	The effective interest rate, maturity dates, repayment terms, collateral for the debt, any restriction imposed by the creditor (such as a limitation on the amount of dividends the company can pay)

Other common descriptive notes relate to pension plans, income taxes, earnings per share calculations, and stock option plans.

OTHER SOURCES OF INFORMATION

Various publications provide general background information

The serious student of financial statement analysis will supplement all the techniques described thus far with several other sources of financial and nonfinancial information. Magazines such as *Business Week* and *Forbes* and financial newspapers such as *The Wall Street Journal, Barrons,* and the *Commercial and Financial Chronicle* provide data on prospects for the economy as a whole and for various industries. In addition, articles on management personnel, company strategy, and significant legislation affecting the business community expand the analyst's background knowledge. Up-to-date quarterly operating results and current stock prices also appear in many of these publications.

THE INSIDERS HAND IS CAUGHT IN THE COOKIE JAR

The affair has quickly become known as Wall Street's Watergate. That hardly seems an exaggerated description of the drama of financial power and corruption that was exploding on both coasts of the U.S. last week. An enormous scandal was spreading at the core of America's investment community, touching some of the biggest money men in the country. . . . There was even the ultimate Watergate touch: the disclosure that for weeks, perhaps months, conversations had been secretly tape-recorded in an effort to plumb the depths of

the worst insider-trading scandal in U.S. history.

All across the U.S., investors were raging at the discovery that Wall Street high rollers had been ripping off millions of dollars by trading on knowledge not available to the general public.

At the center of last week's maelstrom was a shadowy figure whom few people had heard of until last week: Ivan Boesky. On Nov. 14 the Securities and Exchange Commission electrified the financial world with news that Boesky, 49, one of Amer-

ica's richest and savviest stock-market speculators, had been caught in an ongoing insider-trading probe. Boesky had agreed to pay $100 million in penalties, return profits and accept eventual banishment from professional stock trading for life for the alleged wrongdoings. He also faces a single, as yet unspecified, criminal charge, which could lead to a five-year prison term.

Several research firms publish financial services that are available on a subscription basis. These are available in most university and large public libraries. We have already mentioned industry trade associations and credit-reporting bureaus as possible sources of information.

Many large corporations provide interview sessions for professional analysts who work for large stock brokerage firms, trust departments of banks, and other institutions that invest vast sums of money. While these sessions do provide an opportunity for the analysts to ask questions that may interest them and to hear management's hopes for the future of the company, they may not act as a means of communicating secret inside information to a chosen few money managers. Such activities would be illegal.

CHAPTER SUMMARY

The ***auditor's report*** contains the auditor's independent opinion about whether the financial statements are presented fairly in conformity with generally accepted accounting principles. A careful study of this report may alert the reader to weaknesses in financial measurement or disclosure.

Financial statements may be analyzed ***horizontally*** and ***vertically.*** One horizontal approach compares balance sheets of several years expressed in dollars and percentages. A similar comparison is made of income statements of several years. Another horizontal approach, called ***trend analysis,*** compares proportionate changes in selected financial information over time. These proportionate changes are expressed as percentages of a designated base year. A third horizontal approach involves comparing financial ratios for several years in order to detect significant changes in them over time.

Vertical financial statement analysis involves comparing items on financial statements of a single period. ***Common-size financial statements*** state each component of the statements in terms of one other component. A common-size income statement usually states each component as a percentage of sales. A common-size balance sheet presents each item as a percentage of total assets.

Ratio analysis, another form of the vertical approach, may be used to examine earnings performance, debt-paying ability, and liquid position. The following ratios are commonly employed in these evaluations:

Earnings Performance

$$\text{Rate of return on total assets} = \frac{\text{income before interest expense}}{\text{average total assets}}$$

$$\begin{matrix} \text{Rate of return on common} \\ \text{stockholders' equity} \end{matrix} = \frac{\text{net income} - \text{preferred dividends}}{\text{average common stockholders' equity}}$$

$$\text{Earnings per share} = \frac{\text{net income} - \text{preferred dividends}}{\begin{matrix}\text{average number of common shares} \\ \text{outstanding}\end{matrix}}$$

$$\text{Price-earnings ratio} = \frac{\text{market price per share of common stock}}{\text{earnings per share of common stock}}$$

$$\text{Dividend yield rate} = \frac{\text{dividends per share of common stock}}{\begin{matrix}\text{current market price per share of} \\ \text{common stock}\end{matrix}}$$

Debt-Paying Ability

$$\text{Times interest earned} = \frac{\begin{matrix}\text{income before interest expense and} \\ \text{income taxes}\end{matrix}}{\text{annual interest expense}}$$

$$\text{Debt to total assets} = \frac{\text{total liabilities}}{\text{total assets}}$$

$$\text{Stockholders' equity to total assets} = \frac{\text{total stockholders' equity}}{\text{total assets}}$$

Liquid Position

$$\text{Current ratio} = \frac{\text{current assets}}{\text{current liabilities}}$$

$$\text{Quick ratio} = \frac{\text{quick assets}}{\text{current liabilities}}$$

$$\text{Inventory turnover} = \frac{\text{cost of goods sold}}{\text{average merchandise inventory}}$$

$$\text{Accounts receivable turnover} = \frac{\text{credit sales}}{\text{average accounts receivable}}$$

$$\text{Average age of receivables} = \frac{365 \text{ days}}{\text{accounts receivable turnover}}$$

Ratios take on much more meaning when they can be compared to measures of what they "should be." Standards of comparison are usually obtained by analyzing financial statements of companies in the same industry and averaging the ratios thus determined. Industry averages may also be acquired from trade associations and financial research firms.

Ratio comparisons are most useful when the companies studied are in fact in the same industry, are of approximately the same size, and use similar accounting methods.

Notes to the financial statements are an integral part of the statements. Financial analysis is not complete until the notes have been carefully examined. Each company must disclose choices made from among different accounting methods in an *accounting policies note.* The accounting policies note is followed by notes providing detailed information about certain financial statement items such as property, plant, and equipment and long-term debt. Events that may have a significant effect on future financial statements are disclosed in a *contingencies note.* Common contingencies include pending lawsuits and administrative complaints filed by regulatory agencies.

Background information about the firm, its industry, and the economy as a whole may be obtained from business magazines and newspapers, publications of financial research firms, industry trade associations, credit-rating bureaus, and interviews with management.

IMPORTANT TERMS USED IN THIS CHAPTER

Accounting policies note A description of the various accounting methods that the company has selected to use in preparing its financial statements. Disclosure is made of only those methods selected from among several acceptable ones. (page 642)

Auditor's report An independent auditor's opinion regarding the fairness of presentation of the financial statements. (page 626)

Common-size financial statement A financial statement in which each component is stated as a percentage of one other component. A common-size income statement usually states each component as a percentage of sales. A common-size balance sheet presents each item as a percentage of total assets. (page 631)

Comparative financial statements A presentation of financial statements of more than one period in columnar form. Changes between periods expressed in dollars or percentages may also be included. (page 627)

Contingency A future event that may occur but whose occurrence is not certain. (page 643)

Horizontal analysis The comparison of financial data of a single company for 2 or more years. (page 627)

Leverage The use of debt or preferred stock financing in an attempt to earn a higher rate of return on common stockholders' equity than would have been possible without this financing. (page 635)

Ratio The relationship of one number to another that is determined by dividing the first number by the second. (page 633)

Trading on the equity See *Leverage.*

Trend analysis The comparison of proportionate changes in selected financial information over time. These proportionate changes are expressed as a percentage of a designated base year. (page 629)

Vertical analysis The comparison of items on financial statements of a single period. (page 631)

QUESTIONS

1. Does the auditor's report state that the financial statements present a true and correct picture of the company's financial position? Explain.

2. Can a horizontal analysis be made of a single year's financial statements? Explain.

3. What is the analyst attempting to learn by studying comparative financial statements?

4. Jon Investor is calculating trend percentages for sales and net income of Toco, Inc. If he selects 1988 as his base year, what will the trend percentages be for 1988? How will he calculate the trend percentages for 1989?

5. Explain how *vertical analysis* differs from *horizontal analysis.*

6. Which financial statement analysis tool would be most useful in comparing two companies of vastly differing size? Explain how this tool makes the comparison possible.

7. Willco's rate of return on total assets is 11%; explain what this rate tells the analyst.

8. What is meant by favorable leverage? Is favorable leverage present in a company that has a rate of return on total assets of 12% and a rate of return on common stockholders' equity of 10%? Explain.

9. The common stock of Jarax, Inc., has a dividend yield ratio of 8%; Jarax bonds maturing in 20 years offer an effective interest rate of 12%. Explain what the dividend yield rate is. Explain why an investor might prefer the Jarax common stock over the Jarax bonds even though the yield rate on the stock is lower.

10. What does a times interest earned statistic of .95 mean? How would this statistic be evaluated by a long-term creditor? Explain.

11. Why is the quick ratio often a better measure of the very short term liquid position of a company than the current ratio?

12. Explain how inventory turnover is used to evaluate the amount of inventory on hand at the end of a time period.

13. Clyde Co.'s average age of receivables is 35 days. Explain what additional information is necessary before this average can be evaluated as relatively good or bad.

14. List some external standards against which the performance of a company can be compared.

15. Briefly describe the type of information that you will find in an accounting policies note.

EXERCISES

Exercise 14-1
Preparing a common-size income statement

Convert the following income statement into a common-size statement that uses Sales as 100%:

MAYER CORP.
Income Statement
Year Ended September 30, 1989

Sales		$180,000
Cost of Goods Sold		99,000
Gross Profit on Sales		$ 81,000
Operating Expenses:		
Selling Expenses...	$43,200	
General and Administrative Expenses......................	16,200	59,400
Income before Income Taxes.................................		$ 21,600
Income Tax Expense...		9,720
Net Income		$ 11,880

(Check figure: Selling expenses = 24%)

Exercise 14-2
Calculating trend percentages

Pro Foods, Inc., is concerned about the level of its advertising and office salaries expense. Selected income statement data for the past 3 years appear below:

	1989	1988	1987
Sales...	$140,000	$60,000	$37,500
Gross Profit.....................................	89,600	37,200	22,500
Advertising Expense	7,000	3,300	2,250
Office Salaries Expense...........................	22,400	9,000	4,500
Net Income......................................	30,800	13,800	9,000

Calculate trend percentages for Sales, Advertising Expense, and Office Salaries Expense. Use 1987 as a base year. Round to the nearest percent.

(Check figure: 1989 advertising expense = 311%)

Exercise 14-3
Calculating ROR on total assets and on stockholders' equity

The following data have been assembled from the financial statements of Rule, Inc.:

	Dec. 31, 1989	Jan. 1, 1989
Total Assets	$180,000	$140,000
Total Stockholders' Equity...........................	144,000	112,000
Total Preferred Stockholders' equity	30,000	30,000
Preferred Dividends Declared	2,400	—
Net Income	20,000	—
Interest Expense	5,750	—

Calculate the following ratios:
a. Rate of return on total assets
b. Rate of return on common stockholders' equity

(Check figure: 17.96%)

Exercise 14-4
Calculating EPS, price-earnings ratio, and dividend yield rate

Norma Vester is in the process of analyzing the earnings performance of the Boulder Transport Corp. She has gathered the following data from Boulder's financial statements and from a report of the closing market prices of stock:

Net income for 1989.....................	$743,000
Preferred dividends declared during 1989 ...	$60,000
Common dividends declared Dec. 31, 1989....................................	$620,000
Number of shares of Boulder common stock outstanding:	
Jan. 1, 1989	1,100,000 shs
Dec. 31,1989	1,300,000 shs
Market price per share of common stock on Dec. 31, 1989..........................	$15

Calculate the following ratios relating to the Boulder stock:
a. Earnings per share of common stock

(Check figure: $0.569)

b. Price-earnings ratio
c. Dividend yield rate of common stock

Exercise 14-5
Calculating times interest earned, debt to total assets ratio, and stockholders' equity to total assets ratio

The president of Tom's Toys, Inc., has asked you to gather some statistics about his company's debt-paying ability. You have compiled the following data:

Net Income...............................	$900,000
Income Tax Rate.........................	40%
Interest Expense.........................	$100,000
Total Liabilities	$2,048,000
Total Stockholders' Equity.................	$4,352,000

Using the data above, calculate:
a. Times interest earned

(Check figure: 16 times)

b. Debt to total assets ratio
c. Stockholders' equity to total assets ratio

Exercise 14-6
Calculating working capital, current ratio, and quick ratio

The following information was taken from the balance sheet of Ready Corp.:

Cash	$13,250
Accounts Receivable (net).....................	33,000
Merchandise Inventory.......................	40,000
Prepaid Expenses...........................	9,950
Accounts Payable	25,200
Accrued Payables...........................	1,800
Notes Payable (due in 6 months)...............	10,000

Calculate (a) working capital, (b) current ratio, and (c) quick ratio.

(Check figure: Current ratio = 2.6 : 1)

Exercise 14-7
Calculating inventory turnover, accounts receivable turnover, and average age of receivables

You have been assigned the task of evaluating Dorian, Inc.'s management of merchandise and receivables. You decide that inventory turnover, accounts receivable turnover, and average age of receivables statistics will prove valuable in your opinions. The following data are available from Dorian's annual report:

Merchandise Inventory:
Jan. 1	$ 245,000
Dec. 31	375,000

Accounts Receivable:
Jan. 1	250,000
Dec. 31	297,000
Cost of Goods Sold	2,480,000
Cash Sales	1,000,000
Total Sales	5,100,000
Dorian's Credit Terms.....................	Net 30 days

a. Calculate inventory turnover, accounts receivable turnover, and average age of receivables.

(Check figure: Accounts receivable turnover = 15 times)

b. In your opinion, is Dorian doing a good job or a poor job of managing inventory and receivables? Explain.

Exercise 14-8
Finding missing balance sheet amounts using ratios

The following ratios apply to the Turtle Corp. for 1989:

Current ratio.....................	2.7	Inventory turnover	3.4
Quick ratio	1.17	Accounts receivable turnover	6.5

In addition, the following amounts are known:

Cost of Goods Sold for 1989...................	$197,200
Credit Sales for 1989	260,000
Accounts Receivable, Jan. 1, 1989	38,200
Merchandise Inventory, Jan. 1, 1989	62,000

Supply the missing amounts in the schedule below. (Hint: Solve in numerical order—total current assets first, etc.)

TURTLE CORP.
Schedule of Current Assets
and Current Liabilities
December 31, 1989

Current Assets:		
Cash..		$ 5,000
Accounts Receivable...	(2)	?
Merchandise Inventory	(3)	?
Prepaid Insurance		7,200
Total current assets.......................................	(1)	$?
Current Liabilities:		
Accounts Payable	(4)	$?
Accrued Payables...		5,000
Total Current Liabilities.......................................		$40,000

(Check figure: Total current assets = $108,000)

PROBLEMS: SET A

**Problem A14-1
Calculating liquid position, debt-paying ability, and earnings performance ratios**

Poston, Inc.'s income statement and balance sheet for 1989 are presented below:

**POSTON, INC.
Income Statement
Year Ended August 31, 1989**

Sales		$150,000
Cost of Goods Sold:		
Merchandise Inventory, Sept. 1, 1988	$ 24,000	
Purchases (net)	99,000	
Goods Available for Sale	$123,000	
Merchandise Inventory, Aug. 31, 1989	18,000	
Cost of Goods Sold		105,000
Gross Profit		$ 45,000
Operating Expenses		24,000
Income from Operations		$ 21,000
Other Income and Expense:		
Interest Expense		7,000
Income before Tax		$ 14,000
Income Tax Expense		6,400
Net Income		$ 7,600

**POSTON, INC.
Balance Sheet
August 31, 1989**

Cash	$ 6,000
Marketable Securities	3,000
Accounts Receivable (net)	17,000
Merchandise Inventory	18,000
Property, Plant, and Equipment (net)	160,000
Goodwill	6,000
Total Assets	$210,000
Accounts Payable	$ 16,000
Accrued Salaries Payable	2,000
Income Taxes Payable	1,500
Other Accrued Payables	500
10% Note Payable (due in 2000)	70,000
Common Stock ($1 par)	80,000
Retained Earnings	40,000
Total Liabilities and Stockholders' Equity	$210,000

All sales were on credit. On Sept. 1, 1988, Poston had total assets of $240,000 (including accounts receivable of $13,000 and merchandise inventory of $24,000), total liabilities of $127,600, and total stockholders' equity of $112,400.

Required

1. Calculate the following liquid position ratios: current ratio, quick ratio, inventory turnover, and accounts receivable turnover.

2. Calculate the following ratios indicating debt-paying ability: times interest earned, debt to total assets ratio, and stockholders' equity to total assets ratio.

(Check figure: Debt to total assets ratio = 42.9%)

3. Calculate the following earnings performance statistics: rate of return on total assets and rate of return on common stockholders' equity.

**Problem A14-2
Calculating percentage increase and decrease in comparative balance sheets and income statements**

The following financial statements are included in the 1989 annual report of the Federal Company:

**FEDERAL COMPANY
Comparative Balance Sheets
(000s Omitted)**

	June 30	
	1989	1988
Assets		
Current Assets:		
Cash..........	$ 31,600	$ 6,000
Accounts Receivable (net of allowances for uncollectibles of $560 in 1989 and $192 in 1988)	19,200	9,600
Merchandise Inventory	22,100	20,000
Total Current Assets	$ 72,900	$ 35,600
Property, Plant, and Equipment:		
Land	$ 80,000	$ 90,000
Buildings..........	20,000	20,000
Less: Accumulated Depreciation......	(2,700)	(2,500)
Equipment......	15,000	14,000
Less: Accumulated Depreciation......	(2,000)	(1,500)
Total Property, Plant, and Equipment......	$110,300	$120,000
Intangibles:		
Patents	$ 1,500	$ 1,600
Total Assets	$184,700	$157,200
Liabilities & Stockholders' Equity		
Current Liabilities:		
Accounts Payable	$ 20,000	$ 16,600
Accrued Payables	3,500	3,000
Total Current Liabilities	$ 23,500	$ 19,600
Long-Term Liabilities:		
8% Note Payable (due 1992)......	$ 12,000	—
10% Bonds Payable (due 1997)	81,000	$ 81,000
Total Long-Term Liabilities......	$ 93,000	$ 81,000
Total Liabilities......	$116,500	$100,600
Stockholders' Equity:		
Common Stock ($1 par)	$ 10,000	$ 10,000
Paid-In Capital in Excess of Par......	26,400	26,400
Retained Earnings	31,800	20,200
Total Stockholders' Equity......	$ 68,200	$ 56,600
Total Liabilities and Stockholders' Equity......	$184,700	$157,200

FEDERAL COMPANY
Comparative Income Statements
Years Ended June 30
(000s omitted)

	1989	1988
Net Sales	$160,000	$104,000
Cost of Goods Sold	59,200	37,500
Gross Profit on Sales	$100,800	$ 66,500
Operating Expenses:		
Sales Salary Expense	$ 25,800	$ 21,600
Utilities Expense	14,000	11,800
Advertising Expense	27,200	16,800
Other Expenses	5,000	4,200
Total Operating Expenses	$ 72,000	$ 54,400
Other Income and Expense:		
Interest Expense	$ 10,000	$ 8,600
Income before Income Taxes	$ 18,800	$ 3,500
Income Tax Expense	7,200	1,200
Net Income	$ 11,600	$ 2,300

Required

1. Comparative income statements and balance sheets for 1989 and 1988 are presented above. On your solutions paper, prepare columns showing the amount and percentage increase or decrease for each item on the statements.
2. On the basis of your solution for part 1, answer the following questions:
   a. What are the three balance sheet accounts that experienced the greatest percentage change?
   b. What three revenue or expense accounts on the income statement had the highest percentage change?

   (Check figure: Income Tax Expense, Cost of Goods Sold, Advertising Expense)

   c. Does the large increase in current assets appear to have been generated by profits for the year? Explain.
   d. Sales increased as compared with the prior year. Did expenses seem to increase proportionately also? Comment on any exceptions.

Problem A14-3
Completing the balance sheet and income statement

The following financial information is available for the Dallas Machinery Corp.:
a. All sales were on credit.
b. The debt to total assets ratio is 52%.
c. Working capital is $828.
d. Net income is 14% of sales; gross profit is 65% of sales.
e. The only interest paid was on long-term debt.
f. Inventory turnover is 5 (beginning inventory = $150).
g. Accounts receivable turnover is 10 (beginning accounts receivable = $240).
h. 46% of the total cost of the building has been depreciated.

Required

Complete the Dallas Machinery Corp. financial statements shown below. Round all calculations to the nearest dollar. (Hint: Determine the amounts in the order indicated by the numbers in parentheses on the statements.)

DALLAS MACHINERY CORP.
Income Statement
Year Ended December 31, 1989

Sales.	(1)	$?
Cost of Goods Sold.	(3)	?
Gross Profit on Sales	(2)	?
Operating Expenses	(15)	?
Interest Expense	(14)	?
Income before Income Taxes.	(4)	?
Income Tax Expense (34.67% of income before income taxes).	(5)	?
Net Income		$392

DALLAS MACHINERY CORP.
Balance Sheet
December 31, 1989

Assets:		
Cash		$ 418
Accounts Receivable (net)	(6)	?
Merchandise Inventory.	(7)	?
Building	(10)	?
Accumulated Depreciation	(11)	(?)
Total Assets.	(9)	$?
Liabilities and Stockholders' Equity:		
Accounts Payable.	(8)	$?
10% Bonds Payable (due 1995).	(12)	?
Common Stock		500
Retained Earnings	(13)	?
Total Equities		$2,600

Problem A14-4
Selecting data needed
and calculating five ratios

The following financial data have been assembled for World Coatings, Inc., on Dec. 31, 1989:

Average total assets for 1989.	$400,000
Total stockholders' equity (average for 1989)	300,000
Common stock ($2 par).	175,000
8% preferred stock ($50 par).	75,000
Net income.	31,000
Interest expense.	3,000
Income tax expense (40% of income before income taxes)	
Market price of common stock, Dec. 31, 1989.	2.75
Market price of preferred stock, Dec. 31, 1989.	60

Common dividends were paid at the rate of
  $0.10 per share per quarter.
Preferred dividends were declared and paid.
No preferred stock or common stock was issued
  or reacquired during 1989.

Required	Using whatever data you need from the above list, calculate:

1. Rate of return on total assets
2. Rate of return on common stockholders' equity
3. Earnings per common share

(Check figure: $0.286)

4. Price-earnings ratio
5. Dividend yield rate

Problem A14-5
Calculating liquidity ratios for two firms and deciding which should receive a short-term loan

Stan, Inc., and the Oliver Company both sell irrigation equipment for agricultural use. Both companies have applied for a short-term loan. Data from the Dec. 31, 1989, balance sheets appear below:

	Stan, Inc.	Oliver Company
Cash..	$ 27,200	$ 75,000
Marketable Securities.....................	1,800	60,000
Accounts Receivable (net)...............	31,000	44,000
Merchandise Inventory	180,000	120,000
Property, Plant, and Equipment (net)...	350,000	360,000
Intangibles	1,800	—
Total Assets	$591,800	$659,000
Current Liabilities........................	$ 60,000	$100,000
Long-Term Liabilities	100,000	100,000
Common Stock ($10 par)	400,000	400,000
Retained Earnings.........................	31,800	59,000
Total Equities	$591,800	$659,000

Other Information

	Stan, Inc.	Oliver Company
Accounts Receivable, Jan. 1, 1989	$ 39,000	$ 35,000
Merchandise Inventory, Jan. 1, 1989	160,000	130,000
1989 Sales:		
Cash...	258,000	120,000
Credit	342,000	480,000
1989 Cost of Goods Sold....................	528,000	360,000

Required	1. Calculate for each company the current ratio, quick ratio, inventory turnover, accounts receivable turnover, and average age of receivables.

(Check figure: Inventory turnover for Oliver Company = 2.88)

2. Which company would you recommend to receive the short-term loan? Explain.
3. What additional ratios would you consider if the companies were requesting a long-term loan? Explain.

PROBLEMS: SET B

**Problem B14-1
Calculating liquid position, debt-paying ability, and earnings performance ratios**

Milton, Inc.'s income statement and balance sheet for 1989 are presented below:

**MILTON, INC.
Income Statement
Year Ended October 31, 1989**

Sales		$300,000
Cost of Goods Sold:		
Merchandise Inventory, Nov. 1, 1988	$ 27,500	
Purchases (net)	125,000	
Goods Available for Sale	$152,500	
Merchandise Inventory, Oct. 31, 1989	32,500	
Cost of Goods Sold		120,000
Gross Profit		$180,000
Operating Expenses		125,000
Income from Operations		$ 55,000
Other Income and Expense:		
Interest Expense		2,000
Income before Tax		$ 53,000
Income Tax Expense		24,000
Net Income		$ 29,000

**MILTON, INC.
Balance Sheet
October 31, 1989**

Cash	$ 3,750
Marketable Securities	5,400
Accounts Receivable (net)	9,650
Merchandise Inventory	32,500
Property, Plant, and Equipment (net)	80,000
Patents	2,700
Total Assets	$134,000
Accounts Payable	$ 8,100
Accrued Salaries Payable	1,350
Income Taxes Payable	4,800
8% Bonds Payable (due in 1996)	25,000
Common Stock ($10 par)	50,000
Retained Earnings	44,750
Total Liabilities and Stockholders' Equity	$134,000

All sales were on credit. On Nov. 1, 1988, Milton had total assets of $116,000 (including accounts receivable of $10,350 and merchandise inventory of $27,500), total liabilities of $50,500, and total stockholders' equity of $65,500.

Required

1. Calculate the following liquid position ratios: current ratio, quick ratio, inventory turnover, and accounts receivable turnover.

(Check figure: Accounts receivable turnover = 30)

2. Calculate the following ratios indicating debt-paying ability: times interest earned, debt to total assets ratio, and stockholders' equity to total assets ratio.
3. Calculate the following earnings performance statistics: rate of return on total assets, and rate of return on common stockholders' equity.

Problem B14-2
Calculating percentage increase and decrease in comparative balance sheets and income statements

The following financial statements are included in the 1989 annual report of the Aspin Company:

ASPIN COMPANY
Comparative Balance Sheets
(000s Omitted)

	Sept. 30	
	1989	1988
Assets		
Current Assets:		
Cash..	$ 7,200	$ 3,600
Accounts Receivable (net of allowances for uncollectibles of		
$120 in 1989 and $40 in 1988)	5,600	3,800
Merchandise Inventory	15,400	11,000
Total Current Assets	$ 28,200	$ 18,400
Property, Plant, and Equipment:		
Land	$ 50,000	$ 44,000
Buildings...	36,000	36,000
Less: Accumulated Depreciation.........................	(600)	(500)
Equipment	7,000	6,000
Less: Accumulated Depreciation.........................	(200)	(100)
Total Property, Plant, and Equipment.................	$ 92,200	$ 85,400
Intangibles:		
Copyrights	$ 2,900	$ 2,800
Total Assets	$123,300	$106,600
Liabilities & Stockholders' Equity		
Current Liabilities:		
Accounts Payable	$ 2,000	$ 8,000
Accrued Payables	1,300	1,000
Total Current Liabilities	$ 3,300	$ 9,000
Long-Term Liabilities:		
6% Note Payable (due 1991).............................	$ 20,000	$ 20,000
12% Bonds Payable (due 1996)	20,000	—
Total Long-Term Liabilities........................	$ 40,000	$ 20,000
Total Liabilities..	$ 43,300	$ 29,000
Stockholders' Equity:		
Common Stock ($10 par)	$ 20,000	$ 20,000
Paid-In Capital in Excess of Par.........................	8,000	8,000
Retained Earnings	52,000	49,600
Total Stockholders' Equity...........................	$ 80,000	$ 77,600
Total Liabilities and Stockholders' Equity..................	$123,300	$106,600

ASPIN COMPANY Comparative Income Statements Years Ended September 30 (000s Omitted)		
	1989	**1988**
Net Sales	$68,400	$76,000
Cost of Goods Sold	24,472	26,600
Gross Profit on Sales	$43,928	$49,400
Operating Expenses:		
Sales Salary Expense	$10,944	$12,160
Utilities Expense	12,312	9,120
Other Selling Expenses	6,156	6,840
Other General Expenses	2,052	2,280
Total Operating Expenses	$31,464	$30,400
Other Income and Expense:		
Interest Expense	$ 3,600	$ 1,200
Income before Income Taxes	$ 8,864	$17,800
Income Tax Expense	3,988	8,010
Net Income	$ 4,876	$ 9,790

Required

1. Comparative income statements and balance sheets for 1989 and 1988 are presented above. On your solutions paper, prepare columns showing the amount and percentage increase or decrease for each item on the statements.
2. On the basis of your solution for part 1, answer the following questions:
   a. What are the four balance sheet accounts that experienced the greatest percentage change?
   b. What three revenue or expense accounts on the income statement had the highest percentage change?

   (Check figure: Utilities Expense, Interest Expense, and Income Tax Expense)

   c. Does the large increase in current assets appear to have been generated by profits for the year? Explain.
   d. Sales decreased as compared with the prior year. Did expenses seem to decrease proportionately also? Comment on any exceptions.

Problem B14-3
Completing the balance sheet and income statement

The following financial information is available for Waco Sales, Inc.:
a. All sales were on credit.
b. The debt to total assets ratio is 55%.
c. Working capital is $1,310.
d. Net income is 9.0% of sales; gross profit is 30% of sales.
e. The only interest paid was on long-term debt.
f. Inventory turnover is 6 (beginning inventory = $500).
g. Accounts receivable turnover is 12 (beginning accounts receivable = $300).
h. 45% of the total cost of the building has been depreciated.

Complete the Waco Sales, Inc., financial statements shown below. Round all calculations to the nearest dollar. (Hint: Determine the amounts in the order indicated by the numbers in parentheses on the statements.)

WACO SALES, INC.
Income Statement
Year Ended December 31, 1989

Sales.	(1)	$?
Cost of Goods Sold.	(3)	?
Gross Profit on Sales	(2)	?
Operating Expenses	(15)	?
Interest Expense	(14)	?
Income before Income Taxes.	(4)	?
Income Tax Expense (60% of income before income taxes)	(5)	
Net Income		$540

WACO SALES, INC.
Balance Sheet
December 31, 1989

Assets:		
Cash.		$ 310
Accounts Receivable (net).	(6)	?
Merchandise Inventory	(7)	?
Building	(10)	?
Accumulated Depreciation.	(11)	(?)
Total Assets	(9)	$?
Liabilities and Stockholders' Equity:		
Accounts Payable	(8)	$
6% Bonds Payable (due 1997)	(12)	
Common Stock.		800
Retained Earnings	(13)	
Total Equities		$ 4,000

Problem B14-4
Selecting data needed
and calculating five ratios

The following financial data have been assembled for Retton Merchandising, Inc., on Dec. 31, 1989:

Average total assets for 1989.	$250,000
Total stockholders' equity (average for 1989)	200,000
Common stock ($0.25 par).	100,000
8% preferred stock ($5 par).	50,000
Net income.	15,000
Interest expense.	1,000
Income tax expense (40% of income before income taxes)	
Market price of common stock, Dec. 31, 1989.	1.10
Market price of preferred stock, Dec. 31, 1989.	7.50

Common dividends were paid at the rate of
$0.05 per share per quarter.
Preferred dividends were declared and paid.
No preferred stock or common stock was issued
or reacquired during 1989.

Required

Using whatever data you need from the above list, calculate:
1. Rate of return on total assets
2. Rate of return on common stockholders' equity

(Check figure: 7.33%)

3. Earnings per common share
4. Price-earnings ratio
5. Dividend yield rate

Problem B14-5
Calculating liquidity ratios
for two firms and deciding
which should receive a
short-term loan

Front, Inc., and the Center Company both sell machinery for washing large trucks. Both companies have applied for a short-term loan. Data from the Dec. 31, 1989, balance sheets appear below:

	Front, Inc.	Center Co.
Cash..	$ 55,000	$ 150,000
Marketable Securities...............................	3,600	120,000
Accounts Receivable (net)..........................	61,400	90,000
Merchandise Inventory..............................	360,000	240,000
Property, Plant, and Equipment (net)...........	700,000	750,000
Intangibles...	3,000	—
Total Assets...	$1,183,000	$1,350,000
Current Liabilities....................................	$ 120,000	$ 200,000
Long-Term Liabilities................................	200,000	200,000
Common Stock ($10 par)...........................	800,000	800,000
Retained Earnings....................................	63,000	150,000
Total Equities...	$1,183,000	$1,350,000

Other Information

	Front, Inc.	Center Co.
Accounts Receivable, Jan. 1, 1989..........................	$ 78,600	$ 70,000
Merchandise Inventory, Jan. 1, 1989.......................	320,000	260,000
1989 Sales:		
Cash...	516,000	240,000
Credit..	684,000	960,000
1989 Cost of Goods Sold......................................	1,054,000	700,000

Required

1. Calculate for each company the current ratio, quick ratio, inventory turnover, accounts receivable turnover, and average age of receivables.

(Check figure: Inventory turnover for Center Co. = 2.8)

2. Which company would you recommend to receive the short-term loan? Explain.
3. What additional ratios would you consider if the companies were requesting a long-term loan? Explain.

The Statement of Cash Flows

In the previous chapter you learned about numerous financial ratios that external parties use to evaluate the soundness of a company, based on results found in the balance sheet, income statement, and statement of retained earnings. This chapter introduces you to the fourth required financial statement—the statement of cash flows. In preparing this statement, you'll need to use all the accounts that are found in the other three statements. You will learn how to analyze these accounts and determine some new information that none of the other statements (or ratios from Chapter 14 that relate to these statements) show.

A complete set of financial statements must include a statement of cash flows

Generally accepted accounting principles specify that a complete set of annual financial statements must include:

A balance sheet

An income statement

A statement of retained earnings and

A statement of cash flows

This requirement applies to all businesses—no matter how large or small.

Before we proceed with our discussion of the statement of cash flows, let's briefly review the purposes of the other financial statements.

The purpose of the *balance sheet* is to show the resources that a company has—its assets—and where those resources come from: borrowing—liabilities; investments by owners—paid-in capital; and accumulation of earnings—retained earnings. These resources and sources of resources are presented at one instant in time, the end of the accounting period.

The purpose of the *income statement* is to show the expenses incurred matched with the revenues earned. Gains and losses experienced during the period are also included.

The *statement of retained earnings* simply shows the beginning balance of retained earnings, the net income or loss for the period, dividends declared, and the ending balance of retained earnings.

The statement of cash flows provides information not shown in the other financial statements

We may find it difficult, if not impossible, to learn certain things from studying the three major statements. For example, to discover how a company's growth and expansion was financed, or what amount of cash was generated by operations, we would need to make a detailed analysis of the statements. We would also have to make a number of assumptions before we could even attempt to find out this information. The **statement of cash flows** is designed to fill this information gap left by other statements.

The statement of cash flows provides information about cash receipts and payments as well as investing and financing activities

The Financial Accounting Standards Board (FASB) has stated that the objective of the statement of cash flows is to provide information about cash receipts and cash payments and to provide information about the **operating, investing,** and **financing activities** of a business.

The information provided by the statement of cash flows, together with the information contained in the three other financial statements, will help the user of the financial statements to

- Assess an entity's ability to generate positive future cash flows

- Assess an entity's ability to meet its obligations, its need for external financing, and its ability to pay dividends

- Assess the reasons for differences between income and associated cash receipts and payments

- Assess both the cash and noncash aspects of an entity's investing and financing transactions

The statement of cash flows has three sections: operating activities, investing activities, and financing activities

The statement of cash flows is divided into three sections: *net cash flow from operating activities, cash flows from investing activities,* and *cash flows from financing activities.* In order to explain how the statement is prepared and in order to grasp the meaning of the statement we shall work first with a simple example to explain the three sections of the statement.

THE SIMPLE COMPANY

The Operating Section

Operating activities consist of delivering or producing goods for sale and providing services

The operating section of the cash flow statement, as explained by the FASB, consists of the activities of delivering or producing goods for sale and providing services. The cash flows from **operating activities** are generally the cash effects of transactions that enter into the determination of income. In order to see how the operating section is developed let's assume that a small company, we will call it The Simple Company, had the following balance sheet on Dec. 31, 1988:

THE SIMPLE COMPANY
Balance Sheet
December 31, 1988

Cash	$ 9,000	
Accounts Receivable	20,000	
Total Assets		$29,000
Common Stock	$15,000	
Retained Earnings	14,000	
Total Liabilities and Stockholders' Equity		$29,000

The company had just three transactions for the year 1989, these transactions were, in general journal entry form:

Accounts Receivable	40,000	
Sales		40,000
To record sales on account.		

Cash	45,000	
Accounts Receivable		45,000
To record the collection of accounts receivable.		

Expenses	25,000	
Cash		25,000
To record expenses.		

After these transactions have been recorded The Simple Company would prepare an income statement and a balance sheet such as presented below:

THE SIMPLE COMPANY
Income Statement
For the Year Ended December 31, 1989

Sales	$40,000
Expenses.	25,000
Net Income	$15,000

THE SIMPLE COMPANY
Comparative Balance Sheets
December 31, 1989

	1989	1988
Cash	$29,000	$ 9,000
Accounts Receivable	15,000	20,000
Total Assets.	$44,000	$29,000
Common Stock	$15,000	$15,000
Retained Earnings	29,000	14,000
Total Liabilities and Stockholders' Equity	$44,000	$29,000

In addition a statement of cash flows would be prepared and it would look like this:

THE SIMPLE COMPANY
Statement of Cash Flows
For the Year Ended December 31, 1989

Cash Flow from Operating Activities:	
Net Income	$15,000
Noncash Expenses and Revenues Included in Income:	
Decrease in Accounts Receivable	5,000
Net Cash Flow from Operating Activities	$20,000

A decrease in Accounts Receivable is added to net income in determining cash flows from operations

Notice that the statement of cash flows starts with the net income figure. This provides a reconciliation between the two statements. The decrease in Accounts Receivable of $5,000 is added to the net income to determine the amount of cash flows from operating activities for the year of $20,000.

Look on the comparative balance sheets and you can see that cash has indeed increased by $20,000. That's because $45,000 was collected from accounts receivable and $25,000 was paid for expenses. Those were the only transactions involving cash. But when the revenues (sales) were measured on the income statement $40,000 was used in the determination of the $15,000 net income, not the $45,000 collected. Accounts receivable decreased because the company collected $5,000 more cash from its customers in 1989 than it recorded as revenue.

What happened in 1989 was that The Simple Company collected $20,000 cash from 1988 sales, the Dec. 31, 1988, Accounts Receivable balance, and they collected $25,000 cash from the $40,000 1989 sales, leaving $15,000 uncollected as the ending Accounts Receivable balance. So, for the analysis of cash flows when accounts receivable decreases it means that the net income figure must be increased to arrive at the cash flows figure.

Now let's expand the illustration to include accounts payable and inventories. A more elaborate Dec. 31, 1988, Simple Company balance sheet is presented below with these two accounts, Inventory and Accounts Payable, added:

THE SIMPLE COMPANY
Balance Sheet
December 31, 1988

Cash	$ 9,000	
Accounts Receivable	20,000	
Inventory	10,000	
Total Assets		$39,000
Accounts Payable	$ 6,000	
Common Stock	15,000	
Retained Earnings	18,000	
Total Liabilities and Stockholders' Equity		$39,000

During the year 1989, let's assume the following transactions have occurred:

Accounts Receivable.   40,000
    Sales   40,000
To record sales on account.

Cash   45,000
    Accounts Receivable.   45,000
To record collection of accounts receivable.

Inventory.   35,000
    Accounts Payable.   35,000
To record acquisition of inventory.

Expenses (Cost of Goods Sold)   25,000
    Inventory.   25,000
To record the cost of inventory sold.

Accounts Payable.   32,000
    Cash   32,000
To record payment of accounts payable.

After these 1989 activities The Simple Company would record an income statement and a balance sheet as follows:

THE SIMPLE COMPANY
Income Statement
For the Year Ended December 31, 1989

Sales	$40,000
Expenses.	25,000
Net Income	$15,000

THE SIMPLE COMPANY
Comparative Balance Sheets

	Dec. 31	
	1989	**1988**
Cash	$22,000	$ 9,000
Accounts Receivable.	15,000	20,000
Inventory.	20,000	10,000
Total Assets.	$57,000	$39,000
Accounts Payable.	$ 9,000	$ 6,000
Common Stock	15,000	15,000
Retained Earnings	33,000	18,000
Total Liabilities and Stockholders' Equity	$57,000	$39,000

The statement of cash flows would now appear as follows:

THE SIMPLE COMPANY
Statement of Cash Flows
For the Year Ended December 31, 1989

Cash Flow from Operating Activities:	
Net Income..	$ 15,000
Noncash Expenses and Revenues Included in Income:	
Decrease in Accounts Receivable....................................	5,000
Increase in Inventory	(10,000)
Increase in Accounts Payable	3,000
Net Cash Flows from Operating Activities..............................	$ 13,000

An increase in Inventories is deducted from net income in determining cash flows from operating activities

An increase in Accounts Payable is added to net income in determining cash flows from operating activities

The net income figure is again adjusted by $5,000 for the decrease in Accounts Receivable. In addition the increase in Inventory of $10,000 must be subtracted and the increase in Accounts Payable of $3,000 must be added to net income to determine the $13,000 net cash flow from operating activities. The $13,000 is the difference between the Dec. 31, 1989, cash balance of $22,000 and the Dec. 31, 1988, cash balance of $9,000.

The expenses for 1989 amounted to $25,000, the cost of the inventory sold. But the amount of cash *expended* for these *expenditures* was $32,000, a difference of $7,000. And that is precisely the sum of the differences between the Inventory decrease ($10,000) and the Accounts Payable increase ($3,000). We will expand on this later in the chapter when we discuss the conversion of the accrual-basis income statement to the cash-basis income statement.

By adding or subtracting the differences in the Accounts Receivable, Inventory, and Accounts Payable accounts to the net income for the period a reconciliation can be made between the net income figure and the amount of cash flows from operations for the period.

The Investing Section

Investing activities are lending money and collecting loans, acquiring and disposing of securities, and acquiring and selling productive assets

The FASB has defined investing activities as those that include lending money and collecting loans; acquiring and disposing of securities; and acquiring and selling productive assets.

In order to illustrate cash flows from ***investing activities*** we will need to add two more accounts to The Simple Company's balance sheet; Net Property, Plant, and Equipment and Investments. We are using the Net Property, Plant, and Equipment account rather than the individual accounts (Land, Buildings, Equipment, and their related accumulated depreciation accounts) so as to keep the illustration as brief as possible. The substance of the investing activity can be illustrated by using the Net Property, Plant, and Equipment item. Adding these two accounts to the Dec. 31, 1988, balance would result in the following balance sheet:

THE SIMPLE COMPANY
Balance Sheet
December 31, 1988

Cash	$ 9,000
Accounts Receivable....................................	20,000
Inventory..	10,000
Net Property, Plant, and Equipment...................	30,000
Investments...	5,000
Total Assets..	$74,000
Accounts Payable.......................................	$ 6,000
Common Stock	50,000
Retained Earnings	18,000
Total Liabilities and Stockholders' Equity	$74,000

Notice that the addition of the Net Property, Plant, and Equipment account ($30,000) and Investments account ($5,000) was accomplished by increasing the Common Stock from $15,000 to $50,000 to make the balance sheet balance. Now, assuming that the cash flows from operating activities remain the same as before, three additional transactions will illustrate the cash flows from investing activities. They are as follows:

Cash	8,000	
Net Property, Plant, and Equipment		8,000
To record the sale of certain equipment at its book value.		

Net Property, Plant, and Equipment	4,000	
Cash		4,000
To record the acquisition of equipment.		

Investments...	2,000	
Cash		2,000
To record the acquisition of bonds to be held as a long-term investment.		

The sale of the equipment was made at book value. This is to avoid temporarily the problem of dealing with a gain or loss. We will address that issue in a more complex example a little later in the chapter. None of these transactions affect the income statement so net income remains the same. But the 1989 balance sheet will change as will the cash flow statement. These two statements are presented below:

THE SIMPLE COMPANY
Comparative Balance Sheets

	Dec. 31,	
	1989	**1988**
Cash	$24,000	$ 9,000
Accounts Receivable......................................	15,000	20,000
Inventory...	20,000	10,000
Net Property, Plant, and Equipment......................	26,000	30,000
Investments..	7,000	5,000
Total Assets...	$92,000	$74,000

(continued)

Accounts Payable.	$ 9,000	$ 6,000
Common Stock	50,000	50,000
Retained Earnings	33,000	18,000
Total Liabilities and Stockholders' Equity	$92,000	$74,000

The net effect of these investing activities was to add $2,000 ($8,000 − $4,000 − $2,000) to the cash balance, $2,000 to the Investment account, and to deduct $4,000 from the Property, Plant, and Equipment account. This would result in the following cash flows statement:

THE SIMPLE COMPANY
Statement of Cash Flows
For the Year Ended December 31, 1989

Cash Flow from Operating Activities:		
Net Income.		$ 15,000
Noncash Expenses and Revenues Included in Income:		
Decrease in Accounts Receivable.		5,000
Increase in Inventory		(10,000)
Increase in Accounts Payable		3,000
Net Cash Flows from Operating Activities.		$ 13,000
Cash Flow from Investing Activities:		
Proceeds from Disposal of Equipment.	$ 8,000	
Purchase of Equipment	(4,000)	
Purchase of Investment Bonds.	(2,000)	
Net Cash Provided by Investing Activities.		2,000
Net Increase in Cash.		$ 15,000

The disposal of equipment, the purchase of equipment, and the purchase of investment bonds are investing activities

Now you can start to see the statement's usefulness. The statement is telling us that cash has increased by $15,000 this year. Check the comparative balance sheets and it has indeed increased by $15,000 (from $9,000 to $24,000). Specifically, cash has increased by $13,000 resulting from those activities associated with the normal operations of the company. And in addition, cash has increased by $2,000 due to certain investing activities, the purchase of plant and equipment, and the disposal of other equipment.

The Financing Section

The financing activity includes obtaining resources from owners and creditors, providing owners a return on and of their investment, and repaying creditors

The *financing activity,* according to the FASB, would include obtaining resources from owners and creditors; providing owners a return on and a return of their investment, and repaying creditors.

We need add only two more transactions to illustrate the last section of the cash flow statement. And we can use the same 1988 balance sheet as in the previous example. The two transactions are

Cash	10,000	
Common Stock		10,000
To record the issuance of common stock.		

Retained Earnings	3,000	
Cash		3,000
To record the payment of dividends.		

These transactions, together with those from the previous examples, will result in the following balance sheet and cash flow statements:

THE SIMPLE COMPANY
Comparative Balance Sheets

	Dec. 31,	
	1989	1988
Cash	$31,000	$ 9,000
Accounts Receivable	15,000	20,000
Inventory	20,000	10,000
Net Property, Plant, and Equipment	26,000	30,000
Investments	7,000	5,000
Total Assets	$99,000	$74,000
Accounts Payable	$ 9,000	$ 6,000
Common Stock	60,000	50,000
Retained Earnings	30,000	18,000
Total Liabilities and Stockholders' Equity	$99,000	$74,000

THE SIMPLE COMPANY
Statement of Cash Flows
For the Year Ended December 31, 1989

Cash Flow from Operating Activities:		
Net Income		$ 15,000
Noncash Expenses and Revenues Included in Income:		
Decrease in Accounts Receivable		5,000
Increase in Inventory		(10,000)
Increase in Accounts Payable		3,000
Net Cash Flows from Operating Activities		$ 13,000
Cash Flow from Investing Activities:		
Proceeds from Disposal of Equipment	$ 8,000	
Purchase of Equipment	(4,000)	
Purchase of Investment Bonds	(2,000)	
Net Cash Provided by Investing Activities		2,000
Cash Flow from Financing Activities:		
Proceeds from Issuing Common Stock	$10,000	
Dividends paid	(3,000)	
Net Cash Provided by Financing Activities		7,000
Net Increase in Cash		$ 22,000

Issuing common stock and paying dividends are financing activities

The cash flow statement is now complete. It tells us that during the year 1989 The Simple Company has had an increase in its Cash account of $22,000; $13,000 came from operations, $2,000 from investing, and $7,000 from financing activities.

The Simple Company example developed each of the three sections by first showing the transactions that affected that activity. You were then able to follow the transactions into the 1989 income statement and balance sheet and see how the cash flow statement was developed. Such is not the case in real life. The cash flow statement is made after the accounting period has ended and after the income statement and balance sheets have been prepared. This makes it more difficult to prepare the cash flow statement and that's the topic we need to discuss in the remainder of this chapter.

CONVERTING FROM THE ACCRUAL TO THE CASH BASIS

Before we consider a more complex example it is necessary to digress for a moment to consider how the *accrual-basis income* statement can be converted to a *cash-basis income* statement. The concepts used for this conversion will help you understand how the operating activities section of the statement of cash flows is developed.

The revenue realization and matching principles so important to accrual-basis income measurement are ignored in preparing a cash-basis income statement. Since generally accepted accounting principles require income statements for external use to be prepared on the accrual basis, cash from operations is normally derived by adjusting accrual-basis net income as follows:

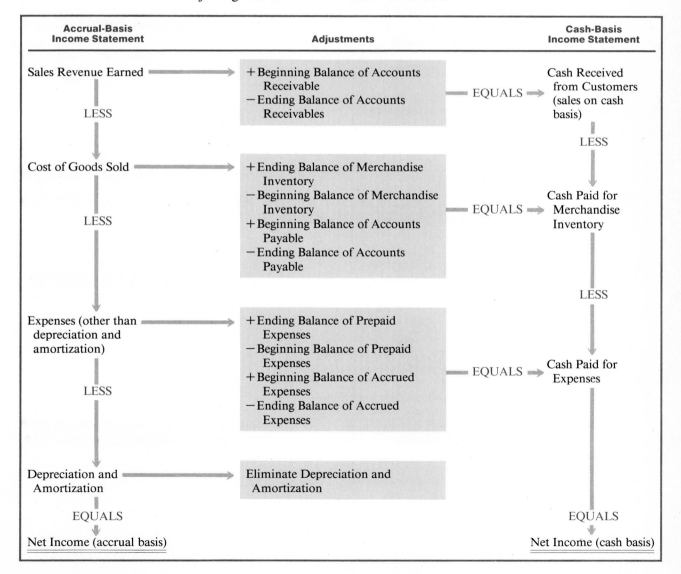

Accrual-Basis Income Statement	Adjustments		Cash-Basis Income Statement
Sales Revenue Earned	+ Beginning Balance of Accounts Receivable − Ending Balance of Accounts Receivables	EQUALS	Cash Received from Customers (sales on cash basis)
LESS			LESS
Cost of Goods Sold	+ Ending Balance of Merchandise Inventory − Beginning Balance of Merchandise Inventory + Beginning Balance of Accounts Payable − Ending Balance of Accounts Payable	EQUALS	Cash Paid for Merchandise Inventory
LESS			LESS
Expenses (other than depreciation and amortization)	+ Ending Balance of Prepaid Expenses − Beginning Balance of Prepaid Expenses + Beginning Balance of Accrued Expenses − Ending Balance of Accrued Expenses	EQUALS	Cash Paid for Expenses
LESS			
Depreciation and Amortization	Eliminate Depreciation and Amortization		
EQUALS			EQUALS
Net Income (accrual basis)			Net Income (cash basis)

Remember as you look at the logic underlying each of these adjustments that we are interested in calculating cash inflows and cash outflows from income-oriented activities.

Cash Received from Customers

To accrual-basis Sales we add the beginning balance of Accounts Receivable. This will include cash collected on accounts receivable during the current year from sales that were reported on the accrual basis in prior years. From accrual-basis Sales we subtract the ending balance of Accounts Receivable. This will exclude credit sales on the current income statement that have not yet been collected.

Cash Paid for Merchandise Inventory

First we calculate net purchases by adding the ending balance of Merchandise Inventory to Cost of Goods Sold and deducting the beginning balance from Cost of Goods Sold.

Now that we know how much merchandise was purchased this year, we must calculate how much was actually paid for. This is accomplished by adding the beginning balance of Accounts Payable—we're assuming that purchases made last year were paid for this year. The process is completed by deducting the ending balance of Accounts Payable—we're removing an amount that is included in purchases this year that won't be paid for until next year.

Cash Paid for Expenses

We must analyze two types of balance sheet accounts in calculating this amount: prepaid expenses (Prepaid Rent, Prepaid Insurance, etc.) and accrued expenses (Salaries Payable, Utilities Payable, etc.).

To accrual income statement expenses we add the ending balance of prepaid expenses—the cash has been paid out this year but the expense won't be reported on the accrual basis until next year. From accrual income statement expenses we deduct the beginning balance of prepaid expenses—we're removing expenses that were included this year but paid for last year.

The beginning balance of accrued expenses is added because we're assuming we paid for these expenses this year even though they were reported on the accrual-basis income statement last year. We deduct the ending balance of accrued expenses—these expenses are on this year's income statement, but they won't be paid until next year.

Depreciation and Amortization

These expenses don't use any cash or any other current asset. We eliminate them in calculating cash from operations.

Cash from Operating Activities — A Shortcut

This method of computing cash flows from operating activities is called the direct method. We can derive cash from operations a little more quickly by using the following shortcut calculation which is commonly used and is called the indirect method:

Cash from operating activities may be derived also by adjusting accrual net income

Accrual-Basis Net Income

Deduct **Increase in Accounts Receivable (or *Add* Decrease in Accounts Receivable)**

Deduct **Increase in Merchandise Inventory (or *Add* Decrease in Merchandise Inventory)**

Deduct **Increase in Prepaid Expenses (or *Add* Decrease in Prepaid Expenses)**

Add **Increase in Accounts Payable (or *Deduct* Decrease in Accounts Payable)**

Add **Increase in Accrued Expenses (or *Deduct* Decrease in Accrued Expenses)**

Add **Depreciation and Amortization Expenses for the Year**

Cash-Basis Net Income

This calculation accomplishes the same thing that we did with the direct method. Now we're beginning with net income and adjusting it instead of adjusting each revenue and expense account on the income statement. The cash flow from operating activities on the statement of cash flows is determined using this shortcut procedure, the indirect method.

THE COMPLEX COMPANY: T-ACCOUNT APPROACH

The T-account and the worksheet approaches are two ways to develop a statement of cash flows

A more realistic example of preparing the statement of cash flows is now needed and The Complex Company example will fill that need. We will demonstrate two approaches to preparing the statement of cash flows: first, the T-account approach, which is easier to understand but less formal, and second, the formal worksheet approach. For both examples we will use the same data which consists of an income statement for the year ended Dec. 31, 1989, a statement of retained earnings for the year ended Dec. 31, 1989, and comparative balance sheets for 1988 and 1989. The statements are presented below and on the next page.

THE COMPLEX COMPANY
Condensed Income Statement
Year Ended December 31, 1989

Sales		$ 290,000
Cost of Goods Sold		(174,000)
Gross Profit on Sales		$ 116,000
Operating Expenses:		
Administrative Expenses	$45,000	
Selling Expenses	20,900	
Depreciation Expenses	12,000	
Patent Amortization Expense	1,000	(78,900)
Other Income and Expenses:		
Interest Expense	$15,400	
Gain on Sale of Land	2,500	(12,900)
Income before Income Taxes		$ 24,200
Income Tax Expense		(9,700)
Net Income		$ 14,500

THE COMPLEX COMPANY
Statement of Retained Earnings
Year Ended December 31, 1989

Balance, Jan. 1, 1989	$ 88,000
Add: Net Income for the Year	14,500
Deduct: Dividends Declared and Paid during 1989	(10,000)
Balance, Dec. 31, 1989	$ 92,500

THE COMPLEX COMPANY
Balance Sheet

	December 31,		Increase (Decrease)
	1989	1988	
Assets			
Current Assets:			
Cash..........	$ 50,000	$ 55,000	$ (5,000)
Accounts Receivable (net).........	109,000	90,000	19,000
Merchandise Inventory.........	175,000	153,000	22,000
Prepaid Expenses.........	15,500	17,000	(1,500)
Total Current Assets.........	$ 349,500	$ 315,000	
Investments:			
Land Held for Investment.........	-0-	$ 27,500	(27,500)
Property, Plant, and Equipment:			
Land Used in Operations.........	$ 148,400	$ 100,000	48,400
Buildings.........	465,000	415,000	50,000
Less: Accum. Deprec.: Building.........	(217,000)	(205,000)	(12,000)
Total Property, Plant, and Equipment....	$ 396,400	$ 310,000	
Intangibles:			
Patents.........	$ 5,000	$ 6,000	(1,000)
Total Assets.........	$ 750,900	$ 658,500	
Liabilities and Stockholders' Equity			
Current Liabilities:			
Accounts Payable.........	$ 69,000	$ 75,000	(6,000)
Accrued Liabilities.........	24,500	20,000	4,500
Total Current Liabilities.........	$ 93,500	$ 95,000	
Long-Term Liabilities:			
Bonds Payable.........	$ 200,000	$ 200,000	-0-
Premium on Bonds Payable.........	29,400	30,000	(600)
Total Long-Term Liabilities.........	$ 229,400	$ 230,000	
Total Liabilities.........	$ 322,900	$ 325,000	
Stockholders' Equity			
Common Stock, no par.........	$ 335,500	$ 245,500	90,000
Retained Earnings.........	92,500	88,000	4,500
Total Stockholders' Equity.........	$ 428,000	$ 333,500	
Total Liabilities and Stockholders' Equity.......	$ 750,900	$ 658,500	

For the T-account approach a T-account is needed for each balance sheet account including a very large T-account for cash

The starting point for the T-account approach is to set up T-accounts for each *balance sheet* account and enter the beginning balance (BB) and ending balance (EB) as illustrated in Exhibit 15-1. Notice the very large T-account for cash, and how the account is divided into the three sections for the cash flow statement. As you may have guessed, the Cash T-account will contain all the information necessary to prepare the cash flow statement when we are done analyzing the T-accounts.

What we are going to do is to analyze the transactions made by The Complex Company in terms of their effects on cash flows. We will enter these transactions in the T-accounts as we analyze them. Beside each transaction we have provided a short version of the T-accounts affected in the margin of the text. The complete T-accounts with all the explanations are shown in Exhibit 15-2; you should be careful to examine

EXHIBIT 15-1

THE COMPLEX COMPANY
Statement of Cash Flows
T-Account Approach
(Before Analysis)

Cash			Accounts Receivable	
BB	55,000		BB	90,000
OPERATING | ACTIVITIES			EB	109,000

Beginning balance

Merchandise Inventory	
BB	153,000
EB	175,000

Entries to explain the changes in cash will be entered here

INVESTING | ACTIVITIES		Prepaid Expenses	
		BB	17,000
		EB	15,500

Entries to explain the changes in accounts other than Cash will be entered in these accounts

FINANCING | ACTIVITIES		Accounts Payable	
		BB	75,000
		EB	69,000

Ending balance

NONCASH INVESTING AND FINANCING		Accrued Liabilities	
		BB	20,000
EB	50,000	EB	24,500

Land Held for Investment		Land Used in Operations	
BB	27,500	BB	100,000
EB	-0-	EB	148,400

Buildings		Accum. Deprec.: Buildings	
BB	415,000	BB	205,000
EB	465,000	EB	217,000

(continued)

	Patents				Bonds Payable		
BB	6,000				BB	200,000	
EB	5,000				EB	200,000	

				Premium on Bonds Payable		
				BB	30,000	
				EB	29,400	

	Common Stock				Retained Earnings		
		BB	245,500		BB	88,000	
		EB	335,500		EB	92,500	

this exhibit to see where the explanations are placed and to see how the completed analysis looks.

Entry Code Letter	Transaction		Cash
A	Cash Flows from Operations.................. 14,500		BB 55,000
	Retained Earnings....................... 14,500		Operating │ Activities
			A 14,500

Description and Analysis

Reported income for the year was $14,500 as seen in the statement of retained earnings. The initial assumption is that all revenue involved is an inflow of cash and all expenses involved an outflow of cash. Adjustments will be made to determine the actual cash flows. Since a positive net income figure is reported, an inflow is the initial assumption. The entry then is to debit Cash (actually Cash in the operating activities section to reflect the assumed increase in cash) and to credit Retained Earnings.

Retained Earnings

BB	88,000
A	14,500

These entries are coded A as a reference. Look at Exhibit 15-2 (page 682).

We recommend that you start your analysis with the income for the year and then adjust this amount by the changes in the current assets and current liabilities. Notice in Exhibit 15-1 that the current accounts were all located near the Cash account.

Please understand that what we are doing is explaining how the accounts changed from the beginning to the ending balances. We are not actually recording the transactions in the accounts of The Complex Company. That has already been done during the course of the year. We are just using T-accounts as accountants do, for analytical purposes!

Entry Code Letter

Transaction

B   Accounts Receivable......................... 19,000

        Cash Flows from Operations..............   19,000

Description and Analysis

We are, in effect, converting from the accrual basis of accounting to the cash basis. Net income on the accrual basis is determined in accordance with generally accepted accounting principles. But cash flows from operations is determined simply by the difference between cash receipts from revenues and cash payments for expenses. Look at entry B in Exhibit 15-2.

When the Accounts Receivable account increases during the year that means that more accrual revenue has been earned than the amount of cash received. Thus, the accrual net income figure would be higher than the cash income figure. For this reason we must deduct the increase in receivables from the net income figure.

Notice the check mark in the Accounts Receivable account. That indicates that we have finished analyzing the account. The beginning balance of $90,000 plus the B adjustment of $19,000 determines the ending balance of $109,000.

Cash			
BB	55,000		
Operating		Activities	
A	14,500	B	19,000

Accounts Receivable		
BB	90,000	
B	19,000	
EB	109,000 ✓	

Entry Code Letter

Transaction

C   Merchandise Inventory....................... 22,000

        Cash Flows from Operations..............   22,000

Description and Analysis

The increase in the Merchandise Inventory account indicates that during the year The Complex Company bought $22,000 more inventory than it sold. The net income figure must be reduced. Look at entry C in Exhibit 15-2.

Cash			
BB	55,000		
Operating		Activities	
A	14,500	B	19,000
		C	22,000

Merchandise Inventory		
BB	153,000	
C	22,000	
EB	175,000 ✓	

Entry Code Letter

Transaction

D   Accounts Payable........................... 6,000

        Cash Flows from Operations..............   6,000

Description and Analysis

A decrease in Accounts Payable indicates that cash was paid out this period for purchases made in a prior period. Income must be reduced by this additional cash payout that does not appear on the income statement. Look at entry D in Exhibit 15-2.

Cash			
BB	55,000		
Operating		Activities	
A	14,500	B	19,000
		C	22,000
		D	6,000

Accounts Payable			
D	6,000	BB	75,000
		✓ EB	69,000

Entry Code Letter	Transaction	
E	Cash Flows from Operations...................	1,500
	Prepaid Expenses........................	1,500

Description and Analysis

A decrease in Prepaid Expenses means that some expenses on this period's income statement were paid for last period. They are noncash outflows for the current period. The decrease, then, must be added to current net income just as any other noncash expense would be. Look at entry E in Exhibit 15-2.

Cash

BB	55,000		
	Operating	Activities	
A	14,500	B	19,000
E	1,500	C	22,000
		D	6,000

Prepaid Expenses

BB	17,000	E	1,500
EB	15,500 ✓		

Entry Code Letter	Transaction	
F	Cash Flows from Operations...................	4,500
	Accrued Liabilities......................	4,500

Description and Analysis

An increase in Accrued Liabilities means that some accrued expenses on this period's income statement will be paid for in future periods. Those expenses that did not require a current use of cash must be added to accrual-basis income. Look at entry F in Exhibit 15-2.

Cash

BB	55,000		
	Operating	Activities	
A	14,500	B	19,000
E	1,500	C	22,000
F	4,500	D	6,000

Accrued Liabilities

		BB	20,000
		F	4,500
		✓EB	24,500

Entry Code Letter	Transaction	
G	Cash Flows from Operations...................	12,000
	Accum. Deprec.: Building	12,000

Description and Analysis

Depreciation expense for the period was recorded by debiting Depreciation Expense, a noncash entry, and crediting Accumulated Depreciation. The analysis debits Cash Flows from Operations to accomplish the objective of adding back this noncash item to net income. Accumulated Depreciation is credited because this was the original noncash account credited. Look at entry G in Exhibit 15-2.

Please, PLEASE understand that depreciation is not, IS NOT, a source of cash. We have simply adjusted the net income figure from the income statement by an item that DID NOT involve cash to determine the income from operating activities on a cash basis.

Look at it this way. Assume a company has cash sales of $6,000 and the only expense it had was $1,000 of depreciation. That would be a net income of $5,000. In order to determine the amount of cash flows from operations (which we know is $6,000 from the cash sales) we would have to add back the $1,000 depreciation to the accrual-basis net income figure of $5,000 to arrive at the $6,000 cash flow from operations.

Cash

BB	55,000		
	Operating	Activities	
A	14,500	B	19,000
E	1,500	C	22,000
F	4,500	D	6,000
G	12,000		

Accum. Deprec. Buildings

		BB	205,000
		G	12,000
		✓EB	217,000

Entry Code Letter	Transaction		
H	Cash Flows from Operations..................	1,000	
	Patents..................................		1,000

Description and Analysis

Patent amortization expense for the period was recorded by debiting the expense account and crediting Patents. Since this too is an expense not using cash, it must be added back to net income by debiting Cash Flows from Operations in the analysis entry. The credit in the analysis entry is to Patents since this was the original noncash credit. Look at entry H in Exhibit 15-2.

Cash

BB	55,000		
	Operating	Activities	
A	14,500	B	19,000
E	1,500	C	22,000
F	4,500	D	6,000
G	12,000		
H	1,000		

Patents

BB	6,000	H	1,000
EB	5,000 ✓		

Entry Code Letter	Transaction		
I	Premium on Bonds Payable	600	
	Cash Flows from Operations...............		600

Description and Analysis

The original entry made by The Complex Company when interest was paid was as follows:

Interest Expense...........................	15,400	
Premium on Bonds Payable	600	
Cash		16,000

The actual cash outflow was $16,000, but only $15,400 was reflected on the income statement as an expense due to the $600 premium amortization. The analysis entry is to debit Premium on Bonds Payable to reproduce the noncash part of the entry and credit Cash Flows from Operations to deduct $600 from income to reflect the correct amount of cash outflows associated with interest. Look at entry I in Exhibit 15-2.

Cash

BB	55,000		
	Operating	Activities	
A	14,500	B	19,000
E	1,500	C	22,000
F	4,500	D	6,000
G	12,000	I	600
H	1,000		

Premium on Bonds Payable

I	600	BB	30,000
		EB	29,400

Entry Code Letter	Transaction		
J	Cash Flows from Investing...................	30,000	
	Cash Flows from Operations...............		2,500
	Land Held for Investment.................		27,500

Description and Analysis

The original entry to record the sale of land was as follows:

Cash	30,000	
Gain on Sale of Land		2,500
Land Held for Investment.................		27,500

The total cash inflow of $30,000 must be shown as an investing activity. Presently, $2,500 of this amount is included on the income statement as a gain. The credit to Cash Flows from Operations in the analysis entry deducts $2,500 from net income. The debit to Cash Flows from Investing for $30,000 shows that this amount will be reported in that section of the cash flow statement. The credit to the Land Held for Investment account of $27,500 reproduces the noncash part of the original entry. Look at entry J in Exhibit 15-2.

Cash

BB	55,000		
	Operating	Activities	
A	14,500	B	19,000
E	1,500	C	22,000
F	4,500	D	6,000
G	12,000	I	600
H	1,000	J	2,500
	Investing	Activities	
J	30,000		

Land Held for Investment

BB	27,500	J	27,500
EB	-0- ✓		

Entry Code Letter   **Transaction**

K
     Land Used in Operations...................... 48,400
         Cash Flows from Investing   48,400

Description and Analysis

A purchase of land for a parking area was recorded during this year. Land Used in Operations is debited to reproduce the noncash part of the entry. Cash Flows from Investing is credited to reflect the outflow of cash. Cash Flows from Operations is not affected since the purchase of land is not reflected on the income statement. Look at entry K on Exhibit 15-2.

Cash

BB	55,000		
	Operating	Activities	
A	14,500	B	19,000
E	1,500	C	22,000
F	4,500	D	6,000
G	12,000	I	600
H	1,000	J	2,500
	Investing	Activities	
J	30,000	K	48,400

Land Used in Operations

BB	100,000	
K	48,400	
EB	148,400 ✓	

Entry Code Letter   **Transaction**

L-1
     Noncash Investing and Financing 50,000
         Common Stock   50,000

L-2
     Buildings 50,000
         Noncash Investing and Financing   50,000

Description and Analysis

A new building was acquired in exchange for common stock having a market value of $50,000. Cash is unaffected by this transaction, but since it is a significant activity it must be shown on the statement of cash flows. This is accomplished by showing the transaction as a noncash investing and financing activity. (Notice the new section included in the Cash account.) An entry to reproduce this transaction in the T-accounts would involve merely debiting Building and crediting Common Stock. This method would bury the entry among the noncash accounts and fail to highlight the data needed for preparation of the statement of cash flows.

The dilemma is solved by arbitrarily splitting the transaction into two parts: (1) issuing the stock and (2) acquiring the building. The two analysis entries above make use of noncash investing and financing activities to show the inflow of noncash resources from issuing common stock (entry L-1) and the outflow of noncash resources in acquiring the building (entry L-2). This procedure keeps all information needed to prepare the statement of cash flows in the analysis account. Look at entries L-1 and L-2 in Exhibit 15-2.

Cash

BB	55,000		
	Operating	Activities	
A	14,500	B	19,000
E	1,500	C	22,000
F	4,500	D	6,000
G	12,000	I	600
H	1,000	J	2,500
	Investing	Activities	
J	30,000	K	48,400
	Financing	Activities	

Noncash Investing and Financing

L-1	50,000	L-2	50,000

Buildings

BB	415,000	
L-2	50,000	
EB	465,000 ✓	

Common Stock

		BB	245,500
		L-1	50,000
		EB	335,500

Entry Code Letter	Transaction
M	Cash Flows from Financing.................... 40,000
	Common Stock 40,000

Description and Analysis

Notice that after transaction L-1 the Common Stock account does not balance to $335,500. That's because there is another transaction involving common stock. Specifically, The Complex Company sold stock for $40,000. This inflow of cash is reflected as Cash from Financing Activities. The analysis entry shows the inflow as a debit and the credit to Common Stock now explains how that account went from a beginning balance of $245,500 to the ending balance of $335,500. Look at entry M in Exhibit 15-2.

Cash

BB	55,000			
	Operating	Activities		
A	14,500	B	19,000
E	1,500	C	22,000
F	4,500	D	6,000
G	12,000	I	600
H	1,000	J	2,500
	Investing	Activities		
J	30,000	K	48,400
	Financing	Activities		
M	40,000			
	Noncash Investing and Financing			
L-1	50,000	L-2	50,000

Common Stock

		BB	245,500
		L-1	50,000
		M	40,000
		✓EB	335,500

Entry Code Letter	Transaction
N	Retained Earnings 10,000
	Cash Flows from Financing............... 10,000

Description and Analysis

On the statement of retained earnings it is indicated that a $10,000 dividend was paid in 1989. This represents an outflow of cash, specifically Cash Flows from Financing Activities. Retained Earnings is debited to reproduce the noncash part of the entry and this will explain, together with the net income entry A, how Retained Earnings went from the beginning balance of $88,000 to the ending balance of $92,500. The credit to the Cash account in the cash flows from financing activities now completes all the transactions for the period. Look at entry N in Exhibit 15-2.

Cash

BB	55,000			
	Operating	Activities		
A	14,500	B	19,000
E	1,500	C	22,000
F	4,500	D	6,000
G	12,000	I	600
H	1,000	J	2,500
	Investing	Activities		
J	30,000	K	48,400
	Financing	Activities		
M	40,000	N	10,000
	Noncash Investing and Financing			
L-1	50,000	L-2	50,000
EB	50,000 ✓			

Retained Earnings

		BB	88,000
N	10,000	A	14,500
		✓EB	92,500

With this last transaction we should be able to add the debits in the Cash account, subtract the credits and have a balance, the ending balance, of $50,000. And that's precisely what we have.

Using the information contained in the Cash account from the analysis prepared

EXHIBIT 15-2

THE COMPLEX COMPANY
Statement of Cash Flows
T-Account Approach
(After Analysis)

Increases   *Decreases*

Cash							Accounts Receivable		
BB		55,000					BB	90,000	
	Operating		**Activities**				A	19,000	
A	Net Income	14,500	B	Increase in					
E	Decrease in			Receivables	19,000		EB	109,000 ✓	
	Prepaid		C	Increase in					
	Expenses	1,500		Inventory	22,000			**Merchandise Inventory**	
F	Increase in		D	Decrease in					
	Accrued			Payables	6,000		BB	153,000	
	Liabilities	4,500	I	Amortization			C	22,000	
G	Depreciation			of Premium					
	Expense	12,000		on Bonds			EB	175,000 ✓	
H	Amortization			Payable	600				
	of Patent	1,000	J	Gain on Sale					
				of Land	2,500			**Prepaid Expenses**	
	Investing		**Activities**						
J	Cash from		K	Cash for			BB	17,000	E	1,500
	Sale of Land	30,000		Purchase of					
				Land	48,400	EB	15,500 ✓	
	Financing		**Activities**						
M	Cash from		N	Cash Used to					
	Sale of			Pay				**Accounts Payable**	
	Common			Dividend	10,000				
	Stock	40,000					D	6,000	BB	75,000
									✓EB	69,000

Cash (cont.)				
	Noncash Investing and Financing			
L-1	Noncash		L-2	Noncash
	Resources			Resources
	from			Used to
	Issuance of			Acquire
	Common			Building	50,000
	Stock	50,000		
EB		50,000 ✓		

Accrued Liabilities		
	BB	20,000
	F	4,500
	✓EB	24,500

Land Held for Investment				
BB	27,500	J	27,500
EB	-0- ✓		

Land Used in Operations		
BB	100,000	
K	48,400	
EB	148,400 ✓	

(continued)

Buildings				**Accum. Deprec.: Buildings**			
BB	415,000					BB	205,000
L-2	50,000					G	12,000
EB	465,000 ✓					✓EB	217,000

Patents				**Bonds Payable**			
BB	6,000	H	1,000			BB	200,000
EB	5,000 ✓					✓EB	200,000

Premium on Bonds Payable			
I	600	BB	30,000
		✓EB	29,400

Common Stock				**Retained Earnings**			
		BB	245,500	N	10,000	BB	88,000
		L-1	50,000			A	14,500
		M	40,000			✓EB	92,500
		✓EB	335,500				

in Exhibit 15-2 we can now prepare a statement of cash flows. This statement is illustrated in Exhibit 15-3.

Notice in Exhibit 15-3, the statement of cash flows, how each section is prepared from the data in the Cash account of Exhibit 15-2. The cash flows from operating activities is a negative $16,600. The credits to the Cash account are listed in the cash flow statement as decreases. Cash flows from investing activities is a negative $18,400, and cash flows from financing activities is a positive $30,000.

Also notice how the noncash investing and financing activities are handled, on the bottom of the statement after the net cash decrease of $5,000 is presented.

The T-account approach is the fastest way to prepare the statement of cash flows

Preparing the statement of cash flows using the T-account approach, once you get used to it, is the fastest way to prepare the statement. The disadvantage of the T-account method is that it does not provide formal documentation of your work which is necessary to have in the files of preparing firms and/or certified public accountants. That's why the worksheet method is used.

THE COMPLEX COMPANY: WORKSHEET APPROACH

A four-column worksheet is used for the worksheet approach to preparing the statement of cash flows

The worksheet approach formalizes the T-account approach. The starting point is to prepare a four-column worksheet with a listing of all the beginning balance sheet debit accounts and all the beginning balance sheet credit accounts entered in the first column. The second and third columns are left for the debit and credit entry analysis.

EXHIBIT 15-3

THE COMPLEX COMPANY
Statement of Cash Flows
For the Year Ended December 31, 1989

Net Cash Flow from Operating Activities:

Net Income..		$ 14,500
Noncash Expenses, Revenues, Losses, and Gains Included in Income:		
Increases:		
Decrease in Prepaid Expenses	$ 1,500	
Increase in Accrued Liabilities.........................	4,500	
Depreciation Expense	12,000	
Patent Amortization	1,000	19,000
Decreases:		
Increase in Accounts Receivable.......................	$ 19,000	
Increase in Merchandise Inventory.....................	22,000	
Decrease in Accounts Payable.........................	6,000	
Amortization of Bond Premium.......................	600	
Gain on Sale of Land	2,500	(50,100)
Net Cash Flow from Operating Activities.........................		$(16,600)
Cash Flows from Investing Activities:		
Increases: Cash from the Sale of Land	$ 30,000	
Decreases: Cash Used to Purchase Land	(48,400)	(18,400)
Cash Flows from Financing Activities:		
Increases: Cash from Sale of Common Stock................	$ 40,000	
Decreases: Cash Used to Pay Dividends	(10,000)	30,000
Net Decrease in Cash		$ (5,000)
Noncash Investing and Financing Activities:		
Acquisition of Building by Issuing Stock		$ 50,000

In the fourth column are entered all the ending balance sheet debit and credits. See Exhibit 15-4 for an illustration of the starting worksheet. Be careful at this stage. The worksheet requires entering the beginning balances in the first column and the ending balances in the last column. This is exactly the opposite from the way these amounts will appear on the balance sheet; the most recent year will appear first (ending balances) on the balance sheet followed by last year's figures (beginning balances). Also, notice that on the worksheet we list all accounts with debit balances first, then those with credit balances. We won't be listing the accounts in exactly the same order that they appear on the balance sheet.

Check the mathematical accuracy of your amounts by adding accounts with debit balances and verifying that this total is the same as the total of the accounts with credit balances. For The Complex Company beginning debits and beginning credits equal $863,500, ending debits and credits equal $967,900. Study Exhibit 15-4 to see how The Complex Company worksheet looks at this point.

After entering the beginning and ending balances on the worksheet you need to write the major headings of the statement of cash flows on the bottom of the worksheet—leave space after each heading to enter the content of the statement as you do your analysis. Look at Exhibit 15-5 to see these headings on the completed worksheet. The headings would be

EXHIBIT 15-4

THE COMPLEX COMPANY
Worksheet for the Statement of Cash Flows
For the Year Ended December 31, 1989

	Jan. 1, 1989 Balance	Summary of 1989 Entries Debit	Credit	Dec. 31, 1989 Balance
Debits				
Cash..	$ 55,000	*This column is for the*		$ 50,000
Accounts Receivable......................	90,000	*beginning balances of the*		109,000
Merchandise Inventory...................	153,000	*balance sheet accounts*		175,000
Prepaid Expenses........................	17,000			15,500
Land Held for Investment...............	27,500			-0-
Land Used in Operations................	100,000			148,400
Buildings................................	415,000			465,000
Patents.................................	6,000			5,000
Total Debits............................	$863,500	*These middle columns are*		$967,900
		for analysis transactions		
Credits		*that explain how the*		
Accumulated Depreciation...............	$205,000	*accounts changed during*		$217,000
Accounts Payable.......................	75,000	*the period*		69,000
Accrued Liabilities.....................	20,000			24,500
Bonds Payable..........................	200,000			200,000
Premium on Bonds Payable.............	30,000			29,400
Common Stock.........................	245,500			335,500
Retained Earnings......................	88,000			92,500
Total Credits...........................	$863,500			$967,900

The bottom section of the worksheet is for adding items that will be used in the statement of cash flows

This column is for the ending balances of the balance sheet accounts

Cash Flows from Operations

   Net Income

      Add:

      Deduct:

Cash Flows from Investing

   Add:

   Deduct:

Cash Flows from Financing

   Add:

   Deduct:

Noncash Investing and Financing

The analysis transactions are entered in the summary debit and credit columns in the following manner: Transaction A, the analysis of net income for the year, is entered in the credit column in the row containing the Retained Earnings account. The

EXHIBIT 15-5

THE COMPLEX COMPANY
Worksheet for the Statement of Cash Flows
For the Year Ended December 31, 1989

	Jan. 1, 1989 Balance	Summary of 1989 Entries Debit	Summary of 1989 Entries Credit	Dec. 31, 1989 Balance
Debits				
Cash	$ 55,000		Z$ 5,000	$ 50,000
Accounts Receivable	90,000	B$ 19,000		109,000
Merchandise Inventory	153,000	C 22,000		175,000
Prepaid Expenses	17,000		E 1,500	15,500
Land Held for Investment	27,500		J 27,500	-0-
Land Used in Operations	100,000	K 48,400		148,400
Buildings	415,000	L-2 50,000		465,000
Patents	6,000		H 1,000	5,000
Total Debits	$863,500			$967,900
Credits				
Accumulated Depreciation	$205,000		G 12,000	$217,000
Accounts Payable	75,000	D 6,000		69,000
Accrued Liabilities	20,000		F 4,500	24,500
Bonds Payable	200,000			200,000
Premium on Bonds Payable	30,000	I 600		29,400
Common Stock	245,500		L-1 50,000	335,500
			M 40,000	
Retained Earnings	88,000	N 10,000	A 14,500	92,500
Total Credits	$863,500			$967,900
Summary Entry Totals		$156,000	$156,000	
Cash Flows from Operations				
Net Income		A$ 14,500		
Add: Decrease in Prepaids		E 1,500		
Increase in Accrued Liab.		F 4,500		
Depreciation Expense		G 12,000		
Patent Amortization		H 1,000		
Deduct: Increase in Receivables			B$ 19,000	
Increase in Inventory			C 22,000	
Decrease in Payables			D 6,000	
Amortization of Bond Premium			I 600	
Gain on Sale of Land			J 2,500	
Cash Flows from Investing				
Add: Cash from Sale of Land		J 30,000		
Deduct: Cash Used to Purchase Land			K 48,400	
Cash Flows from Financing				
Add: Cash from Sale of Common Stock		M 40,000		
Deduct: Cash Used to Pay Dividends.			N 10,000	
Noncash Investing and Financing				
Acquisition of Building for Common Stock		L-1 50,000	L-2 50,000	
Summary Entries Subtotals		$153,500	$158,500	
Net Decrease in Cash.		Z 5,000		
Summary Entries Totals		$158,500	$158,500	

corresponding $14,500 debit is entered in the debit column in the net income row on the bottom of the worksheet under cash flows from operations.

We'll do two more: Transaction B analyzed the $19,000 change in Accounts Receivable. The debit is entered in the accounts receivable row while the credit is entered on the bottom of the worksheet under cash flows from operations in the increase in receivables row. The last transaction from the T-account approach was the payment of $10,000 dividends, transaction N. This is entered on the worksheet in the debit column in the row containing Retained Earnings. And it is entered on the bottom of the worksheet under cash flows from financing as a credit.

All of the other transactions are entered in a similar manner: Study Exhibit 15-5 and trace the transaction analysis entries to their respective debits and credits. With the worksheet approach we need one more debit and credit. After transaction N, the last transaction, we need to add the debit column and the credit column for the bottom portion of the worksheet. The debits total $153,500, while the credits total $158,500, a difference of $5,000. That's the decrease in the Cash account which has yet to be handled on the worksheet. That's why we need one more transaction on the worksheet. We've labeled it transaction Z and it's a debit on the very bottom of the worksheet in the net decrease in cash row and a credit at the very top in the cash row. Now we add the debits and credits for the balance sheet summary entries and get $156,000 proving the equality of the debits and credits.

Once the worksheet is complete it is a simple matter to then prepare the statement of cash flows from the bottom portion of the worksheet.

CHAPTER SUMMARY

The **statement of cash flows** is the fourth major financial statement that must be published for external users. The objective of this statement is to provide information about cash receipts and cash payments and to provide information about the **investing** and **financing activities** of a business. The information provided by the statement of cash flows together with the information contained in the three other financial statements help financial statement users assess: (1) an entity's ability to generate positive future cash flows; (2) an entity's ability to meet its obligations, its need for external financing, and its ability to pay dividends; (3) the reasons for differences between income and associated cash receipts and payments; and (4) both the cash and noncash aspects of an entity's investing and financing transactions.

The statement is divided into three major sections: **cash flows from operating activities, cash flows from investing activities,** and **cash flows from financing activities.** Cash flows from operating activities are generally the cash effects of transactions that enter into the determination of income. Cash flows from investing activities are those that include lending money, collecting loans, and acquiring or selling securities and productive assets. Cash flows from financing activities include obtaining resources from owners and creditors, providing owners a return on and a return of their investment, and repaying creditors.

The statement of cash flows can be prepared in one of two ways, the **T-account approach** or the **worksheet approach.** The T-account approach is easier and faster but it is not as formal as the worksheet approach, nor does the T-account approach provide documentation of the cash flow analysis.

When using the T-account approach you must establish a T-account for each balance sheet item, placing the beginning and ending balances in the T-accounts. A very large T-account must be prepared for cash since this account will eventually contain all the information necessary to prepare the statement. Entries are recorded in the T-accounts to reproduce, in summary form, the transactions that took place during the period. Whenever cash is involved it is placed in the Cash T-account in the appropriate operating, investing, or financing section of that T-account. The corresponding debit or credit is entered into the appropriate balance sheet account. The T-account approach is an orderly, efficient way of handling a large number of transactions in a complex situation.

The worksheet approach requires the preparation of a formal worksheet containing four columns. The first and the last columns contain the beginning and ending balance sheet account balances. The middle two columns are for the summary debit and credit analysis entries. The analysis entries that are entered in the middle two columns explain how the balance sheet account went from the beginning balance to the ending balance and on the bottom of the worksheet where they generate the statement of cash flows.

IMPORTANT TERMS USED IN THIS CHAPTER

Accrual-basis income A measure of income that recognizes revenue as it is earned and matches expenses incurred in earning the revenue reported. (page 671)

Cash-basis income A measure of income that recognizes revenue when cash is received and reports expenses when cash is paid out. (page 671)

Financing activity Transactions entered into by a business entity that would include obtaining resources from owners and creditors, providing owners a return on and a return of their investment, and repaying creditors. (page 669)

Investing activity Transactions entered into by a business entity that would include lending money and collecting loans, acquiring and selling securities, and acquiring and selling productive assets. (page 667)

Operating activity Transactions entered into by a business entity that would include the delivering or producing of goods for sale and providing services. (page 663)

QUESTIONS

1. Why is the statement of cash flows needed when a company already issues a balance sheet, income statement, and statement of retained earnings?

2. How does the statement of cash flows help the user of financial statements?

3. The statement of cash flows contains three major sections. What are these sections and what information is contained in each?

4. When preparing a statement of cash flows net income must be adjusted to derive cash flows from operations. Why is this adjustment necessary?

5. Why is it logical to analyze balance sheet accounts when preparing to construct a statement of cash flows?

6. Towards the end of the chapter another section was added to the statement of cash flows. The section was called noncash investing and financing activities. What is the purpose of this section?

7. A statement in the financial press recently stated that a company had a source of cash flows of $150,000 from depreciation. Comment on this statement.

8. How does the calculation of cash-basis income differ from the calculation of accrual-basis income?

9. Explain the difference between determining cash flows from operations by the *direct* method and the *indirect* method.

10. In calculating cash flows from operations depreciation expense is added back to net income and amortization of premium on bonds payable is deducted from net income. Where are each of these pieces of information found in the T-accounts? (Which T-account, and on which side?)

11. Why is it necessary in the T-account analysis to split a financing and investing activity not affecting cash flows into two parts and analyze it as if it were two transactions?

12. What are the advantages and disadvantages of the T-account and the worksheet approaches to preparing the statement of cash flows?

13. A gain on the disposal of equipment would be reported as a deduction from net income on the statement of cash flows. Explain why?

14. A company recently acquired a desk-top computer, giving a 60-day note for the full price. How is this transaction reflected on the statement of cash flows?

EXERCISES

**Exercise 15-1
Determining the cash-flow effect of changes in account balances on net income**

Explain what effect each of the following changes in account balances would have on net income when determining cash flows from operations. Each item is to be considered independently.

Example: Accounts Receivable decreases by $11,500.
Effect: Net income is adjusted by adding $11,500.

a. Supplies Inventory decreases by $5,690.
b. Accounts Payable decreases by $3,200.
c. Accounts Receivable increases by $24,400.
d. Prepaid Insurance decreases by $1,800.
e. Merchandise Inventory increases by $15,500.
f. Income Taxes Payable increases by $6,100.
g. Allowance for Uncollectibles decreases by $2,800.

**Exercise 15-2
Determining cash flows from operations**

The Dodge Company reported net income for the year to be $27,000. Determine the cash flows from operations assuming the following information:

a. Accounts Receivable increased $3,000.
b. Accounts Payable increased $12,000.
c. Merchandise Inventory decreased $2,500.
d. Depreciation amounted to $5,000.

(Check figure: Cash flows from operations = $43,500)

**Exercise 15-3
Re-creating entries and determining effect on cash flows from operations**

The following transactions are among those entered into by Champion Inc., during 1989. Re-create the entry that Champion should have made and determine the effect of the entry on cash flows.

Example: Champion borrowed $10,000 from the bank on a long-term note.

Entry: Cash.. 10,000
            Notes Payable 10,000

Effect: Cash flows from investing activities increased by $10,000.

a. One hundred shares of Texas-T Oil Inc., was purchased for $21,000 as a long-term investment.

b. An account receivable in the amount of $1,080 was collected.

c. A building was purchased for $170,000. $10,000 cash was paid and a 90-day note was given for the balance.

d. A parcel of land having an original cost of $10,000 was sold for $17,000.

e. A customer's account with a $400 balance was written off as uncollectible (the allowance method is used).

f. Champion issued 1,000 shares of $2 par common stock for $2,460.

Exercise 15-4
Calculating cash flows from operations

The 1989 income statement of Gull Paper Co. appears below:

GULL PAPER CO. Income Statement Year Ended December 31, 1989		
Sales		$240,000
Cost of Goods Sold		90,000
Gross Profit on Sales		$150,000
Operating Expenses:		
Advertising Expense	$14,000	
Depreciation Expense......................................	36,000	
Patent Amortization Expense	5,000	
Salary Expense...	56,000	111,000
Net Income		$ 39,000

Calculate the cash flows from operations for 1989. (Begin with net income and add back expenses not using cash.)

(Check figure: Cash flows from operations = $80,000)

Exercise 15-5
Stating where effect of transactions would appear on statement of cash flows

Each of the following transactions will result in cash flows from investing activities, cash flows from financing activities, or noncash investing and financing activities. Analyze each transaction and state which one of these three categories on the statement of cash flows will be affected.

a. $400,000 was borrowed by issuing bonds that mature in 20 years.

b. A dump truck with a book value of $3,500 was traded for stationery and other office supplies.

c. A $39,400 cash dividend was declared and paid.

d. A machine was acquired by issuing a 60-day note for the $8,000 purchase price.

e. Land was acquired by exchanging 10,000 shares of common stock for the property. The stock had a market price of $98,000.

f. A patent was sold for $12,500. A 30-day note was accepted for the total amount. (The book value of the patent was also $12,500.)

g. Equipment was purchased for $105,000.

h. Used machinery having a book value of $12,800 was traded for 100 shares of stock in another corporation. The stock acquired is to be held for an extended period.

i. An individual to whom the corporation owed $5,000 on a long-term note accepted a used copying machine in full payment of the debt.

j. Five hundred shares of common stock were sold on subscription. The subscription payments were due on the first day of each of the 3 months following the subscription sale. The subscription price totaled $75,000.

Exercise 15-6
Preparing cash flows from operations section of the T-account for cash.

Turbo Products Inc., uses the T-account approach to prepare the working papers for the statement of cash flows. The following T-account was used to gather information about the cash flows from operations.

Cash			
(3) Depreciation Expense	50,000	(1) Net Loss for the Year	24,600
(4) Patent Amortization Expense	6,000	(2) Gain on Sale of Land	8,400
(6) Loss on Sale of Equipment	14,600	(5) Amortization of Premium on Bond Payable	19,000

Prepare the cash flows from operations section of the statement of cash flows.

(Check figure: Cash flows from operations = $18,600)

Exercise 15-7
Converting items from accrual basis to cash basis

Hobbs Inc., is attempting to convert its accrual-basis income into cash-basis income. For each of the following situations, perform the required conversion:

a. Sales on the accrual-basis income statement amounted to $172,500. Accounts Receivable at the beginning and end of the year totaled $97,500 and $115,000, respectively. Determine cash collected from customers on the cash-basis income statement.

b. Advertising Expense on the accrual-basis income statement was $20,750. Prepaid Advertising increased from $7,000 at the beginning of the year to $8,000 at the end of the year. Determine the cash paid for advertising on the cash-basis income statement.

c. Salary Expense on the accrual-basis income statement was $27,900. Accrued Salaries Payable at the beginning and end of the year amounted to $780 and $1,180, respectively. Determine the cash paid for salaries on the cash-basis income statement.

d. Depreciation Expense on the accrual-basis income statement was $12,500. Accumulated Depreciation increased from $62,500 at the beginning of the year to $75,000 at the end. Calculate the Depreciation Expense on the cash-basis income statement.

(Check figure: Cash collected from customers = $155,000)

PROBLEMS: SET A

Problem A15-1
Preparing the cash flows from operating activity section

In each of the three columns below are income statement data for the year ended Dec. 31, 1989:

	Company X	Company Y	Company Z
Sales Revenue.	$200,000	$125,000	$60,000
Cost of Goods Sold Expense	80,000	75,000	20,000
Patent Amortization Expense .ΛE.	3,000	6,000	—
Depreciation Expense: Machinery P.E	9,000	10,000	1,750
Organization Cost Amortization Expense.	750	—	250
Depreciation Expense: Building .ΛE	16,500	9,500	4,200
Income Tax Expense.	26,250	—	12,000
Salary Expense	25,000	15,500	7,500
Utilities Expense	13,500	7,300	3,800
Gain on Sale of Machine	—	—	2,000
Loss on Sale of Land.	—	2,700	—

Required Prepare the cash flows from operating activities section of the statement of cash flows for Company X, Y, and Z, respectively. (Hint: First calculate net income for each of the three.)

(Check figure: Cash flows from operating activities, Company X = $55,250)

Problem A15-2
Preparing a statement of
cash flows

The 1989 financial statements of Asian Products Inc., are shown below:

ASIAN PRODUCTS INC.
Income Statement
Year Ended December 31, 1989
(000's omitted)

Sales.....	$2,000
Cost of Goods Sold....	(960)
Gross Profit on Sales....	$1,040
Operating Expenses:	
Depreciation....	(120)
Other.....	(440)
Net Income....	$ 480

ASIAN PRODUCTS, INC.
Comparative Balance Sheets
(000's omitted)

	December 31,	
	1989	**1988**
Assets		
Cash	$ 60	$ 80
Accounts Receivable (net)	750	500
Merchandise Inventory....	650	700
Land.....	440	416
Building.....	1,680	1,600
Accumulated Depreciation: Building....	(340)	(220)
Total Assets....	$3,240	$3,076
Equities		
Accounts Payable....	$ 384	$ 400
Noncurrent Liabilities....	40	420
Common Stock	1,680	1,600
Retained Earnings.....	1,136	656
Total Equities.....	$3,240	$3,076

Additional information taken from the financial records of Asian Products:

a. Land costing $24,000 was acquired for cash.
b. $380,000 of noncurrent liabilities were paid off with cash.
c. Common stock was issued in exchange for a building with a fair market value of $80,000.

Required Prepare a statement of cash flows in good form for the year ended Dec. 31, 1989. You need not prepare T-account working papers. All the information needed to prepare the statement is given in the income statement, balance sheets, and additional information above.

(Check figure: Cash flow from operating activities = $384,000)

Problem A15-3
Preparing a statement of cash flows

Mainsea's 1989 financial statements appear below:

MAINSEA ENTERPRISES
Income Statement
Year Ended December 31, 1989
(000's omitted)

Sales...		$400
Cost of Goods Sold..		225
Gross Profit on Sales...		$175
Operating Expenses:		
Depreciation..	$33	
Other (including taxes)...............................	92	125
Net Income..		$ 50

MAINSEA ENTERPRISES
Balance Sheet
(000's omitted)

	Dec. 31, 1989	Dec. 31, 1988	Increase (Decrease) in Account Balance
Assets			
Cash..	$ 89	$ 19	$ 70
Accounts Receivable...........................	108	58	50
Merchandise Inventory.........................	123	88	35
Prepaid Expenses..............................	4	5	(1)
Land..	100	70	30
Building......................................	500	400	100
Accumulated Depreciation	(103)	(70)	33
Total Assets..................................	$ 821	$570	
Equities			
Accounts Payable..............................	$ 43	$ 49	(6)
Accrued Payables..............................	16	—	16
Bonds Payable (due 1995)	100	—	100
Common Stock	550	450	100
Retained Earnings.............................	112	71	41
Total Equities...............................	$ 821	$570	

Other relevant data:

a. Land was purchased for $30,000.
b. Bonds Payable in the amount of $100,000 were issued for a new building.
c. A $9,000 cash dividend was declared and paid.
d. Common stock was sold for $100,000 cash.

Required

Prepare a statement of cash flows using either the T-account approach or the worksheet approach as directed by your instructor.

(Check figure: Cash flows from operating activities = $9,000)

Problem A15-4
Preparing a statement of cash flows

Potter Company condensed balance sheets for Dec. 31, 1988 and 1989, and the condensed income statement for the year ended Dec. 31, 1989, are presented below:

POTTER COMPANY
Income Statement (Condensed)
Year Ended December 31, 1989

Sales..		$171,000
Cost of Goods Sold Expense..............................		70,650
Gross Profit on Sales		$100,350
Operating Expenses:		
Depreciation Expense: Building..........................	$12,500	
Depreciation Expense: Machinery........................	3,750	
Patent Amortization Expense............................	600	
Other Selling and Administrative Expenses.............	24,000	40,850
Income before Tax		$ 59,500
Income Tax Expense		26,000
Net Income		$ 33,500

POTTER COMPANY
Comparative Balance Sheets (Condensed)

	Dec. 31	
Assets:	**1989**	**1988**
Current Assets:		
Cash..	$ 16,100	$ 2,650
Accounts Receivable	24,000	28,700
Allowance for Uncollectibles	(1,500)	(1,100)
Merchandise Inventory	40,750	27,250
Current Assets (total).................................	$ 79,350	$ 57,500
Property, Plant, and Equipment:		
Land	$103,500	$ 73,500
Building	210,000	150,000
Less: Accumulated Depreciation.........................	(45,000)	(32,500)
Machinery	112,500	112,500
Less: Accumulated Depreciation.........................	(21,250)	(17,500)
Total Property, Plant, and Equipment.................	$359,750	$286,000
Intangible Assets:		
Patent	$ 8,400	$ 9,000
Total Assets	$447,500	$352,500
Liabilities and Stockholders' Equity		
Current Liabilities:		
Accounts Payable	$ 12,500	$ 18,750
Salaries Payable...	6,500	3,750
Current Liabilities (total).............................	$ 19,000	$ 22,500
Noncurrent Liabilities:		
Bonds Payable (issued at par)............................	50,000	75,000
Total Liabilities.......................................	$ 69,000	$ 97,500
Common Stock (no par)	$290,000	$200,000
Retained Earnings..	88,500	55,000
Total Stockholders' Equity............................	$378,500	$255,000
Total Liabilities and Stockholders' Equity..................	$447,500	$352,500

In addition the following information was compiled from the company's financial records:

a. A plot of land was purchased for $30,000 cash.
b. A new building was purchased for cash, $60,000.
c. Additional common stock was issued for $90,000 cash.
d. Bonds with a maturity value of $25,000 were retired when they matured.

| **Required** |

Prepare a statement of cash flows using either the T-account approach or the worksheet approach as directed by your instructor.

(Check figure: Cash flows from operating activities = $38,450)

Problem A15-5
Preparing a statement of cash flows

Siesta Fashions Inc., condensed balance sheets for 1988 and 1989 and the income statement for 1989 are shown below:

SIESTA FASHIONS INC.
Comparative Balance Sheets (Condensed)
(000's omitted)

	Dec. 31,	
	1989	**1988**
Assets		
Current Assets:		
Cash	$ 115	$ 20
Accounts Receivable	240	200
Allowance for Uncollectibles	(25)	(15)
Merchandise Inventory	450	585
Prepaid Expenses	90	50
Current Assets (total)	$ 870	$ 840
Property, Plant, and Equipment:		
Land	$ 256	$ 156
Building	242	266
Less: Accumulated Depreciation	(84)	(104)
Machinery	300	140
Less: Accumulated Depreciation	(60)	(50)
Total Property, Plant, and Equipment	$ 654	$ 408
Total Assets	$1,524	$1,248
Liabilities and Stockholders' Equity		
Current Liabilities:		
Accounts Payable	$ 260	$ 210
Accrued Liabilities	86	70
Current Liabilities (total)	$ 346	$ 280
Noncurrent Liabilities:		
Bonds Payable (issued at par)	200	200
Total Liabilities	$ 546	$ 480
Preferred Stock	$ 160	$ -0-
Common Stock (no par)	600	600
Retained Earnings	218	168
Total Stockholders' Equity	$ 978	$ 768
Total Liabilities and Stockholders' Equity	$1,524	$1,248

```
                        SIESTA FASHIONS INC.
                      Income Statement (Condensed)
                       Year Ended December 31, 1989
                            (000's omitted)
```

Sales		$840
Cost of Goods Sold Expense		548
Gross Profit on Sales		$292
Operating Expenses:		
Selling Expenses	$152	
Administrative Expenses	64	
Depreciation Expense: Building	16	
Depreciation Expense: Machinery	10	242
Net Income		$ 50

In addition the following was compiled from the company's records:

a. A building was purchased for $40,000 cash.

b. Machinery for a new assembly line was purchased by giving the manufacturer preferred stock. The machinery acquired has a fair market value of $160,000.

c. A building was sold for $28,000. The building had originally cost $64,000 and had accumulated depreciation of $36,000.

d. Land was purchased for $100,000.

Required

Prepare a statement of cash flows using either the T-account approach or the worksheet approach as directed by your instructor.

(Check figure: Net increase in cash = $207,000)

Problem A15-6
Preparing a statement of cash flows

Lott Salt Co. financial statements for 1989 appear below:

```
                          LOTT SALT CO.
                         Income Statement
                     Year Ended September 30, 1989
                            (000's omitted)
```

Sales		$11,892
Cost of Goods Sold		(8,466)
Gross Profit on Sales		$ 3,426
Operating Expenses:		
Depreciation Expense: Building	$ 130	
Depreciation Expense: Equipment	46	
Other Operating Expenses	2,480	(2,656)
Income from Primary Operations		$ 770
Other Income and Expense:		
Interest Expense	$ (58)	*50 paid*
Gain on Sale of Building	32	(26)
Income before Tax		$ 744
Income Taxes		(230)
Net Income		$ 514

LOTT SALT CO.
Statement of Retained Earnings
For Year Ended September 30, 1989
(000's omitted)

Retained Earnings Balance (10/1/88)	$1,024
Add: Net Income for the Year	514
Total	$1,538
Deduct: Dividends Declared and Paid	(194)
Retained Earnings (9/30/89)...	$1,344

LOTT SALT CO.
Comparative Balance Sheets
(000's omitted)

	Sept. 30, 1989	1988	Increase (Decrease) in Account Balance
Assets			
Current Assets:			
Cash	$ 676	$ 608	$ 68
Accounts Receivable (net)	1,280	854	426
Merchandise Inventory..........................	888	1,034	(146)
Total Current Assets........................	$ 2,844	$ 2,496	
Property, Plant and Equipment:			
Land...	$ 1,110	$ 860	250
Buildings	2,102	2,050	52
Less: Accumulated Depreciation	(1,010)	(1,032)	(22)
Equipment	1,460	1,460	-0-
Less: Accumulated Depreciation	(636)	(590)	46
Total Property, Plant, and Equipment	$ 3,026	$ 2,748	
Total Assets.....................................	$ 5,870	$ 5,244	
Liabilities and Stockholders' Equity			
Current Liabilities:			
Accounts Payable..............................	$ 736	$ 900	(164)
Notes Payable.................................	200	280	(80)
Accrued Payables..............................	132	120	12
Total Current Liabilities.....................	$ 1,068	$ 1,300	
Noncurrent Liabilities:			
Notes Payable (due 6/30/95).....................	$ 280	-0-	280
Bonds Payable (due 12/31/99)	600	$ 600	-0-
Discount on Bonds Payable.....................	(72)	(80)	(8)
Total Noncurrent Liabilities	$ 808	$ 520	
Total Liabilities	$ 1,876	$ 1,820	
Stockholders' Equity:			
Common Stock (no par)	$ 2,650	$ 2,400	250
Retained Earnings.............................	1,344	1,024	320
Total Stockholders' Equity	$ 3,994	$ 3,424	
Total Liabilities and Stockholders' Equity	$ 5,870	$ 5,244	

An analysis of Lott's financial records revealed the following information:

a. A building costing $248,000 and having an accumulated depreciation of $152,000 was sold for $128,000. The $32,000 gain appears on the income statement.

b. Common stock was issued in exchange for 10 acres of land. The common stock and the land were fairly valued at $250,000.

c. The entry to record interest expense on the bonds was as follows:

Interest Expense...	58,000	
Cash..		50,000
Discount on Bonds Payable		8,000

(Less cash was used than is reflected in the Interest Expense account.)

d. $280,000 was borrowed from the bank; a note due in 1995 was signed.

e. An addition to the building costing $300,000 was constructed for cash.

f. Dividends of $194,000 were declared and paid.

Required	Prepare a statement of cash flows using either the T-account approach or the worksheet approach as directed by your instructor.

(Check figure: Net cash flows from operations = $154,000)

Problem A15-7
Calculating cash-basis net income

Hamilton Concrete Inc.'s 1989 income statement and comparative balance sheets for 1988 and 1989 appear below:

HAMILTON CONCRETE INC.
Income Statement
Year Ended June 30, 1989

Sales		$360,000
Cost of Goods Sold		150,000
Gross Profit on Sales		$210,000
Operating Expenses:		
Depreciation Expense.....................................	$70,000	
Other Operating Expenses.................................	40,000	110,000
Net Income		$100,000

HAMILTON CONCRETE INC.
Comparative Balance Sheets

	June 30	
	1989	**1988**
Assets		
Cash	$ 60,000	$ 40,000
Accounts Receivable (net)...................................	120,000	160,000
Merchandise Inventory......................................	160,000	70,000
Noncurrent Assets (net)	300,000	110,000
Total Assets..	$640,000	$380,000

(continued)

Equities

Accounts Payable	$ 80,000	$ 50,000
Accrued Salaries Payable	20,000	80,000
Noncurrent Liabilities	210,000	20,000
Total Liabilities	$310,000	$150,000
Paid-In Capital..	$200,000	$200,000
Retained Earnings...	130,000	30,000
Total Stockholders' Equity	$330,000	$230,000
Total Equities..	$640,000	$380,000

Required	Calculate Hamilton Concrete's cash-basis net income for the year ended June 30, 1989.

(Check figure: Cash-basis net income = $90,000)

PROBLEMS: SET B

Problem B15-1
Preparing the cash flows from operations section

In each of the three columns below are income statement data for the year ended Dec. 31, 1989:

	Company A	Company B	Company C
Sales Revenue.....................................	$160,000	$300,000	$400,000
Cost of Goods Sold Expense	60,000	180,000	200,000
Advertising Expense	12,000	16,000	40,000
Sales Commission Expense	6,000	30,000	60,000
Goodwill Amortization Expense	2,000	—	—
Depreciation Expense: Building	3,000	8,000	72,000
Depreciation Expense: Equipment............	1,000	32,000	24,000
Patent Amortization Expense	3,600	40,000	—
Income Tax Expense.........................	18,000	—	1,800
Loss on Sale of Machinery...................	1,600	—	—
Gain on Sale of Land	—	—	20,000

Required	Prepare the cash flows from operations section of the statement of cash flows for Company A, B, and C, respectively. (Hint: First calculate net income for each of the three.)

(Check figure: Cash flows from operations, Company B = $74,000)

Problem B15-2
Preparing the statement of cash flows

The 1989 financial statements of Kord Enterprises Inc., are shown below:

KORD ENTERPRISES INC.
Income Statement
Year Ended December 31, 1989
(000's omitted)

Sales...	$1,600
Cost of Goods Sold.......................................	(820)
Gross Profit on Sales......................................	$ 780
Operating Expenses:	
Depreciation......................................	(40)
Other	(220)
Net Income..	$ 520

KORD ENTERPRISES INC.
Comparative Balance Sheets
(000's omitted)

	Dec. 31,	
	1989	1988
Assets		
Current Assets:		
Cash	$ 120	$ 150
Accounts Receivable (net)	320	80
Merchandise Inventory	560	610
Current Assets (total)	$1,000	$ 840
Property, Plant, and Equipment:		
Land	$ 280	$ 180
Building	1,640	1,500
Accumulated Depreciation: Building	(120)	(80)
Total Property, Plant, and Equipment	$1,800	$1,600
Total Assets	$2,800	$2,440
Equities		
Current Liabilities:		
Accounts Payable	$ 160	$ 80
Salaries Payable	200	220
Total Current Liabilities	$ 360	$ 300
Noncurrent Liabilities	80	400
Common Stock	1,540	1,440
Retained Earnings	820	300
Total Equities	$2,800	$2,440

Additional information taken from the financial records of Kord Enterprises:

a. A building costing $140,000 was aquired for cash.
b. Cash was used to pay off noncurrent liabilities amounting to $320,000.
c. Common stock was issued in exchange for land with a fair market value of $100,000.

Required

Prepare a statement of cash flows in good form for the year ended Dec. 31, 1989. You need not prepare T-accounts. All the information needed to prepare the statement is given in the income statement, balance sheets, and additional information above.

(Check figure: Cash flows from operations = $430,000)

Problem B15-3
Preparing a statement of cash flows.

Maxxco's 1989 financial statements are shown below:

MAXXCO INC.
Income Statement
Year Ended December 31, 1989
(000's omitted)

Sales		$800
Cost of Goods Sold		450
Gross Profit on Sales		$350
Operating Expenses:		
Depreciation	$ 65	
Other (including taxes)	185	250
Net Income		$100

MAXXCO INC.
Balance Sheet
(000's omitted)

A Net Income

	Dec. 31,		Increase (Decrease) in Account Balance
	1989	**1988**	
Assets			
Cash	$ 177	$ 38	$139
Accounts Receivable	217	116	101
Merchandise Inventory	245	176	69
Prepaid Expenses	9	11	(2)
Land	200	140	60
Building	1,000	800	200
Accumulated Depreciation......................	(205)	(140)	65
Total Assets	$1,643	$1,141	
Equities			
Accounts Payable..............................	$ 86	$ 97	(11)
Accrued Payables	33	-0-	33
Bonds Payable (due 1995)	200	-0-	200
Common Stock.................................	1,100	900	200
Retained Earnings	224	144	80
Total Equities	$1,643	$1,141	

Other relevant data:

a. Land was purchased for $60,000 cash.
b. Bonds payable in the amount of $200,000 were issued for a new building.
c. A $20,000 cash dividend was declared and paid.
d. Common stock was issued for $200,000 cash.

Required	Prepare a statement of cash flows using either the T-account approach or the worksheet approach as directed by your instructor.

(Check figure: Cash flows from operations = $19,000)

Problem B15-4
Preparing a statement of cash flows

Raines Inc., condensed balance sheets for Dec. 31, 1988 and 1989, and the condensed income statement for the year ended Dec. 31, 1989, are presented below:

RAINES INC.
Income Statement (Condensed)
Year Ended December 31, 1989

Sales		$970,000
Cost of Goods Sold Expense		630,500
Gross Profit on Sales...		$339,500
Operating Expenses:		
Depreciation Expense: Building	$30,000	
Depreciation Expense: Equipment.....................	28,000	
Copyright Amortization Expense	7,000	
Other Selling and Administrative Expenses	22,500	87,500
Income before Tax		$252,000
Income Tax Expense...		138,500
Net Income...		$113,500

RAINES INC.
Comparative Balance Sheets (Condensed)

	Dec. 31 1989	Dec. 31 1988
Assets		
Current Assets:		
Cash	$ 6,100	$ 3,650
Accounts Receivable	58,500	71,300
Allowance for Uncollectibles	(2,100)	(2,450)
Merchandise Inventory	140,000	127,500
Current Assets (total)	$ 202,500	$ 200,000
Property, Plant, and Equipment:		
Land	$ 196,000	$ 152,000
Building	672,500	610,000
Less: Accumulated Depreciation	(383,000)	(353,000)
Equipment	450,000	450,000
Less: Accumulated Depreciation	(73,000)	(45,000)
Total Property, Plant, and Equipment	$ 862,500	$ 814,000
Intangible Assets:		
Copyright	$ 49,000	$ 56,000
Total Assets	$1,114,000	$1,070,000
Liabilities and Stockholders' Equity		
Current Liabilities:		
Accounts Payable	$ 68,000	$ 89,000
Salaries Payable	12,500	11,000
Current Liabilities (total)	$ 80,500	$ 100,000
Noncurrent Liabilities:		
Bonds Payable (issued at par)	200,000	300,000
Total Liabilities	$ 280,500	$ 400,000
Common Stock (no par)	$ 550,000	$ 500,000
Retained Earnings	283,500	170,000
Total Stockholders' Equity	$ 833,500	$ 670,000
Total Liabilities and Stockholders' Equity	$1,114,000	$1,070,000

In addition, the following information was compiled from the company's financial records:

a. Additional land costing $44,000 was purchased for cash.
b. A new building was purchased for cash, $62,500.
c. Additional common stock was issued for $50,000.
d. $100,000 of outstanding bonds were retired at maturity.

Required

Prepare a statement of cash flows using either the T-account approach or the worksheet approach as directed by your instructor.

(Check figure: Cash flows from operations = $158,950)

Problem B15-5
Preparing a statement of cash flows

Advanced Filters Inc., condensed balance sheets for 1988 and 1989, and the income statement for 1989, are shown below:

ADVANCED FILTERS INC.
Comparative Balance Sheets (Condensed)
(000's omitted)

	Dec. 31, 1989	Dec. 31, 1988
Assets		
Current Assets:		
Cash	$ 12	$ 7
Accounts Receivable	63	59
Allowance for Uncollectibles	(6)	(8)
Merchandise Inventory	135	101
Prepaid Expenses	8	11
Current Assets (total)	$ 212	$ 170
Property, Plant, and Equipment:		
Land	$ 604	$ 428
Building	1,560	1,400
Less: Accumulated Depreciation	(168)	(88)
Equipment	620	660
Less: Accumulated Depreciation	(216)	(200)
Total Property, Plant, and Equipment	$2,400	$2,200
Total Assets	$2,612	$2,370
Liabilities and Stockholders' Equity		
Current Liabilities:		
Accounts Payable	$ 110	$ 60
Accrued Liabilities	26	20
Current Liabilities (total)	$ 136	$ 80
Noncurrent Liabilities:		
Bonds Payable (issued at par)	180	20
Total Liabilities	$ 316	$ 100
Common Stock (no par)	$2,000	$2,000
Retained Earnings	296	270
Total Stockholders' Equity	$2,296	$2,270
Total Liabilities and Stockholders' Equity	$2,612	$2,370

ADVANCED FILTERS INC.
Income Statement (Condensed)
Year Ended December 31, 1989
(000's omitted)

Sales		$700
Cost of Goods Sold Expense		454
Gross Profit on Sales		$246
Operating Expenses:		
Selling Expenses	$70	
Administrative Expenses	40	
Depreciation Expense: Building	80	
Depreciation Expense: Equipment	30	220
Net Income		$ 26

In addition the following information was compiled from the company's records:

a. Equipment having a cost of $60,000 and accumulated depreciation of $14,000 was sold for $46,000.

b. A major addition to the building was constructed. The addition was "paid for" by giving the construction company a bond for $160,000 due in 3 years.

c. Land was purchased for $176,000.

d. Equipment was purchased for $20,000.

Required

Prepare a statement of cash flows using either the T-account approach or the worksheet approach as directed by your instructor.

(Check figure: Cash flows from operations = $155,000)

Problem B15-6
Preparing a statement of cash flows

Unlimited Products Inc., financial statements for 1989 appear below:

UNLIMITED PRODUCTS INC.
Income Statement
Year Ended June 30, 1989
(000's omitted)

Sales.		$12,780
Cost of Goods Sold.		(7,668)
Gross Profit on Sales.		$ 5,112
Operating Expenses:		
Depreciation Expense: Building.	$ 150	
Depreciation Expense: Equipment	75	
Other Operating Expenses.	3,474	(3,699)
Income from Primary Operations		$ 1,413
Other Income and Expense:		
Interest Expense	$ 120	
Loss on Sale of Equipment.	45	(165)
Income before Tax		$ 1,248
Income Taxes.		(609)
Net Income.		$ 639

UNLIMITED PRODUCTS INC.
Statement of Retained Earnings
For Year Ended June 30, 1989
(000's omitted)

Retained Earnings Balance (7/1/88)	$	660
Add: Net Income for the Year		639
Total		$ 1,299
Deduct: Dividends Declared and Paid		(204)
Retained Earnings (6/30/89).		$ 1,095

UNLIMITED PRODUCTS INC.
Comparative Balance Sheets
(000's omitted)

	June 30, 1989	June 30, 1988	Increase (Decrease) in Account Balance
Assets			
Current Assets:			
Cash	$ 1,230	$ 1,155	$ 75
Accounts Receivable (net)	2,520	2,580	(60)
Merchandise Inventory...........................	975	564	411
Total Current Assets	$ 4,725	$ 4,299	
Property, Plant, and Equipment:			
Land......................................	$ 1,455	$ 1,155	300
Buildings	3,210	3,210	-0-
Less: Accumulated Depreciation	(570)	(420)	150
Equipment......................................	2,700	2,565	135
Less: Accumulated Depreciation	(180)	(240)	(60)
Total Property, Plant, and Equipment	$ 6,615	$ 6,270	
Total Assets....................................	$11,340	$10,569	
Liabilities and Stockholders' Equity			
Current Liabilities:			
Accounts Payable.............................	$ 615	$ 720	(105)
Bank Loan Payable	-0-	450	(450)
Accrued Payables.............................	90	129	(39)
Total Current Liabilities....................	$ 705	$ 1,299	
Noncurrent Liabilities:			
Notes Payable (due 9/30/95)...................	$ 690	$ -0-	690
Bonds Payable (due 12/31/99)	3,000	3,000	-0-
Premium on Bonds Payable	600	660	(60)
Total Noncurrent Liabilities	$ 4,290	$ 3,660	
Total Liabilities	$ 4,995	$ 4,959	
Stockholders' Equity:			
Preferred Stock................................	$ 300	$ -0-	300
Common Stock (no par).........................	4,950	4,950	-0-
Retained Earnings	1,095	660	435
Total Stockholders' Equity	$ 6,345	$ 5,610	
Total Liabilities and Stockholders' Equity	$11,340	$10,569	

An analysis of Unlimited's financial records revealed the following information:

a. Equipment costing $405,000 and having an accumulated depreciation of $135,000 was sold for $225,000. The $45,000 loss appears on the income statement.
b. Preferred stock with a par value of $300,000 was issued for 40 acres of land.
c. The entry to record interest expense on the bonds was as follows:

Interest Expense	75,000	
Premium on Bonds Payable	60,000	
Cash..		135,000

(More cash resources were used than is reflected in the Interest Expense account.)
d. Borrowed $690,000 from the bank; a note due in 1995 was signed.
e. Equipment costing $540,000 was purchased for cash.
f. Dividends of $204,000 were declared and paid.

| **Required** |

Prepare a statement of cash flows using either the T-account approach or the worksheet approach as directed by your instructor.

(Check figure: Cash flows used in operations = $96,000)

**Problem B15-7
Calculating cash-basis net income**

Libbey Company's 1989 income statement and comparative balance sheets for 1988 and 1989, are shown below:

LIBBEY COMPANY
Income Statement
Year Ended September 30, 1989

Sales		$180,000
Cost of Goods Sold		75,000
Gross Profit on Sales		$105,000
Operating Expenses:		
Depreciation Expense...................................	$35,000	
Other Operating Expenses...............................	20,000	55,000
Net Income		$ 50,000

LIBBEY COMPANY
Comparative Balance Sheets

	Sept. 30,	
	1989	**1988**
Assets		
Cash	$ 30,000	$ 20,000
Accounts Receivable (net)	60,000	80,000
Merchandise Inventory.....................................	80,000	35,000
Noncurrent Assets (net)	150,000	55,000
Total Assets..	$320,000	$190,000
Equities		
Accounts Payable	$ 40,000	$ 25,000
Accrued Salaries Payable	10,000	40,000
Noncurrent Liabilities	105,000	10,000
Total Liabilities.....................................	$155,000	$ 75,000
Paid-In Capital...	$100,000	$100,000
Retained Earnings...	65,000	15,000
Total Stockholders' Equity	$165,000	$115,000
Total Equities..	$320,000	$190,000

| **Required** |

Calculate Libbey Company's cash-basis net income for the year ended Sept. 30, 1989.

(Check figure: Cash-basis net income = $45,000)

INDEX

INDEX